The Philosophy of John Duns Scotus

The Philosophy of John Duns Scotus

Antonie Vos

EDINBURGH UNIVERSITY PRESS

© Antonie Vos, 2006

Edinburgh University Press Ltd
22 George Square, Edinburgh

Reprinted 2007

Typeset in 11/13pt Adobe Sabon
by Servis Filmsetting Ltd, Manchester, and
printed and bound in Great Britain by
Biddles Ltd, King's Lynn, Norfolk

A CIP record for this book is available from the British Library

ISBN-10 0 7486 2462 7 (hardback)
ISBN-13 978 0 7486 2462 1

The right of Antonie Vos
to be identified as author of this work
has been asserted in accordance with
the Copyright, Designs and Patents Act 1988.

Contents

Preface and acknowledgements

For Boethius, philosophy became a source of comfort. In difficult circumstances, we may set our minds free by focusing on a specific agenda. After having uncovered the infrastructure of John Duns Scotus' theology (*Johannes Duns Scotus*, 1994), I returned to the sphere of philosophy to concentrate on the massive issue of Duns Scotus' own philosophy. I underestimated somewhat the enormity of the task to clean up the research regarding John Duns Scotus' life, works, and philosophical thought. However, my obsession was made lighter and livelier by Marriëtte, Toon, and Elisabeth, my home front and a haven of relief and joy, always fond of keen exchanges of thought to soothe the practical pressures of writing a large book.

I have continually been supported by the wonderful presence of the Research Group John Duns Scotus which gathers regularly in Dordrecht. John Duns' philosophy is a philosophy of individual dignity and goodness, love and friendship. I am grateful for and proud of this unique band of inspirational scholars (Henri Veldhuis, Eef Dekker, Nico den Bok, Klaas Bom, Andreas Beck, Martijn Bac), still going strong in their contributions to Scotist scholarship. Likewise, I enjoy the link between past and present in the Utrecht days of studying and promoting theology (Nico den Bok, Guus Labooy, Arjan Plaisier). We are rediscovering the past in order to infuse present debates with the riches of the classic heritage of Western thought of the past millennium. I am grateful for and proud of such excellent young scholars who started out as students but became my pupils and then my friends who helped prevent me from making mistakes.

Investigating Duns Scotus' thought is a massive undertaking, just as is writing in English. Without the cordial support of Jerry Etzkorn I would certainly not have succeeded in producing an acceptable book. By correcting my *The Philosophy of John Duns Scotus* Jerry saved my book, and hopefully my work. Just as Professor Girard Etzkorn took care of my English, Dr Guus Labooy took care of my computer version. *Mille grazie*. I am also grateful for the financial support I received from the Theologisch Wetenschappelijk Instituut (the Protestant Church in the Netherlands).

Without De Rijk's contributions to philosophical scholarship, I could not have mastered the tools indispensable for reading and analyzing systematic texts of medieval theologians and philosophers. The membership of Medium Aevum is a precious gift to me. I received fine support from Dr Bert Bos in semantic matters and the criticisms Professor H. A. G. Braakhuis bestowed on my work with meticulous care provided me with singular help, particularly in bridging the distance between evidence and conclusions. I feel truly grateful for this assistance.

I am impressed by the sense of responsibility of the staff and the board of Edinburgh University Press and of the referees. Jackie Jones, former philosophy editor, deserves my deeply felt gratitude for her wise encouragement and keen involvement. Working together with her successor Carol Macdonald was always a source of joy. Heartfelt thanks go also to the copyeditor Peter Williams for his hard, efficient, and excellent work. The admirable style and competence of all members of staff I have worked with has surprised me – and surprised me I have to confess in a most pleasant way.

Almost twenty-five years ago in 1981, I showed how the main concepts of Duns Scotus' theory of science constitute a coherent web of ideas based on his central logical and ontological innovations, and utilizing the basic notion of synchronic contingency as a matrix in his theory. The great challenge was to investigate whether this same innovation could be the key to understanding the whole of his philosophy. The journey of this research became a breathtaking adventure, an adventure in retrospect which succeeded due to the quality of Scotus' thought.

The main text of *The Philosophy of John Duns Scotus* was finished in the summer of 2003. I hope to finish *The Theology of John Duns Scotus* in the course of 2005–6.

It is an existential comfort to contribute to coherent philosophy, transcending the subjectivities of individual thinkers. It is a true gift to discover an oeuvre from the past, embodying, in principle, a coherent world of philosophical and theological thought. It is a wonderful experience to discover in addition that this world of theological and philosophical thinking also provided the foundations for the perspectives and dilemmas of mainstream Western thought for centuries.

John Duns Scotus suddenly died in Cologne, in Germany's Rhineland, in 1308, still a young professor of only forty-two years of age. It was a sad blow to the development of Western thought. Nevertheless, we shall have something to celebrate in 2008.

Dordrecht, The Netherlands
Advent 2005
vos-pullen@planet.nl
www.dunsscotus.com

Abbreviations

AFH	*Archivum Franciscanum Historicum* 1 (1908–).
CF	Antonie Vos, H. Veldhuis, A. H. Looman-Graaskamp, E. Dekker and N. W. den Bok, *John Duns Scotus. Contingency and Freedom. Lectura* I 39, Dordrecht/ Boston 1994, I–VIII and 1–206.
CHLMP	Norman Kretzmann, Anthony Kenny, and Jan Pinborg (eds), *The Cambridge History of Later Medieval Philosophy*, Cambridge 1982.
CV	Antonie Vos, H. Veldhuis, A. H. Looman-Graaskamp, E. Dekker and N. W. den Bok, *Johannes Duns Scotus. Contingentie en vrijheid. Lectura* I 39, Zoetermeer 1992, 1–208.
DS	Antonie Vos, *Johannes Duns Scotus*, Leiden 1994, I–X and 1–284.
EP	Paul Edwards (ed.), *The Encyclopedia of Philosophy* I–VIII, New York/London 1967.
ER	Mircea Eliade (ed.), *The Encyclopedia of Religion* I–XVI, New York/London 1987.
FS	*Franziskanische Studien* 1 (1914–).
HCPMA	Étienne Gilson, *History of Christian Philosophy in the Middle Ages*, London 1955.
KN	Antonie Vos, *Kennis en Noodzakelijkheid. Een kritische analyse van het absolute evidentialisme in wijsbegeerte en theologie* (*Knowledge and Necessity*), Kampen 1981, I–XVIII and 1–456. Academic dissertation.
PMA	L. M. de Rijk, *La philosophie au moyen âge*, Leiden 1985.
REP	Edward Craig (ed.), *The Routledge Encyclopedia of Philosophy* I–X, London 1998.

REFERENCE DEVICES

The basic policy has been to arrange the references in the notes in as simple a way as possible. The references reflect the bibliography: surname of the author, including *et al.* if more authors are involved, title or short title, page or pages. If a section is referred to without any title, for example §3.6.8, then it is that section in *The Philosophy of John Duns Scotus* that is referred to.

References to Duns Scotus' writings are also as simple as possible, for example *Lectura* I 39.72: title of the work of Duns Scotus: *Lectura*; number of the book of the *Lectura*: I; number of the distinction of the book of *Lectura* I: 39; and number of the section: 72.

Introduction

1   INTRODUCTION

Over the last ten years I have been constantly aware that momentous decisions and events were taking place in Duns' life seven centuries ago. In 1298–99 John Duns acted as a bachelor lecturing on the *Sentences* in Oxford in the academic year 1298–99.[1] This series of lectures was to change his life. In 1301, rather than become a theological master in Oxford, he sailed for France to become a bachelor lecturing on the *Sentences* and Master of Divinity in Paris, the intellectual capital of Europe.

This move must have been the result of an intervention by the international leadership of the Franciscan Order on John Duns' behalf. All that time the Friars Minor were by far the largest mendicant order. John Duns, born in Scotland, did not go to Paris as a *studens de debito*, nor as a *studens de gratia* (§1.4). He went to become a bachelor of the *Sentences*. However, Parisian Franciscan bachelors reading on the *Sentences* were appointed by the Minister General of the Order (§1.8 and §§2.1–2.2 and §2.4). Duns Scotus became the showpiece of Augustinian thought, the mainstream of Western theology and philosophy, within a few years through the quality of his thought as master of theology at the University of Paris. It had been assumed that he would set the theological and philosophical agenda for years, but it turned out to be that he would do so for centuries, even though he was to die within a short time.

Unfortunately, this picture is not mirrored in our handbooks and introductions to the history of philosophy and theology. Scotus fell from prominence in the nineteenth century, the century in which the study of history came of age. Thus he lost his historical place too, but

---

[1] In addition to the Bible, the twelfth-century *Sentence* (*Sententiae*) of Peter Lombard was the theological standard text during the last stage of studying theology for more than three centuries (until the middle of the sixteenth century). See §1.4: 'A senior theological student.'

amicus Plato, sed magis amicus veritas. When we investigate and interpret the writings of a thinker from the past and their influence, we have to interpret *his* texts and their influence, not our own ideas. If we are researching Duns Scotus' philosophy, what matters is Duns Scotus: *his* life, *his* writings and *his* thinking. Some points of view deserve attention in order to do greater justice to medieval philosophy in general, and to Scotus' philosophy in particular since some modern dualisms are not helpful, if we wish to discover the coherence of the whole of Duns Scotus' philosophical and theological thought and what constitutes his lasting contribution.

Four interpretative points of view

The first point of view concerns the dualistic relationship between *philosophy* and *theology*. The modern dualism separating *philosophy* from *theology* is not at all helpful for understanding medieval thought, including that of Duns Scotus. This first point of view is dealt with in §2 of this Introduction.

The birth of critical historical research in the second quarter of the nineteenth century constituted a true 'scientific revolution' and this historical revolution implies that we have to research *a*-historical ways of thought *historically*. The scientifically academic discontinuity of the historical revolution – giving rise to a new way of thinking: the *historical way of thinking* – confronts us with the task of interpreting texts from an *a*-historical *auctoritates* culture, including Duns Scotus' texts, in a *historical* manner (§3).

The third point of view concerns the modern method of separating early modern philosophy (philosophy during the sixteenth, seventeenth and eighteenth centuries) from medieval thought (§4).

The last dualism we have to deal with rests on the fact that systematic and historical studies in philosophy have become quite different principal subjects. Medieval thought, including Duns Scotus' thought, now belongs to the past. 'Scotism' became almost a purely historical term. This state of affairs forces upon us a gap which separates contemporary developments in philosophy (and theology) from the fruits of the past. When we put aside this kind of isolationism, we may realize that we are able to translate and extrapolate legacies or parts of legacies from our almost forgotten past (§5). The last section (§6) offers an overview of *The Philosophy of John Duns Scotus*.

2 PHILOSOPHY VERSUS THEOLOGY

In order to understand Duns Scotus' philosophy and to uncover what constitutes his lasting legacy, we have to overcome the dualism which separates *philosophy* from *theology*. The modern metaphilosophical dualism separating *philosophy* from *theology* is rooted in Renaissance philosophy as far as it bases itself on a new type of *duplex ordo* ontology. This early modern dualism of *nature* and *super nature* cannot be the key to understanding medieval *simplex ordo* thought, nor most early modern orthodox thought either. This modern intuition does not do justice to medieval thought, nor to Duns Scotus' theology and philosophy, because it takes leave of the Augustinian and Anselmian ideal of *fides quaerens intellectum*. In Duns' time, quite different meanings of *philosophia* and *theologia* were in vogue – roughly stated, *philosophia* indicated non-Christian thought and *theologia* Christian thought, although there were basic philosophical faculties (*facultates artium*) and very important theological faculties. By then, the thought form of theology was philosophical, although it was also interwoven with the interpretation of Scripture. However, in the course of the nineteenth century, theology became a mainly historical discipline; before, it was mainly theoretical and systematic.

Again and again, we have to realize that the most important philosophers of the Middle Ages were professional theologians: the original philosophical work done by medieval theologians was much more important than the philosophical work done by members of the *facultas artium*. Whenever fundamental progress was made *in philosophicis*, it was theological problems which initiated the new developments.[2] Once the time of Lanfranc and Anselm had inaugurated the professionalization of theology, theology would take the lead for centuries.

At the same time, the professionalization of semantics and logic greatly enhanced the development of systematic thought. In the tenth and eleventh centuries, the study of medieval Latin grammar went through a creative stage. In fact, twelfth-century linguistics saw the development of mature grammatical and syntactical theories of Latin. Theories of language (*grammatica*) and logic (*dialectica*) met each other. The combination of logical and grammatical analyses led to a dynamics of analytical thinking: *scholastic* thinking was simply critical and precise thinking developing in the schools.

---

[2] Cf. De Rijk, 'On Boethius's notion of *being*,' in Kretzmann (ed.), *Meaning and Inference in Medieval Philosophy*, 1–29.

Theology and (canon) law also opened their gates to these powerful tools. Logical analysis of language flourished especially in theology, starting as *sacra pagina*. The contextual approach of the functions of words in Latin sentences was the cradle of *terminist logic*: the logic of properties of terms and the uses of terms in propositions.[3] Logical analysis, constructive thought and theology were fused. Duns Scotus' notion of *logical possibility* (*logicum possibile*) may seem the pinnacle of abstract thinking, but this notion was developed within the concrete theological contexts of the doctrine of God Triune and creation theology. Moreover, his notion of (synchronically) *logical possibility* is the cradle of his pervasive idea of *synchronic contingency* (*Lectura* I 39, 49–53). Scotus is not an exception to the rule – he illustrates the rule eloquently (chapters 4–5 and 6–7). We have to analyze and interpret Duns Scotus' world of thought as a whole, even if we select philosophical theories according to our modern understanding of philosophy – as is done in *The Philosophy of John Duns Scotus* where philosophical materials are arranged according to the modern division into principal philosophical subjects.

3   THE DUALITY OF A HISTORY OF WHAT IS A-HISTORICAL

In medieval thought, *theology* and *philosophy* were related to each other in ways quite different from what they are now. However, the relationship between medieval philosophy and theology on the one hand, and *history* on the other, is still more complicated, because, before the historical revolution, there was no *historical* reflection on the past. Certainly there was the past and people from an *a*-historical culture do know there was, but it is the past without critical *historiography*. The fact of the development of the *historical* way of thinking implies that *we* have to research an *a*-historical way of thinking *historically*.

The main point of this cultural and philosophical discontinuity makes us realize that we are unfamiliar with the old ways of handling *auctoritates* – and we have to realize too that the medievals were not familiar with our ways of studying sources and texts critically and *historically*.[4] The fact that surprises us is that the 'curriculum' texts

---

[3] See De Rijk, *Logica Modernorum* II A 95–130. Cf. chapters 4–6, and also chapters 14–16.

[4] We still see the crisis effected by this state of affairs operating in biblical studies. Are biblical texts authoritative, or not? Did this or that truly happen, or not? As far as historical texts – texts from the past – are looked upon as texts of contemporaries, their *historical* dimension becomes invisible.

and set texts were kinds of 'biblical texts', both in antiquity and in the Middle Ages. These cultures were *auctoritates* cultures. However, to the modern mind, *auctoritates* force authority, but in an *auctoritates* culture they enjoy quite a different function – they reveal *truth*.[5] However, the crucial question is now: *whose truth*? If Duns Scotus writes: *Aristoteles dicit* (Aristotle says so), who is this Aristotle? In an *a*-historical culture, 'Aristotle' cannot be the *historical* Aristotle, because, for them, there was no *historical* Aristotle. There was only an Aristotle from the past and Duns Scotus' Aristotle is mainly *Scotus* himself, and it is just this feature which has to be understood *historically*.

The fact that the intellectuals from an *a*-historical culture do not read and interpret *historically* does not mean that they are unable to read in a critical way. They know when they and their neighbors disagree. They read the different sentences and they discover that they differ. In the early Middle Ages, the theologians assumed that the *patrimonium fidei* was unanimous, but when they constructed their *sententiae*, they found out that it was not. Thus they perfected their ways of interpreting *auctoritates* texts with the help of the method of *exponere reverenter*. In general, a culturally 'sacred' text revealed *truth* and for the theologians their texts revealed *profound truth*.

This pattern drastically affected the role of textbooks – and, in particular, the role of the *corpus aristotelicum*. It also affected the history of Duns Scotus' thought substantially. John Duns Scotus did not belong to the Aristotelians of his time. On the contrary, he felt sure that they were wrong and that he was able to prove it. We have to interpret Duns Scotus' texts *from within*, that is in terms of Scotus' own language and philosophical idiom, rooted as they are in late thirteenth-century British thought. John Duns' traditional historical position is primarily Oxonian, although he also became Parisian.

In Paris, Scotus met an array of forces quite different from what was usual in Oxford, ranging from the Christian Aristotelians such as Godfrey of Fontaines and John le Sage to the mystic theologies of the *Meister* Eckhehart and Dietrich. Scotus' *habitat* was the independent dynamics of medieval thought, stamped by the historical development of its own new concepts and theories in a continuous process of renewal based upon tradition. If we want to do justice to medieval

---

[5] On authority, *auctoritas* and *auctoritates*, see PMA §§4.3–4.8. Cf. §14.8: An *auctoritates* culture.

thinkers, we have to return them to their own past and, in particular, if we want to do justice to Scotus, we have to return him to his own past. Then we may make an amazing discovery: a world of thought full of promises for our present. *Present topicality* ensues from *historical identity*.[6]

4   LATER MEDIEVAL VERSUS EARLY MODERN CENTURIES

In order to discover what constitutes Western thought, including medieval thought, we have to free ourselves from some assumptions. We need to pay attention to the third dualism in order to separate early modern philosophy from medieval thought.[7] The development of thought between 1200 and 1500 and 1500 and 1800 had much more of a unity than the developments between the early modern centuries and the nineteenth and twentieth centuries. The entire history of the Western university makes this quite clear.

Scotus lost his status in the nineteenth century. Necessitarianism replaced contingency thought. The victor became a loser and losers become marginal. Duns Scotus' line of thought – the line of thought of Anselm and the Victorines, John of La Rochelle and Bonaventure, John Pecham and Henry of Ghent, Duns Scotus, William of Ockham and Gregory of Rimini – was relegated to a marginal bias for not satisfying the Aristotelian scientific canon. My point is not so much that philosophical alternatives criticize this thought, but that the alternative nineteenth-century view made Duns Scotus' historical place rather invisible. Historiography is often not democratic. Granted, philosophy is not democratic, neither is physics, since simply the best

---

[6] See §5 of this Introduction. For this reason, *The Philosophy of John Duns Scotus* also tries to show how Duns Scotus absorbed previous innovations and radicalized their main tendency at the same time.

[7] Honnefelder's *Scientia transcendens* (1990) is a fine example of what results can be achieved by ignoring the 1500 dividing line. Neither Reformational nor Counter-Reformational thought can be understood cut off from their 'medieval' background. In a sense, the sixteenth century is rather 'medieval.' To my mind, only in Scottish philosophy is the boundary between pre- and post-Reformation thought regularly crossed. A fine example illustrating this strategy may be found in Thijssen and Braakhuis (eds), *The Commentary Tradition on Aristotle's De generatione et corruptione. Ancient, Medieval and Early Modern.* Cf. Thijssen, 'The Commentary Tradition on Aristotle's *De generatione et corruptione*. An Introductory Survey,' in Thijssen and Braakhuis (eds), *The Commentary Tradition*, 15: 'Over time, the imported Greek knowledge came to be totally absorbed and thoroughly transformed in its new Latin context, even in such a way that the Western culture became its new natural home.' See also Lüthy, Leijenhorst and Thijssen (eds), *The Dynamics of Aristotelian Natural Philosophy from Antiquity to the Seventeenth Century* (2002).

have to win. However, historiography ought to be democratic. What's sauce for the goose is sauce for the gander.

It is easy to overlook the legacy of Duns Scotus' thought in later centuries, not only because of his relegation in the nineteenth century, but also by the objective but incidental fact that Scotus was not a man of textbooks. He may have revolutionized systematic thought, but he did not revolutionize the arena of textbooks. No book of his became a set text.

From the second quarter of the thirteenth century, the theological textbook was Peter Lombard's *Sententiae*, but from about 1300 in many cases the conceptualization was broadly Scotist – and 'broadly Scotist means in particular Augustinian, in combination with a *will*-based doctrine of God, including *true contingency* and a central position for *will*, *individuality* and *freedom*. In the sixteenth century, Thomas Aquinas' *Summa Theologiae* replaced Lombard's *Sententiae*, but in many cases the conceptualization was increasingly Scotist. Using Aquinas' *Summa Theologiae* did not imply that the users were Thomists, just as in the Middle Ages using Peter Lombard's *Sententiae* did not imply that they were 'Lombardists', and neither did the fact that they were utilizing the *corpus aristotelicum* imply that they were 'Aristotelians'. The early modern centuries were still centuries of interpretation *per auctoritatem*. In this case, *e mente auctoris* does not refer to the author commented on, but to the author commenting on his *auctoritates*. So, Duns Scotus' *Aristotle* is not the *historical* Aristotle, but mainly *Scotus* himself, and the seventeenth-century Utrecht *Aquinas* is Reformed. From the purely historical point of view, we have to state that much Scotist thought was absorbed in the early modern university.

When Scotus died suddenly in Cologne (Germany) in 1308, no single book of his had been finished – with the exception of the early logical writings, but even they were not published in Duns' lifetime. Scotus' greatest works would still have taken years to finish. It is a sheer miracle that they survived at all. John Duns Scotus' life was an unfinished agenda, his work was an *unfinished agenda*, and his works were an *unfinished agenda*, but, nonetheless, his legacy was for the future – outside the textbook tradition.

5 THE TOPICALITY OF PHILOSOPHICAL LEGACIES

The unity of Duns Scotus' philosophy and theology unlocks the coherence of a whole world of thought. We may see that this is so by integrating the philosophical and theological dimensions which were expressed themselves in the two main faculties of the medieval university. The medieval university, a new type of academic institution, gave rise to a new type of thought: philosophy in a new key and theology in a new key – philosophical theology in a new key. Duns Scotus' contributions have to be understood and analyzed within this context of new concepts and theories in development. The history of concepts and theories has to be set free from the history of terminology. A dominant stability of terms is wedded to an amazing dynamics of concepts and theories and the logic of an *auctoritates* culture accounts for this paradoxical marriage.

Nevertheless, it is still a medieval world of thought we meet in Duns Scotus' oeuvre, expressed with the help of scholastic tools, invented and elaborated on in Latin based semantics and logic. However, this world of thought does not depend essentially on these scholastic tools. We may pile up a list of famous names from modern logic and philosophy who have established theories Duns Scotus' philosophy is definitely in need of: Cantor – Frege, Russell and Beth – Lewis, Kanger and Hintikka – Kripke and Plantinga – Wittgenstein, Ryle and Austin. We can also compose a list of crucial theories: the theory of sets and, in particular, the theory of infinite sets (Cantor), the theory of logical connectives and the logic of quantifiers (Frege, Beth), the logic of relation and identity (Russell, Whitehead). In general, modern standard logic is an excellent tool to translate, to extrapolate and to defend Scotian theories in combination with the 'linguistic turn' (Wittgenstein, Ryle, Austin). Moreover, modal logic (Lewis, Kanger, Hintikka) and the ontology of possible worlds (Kripke, Plantinga) are crucial theories to discuss adequately Duns Scotus' ontology and philosophical and theological doctrines of God.

With the help of such contributions, we are able to translate and to extrapolate, for example, Duns Scotus' theories on negation, the formal distinction, haeceity, common nature, his theories of many kinds of relations and many kinds of distinctions. In general, many theories of Scotus can be explained precisely in terms of modern standard logic, but our present logic is also an excellent instrument to translate many of his philosophical and theological theories which are not semantical or logical themselves. When we overcome the dualisms of *philosophy* and *theology* and of *medieval* and *early modern thought* and when we follow the rules of investigating *a*-historical thinking in a *historical* way, we may arrive at a succint picture of the contents and the impact, the meaning and the value of Duns Scotus' philosophy (Chapter 16). Seeing his thought in the light it deserves elicits new questions concerning its theoretical means and power and its historical effects and meaning.

6 OVERVIEW

By discovering the historical truth of Duns Scotus' thought, we discern that its historical place is embedded in an overall process of Western theology and philosophy emancipating from ancient thought patterns, both in the old-Semitic and in the ancient Greek mould. The Christian faith could not be accounted for rationally in terms of the concepts and theories of ancient *philosophia*. New wine required new skins. Theological dilemmas gave rise to philosophical revolutions eliciting philosophy in a new key. *The Philosophy of John Duns Scotus* consists of three parts:

1. Part I – *Life and works* (Chapters 1–3);
2. Part II – *The philosophy of John Duns Scotus* (Chapters 4–13); and
3. Part III – *Background and foreground: ancient and modern philosophy* (Chapters 14–16): historical and systematic background – ancient philosophy (Chapter 14); and historical and systematic foreground – modern philosophy (Chapters 15–16).

Part I – Life and works

Only a few facts are generally known.[8] At first sight, his life seems to be that of a shadowy academic to overcome which twentieth-century *Scotus* research had to be researched again. This re-investigation has uncovered forgotten contributions, especially from French books and journals before World War II, and filled in many gaps. Moreover, new questions provoke new answers. The result is a more vivid description of John Duns' life – in spite of the scarcity of the sources (Chapters 1–2). The course of his life was not only dramatic after he left Oxford, but the story of his works up to now is dramatic too, and told in Chapter 3. The status of each of the spurious and authentic works and their editions is argued for pointedly, by integrating old results, often hidden in old, inaccessible and mainly

---

[8] See CF 3–9. Cf. Wolter in Alluntis and Wolter, *God and Creatures*, XVIII–XXIV.

forgotten Franciscan publications, and more recent discoveries and arguments.

Part II – The philosophy of John Duns Scotus

Semantics, logic and tools of conceptual analysis

Chapter 4 deals with semantic and logical theories. Apart from Scotus' modal logic, to which much attention was paid, other parts of his logic and semantics have been somewhat neglected. Discoveries by others and new results are integrated into one picture. In two respects, Duns' semantic and logical theories are crucial to understanding his thought. In general, it is true of medieval thought that semantics and logic yield the keys to understanding systematic philosophy and theology because medieval students started with *grammatica* and *dialectica*.[9]

However, in Duns' case, this pattern is even more acute. His oeuvre mainly consists of a unique set of writings on the *corpus aristotelicum* and a unique set of books *in statu nascendi* on the *Sententiae*. The semantic and logical contributions in his early logical writings can be compared with the parallel theories of his great theological works. There have been occasional observations that there seem to be remarkable differences, but the differences constitute a systematic pattern. The very young John Duns is not a 'Scotist', but more or less a kind of a Christian 'Aristotelian', although he was also steeped in British logic during the last quarter of the thirteenth century and in the broad Augustinian tradition. Duns Scotus' ideas on the *ars obligatoria* confirm this outlook (Chapter 5). He contributed distinctively to this fascinating area of medieval logic and his ideas on the *ars obligatoria* are also the key for his theory of argumentation. For Duns Scotus, external inconsistency does not constitute demonstrative proof. Demonstrative proof starts from the hypotheses of the opponent, just as with the *ars obligatoria* practices. He also develops special conceptual tools to elaborate on his ideas (Chapter 6).

Ontology and epistemology

His ontology shows how indispensable his formal tools are in order to be able to follow his long-winded argumentations (Chapter 7).

---

[9] This approach was impressively inaugurated by the early text editions of De Rijk: Abelard's *Dialectica* (1956) and Garlandus Compotista's *Dialectica* (1959), *Logica Modernorum* I (1962) and *Logica Modernorum* II (1967). See *PMA* chapters 3–4.

Most Scotist literature concerns the metaphysical aspects of Duns Scotus' philosophy. Nevertheless, long-standing divergences reign here. In terms of a coherent reinterpretation based on his modal logic and theory of *synchronic contingency*, his main ideas and the main dilemmas they have caused are dealt with. Likewise, the epistemological areas (Chapters 8–9) richly show Duns' emancipation from ancient philosophy and its conceptual patterns. They also gave warning of future developments. Ecclesiastes had already said: *There is a time for everything.* Greek and Hellenistic thought tells the same story of a closed and fixed reality in a philosophical way. Scotus essentially completes a philosophical emancipation from the thought patterns of necessitarianism – an emancipation process which had gone on for centuries. If reality is structurally contingent, the notion of *knowledge* has to be disconnected from the notion of *necessity*. If there is no single web of absolute conceptual connections – no parallelism of *thinking* and *being* (De Rijk) – then a whole new area of epistemological research opens up (Chapter 8).

Science and physics

The philosophy of the *ars obligatoria* and the disconnection of *knowledge* from *necessity* led to quite a new approach to *science*, *proof* and *demonstration*. Duns Scotus' theories of *proof*, *demonstration* and *scientific knowledge* (*scientia*) have to be sketched anew because traditional treatments underestimate their distance from Aristotelian approaches to what constitutes *scientia* (Chapter 9). Because there is an excellent monograph on Duns Scotus' physics by Richard Cross, I also deal with Scotus' physics, taking into account the texts of *Lectura* II 7–44 (Chapter 10).

Individuality, goodness and God

New interests in Duns Scotus' ethics and philosophical doctrine of God have arisen, but a clear insight into his ontology of individuality and his anthropology of will and freedom (Chapter 11) – on the basis of his theory of contingency – is indispensable. New light can be shed on his theories of *good* (Chapter 12) and *God* (Chapter 13), because many traditional expositions have a Thomist or an (extremely) nominalist flavor, neglecting the specific logical and ontological infrastructure of Scotian thinking.

Part III – Background and foreground: ancient and modern philosophy

Duns Scotus specifically shared in the two great worlds of the medieval production of theoretical books: books on the *corpus aristotelicum* (philosophical faculty) and books on the *Sententiae* (theological faculty). The young John Duns wrestled strenuously with Aristotelian thought (compare Chapter 14 with Chapters 4 and 15) and he radicalized in a unique way the emancipation from it. By the time of his premature death, he had become a showpiece of the Augustinian world of Christian learning. The course of historical reassessment (Chapter 15) and systematic extrapolations (Chapter 16) point to a rehabilitation of John Duns Scotus as Scotist studies begin to breathe fresh air. Rediscovering the contents and the impact of Scotus' philosophy also points to revising historically the picture Western history of ideas has designed of itself.

Part I

Life and works

CHAPTER 1

Life I: Duns and Oxford

1.1 INTRODUCTION

Around the turn of the twelfth and thirteenth centuries, the world saw the birth of the very first universities and the thirteenth century was the very first university century in the history of learning. The medieval university enjoyed continuous growth and flourished, as did Europe itself. The thirteenth century has also been characterized as the century of Aristotle. The philosophical faculties were invaded by his works.

From the religious point of view, one is struck by the enormous vitality in the activities of the Church which gave a new dynamics to the development of faith and theology. The thirteenth century was also the century of the evangelical revival of the mendicant orders. A new *évangelisme* flowed over Europe and, in particular, over England and Scotland. From the theological point of view, the thirteenth century was the century of the orders of the poverty movement such as the Austin Friars, the Carmelites, the Friars Preaches and the Friars Minor. It was, above all, the first century of the new orders of the Friars Preacher and the Friars Minor.[1] England turned out to be remarkably sensitive to the charm of the Franciscan branch of the poverty movement. In the twelfth century the poverty movement had fallen into relative desuetude, but it rose again in the thirteenth century and its rebirth could in no way have been foreseen.

1.1.1 Poor for the sake of Christ

The spread of the evangelical movement had an enormous impact on the development of theology. The new theology, professional as it was,

---

[1] See Van den Eijnden, *Poverty on the Way to God,* chapter 1: 'Evangelical Poverty in Aquinas' Time.' In English, members of orders which belong to the poverty movement are called *friars.* A Friar Preacher is a member of the Dominican Order: *Ordo Praedicatorum (OP),* and a Friar Minor is a member of the Franciscan Order: *Ordo Fratrum Minorum (OFM).*

gave birth to a new philosophy during the second half of the thirteenth century. The theological faculty of the thirteenth and fourteenth centuries was a center of scholarly creativity more important for the development of philosophy (in the modern sense of the word) than the 'philosophical' faculties (in the medieval sense of the *facultas artium*). The best minds of Europe opted for theology, just as, in the first decades of the twentieth century, the best minds opted for physics after Einstein's breathtaking discoveries.

Church and faith, mendicancy and theology were Duns' cradle. The young John followed Christ in the footsteps of *il poverello*.[2] He was born in the South of Scotland, named Duns, baptized John in the autumn of 1265 or the winter of 1266 and – later – called *Scotus* (§1.2). For many years, Duns studied theology and philosophy in Oxford and was ordained a priest in 1291 (§1.3). He had already produced many logical writings at an early stage of his theological studies (§1.4). He was selected to become a master of divinity at Oxford and delivered a masterly course on systematic theology which would change his life and interrupt his Oxonian and English career (§1.5). His early *Lectura* I–II are the key to this revolutionary turn in John Duns' life (§1.6). He acted as a *baccalaureus biblicus* and a *baccalaureus formatus* at Oxford University (§1.7). Duns eventually left the pearl of England for Paris and the epilogue to the chapter underlines the synthetic nature of his personal stance and development (§1.8).

1.2   A SCOTTISH BOY

The Franciscan movement reached England in 1224, five years after it had reached Paris, and within twenty years the Friars Minor had settled at the two university towns, fifteen cathedral cities and twenty-five county towns. All over Europe, the Franciscans eventually numbered about forty thousand. Their quantitative success equalled their intellectual achievements. Franciscan theologians creatively contributed to the renewal of Oxonian theology. During the generations

---

[2] The first short and reliable overviews of Duns Scotus' life are by Allan Wolter: 'John Duns Scotus. Life and Works,' in Alluntis and Wolter, *God and Creatures* (1975), XVIII–XXVII, and idem, 'John Duns Scotus,' *The New Encyclopaedia Britannica. Micropaedia* IV ([15]1997) 278f. (= *Macropaedia* V (1976) 1083–1085). Cf. Frank and Wolter, *Duns Scotus. Metaphysician*, 1–16. There is also Stephen Dumont's excellent introductory account: 'John Duns Scotus (*c*.1266–1308),' *REP* III (1998) 153–170. Cf. *CF* (1994) 3–9, especially note 2 (= *CV* (1992) 11–18).

between Richard Rufus and Duns Scotus the professionalization of theology was perhaps less striking, but still very solid. The Franciscan renewal was welcomed both by many families and by inspired individuals. It also touched the gentry family of Duns in the South of Scotland,[3] who supported the Franciscan movement on both the personal and the practical and financial levels.[4]

1.2.1 Iohannes/John

Between November 1265 and March 1266, a new scion was born to the Duns family of Berwickshire: *John*. As in the case of Socrates and Jesus, the suggestion that there never was a John (Duns Scotus) has been totally refuted, although, in the wake of Renan, Allan Wolter rightly pointed out that little biographical material concerning Duns is still available.[5] He was born in the second half of the 1260s and he was baptized *Iohannes*.[6]

1.2.2 Duns *b. 1265/1266*

Proposing a reliable hypothesis concerning the year of Duns' birth is not an easy affair. The upshot of historical research after taking great trouble in order to establish hard facts concludes that the date of Duns' ordination must be the precise point of departure for a reliable hypothesis: 17 March 1291. In the thirteenth century, one had to be twenty-five years of age in order to be ordained a priest. So John Duns must have been twenty-five halfway through March 1291. During mid-December 1290 his bishop had also ordained other young theologians but Duns had not been one of them. While statistically we have to put the date of John's birth between the middle of

---

[3] See Knowles, *The Religious Orders in England* I, part II: 'The Friars 1216–1340,' and Leclercq et al., *A History of Christian Spirituality* II: *The Spirituality of the Middle Ages*, 283–314: 'The Franciscan Spring.'

[4] Cf. Angelus Cardinal Felici in the *Decretum* of Duns Scotus' Beatification by the *Congregatio de Causis Sanctorum*, *Opera Omnia* XIX, X: 'Ortus est in Scotiae urbe Dunsio, ad annum 1265. Eius familia liberaliter beneficia conferebat in Sancti Francisci Asisinatis filios, qui primos evangelizatores imitantes, iam ab institutionis exordio ad Scotiae fines perrexerant.'

[5] Wolter, 'Reflections on the Life and Works of Scotus,' *American Catholic Philosophical Quarterly* 67 (1993) 2–5. Cf. Ernest Renan, 'Jean Duns Scot,' *Histoire littéraire de la France* 25, Paris 1869, 404.

[6] See the occurrence of his Christian name in the list of candidates to be ordained a priest in 1291: Longpré, 'L'ordination sacerdotale du Bx. Jean Duns Scot. Document du 17 mars 1291,' *AFH* 22 (1929) 61 (54–62). For the list of candidates for hearing confessions, see Little, *Franciscan Papers, Lists, and Documents*, 235.

December 1265 and 17 March 1266, we may prudently opt for the
winter of 1266, although we cannot exclude the autumn of 1265.
Historically, the only safe statement is that Duns was born 'in
1265/1266'.[7]

John Duns was a member of the flourishing Franciscan province
of England which included Scotland at that time. The *custodia* of
North England and South Scotland belonged to the English Province.
He was a Duns and there were two branches of the Duns family:
the Dunses of Maxton-on-Tweed, in the Border Countrie, and the
Dunses in Berwickshire, twenty-five miles to the North.[8] The village
of Duns, in the heart of Berwickshire, lies between two chains of
mountains: the Cheviot Hills in the south and the Lammermuir Hills
in the north. It was very much an agricultural area. Father Ninian
Duns was a commoner, a gentleman from the landed gentry in a
world which was a mixture of Scottish-Pictish and Anglo-Norman.
After some preparatory education at home or in a local school a
young friar attended the school of his friary. It was obligatory on all
friars – a word derived from the way Englishmen pronounced the
French *frères* – except the illiterate to devote part of their time to
reading and writing, as the General Chapter of Narbonne (1260)
again confirmed.

Each friary had to have its own school and its own lecturer:

> partly to give the necessary groundwork to novices and young friars,
> but also to deliver lectures to the whole community in order to help
> them in their preaching. Then, in each custody, there was to be set up
> a school for more advanced work, so that younger men who showed
> promise might go ahead with their studies without having to go too
> far afield.[9]

These students had to devote at least three or four years there to
scholastic training before going to the *studium generale* linked up with
a university. The students who were to go to the university attended
the *studium generale* on the authority of the Chapter Provincial and
the Minister Provincial.

According to Longpré, in 1278 John Duns attended a primary
school at Haddington in Berwickshire, presently East Lothian, like

---

[7] Maurice De Wulf felt quite unsure concerning the date of Duns' birth, even in the fifth edition
of his *Histoire de la philosophie médiévale* II (1925). The *Decretum* of Duns' Beatification
has 1265. Allan Wolter opts for the beginning of 1266: see McCord Adams (ed.), *The
Philosophical Theology of Scotus*, 1.

[8] 'Dun' is Celtic for hill or fort.

[9] Moorman, *The Grey Friars in Cambridge. 1225–1538*, 19.

Gifford situated east of Edinburgh.[10] After some mediation from his uncle Elias's side, we meet young John in the Franciscan friary of Dumfries. So the natural thing to expect is that John Duns would have been sent to the principal school of the custody at Newcastle. However, at that time the Scottish Houses were revolting against their inclusion in the custody of Newcastle, and in 1278 the Scottish Houses were allowed to elect a vicar-general to govern them, unanimously electing Elias Duns, guardian of Dumfries. In the 1270s, Elias Duns played an important role in the Franciscan movement of North England and South Scotland.[11] Probably, in his fifteenth year Duns was a novice in the friary of Dumfries, the usual age being eighteen. In addition to the Order's *studia generalia*, there were the preparatory schools of the seven custodies into which the English Province was then divided: London, York, Norwich, Newcastle, Stamford, Coventry and Exeter. My guess would be that, because of the tensions between the Scottish Houses and the custody of Newcastle, Duns went to Oxford at an early age.

At any rate, Duns was born neither in 1245 nor in 1274. Both years are legendary, 1245 being the year that Alexander of Hales died and 1274 that both Bonaventure (1217–74) and Thomas Aquinas (1225–74) died. This view of older biographers throws legendary light on the birth of John Duns: when the suns of a previous generation go down, a new star is born. The legend implies that the theological riches of a recent past can be salvaged in a new synthesis. The theological life of Iohannes Duns Scotus is a moment in the scientific tradition of the Church. The symbolism of the legend is clear.

1.2.3   Do(u)ns/*Duns*

In family and village life he was simply called *John*. However, meticulous research has uncovered a few more facts. In three old documents

---

[10] Longpré, 'Nouveaux documents franciscains d'Écosse,' *AFH* 22 (1929) 588.
[11] See Béraud de Saint-Maurice, *Jean Duns Scot. Un docteur des temps nouveaux*, 76–78. Until the middle of the 1960s, Little, 'Chronological Notes on the Life of Duns Scotus,' *English Historical Review* 47 (1932) 568–582, dominated accounts of the chronology of Duns' life. Following the *Brockie Forgeries* he linked the Duns family with Maxton-on-Tweed. The historical value of Brockie's story has been reduced to almost zero by Henry Docherty: 'The Brockie Forgeries,' *The Innes Review* 16 (1965) 79–129, and idem, 'The Brockie MSS. and Duns Scotus,' *De doctrina Ioannis Duns Scoti* I 329–360. Wolter mainly follows the view of John Maior, *History of Great-Britain* (1521), in his *Scotus. Philosophical Writings*, XI f. See also Wolter, 'Reflections on the Life and Works of Scotus,' *American Catholic Philosophical Quarterly* 67 (1993) 6–7.

Duns is mentioned, and these occurrences are the backbone of reconstructing his career in England. For the moment, let us focus on the
way his name was spelled:

> Fr. *Iohannes Dons*[12]
> *Iohannem Douns*[13]
> *Duns*[14]

The first occurrence is from an official list of candidates, including
John Duns, ordained in March 1291. The other occurrences are both
connected with 1300: the second is from a list of candidates including Duns to be licensed in July 1300 to hear confessions and the third
reports that he was a bachelor under Bridlington in 1300.

We are struck by two features. Both lists name him 'Iohannes
Do(u)ns': they explicitly give his Christian name and his family name.
In an English context, he is called *Iohannes* (*John*) and *Dons/Duns/
Douns*. These variants are to be expected from the viewpoint of pro-
nunciation. 'Scotus' is missing in the English lists.

1.2.4   Scotus

We have to separate the issue of name from the issue of origin and
make a decision on independent grounds. A name like 'Duns' might
be a family name or a place-name. The name itself is not sufficient
reason to infer that *Duns* be from Duns. It took some effort to establish his year of birth and his native soil. The great Irish scholar Luke
Wadding, the seventeenth-century editor of Duns Scotus' *Opera
Omnia*, took a pride in telling us that Duns Scotus was an Irishman,
as several great Scotists, like Maurice O'Fihely and Wadding
himself, were.

In general, nineteenth-century literature was not only confused on
doctrinal but also on biographical issues, including the issue of Duns'
native soil. In 1917, Callebaut did away with this confusion. England,
Scotland and Ireland claimed to be the native soil of Duns. Callebaut's
first point was that the candidature of England is eliminated by Duns'
famous surname *Scotus* which he already enjoyed during his lifetime. A person *de Anglia* was never called *Scotus*. The candidature of

[12] Longpré, 'L'ordination sacerdotale du Bx. Jean Duns Scot,' *AFH* 22 (1929) 61.
[13] Little, *Franciscan Papers, Lists, and Documents*, 235. See §1.6.
[14] Longpré, 'Philippe de Bridlington, O.F.M. et le Bx. Duns Scot,' *AFH* 22 (1929) 588.

Ireland has to be cancelled because of the thirteenth- and fourteenth-century meaning of 'Scotus' and the Ireland hypothesis itself is only a seventeenth-century suggestion.[15]

Callebaut's line of argumentation runs parallel to the approach adopted by Ehrle, but his very early contribution was only published much later by Pelster.[16] The main idea is to derive the evidence for the name of 'Duns' from original lists where *Duns* is named, and similar lists of candidate priests, confessors, members of a faculty or a university, and the like, linked with a place-name. By 1920, with regard to Duns, the harvest was still very small. However, Callebaut was aware that the list of theologians siding with King Philip the Fair in June 1303 at Paris shows systematically, as many other documents do in a more individual way, that people were often named after their place or country of origin. His main point was that 'Scotus' proves that Duns is from Scotland, because *Scotia* is clearly distinguished from *Anglia* and *Hibernia*.

Let us consider a number of documents concerning Duns' short life: his ordination to become a priest, his being presented to the bishop as a candidate for hearing confessions and his appearance as *baccalaureus responsalis* under Bridlington at Oxford on the one hand, and his siding against Philip IV and his appointment to prepare as doctor of divinity at Paris on the other. The list showing the names of the Franciscans siding against Philip IV was discovered by Longpré.[17] The appointment to prepare as doctor of divinity is related to the Parisian faculty of theology, while in a letter from Gonsalvo of Spain, the new Minister General of the Franciscan Order in 1304, we read: 'patrem Ioannem Scotum'.[18] We conclude from this that Duns is said to be *a priest* called *Ioannes*, namely the John who originated from Scotland: *Scotus*.

In this letter the family name 'D(o)uns' is missing; in the English documents 'Scotus' is missing. Nevertheless, the identification is certain. The copyist of *Codex A* of the *Ordinatio* also informs us that he has made use of the 'liber Scoti'. Much other early evidence

---

[15] Callebaut, 'La patrie du B. Jean Duns Scot,' *AFH* 10 (1917) 3–7. The first part of Callebaut's contribution creatively highlights the usage of naming academic foreigners at work abroad after their place of origin or country of origin. André Callebaut established that Duns originated from Scotland.

[16] Pelster, 'Handschriftliches zu Skotus,' *FS* 10 (1923) 1 f.

[17] See Longpré, 'Le B. Jean Duns Scot. Pour le Saint Siège,' *La France franciscaine* 11 (1928) 150.

[18] See Denifle and Chatelain, *Chartularium Universitatis Parisiensis* II 1, 117. This letter from the autumn of 1304 contains a lovely characterization of Duns.

names Duns likewise *Scotus*. Thus we have two very early continental occurrences:

> *fr. johannes scotus* (1303)
> *patrem Ioannem Scotum* (1304).

However, there is also the possible early medieval meaning of
'Scot(t)us' which we find in 'Johannes Scottus Eriugena'. In those centuries, or at any rate before about 1000, 'Scotus' could refer both
to a Scot(sman) and to an Irishman, as 'Eriugena' itself explicitly
indicates: *born in Ireland* (= Eriu). However, in thirteenth- and
fourteenth-century Latin 'Scotus' only means *Scottish*. Here, the decisive contribution made by Callebaut lies in the proof that thirteenth-
and fourteenth-century usage did distinctively distinguish between
Y(m)bernia (= Ireland) and *Scotia* (= Scotland). Likewise, the list
(*rotulus*) from June 1303, discovered by Longpré, unambiguously
proves this usage: in the list of the dissenting brothers where Duns'
name occurs, Franciscans from England, Scotland and Ireland are distinctively mentioned:

> *fr. johannes scotus – fr. thomas anglicus – fr. ricardus yberniensis.*

This list clearly distinguishes between friars from Scotland, England
and Ireland,[19] a usage which is different from the early medieval. The
identification of the Duns family also points to Scotland and, likewise,
both the present inscription on Duns' tomb in Cologne and the original epitaph tell us: *Scotia me genuit* = Scotland brought me forth.[20]
In fact, there was no medieval tradition at all that Duns originated
from Ireland, *pace* Wadding.[21] In the fourteenth century, although the
English population in Paris dropped dramatically as an effect of the
wars between England and France, scores of Scotsmen studied at
Paris and many of them added their native place-name to *Scotus*. A
striking example of this phenomenon is *Thomas de Dunz Scotus*.[22]

---

[19] Longpré, 'Le B. Jean Duns Scot,' *La France franciscaine* 11 (1928) 150 f., where both a tran-
scription and even a photocopy are found.
[20] In 1917 Callebaut had already proved that Duns was called *Scotus* in his own time and that
by about 1300 'Scotus' did not mean Irish any more. See Callebaut, 'La patrie du B. Jean
Duns Scot,' *AFH* 10 (1917) 7–9 and 10–16, respectively.
[21] See Callebaut, 'L'Écosse: Patrie du Bx Jean Duns Scot', *AFH* 13 (1920) 79–84.
[22] See Denifle and Chatelain, *Auctuarium chartularii Universitatis Parisiensis* I col. 130[36]. The
combination of the surname *Scotus* and the place-name *Dunz* is found here: de Dunz Scotus.
For *de* indicating *originating from*, see also Chapter 2, notes 46 and 56.

1.2.5 Duns

'Duns' is a family name, linked with the little place of the same name in the South of Scotland. If someone's place of origin has to be expressed in Latin 'de' is usually added to the place-name, but John Duns is called Duns, not *de* Duns. While there are cases of fourteenth-century people *from* Duns named 'de Duns', in the case of John Duns, 'Duns' has to be considered a family name. From the simple combination of the Christian name *Iohannes* and the family name *Duns* it should not be assumed that Duns originated from Duns nor, therefore, that Duns was a Scotsman – this was just the point correctly made by Ehrle and Pelster. However, from all the data available, it is clear he was. The oldest documents certify that a Franciscan *John Duns* from Scotland lived and studied at Oxford during the last decades of the thirteenth century.

1.2.6 Subtilis

The title *subtilis* (subtle) occurs in several works of William of Alnwick and is also found in the commentaries on the *Sentences* of Peter Auriol, Robert Cowton and William of Ockham. The oldest evidence is found in Gonsalvo's exceptionally appreciative letter (autumn 1304), which dates right from the beginning of the fourteenth century: 'I am fully acquainted with his praiseworthy life, excelling knowledge and most *subtle* ingenuity' (see §2.4).

1.3   STUDENT OF DIVINITY AT OXFORD

There exists little direct documentation regarding Duns' life. We depend on documents, usually of a later date, regulating institutional life. Thus we extrapolate from the general regulations what John Duns as a member of these institutions had probably gone through, after we have clarified which institutions John Duns (Scotus) must have belonged to.[23] At the end of the thirteenth century, studying theology at Oxford was a massive undertaking. However, we know that 1300–1 was the last year of his theological studies at Oxford and at

---

[23] See Roest's excellent survey, *A History of Franciscan Education*, 1–117: '*Studia* students, lectors, and programs.' See also Courtenay, 'The instructional programme of the mendicant convents at Paris in the early fourteenth century,' in Biller and Dobson (eds), *The Medieval Church: Universities, Heresy, and the Religious Life*, 77–92.

Oxford, secular students in theology spent an initial seven-year period
before advancing to a baccalaureate period of four years.

> Students from the religious orders, instead of the favored treatment
> they received at Paris, were required at Oxford to study two years
> longer than their secular counterparts – probably to balance the two
> years of required regency for those who had 'reigned in arts'.[24]

After a program of twelve or thirteen years, Duns would have fulfilled
almost all the requirements for the doctorate in theology. So he must
have finished his philosophical studies about 1289, which usually
required eight years at Oxford, so that he would have become a theological freshman at the end of the 1280s. Bonaventure was over
twenty-five and Thomas Aquinas twenty when they had finished their
philosophical studies, Duns about twenty-two.

> Custodial and provincial theological schools (*studia particularia
> theologiae*) formed the top of the subprovincial educational system.
> Contrary to the arts schools, which came into being when the average
> age of new postulants dropped and the pursuit of university degrees
> asked for a proper grounding in the profane sciences, these interme-
> diate theology schools sometimes can be traced back to the late 1220s
> and early 1230s.[25]

Such theological schools might become prestigious centers of learning.
With regard to England, the educational organization was due to the
second Minister Provincial, Albert of Pisa, the fourth Minister General,
who appointed lecturers at London, Canterbury, Hereford, Leicester,
Bristol, Cambridge and Oxford. The work was continued by William
of Nottingham. In John Duns' days, the English Province already had
a higher academic school of theology in each of its seven custodies:
London, Norwich, Stamford, Exeter, Coventry, York and Newcastle.[26]

These custodial and provincial schools and the *studia generalia*,
spread over the whole of Europe, were the tip of an iceberg. The
astounding growth of the Franciscan Order in the middle of the thirteenth century resulted in a huge number of convents and convent
schools. There was excellence in abundance because this Franciscan
world was first class from the human and spiritual points of view.
Duns was involved in a most promising youth movement. Finishing
one's theological studies was a most exciting affair. The mendicant

---

[24] Courtenay, 'Programs of Study and Genres of Scholastic Theological Production in the
   Fourteenth Century,' in Hamesse (ed.), *Manuels, programmes de cours*, 332.
[25] Roest, *A History of Franciscan Education*, 71.
[26] See Roest, *A History of Franciscan Education*, 72 f.

orders were very popular with a host of powerful young men. On top
of this, the mendicant orders abounded in bright students. The most
talented got a chance to study in the theological faculties at Paris and
Oxford, but it was Oxford that was extraordinarily popular with the
poverty movements and their students. The hinterland was huge. In
England there were already 34 lectors for the 43 Franciscan convents
in 1254. Soon after 1230 the German Province was split into the
provinces of Cologne (which still exists), Saxony and Strasbourg.

> The situation in the Umbrian province sheds some additional light on
> the distribution of convent schools. Aside from the more important
> *studia* in Perugia, Assisi, Todi, Gubbio, Città del Castello, Spoleto
> and Borgo Sansepolcro [. . .], the province seems to have had a range
> of convent schools with only one lector each by the early fourteenth
> century.[27]

For the year 1282, when Duns had started his philosophical studies
in his *studium*, 669 Franciscan convents can be traced in Italy and
there would have been more than 400 Italian convent schools
throughout the fourteenth century.

> It is in the conventual school context that nearly all adult friars were
> immersed in straightforward lectures on dogmatic and moral the-
> ology, where they would hear countless numbers of sermons, and
> would receive additional training in forensic skills on a daily basis.
> Together with the custodial schools, the convent schools provided by
> far the most important context for the regulated permanent educa-
> tion of the friars, most of whom would never leave their province for
> higher studies at a *studium generale*.[28]

In general, the best theological students of the custodial schools were
sent to the *studia generalia theologiae* of the Order to get qualified for
the *lectorate*, the teaching licence for theology within the Order. 'The
"non degree" status of these schools derived not so much from their
inferior curriculum, but was due to the absence of a public chair of
theology attached to a university.'[29] There might have been various
reasons for the absence of a chair of theology: there was no university
in the neighborhood, the neighboring university did not have a theological faculty, or the Franciscan school in question was not willing to
align itself with such a local institution. In addition to the degree
studia of Paris, Oxford and Cambridge, at the end of the thirteenth

---

[27] Roest, *A History of Franciscan Education*, 85.
[28] Ibid., 86 f. (84–86: on Italy).
[29] Ibid., 30 (28–38 on *studia generalia*, and 97–107 on the degree program).

century, the Franciscan Order had more than ten such non-degree *studia generalia*, for example Bologna, Pisa, Venice, Milan, Lisbon, Toulouse, Magdeburg and, soon, Cologne. Already by the second half of the thirteenth century there was a papal privilege of the mendicant orders that friars who had finished the lectorate courses at such a non-degree *studium generale* received the *licentia docendi* in all non-degree schools.[30]

The continuous process of assessment and selection implies that it does not make sense to say of the postgraduate student John Duns that, at the end of the 1290s, he started to study theology at the university. At the end of the 1280s, he started to study theology at the *studium generale* and remained in that position until the end of his stay at Oxford. Through the first half of the 1290s he also became a degree student at the university and by 1297 his baccalaureate candidacy was quite clear. Courtenay's thesis that the common practice was to send a friar for the lectorate course where he would eventually seek his mastership may be true of the candidates who eventually earned a doctorate but, in general, it is not correct. It cannot be true, because in most *studia generalia* where a student could qualify for the lectorate, there was no opportunity to pursue a doctoral degree. Because most professorial candidates in Oxford and Cambridge came from the British Isles, the lectorate-mastership rule would only be applicable to Paris. However, in Duns' case, there is no reason to assume this, because the Parisian Franciscan bachelors were appointed by the Minister General. Everything was a matter of strategy and policy, not a question of individual students pursuing studies with a view to promoting their personal careers. Although in the end Scotus became a Parisian master, originally there was definitely no plan to send him to Paris. A Parisian *studens de debito* only returned after a few years to his mother province if it were clear that the baccalaureate degree would not be granted. John Duns' appearance as *sententiarius* in Paris in 1302 can only mean that he was not a *studens de debito*.[31]

The important orders of the poverty movement had stipulated that their students of theology would be exempted from the regular program of philosophy in the *facultas artium* and had gained this dispensation from the preparatory general and philosophical studies

---

[30] See Pou y Marti (ed.), *Bullarium Franciscanum* II 208b note 317. At the end of the fifteenth century, there were more than a hundred Franciscan *studia generalia* – see Roest, *A History of Franciscan Education*, 32–36.

[31] On *studentes de debito*, see Roest, *A History of Franciscan Education*, 15, and on *studentes de gratia*, see Roest, *A History of Franciscan Education*, 16.

at the university. The two 'student orders' had in the meantime built up their own academic system. The philosophical courses were partly attended in the *studium* of the involved province of the order the student belonged to. For Duns, this center of higher learning was the Franciscan *studium* at Oxford.

> There were to be the schools in the Universities to which the most apt pupils could be sent in order that they might graduate in theology and themselves become lecturers in the other convents. It was thought desirable that each community should have always one friar as a lecturer, and one in training to take his place when the time came.[32]

Duns was educated at the Franciscan *studium* at Oxford in every sense of this precious word *educated*, staying there for about twenty years. So he was every inch an Oxford man whose daily life revolved around the liturgy and the routine, the spirituality and the sphere of debate in a life of study and prayer in a Franciscan friary. His was also a world of semantics and logic, analytical methods and philosophy.

1.3.1 The Oxonian Studium

The Franciscans reached Oxford as early as 1224 and settled south of Carfax in St Ebbe's parish. In the year of the great Paris dispersion (1229–30), they moved into a larger house and it was probably Agnello da Pisa who started to build a school. The lands of the Minors lay behind St Ebbe's Church, in a triangular area enclosed by Pennyfarthing Street and running from St Aldate's to the Castle, the Baley and the old wall. Eventually they bridged the city wall, covering an area of more than 30,000 m². Even more noteworthy is the size of their buildings. The large church was built in seven stages between 1245 and 1480.[33] 'The prestige of the Oxford *studium* stimulated the growth of the Oxford convent from 63 students and other friars in 1277 to 84 in 1317 and 103 in 1377. The majority of the students would have been enrolled in the non-degree theology program.'[34]

---

[32] Moorman, *The Grey Friars in Cambridge. 1225–1538*, 19 f. (19–38: 'The Friars and the University: 1225–1306').

[33] See the fine maps of Oxford in 1279 and 1313, respectively, in Catto (ed.), *The History of the University of Oxford* I, XXXIV f. and XXXVI f. The Franciscan area must have been located between New Road and Castle Street and the River Thames.

[34] Roest, *A History of Franciscan Education*, 23 (21–24). The Oxonian figures for 1317 were: Dominicans 90, Franciscans 84, Carmelites 45, Austin Friars 43; and for 1377: Dominicans 70, Franciscans 103, Carmelites 57, Austin Friars 49. See Little, 'The Franciscan School at Oxford,' *Franciscan Papers, Lists, and Documents*, 65.

Duns joined the community of this *studium* but in Paris he would live in an even larger house.

By 1229 the English province already counted a number of distinguished *magistri*, probably including Grosseteste's friend Adam Marsh, and a number of young Oxford scholars. At that time, Grosseteste had already become lecturer to the Friars Minor and the initiative must have lain with the chancellor himself. The Oxford Friars were engaged in learning almost from the beginning of their Oxford days.[35] They brought a radical type of spirituality to it, resolved to preserve the purity of their Rule. 'Spiritual simplicity, [. . .] a spirit of prayer, of frankness, of poverty and of fidelity to the Rule did not go so early, and, for some fifty years at least there were among the Friars Minor in England many examples of unusual fervour and sanctity.'[36]

In general, the Franciscan order made enormous efforts to build a network of high quality educational centers from the middle of the thirteenth century.

> The Franciscan *studia generalia*, where the intellectual elite was trained, quickly evolved into prestigious centres of learning. The level of theological and philosophical education in the study houses of Paris, Oxford, and Cambridge was very high, as is reflected in the Franciscan academic output of quodlibetal questions and commentaries on the Bible and the Sentences, as well as in the influence of Franciscan theologians and their theological and philosophical positions on the major academic debates.[37]

1.3.2 The study of theology

At the time, studying theology in England was quite an extraordinary matter, especially for the Franciscans, as there were plenty of schools of higher learning and plenty of students. This needs to be emphasized in the case of John Duns. In general, the choice of which students were to be trained at the universities was in the hands of the Provincial Chapters, such students being known as *studentes de debito*. As far as the English Province was concerned, there was much to decide on

---

[35] See Vos, 'Ab uno disce omnes,' *Bijdragen* 60 (1999) 176–181.

[36] Knowles, *The Religious Orders in England* I 137 (114–145), cf. 171–193 and 205–232: 'The Friars Minor.' See Leclercq et al., *The Spirituality of the Middle Ages*, 283–314, and the excellent studies by Edith van den Goorbergh and Theo Zweerman, *Light shining through a veil*, and *Yours Respectfully. Signed and Sealed: Saint Francis*.

[37] Roest, *A History of Franciscan Education*, 327.

for the Chapter Provincial. The convents proposed candidates and the Chapter and the Minister Provincial made the appointments. We have seen that Duns was sent from Scotland at the beginning of the 1280s, his uncle Elias Duns being the Vicar General for the Scottish houses. For the English there was a wide choice. They could send their students either to Oxford or to Cambridge,[38] but at Paris two out of every three candidates to graduate there had also to be 'foreigners,' friars not originating from the French Province. This shared responsibility created a rich pool of gifted students.

The next stage is the decision to appoint the bachelors and, in particular, the *baccalaureus formatus/responsalis*, the next bachelor to graduate and go on as regent master. Consider, for example, the year 1297–98, when Duns was preparing his course on the *Sentences*: at the same time, there was a *sententiarius* lecturing on the *Sentences* in addition to a *biblicus* and a *formatus*. The *master* worked, as it were, together with four assistant professors. In all this the English Minister Provincial had a formidable say.

John Duns studied at one of the best *studia generalia* of that time, connected with one of the only three theological faculties of Europe's universities, in order to get the degree of doctor of divinity. This degree was a very special one. Indeed, Duns may have met John Pecham, the keen archbishop of Canterbury (1279–92). There was a long-standing tradition of teaching of kindred spirits, and Oxford was in wholehearted agreement with the course Bonaventure and Henry of Ghent, Robert Kilwardby and John Pecham had struck out on in the 1270s. The Parisian Articles of 1270 and 1277 and the Oxonian Articles of 1277 and 1284 are evidence of this commitment. Under the leadership of the Dominican Robert Kilwardby OP, at that time the dominant ecclesiastical statesman, the theological *doctores* followed Paris on 18 March 1277. They rejected logical, semantic and ontological propositions, including the metaphysics of the unity of the form advocated by Thomas Aquinas.[39]

For the whole of the thirteenth century, studying theology at a university was a remarkable occupation, but majoring in theology at

---

[38] See §2.4.2. The *studia* at Oxford and Cambridge had substantial numbers of foreign students, although at Cambridge a disproportionate number came from the custody of Norwich/Cambridge. See Little, 'Friars and Theology at Cambridge,' *Franciscan Papers, Lists, and Documents*, 139, and Moorman, *The Grey Friars in Cambridge*, 6, 13 and 21 f.

[39] See Catto, 'Theology and Theologians 1220–1320,' *The History of the University of Oxford* I 496–501, and Lewry, 'The Oxford Condemnations of 1277 in Grammar and Logic,' in Braakhuis and De Rijk (eds), *English Logic and Semantics*, 235–278.

Oxford at the *fin de siècle* was even more so. If we look at the map of Europe, we see that in this 'century of the university' there were only a few universities. There were still no universities in Germany and Switzerland, the Netherlands or Scotland. The jewel in the crown of the thirteenth-century university was the faculty of theology, if there were such a faculty in the university at all. The special nature of the doctoral degree can be pointed out on many levels. Simply finishing a theological study was a spectacular achievement. A doctorate (mastership) of divinity could only be obtained from the 'big three': – Paris, Oxford and Cambridge – for it was only at these universities of the thirteenth century that theological faculties could be found. Indeed, Bologna, probably the world's oldest university city, only received a theological faculty in 1365.

Quantitatively, the University of Paris was the alma mater of thirteenth-century Europe. Qualitatively, its theological faculty in fact constituted the intellectual capital of Europe: at the beginning of the 1270s there were about twenty-five professors of theology affiliated with about a hundred brilliant bachelors, all being over the age of thirty. While two of the three theological faculties were English, Oxford and Cambridge were much smaller than Paris, but during the course of the 1280s and 1290s, the Oxford masters were making contributions to theology on a par with their Parisian colleagues, and these faculties cherished exceptionally high standards.[40]

1.4   A SENIOR THEOLOGICAL STUDENT

The cumulative combination of philosophy and theology implied that it was necessary to be a 'professor of philosophy' to become a 'student of theology.' The highest quality in philosophy was a necessary condition for studying theology. Moreover, many a student found a job as master of arts (*magister artium*). Likewise, many theological students found appropriate positions in the course of their endless theological journey which, at Oxford, would take thirteen years to arrive at the doctorate when Duns was a graduate there.

A Franciscan student of theology was not only active in Church and faculty. An advanced student of theology usually trained younger students in doing logic and philosophy and he often taught in his own *studium*. He may have lectured in logic and philosophy

---

[40] See Cobban, *The Medieval English Universities*, 209–238.

for the benefit of the undergraduates and supervised exercises in debate and disputation. Although, in contrast with Bonaventure, Thomas Aquinas and Henry of Ghent, Duns was no *magister artium* – even in 1930 it was still believed that Duns produced his logical works in his capacity as *magister artium* – we cannot discern a difference, for all this was very much to the taste of the majoring student of divinity which Duns was. Faith and knowledge, theology and philosophical logic go hand in hand. From the second half of his twenties onwards John Duns was extremely productive, but the traditional hypothesis that Duns died at an age – the age of thirty-four – when one in general is only beginning to write is simply unfounded. Nevertheless, his productivity remains as mysterious as his genius. However, the theological world of the thirteenth century abounded in such mysteries.

1.4.1 Becoming a priest

It was in 1288 that Duns probably started his theological studies, and during the period around 1290 he experienced another high point of his life. He belonged to a university and a famous city, but was also linked with national and international life through his order and the Church. He loved it all very much. In the priesthood many aspects of this life were combined. Medieval church and society were protective of young lives. One had to be twenty-five in order to become a priest and about thirty-five to become a don of divinity. And so, on 17 March 1291, Duns was ordained a priest by Oliver Sutton, Bishop of Lincoln, in Northampton's St Andrew's Church, in the company of some colleagues, at the age of twenty-five.[41] Thus during Lent 1291 a boy's dream came true.

Franciscan spirituality turned around Christ, the eucharist and the priesthood. However, his ordination did not take place at Oxford as in the Middle Ages, there was no cathedral in the city.[42] It was not until 1542, during the reign of Henry VIII (1509–47), that Oxford became an independent diocese. The medieval Oxford was part of the very large diocese of Lincoln and consequently the University of Oxford did not originate from a cathedral school as did Paris University from the Cathedral School of the Notre Dame.

---

[41] See Longpré, 'L'ordination sacerdotale du Bx. Jean Duns Scot. Document du 17 mars 1291,' *AFH* 22 (1929) 54–62.
[42] See Cobban, *The Medieval English Universities*, 10–12 and 19–30.

1.4.2   The early logical writings

A senior student of theology could teach logic and philosophy, because he had himself already studied the arts and philosophy before beginning with theology. Although the theological students of the mendicant orders were granted dispensation from doing philosophy in the faculty of arts, they had to study philosophy thoroughly within their own *studium*. So, for Duns, the 1280s were also much occupied with studying the arts and philosophy.

When Duns had become a senior student of theology in the mid-1290s, he invested enormously in logic. The traditional approach to the philosophical works of a medieval theologian suggests that the works date from an early stage of his career and are considered to be the key to understanding the theological writings. This view does not hold generally, but dating Duns' logical works in this way must do so. Admiring Paris would soon call him the subtle teacher, but, as a student, he was already subtle, and working hard. During the first half of the 1290s he produced a long series of logical writings *per modum quaestionis*, not avoiding profound methodological and philosophical problems. His logical *Quaestiones*, occasioned by the logical writings of Aristotle and Porphyry, contain thorough and detailed logical investigations which offer a fascinating view of the frontline in contemporary logic and conceptual analysis.[43] Although many logical and philosophical works in the old editions turned out not to be authentic, the following logical writings survived modern textual criticism:

1. *Quaestiones super librum Porphyrii Isagoge*;
2. *Quaestiones super Praedicamenta Aristotelis*;
3. *Quaestiones super libros Perihermenias*;
4. *Quaestiones super librum Perihermenias. Opus alterum*;
5. *Quaestiones super librum Elenchorum Aristotelis*.[44]

---

[43] On the phenomenon of logical *quaestio*-'commentaries,' a rather recent introduction in about 1290, see Andrews, 'Andrew of Cornwall and the Reception of Modism in England,' in Ebbesen and Friedman (eds), *Medieval Analyses in Language and Cognition*, 107–113.

[44] See *Opera Omnia* I 153*–154* and §§3.6.2–3.6.6. Cf. §4.2 in particular, and Chapter 4 in general. Gedeon Gál thought that Duns wrote his logical works in Paris, around 1295–97. Both hypotheses I deem improbable. The alternative hypothesis that he wrote them in England between 1281 and 1287 is improbable too, because this hypothesis implies that Duns was about twenty years of age when he composed them. Cf. Andrews, 'Andrew of Cornwall,' in Ebbesen and Friedman (eds), *Medieval Analyses*, 105 note 1.

The general background of these logical works was primarily British. The young Duns was familiar with, among others, William of Sherwood, Kilwardby, Simon of Faversham and Andrew of Cornwall. 'Scotus was not a modist,'[45] and not a 'Scotist' either, because these writings, together with Duns' *Quaestiones super libros Metaphysicorum Aristotelis*, deliver a systematic riddle. The logic and semantics, epistemology and ontology of a medieval theologian are often the hermeneutical key to understanding his theological works, but where is this philosophy to be found? The philosophy of Robert Kilwardby offers much help for understanding his dogmatics and the same can be said of Henry of Ghent's *Syncategoreumata*, but this assumption does not work in the case of Duns' logical writings. Many problems, strategies and ideas may be recognized, but they are not close to the systematic fabric of *Lectura* I–II. The logical theories of *Lectura* I–II, which turn around his personal notion of *synchronic contingency* and play a decisive part in the *Lectura* reconstruction of theology, are missing in the early logical writings (see §1.6). The last three questions of Duns' early booklet *Quaestiones super librum Perihermenias. Opus alterum* discuss the possible truth value of several propositions.[46] In *Quaestio* 8.8 he deals with the thesis that

This will be the case and
It is possible that this will not be the case

are incompatible.[47] Two propositions are at stake:

It will be the case tomorrow

and

It is possible that it is not the case tomorrow.

---

[45] Andrews, 'Andrew of Cornwall,' in Ebbesen and Friedman (eds), *Medieval Analyses*, 114. According to Robert Andrews's hypothetical scenario, modistic ideas were first transmitted to England by Simon of Faversham, where they 'were criticized by Andrew of Cornwall, who then helped to shape Scotus' attitude towards modism' (ibid.). Pinborg looked on Scotus, the logician, as a modist: Pinborg, 'Speculative grammar,' *CHLMP* 262. See also Irène Rosier-Catach, 'Modisme, pré-modisme, proto-modisme: vers une définition modulaire,' in *Medieval Analyses*, 45–81, and Marmo, 'The Semantics of the Modistae,' in *Medieval Analyses*, 83–104.

[46] Wadding, *Opera Omnia Iohannis Duns Scoti* I 211–223 (= Vivès I 581–601).

[47] *Quaestiones super librum Perihermenias* 8.8: 'Ad aliud dico, quod non stant simul quod haec nunc sit determinative vera *hoc erit et hoc potest non fore.*' For the term 'synchronic contingency', see §§1.5–1.6.

The incompatibility of both propositions is argued for by Duns on the
basis of excluding synchronic contingency for the present:
Just as

> *You are white now*

and

> *It is possible that you are not white now*

are not compatible now, in the same way

> *It is true now that you will be white tomorrow*

and

> *It is true now that it is possible tomorrow that you are not white*

are not compatible. (ibid.)

Diachronic possibilities are acknowledged by Duns, but synchronic
alternatives are straightforwardly denied for the present and the
denial of synchronic alternatives for the future is based upon this
impossibility for the present.

The *Quaestiones super librum Elenchorum Aristotelis* present the
same world of thought.[48] The same view is presupposed in the theory
which is rejected in *Quaestio* 8.7–8. In fact, this theory utilizes intuitively ideas of synchronic contingency for the present and for the
future, but they are rejected by Duns. Finally, the research note in
Quaestio 8.11–14 explicitly tells us about an alternative theory
solving the problems Duns dealt with in the last three questions of his
booklet, by assuming that a proposition about the future is determin-
ately true. This theory links the idea of a definite truth value of a
proposition about the future with contingency. Duns notes himself
that in terms of this alternative theory the objections to be considered
can be handled in an alternative way, but in the last section of
Quaestio 8.14 it turns out to be that Duns is still not convinced.
However, in the near future he will embrace these ideas under the
pressure of his theological dilemmas. It is the same story again.
Theological dilemmas give birth to a new and alternative way of
thinking, but the moral of Duns' personal intellectual biography is
even more striking than the old story itself.

---

[48] Wadding, *Opera Omnia Iohannis Duns Scoti* I (= Vivès II 1–80). Ebbesen suggests the
approximate date of 1295 for Duns' *Quaestiones super librum Elenchorum* in his
Incertorum auctorum Quaestiones super Sophisticos Elenchos, XLII, cf. XXXVI.

On account of their contents, we conclude that the logical *quaestiones* originate from the years prior to the *Lectura*. Brampton has suggested that 'during this year 1301–2 Scotus probably lectured on the Porphyry, the Predicaments, the Perihermenias and the Elenchi, just as Ockham did in similar circumstances.'[49] This is unlikely.[50] According to this suggestion, Duns would have espoused quite different theories from the *Lectura* and the *Ordinatio* in between these works (see §1.8 and §2.2.1). The fact that Antonius Andreas witnessed Duns lecturing *super cathedram magistralem* on the *Isagogè* of Porphyry and the *Categoriae* of Aristotle as a master does not prove that Duns' logical writings on the works of the *logica vetus* date from the Parisian year of Duns' regency.[51] Duns' logical *quaestiones* form a marvellous starting point for investigating his development. If the view of medieval thought as an ongoing emancipation from ancient philosophy has some point, Duns himself symbolizes this development *in excelsis*. He wrestled so much with Aristotle that he missed Paris initially. Eventually, he overcame the basic dilemmas (see §1.8).

1.4.3 In sum

Becoming a *baccalaureus sententiarius* in the favorite Franciscan *studium* was as such a marvellous achievement. As a teaching 'apprentice' in about 1295 and the bachelor *designatus* of theology which he became in 1297, John Duns was a remarkable figure. While there were many excellent academic centers, there were only a few universities, particularly during the first century in the history of the university, and there were even less theological faculties than universities.

So becoming a master of theology was a true achievement and, in the medieval university, employment was guaranteed for such qualified doctors. Those who had fulfilled all the requirements for such a doctorate went on as *magister*. There was academic excellence in abundance. In addition to these assets, this Franciscan world was also first class from the human and spiritual points of view. Duns was involved in a most promising youth movement.

---

[49] Brampton, 'Duns Scotus at Oxford, 1288–1301,' *Franciscan Studies* 24 (1964) 17.

[50] Ockham's and Duns' circumstances were different. The Parisian requirements, conducting the *Collationes Parisienses*, and the revision of *Ordinatio* I are not taken into account, apart from the invincible obstacle of varying doctrines.

[51] See *Opera Omnia* I 151*. Compare Wolter, *God and Creatures*, XXIII, where he seems to place the philosophical works in the Parisian years. See also Chapters 14 and 16.

Finishing one's theological studies was an exciting affair. The competition – of which there is no longer any visible trace – must have been enormous, because a professor of theology was the tutor of only one *baccalaureus* in every baccalaureate year – there was only one *baccalaureus formatus* a year per chair. The last four years of Duns' Oxonian theological studies were related to his baccalaureate. In the University of Oxford a mendicant order enjoyed only one chair. This is the intellectual profile of Duns and his circle at the end of his twenties and at the beginning of his thirties in the mid-1290s.

However, there is more to the world than university life and scholarship. In the middle of the thirteenth century, the reign of the incompetent King Henry III (1234–58) led to a characteristic reconstruction of the English monarchy. Since 1254 the 'parliaments' played a role on their own. During the reign of King Edward I (1272–1307), the 'English Justinian,' the national consciousness was growing and successful reforms enhanced efficient goverment. Noble feudalism was transformed and embedded into a monarchial style. England started to become 'Great Britain': rule over Wales was effectuated and Edward I tried to establish his personal 'suzerainty' (sovereignty) over Scotland.[52] When Duns Scotus taught at Paris, the English king was forced to keep peace with France, but in the 1290s a century of peaceful relations between England and Scotland came to an end and those between England and France were still very tense. King and church were still at war because of the vehement conflicts between the king and the great archbishops of Canterbury: John Pecham OFM (1279–92) and Robert Winckelsey (1293–1313).

1.5 BACHELOR OF DIVINITY

A bachelor was a kind of assistant professor and his teaching was a substantial part of the theological curriculum. We incidentally know that Duns became *baccalaureus formatus* in 1300.[53] We have to remind ourselves that the degree student was a very exceptional figure, especially degree students of secular masters, but degree students of Franciscan masters as well, in comparison with the huge numbers of theological students in the numerous schools. The *sententiarii*

[52] See Treharne, 'Edward I of England,' *Encyclopaedia Britannica. Macropaedia* (1976), VI 434–436, and Powicke, *The Thirteenth Century*, on the wars between England and France. In 1294 Edward I forbade all shipping traffic between England and France.

[53] Cf. *PMA* 99. See Longpré, 'Philippe de Bridlington et le Bx. Duns Scot,' *AFH* 22 (1929) 587–588, and Little and Pelster, *Oxford Theology and Theologians*, 310 and 345.

'initiated this course with a solemn introductory sermon (the so-called *principium* or *introitus*, which could also comprise an additional disputation), and an act of commitment to orthodoxy.'[54]

The last stage of Oxonian theological studies may be sketched as follows: a student who was selected to become a bachelor of divinity started his first year of the last four by preparing the advanced course he had to deliver after one year of preparation as *baccalaureus sententiarius*. The next task the bachelor had to cope with was lecturing on the Bible in his capacity of *baccalaureus biblicus* in the penultimate year of his baccalaureate. During the last year he acted as *baccalaureus formatus,* supervising disputation exercises and assisting his own professor of theology in ordinary disputations, while he also had to participate in disputations and ceremonies of colleagues of his professor. According to this scheme we get the following picture:

1297–1298: preparing the course on the *Sententiae*;
1298–1299: *baccalaureus sententiarius* delivering his sentential course;
1299–1300: *baccalaureus biblicus*;
1300–1301: *baccalaureus formatus.*[55]

In Oxford the baccalaureate took three years and the *baccalaureus* first acted as *baccalaureus sententiarius*. The two first years of the last four years were occupied with the *Sententiae*. A *Sentences* collection presents systematically patristic texts in order to probe more deeply into the mysteries of faith. Thus *Sentences* are an arrangement of patristic views (*sententiae Patrum*) touching on all major Christian teaching. In systematic theology, the *Sententiae* of Peter Lombard (*c.*1100–60) had become the main text. The theological perspective of this dogmatic handbook lies in its Augustinian character. From the didactic point of view it was superior to alternative books which may have sprung from more creative minds, for example Robert of Melun's. At Paris Alexander of Hales started to use the *Sententiae* as his standard text for systematic theology in the beginning of the 1220s and by halfway through the thirteenth century this innovation had become a tradition in the Parisian faculty. The assistant professors had to show that they were able to handle the explicit, and implicit, problems of this handbook in an independent way.

[54] Roest, *A History of Franciscan Education*, 98 (98–99).
[55] The pattern of Oxford's study of theology was efficiently researched by Brampton: 'Duns Scotus at Oxford, 1288–1301,' *Franciscan Studies* 24 (1964) 5–20, who is also followed by Wolter, in Alluntis and Wolter, *God and creatures*, 19–21.

An attractive feature of the Oxford baccalaureate in theology was
that the future *baccalaureus sententiarius* had to study the whole
intricate web of theological theories in order to prepare his first grand
theological course. It was a sabbatical year in order to prepare the
course and this preparation took place during the year preceding the
first year of his baccalaureate.[56] Preparing the course was not a part
of the office of being a bachelor: it was just what had to be done
for the course required by the office of the baccalaureate.[57] This point
is very much reinforced by the mysteries surrounding Duns'
Quaestiones super libros Metaphysicorum Aristotelis (= *Quaestiones
Metaphysicae*). Duns had turned to the great spokesmen of non-
Christian philosophical thought – Aristotle, Avicenna and Averroes.
His early philosophical works testify to this fact in a remarkable
way. We know that the young Duns was very much impressed by
Aristotle – even in a boyish way – and by Avicenna as well. At the
level of explicit individual references, the great theologians are absent
in his logical writings but, from the start, the great theologians (*doctores nostri*) go side by side with the great philosophers in Duns'
Quaestiones Metaphysicae. Although Thomas Aquinas does not
seem to play a major role in the *Lectura*, the first theory to be discussed in the *Quaestiones Metaphysicae* is a contribution of Thomas
Aquinas. We know of Duns' fervent admiration of Aristotle and we
see the unique concentration of a young Augustinian scholar
wrestling with his thought. The scene of the problems facing Duns in
his first theological course is set by metaphysical questions, because
the first major project after the logical writings are his metaphysical
quaestiones. The tension is mirrored in the literature on the subject
for, in spite of their important role, from the start the contents and
nature of these *Quaestiones Metaphysicae* have given rise to wonder
and doubt.

Great theologians such as Augustine and Henry of Ghent are at
odds with the grand philosophical past of Western history.[58] To the
minds of Thomas Aquinas, Duns Scotus and many others in the
second half of the thirteenth century, the term 'philosophi' refers to
non-Christian thinkers. For them it is not a word signifying an

---

[56] See Vos, 'Johannes Duns Scotus,' *Kerk en Theologie* 36 (1985) 182. The same conclusions
are drawn by Catto, 'Theology and Theologians 1220–1320,' *The History of the University
of Oxford* I 505–506. Cf. Balic, 'The Life and Works of John Duns Scotus,' in Ryan and
Bonansea (eds), *Studies in Philosophy* III (1965) 10–11.

[57] Courtenay makes this point well: 'Scotus at Paris,' in Sileo (ed.), *Via Scoti* I 152.

[58] See *Lectura* I 3.339–341 and 412. Cf. Chapter 14.

implicit code or value of rationality, but a quasi-historical indication of thinkers in the context of an *auctoritates*-culture: 'philosophi' refers not so much to these thinkers in their historical setting as to their *texts*. According to post-1270/1277 theological thought, these texts represented a way of thought belonging to the past – an impressive past but, nevertheless, a dated past which had definitely gone. *Philosophy* stood for ancient philosophy as represented by Plato and Aristotle, by neoplatonism and the mistaken way of thought defended by Avicenna and Averroes.

Duns concentrated on the principal issues raised by the *philosophi* who followed a way of thought which excludes the very possibility of the Christian view of reality and of contingent revelation. What was at stake in this pervasive debate between non-Christian *philosophy* and the thought form of the theology of the church is whether Christian talk on God and theological theories are possible and tenable at all. John Duns was to challenge the non-Christian *philosophical* way of thought in quite a fundamental way and Duns himself was not so much interested in the question whether a position is incompatible with the views of a fundamental opponent, but whether a theory be inconsistent in itself and whether it be tenable at all. Therefore his dream was to meet the demands of the theology of salvation history and the trinitarian doctrine of God. He focused on a renewal of classic theology. In the wake of this tradition, Duns developed a well-reasoned refutation of the usually implicitly held view: everything is necessary and all states of affairs are necessary. Within this context, he discovered the potential of what I have named *synchronic contingency*.[59]

There was certainly a dream which guided and governed Duns' daily life, but because his life was an unfinished one we can only guess what his dream had been from the remnants of his output, and his output is very remarkable. Surely, this is a platitude. My generation was mainly trained according to the myth that medieval culture was simply monolithic and the lives of those remarkable women and men were simply 'more of the same.' It took me some time to see that my teachers – De Rijk being the great exception to this rule – and my textbooks meant only Aquinas when they said 'in the Middle Ages this is what one thought . . .', but we know now that there were many remarkable individuals, not just one. Duns' life is difficult to understand because the sources are scarce and because of its brevity – short

[59] See CV 13–14 and 27 ff. and CF 4–6 and 18 ff. Cf. KN 81–87 and 269–273.

lives hardly comment on themselves. Comment, reflection and interpretation are gifts which grow as we grow older, and Duns never grew
old. Although he understood most things better than we do, he never
became familiar with this aspect of life.

Great oeuvres are enigmatic, but we often forget this because they
are famous and great. Duns' oeuvre is enigmatic because it only consists of unfinished writings, and because it mirrors the terms of
medieval systematic culture during its last three centuries. The thirteenth, fourteenth and fifteenth centuries are the centuries when the
university flourished. In this academic world, the emphasis on
Aristotle in the general pool of systematic writers on philosophy and
theology is about 14 percent and the general Franciscan emphasis on
Aristotle is about 9 percent.[60] Duns' emphasis on Aristotle is about
50 percent in terms of the number of his works, with the large number
of eight on Aristotle and Porphyry and also eight theological works.
This emphasis is paralleled by the four works on the *Sentences*, again
a relatively large number (see Chapters 14 and 16).

The numbers of works on the *Sentences* discovered in medieval
manuscripts are nevertheless misleading because many secular teachers, even great masters, have left no 'commentaries' on the *Sententiae*,
for example Henry of Ghent or Godfrey of Fontaines, although they
must have delivered fascinating courses on the *Sentences*. It is in fact
quite noticeable if an author on the *Sententiae* turns out to have
written more than one sentential commentary or more than one
version of his commentary on the *Sententiae*. However, Duns Scotus'
case is very rare, both with respect to the *corpus aristotelicum* and to
the *Sententiae*. A general characteristic of systematic authors focusing on the *corpus aristotelicum* and on the *Sententiae* is mirrored by
Duns Scotus' works in a remarkable way. His oeuvre is just focused
on works on Aristotle and works on the *Sentences*, and in quite considerable numbers.

1.5.1 In sum

John Duns Scotus embodies the bipolar tension between medieval
theological and philosophical teaching. Within the context of his
theological and philosophical studies, he starts with Aristotle and
takes him utterly seriously. In reconstructing systematic theology he

---

[60] See Livesey, '*De viris illustribus et mediocribus*', *Franciscan Studies* 56 (1998) 201–237. Cf.
§16.3 where Livesey's research is dealt with. Nine percent of the books of the Franciscan
authors in Livesey's database are on Aristotle which is a low score.

continues to concentrate on eliciting philosophical answers from faith and theology. His personal movement from logical and philosophical questions and answers through theological questions to new philosophical answers is quite exceptional. The upshot is exceptional too. It was John Duns who, standing amid the collision of *fides* and *intellectus*, contributed most to the articulation of Christian thought, realizing that this was his calling. The study of the history of medieval philosophy which commenced in the nineteenth century by banning Scotus from the realm of rationality and philosophy can only be assessed to have been wrong (see §§15.1–15.3).

1.6 LECTURA I–II

Lectura I 39 presents the ramified systematics of the central notion of a specific type of *contingency* (see §7.3) which Gilson and Boehner have termed *radical contingency*. De Rijk called it also *Franciscan contingency*. It is precisely this scientific revolution that classic theology needed in order to become successful as consistent philosophy. This great enterprise took place in the course of 1297–98 – or shortly before – when Duns was preparing his course on the *Sententiae*. In the logical works, the theory of *synchronic contingency* is conspicuous by its absence or is even rejected, while during the second half of the 1290s the very idea will bloom into a fully ramified theory and become the conceptual nucleus of the whole of Duns' mature thought. In *Lectura* I–II Duns' insights into this type of *radical contingency* are present from the start, even in the *Prologus*. It intuitively pervades the entire book rather than appearing unexpectedly, although in *Lectura* I 39 we find the first clear theoretical presentation of it. Before the middle of the 1290s the concept was not even considered by Duns (see Chapters 15–16). In between, in the year during which he prepared his course – 1297–98 – his ideas took definite shape.

The theory of *synchronic contingency* is a view which classic theology was in great need of. The heart of this view is that our factual reality could have been different from what it is in fact and that it should often have been different. God's real activity is the focus. He acts contingently. God is essentially free. His world is created reality. Therefore, his acts of creation and recreation are free. Patristic theology had beaten ancient necessitarianism. It had already replaced philosophical cosmology by creation thought. The world turns, but the world could have turned otherwise. Things are now factually so, but it is possible at the same moment that they are not so. So, people are essentially free too. They could have acted differently and they often should have acted otherwise. This experience and insight revolutionized the understanding of human existence, the nature of nature and the nature of history.

Lectura I–II are the notes the young John Duns jotted down in preparing his first systematic course in theology. Because they are a teacher's notebook, they have been jotted down before the course to be given and because they are the notes of a *Sentences* course, they have been prepared before the course on the *Sentences* to be given by a bachelor of divinity. Here, we meet John Duns as assistant professor. In these personal notebooks (*cahiers*, *quaterni*) he also pencilled his additions and corrections. It is a youthful work to be considered a unique contribution to the history of Western thought and *Lectura* I 39 is its brilliant ontological kernel, permeating through the whole of the systematic fabric of the *Lectura*. However, *Lectura* I–II was forgotten for six centuries until Balic rediscovered it midway through the 1920s.[61] The *Lectura* is the key source for studying Duns Scotus. It is a presentation of his systematics from his doctrine of God and his ethics to his metaphilosophy, his logic and theory of science.

Lectura I–II is a thoroughly theological work. Nevertheless, it is a fact that it contains important insights belonging to logic and semantics. It is a song of faith in a logical-philosophical key, but there are also many provoking ontological solutions which arise from theological dilemmas as well. The tension originates from the familiar limitations and modal simplisms of Aristotelian conceptual structures. At the end of the thirteenth century, there is a concrete mixture of *logica modernorum* and *theologia antiqua* full of philosophical innovations. The faith of John Duns and his brothers, the followers of the little *poverello*, cannot be accounted for in terms of semantic, logical and ontological presuppositions which are basic to any form of necessitarianism. When one sticks to such views, the theory of divine properties and the doctrine of the incarnation reveal glaring inconsistencies. Philosophical theology and church dogmatics would be incoherent if Aristotle's logic, semantics and ontology were right. The logical differences between Duns' early logical and philosophical writings and his early theological master work illustrate this point.

---

[61] See Balic, *Les commentaires de Jean Duns Scot*, 56–87, where he only deals with the manuscripts V, P and R, and 117–127, where also *Codex Q II 21* of the Saint Francis Convent in Rome is dealt with. Nature and year of this Oxford Commentary are here undecided. See §3.6.8 and §3.6.12.

There is one puzzle we have still to face. Is John Duns' personal scientific revolution as sketched above not an intellectual *tour de force* simply beyond imagination? Again, if we look at Duns Scotus' texts we can see they divide into three kinds:

1. texts I call 'Aristotelian': the logical writings dating from the first half of the 1290s, showing no theological expertise and being doctrinally different from the *Lectura*;
2. texts we may call 'Scotist': displaying the world of thought, world-famous and prominently present in Western thought for half a millennium (*c*.1300 – *c*.1800); and
3. philosophical writings: showing off definite theological expertise but on main points different from the *Lectura*, namely the four first books of the *Quaestiones Metaphysicae* and the *Quaestiones de Anima* (see §1.5 and §§3.6.6–3.6.7).

The puzzle we have to consider seriously is the huge philosophical jump from the first group to the first 'Scotist' text, *Lectura* I–II, since there are only at the most five years in between. In the intermediate years before 1297–98 Duns' personal scientific revolution must have taken place. Evidently, the decisive factor consists in mature theological studies. This fact implies that John Duns stood on the shoulders of the preceding generations, particularly the generation of Richard of Middleton (d. *c*.1300) and Roger Marston (d. *c*.1303), Olivi (d. 1298) and Matthew of Acquasparta (d. 1302). However, a remarkable discovery, made by Stephen Dumont and published in 1995, contributes to narrowing the gap. More and more, it becomes clear how tremendous the 1290s must have been and Dumont was able to link Duns' innovations with some discoveries of Olivi. Olivi was a crucial link between Bonaventure and Duns Scotus. Probably, Olivi's discoveries date from the decade before 1297.

> The conception of the will as a power for opposites without succession is found, together with its argument, in Olivi. Indeed, the scenario of the instantaneously existing will, used by Scotus to argue for his new conception of possibility, is quite evidently nothing more than a restatement of the angel willing in the first instant of its creation. [62]

The extraordinary creativity of Olivi in this respect comes to the fore, if we compare his views with the parallel theories of Richard of Middleton who published his Commentary on the *Sententiae* in the

---

[62] Dumont, 'The Origin of Scotus's Synchronic Contingency', *The Modern Schoolman* 72 (1995) 167. See §7.10.

first half of the 1290s. The English Minor Middleton also subscribes
to the primacy of the will and there is a substantial consensus between
him and his younger Scottish *confrère*. The senior theological student
Duns must have been extraordinarily keen to master the most recent
literature, although he was weighed down sometimes under the bur-
den of so many massive commentaries on the *Sentences* and volumes
of disputed questions and quodlibets. Richard of Middleton's representative thinking is still beset with many a deadlock, most of which
dilemmas Duns is to solve in the very near future. Olivi opened up the
theoretical road, by solving the master dilemma of Christian thought
in his own way, but there is a snake in the grass. While Dumont did
prove textual dependence with regard to the Parisian text *Ordinatio* I
39, he did not with regard to *Lectura* I 39, where the argumentation
does not follow Olivian patterns.

1.7   *Baccalaureus biblicus and baccalaureus formatus*

Most theological faculties kept to the order of *baccaulaureus biblicus – baccalaureus sententiarius*, but in Oxford degree students were
engaged in lectures on the *Sentences* before moving on to cursory
and ordinary readings on the Bible.[63] In 1299 at the age of thirty-
three Duns acted as a biblical *baccalaureus*,[64] and had to lecture on
the Bible where everything had started a millenuim previously.
Theological scholarship had started with the Bible in the eleventh and
twelfth centuries as *sacra pagina*. The main task of the master of theology was to teach biblical theology. Here, the great decisions were
to be made. Biblical *auctoritates* held sway in the *sed contra*'s. In
1299–1300 Duns was teaching biblical theology before he moved on
to his duties as *baccalaureus formatus* in order to give guidance to
public disputations. Some fruits of the appointment to act as the *biblical bachelor* are found in the revised first part and the new second
part of the *Prologus* of his *Ordinatio*.

In the transition period between the academic years 1299–1300
and 1300–1301, say in the course of late spring and summer of 1300,
John Duns made a weighty decision: he decided to embark on a great

[63] See Roest, *A History of Franciscan Education*, 98.
[64] For the structure of the bachelor years in Oxford, see Brampton, 'Duns Scotus at Oxford,' *Franciscan Studies* 24 (1964) 18. For the Parisian curricula, see *PMA* 89–96 and 99–102. Cf. Catto, 'Theology and Theologians 1220–1320,' in Catto (ed.), *The History of the University of Oxford* I 505–507, and Wolter, 'Life and Work,' in Alluntis and Wolter, *God and Creatures*, XX.

new project. He started to write a new *Sententiae* book instead of simply revising his *Lectura*. In this far-reaching decision the conviction shines forth that he had to produce something new and something definitive. When we look at the tremendous revisions of the *Prologue* and the first distinctions of *Book* I, found in *Ordinatio* I, then we are aware of the immense task Duns had committed himself to. Moreover, the balance of discontinuity and continuity of this new program has to be stressed: there is a decisive systematic gap between *Lectura* I–II and the logical writings and *Ordinatio* I–II is based on *Lectura* I–II, but how do we know that Duns started to write his *Ordinatio* halfway through 1300?

There is the remarkable and unique fact that the *Prologus* of the *Ordinatio* mentions the name of Mohammed four times, while *Mahometus* is only mentioned in the *Prologus* and not in either *Lectura* I–II or *Ordinatio* I–II. Morover, in *Ordinatio Prologus* 112, Duns informs us that the cause of the Islam has been weakened very much in 1300 and that the end of it can be expected.[65] This statement reflects the short-term effects of the battle of Hims (23 December 1299). The news of this battle reached England in the summer of 1300 and the optimistic expectations did not last long.[66]

Prologus 112 belongs to the new second part, dealing with the sufficiency of Holy Scripture: this part reflects teaching Duns must have given during his biblical baccalaureate (1299–1300). The *Prologus* numbers 366 sections and when Duns left Oxford for Paris, he had arrived at *Ordinatio* I 10 (see §2.2.1). So, John Duns had only recently started to work on his *Ordinatio* when he jotted down the statement of *Prologus* 112, linked up with the summer of 1300.

1.7.1 Baccalaureus formatus

In 1300 Duns became *baccalaureus formatus*. There is a note in *Codex Q* 99 of the Library of Worcester Cathedral which reveals that 1300–01 was the final year of Duns' baccalaureate.[67] This perfectly refutes the hypothesis of Callebaut that Duns would have studied

---

[65] *Ordinatio Prologus* 112: 'In brevi [. . .] finietur, quia multum debilitata est anno Christi millesimo trecentesimo, et eius cultores multi mortui, et plurimi sunt fugati.'

[66] See Balic, *Les commentaires de Jean Duns Scot*, 41–43.

[67] See Catto, 'Theology and Theologians 1220–1320,' in Catto (ed.), *The History of the University of Oxford* I 506. The year of the course is, according to Catto, 1298–99. I have defended 1298–99 since 1982. The plan to write *The Philosophy of John Duns Scotus* arose in 1999.

at Paris in the 1290s as Jeremy Catto also pointed out (ibid.).[68]
'The University recognized only one regent at a time for each of
the Mendicant Orders,' while four mendicant orders held a chair in
the theological faculty: the Friars Preacher, the Friars Minor, the
Carmelites and the Austin Friars.[69] 'Necessary regency normally
lasted two years from the date of the conferment of the degree of
master or doctor in theology. The rule was not very strictly enforced,
and the period seems to have varied in practice from three years to a
year and a half or less' (ibid.). This 'necessary regency' system of the
theological faculty was derived from the 'necessary regency' system
of the faculty of arts, 'whereby every new master of arts had to teach
for the remainder of the year in which the degree was taken and for
one year further.'[70] So, the formed bachelor could only become the
successor of his master if that master resigned after a year and the
Minister Provincial and the Provincial Chapter appointed him.

1.7.2   *Ordinatio* I *and Collationes Oxonienses*

In *Ordinatio* I 2, we find a note which contains an unspecified reference to Duns' *collationes*: 'and elsewhere [. . .] in the *Collationes*.'[71]
This reference concerns an Oxonian *collatio*, but in a fascinating
research note appended to *Ordinatio* I 5.118 we meet the phrase '*in
Collationibus Oxoniensibus quaestione 1*':

> There is an argument against the thesis of the first difficulty in the
> *Collationes Oxonienses, quaestio* 1, and in *quaestio* 14, where its first
> part is found.[72]

What conclusions can be derived from this piece of evidence? The first
point to be made derives from the fact that the *collationes* are called
Oxonienses which implies that Duns did not live in Oxford at the time
of scribbling down this note, for it does not make sense to call a
writing *Oxonian* in Oxford. This comment must originate from Paris.

---

[68] See Callebaut, 'Le B. Jean Duns Scot étudiant à Paris vers 1293–1296,' *AFH* 17 (1924) 3–12,
and idem, 'Les séjours du B. Jean Duns Scot à Paris,' *La France franciscaine* 12 (1929)
353–374. See §2.2 and §2.4, cf. *DS* 30–33: Duns spent 1301–02 at Paris, while Catto opts
for a year at Cambridge (ibid.).

[69] Little, 'The Franciscan School at Oxford,' *Franciscan Papers*, 67.

[70] Cobban, *The Medieval English Universities*, 100, cf. 171–174.

[71] *Ordinatio* I 2.303: 'et ibi [. . .] in *Collationibus*.' On the function of a *collatio*, see Hamesse,
'" Collatio" et "reportatio": deux vocables spécifiques de la vie intellectuelle au moyen âge,'
in Weijers (ed.), *Terminologie de la vie intellectuelle au moyen âge*, 78–82.

[72] *Ordinatio* I 5.118: 'Contra conclusionem primae difficultatis, hic arguitur in *Collationibus
Oxoniensibus quaestione* 1, et in *quaestione* 14, ubi habetur pars eius prima.'

Second, referring to Oxonian *collationes* presupposes that by that time Duns had already written other reports. If there were only Oxonian *collationes*, then he would have referred to them simply as his *collationes*. So, when Duns added this note, he had already conducted some *collationes Parisienses*. Moreover, we have to assume that he had already finished all his Parisian *collationes* at that stage, because he refers to his *last* Parisian *collatio* in *Ordinatio* I 10.36. Third, *Collationes Oxonienses* 1 and 14 must be later than *Ordinatio* I 5, for Duns would not have appended a note if he had already written *Collationes Oxonienses* at the time of writing *Ordinatio* I 5. Otherwise, he would have referred to them in the basic text of his *Ordinatio*. Of course, he must have finished all his *Oxonian* reports when he added his Parisian notes.

In sum, the huge collection of Duns' *Collationes Oxonienses* is later than *Ordinatio* I 2–5 and the note belonging to *Ordinatio* I 5.118 not only presupposes a Parisian stay, but also Parisian *collationes*.[73] Most of the Oxonian part of *Ordinatio* I precedes the set of *Collationes Oxonienses*. A continuous series of references to both sets of Duns' *Collationes* is only found in *Ordinatio* I 2–10. Apparently, this points to *Ordinatio* I 10 as the borderline between the Oxonian and Parisian parts of *Ordinatio* I.[74] Therefore, I place *Ordinatio Prologus* and *Ordinatio* I 1–10 between the summer of 1300 and the period of the *collationes* conducted at Oxford and, so, *Collationes Oxonienses* have to placed in the first half of 1301: spring 1301 is the latest possible date for any Oxonian *collatio* (see §2.2.1).

The *Collationes Oxonienses* are testimony to Duns' argumentational acumen and theological creativity. The issue of divine knowledge is the central theme of the *Collationes Oxonienses*, while the future *Collationes Parisienses* focus on the divine will. In 'private' disputations in the Franciscan College additional training was given. Analysis of the *Collationes* is not an easy process because the *ars obligatoria* marks the line of argumentation in these exercises even more than in the *Lectura*, with the effect that it is often difficult to find the doctrinal solutions. Of course, those involved in the factual disputes were not aware of any complications because all participants knew quite well the rules of the game. So, they were able to identify immediately the moment the game was over and the bachelor had to

---

[73] The note was both appended and cancelled in Paris – cancelled, because *Ordinatio* I 5.119ff. offer the exposition asked for in the note.

[74] For a more elaborate defense of this hypothesis and of 1301–02 as the first year in Paris, see §2.2.1.

finish it by his final solution, although this is not easy to do for the present reader. It was vital to this type of theological training that the theological graduate was able to take seriously the insights and arguments of a view he did not share himself. This academic style is not self-centered.

1.7.3   The Bishop and the Franciscans

The year 1300–01 marked the regency of Philip of Bridlington, the twenty-ninth Franciscan master at Oxford, while Adam of Howden had been the twenty-eight master. Adam would soon teach at Cambridge, as the twenty-ninth Franciscan *lector* (1303).[75] However, the year of Philip's regency in Oxford was Duns' final year, for he acted as the *baccalaureus responsalis/formatus* under Bridlington, passing through the last stage of his theological studies.[76]

Both Adam and Philip were included in a list of twenty-two Franciscans at the Dorchester gathering presented by the English Provincial Hugh of Hertilpole to Dalderby, Bishop of Lincoln, on 26 July 1300. For all these Franciscan priests Hugh claimed a licence to hear confessions in their crowded church at Oxford.[77] In the summer of 1300 Duns is named *Iohannes Douns*.[78] We conclude that Duns was not only at Oxford at the time, but 'the very presence of Scotus' name on the list seems a solid argument that he would be in Oxford during the coming academic year at least, if not longer.'[79] Neither would it make much sense to act as *baccalaureus responsalis* and then leave for Paris in a few months time. Moreover, the system does not tolerate such arbitrary measures.

---

[75] See Moorman, *The Grey Friars in Cambridge*, 144 (and plate II) and 184.

[76] See Longpré, 'Philippe de Bridlington et le Bx. Duns Scot,' *AFH* 22 (1929) 587–588. The evidence is contained in *quaternus* VI, *quaestio* 20, in *MS Q* 99 of Worcester Cathedral. See Little and Pelster, *Oxford Theology and Theologians*, 310 and 345.

[77] See Little, *The Grey Friars in Oxford*, 63–64. We find this fact documented in the *Liber memorandorum* of John Dalderby, Bishop of Lincoln, who licensed six Franciscan brothers to hear confessions. Relevant extracts of this *Liber memorandorum* have been edited by Little, 'Documents I,' *Franciscan Papers*, 230–243 and 262.

[78] In 1892, Little identified the name 'Iohannes Douns' as the name of the famous Scotus. For the text concerning the Oxford Friars Minor (26 July 1300), see 'Documents I,' *Franciscan Papers*, 235, starting with the tenth name: '(. . .) Iohannem de Stapelton, Adam de Corf, Petrum de Todeswrth, Willelmum de Schirburn, Petrum de Baldeswell, Martinum de Alnewyk, *Iohannem Douns*, Fratrem Walterum Boseuille, Robertum de Couton, Rogerum de Alnewyk, Iohannem de Horley, Ricardum de Conigton, Thomam de Pontefracto.' Compare Emden, *A Biographical Register of the University of Oxford* I 607, and Catto, 'Theology and Theologians,' *The History of the University of Oxford* I 506.

[79] Wolter, 'Duns Scotus at Oxford,' in Sileo (ed.), *Via Scoti* I 187–188.

As to the request of Hertilpole, Duns was not a successful nominee, nor were any of the other candidates, including the bachelors. The Bishop was amazed at the large number of confessors the Provincial was asking for. He wondered whether this number was meant for all Franciscan houses in his large diocese, but according to the English Provincial all these twenty-two candidates were needed for the Friars' church at Oxford. To the Bishop four priests was a more rational number than twenty-two, but to show his understanding of the situation in Oxford he granted six confessors. The first name on the list was that of the Guardian of the House, John of Codington, and the next two were those of the outgoing and incoming masters of theology. Initially, the Bishop ignored them and chose the first six of the remaining list of nineteen, all experienced priests working exclusively in the ministry. Then the Bishop, himself a former master of theology, added Adam of Howden and Philip of Bridlington to his list.[80] In spite of all this, the careers of the thirteen rejected priests were nevertheless impressive: six became masters at Oxford or *lectores* and two bachelors eventually incepted at Paris: *Iohannes Douns* and Robert Cowton.[81]

'This group contained a number of prominent theologians working together at Oxford as masters and bachelors. [. . .] The activity and interaction of this impressive line of theologians is attested in the *Sentences* of William of Nottingham, who was just junior to the last of this group to become master at Oxford, William of Shirebourne.'[82] In fact, William of Shirebourne was the thirty-eighth Franciscan *lector* in Oxford.[83] Within the ranks of the poverty movement so greatly interested in Oxonian theology, there existed a network of brilliant young but not angry men, although in the fourteenth century the position of the English universities would become more isolated; for instance, 'before the 1380s [. . .] there were very few Germans who crossed the Channel for degrees in arts and theology at Oxford,'[84] nor did many Frenchmen either. Theology was a joyful science, academic activity a feast, surrounded by faith and

[80] See Clark (ed.), *Survey of the Antiquities of the City of Oxford composed in 1661–6, by Anthony Wood*, 386–387.

[81] See Little, 'Documents I,' *Franciscan Papers*, 231–235.

[82] Dumont, 'William of Ware, Richard of Conington and the *Collationes Oxonienses* of John Duns Scotus,' in Honnefelder, et al. (eds), *Metaphysics and Ethics*, 69.

[83] Dumont, 'William of Ware, Richard of Conington and the *Collationes Oxonienses* of John Duns Scotus,' in Honnefelder et al. (eds), *Metaphysics and Ethics*, 69.

[84] Courtenay, 'Study Abroad: German Students at Bologna, Paris, and Oxford,' in Courtenay and Miethke (eds), *Universities and Schooling in Medieval Society*, 29.

liturgy. The request of the English Minister Provincial also implies that they were eager to win souls for Christ. Their inspired ministry was accompanied by a vast popularity as their crowded church in South Oxford attested.

1.7.4 A theological debate

Stephen Dumont has ably shed new light on a ray of theological debate, elicited by Henry of Ghent's position on divine generation. Duns was not happy with Henry's solution, but many young colleagues stood firm to defend the leader of the previous generation during the first decade of the fourteenth century, among them William of Ware, Robert Cowton, Richard of Conington and William of Alnwick. In Paris, the influence of Henry of Ghent was less pervasive and the much more Aristotelian counterforce of thinkers like Godfrey of Fontaines and John of Pouilly was not only stronger but also more creative. There, the problem-solving power of Duns Scotus would be more existentially felt.

In Oxford, we meet Richard of Conington as one of the younger *fratres* of the *studium*. Richard of Conington would become the thirty-fourth *lector* at the Oxford convent. Indeed, John Duns himself might have been the thirtieth *lector*, were he not to have left Oxford for Paris in 1301. Robert Cowton might have been *sententiarius* at Oxford during the academic year 1299–1300 and so Richard of Conington might have been *sententiarius* in 1300–01.[85] Richard of Conington became master of theology at Oxford in 1305 at the earliest. We meet him again as the thirty-first master of theology at Cambridge, at the earliest in 1306–07.[86] He even rose to prominence as English Provincial (1310–16), immediately preceding William of Nottingham, at which time there were still strong links between Oxford and Cambridge. Therefore Little's thesis, that 'from about 1300 the practice [of strengthening Cambridge by sending distinguished teachers] entirely ceases,' is not completely true.[87] In fact, Duns' unexpected stay at Cambridge in 1304 fits in with a well-established tradition. A strand of lively debate is testified to by Duns' *Collatio* 27. According to my reconstruction of the debate,

---

[85] On Cowton, see Brown, 'Robert Cowton, O.F.M. and the Analogy of the Concept of Being,' *Franciscan Studies* 31 (1971) 5–40.

[86] See Moorman, *The Grey Friars in Cambridge*, 165, cf. 144–144a and 96 f.

[87] Little, 'The Friars and the Foundation of the Faculty of Theology in the University of Cambridge,' *Franciscan Papers*, 135.

Conington responded in his *Sententiae* course to Duns' criticisms of Henry of Ghent, documented in *Lectura* I 5. Duns' *Collatio* 27 (1301) is in turn a reply to Conington's *Sententiae* course. [88]

1.7.5 Magister Scoti

Since Adam of Howden came first, followed by Philip of Bridlington, we may conclude that Adam of Howden was the outgoing and Philip of Bridlington the incoming master of 1300. This fact throws light on the problem as to who was Duns' teacher in theology, though posing this problem is typically modern. In the *auctoritates* culture, manuscript society and university milieu of the thirteenth century things were rather different. Adam and Philip must have been slightly John's seniors. As bachelors they had been colleagues. In 1923, Pelster observed that we have some reason to say that there had been at least two masters of Duns Scotus at Paris: Alan of Tongeren and Giles of Loigny.[89] The same observation can be extended to the parallel situation at Oxford in 1300: Adam of Howden and Philip of Bridlington were Duns' masters at Oxford. By tradition, William of Ware was held to be Duns' *magister*. This view rests on the information found in the *Liber de Conformitate* (1399) of Bartholomew of Pisa (Pisanus) though Ehrle had refuted this view some twenty years before Pelster published his findings.[90] At the end of the fourteenth century and in the fifteenth century it was commonly held that Ware was the *magister Scoti*. However, this information is not confirmed by early

---

[88] According to Dumont, Scotus' *Collatio* 27 is a response to Conington's *Quodlibet*, probably 1305–06 ('William of Ware, Richard of Conington,' in Honnefelder et al. (eds), *Metaphysics and Ethics*, 77–85). The connection of Duns' *Collatio* 27 with 1305 or 1306, however, is improbable. Scotus was then the theological key figure of the Franciscans at Paris, involved in becoming doctor of divinity or acting as their new, long-expected *magister regens*. There was no occasion for a conference trip to Oxford. Unfortunately, the connection with Conington's *Sententiae* course I am assuming cannot be proven, because we are not in possession of his commentary. Nevertheless, the connection can be confirmed, since *Reportatio Parisiensis* I 5 informs us that Richard was *baccalaureus* at the time of his criticisms of Scotus' view. Of course, he was master when conducting his *quodlibet*. So, these criticisms must have been anterior to Duns' *Collatio* 27, anterior to his last half a year at Oxford, and anterior to his Parisian stay. See the evidence with Dumont, 'William of Ware, Richard of Conington,' in Honnefelder et al. (eds), *Metaphysics and Ethics* ,68 note 18.

[89] Pelster, 'Handschriftliches zu Skotus,' *FS* 10 (1923) 15.

[90] See *AFH* 4 (1906) 545 f., cf. 337, and the *explicit* of the Viennese *MS* 1424: 'Explicit 4us liber Varronis qui fuit magister Scoti sive doctoris subtilis.' This manuscript dates from the end of the fourteenth century. Cf. Pelster, 'Handschriftliches zu Skotus,' *FS* 10 (1923) 2–3. De Wulf dropped immediately the idea that Ware was the teacher of Duns. On Bartholomew of Pisa, see Moorman, *The Grey Friars in Cambridge*, 99 ff.

manuscripts. Moreover, Ehrle discovered too that early manuscripts do not ascribe the relevant *Sententiae* commentary to William of Ware but to William of la Mare.

1.7.6 Inceptor

Ehrle unearthed the meaning of *inceptor*. Apart from William of Ockham and Walter of Chatton, William of Ware and Robert Cowton had also been *inceptores*.[91] *Incipere* is a institutional term at Oxford and Paris. In Oxford a *baccalaureus formatus* is titled *inceptor*. After having read on the *Sententiae* the bachelors who set out for the doctorate had to participate in disputational exercises and to give guidance in debates and they had to preach during their last year before they could admitted to the *magisterium*.[92] William of Ware was posthumously called *inceptor*, so he was never a *magister theologiae*. Because he was no *magister theologiae*, he cannot have been the *magister Scoti*. Longpré failed to prove that William of Ware got his doctorate from Paris while Pelster presented a case for Ware not having published his Commentary on the *Sententiae* until about 1304–06.[93] So Ware must have been a younger Oxonian contemporary of Duns but, in its turn, this hypothesis is not probable either, because the name of William of Ware is missing from the list presented by Hertilpole to the Bishop of Lincoln.[94]

In sum, on the one hand, the theological bachelors worked every year under a different 'professor.' This pattern obtains for Adam of Howden, Philip of Bridlington and John Duns at Oxford and for Alan of Tongeren, Giles of Loigny and John Duns at Paris. Posing the problem in the modern way stems from the modern pre-eminence of the professor in the university system. This was not the medieval approach. The effect of the system of quick succession practised by the Dominicans and the Franciscans was in fact that the bachelors and the professors functioned as a single peer group. In the case of the famous secular masters, for example Henry of

---

[91] See Ehrle, *Der Sentenzenkommentar Peters von Candia, des Pisaners Papstes Alexanders V*, 3–6 and 81–83.

[92] The Statutes distinguish between *incipere in theologia* and *ad magisterium* (Ehrle, *Der Sentenzenkommentar Peters von Candia*, 81–82).

[93] See Pelster, 'Duns Scotus nach englischen Handschriften,' *Zeitschrift für katholische Theologie* 51 (1927) 67–68.

[94] The names after *Johannes Douns* are to be recognized as future bachelors. Moreover, it is one of the specialities of Cross's research to point out on a regular basis that Duns discusses the contributions of William of Ware. On Ware, see *HCPMA* 697–700.

Ghent and Godfrey of Fontaines, it would make much more sense to talk in terms of *the master of* . . ., but in this situation their bachelors were unable to incept because of the long tenure of these long-term masters. Because a secular master acted outside the context of an order, the chair was the only institutional factor which could protect him. The upshot is rather paradoxical: the great teachers and doctors did not have 'pupils' while those who were teachers for only a short while did. There was the enomous influence of the *doctores antiqui* like Bonaventure and Henry of Ghent. *Being the master of* . . . and *being the disciple of* . . . describes a custom much more from antiquity or the nineteenth century than it is a medieval idea related to the life of the university. In any articulated sense of being *the master of* . . ., there was no *magister Scoti*. However, Scotus himself would become *a* master, even *the* master, for many of his students, although this was not institutionally but personally motivated. In Paris he had to start again, from scratch as it were, since the achievements of his Oxonian baccalaureate did not count institutionally in Paris.

1.8   OXFORD AND PARIS

Apart from a few famous exceptions, such as Peter Abelard and his Héloïse, medieval scholarship is slow in discerning drama in the lives of medieval intellectuals. The big question of John Duns' biography arises from an odd mixture of stability and being on the move. The Scottish and English years stand out in terms of rest and stability. His family loved Saint Francis so he naturally espoused the optimistic Franciscan ideals and joined the celebrated ranks of the friends of Saint Francis. The focus of the three first decades of his life was dynamic and coherent development the culmination of which was the birth of consistent Christian thought. In fact, coherent creativity is the constant strain of Duns at Oxford. When John Duns was acting as *baccalaureus sententiarius* at Oxford, he was preparing himself for the Oxonian doctorate. He had not been selected for Parisian training for the theological doctorate, although the English Province was allowed to send two students to the Parisian *studium* at the expense of the Order.

> The choice of those who were to be trained at the Universities was in the hands of the Provincial Chapters, while the selected friars were known as *studentes de debito*. This, however, was not intended to prevent any individual convent from sending one or more of its men

to the University if it could afford to do so. Such students were known as *studentes de gracia.*[95]

Within this framework the English situation was unique. The system was also applicable to the theological faculties of the English universities but, as things stood, the English Province sent likewise two students *de debito* to the University of Paris. The English Minister Provincial had a powerful say in the decision to be made by the Provincial Chapter to select the candidates for Paris, but it was up to the Minister General to select the Parisian bachelors and to appoint the *baccalaureus formatus* in order to get the doctorate. In the flourishing theological societies of Oxford, Duns was acknowledged to be 'masterly.' However, although he belonged to the top echelons at Oxford, he had not been sent to the *studium* at Paris by the middle of the 1290s so was not considered absolutely theologically top-class at that point in time. Because John Duns initially prepared himself for the Oxonian doctorate and only went to Paris for the final baccalaureate stage, it has to be concluded that he had not been selected as a *studens de debito* in the mid-1290s. So, in the 1290s Duns did not go to Paris and, therefore, was never a *studens de debito* or a *studens de gratia* in the 1290s. Nor was he in 1301, for in 1301 he was destined to lecture on the *Sentences*. New questions require new anwers, and the crucial new questions concern the riddles of John Duns' life: why was he not sent to Paris in the mid-1290s and why was he sent in 1301?

In the surroundings of Oxford we meet the impressive Oxonian theologian Roger Marston who had already taught theology at Cambridge and Oxford.[96] He was the English Minister Provincial (1292–98) before John Duns became *sententiarius* in 1298. So it was Marston who initially passed over Duns. I have already suggested that this fact probably has to be linked with Duns' early obsessive interest in logic and Aristotle. Such interests were not at the top of Marston's list, and even after having resigned as Minister Provincial in 1298, he must have continued to be a powerful influence in his *studium* in Oxford.

At any rate, at the end of the 1290s the Franciscan leadership in England must have realized their mistake and sought opportunities to put right their decision. The change must have been caused by the

---

[95] Moorman, *The Grey Friars in Cambridge*, 20. On *studentes de gratia*, see Roest, *A History of Franciscan Education*, 20 f. and 31.

[96] See Etzkorn, 'Roger Marston,' *EP* V 168f., cf. Gilson, *HCPMA* 343 f. and 690 f. Cf. Pelster, 'Roger Marston O.F.M.,' *Scholastik* 3 (1928) 526–556.

impression the brilliant logician John Duns made in the field of theology in his quality as *sententiarius*. Now it was clear he was not only a very smart researcher, but that he was also a thinker. The moves needed to launch a new strategy must have been welcomed by the international leadership of the Order at Paris, because, according to the by-laws of the Franciscan Order, the appointment of the bachelors and, in particular, the *baccalaureus responsalis* and the new holder of the Franciscan chair at Paris University was under control of the Minister General.[97] When England sent a *baccalaureus formatus* of thirty-five years of age, it is clear that the Minister General must have been involved in this decision in order to safeguard its efficiency. His was the right to appoint. It is at this point we meet John Minio of Morrovalle (Minister General 1296–1302, Vicar General 1302–04) and Gonsalvo of Spain (Minister General 1304) who were to exert a decisive influence on Duns' personal life (§2.2.2 and §§2.4–2.5).

From the 1250s until the end of the 1320s, the Franciscan Minister General was usually a former Parisian master of divinity. This academic tradition for the Order's leadership had started with the distinguished example of Bonaventure, although even before Bonaventure several Ministers General were familiar with theological teaching. With Roest, we may relegate the alleged anti-rational origins of the Franciscans to the realm of fantasy. The triangle of the Cardinal Protector, the Minister General and the Parisian Master of Theology formed the centers of power within the Franciscans. Matthew of Acquasparta, John Minio of Morrovalle – both Cardinal Protector on the Franciscan side, linked by Matthew Rubei, advising the Pope and looking after the interests of the movement – and Gonsalvo of Spain must have paid attention to the case of John Duns over the years. In the spring of 1301, *Iohannes Duns*, thirty-five years of age, had satisfied the requirements for becoming a *magister* at Oxford. Nothing stood in his way to incept except the illustrious plans the leadership of the Order had for Duns in the future by sending him to the more prestigious university at Paris, Europe's *alma mater*.[98]

The form and contents of Duns' personal copy of Oxonian lecture notes in preparation in 1298–99, which have come to us as the

---

[97] See Denifle and Ehrle, *Archiv für Litteratur- und Kirchengeschichte des Mittelalters* VI 107: 'De fratribus lecturis sententias et ad magisterium praesentandis Parisius, minister provideat generalis'; cf. Denifle and Ehrle, *Archiv*, 55.

[98] Now I side with Courtenay that the hypothesis of a great number of bachelors waiting for inception is a speculative one. In CV 14–15 and CF 6, we accepted without question the view of Brampton and Wolter. Cf. Courtenay, 'Scotus at Paris,' in Sileo (ed.), *Via Scoti* I 152.

Lectura, testify to the quality of the schools and University of Oxford around 1300. Methodologically and systematically, new roads were being opened up. The years of Duns' baccalaureate meant the start of a new theological enterprise which would quickly spread all over Europe through the courageousness of its new ideas and the independence of its method. John Duns was a son of Oxford, and although he never taught in his capacity of *doctor theologiae* there:

> With Scotus the Oxford school of theology reached its zenith, for the first time it was the equal of Paris as a centre of original thought. He was the first of the Oxford masters strongly to influence thought in the older university, and the critical, independent spirit of fourteenth-century Oxford begins with him.[99]

Alan Cobban places this flourishing within a wider context:

> For most of the thirteenth century, Oxford theologians, it seems, followed in the intellectual wake of those of Paris, but by the 1280s, Oxford masters were making contributions to theological debates on a par with those made by their Parisian colleagues. Oxford's markedly original theological phase was inaugurated by Duns Scotus towards the close of the thirteenth century and reached its zenith in the first half of the fourteenth century. The intellectual distinction which this generated, combined with the fact that only Paris, Oxford and Cambridge, from their origins, Florence, from 1359, and Bologna, from 1364, had the right to promote to the doctoral degree in theology, made Oxford, and indeed Cambridge, attract a migratory stream of continental friars, and this influx was accentuated when Paris University fell into one of its recurrent states of disorder.[100]

---

[99] Catto, 'Theology and Theologians,' in Catto (ed.), *The History of the University of Oxford* I 505.

[100] Cobban, *The Medieval English Universities*, 214. For Duns' move from Oxford to Paris, see Wolter, in Alluntis and Wolter, *God and Creatures*, XX–XXI.

CHAPTER 2

Life II: Paris, Oxford, Cambridge, and Cologne

2.1 INTRODUCTION

The fourth Lateran Council coincided with the rise of the universities and of the new orders of friars, those of St Francis and St Dominic, and marked the beginning of a new era in the pastoral life of the church. When it called the direction of souls 'the art of arts' it made clear the purpose of the pastoral programme which its decrees laid upon bishops and clergy: an informed laity instructed by a reformed clergy. The clergy, who had to be disciplined, educated, orthodox and fitted by character and training for the direction of souls, were the key to its success. They had, in effect, to live good lives and to study theology. The friars grasped the full implication of the conciliar decrees and made a determined effort to put them into practice. Their studies always had a practical side: 'the purpose of study is preaching, and of preaching the salvation of souls', as Humbert of Romans (master general of the Dominicans 1254–63) put it. The studies of the friars were aimed at their apostolate of preaching in the pulpit and instruction in the confessional. This combination of learning and its practical application to Christian life made them indispensable to those committed to making a reality of the conciliar decrees.[1]

The young John Duns was committed to the ideals and expectations of his Order and the renewal program of the Church. Initially, he had missed Paris. At Oxford he had already been *professor designatus*. Now, after about twenty years in Oxford, he sailed for France. He would again be a teacher-student for years to come, going through a very tough program in the capital of Western learning. The years 1303–08 would see a series of events no one could have dreamt of in 1301: exile (1303–04); a new effort as *baccalaureus sententiarius* in Cambridge; a new chance in Paris (1304–06); a short Parisian professorship (1306–07), a last year in Germany because of an early

---

[1] Sheenan, 'The Religious Orders 1220–1370,' in *The History of the University of Oxford* I 193. See Roest, *A History of Franciscan Education*, chapter 7 (272–324): 'Preaching: Cornerstone of the Franciscan Educational Project.'

death – and all this happened within five years: Paris, Oxford, Cambridge, Paris again, Cologne. At the time, Duns did not know nor could he have known.

The Franciscan leadership had made a momentous decision and John Duns went to the Franciscan friary at Paris. The case of Duns teaching at Paris is a rather unique one. Usually, a foreign Franciscan *sententiarius* at Paris (a foreign *sententiarius* is a one who does not originate from the Franciscan Province *Francia*) had not already read on the *Sententiae* at another university before he went to Paris. When Duns started to read on the *Sentences* at Paris, he was already thirty-six of age. In comparison, Bonaventure had been thirty-three and Thomas Aquinas only twenty-seven when they embarked on their *Sententiae* courses in Paris.

Relatively speaking, then, Duns' arrival at Paris was a late one. Duns was a second choice for Paris, but once he had got his second chance, he believed in the power of new effort, although sending a professorial candidate to Paris at an earlier and a more convenient date would have been an easier move. This new development resulted in a pile of works, but these would remain unfinished. Nevertheless, they would change the trajectory of Western thought. Duns was a theological latecomer. Biographically, his life was short. Time battled with eternity.

It is clear that the leadership of the Franciscan movement took a huge interest in the personal career of John Duns after he had delivered his *Sententiae* course in Oxford, important as scientific theology was considered to be. The consequences for Duns' personal life were far-reaching. When he crossed the Channel in the late summer of 1301, nobody would have guessed at his funeral in November 1308.

Let us remind ourselves of the five distinct periods in the life of Duns constantly on the move: Paris I: two years (§2.2); Oxford: six months (§2.3.1); Cambridge: six months (§2.3.2); Paris II: about two and a half years (§§2.4–2.5 and §2.7); and Cologne: one and a half years (§2.7). The complicated literature on the subject is surveyed in §2.6. Duns' sojourns lasted from six months to two and a half years. In contrast to the maximum stability of his years in England, he had to cope with maximum instability during his years on the continent.

2.2   At Paris I: 1301–03

2.2.1   1301–02: the first Parisian year

Duns probably enrolled at Paris in the late summer of 1301 (see §2.2.2). By 1298, there were about 140 Franciscans living in the

Great Convent of the *Cordeliers*.[2] Since the days of Alexander of Hales (d.1245), the role of the Franciscans within theology had changed. His decision to enter the Franciscan Order caused a sensation in the academic world.[3] The Friars Minor had already arrived in 1219, just two years after the Dominicans, and even as early as 1217 has been suggested.[4] In 1223 the Franciscans received full confirmation from Honorius III (1216–27) and in 1228 there were thirty Friars living on grounds of the Benedictines of St Denis, preaching and saving souls. 'Already in 1230, they received episcopal permission to start with a new building program, now on a new site *intra muros* received from the Abbey of Saint-Germain-des-Prés,'[5] which itself was outside the city like Saint Victor.[6] Their site, near the university quarter, was enlarged in 1240, just four years after the world-famous theologian Alexander of Hales had received the Franciscan habit, and the Grand Couvent des Cordeliers was built. The church was consecrated in 1263, Bonaventure having being Minister General then for six years, and became one of the academic churches for preaching university sermons. Eventually, the street of their convent was renamed Rue des Cordeliers, intersecting the Rue de Saint Jacques at the Dominican Priory of Saint Jacques.[7] Both the street and the gate

---

[2] Moorman, *A History of the Franciscan Order*, 132.
[3] See Van Winden and Smits, *Bonaventura. Itinerarium*, 1–7. According to Weisheipl, there was hardly any theological teaching at all before Alexander became a Franciscan – see Weisheipl, *Friar Thomas d'Aquino*, 64 f. An alternative thesis states that John of La Rochelle had already been lecturing to the Franciscan community before 1236: see Roest, *A History of Franciscan Education*, 14.
[4] Cf. F. de Sessevalle, *Histoire générale de l'Ordre de Saint François* I 425.
[5] Roest, *A History of Franciscan Education*, 13 (11–21). The area of the *Grand Couvent des Cordeliers* is to be located between the following streets of the present district Saint-Germain-des-Prés: Rue Hautefeuille, Boulevard Saint Germain, Rue de l'Odéon, Rue Vaugirard, Rue Monsieur le Prince, Boulevard Saint Michel and Rue de l'École de Médecine. Only the old Refectory (*Réfectoire*) has survived, an impressive building of 20 by 60 metres with three floors in a style now very rare. It is to be found at the entrance of the *Ancienne Faculté de Médecine* (on the corner of Rue Hautefeuille and Rue de l'École de Médecine). A plaquette informs: 'Ici s'élevait l'ancien Couvent des Cordeliers où la Société des droits de l'homme et du citoyen connue sous le nom de Club des Cordeliers tint séance du 1791 à 1794.' I owe crucial information to Père Dr Luc Mathieu (Paris, 3 September 2002). Cf. Smits, 'Inleiding,' in Van Winden and Smits, *Bonaventura. Itinerarium*, 2 f., and consult the maps of medieval Paris on pp. 29 f.
[6] At the beginning of the French Revolution, the *Grand Couvent* was suppressed. The church was destroyed in 1795 and the friary itself in 1877. A simple restoration of the *Réfectoire* is now under way.
[7] See Weisheipl, *Friar Thomas d'Aquino*, 64 f. Now, there is a plaquette on the corner of Rue Soufflot and Rue Toullier (very near to Rue Saint Jacques) which indicates the site of the former Dominican friary: 'Emplacement du Couvent des Jacobins 1217–1790.'

of Saint Jacques owed their names to the many pilgrims on their way
to Santiago de Compostela in Spanish Galicia.

Innocent III (1198–1216) had allowed the university eight chairs
of theology in 1207 and by 1218 the theological faculty had twelve
chairs. After the 'Great Dispersion' (1229–31) the Friars Preachers
held two chairs and the Friars Minor one following 1236, because
Alexander of Hales retained his former chair. In 1258 three
more chairs were authorized to accommodate the Cistercians, the
Benedictines and the monks of Val-des-Écoliers. The faculty numbered about twenty-five chairs in the 1270s. Some thirty to forty students lived in the smaller convents, the Friars Preacher holding
position in between the smaller convents and the Franciscan friary
which was by far the largest. The Franciscan community numbered
173 members in 1303, while about forty-five students may have been
professional philosophical and theological scholars.[8] John Duns, soon
surnamed *Scotus*, must have felt impressed in the scholarly capital of
Europe with a population of more than 100,000 including over
10,000 students, while a population of no more than 25,000 inhab-
ited Rome, in sharp contrast to the half a million during her ancient
prosperity.

Nevertheless, we still need to discuss where Duns spent the year
1301–02. The evidence at our disposal tells us that at the end of the
year 1300–01, he had satisfied all baccalaureate requirements in
order to become a master at Oxford. At the beginning of the academic year 1302–03, he was teaching on the *Sentences* at the University
of Paris (see §2.2.2). Courtenay has defended the thesis that Duns was
at Paris during 1301–02. Why should Duns not have acted as a *magister regens* at Oxford during 1301–02, if he could not have started
at Paris before the year 1302–03 or if the Franciscan leadership did
not need him at Paris?

One might wonder when Duns would have been *baccalaureus biblicus* at Paris if he had not spent 1301–02 there, since at Paris one read
cursorily on the Bible before lecturing on the *Sententiae*. However, a
dispensation from the lectureship on the Bible was probably readily
granted to John Duns when he enrolled there, because he had already
become familiar with the text of the Bible.

> The normal course for a secular cleric at Paris was this: on becoming
> a bachelor, he was a *cursor biblicus* for one or two years before going

---

[8] Courtenay, 'The Parisian Franciscan Community in 1303,' *Franciscan Studies* 53 (1993)
163–165.

on to the *Sentences*. [. . .] Even from what little we know now, we can say that no Dominican ever lectured on the Bible when he came to Paris. A dispensation from this first lectureship was readily granted to Dominicans. [. . .] The purpose of the *cursor biblicus* was to familiarize himself and his students with the text of Scripture.[9]

However, the students of the orders were already familiar with the Bible. The policy of dispensation also bears on the Franciscans and the other orders. How did Duns proceed in writing his *Ordinatio*? In 1300 John Duns had decided to compose a new large-scale *Sententiae Book*, and not only to improve on his *Lectura*. During the summer of 1300 he was busy revising the Prologue. The collection of Duns' *Collationes Oxonienses* is at any rate later than *Ordinatio* I 5 and the relevant evidence to be found in *Ordinatio* I 2–10 presupposes Parisian *Collationes*. What point of *Ordinatio* I had Duns arrived at when he moved to Paris? Let us turn to *Ordinatio* I 10.

Ordinatio *I 10*

In *Ordinatio* I 5.118, Duns refers to some Oxonian debate reports (*collationes*), although the precritical tradition of his oeuvre did not know of any *collationes* conducted in Oxford at all (see §3.6.9). Wadding believed that all *collationes* were Parisian ones. The reference in *Ordinatio* I 5.118 implies that there were Oxonian *collationes*, but it also implies that Duns had other *collationes* not held at Oxford.[10] The alternative set of *collationes* must originate from Paris and this probable assumption is confirmed by the manuscript tradition (§3.6.10). The *liber Scoti* refers twice to *Collat. Paris*: in *Ordinatio* I 5 and I 10,[11] but there are already references to Parisian *collationes* in *Ordinatio* I 3. Duns' second reference to his *Collationes* in *Ordinatio* I 10 is also an unspecified one. In a note appended to *Ordinatio* I 3.370 it may be found – *Collationes*. It is, in fact, a reference to a Parisian *collatio*, while the first reference concerned an Oxonian *collatio*. Viewed in this light, the following reference found in a note added further on in *Ordinatio* I 3 is quite interesting: 'Look for an analysis of it in the *Collationes Parisienses*.'[12] After two

---

[9] Weisheipl, *Friar Thomas d'Aquino*, 50.

[10] For the chronological order of the Oxonian part of *Ordinatio* I and the *collationes Oxonienses*, see §1.7.

[11] See *Opera Omnia* I 20* and 22* (15*–28* list the critical notes of *Codex* A which are based on the *liber Scoti*).

[12] The note added to *Ordinatio* I 3.492 reads: 'Quaere in *Collationibus Parisiensibus*.'

unspecified references – one related to Oxford and one to Paris – Duns must have realized that such references are not very helpful. The result is that the remaining references to his *collationes* in *Ordinatio* I 3–10 and in the margins of the *liber Scoti* are all specific. Finally, there is a reference found in *Ordinatio* I 10.36. *Ordinatio* I 10 is a remarkable chapter. The references to Duns' *Collationes* come to an end after *Ordinatio* I 10. The first version of *Ordinatio* I 10 is a rather unfinished text form so that, in fact, Duns' own additions smoothly finish the chapter. Within the whole of the fascinating integral addition *Ordinatio* I 10.30–38, we read in *Ordinatio* I 10.36: 'Consult the last Parisian *collatio*.'[13]

Duns Scotus' Oxonian *collationes* reference in *Ordinatio* I 5 implies that Duns did not work in Oxford at the time when he pencilled down that note and that he had possession of a complete set of *Collationes Oxonienses* by then. However, the phrase 'the last Parisian *collatio*' does not imply that Duns did not live in Paris when he added this note: it only serves to distinguish the *Collationes Parisienses* from the *Collationes Oxonienses*. Here, the striking point is that it is the *last* Parisian *collatio* that is referred to. So, at the time of finishing *Ordinatio* I 10, Duns had a complete set of Parisian *Collationes* and these *Collationes Parisienses* must be prior to the present text form of *Ordinatio* I 10.

Moreover, Duns continued to work on his massive *Ordinatio* I when he had finished his Parisian series of *collationes*. Some distinction before *Ordinatio* I 10, or *Ordinatio* I 10 itself, must be the borderline between the Oxonian and Parisian parts of *Ordinatio* I. The whole of *Ordinatio* I 10 ff. is no Oxonian text, let alone an immature Oxonian text. It may be suggested that Duns picked up the thread of composing his *Ordinatio* by revising the Oxonian part of *Ordinatio* I – witness the references to his *collationes* which he had produced in the meantime all over *Ordinatio* I 2–10. However, the revision of *Ordinatio* I 10 was more than simply executing some alterations. The revision of the last part of *Ordinatio* I 10 simply boils down to finishing it. The fact that there are no added references to the *collationes* after *Ordinatio* I 10 can be explained in a simple way: there are no further additions for there was no text he could add to new references. Duns continued to work on his *opus magnum*,

[13] *Ordinatio* I 10.36: Quaere *in ultima collatione Parisiensi* (= *Collationes Parisienses* 19). The references to the *Collationes* are missing in *Opus Oxoniense* I (Wadding/Vivès). According to the Vatican counting, the last Parisian *collatio* is *Collatio* 13 (= Wadding/Vivès 20). See §3.6.10.

absorbing his earlier discoveries, and so his *Lectura* and *Collationes* are no longer referred to.

Oxford and Paris: 1301 and 1302

Before the *Reportatio Parisiensis* I course on systematic theology, Duns Scotus was busy creating *Ordinatio* I 10 ff., based on *Lectura* I 10 ff. Because of the chronological order *Collationes Parisienses* – the Parisian part of *Ordinatio* I – I place *Collationes Parisienses* in the autumn of 1301. For some time, Duns was so heavily involved in conducting his *collationes*, both at Oxford and at Paris, that working on his new *Sententiae Book* almost came to a standstill. The year of his move to Paris, 1301, was mainly the year of his *collationes*, both at Oxford and Paris, and 1302 was again a year devoted to *Sententiae* I, bringing to light both the largest part of *Ordinatio* I and the basis of *Reportatio Parisiensis* I. The production of *Collationes Parisienses* and the transformation of the largest part of *Lectura* I into *Ordinatio* I 10 ff. and of the beginning of *Lectura* II are arguments which compellingly support the hypothesis that Duns stayed at Paris during the academic year 1301–02. Finally, there is no room for them in the years to come.

Now, Duns adopted a different strategy. The Oxonian part consists of massive extensions, witness the voluminous Prologue and the first distinctions of *Ordinatio* I. With some exceptions, for example *Ordinatio* I 17 and the later distinction *Ordinatio* I 39, the revision is continued on a more modest scale, but the transition from Oxford to Paris also shows continuity. The chronology of 1301–02 makes understandable why Duns kept to his original plan to rewrite his *Lectura*, for he did so before his Parisian *Sententiae* I course. Moreover, we can grasp why *Reportatio Parisiensis* I covers much new ground. If Duns Scotus had decided to provide surplus value to his Parisian teaching on *Sententiae* I, then the strategy of dealing substantially with new issues is a natural one. However, at what point of the *Ordinatio* might Duns Scotus have arrived before resolutely embarking on his great *Reportatio Parisiensis* I and IV project?

Ordinatio *I–II and the* liber Scoti

There is the remarkable fact that *Codex* 137, to be found in the Municipal Library of Assisi (*Codex* A), closely follows the *Ordinatio* text of Book I and Book II up to *Ordinatio* II 2.485. When the copyist had finished the second part of *quaestio* 6, he no longer offers references to the *liber Scoti*, although he continued to write a fine *Ordinatio* version.[14] At that point, Duns' Parisian 1302 *Ordinatio* must have ended and the much more demanding *Reportatio Parisiensis* course took over. In §2.2.2, we shall see that Duns Scotus enjoyed the help of a *socius* in his first sentential year in Paris. Because there was no longer any need to continue this time-consuming task personally from the autumn of 1302 onwards, the most obvious conclusion to be drawn is that Duns had dropped this burdensome piece of work in Paris by then. So, two striking theses force themselves upon us: the largest part of *Ordinatio* I – in company with *Ordinatio* II 1–2 – and the basic text of *Reportatio Parisiensis* I belong to one and the same year and in Paris Duns Scotus no longer continued to write out his texts personally following that same autumn. Incidentally, the suggestion that there is a world of difference between the teaching of *Ordinatio* I as if it were immature Oxonian writing and *Reportatio Parisiensis* I is unfounded. Likewise, this hypothesis implies that *Lectura* I–II is an immature Oxonian work. Such views are the result of chronological confusion, overlooking a most striking scientific revolution.

2.2.2   1302–03: the second Parisian year

In 1301 Duns became acquainted with Gonsalvo of Spain, the future Minister General of the Franciscan Order (1304–13) and the academic year 1302–03 was the year of Gonsalvo's regency at Paris.[15] So, Gonsalvo was *baccalaureus responsalis*, or perhaps already regent master, when, among other things, Duns conducted his *collationes* during his first year at Paris. Gonsalvo, originating from Galicia (Spain) and Minister Provincial of the Franciscan Province of Santiago di Compostela (= Galicia) from 1290 until about 1297, would enjoy a meteoric rise in the Order in the years to come after the choice of a self-selected exile (June 1303). He had already become

---

[14] *Opera Omnia* VIII 4* f. The *Commissio Scotistica* assumes that the scribe utilized another reliable and kindred manuscript after *Ordinatio* II 2.485.

[15] Longpré, 'Gonzalve de Balboa et le B. Duns Scot,' *Études Franciscaines* 36 (1924) 640–646. Callebaut – and Gilson – followed Longpré in identifying the Spanish Minister General with a different Spanish Franciscan Gonsalvo of Balboa. See Callebaut, 'La maîtrise du Bx. Jean Duns Scot en 1305,' *AFH* 21 (1928) 209 note 1, and *HCPMA* 698. Amorós proved that Gonsalvo is not identical with Gonsalvo di Vallebone = Balboa (= Bilbao), who turned out to be a *procurator* of the Order in the fifteenth century – see his *Gonsalvi Hispani Quaestiones disputatae*, XIV–XXII. Cf. Longpré, 'Le primat de la volonté. Question inédite de Gonzalve de Balboa, O.F.M.,' *Études Franciscaines* 37 (1925) 170–181.

Minister Provincial of Castile in 1303 (1303–04).[16] The friendship between Gonsalvo and John Duns turned out to be very inspiring and of decisive importance to the future course of Duns' career, for Gonsalvo was a heartfelt admirer of his younger colleague.

At Paris, Duns had to teach courses on the *Sententiae* for the second time and during the academic year 1302–03 he read on *Sententiae* I and IV. *Lectura* I (1298) is the '*Vorlage*' of *Ordinatio* I and *Ordinatio* I must have been largely finished by the autumn of 1302 when Duns embarked on the ambitious project of his Parisian course on the *Sententiae*. Now, we meet another literary phenomenon: the *reportatio* – the lecture notes of a student or a secretary.[17] If a *reportatio* has been checked and supervised by the teacher himself, it is called a *reportatio examinata*. We are in possession of such a notebook of Duns' Parisian course on *Sententiae* I. In contrast with Oxford, the Parisian *baccalaureus sententiarius* enjoyed the assistance of a *socius* and Duns' first secretary was called Thomas. The achievement of writing the text of *Reportatio Parisiensis* I *Examinata* must be due to Duns' Parisian *socius* Thomas. The assistant (*socius*) prepared the copy, tracked down quotations and filled in arguments.[18]

Dating *Reportatio Parisiensis* I in the autumn and early winter of 1302–03 is due to the important colophon of the excellent *Codex F 69* of Worcester Cathedral, written only a few years after Duns' death, which reads concerning *Book* I as follows:

> Here end the *questions* on the first book of the *Sentences* given by brother J. of the Order of the Friars Minor at Paris in the year of the Lord thousand three hundred and two and the beginning of the third.

This colophon offers precious information on Duns lecturing on the first Book of the *Sententiae* at Paris in the autumn of 1302 and the beginning of 1303, the term ending in the first half of January. There is still another interesting colophon in the crucial Worcester *Codex F 69* which concerns Book IV and runs as follows:

> Here end the *questions* of *Sentences* (IV) given by the afore-mentioned brother J. in the House of Studies at Paris in the year of the Lord M CCC IIJ.[19]

---

[16] See Gál, 'Gonsalvus Hispanus,' *New Catholic Encyclopedia* VI 608 f.

[17] On *reportationes*, see Courtenay, 'Programs of Study and Genres of Scholastic Theological Production,' in Hamesse (ed.), *Manuels, programmes de cours*, 338–341.

[18] On Brother Thomas, see the end of this section. On the functions of a *socius*, see Courtenay, 'Programs of Study and Genres,' in Hamesse (ed.), *Manuels, programmes de cours*, 342 ff. See §3.6.11.

[19] See §3.6.11, and compare §3.2.

Duns taught on Book IV in the first half of 1303. So, the order of the books of the *Sententiae* to be lectured on is not the chronological one. Pelster was also able to prove on internal grounds that *Reportatio Parisiensis* IV is earlier than *Reportatio Parisiensis* II by pointing out that Duns extensively quotes from *Reportatio Parisiensis* IV 1 *quaestio* 1 in *Reportatio Parisiensis* II 1 *quaestio* 1 in replying to his Dominican *baccalaureus socius*. *Reportatio Parisiensis* II has to be referred to the autumn of 1304. This fact also mirrors the lively debate going on among bachelors belonging to different chairs.

The years 1300–02 were dominated by doctrines and problems lurking in *Sententiae* I, but in the first half of 1303 Duns had to lecture on *Sententiae* IV. The Parisian adventure constituted a real challenge for Duns. He had already written two substantial books on *Sententiae* I: *Lectura* I and *Ordinatio* I (1297–1302) and at the beginning of the academic year 1302–03 he decided to strike out on a new course. The next stage of his *Sententiae* courses offered an even more thrilling challenge to him, for now he had to lecture on *Sententiae* IV and the attention paid to *Sententiae* IV at Oxford must have been rather poor. Duns was eager to cope with a wealth of new problems. The courses of 1302–03 show an enormous amount of new materials: many new *quaestiones* in *Reportatio Parisiensis* I which do not run parallel with *Lectura* I, and a brand-new text on *Sententiae* IV. *Reportatio Parisiensis* I has much new material: fifty-two out of 129 *quaestiones* of the *Prologus* and *Book* I have no counterpart in *Lectura* I and *Ordinatio* I.[20] The Parisian course was not just 'more of the same.' Duns did everything possible to prove that he was the right choice, covering new ground both in *Reportatio Parisiensis* I and in *Reportatio Parisiensis* IV. Judging by *Reportatio Parisiensis* I and IV, he was already quite familiar with the Parisian scene.

Maestro *Gonsalvo* and Meister *Eckhart*

Not only were Gonsalvo's colleagues in the Franciscan *studium* remarkable men, but his colleagues in the neighboring Dominican *studium* of Saint Jacques were also worthy of note. In the academic year 1302–03 the Dominican chairs were held by Dietrich of Freiberg and Johannes Eckhart of Hohenheim – *Meister* Eckhart (b. c.1260), slightly Duns' senior. It was Gonsalvo's first year of regency and Eckhart's first year of regency as well, but Dietrich of Freiberg had

---

[20] See *Opera Omnia* XIX 35*. See also ibid., 55*–66*.

already acted as master since 1297.[21] These two theologians from Germany did not follow the mainstream of Dominican theology of those who taught in the wake of Saint Thomas Aquinas (*communiter loquentes*). They adhered to the *via Alberti* in a very specific form, embracing a mystical way of religious knowledge. *Meister* Dietrich was not only an influential mystic, but also an excellent physicist. His theory of individuality has points of contact with that of Duns Scotus.[22] Like Gonsalvo of Galicia and Duns Scotus, *Meister* Eckhart and *Meister* Dietrich would also leave Paris at the beginning of the summer of 1303. The Parisian professorial careers of both *Meister*s suffered from a sudden death in the King Philip the Fair crisis. Both *Maestro* Gonsalvo and *Meister* Eckhart already became provincial heads in their respective orders in the same year 1303: Gonsalvo in Spanish Castile and Eckhart in German Saxony. In contrast to Duns, Eckhart would teach in the Parisian chair, once held by Thomas Aquinas, for a second time (1311–13) but, in parallel with Duns, his last job was teaching at the Cologne *studium* of his order. *Meister* Eckhart probably died in Avignon (1327/1328).[23]

Duns Scotus, one of Gonsalvo's bachelors on the *Sentences*, must have known *Meister* Eckhart shortly before back in the city, but several scholars assume that a lively interaction had gone on between these two Parisian stars. Thomas Aquinas had defended the thesis that in God *existence* (*esse*) and *knowing* are identical, because *esse* is the ground of his knowing.

> This argument presupposes the primacy and excellence of *being* with respect to *knowing*. Eckhart was certainly aware that this was the doctrine of Aquinas; and he must have known that Duns Scotus also defended the primacy in God of being over knowledge, for in the very year that Eckhart was disputing this question at Paris (1302), the Subtle Doctor was in that city upholding this position in his commentary on the *Sentences*.

Maurer refers to *Reportata Parisiensia* I 8 in order to substantiate this claim.[24]

Klibansky and Maurer drew attention to a debate between Gonsalvo and *Meister* Eckhart on the primacy of the intellect or the

---

[21] See *HCPMA* 433–437 and 753–755, and Somerset, 'Dietrich of Freiberg,' *REP* III 69–71.

[22] See Krebs, *Studien über Meister Dietrich*, 38–40. Cf. Krebs, *Meister Dietrich*.

[23] See *HCPMA* 438–442; Beck, *Early German Philosophy*, 41–56; Schmidt, 'Theologen des Übergangs,' in Andresen (ed.), *Handbuch der Dogmen- und Theologiegeschichte* I 698–702; Fischer, *Meister Eckhart*; and Zum Brunn et al., *Maître Eckhart à Paris*.

[24] Maurer, *Master Eckhart. Parisian Questions and Prologues*, 15.

will. 'As Klibansky pointed out, Scotus would undoubtedly have participated as opponent, or more probably respondent, in the famous
dispute between Gonsalvus and Eckhart that year.'[25] Wéber even enumerates a series of points of doctrinal divergence to which Eckhart
would have critically reacted. This hypothesis assumes that Eckhart's
general target was not only the Franciscan view, but that Eckhart also
knew Duns' thought quite well.[26] For these authors, Duns is the *subtle
doctor*, but although he was *subtle* right from the start, he was not a
doctor then.

Maurer assumes that Eckhart immediately became familiar with
the results of Duns Scotus' ongoing courses on the *Sentences*.
However, this is highly improbable. At the University of Paris, dozens
of bachelors were lecturing on the *Sentences* at the time, piling up
every year thousands of pages crammed with brilliant notes. It takes
enough time to read the hundreds of pages of Duns' *Reportatio
Parisiensis* I and IV.[27] It was simply out of question that any master,
no matter how brilliant or how much of genius he might have been,
could have known what was going on in the world of the bachelors,
a dynamic group who had to discuss important issues with one
another continuously. Wéber utilizes the whole of Duns' oeuvre in
order to look for points of contact between Duns and Eckhart, but at
the time Duns had published nothing at all.

Maurer's view amounts to the hypothesis that Eckhart attacked
Duns' 'ontothéologie,' but this hypothesis cannot be true because
Duns' way of thought is no 'ontothéologie.' It is no 'ontothéologie',
simply because Duns claims that God's existence can be demonstrated
and, for that reason, existence cannot be the starting point of Duns'
way of thought on God. Duns' doctrine of God is not an explication
of his notion of *existence/being*. The transcendent nature of *being*
(*ens*) has in Duns' ontology quite a different importance. It bears on
the meaningfulness of theological language, since the denial of Duns'
approach simply entails the statement that God does not exist. So,
Klibansky's and Wolter's 'without any doubt' are rather exaggerated.

---

[25] Wolter, 'Duns Scotus at Oxford,' in Sileo (ed.), *Via Scoti* I 185. The Klibansky reference concerns Klibansky, *Commentarium de Eckardi magisterio. Magistri Eckardi Opera Latina*
   XIII, XXX–XXXIII. See also Boulnois's more prudent verdict in his excellent *Duns Scot*, 8.
[26] Wéber, 'Eckhart et l'ontothéologisme,' in Zum Brunn et al., *Maître Eckhart à Paris*, 13–83.
   See also A. de Libera, 'Les 'Raisons d'Eckhart,' ibid., 109–140, and Vignaux, 'Pour situer
   dans l'école une question d'Eckhart,' ibid., 141–154.
[27] Cf., for example, Balliol College: *Codex* 205, ff. 1–185 and *Codex* 206, ff. 143–269,
   respectively.

The *baccalaureus responsalis* of 1302–03 was the *baccalaureus formatus* during Gonsalvo's regency and by then Duns was certainly not a *baccalaureus formatus*, because – as *baccalaureus incipiens* – he had only started as a *baccalaureus sententiarius*. My guess would be that the next holder of the Franciscan chair – Alan of Tongeren – acted as *baccalaureus formatus* in that year and that Alexander of Alessandria or Albert of Metz was the first *baccalaureus sententiarius* and John Duns the second (see §2.4). We may assume that Duns had been present and had also participated in the course of the ongoing debate, but, as the beginning *baccalaureus sententiarius*, he was certainly not one of the main participants.

No historical evidence has been established regarding a possible exchange of ideas between *Meister* Eckhart and John the Scot. A clash between these great minds of European thought is surely an attractive fancy, but – *pace* Klein – the bare naked facts do not show any traces of Eckhart in Duns' oeuvre. Duns Scotus was very eager to keep in touch with the thought of the grand old men of the previous generation – not only with the doyens of his own preference, but also, for example, with Godfrey of Fontaines, certainly not a kindred spirit, and the colleagues who were slightly his juniors. However, no trace of Eckhart is found. Duns was not a character spontaneously to be drawn into easy conlicts. Duns simply let the matter drop. In terms of the Scotian design of systematic thought, the presumption that God is essentially only knowledge is patently false and simply incompatible with Trinitarian theology. He was very eager to analyze this central topic, but his target was the great representatives of non-Christian *philosophia* – Aristotle and Avicenna – not theologians. At any rate, it is evident that his master Gonsalvo was rather critical of *Meister* Eckhart's ideas, but Duns Scotus' style was different.

'The outrage of Paris'

In order to discover who were members of staff in the Franciscan *studium* of the *Cordeliers* we have to study the lists (*rotuli*) of the members of that House of Studies at that time. The key relates to the unpleasant tensions during the spring of 1303. In the *Archives Nationales* at Paris, Longpré discovered the documents containing the names of the friars who sided against Philip IV at the end of the academic year 1302–03.[28] Before Longpré's discovery, we were only

[28] Longpré, 'Le B. Jean Duns Scot. Pour le Saint Siège,' *La France franciscaine* 11 (1928) 137–162.

acquainted with the list which mentioned the theologians who agreed with the King. However, Little, Pelster and Harris, following Pelster, did not realize that the list they paid attention to only dealt with the King's supporters. So, they offered an incorrect interpretation of the list, convinced that Duns was also on its, including all the Franciscans of the *studium*. According to this interpretation, Duns would have supported Philip IV, but then we would no longer be able to explain why Duns had to go into exile. So, we have to look again at the list known to Little and Callebaut, and Pelster and Harris: there we meet the names of the masters Alan of Tongeren and John of Tongeren, and of the bachelors Giles of Loigny and Martin of Abbeville.[29] In addition to these names on the traditional list, we find the names of Gonsalvo and his *socius* and John Scotus and his *socius* in the list discovered by Longpré.[30]

All in all, we meet the former master Gonsalvo of Spain and his *socius*, the masters Alan of Tongeren and John of Tongeren and their bachelors Giles of Loigny and Martin of Abbeville, and Gonsalvo's favorite Duns Scotus and his *socius* Thomas. In 1303, John of Tongeren was also master of theology and a Franciscan. Nevertheless, it would be wrong to insert John into the succession line of holders of the Franciscan chair at Paris. John of Tongeren was already master of theology before 1300 and was elected Premonstratensian abbot of Vicoigne in 1301. The next year, he entered the Franciscan Order and returned to Paris. His fellow townsman, Alan of Tongeren, regent master from 1303 to 1305 (but not teaching at Paris from June 1303 to the summer of 1304), might have been instrumental in the transition of John of Tongeren to the Franciscans.[31] Gonsalvo of Spain was the regent master during the academic year 1302–03, but in June 1303 Alan of Tongeren was already the upholder of the Franciscan chair. The fact that Alan of Tongeren is called *magister* indicates his role at that time. There is the characteristic feature that Gonsalvo is said to be in company with his *socius*, and not in company with his *baccalaureus*, as is said of Alan and John of Tongeren. This feature points to the fact that he was no longer regent master at the time of

[29] See Callebaut, 'La patrie du B. Jean Duns Scot,' *AFH* 10 (1917) 5 (5–7): '[. . .] Religiosi viri fratres *Alanus* et *Iohannes de Tongres*, ordinis fratrum minorum, magistri in theologia, de conventu eiusdem ordinis Parisius; item fratres *Egidius de Longniaco* et *Martinus de Abbatisvilla*, baccalarii in theologia eiusdem conventus.' Cf. Harris, *Duns Scotus* I 31 note 3.

[30] See the list published by Longpré, 'Le Bx. Jean Duns Scot. Pour le Saint Siège,' *La France franciscaine* 11 (1928) 147–149. See also §1.2.

[31] See Glorieux, *Répertoire des maîtres en théologie de Paris au XIIIe siècle* II, 202 f.

the expulsion. In the winter or Lent of 1305 we shall meet Alan of Tongeren again in his role of outgoing master (see §§2.4–2.6).

From 1296, problems beset the relationship between Boniface VIII and the French King Philip IV the Fair and such political and military events were to affect Duns' life very much in the years to come. After the abortive Council of Rome in November 1302, the tensions between these two opponents culminated in a vehement conflict. The bull *Unam Sanctam* was soon answered by Philip IV the Fair who rallied national opinion during the spring of 1303. At the end of June 1303, the king commanded the theologians who disagreed with his policy to leave the country within three days (25–28 June). Duns Scotus was among them. In August, Boniface VIII responded by suspending the university's right to to grant degrees. The ban against the university paralyzed its life. The King even arranged a violent attack on the person of the Pope – 'the outrage of Anagni.' Boniface's sudden death in the autumn of 1303 drastically changed the course of events again.

The lists (*rotuli*) mentioned above provide some fascinating details. First, we get a marvelous idea of the entire population of the Parisian *studium*, for they reveal that there were 173 residents. Second, we conclude from an analysis of these lists that a small group of about ten friars was involved in the last stages of the degree program of the theological faculty, while dozens of them were involved in professional academic studies.[32] Third, we see on which side Duns' sympathies lay, being definitely against the quasi-enlightened despotism of Philip IV. Duns shares the viewpoint of Gonsalvo of Spain and Albert of Metz, Matthew of Acquasparta (d.1302) and his cardinal successor, John Minio of Morrovalle, Minister General (1296–1302) and the Vicar General of the Franciscan Order at that time.[33] Fourth, it is to be observed that the Franciscan Tongeren party opted for the King and that the Gonsalvo party was against. There is also the interesting detail that there is no trace of any tension between these two parties.

We also meet three English brothers: *Fr. guillermus anglicus, Fr. johannes crombe* and *Fr. thomas anglicus.* Little and Wolter,

[32] See Courtenay, 'The Parisian Franciscan Community in 1303,' *Franciscan Studies* 53 (1993) 155–173, and idem, 'Between pope and king. The Parisian letters of adhesion of 1303,' *Speculum* 71 (1996) 577–605.

[33] Matthew of Acquasparta was professor of theology at Paris (1276–77), lector *Sacri Palatii*, as successor of John Pecham (1279–87), Minister General 1287–89, cardinal from 1288, and the Cardinal Protector of the Order. See Brown, 'Matthew of Aquasparta,' *REP* VI 201–203.

among others, identified *Fr. guillermus anglicus*, listed among the consenting party, with William of Alnwick.[34] However, it is utterly improbable that an English friar who was a friend and devoted kindred spirit of John Duns sided with King Philip the Fair, and it has also been proven that William of Alnwick was not in Paris at the time. Neither had he been Duns' *socius* in Oxford, because an Oxonian *sententiarius* did not have a *socius*.[35] The hypothesis that Duns was not a *studens de debito* is also confirmed by the lists, because there were already three Englishmen, the maximum number of students originating from one and the same province.

Apart from the nature of Duns' commitment in this political drama, there is quite an interesting detail to be observed in the *rotulus* which mentions Duns:

> *Fr. johannes scotus*
> *Fr. thomas eius socius.*[36]

As well as the theological masters Gonsalvo and Alan of Tongeren and John of Tongeren, Duns too had a *socius*. The position of *sententiarius* which Duns held at that moment was that of a privileged bachelor. At Paris the *baccalaureus sententiarius* of the Franciscans and Dominicans was accompanied by a *socius*, while, usually, only theological masters enjoyed such company.[37] Without the assistance of his Parisian *socii*, Duns Scotus could never have achieved what he in fact did in his Parisian years. It seems a reasonable guess that the so-called *reportatio maior* of the Parisian course on *Book* I, which is a very long text, has to be linked up with Duns' personal assistant Thomas. The *reportatio maior* is much longer than other *reportationes* which are still extant and it gives a carefully corrected and enlarged text. This also explains the several kinds of differences between the known *reportationes*. Moreover, it is a *reportatio examinata*, from which fact

---

[34] Little, 'Chronological Notes on the Life of Duns Scotus,' *English Historical Review* 47 (1932) 576. Consult the lists published by Longpré, 'Le Bx. Jean Duns Scot. Pour le Saint Siège,' *La France franciscaine* 11 (1928) 147 and 149.

[35] Compare the size of *Lectura* I and II with the size of, for example, *Reportatio Parisiensis* I and *Reportatio Parisiensis* IV. The absence of *Sentences Commentaries* in the biographies of theological masters who were secular priests, for example Henry of Ghent and Godfrey of Fontaines, indicates the importance of the *socius* in the life of the bachelors of the grand mendicant orders.

[36] See Longpré, 'Le B. Jean Duns Scot. Pour le Saint Siège,' *La France franciscaine* 11 (1928) 150, and compare the photocopy on p. 151: lines 12 and 13.

[37] Cf. Longpré's comments, 'Le B. Jean Duns Scot. Pour le Saint Siège,' *La France franciscaine* 11 (1928) 156.

we may derive several conclusions. The history of Duns Scotus' life and works is a history of misnomers. The *Reportatio Examinata* is rooted in the genre of the *reportationes*, but it is in fact no *reportatio*, just as the *Ordinatio* is not an *ordinatio*. This *reportatio examinata* has the value of an *ordinatio*.

The availability of such a definitive version implies that Duns Scotus never intended to integrate most of these *reportatio* materials into the *Ordinatio*. Such a plan would have been impracticable. Duns' decision to write a definitive *Sententiae* commentary was made when he had only written *Lectura* I–II. The new Parisian baccalaureate created new challenges and opportunities and new problems. Duns saw that dropping the original plan of revising his early *Lectura* would have been the end of his ambitious *Ordinatio* project. Even if we abstract from the circumstances of the summer of 1303, I do not think that Duns ever resolved to prepare a *Reportatio Parisiensis* IV *examinata*, for he did not have a *Lectura* IV: *Reportatio Parisiensis* IV is the foundation of *Ordinatio* IV. Both the course and the book *Reportatio Parisiensis* I *examinata* belong, I think, to the year 1302–03. Duns received in his capacity of *sententiarius* a great deal of support from his *socius*. The fact that he was given such an able *socius* testifies to the special interest the Order invested in its precious Parisian members.

2.3 OXFORD: AT HOME AGAIN AND *BACCALAUREUS SENTENTIARIUS* AT CAMBRIDGE

What happened to Duns amid all these stormy affairs? The 1303 exile of Duns not only upset Duns' personal expectations, but also the expectations, calculations and scholarly ambitions of the Franciscan Order. When Duns was suddenly banished from Paris, and France, he had nowhere to stay. From Gonsalvo's letter of November 1304 we deduce that Albert of Metz was still not back in town at the end of 1304 (§2.4). Gonsalvo himself had gone to Spain. The first thing a friar in such a troubled situation could do was to return to his original House of Studies. So, Duns spent the next period of his life at Oxford. However, Oxford was unable to solve the new pressing problem in his life. What could be done? Let us look at the first provisional move and at the strategy employed by the Franciscan Order in coping with John Duns Scotus' dilemma.

2.3.1   Oxford: at home again (1303)

The world of the Franciscan *studium* at Paris in general, and the Duns
Scotus circle in particular, were disappointed by the main academic
effect of the war beteen King and Pope: the University of Paris was
closed. For Duns, the most reasonable thing to be done was to return
to Oxford, to his own original *studium*, where disillusions beset him.
During the autumn, the leading circles of the Order had to overcome
the deadlock, but what did John Duns himself do in the meantime?
What might he have done, now that he was back in his mother house,
an exulant without a specific appointment and without the valuable
degree of being a *magister theologiae*. For the moment, he was a
former *baccalaureus formatus* of Oxford and an ex-*baccalaureus sententiarius* of Paris. What did he have on his desk, either at Oxford or
in the library of the Parisian *studium*? An already impressive list of
manuscripts can be shown: logical works, the *Quaestiones super
libros Metaphysicorum Aristotelis*, the *Collationes* collections,
Lectura I–II, *Ordinatio* I, *Reportatio Parisiensis* I and *Reportatio
Parisiensis* IV. So, one aspect of Duns' *Sententiae* production is conspicuous by its absence: a treatment of *Sententiae* III is still missing in
Duns Scotus' pile of contributions on the *Sententiae*, for he had still
not lectured substantially on *Sententiae* III.

   One of the challenges of Scotist scholarship consists in having to
account for the remarkable and enigmatic fact that two Oxonian
Reportatio Parisiensis codices and a Polish manuscript have a double
Sententiae III text. Balliol's *Codex* 206, ff. 105–151, and Merton's
Codex 62, ff. 229–260, have excellent text forms of *Reportatio
Parisiensis* III 1–17 (see §3.6.11). Both manuscripts – *Codex* 206,
ff. 1–104, and *Codex* 62, ff. 124–228 – also contain a second text,
covering the whole of the material of *Book* III (see §3.6.12). Let us
term this *Sententiae* III text *Sententiae* III*.

   It is a remarkable fact that *Sententiae* III* is quite different from
Reportatio Parisiensis III 1–17 and so it cannot be identical with
Reportatio Parisiensis III. However, *Sententiae* III* can neither be
identified with *Ordinatio* III (= *Opus Oxoniense* III), although there
are many links. Is it then possible to frame a hypothesis so that
Sententiae III* fits in somewhere in Duns Scotus' biography? Duns
lectured no less than three times on the *Sententiae*: in Oxford, Paris
and Cambridge. At any rate, *Sententiae* III* does not belong immediately to the unit *Lectura* I–II. The manuscript traditions are entirely
different, because *Sententiae* III* is missing in the codices which

contain *Lectura* I or II texts (see §3.6.8). Moreover, *Sententiae* III* presupposes that Duns had already worked in Paris, for in *Sententiae* III* 5.14 Duns informed the listener that he had already dealt with the issue under consideration at Paris: 'I have said so and so in Paris.'[38] So, this piece of evidence rules out the *Lectura* I–II years. However, dating *Sententiae* III* after his *second* Parisian stay (1304–07) is an impossible option, because it would lead us to Cologne where Duns Scotus must already have written *Ordinatio* III (= *Opus Oxoniense* III). It has to be concluded that *Sententiae* III* must be placed in the period between the two Parisian stays: the year 1303–04. Moreover, *Sententiae* III* cannot be linked with Cambridge where Duns only lectured on *Sententiae* I (see §2.3.2). This hypothesis also fits in with the facts that by 1303 Duns had still not lectured on *Sententiae* III and that *Sententiae* III* is neither identical with *Reportatio Parisiensis* III not with *Ordinatio* III (= *Opus Oxoniense* III).

So, hypothetically *Sententiae* III* fits in here remarkably well. However, the formal critical device of introducing the *quaestio* of a distinction is here *quaeritur*, not *quaero*, which presupposes that these lectures have been delivered by a *baccalaureus*, as *quaero* is the form used by a *magister*. So the text must belong to Duns' *pre*-master period in so far as it has to be placed after June 1303. Moreover, the formal critical devices of introducing a *distinctio* by adding *circa* (prim)*am distinctionem* and *quaeritur* (in the case of a bachelor) refers to the Oxonian setting.[39] So, *Sententiae* III* has to be styled *Lectura* III or *Lectura Oxoniensis* III, to be placed *after Paris* I. Oxford 1303–04 is the only possibility. We have arrived at Duns Scotus' year of exile in England, but since we also have to assume a sojourn in Canterburg (§2.3.2), the order Oxford sojourn – Canterburg sojourn is much more probable than the other way round. Therefore, *Lectura* III dates from the first half of the academic year 1303–04 (the autumn of 1303) in Oxford. Finally, the item of information: 'I have said so and so in Paris' (*Lectura* III 5.14: 'Dixi Parisius') also entails that *Lectura Oxoniensis* III is in fact a *reportatio*, because it has been written as a *reportatio*. Moreover, there is a moving personal testimony to be identified and, particularly, to be listened to.

---

[38] *Lectura* III 5.14: 'Dixi Parisius' (*Opera Omnia* XX 161). See also Balic, *Les Commentaires de Jean Duns Scot*, 153. Cf. *Opera Omnia* XIX 33* note 4 and *DS* 55 f.

[39] The elements *circa* (prim)*am distinctionem* and *quaeritur* are usually missing in the Parisian texts. They begin straightforwardly with the pattern *utrum . . ., an . . . .*

Comfort in disaster

At the peak of his personal disaster, Duns' spirituality makes an entrance and the way it does so is unique. His theological foundation has its own existential color. God is good and his doing is doing well. All the same we have to be made free *for* God. We have to love Him for Himself, without immediate self-interest, inspired and absorbed by the endless goodness and attractiveness of his character. In Duns' expositions on hope, charity (love) and faith he indirectly sketches his own spiritual life. The argument regularly passes on to the personal 'I' and is supported by his own longing and intense expectation in order to reach out to Him who is absolutely good and infinitely communicative.

The experience of faith shows that hope is distinctive. We live from expectation and what we expect is as such something good. Expectation is built on desire. He who is infinitely good arouses our desire most intensely. Such a desire can be hope or can be despair. In the experience of faith God is present, in the experience of hope He is absent, but He who cannot disappoint is then present in our expectations of the One who is hoped for, just as an expected one is – as the expected one – present in our longings for her or for him: that is hope. We are longing for Him to be ours. He has to be our God. Then there is the very personal sentence: 'I do not give up the act of desiring.'[40] Thus hope is a very personal act of the will as is love.[41] However, this existential solution did not solve the urgency of Duns' scholarly life. Still, Scotus was not a master of theology.

Conclusion

John Duns did cope with the pressing dilemmas of his personal biography by concentrating on his only great lacuna, *Sententiae* III, during the autumn of 1303. The text must be Oxonian and is a mature

---

[40] *Lectura* III 26.14 (*Codex 206*, Balliol College, 82r): 'Spes est virtus theologica alia a caritate et fide, quod ex actu patet. Experimur enim in nobis nos posse habere aliquem actum expectandi bonum infinitum et desiderandi summum bonum ut liberaliter se communicans [. . .], sed ille actus non est actus caritatis, nec fidei, nec aliquius virtutis moralis et est actus ordinatus, igitur est alicuius alterius virtutis quam dico *spem*. Est theologica, quia habet Deum pro obiecto immediato, quia per hunc actum desidero bonum infinitum, nec per aliquid additum distrahitur quin sit obiectum illius actus. Licet enim desidero istud bonum esse *meum*, ad huc bonum infinitum est obiectum, quia *non recedo* ab actu desiderandi ipsum.' See §12.11.

[41] *Lectura* III 26 (*Codex 209*, 82v ff.). See Vos, 'Ein Profil der Scotischen Spiritualität,' in Schneider, (ed.), *Scotus. Seine Spiritualität und Ethik*, 97 ff.

prolongation of *Lectura* I–II. In contrast to *Ordinatio* IV, which has to be linked with *Reportatio Parisiensis* IV, *Ordinatio* III is based on *Lectura* III, just as *Ordinatio* I–II are based on *Lectura* I–II.

2.3.2   Baccalaureus sententiarius at Cambridge (1304)

The University of Paris had almost a monopoly on theological degrees on the continent in the thirteenth century, but it is remarkable that both English universities also enjoyed this rare privilege. There existed a Faculty of Theology at the University of Cambridge in the middle of the thirteenth century, the Franciscans having been quite instrumental in achieving this.[42] Against this background, a hypothesis can be framed in order to solve the question where Duns may have spent the second half of the academic year 1303–04.

The administrative bodies of the international Franciscan Order and the English Province also had to face the case of John Duns. Where could he go? Everyone was eager to see him as a professor of theology, but Oxford was over and Paris had been blocked. There were only three university faculties of theology where brilliant upcoming men in theology could take their degree of *doctor theologiae*. So the only possibility left was Cambridge.

The assumed Cantabrigian solution is a natural one. The Franciscans had a *studium generale* at Cambridge.[43] They had founded a *studium generale* in Oxford (1229–30), soon after they had arrived in England, and the fourth Minister Provincial of the English Province, William of Nottingham (1240–54), bestowed the same status on the School in Cambridge. Such a *studium generale* functioned as a theological research college where, in general, logic and philosophy were also taught to a very high standard. The way Franciscan masters were recruited at Cambridge in the thirteenth century differed from the way practised in the fourteenth century:

> What strikes one about these early masters of the Friars Minor at Cambridge is the very large proportion of men who had taken their degrees elsewhere. It looks as if the position of the Faculty of Theology at Cambridge were not firmly established and the rulers of

---

[42] On the Cambridge *studium*, see Roest, *A History of Franciscan Education*, 24–27.

[43] Little, 'The Friars and the Foundation of the Faculty of Theology in the University of Cambridge,' *Franciscan Papers*, 131 and 137–138. For the *studia generalia* in Oxford, see Sheehan, 'The Religious Orders 1220–1370,' in *The History of the University of Oxford* I 193–201.

the Franciscan Province of England were strengthening it by sending
a succession of their most experienced and distinguished members,
who had already had the *jus ubique docendi*, as teachers.[44]

However, this policy seems to have ceased only after the mastership
of Richard of Conington (see §§1.6–1.7). From the list of
Cantabrigian Franciscan masters we learn that Adam of Howden, the
outgoing Oxonian master of 1300, was the twenty-ninth master and
Richard of Conington, slightly Duns' junior in Oxford and Oxonian
master during the academic year 1305–06, was the thirty-first
master.[45] In the Cantabrigian succession, Richard of Sloley was the
thirty-eighth *lector* and Henry of Cossey, Ockham's contemporary,
the forty-sixth.[46] In the year 1303 Roger Marston died at Cambridge
and the academic year 1303–04 was by any account a stormy one for
the Franciscan community at Cambridge, because it was Cambridge's
turn to suffer in the series of conflicts between secular and mendicant
masters in 1303.[47]

Eventually, the leadership of the Franciscan Order probably opted
for a completion of Duns' theological studies in the only theological
faculty of Europe left open to him. The natural answer to the question where Duns was to go seems to be to the Franciscan *studium* at
Cambridge, but is there evidence to confirm the hypothesis that Duns
delivered a course on the *Sententiae* at Cambridge?

First of all, there is a text added to the beginning of *Ordinatio* I 4.
In fact, the whole of the first part (*Ordinatio* I 4.1–6) is added to the
original pattern of *Lectura* I 4 which runs parallel to *Ordinatio* I 4
from *Ordinatio* I 4.7 onwards, containing references to Cantabrigian
and Parisian *quaestiones*. *Ordinatio* I 4.1 runs as follows:

> Another question concerns '(an)other'. It is found in the *Cantabrigian
> quaestio*: just as in the case of all concrete terms, whether they are sub-
> stantival or adjectival. Therefore, they are not counted as possessing

---

[44] Little, 'The Friars and the Foundation of the Faculty of Theology in the University of
Cambridge,' *Franciscan Papers*, 135. The whole list is given at pp. 133 f.

[45] For Richard of Conington's works, see Doucet, 'L'oeuvre scolastique de Richard de
Conington O.F.M.,' *AFH* 29 (1936) 396–442. See also §1.7, including notes 75 ff.

[46] Little, 'The Friars and the Foundation of the Faculty of Theology in the University of
Cambridge, *Franciscan Papers*, 133: '*Magistri Fratrum Minorum Cantabrigie*. [. . .] 29ᵘˢ
Fr. *Adam de Houeden*' sed incepit Oxon'. 30ᵘˢ Ricardus de Trillek. 31ᵘˢ Fr. *Ricardus de
Coniton*', sed incepit Oxon'. et resumpsit Cant'. 32ᵘˢ Fr. Symon de Saxlinham. 33ᵘˢ
Fr. Ricardus de Grymeston'. 34ᵘˢ Fr. I. de Wateley. 35ᵘˢ Fr. W. de Doffeld. 36ᵘˢ Fr. Rogerus
Dunemede. 37ᵘˢ Fr. Walterus Beafou. 38ᵘˢ *Ricardus de Slolee*.'

[47] See Moorman, *The Grey Friars in Cambridge*, 35 ff., and Roest, *A History of Franciscan
Education*, 62–64. On Paris and Oxford, cf. Roest, ibid., 51–62.

a form. There is still another question, which is a well-known one, whether 'God generates God', and that *Cantabrigian quaestio* can be an article of it.[48]

Therefore there is a Cantabrigian commentary on *Sententiae* I, for Duns himself refers to a Cantabrigian question, even indicating that its text had to be integrated into the definitive text of *Ordinatio* I 4, just as he refers to Parisian questions. A *Sententiae* commentary usually presupposes the teaching activity of a *sententiarius* – directly or indirectly.

Second, the Cantabrigian adventure gave rise to a rather special contact Duns evidently appreciated very much. He became acquainted with the secular priest Henry of Harcley who became one of the most important English innovators between Duns Scotus and William of Ockham. He was born near London about 1272 and was ordained a priest in 1297. He must have been acting as an Oxonian bachelor around 1303–04 when, quite unexpectedly, Duns spent a year in England.[49] For Henry of Harcley, Duns Scotus must already have been a celebrity, but the striking fact is that Duns also took very seriously the new Oxonian star. All this can be gleaned from some enigmatic features of the Oxonian part of *Ordinatio* I.

During his long search for the meaning of the abbreviation *q. cant'*, Balic also collected a series of other enigmatic abbreviations which are absent in *Lectura* I but occur in *Ordinatio* I, namely in *Ordinatio* I 2,242, *Ordinatio* I 3.44 and 123 f. and *Ordinatio* I 8.184 f.[50] In most cases, Balic took *artil'/arcl'* and so on to mean *articulus*.[51] This must be wrong, for this interpretation cannot explain *artil'/arcil'* (*Cant'*) in *Ordinatio* I 2.242 where, eventually, Balic himself read *Harcley* (= *Arcellinus*), *Cantabrigiae*. For the copyist of *Codex A*, the meaning of *artil'/arcil'* is evidently a riddle, although *A* has *arcl'* several times. So there is scarcely any reason to read *articulus* on the basis of the

---

[48] *Ordinatio* I 4. 1: 'Alia quaestio, de "alius". Habetur *in quaestione cantabrigiensi*, sed sic, sicut in omnibus concretis, sive substantivis sive adiectivis – quare non numerantur sicut habens formam. Alia quaestio, communis, "an Deus generet Deum," cuius *illa cantabrigiensis* potest esse articulus.'

[49] See *HCPMA* 480–484; Molland, 'Henry of Harclay,' *REP* III 360–363; Balic, 'Henricus de Harcley et Scotus,' *Mélanges offerts à Étienne Gilson*, 93–121. Cf. Pelster, 'Heinrich von Harclay,' *Miscellanea Francesco Ehrle*, 307–356, and Maurer, 'Henry of Harclay,' *EP* III 476f.

[50] For example, *artil'/arcil'* (*Cant'*), *artlᵖ/arclᵖ*, *arˡᵘˢ*, *arcl'* (especially in *Codex A*), *arˡ* (*cant'*) (especially in *R*, but also in several other manuscripts) and *har.* (*cant'*) and *Harkeley* in *Codex D*. Consult the §§ of *Ordinatio* I referred to and Balic's final elaborate exposition in *Opera Omnia* IV (1956) 6*–46*.

[51] *Ordinatio* I 8.185, addition *a*, however, simply reads: *Arcl'inus*.

occurrences of the enigmatic *artil'/arcil'* and other manuscripts are familiar with the name of the author meant by the curious abbreviation *arcl'* or the mysterious name *Arcellinus*, which was still a puzzle in the 1930s and 1940s.[52]

The upshot of all this is an outstanding series of six references to Henry of Harcley, all found in later additions to the original main text of the Oxonian part of *Ordinatio* I, which mostly concern the issue of the nature of divine self-knowledge. Henry's output can hardly be linked with John Duns' final years at Oxford. Here the enigmatic abbreviation *artil'/arcil' Cant'* comes in. It cannot mean: *the Cantabrigian Harcley*, for there was no Harcley from Cambridge. However, the desperate search for the meanings of *q. cant* and *artil'/arcil'* (*Cant'*) led to Balic's discovery of Henry of Harcley's *Sententiae* I in *Codex Vat. latinus 13687* and *Sententiae* II in *Codex Vat. Borghese 346, ff. 1–94*.[53] In his *Sententiae* I, Harcley again and again discusses views of *Ioannes* (= John Duns), but when Duns replies to Harcley in *Ordinatio* I 2.242 ff., he also made use of his own *Cambridge* text on *Sententiae* I, as textual agreements between *Ordinatio* I 2.223 and 242 ff. and the *Reportatio Cantabrigiensis* I 2 text, as the editors of the critical edition have styled it, make clear.[54] Duns' note must mean that he discussed a proposal taken from Harcley's *Sententiae* I Commentary which had examined a theory from Duns' *Cantabrigian* I 2. Revising a rather old part of *Ordinatio* I, Duns made use of his own *Cantabrigian* I. In short, when Duns was finally revising his *Ordinatio* I, he paid attention to Harcley who had used parts of Duns' Cantabrigian Commentary in his course on the *Sententiae*. In the eyes of Henry of Harcley (1272–1317), later to be a Chancellor of the University of Oxford, John Duns was already a celebrity by 1304. Harcley quickly adopted many of Duns' conclusions and was one of the first to lecture on them and to spread Duns Scotus' fame in England.[55]

[52] The combination of, for example, Aristotle and the mysterious abbreviation also shows that an author must be meant, just as *Ordinatio* I 3.123 shows: 'Concordant Aristoteles et Arcl.'

[53] See *Opera Omnia* IV 7*–15*. For the relationship between Harcley and Duns Scotus' disciple Alfred Gonter, see *Opera Omnia* IV 15*. Cf. also Pelster, 'Theologisch und philosophisch bedeutsame Quästionen des W. van Macclesfield O.P., H. von Harclay in *Cod. 501* Troyes,' *Scholastik* 28 (1953) 222–240.

[54] For the exact evidence, see *Opera Omnia* IV 29*–31*.

[55] Harcley also indicated that Duns acted as *sententiarius* at Cambridge, for he quotes from Cantabrigian lecture notes on *Sententiae* I; cf. Catto, 'Theology and Theologians 1220–1320,' in *The History of the University of Oxford* I 511, and Wolter, 'Reflections about Scotus's Early Works,' in Honnefelder et al. (eds), *Metaphysics and Ethics*, 49 f.

Third, the hypothesis of a temporary stay at Cambridge is confirmed by an interesting note appended to *Ordinatio* II 1.277, where Duns Scotus discusses the issue of transcendent terms. At the end of this paragraph, Duns adds an objection to what he has defended in that same paragraph in an inserted note, referring to *Richardus Sloley*.[56] Richard of Sloley (or Slolee) OFM, originating from Sloley in present-day Norfolk, worked during the first decades of the fourteenth century at Cambridge, where he also became master of theology – the thirty-eighth master.[57] No works of his have yet been found, and this reference can only be explained by assuming that Duns became familiar with Sloley's ideas at Cambridge where he must have taught on the *Sentences*. This is also in line with Duns' eagerness to discuss points with colleague bachelors.[58] The teaching of Richard of Sloley – who came from Norfolk, being in the custody of Cambridge, together with fifteen others out of the first forty-six masters – was exclusively linked with Cambridge, so Duns can only have known him in Cambridge.

Fourth, the editors identify the reference *in quaestione cantabrigiensi* in *Ordinatio* I 4.1 as referring to a *Sententiae* I text, to be found in *Codex 12* of the Public Library of Todi (Italy).[59] To my mind, it is a *lectura*, not a *reportatio*, because by then Franciscan bachelors did not work with a *socius* in Cambridge (see §3.6.13) – so though I would like to term it *Lectura Cantabrigiensis* I, I shall follow the common tradition: *Reportatio Cantabrigiensis* I.

For all these reasons, I opt for Cambridge as the university city where Duns taught during the second half of the academic year 1303–04.

---

[56] *Ordinatio* II 1.177ª: '*Adnotatio interpolata*: *Richardus Sloley* – contra primam responsionem.' Cf. Index Nominum s.v. *Richardus de Sloley* (*Opera Omnia* VII 622). The editors take *Sloley* as the name of a place by adding *de* to *Sloley*. It is to be noticed that Duns only writes *Sloley*.

[57] See §2.3.2, note 46.

[58] See Little, 'The Friars and the Foundation of the Faculty of Theology in the University of Cambridge,' *Franciscan Papers*, 133 and 139. On Richard de Sloler or Slolee, see also Moorman, *The Grey Friars in Cambridge 1225–1538*, 144: 'Richard de Slolee 1318–1319' (143–145 (Appendix A): the list of the Cambridge *lectores*, taken from Little (ed.), *Thomas Eccleston. De Adventu Fratrum Minorum in Angliam*, 73); cf. the potted, but empty, biography on p. 210. Moorman's date is rather late. I like to suggest the first half of the 1310s.

[59] See *Opera Omnia* IV 1, note 3: namely in *Reportatione Cantabrigiensi* (= Rep. IC; cf. infra nota 5). Note 5 provides the evidence takem from Cod. Tudert. comm. 12, f. 140*va*. On *Reportatio Cantabrigiensis* I being identical with *Reportatio IC* see *Opera Omnia* I 145*: *Quaestiones in* I *Sententiarum* e) opus ineditum. Cod.: Tuderti (= at Todi), bibl. commun. (= Public Library), cod. 12, ff. 121*ra*–192*vb*.

2.4   AT PARIS II: *BACCALAUREUS* 1304–06

Fortunately, new events in Paris in the spring of 1304 rendered the Cantabrigian solution of a future mastership for Duns superfluous. As soon as the situation between the new Pope Benedict XI (1303–04) and the French King Philip IV improved, the ban against the University of Paris was lifted in April 1304 so that the university could be reopened. The Pentecost Assemblies of the Dominican and the Franciscan Orders made arrangements to deal with the troubled situation. The Dominican General Chapter at Toulouse was also attended by Dietrich of Freiberg, former master of theology at Paris, and at that time *diffinitor* (also *elector?*) of his German Province (see §2.2.2). At that moment, the *Meister* Dietrich and Eckhart were no longer Parisian *magistri regentes*. Both versatile men already held high offices in their order. Hypotheses which assume that the predicaments of the Franciscans and Dominicans in Paris ran parallel overlook how different the Franciscan situation was. The Dominican Order had lost both upholders of the Dominican chairs in the battle, but the Franciscan master – Alan of Tongeren – had not left Paris and was again in office, Gonsalvo having already resigned from office before the big clash. In the meantime, at Pentecost 1304, Scotus' beloved *magister Gonsalvus* had become Minister General of the Order, successor to John Minio of Morrovalle.

Gonsalvo was part of a grand Franciscan tradition of Parisian masters of theology who became Minister General of the Order. Let us frame the rather impressive list: Saint Bonaventure ((1253–)1257: *magister regens*) Minister General 1257–73; Arlotto da Prato (1284–85: *regens*) Minister General 1285–86; William of Falguières (1280–82 *regens*) Vicar General 1286–87; Matthew of Acquasparta (1276–77: *regens*) Minister General 1287–89; Ramon Godfrey (1292: *regens*) Minister General 1289–95; John Minio of Morrovalle (1289–90: *regens*) Minister General 1296–1302; Gonsalvo of Spain (1302–03: *regens*) Minister General 1304–13; Alexander of Alessandria (1307–08: *regens*) Minister General 1313–14 and Michael of Cesena (1316: *regens*) Minister General 1316–28. So, after 1257, for almost sixty out of seventy years dons of divinity had served the Order at the level of the international leadership. Three ministers general must have been personally known to Duns: John Minio during Duns' first Parisian stay; Gonsalvo, his theological teacher; and Alexander of Alessandria, perhaps his co-bachelor on the *Sentences* during 1302–03, his immediate successor.[60]

Duns was soon able to return to the Continent and he must have again sailed for France in the (late) summer of 1304 – now in the company of William of Alnwick. 'Between 1303 and 1308 he (= Alnwick) was closely associated with Scotus, attending his lectures at Paris and Oxford and acting as his secretary at Paris.'[61] They may have become acquainted with one another when Scotus had sought refuge in his mother *studium*. During the years to come Alnwick was wholeheartedly dedicated to the cause of Scotus and may have joined Duns in order to study theology as a *studens de debito*, determined to work with him. Because he was not in Paris in 1303 (see §2.2.2) but lectured there on the *Sententiae* in about 1313, he must have finished his regular theological studies in 1308, afterwards sacrificing important years of his own life to save Duns' heritage (1309–13): 'After Scotus' death in 1308, he oversaw the definitive edition of the *Opus Oxoniense* and the *Reportatio Parisiensis.*'[62] Alnwick must have acted as regent master in Oxford before he taught as master in Paris (1317–18).[63]

In the autumn of 1304, Gonsalvo, the new Minister General (1304–13), recommended *Joannes Scotus* as the first bachelor to inaugurate as professor of theology after Giles of Loigny. Gonsalvo acted as Minister Provincial of Castile (1303–04), when he found himself chosen to be the fifteenth Minister General at the Assisi General Chapter of Pentecost 1304 (17 May).[64] The President of this General Chapter was John Minio, Minister General until 1302, Cardinal since 1302, then Vicar General of the Order (1302–04).[65] The new Minister General was chosen by general consent. From ancient testimonies we may deduce he had an impressive and formidable personality. Gonsalvo's merit as Minister General lies in

---

60 Veuthey, 'Alexandre d'Alexandrie,' *Études Franciscaines* 43 (1931) 145–176, 319–344, and 44 (1932) 21–42, 193–207, 321–336 and 429–467. Cf. *HCPMA* 8. Alexander probably spent 1301 at Paris.

61 Courtenay, *Adam of Wodeham*, 58. Alnwick came from North England, from the custody of Newcastle. For biographical data, see Emden, *Biographical Register of the University of Oxford* I 27. See also §3.3.10 and §3.6.18.

62 Courtenay, *Adam of Wodeham*, 58.

63 His regency is dated there as 1317–18, while he remained in southern France and in Italy thereafter. He was the forty-second lector in Oxford while John of Reading was the forty-fifth there around 1320.

64 For the Assisi meeting, see Amorós, *Gonsalvi Hispani Quaestiones disputatae*, XXIXf.; on the general chapters of that period held every three years, see ibid., XXXIVf.

65 See Amorós, *Gonsalvi Hispani Quaestiones*, XXXIIIf. Cf. the last paragraph of §2.4.

the fact that he succeeded to save the Order from the dissolution that threatened it in a very difficult period. The recommendation of Duns Scotus by this exceptional Minister General was unusually personal:

> By this appointment I assign to your love Father *John Scotus*, beloved in Christ. I am fully acquainted with his praiseworthy life, excelling knowledge and most subtle ingenuity, as well as with his other remarkable qualities, partly through my long personal experience, and partly because his fame has spread everywhere.[66]

We have some idea of the ins and outs of Duns' last years of acting as a *baccalaureus* at Paris. First, when the university had been reopened and Duns had returned from England, he had still to lecture on Book II (autumn 1304) and Book III of Peter Lombard's *Sentences*. According to Wolter:

> Before the summer of 1304 Scotus was back in Paris, for he functioned as bachelor respondent in the disputation *in aula* (in the hall of the bishop) when his predecessor, Giles of Loigny, was promoted to being master. Meanwhile, Gonsalvo had become Minister General, or head, of the Franciscan order during the Pentecost General Chapter of 1304. On November 18 of that same year 1304 he wrote to the Franciscan superior at the Paris friary that the next bachelor to be licensed as regent master was Friar John Scotus.[67]

However, this same letter of the Minister General refutes Wolter's reconstruction of the facts. The theological masters Alan and John of Tongeren and the bachelors Giles of Loigny and Martin of Abbeville had sided with King Philip IV the Fair on 25 June 1303. The university had been closed in the summer of the same year. It is not quite clear where the theologians who had given way under pressure from the king spent the academic year 1303–04. Gonsalvo stressed in his letter that it was the accepted right of the Minister General to appoint the next master at the University of Paris. It was his prerogative, and not a prerogative of the general chapter, the theological faculty or the

---

[66] The text of Gonsalvo's letter was reprinted by Little, *The Grey Friars in Oxford*, 220: 'Baccalaureus hujusmodi praesentandus ad presens debeat esse de aliqua provincia aliarum a Provincia Francie dilectum in Christo Patrem Joannem Scotum, de cujus vita laudabili, scientia excellenti, ingenioque subtilissimo, aliisque insignibus conditionibus suis, partim experientia longa, partim fama, quae ubique divulgata est, informatus sum ad plenum, dilectioni vestre assigno, post dictum patrem Egidium, principaliter et ordinarie praesentandum.' See Callebaut, 'La maîtrise du Bx. Jean Duns Scot en 1305,' *AFH* 21 (1928) 206–239. The source is: Denifle and Chatelain (eds), *Chartularium Universitatis Parisiensis* II 1, 117.

[67] Wolter, in *God and Creatures*, XXII.

university, to appoint (former) brothers of the Franciscan *studium generale* at Paris to prepare for the mastership in theology.[68] The letter from Gonsalvo implies that, at that time, Giles of Loigny was still a bachelor of theology, the *baccalaureus responsalis* of that academic year. Gonsalvo confirmed that Giles would be the first to incept or inaugurate as a professor of theology and, *then*, it would be Duns' turn.[69] If the Lord Chancellor would be prepared to license two brothers at the same time after Giles of Loigny, and if Albert of Metz could return to the convent in time, then Albert and *John from Scotland* had to incept, successively, because of the age of Albert of Metz.[70]

Conclusion

We conclude that, at the end of 1304, Gonsalvo was eager to see Duns Scotus as a future master of theology, but that he was also committed to moral rules and the bylaws of the Order. At the time when he wrote his famous letter, Duns Scotus was only a *baccalaureus sententiarius*. Giles of Loigny, being *baccalaureus formatus* at that time, had still to act as master before him. By then, Giles was no doctor of divinity. If he were to have incepted before the summer of 1304 (according to Wolter), then Duns would already have acted as the *baccalaureus responsalis* during that same time. If so, then Alan of Tongeren would hardly have acted as *magister regens* at Paris. In this case, it would have made no sense for the Minister General to appoint Duns in the middle of November 1304 to prepare for the mastership through the office of Giles's *baccalaureus responsalis*. All this would already have been decided, or to put it the other way around, if Giles of Loigny were to have incepted in June or September – being odd months for such an official ceremony – then Duns Scotus would already have read on *Sententiae* II–III, and then the question *when?* would arise. However, Duns cannot have returned to Paris before the summer of 1304 and he cannot have finished such tasks before November 1304.

---

[68] Originally, the Dominicans cherished the same policy, as is known from the biography of Thomas Aquinas who was appointed by John of Wildeshausen (= John the Teuton (= German)), the Master General of the Dominican Order, in 1252. Appointing the next candidates for the mastership in theology became later the prerogative of the Dominican general chapter. Every order had its own set rules.

[69] Little, *The Grey Friars in Oxford*, 220: '[. . .] post dictum Patrem Egidium, principaliter et ordinarie praesentandum.' See note 66.

[70] See the last passage of Gonsalvo's letter in note 66.

2.5　At last: *Magister* at Paris

Before the new, revolutionary insights of the mid-1920s (§§3.2 and 3.4–3.5), it was commonly held that the *Opus Oxoniense* was Scotus' first commentary on the *Sentences* written at Oxford, and the so-called *Opus Parisiense* was seen as a kind of summary of the Oxford Commentary written in Paris. The idea was that at the time Duns had reached the eighteenth distinction of Book III in his Parisian course, he was called away to Cologne. However, at the end of *Reportata Parisiensia* III 18.3, we find the following note:

> This is the end of the disputation in the hall of the Bishop [et sic finis disputationis in aula].[71]

Duns had returned to Paris in the summer of 1304 while Giles of Loigny was not yet master of theology. The *disputatio in aula* belongs to the ceremonies celebrating the attainment of the master's degree. It points at a *principium* of a new master. In Paris, the *disputatio in aula Domini Episcopi* counts four actors: a *baccalaureus responsalis* who was the *baccalaureus formatus* of the same year, the *magister novus aulandus*, the *magister aulator* and the *Lord Chancellor*. Pelster proposed an identification of the four actors referred to in the account of the disputation. Three actors are mentioned by name: *Goffredus* (Godfrey of Fontaines), *Alanus* (Alan of Tongeren) and *Egidius* (Giles of Loigny). Alan of Tongeren (the *magister aulator*) and Giles of Loigny (the *magister novus aulandus*) were, successively, the outgoing and the incoming Franciscan professor of theology, while the outgoing master usually presided over the disputation. Godfrey of Fontaines had never been the Chancellor of the Parisian University – this famous *doyen* of the Faculty of Theology must have replaced the Chancellor as his representative. Duns acted as the *baccalaureus responsalis*.

However, the respondent bachelor did not participate in the first part of the inception of the new master, which took place in the afternoon

---

[71] See Pelster, 'Handschriftliches zu Skotus,' *FS* 10 (1923) 11–15. The source is: *Codex F 69* of Worcester Cathedral: *Reportatio Parisiensis* III 18.3: 'Utrum sit necessarium ponere habitum caritatis in anima Christi propter actum fruitionis vere? [. . .] Respondeo exponendo intellectum questionis quod non querit de potentia absoluta [. . .]. Intelligitur ergo de necessitate indigentie [. . .] et secundum hoc dico quid anima Christi indiget habitu caritatis respectu fruitionis vere. [. . .] Tunc arguit frater Egidius primo sic [. . .], secundo sic [. . .]. Contra arguit frater Egidius sic [. . .]. Tunc arguit magister Alanus primo sic [. . .], secundo sic [. . .], tertio sic [. . .]. Tunc arguit Goffredus [. . .].' The *disputatio in aula*, mentioned in the old *Reportata Parisiensia* III edition, is confirmed by the impressive Worcester Cathedral *Codex F 69*.

of the day before, after vespers, except during Lent. *Reportata Parisiensia* III 18.2 informs us about this event, for it belongs to Giles of Loigny's *vesperies* disputation of the previous day, called after the vespers of that day. Only *seniores magistri* were allowed to dispute with the incoming master. The bachelor of the incoming master joined in on the next day during the *disputatio in aula*, documented by *Reportatio Parisiensis* III 18.3, when the second set of questions put forward by the incoming master was discussed.[72]

> The *aula* was held in the morning at about tierce, no other lecture or disputation being permitted. The licentiate sat among the chancellor and masters. The presiding master (*magister aulator*), just as was the case in the ceremony for inception in the arts, placed the master's hat (*biretta*) on the new master's head.[73]

The debate on the third of the four questions was opened by a formed bachelor and then the new master, the outgoing master and the chancellor or his representative joined in. The last question was only discussed by masters.

We have established that at the end of 1304, Giles of Loigny was still bachelor of theology, Duns' *Reportatio Parisiensis* II and III belonging to the academic year 1304–05. *Reportatio Parisiensis* III does not suddenly break off after III 17 because of a call to Cologne, but because of the inauguration of Giles of Loigny. The striking coincidence is that the *baccalaureus sententiarius* Duns, as he was still at the time, had not yet finished his task when he had to act as *baccalaureus responsalis*. The Franciscan leadership was eager to arrange excellent representation in the theological faculty. It is clear from the letter of Gonsalvo, a former Parisian professor of theology himself, that he cherished a particular interest in the course of events in the faculty. His interest in John the Scot is clear. He also recommends Albert of Metz. If he were to return in time and the Lord Chancellor were to accept an additional Franciscan professor, Albert of Metz should incept before Duns because of his age. Involvement is mixed with fairness. I interpret the acceleration of Giles's inception and Duns' breaking off his course and responding at the occasion of Giles's inception as a sign of special involvement on the side of the

---

[72] See Balić, 'Henricus de Harcley et Ioannes Duns Scotus,' in *Mélanges offerts à Gilson*, 95–101 and 117.

[73] Leff, *Paris and Oxford Universities in the Thirteenth and Fourteenth Centuries*, 170 (168–171); on Bologna procedures, see Roest, *A History of Franciscan Education*, 108–115. Cf. §2.6.

Franciscans. We have to assume that Duns Scotus interrupted his systematic course on christology, for we have to explain why the manuscripts of *Reportatio Parisiensis* break off after III 17, as far as the normal course is concerned. Duns' commenting on *Sentences* III smoothly passed on into his responding on the same christological material in his capacity as *baccalaureus responsalis* at the occasion of Giles's *disputatio in aula*.

I conclude therefore that 1305–06 was the year of the regency of Giles of Loigny. Duns had still to fulfil the final requirements for the theological mastership embodied in the office of *baccalaureus formatus* and a master wants to be a master at least for one year. In this light, I expect that it was only during the winter of 1306 at the earliest or in Lent 1306 that Duns started in his capacity as *magister actu regens* and, so, Duns' only *Quodlibet* cannot be reasonably linked up with Easter 1306. We sum up the years of the Franciscan *magistri* as follows:

> Gonsalvo of Galicia/Spain (1302(?)–03)
> Alan of Tongeren (1303–05)
> Giles of Loigny (1305–06)
> John Duns Scotus (1306–07)
> Alexander of Alessandria (1307–08).

However, all this could not have taken place without the sincere support of the Chancellor and his main adviser Godfrey of Fontaines. There is a striking coincidence between Duns' last week of lecturing on the *Sententiae* and his responding in a *disputatio in aula*: the last normal distinction of his last sentential course is *Reportatio Parisiensis* III 17. *Reportatio Parisiensis* III 18.2 concerns the *disputatio* of Giles's *inceptio*, accompanied by a striking participation on the part of Godfrey of Fontaines. There is an impressive theoretical distance between the up and coming Duns and the old *nestor* of the theological faculty, in some respects even more an Aristotelian than Aquinas, but Godfrey fairly supports the acceleration of the career of Duns Scotus who had had the utmost respect for Godfrey of Fontaines for many years (see the end of §2.6).

On the one hand, the Franciscan circles felt critical of Meister Eckhart's thought and, on quite the opposite, Godfrey of Fontaines felt critical of the Franciscan way. Godfrey's personal metaphysics is too original to be reduced to any of the other Aristotelian movements of Siger of Brabant and Thomas Aquinas and their followers, nor of course to the Neo-Augustinian philosophical movement. Godfrey was evidently far more sympathetic to Siger's way of philosophizing and to that of Aquinas than to that of the Neo-Augustinians. [. . .] His metaphysics stands out [. . .] as the most striking and the most powerful form of a purer kind of Aristotelianism to be developed at Paris during the period between the death of Thomas Aquinas in 1274 and the highly original synthesis created by John Duns Scotus at Oxford and Paris around the turn of the fourteenth century.[74]

Godfrey's thought is just the type of philosophy Duns Scotus would have to face from his own point of view, and so he did.

Traces of Godfrey's criticisms of Gonsalvo of Spain we meet in his *Quodlibet* XV.[75] When D. De Bruyne had discovered a fifteenth quodlibet conducted by Godfrey, he requested Lottin to examine it.[76] Lottin established its authenticity but was unable to date it.[77] Lottin edited this quodlibet in 1937 and Palémon Glorieux soon managed to date *Quodlibet* XV, because there are identifiable references to the *Quaestiones Disputatae* 11 and 13 of Gonsalvo of Spain, while the whole series of Gonsalvo's *Quaestiones Disputatae* consists of sixteen *quaestiones*.

> Since the latter had been debated at Paris in 1302/1303, Glorieux concluded that Godfrey's *Quodlibet* XV could be no earlier than Easter 1303, and should more likely be placed in the academic year 1303/1304, either at Christmas or Easter. Since it was apparently not included in the University stationer's list of *exemplaria* of Godfrey's Quodlibets dating from February 25, 1304, Glorieux also suggested that it had not been released for public circulation by that time.[78]

So, both Glorieux and Wippel place Godfrey's *Quodlibet* XV in the academic year 1303–04.

---

[74] Wippel, *The Metaphysical Thought of Godfrey of Fontaines*, 381 and 385, respectively.

[75] For criticisms of Franciscan masters by Godfrey, see Pelzer, 'Étude sur les manuscrits des Quodlibets,' in Lottin, (ed.), Hoffmans and Pelzer (intro.), *Le Quodlibet XV et trois Questions ordinaires de Godefroid de Fontaines*, 235 f. (231–244: Codex Vat. latinus 1032). Cf. Wippel, *The Metaphysical Thought of Godfrey of Fontaines*, 276–285 (on Gonsalvo of Spain) and 371–386: 'Concluding remarks.'

[76] See Hoffmans, *Le Quodlibet* XV, 305–307, and on the Louvain Codex G. 30, ff. 241–253, which contained *Quodlibet* XV before it was destroyed in the Library fire of 1940, see Hoffmans, *Le Quodlibet* XV, 301–307.

[77] Lottin, 'Une question quodlibétique inconnue de Godefroid de Fontaines,' *Revue d'Histoire Ecclésiastique* 30 (1934) 852–859.

[78] Wippel, *The Metaphysical Thought of Godfrey of Fontaines*, XXVII. See also Glorieux, 'Notations brèves sur Godefroid de Fontaines,' *Recherches de théologie ancienne et médiévale* 11 (1939) 171–173.

This dating was challenged by Antonio San Cristóbal-Sebastián who placed it at Christmas 1286, but his proposal has been refuted by Wippel.[79] Godfrey and his disciple John of Pouilly (Ioannes Sapiens, Jean le Sage) were standard targets in Gonsalvo's teaching in 1302–03 when John of Pouilly was still *magister regens*, because they constantly attacked the independence and priority of the will and its freedom.[80] Gonsalvo's *Quaestiones Disputatae* 3, 4, 5 and 12 incisively criticize *Quodlibeta* VI, VIII and XIII, and occasionally I, II and X, of Godfrey of Fontaines.[81]

In the following year – the year of Duns Scotus' exile – Godfrey of Fontaines must have attended a meeting of 26 February 1304 connected with the Sorbonne, several other secular masters also being present.[82] The day before, 25 February 1304, the *librarius* – the 'bookmaker', that is the official publisher of the university – had listed all *quodlibeta* of Godfrey of Fontaines available at that time, but *Quodlibet* XV is not included in that official list.[83] Godfrey himself must have utilized his visit to Paris to make sure the publication of the impressive series of his *quodlibeta*, the heart of his productivity and his vital contribution to theology and philosophy. The elaborate and contrived attempts of San Cristóbal-Sebastián to place *Quodlibet* XV at Christmas 1286 are simply incompatible with this official list. Godfrey would certainly not have overlooked this quodlibet. He had invested into his quodlibetal disputations all that he had to offer.

However, the proposed date 1303–04 must also be wrong, because no quodlibetal questions were conducted in this academic year, the year of the exile when the university was closed (see §§2.2–2.4). Godfrey had been absent from the university for a time after 1298–99 but he did return to Paris to resume his functions by February 1304, but not in order to lecture. It seems reasonable to suggest that it was the turmoil of 1303–04 which occasioned Godfrey to return in the winter of 1304, and his *Quodlibet* XV must be deferred to Christmas 1304 or Lent 1305.

---

[79] San Cristóbal-Sebastián, *Controversias acerca de la volundad desde 1270 a 1300*, 109–118, and Wippel, 'Godfrey of Fontaines: the Date of *Quodlibet* 15,' *Franciscan Studies* 31 (1971) 300–369.

[80] For John's *Quodlibet*, see Glorieux (ed.), *Jacques de Thérines. Quodlibets I et II. Jean le Sage. Quodlibet I*, and on Gonsalvo's *quaestiones*, see Amorós, *Gonsalvi Hispani Quaestiones*, 427–450.

[81] See Amorós, *Gonsalvi Hispani Quaestiones*, 29–46, 53–68, 74–78 and 227–241.

[82] See Denifle-Chatelain, *Chartularium Universitatis Parisiensis* II n. 617.

[83] See Denifle-Chatelain, *Chartularium Universitatis Parisiensis* II n. 642. See also Wippel, 'Godfrey of Fontaines: the Date of *Quodlibet* 15,' *Franciscan Studies* 31 (1971) 300–369.

2.6 A PROBLEMATIC HISTORICAL INTERLUDE

For centuries, the vicissitudes and tensions of Duns' short life were virtually unknown. The logical works were considered to be the brilliant exercises of Duns as a *magister artium* at Oxford. However, Duns was no *magister artium* at all. The *Lectura* was unknown and the *Opus Oxoniense* was thought to be a large finished work of Duns in his capacity as an Oxonian don of divinity, but Duns was no master of theology at Oxford either. Having become professor of theology at Paris in 1304 or 1305, he wrote the *Opus Parisiense*. The *Opus Parisiense* was thought to be one of his last main works, being a summary of the *Opus Oxoniense*. It was known that he had died at Cologne, but during the 1920s his date of birth and his age were still enigmas.

Pelster reversed the chronological order of the *Opus Oxoniense* and the *Opus Parisiense*. His hypothesis implies that the *Opus Oxoniense* embodies the final stage of Duns' thought. This view is usually wedded to the seven outstanding volumes of *Editio Vaticana* I–VII (1950–73). The old-fashioned tradition exclusively connected the *Opus Oxoniense* with Oxford and the modern tradition mainly links it with Duns' last years at Paris. However, it is a 'serious and inexcusable mistake for scholars writing on Scotus today to regard his *Ordinatio* as a seamless garment rather than a work begun in Oxford and left unfinished when he left Paris for Cologne.'[84] Wolter stresses the early and rather immature nature of *Ordinatio* I–II 3. Nevertheless, we must conclude that these theses are vulnerable in the light of the available evidence. There is, indeed, a true *opus Oxoniense*, namely *Lectura* I–II, not the *Ordinatio*. Duns was composing and revising his *Ordinatio* for more than eight years (1300–1308) and *Reportatio Parisiensis* I–IV and II–III have to be placed in the academic years 1302–03 and 1304–05, respectively.

2.6.1 The problem of the Parisian years

Many authors have assumed Duns stayed at Paris during the 1290s in order to be able to explain the knowledge of recent Parisian theology his *Opus Oxoniense* displayed. This was mainly due to the influence of Callebaut's proposals and to the phenomenon of continental myopia. Callebaut's claim that Scotus studied at Paris between

---

[84] Wolter, 'Reflections about Scotus's Early Works,' in Honnefelder et al. (eds), *Metaphysics and Ethics*, 39.

1293–1297 was immediately accepted by De Wulf and many others, including even A. G. Little and Carlo Balic.[85] Callebaut did not take into account the Oxonian background of Duns Scotus' systematic thought, logic and spirituality and he ignored the internal requirements of the system of courses preceding the baccalaureate at Oxford. Brady and Etzkorn added the following criticism to this type of reasoning: King Philip IV the Fair decreed in the year 1293 that all Scottish and English scholars were to leave France.[86] Moreover, King Edward I declared war on France in 1294 and forbade all shipping traffic to the Continent.[87] There is no evidence that Duns studied elsewhere in the middle of the 1290s.[88] Such a stay would run against the statutes of Oxford's university. Experts as varied as Ignatius Brady, Brampton, Wolter and Courtenay now agree that there is no good reason to assume that Duns went to Paris before 1301 or 1302.[89] Moreover, with the exception of William Courtenay – and Giovanni Lauriola – the modern scholarly tradition looks on 1302–03 as Duns' first Parisian year.[90]

The year 1301–02 is not a candidate for Cambridge, because it is quite probable that Duns had already left for Paris in the late summer of 1301 and some of the arguments proving that Duns enjoyed a Cantabrigian stay also point to 1303–04 (see §2.2.1 and §2.3.2). Duns' stay at Paris is also required, when we take into account the future events of 1305–06. At the end of 1304, the leadership of the Franciscan Order felt certain that Duns would soon go further along on the path leading to the mastership in theology. Paris devoted two years to the course on the *Sententiae*, a term of about five months, including holidays, devoted to each book of the *Sentences*. Duns lectured on *Book* I and *Book* IV during the academic year 1302–03, before he conducted his *collationes* and produced *Ordinatio* I 10 ff. Therefore, the obvious solution is to assume a stay in Paris in 1301–02.

[85] Cf. *HCPMA* (1955) 454: 'John studied at Oxford shortly before 1290, was ordained a priest at Northampton March 17, 1291, and studied at Paris (1293–1296).'

[86] See Etzkorn and Brady, *Marston. Quodlibeta quatuor*, 34*–36*.

[87] See Powicke, *The Thirteenth Century*, 648.

[88] Cf., for example, De Wulf, *Histoire de la philosophie médiévale* II 25 (⁵1925), Knowles, *The Religious Orders in England* I 235, and *New Dictionary of Theology*, Leicester 1988, 211.

[89] See Wolter, 'Duns Scotus at Oxford,' *Via Scoti* I 183–192, but there are still authors following Callebaut, for example Esser, *Johannes Duns Scotus. Leben, Gestalt und Verehrung*, 17–28. Lauriola even opts for 1286–89 and 1292–97 as Parisian years in his *Duns Scoto. Antologia*, 112–121.

[90] See Wolter, 'Duns Scotus at Oxford,' in Sileo (ed.), *Via Scoti* I (1995) 183–192. Cf. Lauriola, *Duns Scoto. Antologia*, 121: '1301–1303: baccelliere *formatus* a Parigi.' Cf. Courtenay, 'Scotus at Paris,' in Sileo (ed.), *Via Scoti* I 149–163.

2.6.2 When did Duns complete his studies at Paris? The hypothesis of Callebaut

The traditional view that Duns only moved to Paris in 1304 or 1305 was effectively demolished by Ehrle's and Pelster's discovery that Duns read the Sentences at Paris during the academic year 1302–03.[91] Pelster rightly concluded that Duns must have gone to Paris in the autumn of 1302 at the latest. In 1928 André Callebaut proposed a different hypothesis in a learned contribution concerning the promotion of Duns Scotus.[92] His starting point is the letter of the new Minister General of the Franciscan Order: Gonsalvus Hispanus. First, Callebaut sketched the historical background. During the early summer of 1303 Duns had taken sides in the fierce conflict between Pope Boniface VIII and the French King Philip IV the Fair. In contrast to master John of Tongeren and Martin of Abbeville, bachelor of master John, and master Alan of Tongeren and his bachelor Giles of Loigny, Duns did not stay on at Paris after the end of June.[93] Support given by the university to Philip IV was countered by Boniface VIII in his Bull of 15 August, but Benedict XI, Boniface's successor, had lifted the ban by 13 April 1304. The Orders concerned reacted immediately. The Dominicans, gathered on the occasion of their General Chapter at Toulouse at Pentecost, appointed John Quidort and William Peter of Godin to be the next Dominican masters at Paris (see §2.2.2 and §2.3.2), which according to Callebaut, they became in 1304. The difficult situation the Dominicans found themselves in can also be implied from the fact that they had appointed John Quidort (John of Paris) who was already over fifty years of age, a colorful and able man but with a penchant for ideas not very welcome in the Order. By 1305 he already stood accused, but after his self-defense in Rome he soon died in 1306 and it was Godin who acted as a *lector* at the *Curia* in 1306. These were not easy years for the Dominican chairs.

According to Callebaut, Duns returned to Paris in order to continue his lectures on the *Sentences*, for, in contrast to the Dominicans, the Franciscans still had a master in Paris so Duns continued his career

---

[91] Pelster, 'Handschriftliches zu Skotus,' *FS* 10 (1928) 7–10. Pelzer immediately adopted Pelster's results – see Pelzer, 'A propos de Jean Duns Scot,' in Pattin and Van de Vyver (eds), *Études d'histoire littéraire*, 416 ff.

[92] Callebaut, 'La maîtrise du Bx. Jean Duns Scot en 1305,' *AFH* 21 (1928) 206–239.

[93] See Callebaut, 'La patrie de B. Jean Duns Scot,' *AFH* 10 (1917) 5–7.

under master Alan of Tongeren late during the following summer, while Giles of Loigny had to prepare himself for the doctorate. Callebaut also suggested with reason that the Franciscan General Chapter taking place at the same time ordered this. With the Franciscans, the prerogative of appointing the next Parisian master rested with the Minister General. Giles was already thought to be master of theology when Gonsalvo of Spain dispatched his famous letter to the Parisian headquarters on 18 November 1304, having incepted in mid-September. Around about Christmas 1304, Scotus would have had to present himself to the Chancellor of the University, Simon of Guiberville. Easter was early in 1305. The inception of Duns Scotus must have taken place in the course of April 1305 and Duns must have left Paris in the summer of 1307.

We have to conclude that, in terms of this theory proposed by Callebaut, the successive order of the Franciscan masters of theology must have been as follows: Gonsalvo of Spain (1302–03), Alan of Tongeren (already master in June 1303), Giles of Loigny (1304–05), John Duns Scotus (1305–07) and Alexander of Alessandria (1307–08). Let us spell out the difficulties implied in this view. Callebaut presupposed that the *expeditio* of Giles entails that he was already master of theology in November 1304. The only decision the Minister General had to make was appointing one or two bachelors to safeguard the next succession or successions of Franciscan masters in the important Parisian chair. Incidentally, Callebaut claimed that Duns acted as *baccalaureus responsalis* under Giles of Loigny, referring to *Reportatio Parisiensis* III 18.3, but he did not spell out the implications of this fact. If Giles had already incepted in mid-September 1304, then, of course, he would have been master of theology in November 1304, but does it really make sense to present Giles of Loigny if he already was a regent master? Consequently, Alan of Tongeren would not have *acted* as a regent master. This thesis also implies dating the *disputatio in aula* in the early autumn of the same year. There is then no longer any room for Duns' *Reportatio Parisiensis* II 1 – III 17 (§2.4).

2.6.3   Pelster on the inception of Giles of Loigny

The old university of Bologna did not receive a theological faculty until 1365. Hugoline of Malabranca, who had been a Parisian master of theology, drafted the statutes of the new faculty according to the Paris model. A *disputatio* such as Duns' Parisian *disputatio in aula Domini Episcopi* required four actors:

1. a *baccalaureus responsalis* who was the *baccalaureus formatus* of that same year;
2. the *magister novus aulandus*;
3. the *magister aulator*; and
4. the Lord Chancellor.

Pelster proposed an identification of all four actors in the case of the *disputatio* text in *Reportata Parisiensia* III 18.3. There is a specific order of entrance. The last in the row is the Lord Chancellor or his representative (Godfrey of Fontaines). The last actor but one is the *magister regens*: the *magister aulator* (Alan of Tongeren); counting the other way around, the first opponent must be the new professor (Giles of Loigny).

The traditional view considered the course on the *Sententiae* to be the task of the *magister* and assumed Duns stayed in Paris rather late in his short life thus putting *Reportata Parisiensia* I–IV in the years 1306–07. Pelster saw that *Reportata Parisiensia* III 1–17 belonged to an earlier period and ascribed the *Reportata Parisiensia* to the years 1302–04, not to the years 1305–07, although Pelster left undecided whether the disputation *in aula* took place before or after the letter of Gonsalvo of Spain.[94] Pelster identified Alan of Tongeren and Giles of Loigny in terms of the royal list of June 1303. His identification rested on the list of the Franciscans siding with Philip IV. Pelster added an attempt to identify Duns in terms of the same list and proposed to identify *Iohannes de Anglia* as Duns Scotus.[95] However, this identification does not fit in with Pelster's acceptance of Ehrle's and Callebaut's readings of academic lists: the scholars are named after their place or country of origin. Because according to Pelster it has been proven that Duns is a Scotsman and not an Englishman, 'de *Anglia*' must indicate the Franciscan province of

---

[94] Pelster, 'Handschriftliches zu Skotus,' *FS* 10 (1923) 14 note 2: 'Die Disputation fand Ende 1304 oder spätestens Anfang 1305 statt; denn der Brief des Generalministers vom 18. November 1304 setzt die Promotion des Aegidius entweder als schon vollzogen oder doch als unmittelbar bevorstehend voraus.' The first possibility is incompatible with Gonsalvo appointing Duns to become Giles's successor, because in that case Duns would already have acted as his succcessor and then there would be no need for Duns to be designated as Giles's successor.

[95] The third section of 'Handschriftliches zu Skotus' is Pelster's first independent contribution: the discovery of the nature of the *disputatio in aula* and its disputants on the basis of Ehrle's dating of Duns commenting on *Sententiae* I and IV (1302–03). The first sections stem from Ehrle: Pelster, 'Handschriftliches zu Skotus,' *FS* 10 (1923) 2–10. Later Pelster corrected the wrong identification of *Johannes de Anglia* in 'Ein Münchener Handschrift des beginnenden 14. Jahrhunderts,' *FS* 17 (1930) 254 note 2.

Duns, and not his native soil, which contradicts the theory advocated by Pelster himself.

Moreover, this identification shows that the identity of the royal list was still unclear. If Duns' year of exile were then the paradoxical ring of this interpretation would be clear. If Duns were among those choosing exile, how could his name have occurred on the list of the consenting Friars Minor? This paradox was pointed out by Callebaut in 1926 who delved deeply into the connections between the Franciscan order and the policy of Boniface VIII.[96] However, the puzzle was solved in 1928 by Longpré: together with Gonsalvo of Spain, Duns was among the dissenting Franciscans very much opposed to the leanings of Philip IV.[97] However, the mistaken interpretation of the list does not endanger Pelster's identification of the actors of the *disputatio in aula*.

2.7 PROFESSOR AT PARIS (1306–07) AND COLOGNE (1307–08)

By Lent 1306, *Magister* Duns Scotus was about forty years of age. Duns eventually was granted the foreigner's chair in theology as *magister actu regens*. His inception marked the beginning of a period of intense activity. Surrounded by a staff of a secretary – Duns' *socius* – and some assistants, he lectured in theology, led disputations, taught logic and worked hard at elaborating a comprehensive and definite 'commentary' on the *Sententiae*. This elaborate revision is the so-called *Ordinatio*, a work meant to become a new map of the entire field of systematic theology and philosophy of religion. *Ordinatio* I–III is mainly based on *Lectura* I–III and on his notes from his courses in Paris and Cambridge as well. *Ordinatio* IV rests on *Reportatio Parisiensis* IV. New material was continuously added to his *Ordinatio*.

In 1306 Duns Scotus must also have crossed swords with the Dominican master Godin, against the thesis that matter is the principle of individuation.[98] To date no publicly disputed questions have been found, but certainly some questions of this sort must have been incorporated in the *Ordinatio*.

---

[96] Callebaut, 'Le Bx Jean Duns Scot. Bachelier des *Sentences* à Paris en 1302–3,' *La France franciscaine* 9 (1926) 293–317.

[97] See Longpré, 'Duns Scot. Pour le Saint Siège,' *La France franciscaine* 11 (1928) 137–162.

[98] See Noone, 'Scotus's Critique of the Thomistic theory of Individuation and the Dating of the *Quaestiones super libros Metaphysicorum* VII q. 13,' in Sileo (ed.), *Via Scoti* I 391–406. See also §10.2 and §11.2.

Duns Scotus also produced a monumental series of *Quaestiones Quodlibetales* – Advent 1306. Wadding and modern researchers agree that Duns conducted only one quodlibetal disputation. Wolter and Alluntis opt for Advent 1306 or Lent 1307. Lent 1306 is incompatible with a simultaneous inception and Lent 1307 seems too late taking into consideration the vast amount of redrafting Duns had already invested in his *Quaestiones Quodlibetales* when he died. So, I opt for the second or third week of Advent 1306. The Cistercian master James of Thérines (d.1321) also conducted his first quodlibetal disputation in the second or third week of this same Advent before Christmas 1306.[99] There is a considerable overlap of themes in these two *quodlibeta*. The *Quodlibet* of James of Thérines is one of the earliest testimonies of Duns Scotus' influence spreading over the theological faculty of Paris.

Quodlibetal disputations reflected the theoretical interests and preoccupations of the day. Published *quaestiones quodlibetales* give a topical impression of the problems of the day and of the way the leading masters reacted to them. They enable us to gauge the currents of ideas prevalent in different subjects of academic teaching and faculties of the universities. In general, *quodlibeta* 'contain valuable insights into the personal opinions of a master and often expressed his mind on a score of topics never touched upon in any other work.'[100] The solemn quodlibetal disputations were only held before Easter and before Christmas. They offered something for everybody.

> A particular type, the so-called *questio de quolibet* (= *questio* regarding an arbitrary topic) developed within the genre of the *questio disputata*. Twice a year, in the academic holiday before Easter and Christmas, the *magistri* (especially those of the theological faculty) were allowed to arrange a disputation where the audience chose the themes. This might be 'anything under the sun' (*de quolibet ad voluntatem cuiuslibet*).[101]

The meeting started at nine o'clock in the morning or at noon. Because the *magister* was unable to control the questions and the topics, he was sometimes unable to prevent chaos. At any rate, it was risky for him.

---

[99] See Glorieux (ed.), *Jacques de Thérines. Quodlibets I et II. Jean le Sage. Quodlibet* I, 11.

[100] Alluntis and Wolter, *God and Creatures*, XXVI, referring to Glorieux, *La littérature quodlibétique* II 45 ff., and idem, 'Où en est la question de quolibet?,' *Revue du moyen âge latin* 2 (1946) 411.

[101] PMA 101 (99–102). Cf. CV (1992) 16 and CF 12–14.

Duns Scotus' *Quodlibet* presents us with quite a special surprise. In a sense, his *Quodlibet* is not a source of new and surprising insights, but more a kind of dense Scotist handbook. It is an accumulation of crucial ideas already exposed in detail in the *Lectura* and the *Ordinatio*, but, in the light of the general nature of the quodlibetal genre, this is quite revealing. Duns did not select his personal preferences for discussion before hand: it was the audience which framed the questions, not the master. Nevertheless, it is the only 'Scotist' monograph Duns Scotus produced, although he was invited to conduct the *disputatio quodlibetalis*. He did not select his questions himself; rather this audience did so, apparently led by interest in Duns Scotus' innovations. The audience asked for a detailed exposition of the bottlenecks of his universe of ideas and they got it in clear and precise, dense and surveyable teaching. When we compare the Munich manuscript *Clm 8717* with the last but one draft to be found in modern editions, we can still sense how Scotus made an effort to be clear and complete.[102] The *quodlibet* testifies to the fact that Scotus himself was becoming the flavour of the day. The fact that the audience danced attendance on him shows that the guiding interest was Duns' personal approach. The scholars present had carefully prepared themselves in order to use the opportunity to the full and asked for what was new to them, not to Duns Scotus. Scotus was new to them and they were very much interested.

Scotus' *Quodlibet* is a unique source of systematic information. One is struck by the fact that we find here just the bottlenecks of the *Lectura* and the *Ordinatio*. In particular, I point at the Trinitarian issues in *Quodlibet* 1–6 and matters of divine omnipotence in the *quaestiones* 7–11. From *quaestio* 12 onwards, theology of creation and anthropology are dealt with.[103] Here, in addition to argumentative depth, Duns Scotus' language is more concise than in his *Sententiae* Commentaries, but the doctrinal continuity with the *Lectura* is decisive. The *Quaestiones Quodlibetales* are an almost Scotist monument, unique for John Duns Scotus.

At this stage of his development, Duns Scotus received much admiration and support. However, again there is a paradoxical shadow. On the one hand, there had already been the exile during the year 1303–04, while on the other hand, he had to leave Paris again helter-skelter in 1307. The Knights Templar had to be wary of dangerous

---

[102] See §3.6.14. Cf. Alluntis and Wolter, *God and Creatures* XXIV–XXVII and *DS* 75f.
[103] See Alluntis and Wolter, *God and Creatures*, XXVII–XXXI.

lawsuits because they would suffer from the harsh actions of the French king against them.[104] Paris was still full of unrest. Theological creativity could easily be interpreted as heresy. Then there was his sudden death. The whole of Duns Scotus' oeuvre is complicated, almost beyond imagination. Not a single book was published during his lifetime, and worse, every individual work was unfinished at his untimely death.

Duns Scotus must have realized himself how complicated the collection of all these works *in statu nascendi* already was. However, the tendency for integration is of great help, and anyone who has once observed the inner structure and dynamics of Duns Scotus' method in his semantics and logic, in his theory of knowledge, anthropology and ethics, and in his ontology and theology, will gain much support from the center of his systematic thought for their understanding of the many complicated and specific parts. Anyone who has grasped the inner coherence of one vital area of his thought has a key for understanding many other parts of his philosophy and theology. The *quaestio* technique practised in the universities of Scotus' time was aimed at profound examination when complicated dilemmas arise, but the technique is not well suited for presenting an overview of someone's thinking. The monographic style is missing. Duns Scotus set out using this solution, but he died too early to solve the problem in a representative manner. It is for this very reason that the monographic tendency of his 'commentaries' offers much help.

Again and again, Duns treatment of issues is so extensive that small monographs come into existence. Such extensive digressions give a formidable training in philosophical and theological thinking. The contents are very rich and have a theocentric orientation. The style has a philosophical ring. The *Prologue* of the *Lectura* deals with the methodology and theory of science, while other fascinating examples of philosophical wealth are: philosophical doctrine of God (*Lectura* I 2), epistemology (*Lectura* I 3), semantics (*Lectura* I 8 and I 2), the doctrine of grace (*Lectura* I 17), ontology (*Lectura* I 39 and I 8) and the theory of the individual (*Lectura* II 3). For all these subjects, the *Ordinatio* offers important counterparts.

With reference to the monographic tendency of Duns Scotus' authorship, during his last two years Duns drafted a new kind of monograph. His last work, *De primo principio*, which contains his

---

[104] See Wolter, 'John Duns Scotus,' *The New Encyclopaedia Britannica: Macropaedia* V (1976) 1084, and Little, 'Chronological Notes,' *English Historical Review* 47 (1932) 577–582.

philosophical doctrine of God, shows an important tendency in his writings. We observe an enormous development of the *quaestio*. There is not only a substantial quantitative growth of the analytical dimension with many arguments and counter-arguments put forward and analyzed with endless patience. There is also a remarkable concentration on the problem-solving potential of the alternatives he embarks on himself. A broad texture of semantic, logical, ontological and theological solutions is elaborated on in scriptural, theologically historical (Augustine and Anselm) and systematic ways. We also know that there were plans for a booklet called *De Creditis*. The central theme of the Creed is God Triune. This unwritten monograph would have dealt with the theology of the Trinity. Again, much material was already to be found in the *Ordinatio*. A new way of dealing with the central issues was taking shape. The whole of philosophy and theology was to be presented according to the new systematic discipline and carried out with a new sense of oversight.

The last years of this remarkable short life throw new light upon its exceptional richness. Every year specific challenges had to be faced and new output was seen. His theological production lasted for only a decade or so. When he was forty years of age, he was still working as an assistant professor. His duties almost always came from the outside, from superiors. He had been a student of divinity at Oxford for more than fifteen years. The span of his baccalaureate, which had encompassed Oxford, Paris, Cambridge and Paris again, numbered almost nine years. As an ordinary don of divinity he taught for two and a half years: well over a year at Paris and one and a half years at Cologne.

It was a career exceptionally short, institutionally marginal in duration, though powerful in its effects – the unique career of a unique theological genius, second to none in philosophy. He creatively touched every systematic spot, for the most gifted young scholars in systematics, from every European corner, hung upon his words with absorbed attention at Oxford and Cambridge, Paris and Cologne, the four most important theological centers in Europe at that time. In spite of all difficulties, his unique journey reached far and wide.

In short, 1305–06 had been the last year of a very long baccalaureate period (1297–1306). During the winter of 1305 he had presented his treatment of christology after having taught the theology of creation during the autumn of 1304. *Reportatio Parisiensis* III suddenly ends with distinction 17. The year 1306–07 was that of the *Quodlibet*. In the second or third week of Advent 1306 he unfolded his ideas regarding the whole of theology for a broad theological audience. In 1307 a new type of plan matured. He embarked on reconstructing the philosophical theory of divine attributes along new methodological lines with a new weft which dealt with the theoretical contents in an axiomatic way, arguing from evident or proven premisses to long strings of new conclusions. Then he had to leave Paris again and in 1308 Cologne would hold him.

A new world of theological thought arose. His fellow friars worked with all their strength. Superiors and students were attached to Duns and his disciples were enthusiastic. However, in November 1308 grief and panic took over at Cologne and Oxford, in France and England. His genius still had the radiance of youth and there was also the admiration of a beloved tutor. We can still feel the panic in the old printed editions. However, who was able to grasp fully what seemed to be so compelling in the lecture room? Nothing was finished and then he was buried in the Franciscan church near the Cathedral of Cologne:

> *Scotland brought me forth,*
> *England taught me,*
> *France received me,*
> *Cologne holds me.*

> Scotia me genuit,
> Anglia me docuit,
> Gallia me recepit,
> Colonia me tenet.[105]

Before Duns Scotus was buried in the sarcophagus which has the more recent version of the inscription, he had been interred from 1643 to 1946 before the main altar of the Minoritenkirche (church of the Friars Minor) which belonged to the old friary.[106] After the Second World War, Duns Scotus' mortal remains were saved in the famous Cathedral of Cologne (1946–56), as the Minoritenkirche had been destroyed almost entirely by the end of the war (March 1945).

---

[105] The present sarcophagus dates from 1957. Its inscription runs as follows:

Scotia me genuit, / Anglia me suscepit,
Gallia me docuit, / Colonia me tenet.

This historically incorrect epitaph goes back to a text of William Worilong (about 1440). The original version, quoted in the main text, is found in Abato, 'La tomba del Ven. Giovanni Duns Scoto, o. min. nella chiesa di S. Francesco a Colonia,' *Miscellanea Franciscana* 45 (1945) 63 (29–79) – see CF 9. For the history of Duns Scotus' grave, see Esser, 'Das Grab des seligen Johannes Duns Scotus in Köln,' *Johannes Duns Scotus. Untersuchungen zu seiner Verehrung*, 165–204.

[106] The friary stood where the Wallraf-Richartz museum was found until 1986.

In 1980 Pope John Paul II visited Scotus' tomb, describing Duns Scotus as 'a spiritual tower of faith'. The beatification of John Duns Scotus was declared and confirmed by John Paul II as the celebrant in the evening prayer of 20 March 1993, in Saint Peter's Church at Rome.[107]

2.8 EPILOGUE

Duns Scotus' early death is wedded to a long-term perspective of eternal richness. However, the poetry of Thomas Merton sings its own song:

> Striking like lightning to the quick of the real world
> Scotus has mined all ranges to their deepest veins:
> But, where, oh, on what blazing mountain of theology
> And in what Sinai's furnace
> Did God refine that gold?
>
> Until the firmament, with high heavenly marvel
> Views in our crystal souls her blue embodiment,
> Unfurls a thousand flags above our heads –
> It is the music of Our Lady's army!
>
> For Scotus is her theologian,
> Not has there ever been a braver chivalry than his precision.
> His thoughts are skies of cloudless peace
> Bright as the vesture of her grand aurora
> Filled with the rising Christ.
>
> Language was far too puny for his great theology:
> But, oh! His thought strode through those words
> Bright as the conquering Christ
> Between the clouds His enemies:
> And in the clearing storm, and Sinai's dying thunder
> Scotus comes out, and shakes his golden locks
> And sings like the African sun.[108]

---

[107] See *Opera Omnia* XIX (1993) XIIIff. Cf. Schneider, 'Die Aktualität des seligen Duns Scotus,' in Schneider (ed.), *Johannes Duns Scotus. Seine Spiritualität und Ethik*, 76–83, and Pauli Papae VI *Epistula Apostolica 'Alma Parens'* (1966), in *De doctrina Ioannis Duns Scoti* I 33–39, cf. pp. III–VI.

[108] Merton, 'Duns Scotus,' from *Figures for an Apocalypse* (1947), in *The Collected Poems of Thomas Merton*, 164 f.

CHAPTER 3

Two critical text revolutions

3.1 THE FATE OF AN OEUVRE

The legacy of Duns Scotus' works is a complicated affair due to a number of different causes. His life was short. He studied and taught in all the theological faculties the universities of the thirteenth century possessed. He spent the last year of his life in the important academic center that Cologne had already become. The extraordinary brevity of his life is combined with a unique range of work. The specific nature of university education in these times, the stature of the University of Paris, the policy of the Franciscan Order and the academic legislation of the University of Paris transformed Duns Scotus' life. Unexpected events in his life led to the unique fact that he even acted as *sententiarius* in all the theological faculties he studied at. The period of Duns Scotus' theological productivity and his baccalaureate years (1297–1306) almost coincided. He died suddenly at Cologne, forty-two years of age. The world of the Franciscans was desolate. The early death of brother John in 1308 was felt in the whole of academic Europe. One of the brightest stars of the thought of mankind had gone dim.

The death of Duns Scotus was the end of an improbable individual history of thinking. His personal fate was an institutional disaster. The individual thinker John Duns managed to absorb the whole of the *philosophia christiana* and systematic theology but managed also to reconstruct it from a new semantic, logical and ontological perspective. In fact, his thought was philosophy from a new perspective, but everything was unfinished at his untimely death. There is an immense loss – loss of meaning of individual life and loss of institutional meaning, if, historically, a personal loss can have an international impact. Here, the 'Unvollendete' of an individual life is at the same time the 'Unvollendete' of an unfinished oeuvre.

Duns not only left behind an unfinished oeuvre, but each individual work was also unfinished. Some of his books could almost have been sent to the publisher, the *librarius* (the 'book-maker'). Other works would have required years of further sustained efforts, like the *Ordinatio*, his definitive Commentary on the Sentences, the *Quaestiones super libros Metaphysicorum Aristotelis* and the planned series of monographs. Then, *De primo principio* would have been the first monograph and *De creditis* the next.[1] His was an unfinished agenda.

However, every book unfinished in 1308 is still important. It is clear that his friends in mourning realized how important was what was going on. They did everything in their power to make it possible that his unfinished legacy would survive. Not only did they do everything possible to save all these works, particularly the *Ordinatio*, but they also collected the notebooks (*quaterni*) of the *Lectura*, the *reportationes Parisienses* and other notes and annotations on all the courses ever given at Oxford and Paris, Cambridge and Cologne – countless piles of jottings, marginal notes, and sets of digressions.

The effect of all these complexities was that Scotus was not forgotten during the next half a millennium (§3.2). Many editions were published every century. However, many of the older editions turned out not to be authentic: §3.3 deals with these spurious works. Section 3.4 describes the second revolution in textual criticism concerning the authentic works and §3.5 sketches the tragic paradoxes connected with the tensions of the 1930s. Section 3.6 goes on to discuss the authentic works and some concluding observations are made in §3.7.

3.2   FROM THE HISTORY OF DUNS SCOTUS' OEUVRE

The works of Duns was paid much attention during the fourteenth and fifteenth centuries, though the contribution of the fifteenth century is ambivalent. On the historical level, many legends were added to the Scotus traditions and, on the textual level, many spurious works were inserted into his canon. The fifteenth century was a period of growing interest in Scotist thought and its second half became the age of the new art of printing, achieving an immense importance for the *Wirkungsgeschichte* of Duns Scotus' books. The new art of producing books was immediately put into the service of Scotus' legacy. Around 1455 the first large-scale book was printed by Gutenberg in Mainz, the so-called *42-lines Bible*. By 1472 the two first editions of Scotus' *Opus Oxoniense* I appeared in Venice, as a result of the careful oversight of Rufini (5 November) and Antonio Trombetta (19 November) and their

---

[1] See Vos, 'Johannes Duns Scotus,' *Kerk en Theologie* 36 (1985) 184 f.

collaborators and the creativity of some of the first Italian publishers. The first Scotus book is older than the oldest Dutch book, the *Delft Bible* (1477), although the Netherlands are one of the very first areas where printing was available. The oldest Dutch publication is older than the book production in Mainz. 'However, it was Thomas Penketh, an English Augustinian Hermit and professor of theology at Padua, who first edited all four books of Scotus' *Opus Oxoniense*. Editions were issued at Venice in 1477–1478 and 1481.'[2] Thirteen editions of *Opus Oxoniense* appeared between 1472 and 1500 and the number of Duns Scotus' books published during the next three centuries is quite substantial.[3] Early modernity served Duns Scotus well until the end of the eighteenth century.

The books of Duns, collected by the Scotus circle, constituted a chaotic library. The art of printing served the *Wirkungsgeschichte* of this 'library' well. However, no solution was found before Balic and his team applied modern textual criticism to the complete works of Duns Scotus. The dissolution of the monastic orders and the destruction of the Franciscan monastery in Oxford also occasioned the destruction of Duns' *autographa* in 1535. Neither the *Ordinatio* nor the *Lectura*, nor even the meanings of the words *ordinatio* and *lectura*, escaped oblivion.

Many spurious works sailed under Scotus' colors. Even the splendid edition of Luke Wadding OFM was far from a critical edition.[4] Apart from many works being spurious some books were printed on the basis of reliable old editions or good manuscripts; other works, or parts of them, have been badly edited. The text of the *Opus Oxoniense* is reliable in parts, but not so in general. The older *Opus Oxoniense* edition of Maurice O'Fihely (Mauritius Hibernus) is better than Wadding's and Wadding's *Reportata Parisiensia* is certainly no improvement when compared with the Paris edition of 1517. *Lectura* I–II is conspicuous by its absence in the old printed editions.

The Vivès edition (1891–95) was an important event but did not improve anything from the critical textual point of view: this late nineteenth-century edition is almost simply a corrected reissue of Wadding's in twenty-six volumes, because only the spurious *De*

---

[2] Mahoney, 'Duns Scotus and the School of Padua around 1500,' *Regnum Hominis et Regnum Dei* II 216 (215–219). Cf. Balic, 'Die Frage der Authentizität und Ausgabe der Werke des J. Duns Skotus,' *Wissenschaft und Weisheit* 2 (1935) 136–143.

[3] For lists of old editions and their descriptions, see *Opera Omnia* I 127*–139* and Harris, *Duns Scotus* I.

[4] *Opera omnia Ioannis Duns Scoti* I–XII, Lyons 1639, reprint Hildesheim 1968.

perfectione statuum was added to Duns' oeuvre.[5] Only in the 1920s did we see a true revolution in the critical research on Duns Scotus' texts. There is an impressive record of discoveries to be registered, particularly to the account of Pelster, Pelzer, Michalski and Balic. In 1915 Überweg-Baumgartner was still presenting a simple picture: Duns Scotus' oeuvre was to be found in Vivès, apart from a few exceptions. The historical picture lacked sophistication too: Scotus taught at Oxford until 1304; there he wrote the *Opus Oxoniense* in the years 1301–04. He then acted as a master at Paris from 1305 to 1308, when the *Opus Parisiense* came into existence.

It was not until 1923 that Pelzer and Pelster published singularly new results. Within the space of a few years, many works were shown to be spurious.[6] Moreover, Balic rediscovered the *Lectura* and also uncovered the true relationship between the *Lectura*, the *Ordinatio* and the *Opus Oxoniense*. Brave plans were made aimed at a critical edition of Duns' Commentaries on the *Sententiae* to be finished before the outbreak of the impending Second World War, preferably in 1939, three hundred years after the famous edition of Wadding. In the meantime Balic's dreams have dissipated. More than sixty years later, eighteen volumes of the definitive edition have been published: eight volumes containing *Ordinatio* I–II and six containing *Lectura Oxoniensis* I–III, and four volumes of *B. Ioannis Duns Scoti Opera Philosophica*, comprising his important *Quaestiones super libros Metaphysicorum Aristotelis* (volumes III–IV, 1997), *Quaestiones in librum Porphyrii Isagoge et Quaestiones super Praedicamenta Aristotelis* (volume I, 1999), and *Quaestiones in libros Perihermenias Aristotelis, Quaestiones super librum Elenchorum Aristotelis et Theoremata* (volume II, 2004).

3.3   THE FIRST REVOLUTION IN TEXTUAL CRITICISM: THE SPURIOUS WORKS

From the beginning of the twentieth century, the picture of Scotian authorship was changing at a good pace. One work after another disappeared in a critical textual drama, but the entirety of the results of the critical textual research was never summarized argumentatively in the modern literature. We know what we need not study when we

---

[5] *Opera omnia. Editio nova iuxta editionem Waddingi*, Paris: L. Vivès 1891–1895.

[6] Pelster informs us that his and Pelzer's new insights arose from analyzing Munich and Vatican manuscripts, containing Duns Scotus' *Opus Oxoniense*, between 1915 and 1920: 'Zur Scotus-Forschung,' *Theologische Revue* 28 (1929) 146. See §3.3.

study Duns, although these inauthentic works are important witnesses to a wider tradition. Section 3.3 surveys the fate of the spurious books and §3.6 deals with the authentic works.

3.3.1 *De rerum principio*

Wadding III 1–207 and Vivès IV 257–471

De rerum principio played an important role in the history of modern Scotism. In the Wadding edition *De rerum principio* is called *Quaestiones disputatae De rerum principio sive Quaestiones universales in philosophiam*. In twenty-six *quaestiones* this treatise deals with the doctrine of God, the theory of matter, anthropology and epistemology and issues of number, time and eternity. Wadding ascribed it to Scotus on the basis of the testimony of one manuscript: *Codex* 15 of the College St Isidore in Rome. In a paradoxical way, particularly during the last hundred years, this work was a privileged source for reconstructing the thought of Duns Scotus. It was reprinted in the Vivès edition and edited by Mariano Fernàndez Garcia: *Quaestiones disputatae De rerum principio et Tractatus De primo omnium rerum principio* (1910). This edition earned some severe criticism from Auguste Pelzer (1923): unfortunately, without recourse to the manuscript tradition.[7] De Wulf stuck to the traditional ascription of *De rerum principio* until the fifth edition of his *Histoire de la philosophie médiévale*, while Harris tenaciously defended it against Longpré in his *Duns Scotus* I (1927). Parthenius Minges had already thrown doubt on the authenticity of *De rerum principio*.[8] He believed it to be possible that it was the work of an early Scotist. According to Carreras y Artau, *De rerum principio* had to be spurious because some passages are incompatible with the authentic works.[9] In the years of refuting Landry, Longpré urged the inauthenticity of both the *Theoremata* and *De rerum principio*.[10] Nevertheless, the work was still something of an enigma. A couple of years later, Longpré returned to the theme of the authorship of *De*

---

[7] Pelzer, 'A propos de Jean Duns Scot et des études scotistes,' *Revue Néo-Scolastique de Philosophie* 25 (1923) 411 f., reprinted in Pattin and Van de Vyver (eds), *Études d'histoire littéraire*, 413.

[8] Minges, 'Die Skotistische Litteratur im XX. Jahrhundert,' *FS* 4 (1917) 185. Cf. idem, *Ist Duns Scotus Indeterminist?*, IX.

[9] Carreras y Artau, *Ensayo sobre el voluntarismo de J.D. Scot*, 74–84.

[10] See Longpré, *La philosophie du B. Duns Scot*, 19, 22–48 and 290–291.

rerum principio and ascribed it to the Franciscan theologian Vital du Four (Vitalis a Furno).[11] In the meantime, Ferd. -M. Delorme had proven that crucial theses of *De rerum principio* occurred among the *quaestiones* of Vital du Four.[12] Thus the essence of a new solution had been established by Delorme.

Delorme's analysis of De rerum principio

De rerum principio consists of three parts: *A – quaestiones* 1–15; *B – quaestiones* 16–24 and *C*, the last small group of two questions: 25 and 26. Delorme was able to identify the first fifteen questions as *quaestiones* written by Vital du Four. *Manuscript 95* of Todi contains a chronological series of disputed questions and quodlibets of du Four: his first *quodlibet*, seven disputed questions *De primo rerum principio*, one *quaestio disputata: de productione creaturarum*, six disputed questions on the soul and its powers, his second *quodlibet*, seven disputed questions *de cognitione* and his third *quodlibet*.[13]

Group A

The first fifteen questions of *De rerum principio* are simply an arbitrary selection from du Four's disputed questions: the *quaestiones disputatae* 1, 2, 3, 4, 6 and 7 of the series *De primo rerum principio*, the six anthropological questions and the epistemological *quaestiones disputatae* 1, 2 and 4.[14] Glorieux established the *terminus a quo* and the *terminus ad quem* on the basis of these disputations: the first anthropological question refers to *Quodlibet* XIII *quaestio* 4 of Henry of Ghent, which dates from 1289, and the fourth and sixth anthropological questions deal with theses of Peter Olivi who died in March 1298.[15] They belong to the years of du Four's regency at Paris, probably 1292–95.

---

[11] Longpré, 'Pour la défense de Duns Scot,' *Rivista di filosofia neoscolastica* 18 (1926) 35–36. Cf. Gölz, 'Die echten und unechten Werke des Duns Scotus,' in *Sechste und siebte Lektorenkonferenz*, 53 f. See §§3.4–3.5.

[12] See Delorme, 'Autour d'un apocryphe scotiste,' *La France franciscaine* 8 (1925) 279–295, and idem, 'L'oeuvre scolastique de maître Vital du Four d'après le Ms. 95 de Todi,' *La France franciscaine* 9 (1926) 428–430. The debate was rounded off by Palémon Glorieux, 'Pour en finir avec le *De rerum principio*,' *AFH* 31 (1938) 225–234.

[13] See Delorme, *Vitalis de Furno SRE. Card. Quodlibeta tria.*

[14] See Delorme, 'Le Cardinal Vital du Four. Huit questions disputées sur le problème de la connaissance,' *Archives d'histoire doctrinale et littéraire du moyen âge* 2 (1927) 151–337.

[15] Glorieux, 'Pour en finir avec le *De rerum principio*,' *AFH* 31 (1938) 226 f.

Group B

The nine questions of group *B* (16–24) deal with topics of number (16–17), time and duration (18–21) and moment (= *instans* (22–24)). Glorieux found group *B* in the Vatican codex *MS. Borghese 192* Fol. 93a–129a, described by Pelzer in his study on the manuscripts of *Quodlibeta* of Godfrey of Fontaines. The text of the Wadding edition is similar to the text of this manuscript. Even the last question 24 ends in both text forms in the same way. There is contact with a quodlibet of Godfrey of Fontaines: systematic points of his *Quodlibet* VI 5 are dealt with in *quaestio* 17. Ideas and formulations of *quaestio* 8 and *quaestio* 17 are very similar. For internal reasons, the author of group *B* must be the author of group *A* and Vital du Four is the author of group *A*. So, we conclude that du Four is the author of group *B*. In these terms we may also establish the *terminus a quo* of these expositions: *Quaestio* 17 refers to Godfrey's *Quodlibet* VI 5 (1289) and *quaestio* 21 refers to *Quodlibet* XIII 7 of Henry of Ghent, likewise dating from 1289. Group *A* and group *B* belong to the same period.

Group C

The story of the small last group is rather different. Delorme also discovered that *quaestio* 25 is a simple excerpt of *Quodlibet* VIII 1 of Godfrey of Fontaines and, likewise, *quaestio* 26 of Godfrey's *Quodlibet* VIII 3. Moreover, *MS. Borghese 192*, fol. 130–145v, contains a collection of 28 extracts, taken from the *Quodlibeta* of Godfrey of Fontaines, beginning with *Quodlibet* VIII 1 and VIII 3, as is shown by Glorieux.[16] Again, this is a complete surprise. *De rerum principio* breaks off after *quaestio* 26, but Glorieux discovered that *quaestio* 26 is the second question of an independent collection of extracts, the two first extracts of which are *quaestiones* 25 and 26 of *De rerum principio* and, so, the last two questions of *De rerum principio* originate from an independent collection of *quaestiones* of Godfrey's *Quodlibeta*. Glorieux does not ascribe the *quaestiones* 25 and 26 to du Four.

Conclusions

Our conclusions are the following: *De rerum principio* is a remarkable and paradoxical text. Certainly, it is not a work of Duns', but

---

[16] Glorieux, 'Pour en finir avec le *De rerum principio*,' *AFH* 31 (1938) 231, refers to *Quodlibet* VIII 1, 3–7, XI 1–5, XII 1, V 1–6, XII 2–7, 9, 11–13.

neither is it a work of Vital du Four. *De rerum principio* is a collection of selections of rather different pieces of work, mainly by du Four who definitely did not want to publish such a compilation of writings, notes and excerpts. Thus *De rerum principio* belongs to the *spuria* of Duns, but neither is it a work *of* du Four, although *quaestiones* 1–24 are *by* du Four. *Quaestiones* 1–15 are *quaestiones disputatae* and *quaestiones* 16–24 do not reflect *quaestiones disputatae* of du Four: they are only personal notes. But are the last two questions by du Four?

De rerum principio suddenly breaks off after *quaestio* 26. Within the whole of the questions of *De rerum principio*, the summaries of *quaestiones* 25 and 26 are summaries of texts of Godfrey of Fontaines. This is quite confusing, because a different world of ideas comes to the fore. The thrust of the ideas of Godfrey of Fontaines is quite alien to Franciscan thought and diametrically opposed to the Scotian way. Nor are these excerpts found among the works of Vital du Four. I also conclude that Delorme and Glorieux do not ascribe them to du Four explicitly, although at this point they started researching after the historical origin of the *De rerum principio* pieces.

This spurious writing played an important role in the traditional expositions of Duns Scotus' metaphysics and caused much confusion. In particular, *De rerum principio* VIII 4 has been a target: 'As for me, I go back to the position of Gabirol.'[17] It is fitting to conclude with Gilson's ironic comment: 'This statement, bitterly reproached to Duns Scotus, who never made it, will probably sound harmless now that its author is merely Vital du Four.'[18]

3.3.2   *Conclusiones Metaphysicae*

Wadding IV 463–495 and Vivès VI 601–667

The authenticity of *Conclusiones utilissimae ex* XII *libris Metaphysicorum Aristotelis collectae* was generally accepted during the sixteenth and seventeenth centuries. John Camers provided for the first printed edition of *Conclusiones Metaphysicae* (Venice 1503) and ascribed it to Scotus. Maurice O'Fihely, Hugh Cavell and Wadding followed this move and the scholarship of the nineteenth century was no exception, but doubts regarding its authenticity appear as early as Sbaralea.[19]

---

[17] Vivès IV 378: 'Ego autem ad positionem Avicembroni redeo.'
[18] HCPMA 694.
[19] See the important, modern reprint of Sbaralea, *Supplementum et castigatio ad Scriptores trium Ordinum S. Francisci* II 67: 'Opus fortasse alicuius ex Scoti discipulis.'

According to Seeberg, it was a summary of the interpretation of the Aristotelian metaphysics in terms of the Scotist school.[20] The authorship was discovered by Fedele da Fanna, preparing the edition of Bonaventure's complete works.[21] Da Fanna showed that these interesting theses on ontology are a work of Scotus' teacher Gonsalvo of Spain at Paris where he acted as *magister regens* during the academic year 1302–03 (§2.2). The *explicit* of these *Conclusiones metaphysicae* in the manuscript *MS. M.* III 26 of the Library of the Patriarchal Seminary at Venice, discovered by da Fanna, runs as follows:

> Expliciunt collationes metaphysice secundum magistrum *Gunsa*(n!)-*lvum*, tunc Parisiensem lectorem ac demum ordinis Minorum generalem atque lectorem.[22]

Ten manuscripts are still available, to be found in Venice, the Vatican Library (three codices), Erfurt (two codices), Lisbon, Cambridge, Paris and Bruges.[23] No codex mentions Scotus as the author. It is not clear why John Camers believed that the *Conclusiones Metaphysicae* were by Scotus.

3.3.3 *Expositio in XII libros Metaphysicorum Aristotelis*

Wadding IV 1–462 and Vivès V 435–775 and VI 1–600

Ferkic (= Matteo Ferchio) had already contested the authenticity of this work and ascribed it to Antonius Andreas. Seeberg agreed with Ferkic and assumed that Antonius Andreas extensively utilized notes jotted down by Duns.[24] This *Expositio in XII libros Metaphysicorum Aristotelis* is also called *Metaphysica textualis*. In the meantime, it has been shown to be a work of Antonius Andreas, commenting on the text of Aristotle's *Metaphysics*.[25] Antonius Andreas must have known

---

[20] Seeberg, *Die Theologie des Johannes Duns Scotus*, 61.

[21] *Catalogus Bibliothecarum* (College of Saint Bonaventure) XIX 22.

[22] Amorós, *Gonsalvi Hispani Quaestiones disputatae*, L (XLVIII–LII: §II C1: *Conclusiones Metaphysicae*). The first publication of this colophon was due to Longpré, 'Les *Conclusions métaphysiques* de Gonzalve de Balboa,' *La France franciscaine* 5 (1922) 433. Cf. the colophon of *Codex Ottoboniani Lat.* 1816 of the Vatican Library, fol. 15r: 'Explicit Collectio conclusionum libri metaphisici cum initiis suis, edita a magistro *Gunsalvo*, tunc Lectore Parisius et postea generali ministro ord. Minorum fratrum, de provincia Sancti Iacobi oriundo' (ibid.).

[23] See Amorós, *Gonsalvi Hispani Quaestiones disputatae*, XLVIII–XLIX.

[24] See Ferkic, *Discussiones Scoticae*, 46–50, joined by Balic and Seeberg, *Die Theologie des Johannes Duns Scotus*, 60–61.

[25] See Marti de Barcelona, 'Fra Antoni Andreu, OFM, "*doctor dulcifluus*" (s. XIV),' *Criterion* 5 (1929) 321–346, and Bérubé, 'Antoine André,' *Antonianum* 54 (1979) 369–446. Cf.

Duns' personal literal comments or *expositiones*. In general, *expositio* texts were originally combined with a *quaestiones* text.[26]

3.3.4 *Grammatica speculativa*

Wadding I 43–76 and Vivès I 1–50

The biography of Martin Heidegger is disastrously involved in the first revolution in textual criticism regarding Duns Scotus' oeuvre. The young Heidegger wrote a fine piece of work on the so-called *Grammatica speculativa* and considered specializing in Scotus' philosophy: *Die Kategorien- und Bedeutungslehre des Duns Scotus.* Moreover, in his still interesting *Habilitationsschrift*, Heidegger succeeded in showing that the semantics of the *modistae* still presents a worthwhile alternative.[27] Six years later Grabmann discovered that the *Grammatica speculativa* was not a work of Duns Scotus at all. It has to be attributed to Thomas of Erfurt.[28]

3.3.5 *In librum primum et secundum Priorum Analyticorum Aristotelis Quaestiones*

Wadding I 273–341 and Vivès II 81–197

Seeberg still felt perfectly certain as to the authenticity of the interesting logical writings on Aristotle's *Analytics.*[29] At the beginning of

---

Pelster, 'Duns Scotus nach englischen Handschriften,' *Zeitschrift für katholische Theologie* 51 (1927) 65–80, and idem, 'Handschriftliches zu Skotus,' *FS* 10 (1923) 1–32.

[26] Consult the excellent contributions of Giorgio Pini, 'Una lettura scotista delle *Metafisica* di Aristotele: l' *Expositio in libros Metaphysicorum* di Antonio Andrea,' *Documenti e studi sulla tradizione filosofica medievale* II 2 (1991) 529–586, and idem, 'Scotistic Aristotelianism,' in Sileo (ed.), *Via Scoti* I 374–389, especially 379–382. See also *Opera Philosophica* III xxxix–xlii. Cf. §3.6.7.

[27] Tübingen 1916. Cf. De Rijk, 'Die Bedeutungslehre der Logik im 13. Jahrhundert und ihr Gegenstück in der metaphysischen Spekulation' (1970), in Bos (ed.), *De Rijk. Through Language to Reality* VII 2: 'Seine Ausführungen sind darum so wichtig, weil die modistische Lehre von ihm in direkten Zusammenhang mit den semasiologischen Aspekten der zeitgenössischen philosophischen Spekulation gebracht wurde.'

[28] Grabmann, 'De Thoma Erfordiensi auctore *Grammaticae* quae Ioanni Duns Scoto adscribitur *speculativae*,' *AFH* 15 (1922) 273–277. As to the same discovery, see also Grabmann, 'Die Entwicklung der mittelalterlichen Sprachlogik IV: Die *Tractatus de modis significandi*,' *Philosophisches Jahrbuch* 35 (1922) 132–135 and 199–202. This last contribution has also been gathered in: *Mittelalterliches Geistesleben* I 118–125. As to Thomas of Erfurt, see Meier, 'Erfurter Franziskanerschule,' *FS* 18 (1931) 109–150, and idem, 'Erfurter Schulen,' *Antonianum* 5 (1930) 57–94, 157–202, 333–362 and 443–474.

[29] Seeberg, *Die Theologie des Johannes Duns Scotus,* 58.

the 1930s, the *sectio scotistica* doubted the authenticity of the *Quaestiones* on the *Prior Analytics*.[30] This writing is now attributed to Pseudo-Scotus, although Courtenay ascribed it to John of Cornwall.[31] Bendiek dated the *In librum Priorum Analyticorum Aristotelis Quaestiones* to about 1350 and Stephen Read believes it to have been written between the middle of the 1340s and about 1355.[32] Lagerlund argues for the first half of the 1330s, because the similarities with John Buridan's *Quaestiones in Analytica Priora* are striking although the author is unfamiliar with his more mature logical theories.[33]

3.3.6 *In librum primum et secundum Posteriorum Analyticorum Aristotelis Quaestiones*

Wadding I 342–430 and Vivès II 199–347

According to Parthenius Minges and Smeets, the author is certainly John of Cornubia,[34] for this work is attributed by an Oxford manuscript to John of St Germain of Cornwall who studied at Oxford in about 1300 and taught theology at Paris from 1310 to 1315.[35] At any rate, the logical analyses are brilliant.

3.3.7 *In libros Meteorologicorum Aristotelis quaestiones*

Wadding III 1–130 (first part of volume III) and Vivès IV 1–263

The commentaries on Aristotle's *Physics* and *Meteorology* attributed to Duns are not authentic works as is shown by Pierre

---

[30] See Gölz, 'Die echten und unechten Werke des Duns Scotus,' *Lektorenkonferenz*, 56. Cf. Smeets, *Lineamenta bibliographiae scotisticae*, 8 f., and Dermott, 'Note on the Assertoric and Modal Propositional Logic of the Pseudo-Scotus,' *Journal of the History of Philosophy* 10 (1972) 273.

[31] See Courtenay, *Schools and Scholars in Fourteenth-Century England*, 228.

[32] See Bendiek, 'Die Lehre von den Konsequenzen bei Pseudo-Scotus,' *FS* 34 (1952) 206, and Read, 'Self-reference and Validity Revisited,' in Yrjönsuuri (ed.), *Medieval Formal Logic*, 183 f. For Yrjönsuuri's translation of *Question* X of Pseudo-Scotus' *Questions on Aristotle's Prior Analytics*, see ibid., 225–234.

[33] See Lagerlund, *Modal Syllogistics in the Middle Ages*, 165–167: The Pseudo-Scotus. On Pseudo-Scotus on induction, see Bos, 'A Contribution to the History of Theories of Induction in the Middle Ages,' in Jacobi (ed.), *Argumentationstheorie*, 567–570.

[34] Minges, *Doctrina Scoti*, VI. Cf. Smeets, *Lineamenta bibliographiae scotisticae*, 8–9.

[35] See Lohr, 'Medieval Latin Aristotle Commentaries: Authors Jacobus-Johannes Juff,' *Traditio* 26 (1970) 178 (135–216). Cf. Emden, *A Biographical Register of the University of Oxford*

Duhem.[36] Thomas Bradwardine's *De proportionibus* (1328) is quoted in this work on meteorology attributed to Scotus.

3.3.8   *Dilucidissima expositio et quaestiones in VIII libros Physicorum Aristotelis*

Wadding II 1–475 and Vivès II 352–677 and III 1–470

These expositions are spurious as Wadding had already conceded. *De causa Dei* of Thomas Bradwardine was used by the author as was pointed out by Daniels in 1909. The author is the Dutch theologian and first rector of the University of Heidelberg Marsilius of Inghen.[37] Wadding had already revealed that a Neapolitan codex ascribed this work to Marsilius of Inghen (*Opera Omnia* II *prologus* 3r).

3.3.9   *De perfectione statuum*

Vivès XXVI 499–561

The *Tractatus De perfectione statuum* forms the textual difference between the Wadding and Vivès editions. *De perfectione statuum* was not accepted by Wadding, but it occurs in Vivès.[38] The theme is whether the status of a person following the footsteps of the apostles is superior to the status of prelates from a religious point of view, or not. The general background of Duns' personal views is clear: the Friar Minor has to live in conformity with the advice of Christ. It is the same concept from Alexander of Hales to Duns Scotus. The mendicant brother has to be poor and live without money or property.

Longpré discussed the authenticity of *De perfectione statuum* because it had been used by Bernard Landry. His criticisms are mainly based on arguments from internal evidence and psychological

---

III col. 1626. This ascription is no proof that both sets of *Analytica Quaestiones* stem from John of Cornwall: there is no evidence that both treatises have the same author.

[36] Duhem, 'Sur les Meteorologicorum libri quattuor, faussement attribués à Jean Duns Scot,' *AFH* 3 (1910) 626–632. Baumgartner adopted this conclusion in 1915.

[37] See Daniels, *Quellenbeiträge und Untersuchungen zur Geschichte der Gottesbeweise im dreizehnten Jahrhundert*, 162 and 164. Cf. Minges, *Scoti doctrina philosophica et theologica*, VI.

[38] See Innocenti, 'Il *De perfectione statuum* del B. Giovanni Duns Scoto (Saggio storico-critico),' *Luce e amore* 6 (1909) 498–508, Longpré, *La philosophie du B. Duns Scot*, 16–17 and 20–22, and Kirby, 'The Authenticity of the *De perfectione statuum* of Duns Scotus,' *The New Scholasticism* 7 (1933) 134–152.

arguments. However, we are also able to base our argumentation on external evidence for the Cambridge manuscript *University Library MS* 134 from the fifteenth century and the sixteenth-century *Codex* 65 of Oxford's Merton College (1456) – used by Vivès – and a Florentine fragment are late.[39] In general, just as in the case of Albert the Great and Thomas Aquinas, it is not advisable in Duns' case to use the testimony of fifteenth-century manuscripts. At any rate, the tract does not play any part in the debates on poverty during the first half of the fourteenth century.

Most authors have followed Longpré. However, Gerald Kirby was not convinced and critically concentrated on the arguments from internal evidence. In general, the tenor of such an approach is right. One cannot argue from the presence of a counter-argument to the inauthenticity of a work. Even the *Sententiae* commentaries abound in counter-arguments. The duality of arguments for and against belongs to the culture of university training of the time. Moreover, Duns' logical treatise *Quaestiones super librum elenchorum Aristotelis* rejects the concept of synchronic contingency. However, this fact does not prove that the *Quaestiones de sophisticis elenchis* is spurious. External evidence is the decisive factor. However, Kirby reversed the methodological order, stating that late medieval provenance does not *prove* that a work is spurious,[40] but sound methodology states that early provenance proves authenticity and that late medieval provenance does not.

3.3.10 *Additiones Magnae*

Wadding XI and Vivès XXII 1–512

The *Additiones Magnae* is a curious case and it might seem exceedingly critical to refer to them as spurious works. The famous research reports by Longpré from the beginning of the 1930s still consider the *Additiones Magnae* as an authentic work. Its critical edition would constitute a true contribution to Scotist scholarship, for though inauthentic in the strict sense that it had been composed by William of Alnwick, it is second to none as far as care for Duns' legacy is

---

[39] See Longpré, *La philosophie du B. Duns Scot*, 21. As for the *censura* of the Vivès Fathers, cf. Vivès XXVI 499–500.

[40] Kirby, 'The Authenticity,' *The New Scholasticism* 7 (1933) 144. The external evidence is discussed on pp. 143 f.

concerned. *Reportata Parisiensia* I in Wadding and Vivès is not a text by Duns, nor is it a set of lecture notes in preparation of the Parisian course on *Sententiae* I (autumn 1302 – beginning 1303). It is a text based on the *Summary* of William of Alnwick, doctrinally an important author for understanding Duns, and it would seem to be a gross exaggeration to say that it would cause much damage to the interpretation of Duns' thought.[41] However, this does not alter the fact that these notes were not written by Duns himself but by someone else, even if that person had been a secretary of Duns during his magisterial year. Moreover, the incunable edition (Bologna 1478) is highly problematic, though Wadding emended this *editio princeps* on the basis of the Vatican codex *Latinus 876*. *Reportata Parisiensia* I is not a text to be recommended from the critical point of view, for it is spurious and a mixture of ingredients taken from different sources. However, it is doctrinally reliable.[42] Because we do not have a critical edition, it would be rather speculative to identify Alnwick's motives for composing this work, based on *Lectura* I–II and the Parisian notes. Pelzer's suggestion that the *additiones magnae* were to improve on the minor marginal notes Duns made to his earlier *ordinatio* is out of place. Pelzer did not have, and could not have, any idea of the interaction between *Lectura* I, *Ordinatio* I and *Reportatio Parisiensis* I.[43]

3.3.11 Conclusion

The results of critical textual research conducted concerning the spurious works, some of which may be prominent in the old editions, may be summarized in the following list of works which are not authentic:

1. *Grammatica speculativa* and *De rerum principio*;
2. *Conclusiones Metaphysicae* and *Expositio in* XII *libros Metaphysicorum Aristotelis*;

[41] See Pelzer, 'Le premier livre des *Reportata Parisiensia* de Jean Duns Scot,' *Annales de l'Institut Supérieur de Philosophie* 5 (1924) 460 f., reprinted in Pattin and Van de Vyver (eds), *Études d'histoire littéraire*, 434–435, and for his criticisms, see pp. 453–464. Cf. Balic, *Les commentaires de Jean Duns Scot*, 25–33 and 44–55. Balic sees in this notebook of William of Alnwick, that is the *Additiones Magnae*, a *reportatio* of a *Sententiae* course of about 1305.

[42] Pelzer, 'Le premier livre des *Reportata Parisiensia*,' in Pattin and Van de Vyver (eds), *Études d'histoire littéraire*, 429, 441 ff. and 459–464.

[43] Pelzer, 'Le premier livre des *Reportata Parisiensia*,' in Pattin and Van de Vyver (eds), *Études d'histoire littéraire*, 446. Pelzer's *Opus Oxoniense* is something quite different from Wolter's idea of an Oxonian *ordinatio* covering *Sententiae* I–II, although Wolter embraces Pelzer's suggestion – see Wolter, 'Reflections,' in Honnefelder et al. (eds), *Metaphysics and Ethics*, 47–49.

3. *In librum primum et secundum Priorum Analyticorum Aristotelis quaestiones* and *In librum primum et secundum Posteriorum Analyticorum Aristotelis quaestiones*;
4. *In libros Meteorologicorum Aristotelis quaestiones* and *Dilucidissima expositio et quaestiones in* VIII *libros Physicorum Aristotelis*;
5. *De perfectione statuum* and *Additiones Magnae*.

3.4 THE SECOND BREAKTHROUGH IN TEXTUAL CRITICISM DURING THE 1920S

Everything started with new research concerning the *Reportatio Parisiensis*. In the first quarter of the twentieth century, the problem of authenticity in Duns Scotus' works was given much attention and the results were fascinating. At the same time, discovering that many works were not authentic was also a threat to the continuity of Scotus research. However, in 1923 and 1924 Auguste Pelzer published his searching and pioneering investigations regarding manuscripts which contain texts related to Duns Scotus' Parisian course on *Sententiae* I and these important contributions were even more shocking. Textual criticism of a new style now caught on through Pelzer's 'A propos de Jean Duns Scot et des études scotistes' and 'Le premier livre des *Reportata Parisiensia* de Jean Duns Scot.' He pointed out the importance of the Worcester and Utrecht codices of the *Reportatio Parisiensis*.[44] 'Le premier livre des *Reportata Parisiensia* de Jean Duns Scot,' concluded on 24 August 1923, is very critical of the text of Wadding. The main result was the thesis that *Reportata Parisiensia* I from the Wadding edition did not constitute a text by Duns Scotus himself.

In terms of his results, Pelzer sharply criticized the text of the Wadding edition. The Franciscan world, including the Scotist circles, were upset. Bertoni, the editor of the *Acta Ordinis Fratrum Minorum*, immediately expressed his doubts whether the highly respected *Scriptor* had adequately examined the codex under consideration.[45] Pelzer himself wondered how long such vulnerable sources could still be used,[46] and invited the College of Saint Bonaventure in Quaracchi

---

[44] Pelzer, 'A propos de Jean Duns Scot,' in Pattin and Van de Vyver(eds), *Études d'histoire littéraire*, 416 f. See also §2.2.2 and *DS* 50–52.
[45] See Bertoni's reply in *Acta Ordinis Fratrum Minorum* 42 (1923) 305–306.
[46] Pelzer, 'Le premier livre des *Reportata Parisiensia*,' in Pattin and Van de Vyver (eds), *Études d'histoire littéraire*, 463: '[. . .] ma curiosité, jugée peut-être indiscrète ou révolutionnaire.'

to publish a critical edition rather quickly. The intended Louvain pro-
moter of Balic and Bernardinus Klumper, the Dutch Minister General
of the Franciscan Order, were alarmed when they learned about the
results of Pelzer's research and, as a result, new initiatives were taken
at Quaracchi. Even more dramatically, all this happened in the wake
of the failure of the beatification process of Duns Scotus (1920–21).[47]
Pelzer was also convinced that both *De rerum principio* and the
Theoremata were authentic.

3.4.1   Quaracchi

The Bonaventure College was founded by the leadership of the
Franciscan Order at Quaracchi (*Ad Claras Aquas*), a small village near
Florence in the valley of the Arno, in 1877. The driving force behind
this project was Bernardino dal Vago da Portogruaro, at that time the
Minister General of the Order (1869–89), who was looking for
someone to edit the complete works of Bonaventure.[48] With a view to
this ideal he appointed Fedele Maddalena da Fanna (1838–81) in
1870 to search for and to collect manuscripts containing works of
Bonaventure and to explore the complicated situation of the medieval
manuscripts and the early editions.[49] Da Fanna, having been ordained
a priest in 1861, was a systematician by profession and he became a
Bonaventure scholar during the 1860s. From 1870 he devoted himself
entirely to the new critical edition of Bonaventure's *Opera Omnia*.
During the 1870s Fedele da Fanna visited scores of libraries in Italy
and France, Germany and Austria, Switzerland and Belgium, England,
Spain and Portugal. In 1875–76 – after the beginning of the German
Kulturkampf – da Fanna visited many libraries in North Germany,
Denmark and Central Germany in the company of Jeiler. According
to Grabmann, da Fanna visited almost 400 libraries during about

According to Pelzer, the text is based on bad lecture notes and this text is believed to contain
'l'expression la plus pure et la plus complète du véritable enseignement parisien du Docteur
subtil sur le Ier Livre des Sentences' (ibid.).

[47] See Balic, 'Note per la Storia della Sezione e poi Commissione Scotista,' in Almagno and
Harkins (eds), *Studies Honoring Ignatius Charles Brady Friar Minor*, 17–44. The interest of
the objective and imperturbable Pelzer in matters of textual criticism regarding Scotus'
works was rather ambivalent – see Balic, ibid., 18–28. Cf. Van Steenberghen, *Introduction
à l'étude de la philosophie médiévale*, 166–168.

[48] See Oliger, 'P. Ignatius Jeiler in Quaracchi,' *Franziskanische Studien* (1923), 50–61.

[49] See Oliger, 'Ignatius Jeiler,' *Franziskanische Studien*(1923), 50–53, and Grabmann, 'Das
Bonaventurakolleg zu Quaracchi,' *Mittelalterliches Geistesleben* I 62–71. Grabmann's personal report has been reprinted in his *Mittelalterliches Geistesleben* I 50–64.

eight years and surveyed about 50,000 manuscripts, described in twenty large folio volumes.[50] He also discovered fifty-nine Duns Scotus manuscripts.[51]

Library research was in fact established by da Fanna. According to him, the new edition of Bonaventure had to be based on the whole of his manuscript tradition. In the course of his search for Bonaventure manuscripts he stated the fundamental rules for approaching catalogues and library collections. Visiting a library, the first thing to do is to find out whether there is a reliable catalogue. Lacunae in a catalogue mean that the manuscripts themselves must be consulted, and in the absence of a functional catalogue, the manuscript collection itself must be surveyed personally. One has always to be on one's guard: the best manuscript of a particular work might be kept in an unimportant and remote library. In 1874 he published his results in a pioneering work: *Ratio novae collectionis*. This achievement earned da Fanna corresponding membership of the *Real Academia de la Historia* (Madrid) in 1877.[52]

Fidelis da Fanna, who had moved into the newly founded *Collegium Sancti Bonaventurae* at Quaracchi in the company of eight brothers in 1877, was the first director of the Bonaventure College founded to edit Bonaventure's *Opera Omnia* (1882–1902). Only forty-three years of age, he died at Quaracchi having exhausted all his strength. After his early death in 1881, Ignatius Jeiler (1823–1904), who had joined the Quaracchi team in 1879, immediately became his successor.[53] In the time span of twenty-five years Ignatius Jeiler and Elpidio Rocchetti brought the huge project to a favorable conclusion in 1902, when the eleventh volume of *S. Bonaventurae Opera Omnia* appeared.[54] In the new series *Bibliotheca Franciscana Scholastica* (1904–) crucial works of many important thinkers were edited – among others, Matthew of Aquasparta, Peter Aureoli, Peter John's Olivi, Alexander of Hales

---

[50] See Grabmann, 'Das Bonaventurakolleg zu Quaracchi,' *Mittelalterliches Geistesleben* I 51–52.

[51] See *Opera Omnia* I 138*. The Committee's formulation is only fifty-nine codices.

[52] *Ratio novae collectionis omnium operum sive editorum sive anecdotorum Seraphici Ecclesiae Doctoris S. Bonaventurae proxime in lucem edendae manuscriptorum bibliothecis totius Europae perlustratis.* See Grabmann, *Mittelalterliches Geistesleben* I 51–56.

[53] Cf. also Baeumker, 'Erinnerungen an P. Ignatius Jeiler,' *Franziskanische Studien* (1923), 33–49. This memoir informs us of the philosophical stance taken by Jeiler: modern science is rooted in nominalism and Bonaventure's theory of divine illumination is considered to be the true cornerstone of modern thought and science.

[54] Oliger, 'Ignatius Jeiler in Quaracchi,' *Franziskanische Studien* (1923), 53.

and his immediate successors and the important edition of the *Sententiae* of Peter Lombard.

Finally, a grand succession of directors of the *Collegium Sancti Bonaventurae* must be mentioned: Fedele da Fanna, Ignatius Jeiler, Leonard Lemmens, Aubain Heysse, Éphrem Longpré and Van de Woestyne, up to the Scotus edition passed on to the *Commissio Scotistica* headed by Carlo Balic.[55]

3.5 TRAGEDY AND PERSPECTIVE

The Wadding edition contained *De rerum principio* which was not only reprinted in the Vivès edition, but was also edited by Mariano Fernàndez Garcia: *Quaestiones disputatae De rerum principio et Tractatus De primo omnium rerum principio* (1910). This new edition earned severe criticisms from Auguste Pelzer (1923): it was considered to be an unfortunate achievement, because it was done without recourse to the manuscript tradition.[56] There is a paradox to be observed in the Franciscan way of handling the challenge of editing Duns Scotus critically. The Franciscans had made a splendid start in textual criticism and were credited with the first great critical edition in the historical project of editing texts of medieval thinkers: the *Opera Omnia S. Bonaventurae*. However, there is a gap to be observed between the manuscript expertise of the Bonaventure tradition of Quaracchi and Scotist experts like Garcia and Minges still working with old and unreliable editions. This latent tension led to the conflicts in the 1920s when illustrious experts like Pelster and Pelzer got involved, and painful decisions had to be made in the 1930s concerning Longpré and Balic. The tragic outcome of a review of what happened almost a century ago is that we still do not have a complete critical edition of the medieval oeuvre we need mostly from a systematic and philosophical point of view: *Scotus' complete works.*

---

[55] Grabmann, 'Das Bonaventurakolleg zu Quaracchi,' *Mittelalterliches Geistesleben* I 58. On the *Commissio Scotistica*, see Capkun-Delic, 'Commissio omnibus Operibus Ioannis Duns Scoti critice edendis,' *De doctrina Ioannis Duns Scoti* I 361–373.

[56] Pelzer, 'A propos de Jean Duns Scot,' in Pattin and Van de Vyver (eds), *Études de l'histoire littéraire*, 413. There is a bias in Pelzer's research contributions (1923) – a bias consisting of the issue of Duns Scotus' beatification. There are no contributions by Pelzer before 1923 and no more thereafter when he suddenly retreats from Scotist studies.

3.5.1   Tragedy and paradox: Éphrem Longpré (1890–1965)

When Longpré started to compose his long series of contributions on the thought of Duns Scotus being published in *Études Franciscaines* during the years 1922–24, one could have said a new star was born. *La philosophie du B. Duns Scot* is still a milestone in the history of Scotist scholarship. In fact it was as improbable an achievement as the work of Parthenius Minges in the previous generation had been. Minges and Longpré must have known one another well, but here mystery reigns in the history of scholarship. Longpré is one of the most fascinating Duns Scotus scholars. This precocious scholar (b. 1890) published a masterpiece on Duns Scotus' thought when he was only thirty-three. Landry had aggressively attacked the philosophy of Duns Scotus which was both the enemy of traditional Augustinianism and of new Thomism.[57] The young Longpré turned out to be a staunch defender of Scotus. He edited the first volume of the so-called *Summa fratris Alexandri* in the same year 1924, but did not publish much more on Scotus after 1935, although he lived for a further thirty years (d. 1965).

Born 24 August 1890 at Woonsocket (Rhode Island, USA), Zéphirin Eugène Longpré was raised at Saint-Éphrem d'Upton, in the county of Bagot (Quebec). He entered the Franciscan college in Montreal in September 1902 and started as a novice in August 1911. At the age of twenty-five he took his vows at Quebec in August 1915.

Longpré left for New York in order to sail for Rome on 9 November 1918, and enrolled as one of the first students in the recently founded Pontifical Oriental Institute. By 1920 he had achieved his doctoral degree, thus the first doctor of this Institute, so dear to Benedict XV, was a French-speaking Canadian. By the end of December 1920 he lived at Quaracchi and he would stay there until 27 February 1939. The years 1920–35 mark the period of Longpré's greatest scientific output.

Longpré arrived at Quaracchi at the end of 1920, thirty years of age. At a great pace, he conquered the secrets of paleography. What he achieved in five years is almost beyond belief and only his most striking achievements are mentioned here: *La théologie mystique de S. Bonaventure*, his series on the philosophy of Duns Scotus in *Études franciscaines* (1922–24), resulting in *La philosophie du B. Duns Scot* (1924), and a substantial contribution to the critical edition of the

---

57 Bernard Landry, *Duns Scot*, Paris 1922.

so-called *Summa fratris Alexandri*, including the doctrinal introductions of volumes I and II (1928). In addition, in a long series of important essays on Franciscan thinkers, his admiration for Walther of Bruges (d. 1307) shines out.[58]

In the meantime, the involvement of the leadership of the Franciscan Order in order to foster a critical edition of Scotus' works steadily increased. During these years, Longpré was on the team considering the work of Alexander of Hales, but on 6 November 1923, the Dutch Minister General, Bern. Klumper, charged Longpré with the task of solving the pressing problems of the manuscript tradition of Scotus' works highlighted by the alarming article by Pelzer on *Reportata Parisiensia* I. However, in January 1927 Longpré wrote to Balic that he was still mainly editing the *Summa* of Alexander of Hales.[59] Moreover, the president of the Quaracchi team, Aubain Heysse, an excellent photographer, was to support Longpré to the best of his ability and, according to Wolter, in April 1925 Heysse and Longpré had already microfilmed the most important Scotus manuscripts at the Vatican. Longpré also discovered *Codex Assisi* 137. On 13 June 1927, the year of Balic's dissertation, the General Chapter founded the *sectio scotistica* at Quaracchi. Bonaventura Marrani, the Minister General, appointed Longpré to lead this *sectio* and released him from his other tasks. Ten years later, this small team had produced almost 30,000 photographs of works of Duns Scotus.[60] In the spring of 1938, Victorin Doucet, one of the many French-speaking Canadians of the Quaracchi college at the time, was able to produce a list of almost 450 Duns Scotus manuscripts.[61] In 1938 the *Commissio Scotistica* was founded to work in Rome and to edit Scotus' works.[62] The Minister General Leonardo Bello played a decisive role to achieve this result.

[58] Longpré, 'Gauthier de Bruges O.F.M. et l'augustinisme franciscain au XIIIᵉ siècle,' *Miscellanea Francisco Ehrle* I 190–218, and idem, *Quaestiones disputatae du B. Gauthier de Bruges.*

[59] See Wolter, 'Reflections,' in Honnefelder et al. (eds), *Metaphysics and Ethics*, 20 note 82: 'Personellement je travaille à Alexandre de Halès. Ceux qui ont le désir de travailler sur Scot feront bien de ne pas s'engager dans la voie qui mène ici: c'est impossible de réaliser.' By then, Balic had already been invited to become a member of the Quaracchi team. In 1927, Balic's *Les commentaires de Jean Duns Scot* was published and he also wrote *Theologiae Marianae Elementa* (1926–27), not published until 1933.

[60] Anselme Longpré, *Éphrem Longpré*, 54–55. This fraternal contribution is a moving memoir of a life entirely devoted to Christ and the Franciscan testimony to Him. As he confessed himself, his was a happy life.

[61] Doucet, *De editione Operum omnium Ioannis Duns Scoti*, 1–24.

[62] See *Opera Omnia* I ix–xi.

3.5.2 Tragedy and perspective

We appreciate the literary legacy of one of mankind's greatest thinkers, but it is a mysterious legacy. There are old impressive editions, but they are by no means critical. There was a huge distance between the certainties cherished by the scientific establishment and the brute facts regarding this historical legacy and its editions. This was the situation at the beginning of the 1920s. There was some fierce longing in Franciscan and sympathetic circles in the Catholic Church to enhance the official position of Duns Scotus in Church and theology. In these tensions we feel the effects of Duns' sudden death centuries ago, in 1308 in Cologne. It was an unexpected blow bearing extreme consequences, even in the twentieth and twenty-first centuries. We discern uncertainty and diversity of opinion. Many scholars trusted the old-fashioned views. They were terrified by the revolutionary changes in Scotist scholarship. Not every scientific revolution is to the benefit of its subject: if the discoveries are too drastic, a scientific revolution can become a disaster to the field because it may wreck the achievements of the older generation. It may cause discontinuity so that a constructive development of the subject is seriously endangered. In fact, this was exactly what was at stake in what was going on in the revolution within Scotist studies. Pelzer, among others, felt rather critical of the traditional text form. Pelster refused to take seriously the newly discovered *Lectura*. According to his view it was not a work of Duns at all and was neither produced in Oxford nor in Duns' lifetime. In 1929 Pelster and the young Balic were crossing swords with one another, though eventually Pelster gave in.[63] To be fair to Pelster, in 1936 Pelster publicly acknowledged that he had been mistaken: 'Balic found the last one (*Lectura Oxoniensis*). I like to acknowledge this after my resistance in the beginning.'[64]

The story of the development of the work of Éphrem Longpré, then president of the *Sectio Scotistica* of the Franciscan Center of Studies at Quaracchi, is even more tense. In 1930 Longpré rejected the view that the so-called *Lectura* is a work of John Duns, claiming that, on the contrary, it is a simple abbreviation. However, in 1933 Longpré

---

[63] Cf. Balic, 'Erwiderung,' with Pelster, 'Antwort,' *Theologische Revue* 29 (1930) 225.

[64] Pelster in *Scholastik* 11 (1936) 134: 'Balic hat die letzte (*Lectura Oxoniensis*) gefunden, wie ich nach anfänglichem Widerstreben gern anerkenne,' in reply to Balic, 'Die Frage der Authentizität und Ausgabe der Werke des I. Duns Skotus,' *Wissenschaft und Weisheit* 2 (1935) 136–158. Cf. *Opera Omnia* XVII 1*–4*.

acknowledged the authenticity of the *codices* of the *Lectura*,[65] although at the beginning of the 1950s Longpré retracted this view one more time.[66]

3.6   THE AUTHENTIC WORKS

There was much news from the critical textual front from the crucial year 1923 until the middle of the 1930s. When the storm was over and the new strategy established, the new *Commissio Scotistica* relieved the old team of Quaracchi College. Balic moved into the *Antonianum* with an impressive team in 1938. It wasn't until 1950 that the first beautiful volumes of the *Editio Vaticana* appeared; by 2005 eighteen volumes of the critical edition were available.

3.6.1   The early logical writings

During the first half of the 1290s Duns produced a long series of logical writings *per modum quaestionis*, which did not avoid profound methodological and philosophical problems. His logical *Quaestiones*, occasioned by the logical writings of Aristotle and Porphyry, contain detailed logical investigations, which offer a fascinating view of the front line in contemporary logic and conceptual analysis. A substantial interest in Duns' logic had already started in the fourteenth century, but interest in Duns' logical *quaestiones* on Aristotle is to be contrasted with the continuous interest in his great theological works such as the *Opus Oxoniense* and the *Quodlibet*. We may even say that interest in Duns' logical writings was dependent on interest in the theological works. Although many logical and philosophical works in the old editions turned out to be spurious, the following survived modern textual criticism: *Quaestiones in librum Porphyrii Isagoge, Quaestiones super Praedicamenta Aristotelis, Quaestiones super libros Perihermenias, Quaestiones super librum Perihermenias. Opus alterum* and, last but not least, *Quaestiones super librum Elenchorum Aristotelis.*[67] In contrast to some other works, such as the *Opus Oxoniense* and the *Quaestiones super libros Metaphysicorum Aristotelis*, the old editions of the logical writings offer a workable text form while critical editions

---

[65] See Müller, 'Stand der Skotus-Forschung 1933. Nach Ephrem Longpré, O.F.M.,' *Wissenschaft und Weisheit* 1 (1934) 63–71.

[66] Longpré, 'Duns Scot,' in *Catholicisme hier, aujourd'hui, demain* III, Paris 1952, 1174: 'un médiocre abrégé de l'*Opus Oxoniense*'. Cf. *Opera Omnia* XVII 1*–4*.

[67] See *Opera Omnia* I 153*–154*. See also §1.4 and Chapter 4.

of the questions on the *Isagoge* and the *Categories* and the questions on Aristotle's *Metaphysics* are now available. The blue volumes of *Quaestiones super libros Perihermenias, Quaestiones super librum Perihermenias. Opus alterum, Quaestiones super librum Elenchorum Aristotelis, Theoremata* and *Quaestiones de Anima* are to be expected in the near future. In general, the manuscripts containing Duns Scotus' logical writings are late, most of them stemming from the fifteenth century. All of the codices containing the *Quaestiones super Praedicamenta Aristotelis* have the *Quaestiones in librum Porphyrii Isagoge*. The numbers of the available manuscripts of the logical writings differ substantially. A richest harvest holds for *Quaestiones in librum Porphyrii Isagoge* which have survived in twenty complete and three incomplete manuscripts, while *Quaestiones super librum Elenchorum Aristotelis* have only survived in two manuscripts.[68] Nevertheless, about every logical writing a different individual story can be told.

3.6.2 *Quaestiones in librum Porphyrii Isagoge*

Wadding I 87–123 and Vivès I 51–421
Opera Philosophica I 1–245

The family relations of the manuscripts are remarkably complex, in a manner similar to the codex tradition of the *Quaestiones super libros Metaphysicorum Aristotelis*. There are two groups each consisting of two fifteenth-century manuscripts and a third group of three fourteenth-century manuscripts together with a fifteenth-century witness, but

> although three of the four manuscripts in group 3 of the collated manuscripts belong to the fourteenth century, the failure of this group of manuscripts to read consistently together and their tendency to vary widely from the other two groups pose problems for constructing a critical text based on them, and pose similar problems for establishing a justifiable *stemma codicum*.[69]

I take this complex fact of textual criticism to imply that there was a heterogeneous interest in the logical writings of Duns Scotus in the

---

[68] See Andrews, Etzkorn et al. (eds), *Opera Philosophica* I. *Quaestiones in librum Porphyrii Isagoge et Quaestiones super Praedicamenta Aristotelis*, vii; pp. vii–xxiii list the manuscripts. Cf. *Opera Omnia* I 153*.
[69] *Opera Philosophica* I xxv. Cf. §1.4 and §4.5.

fourteenth century, caused by the combination of Duns Scotus' celebrity and the fact of the doctrinal divergence. Just for this reason, I assume that Duns Scotus never published these works, but because of his celebrity and the presence of autographs in the Oxonian *studium* quite different copies could be made. The increase of Duns Scotus' importance in the fifteenth century occasioned a more consistent interest in *all* of his works so that in this case the fifteenth-century witnesses have to be taken more seriously than would be profitable in the main. The group of collated manuscripts numbers twelve in all, five being Oxonian: *Codex* 291, ff. 1–20v (Balliol College); *Codex* 643, ff. 69v–87v (Bodleian); *Rawls D.* 235, ff. 1r–42r (Bodleian); *Seville* 18, ff. 5r–32r (Bodleian); and *Codex* 162, 77r–100r (Magdalen College).[70]

The Oxonian manuscripts have a substantial degree of correlation. So, my advice would be to consult the critical apparatus continually to see whether these witnesses are quoted. Early modern scholars such as O'Fihely and Naveros had already observed tantalizing doctrinal differences between Duns Scotus' philosophical and theological works. James Naveros tried even to alleviate the tensions by suggesting that denying the authenticity of the logical writings would help.[71] In our day, Vladimir Richter argued that probably none of the logical writings belong to Duns Scotus, because only one manuscript would have dated from the fourteenth century and these works would not have been referred to by the next generation. However, 'altogether sixteen of the twenty-three surviving manuscripts containing the questions on the *Isagoge* ascribe them to Scotus.'[72] The Belgian *Codex* 2908 going back to the first half of the fourteenth century explicitly considers both *Quaestiones in librum Porphyrii Isagoge* and *Quaestiones super librum Elenchorum Aristotelis* as *quaestiones doctoris subtilis*.

Antonius Andreas offers summaries of the questions on the *Isagoge* and the *Praedicamenta* in works of his going back to the second decade of the fourteenth century. Adam Wodeham, very eager to utilize the full harvest of recent Franciscan heritage and

---

[70] See *Opera Philosophica* I ix–xiii: codices 4–8. Cf. *Opera Omnia* I 153*.

[71] See Ashworth, 'Jacobus Naveros (fl. ca. 1533) on the Question: "Do Spoken Words Signify Concepts or Things?," in De Rijk and Braakhuis (eds), *Logos and Pragma*, 204. Cf. *Opera Philosophica* I xxvii note 49, and §4.5.

[72] *Opera Philosophica* I xxvii. On *Codex* 2908, ff. 131v–421v, circa 1325–1350, of the Bibliothèque Royale (Brussels), see op. cit., viii f. Cf. Richter, *Studien zum literarischen Werk von Johannes Duns Scotus*, 16.

familiar with Oxonian autographs of Duns, has two quotations from Duns' questions on the *Perihermenias* which are internally linked with the questions on the *Isagoge* and the *Praedicamenta* in his *Lectura secunda in primum librum Sententiarum* (about 1330).[73] There is no good reason at all for doubting the authenticity of the logical writings. Moreover, attacking the authenticity of the logical writings only on the basis of doctrinal divergence is simply mistaken from the historical point of view, because such facts ought not to be explained away but explained in a historical manner (see §§1.4–1.6).

We may conclude that *Quaestiones in librum Porphyrii Isagoge* is John Duns' first writing, because other writings of his are not referred to in it. This hypothesis is confirmed by the fact that *Quaestiones super Praedicamenta Aristotelis* refer twice to the questions on Porphyry's *Isagoge*.[74]

3.6.3   *Quaestiones super Praedicamenta Aristotelis*

Wadding I 124–185 and Vivès I 437–538
Opera Philosophica I 247–566

The *Praedicamenta* questions have survived in eleven complete and three incomplete manuscripts. *Codex* 291, ff. 21r–57r (Balliol College), *Rawls D.* 235, ff.43–47v (Bodleian) and *Codex* 162, ff. 122r–165r, 247r–v (Magdalen College) again put in an appearance. The relations between them are to be compared with those of the *Isagoge* questions. The text of the Venice (1492) and the Wadding editions (1639) was already a workable one. The new critical edition is found in the second part of Scotus' *Opera Philosophica*. 'Six of the surviving manuscripts containing these questions ascribe them to Scotus.'[75] As to the authenticity issue, the general text tradition and in particular the Oxonian tradition exclude reasonable doubt. The natural background of Duns' *Questions on the Isagoge* and *Questions on the Categories* is the British logical tradition of the final decades of the thirteenth century.[76]

---

[73] See *Opera Philosophica* I xxvii f. Cf. Courtenay, *Adam Wodeham*, chapter 2: 'Oxford Thought in the Age of Wodeham: His Sources.'
[74] See *Opera Philosophica* I xxxvii.
[75] *Opera Philosophica* I xxvii. See also *Opera Omnia* I 153*.
[76] See the *Introduction* in *Opera Philosophica* I xxxi ff. and xxxvi–xliii.

3.6.4a   *Quaestiones super libros Perihermenias*

Wadding I 186–210 and Vivès I 539–579

3.6.4b   *Quaestiones super librum Perihermenias. Opus alterum*

Wadding I 211–223 and Vivès I 581–601

In general, the view that the logical works only came down to us in a few fourteenth-century codices is unfounded. Even in the case of the two sets of the *Quaestiones super librum Perihermenias*, the number of manuscripts can compete with the number of manuscripts which contain the commentaries on the same work by other logicians who are generally recognized to have been influential. However, only five manuscripts contain the *Opus alterum*, namely *Codex Vat. latinus* 870, ff. 47–52 (Bibliotheca Apostolica), *Codex Vat. latinus* 9402, ff. 146–152, *Codex* 291 of the Library of Balliol College (Oxford), *Codex e. Mus.* 167, ff. 103–108 of Oxford's Bodleian, and *Codex latinus* 284, ff. 112–123 of the *Biblioteca Marciana* of Venice.

Eight of the thirteen manuscripts containing the first set of questions on the *Perihermenias* ascribe them to John Duns.[77] There is no reasonable doubt as to its authenticity.

> The first commentary [. . .] was written before the other one [. . .]; there are references in *opus* I to a later work, *viz. opus* II, *e.g.* for the discussion of the so-called *res verbi*. [. . .] Both *opera* are considered authentic by modern scholarship and date from an early period of Duns Scotus' life.[78]

Both sets of *Quaestiones super librum Perihermenias* will appear in *Opera Philosophica* II in the near future.

3.6.5   *Quaestiones super librum Elenchorum Aristotelis*

Wadding I 224–272 and Vivès II 1–80

These important *Quaestiones super Librum Elenchorum Aristotelis* are not as strongly represented in the manuscript tradition than the

---

[77] See *Opera Philosophica* I xxvii. Cf. *Opera Omnia* I 153*. See also §1.4 and §4.5. Vivès I–II comprising the logical writings were reprinted in 1965 by Gregg International Publishers.

[78] Bos, 'The Theory of the Proposition,' in De Rijk and Braakhuis (eds), *Logos and Pragma*, 123. The *Notabilia Scoti in libros Topicorum* present the most mysterious case. Pini is convinced that it is not a spurious writing, but although this sense of certainty is premature, it

other logical writings. The solid evidence from the fourteenth century shows only two codices so this harvest is even poorer than in the case of the *Theoremata*, namely *Codex* 2908, ff. 101–119, of the *Bibliothèque royale* in Brussels and *Codex* 260, ff. 100–153, of the Library of Merton College (Oxford).

The fourteenth-century Brussels *Codex* 2908 also contains *Quaestiones super libros Metaphysicorum Aristotelis* (ff. 1r–100v), *Quaestiones in librum Porphyrii Isagoge* (ff. 119v–131v) and *Quaestiones super Praedicamenta Aristotelis* (ff. 131v–142v).[79] The *Quaestiones super librum Elenchorum Aristotelis* will appear in *Opera Philosophica* II in the near future.

3.6.6 *Quaestiones super libros Aristotelis de Anima*

Wadding II 477–582 and Vivès III 475–641

Éphrem Longpré not only contested the authenticity of *De rerum principio* and the *Theoremata*, but also the authenticity of the *Quaestiones de Anima*. Pelster defended the authenticity of the *Quaestiones de Anima* against Longpré on the basis of the testimonies of *Codex Vat. lat.* 890, *Codex* 173 of the Library of Saint Anthony in Padua (fourteenth century), the much older *Codex lat.* 8717 (Munich) and early lists of questions.[80]

The *Quaestiones super libros Aristotelis de Anima* have survived in twenty-seven manuscripts which fall into four major groups, one group diverging substantially from the rest. However, colophons of all four groups ascribe these *Quaestiones de Anima* to Duns in quite similar wording. So it is to be concluded that they go back to the original colophon. Moreover, Adam Wodeham cites these *Quaestiones de Anima* as a work of the subtle doctor in his *Lectura secunda*. In contradistinction to the logical writings, *Quaestiones super libros Aristotelis de Anima* shows substantial theological expertise. Giles of

---

is not impossible that it will turn out to be an authentic work: see Andrews, 'The *Notabilia Scoti in libros Topicorum*,' *Franciscan Studies* 56 (1998) 65–75 and Pini, 'Duns Scotus' Commentary on the *Topics*: New Light on His Philosophical Teaching,' *Archives d'histoire doctrinale et littéraire du moyen âge* 66 (1999) 225–243.

79 On *Codex* 2908 (Brussels), see *Opera Philosophica* I viii f. *Codex* 260 (Merton College) also contains *Quaestiones super libros Perihermenias* (ff. 62r–95v). Cf. *Opera Omnia* I 154*. See §1.4.

80 Pelster, 'Eine Münchener Handschrift des beginnenden vierzehnten Jahrhunderts (*Cod. lat. Monac.* 8717),' *FS* 17 (1930) 264 f. See also Fleig, 'Um die Echtheit von Duns Scotus' *De Anima*,' *FS* 16 (1929) 236–242.

Rome, *De cognitione angelorum* (about 1288–90), *Quodlibeta* V–VII of Godfrey of Fontaines and Olivi's *In II Sententiarum* are among its sources. According to the editors, it precedes *Lectura* I–II and must have been composed rather soon after 1293. *Quaestiones super libros Aristotelis de Anima* will appear in *Opera Philosophica* V.[81]

3.6.7a *Quaestiones super libros Metaphysicorum Aristotelis*

Wadding IV 497–848 and Vivès VII 2–620
Opera Philosophica III–IV

Duns Scotus' *Quaestiones super libros Metaphysicorum Aristotelis* (*Quaestiones Metaphysicae*) show a medieval harvest of seventeen fairly complete manuscripts: twelve from the fourteenth century, three from the late fourteenth century or the beginning of the fifteenth and two from the fifteenth century. The team of editors collated eleven fourteenth-century manuscripts which may be divided into five groups (vii–xxi):[82]

  I   *Codex* 292 (Merton College) // *Codex Lat.* 16110 (Bibliothèque Nationale, Paris);

  II *Codex* 234 (Balliol College) – an independent source;

  III *Codex* 186 (Biblioteca Antoniana, Padua) // *Codex Amp.* Q 291 (Stadtbibliothek, Erfurt);

  IV *Lat. Fol.* 420 (6822) (Staatsbibliothek, Berlin) // *Codex Plut.* XXXI *dextr.* 9 (Biblioteca Laurenziana, Florence) // *Codex* 64 (Peterhouse, Cambridge);

  V   *Codex CLM* 15829 (Bayerische Staatsbibliothek, Munich) // *Codex* 201 (Biblioteca Catedral, Tortosa) // *Codex* 2908 (Bibliothèque Royale, Brussels).

According to the editors, no single manuscript is truly superior to the text of the other codices.

It is impossible to establish a *stemma codicum*. The problem of sections and additions can reasonably be solved by the convergence

---

[81] The unique information found in this section is the result of a communication by Prof. Tim Noone, the Catholic University of America, dated 20 November 2001.

[82] See the Introduction of *Opera Philosophica* III (1997) vii–xxi.

of three of the families of manuscripts, namely groups I, IV and V, if possible.

> With regard to a goodly number of questions, there is a wide divergence between manuscripts and families of manuscripts as to the order of paragraphs. There is no codicological evidence which would allow us to discern whether such reordering was done at the behest of Scotus himself or undertaken by a disciple or a scribe. We have tried to follow the *meaning* of the text, corroborated – if possible – by the convergence of *A*, *E* and *G*.[83]

A parallel solution to the problem of textual variants is not possible and, for this reason, the team of editors opted for the so-called 'rational method.'[84]

Authenticity

The fourteenth-century manuscripts – particularly the earliest ones – leave no room for reasonable doubts as to who is the author of the *quaestiones* on Book I–IX. The questions on Book X and XII (Wadding/Vivès) are a work of John Dymsdale.[85] Antonius Andreas continually quotes from Duns' *Quaestiones Metaphysicae* in his own *Quaestiones super duodecim libros Metaphysicae* (xxxvii–xl). Early references to Duns Scotus' *Quaestiones Metaphysicae* deliver an interesting picture. John Reading quotes from Duns Scotus' *Quaestiones Metaphysicae* VI 1.13–19 and 66 in his *Scriptum in Sententias* I *Prologus* 66 (xxiv–xxvi). Petrus Thomae quotes from *Quaestiones Metaphysicae* VII 17.23 (xxvi f.) and William of Ockham from

---

[83] See *Opera Philosophica* III xxxvi (xxviii–xxxvii).

[84] It is to be regretted that the fifteenth-century *Codex* 35 (Oriel College, Oxford) and *Codex* 291 (Balliol College) – 1464 – have not been collated. *Codex* 291 is a late manuscript – for this reason the editors decided not to collate it – but it was written by the famous copyist John Reinbold who copied a great many Duns Scotus codices for Bishop William Gray in the middle of the fifteenth century. The Scotus codices written by Reinbold do not contain any spurious work. *Codex* 291 contains *Quaestiones super librum Porphyrii Isagoge* (ff. 1r–20v), *Quaestiones super Praedicamenta Aristotelis* (ff. 21r–57r), *Quaestiones super libros Perihermenias* (ff. 57v–67r and 74v–78r) and *Quaestiones super librum Perihermenias* (ff. 67v–74v), concluding with the *Quaestiones super libros Metaphysicorum Aristotelis* (ff. 79–229). At that time, Duns Scotus' autographs still were in the Franciscan *studium*. These manuscripts were in private hands and escaped the unwelcome attention of Thomas Cromwell. Here, the Oxonian tradition seems to be crucial.

[85] See Ermatinger, 'John of Tytynsale (d. ca. 1289) as the Pseudo-Scotus of the Questions on *Metaphysics* X and XII,' *Manuscripta* 23 (1979) 7, and Thro and Ermatinger, 'Questions on Aristotle, *Metaphysics* X and XII, by Master John Dymsdale,' *Manuscripta* 36 (1992) 71–124 and 37 (1993) 107–167.

Quaestiones Metaphysicae VI 1.21 (xxvii), while Adam Wodeham refers to *Quaestiones Metaphysicae* VI 3.38–39 in his *Lectura secunda* I 1 *quaestio* 1.4 (xxvii). These quotations are characterized by the fact that they only concern the last four books of Duns' *Quaestiones Metaphysicae*. There are no quotations from the first half of the *Quaestiones Metaphysicae*, doctrinally deviating from *Lectura* I–II (see §1.5).

Expositio in libros Metaphysicorum Aristotelis

Antonius Andreas's ontology dominated late-medieval metaphysics. Departing from Thomas Aquinas' *Expositio* he built up a standard Scotist interpretation of Aristotle's *Metaphysics*.[86] His own *Quaestiones super duodecim libros Metaphysicae* enjoyed great reputation. The forty-four manuscripts of these *quaestiones* and the twenty-one editions from 1471 to 1523 testify eloquently to their fame.

> The *Quaestiones super Metaphysicam* of the Scotist Antonius Andreas was the overwhelming favorite in this field. Organized for ready adaptation to disputations, it was virtually unchallenged in the later Middle Ages. Aquinas' commentary ran a poor second, followed by Averroës and Duns Scotus.[87]

Ordinatio IV 11.47 clearly tells us that Duns himself wrote an *expositio* of Aristotle's *Metaphysica* and Duns' *Quaestiones Metaphysicae* refer at least five times to his own *expositio litteralis*. The most interesting reference is *Quaestiones Metaphysicae* IV 2.127 where he notes: *require expositionem ibi in* X (xxxix).[88] The traditional view assumes that Duns' *expositio litteralis* was lost.

However, Giorgio Pini revealed a truly fascinating discovery in his review of the critical edition of Duns Scotus' *Quaestiones super libros Metaphysicorum Aristotelis*.[89] He not only believes the *expositio litteralis* of the Wadding/Vivès editions was written by Antonius Andreas,[90] but he also claims that he discovered Duns Scotus'

---

[86] See Pini, 'Una lettura scotista delle *Metafisica* di Aristotele: l' *Expositio in libros Metaphysicorum* di Antonio Andrea,' *Documenti e studi* II 2 (1991) 529–586. Cf. §3.3.3.

[87] Leader, *A History of the University of Cambridge*, 168.

[88] See *Quaestiones Metaphysicae* VII 1.35, VII 19.58, VII 16.46, VII 7.19, and VIII 4.10. Cf. *Opera Philosophica* III xxxix.

[89] Pini, 'Critical study. Duns Scotus's *Metaphysics*,' *Recherches de théologie et philosophie médiévale* 65 (1998) 353–368.

[90] See his pioneering study 'Una lettura scotista: l' *Expositio in libros Metaphysicorum* di Antonio Andrea,' *Documenti e Studi* II 2 (1991) 529–586.

expositio litteralis in the Milanese library *Biblioteca Ambrosiana*, and also partially in a Vatican manuscript.[91]

> Consequently, these *Notabilia* should be regarded as Duns Scotus' *expositio*, or as what is now extant of it. [. . .] An examination of the cross-references between *Notabilia* and *Quaestiones* shows that the questions were likely originally interspersed with the literal explanation of the *Metaphysics*.[92]

The *Notabilia* also deal with *Books* X and XII.

3.6.8   *Lectura Oxoniensis* I–II

Opera Omnia XVI–XIX

In the mid-1920s Balic discovered a new *Sentences Commentary* which he attributed to Duns (see §§1.5–1.6 and §3.4). The four splendid volumes of the critical edition are based on four manuscripts. The two volumes containing *Lectura* I are based on three manuscripts: *Codex latinus* 1449 (*V*) of the Nationalbibliothek in Vienna, *Codex* 178 (Bibliotheca Antoniana, Padua) and *Codex pal. lat.* 993 (Bibiotheca Vaticana, Rome). The two volumes containing *Lectura* II are based on two manuscripts: *V* and *Codex Q* II 21 of the Library of the Friary *Sanctus Franciscus ad Ripas*.[93]

Lectura I–II is a *Sentences* 'Commentary', but such a 'commentary' is not *a commentary* in the modern sense of the word. The author must have been a *baccalaureus sententiarius*. Because of its relationship with a university course, the text may be the notebook of a teacher, a secretary or a student or the text form prepared with an eye on publication. In Duns Scotus case, we have the unfinished *Ordinatio*, *Reportatio Parisiensis* I and IV (1302–03) and II and III (1304–05) and *Lectura Cantabrigienis* I (1304). Thus we have to conclude that the only place left to incorporate *Lectura* I–II into Duns' biography is his Oxonian course on the *Sentences* (1298–99). In addition to this argument the

---

[91] See Pini, '*Notabilia Scoti super Metaphysicam*: una testimonianza ritrovato del'insegnamento di Duns Scoto sulla *Metafisica*,' *AFH* 89 (1996) 137–180, and idem, 'Duns Scotus' Literal Commentary on the *Metaphysics* and the *Notabilia Scoti super Metaphysicam* (Milan, Biblioteca Ambrosiana, C 62 Sup., ff. 51r–98r),' *Bulletin de philosophie médiévale* 38 (1996) 141–142.

[92] Pini, 'Critical study: Duns Scotus's *Metaphysics*,' *Recherches de théologie et philosophie médiévale* 65 (1998) 367.

[93] For descriptions of the manuscripts, see *Opera Omnia* XVII 4*–8* and XIX 6*–8*, cf. XIX 1*–6*. See also *Opera Omnia* I 144*–148*, and the *Lectura* I–II volumes: XVI (1960) IX–XI, XVIII (1982) XI f., and XIX (1993) 1*–15*.

decisive point can be gleaned from a text by William of Alnwick, the personal secretary of Duns in Paris. The evidence is found in the *Explicit* of the old manuscripts of his *Additiones Magnae libri secundi* which tells us that these *additiones* are summaries or excerpts *de lectura parisiensi et oxoniensi*.[94] This summarizing work clearly presupposes *Lectura* II and *Lectura* II builds on *Lectura* I. The decisive point is that Alnwick explicitly tells in these *Additiones Magnae* that it is Duns who read this material in Oxford (*Oxoniae*), even attacking theories of Henry of Ghent, for instance his theory of will.[95]

We can also prove that *Lectura* I–II was his personal notebook. 'The third theory is of John's Peter. I left off writing it down because of a certain affair.'[96] So, these notes originate from Duns himself. The '*Lectura*' is a true *lectura*, and not a student's *reportatio*. In his personal notebooks (cahiers, *quaterni*) he also pencilled his additions and corrections. The editors were able to discover that an unknown amanuensis had seen the author's autograph and copied these notes. The apograph is the basis of the text of the manuscripts we still have.[97]

3.6.9   Collationes Oxonienses

Wadding III 339–430 and Vivès V 131–317

The Wadding and Vivès editions make no mention of *Collationes Oxonienses*. All *Collationes* are entitled *Collationes Parisienses*. In his *Les commentaires de Jean Duns Scot* Balic pointed out that Wadding was wrong in giving to all Duns'*collationes* the title *Collationes Parisienses*. He also noticed that Wadding's view was commonly held but, nevertheless, mistaken, for the greater part of the *Collationes* originated from Oxford.[98] Balic promised a contribution on this mystery and had redeemed his promise by 1929, making use of six manuscripts.

---

[94] *Codex* 208, f. 40va (Balliol College) and *Codex latinus* 876, f. 310va (Bibliotheca Vaticana). See Balic, *Les commentaires de Jean Duns Scot*, 93 ff., and *Opera Omnia* XIX 17*–18*. It is not clear to me why the *Commissio Scotistica* talks of *codices* from which can be simply concluded: ' "*Lectura Oxoniensis*" seu brevius "*Oxon*" ' (*Opera Omnia* XIX 33*). Conclusive proof is only to be gathered from Alnwick's evidence. See the introduction in the forthcoming edition of William of Alnwick's *Determinationes* by Gál, Wolter and Noone.

[95] See *DS* 109–111. The *Additiones Magnae* also summarize *Lectura* II 25.

[96] *Lectura* I 26.46. Cf. §§1.4–1.6. John's Peter is: *Petrus Ioannis Olivi.*

[97] *Codex* 66, f. 32rb (Merton College, Oxford) comments on a quotation from *Lectura* I 3.56 in a critical addition to *Ordinatio* I 3.61 as follows: 'Illud invenitur in quaterno qui fuit scriptus post quaternum fratris Ioannis Duns'. Consult *Opera Omnia* XVII 8*, 10* and 13*–14*.

[98] *Les commentaires de Jean Duns Scot*, 5 note 2: 'C'est une erreur; une moitié de ces textes provient d'Oxford.'

The new view is attested by the precious *Codex 137* of the Municipal Library of Assisi. In 1927 Balic also mentioned *Codex 65* of Merton College which contains the *Collationes Parisienses*, and *Codex 90* of Merton College which contains both *Collationes Parisienses* and *Collationes Oxonienses*.[99] In 1929 Balic added four manuscripts to this Mertonian couple: *Codex 209* of Balliol College, likewise in Oxford, *Codex 241* of Peterhouse (Cambridge), *Codex 7969* of the British Museum and *Codex Vaticanus Latinus 876* which only contains the Parisian *collationes*. In the same year Longpré published a short communication on a seventh codex he attached great value to: *Codex 194* of Magdalen College (Oxford). Not all the twenty-four *collationes Oxonienses* are present in the Wadding/Vivès editions. The text form and the order of the manuscripts deviate from the printed text. Both the *Collationes Oxonienses* and the *Collationes Parisienses* date from 1301 when John Duns sailed for France in the late summer (see §1.7 and §2.2.1).

I appreciate most the order given by Pelster: *Collationes Oxonienses* according to the order of *Codex 194* of Magdalen College and for the *Collationes* numbers *15–24* according to the order of *Codex 65* of Merton College // *Codex 209* of Balliol College. The order of the twenty-four Oxford *collationes* corresponds as follows with the Wadding/Vivès (WV) counting and the *collationes* in Harris, *Duns Scotus II (CH)*:[100]

1 – WV 23	9 – WV 33	17 – WV 35
2 – WV 26	10 – WV 31	18 – WV 14
3 – WV 19	11 – WV 21	19 – WV 16
4 – CH	12 – WV 13	20 – CH
5 – WV 30	13 – WV 22	21 – (–)
6 – WV 34	14 – WV 27	22 – CH
7 – WV 12	15 – WV 25	23 – WV 15
8 – WV 32	16 – WV 24	24 – WV 28–29

[99] Ibid.: *Codex 90* reads on F° 155r: '*Collationes Parisienses* secundum doctorem subtilem,' and on F° 200r: '*Collationes Oxonienses* sec doctorem subtilem.'

[100] The sets of *Collationes* in *Codex 209*, ff. 114r–173v, of Balliol College, and *Codex 65*, ff. 66r–110v, and *Codex 90*, ff. 155r–216r, of Merton College, are beautiful. *Codex 209*, ff. 142–173v, contains the *Collationes Oxonienses*, while the first half of this part of the *Codex* contains the Parisian *collationes*. There are also good manuscripts containing only Parisian *collationes*, for example *Codex Vaticanus Latinus 876*. In Harris, *Duns Scotus* II 371–378, three *Collationes Oxonienses* have been edited which do not occur in the Wadding/Vivès editions. See Balic, 'De *collationibus* Ioannis Duns Scoti,' *Bogoslovni Vestnik* 9 (1929) 185–219, and Pelster, 'Handschriftliches zur Überlieferung,' *Philosophisches Jahrbuch* 44 (1931) 79–92.

3.6.10   *Collationes Parisienses*

Wadding III 339–430 and Vivès V 131–317

Pelster's list from 1923 simply enumerates seventeen *Collationes Parisienses* of Duns', although Pelster could not know so at the time, because one did not yet distinguish *Collationes Parisienses* from *Collationes Oxonienses*.[101] The Vatican order, compared with the enumeration in Wadding/Vivès (WV), is confirmed by the Oxonian manuscripts. In fact, Pelster presented the same list in 1931, but then he added the two last Parisian *collationes*, numbers *18* and *19*, which were not known from the printed tradition and which curiously enough are also missing in the *Codex Vaticanus Latinus 876*. However, *Collationes Parisienses 18* and *19* had, in the meantime, been edited by Harris.[102] The Vatican order of the nineteen *Collationes Parisienses* corresponds as follows with the Wadding/Vivès counting:

1 – WV 1	*8* – WV 17	*15* – WV 37
2 – WV 8	*9* – WV 18	*16* – WV 38
3 – WV 6	*10* – WV 9	*17* – WV 39
4 – WV 7	*11* – WV 10	*18* – CH
5 – WV 2	*12* – WV 11	*19* – CH
6 – WV 3	*13* – WV 20	
7 – WV 4	*14* – WV 36	

3.6.11   *Reportatio Parisiensis* I–IV

Wadding XI and Vivès (*Reportata Parisiensia* II–IV) XXII 513–XXIV

Two extraordinary explicits

At Paris Duns taught courses on the *Sententiae* for the second time to get his theological doctorate. We have a *reportatio examinata* of Duns' Parisian course on *Sententiae* I and, in contrast with Oxford, at Paris *the baccalaureus sententiarius* enjoyed the assistance of a *socius* (see §2.2.2).

Critical research into authentic *scotiana* started with research into *Reportatio Parisiensis* I. In 1880 (!), Fr. Ehrle (b. 1845) took down

---

[101] Pelster, 'Handschriftliches zur Überlieferung,' *FS* 10 (1923) 21 f. See §3.6.9.

[102] Although Harris took the names of '*Collationes Parisienses*' and of '*Collationes Oxonienses*' from the manuscripts he made use of, he did not face the problem of the historical identity of the Oxonian *collationes*, in contrast with Wadding's view. Cf. §2.2.1.

some fascinating quotations from an excellent *Reportatio Parisiensis* codex he had discovered in the library of Worcester Cathedral, *Codex F. 69*, one of the oldest manuscripts of the Scotian tradition: he transcribed a colophon belonging to *Reportatio Parisiensis* I and a colophon belonging to *Book* IV (see §3.4). These explicits were not published by Pelster until 1923.[103] Pelster had 'inherited' notes from Ehrle[104] but at that time had not seen the Worcester codex himself.[105] Pelzer immediately adopted the conclusions drawn by Pelster. In 1923 he pointed out the importance of the Worcester and Utrecht codices of the *Reportatio Parisiensis*, stressing the unreliability of the old editions containing the so-called *Opus Parisiense* as a masterly contribution. The famous results of this article were immediately accepted by, among others, Callebaut, Bihl, De Wulf and Harris. All this took place in the same year that Balic was ordained a priest and started his doctoral studies at Louvain.

Reportatio Parisiensis I

The codex of Worcester Cathedral *F. 69* was written only a few years after Duns Scotus' death.[106] The important colophon of *Book* I reads as follows:

> Here end the questions on the first book of the Sentences delivered by brother J. of the Order of the Friars Minor at Paris in the year of the Lord thousand three hundred and two and the beginning of the third.[107]

This colophon gives precious information on Duns lecturing on *Sententiae* I at Paris in the autumn of 1302 and the beginning of 1303.

---

103 Pelster, 'Handschriftliches zu Skotus,' *FS* 10 (1923) 8–9, cf. p. 1. Here, his readings of the colophons are as follows: *Questiones in I Sententiarum a fratre . . . to ord fratr min Parisius aD MCCCII° intrante III°*, and *Questiones [in IV] Sententiarum date a fr Iohanne . . . in studio Parisiensi aD MCCCIII°*.

104 See Pelster, 'Zur Scotus-Forschung,' *Theologische Revue* 28 (1929) 146–147.

105 Cf. Pelster, 'Duns Scotus nach englischen Handschriften,' *Zeitschrift für katholische Theologie* 51 (1927) 68 and 66. In the meantime, the *explicits* had also been published by the librarian of Worcester Cathedral: Kestell Floyer, *Catalogue of mss preserved in the Chapter Library of Worcester Cathedral*, 33.

106 The last questions of *Book* IV which were originally missing have been taken from Worcester's Q 99 which dates from about 1310: see Pelster, 'Duns Scotus nach englischen Handschriften,' *Zeitschrift für katholische Theologie* 51 (1927) 71–72.

107 'Expliciunt questiones super primum sentenciarum date a fratre J. [erased space + correction: Duns Scoto] ordinis fratrum minorum Parisius *anno domini M° trecentesimo secundo intrante tercio*' (Fol. 158v). See Pelster, 'Duns Scotus nach englischen Handschriften,' *Zeitschrift für katholische Theologie* 51 (1927) 69.

Reportatio Parisiensis IV

The second colophon in *Codex F. 69* concerns *Book* IV and runs as follows:

> Here end the questions (on the fourth book) of the Sentences, delivered by brother J. mentioned above in the House of Studies at Paris in the year of the Lord M CCC IIJ.[108]

Likewise, this explicit was not published by Pelster until 1923, although it also occurs in the catalogue of the Worcester Library. Neither of these solid early ascriptions leave room for any doubt as to Duns' authorship. So, Duns taught on *Book* IV in the first half of 1303. Fortunately we have a checked and amended notebook (*reportatio examinata*) of *Reportatio Parisiensis* I, in *Codex latinus* 1453 of the Viennese Nationalbibliothek (ff. 1–125). This notebook enables us to put together a privileged group of *Reportatio Parisiensis* manuscripts. Other members of this select group are *Codex F.39* and *Codex F.69* of the Library of Worcester Cathedral, *Codex 205* and *Codex 206* of Balliol College and *Codices 61–63* of Merton College (Oxford), *Codex Vat. Borghese latinus 325* of the Bibliotheca Apostolica (Rome), *Codex K. II 26* of Turin's University Library and *Codex 105* of the Library of Utrecht University (see §3.3.11). Concerning *Reportatio Parisiensis* II, we have to turn to the same group: *Codex 205* of Balliol College and *Codex 61* of Merton College in Oxford. This text is in fact found in *Reportata Parisiensia* II of Wadding XI and Vivès XXII 513–XXIII 233. Wadding's text is based on the acceptable Maior edition (Paris 1517).[109]

The story of *Reportatio Parisiensis* III is again a different one. We stick to the same group: *Codex F. 39* and *Codex F. 69* of Worcester Cathedral, *Codex 206* of Balliol College and *Codex 62* of Merton College. *Reportatio Parisiensis* II–III belong to the academic year 1304–05, but *Reportatio Parisiensis* III has only distinctions 1–17, *Sententiae* III numbering forty distinctions. During the winter of 1305 Duns had to read on christology. A useful text is found in *Reportata Parisiensia* III 1–17 (Wadding XI and Vivès XXIII 234–530).[110]

---

[108] 'Expliciunt questiones sentenciarum date a fratre J [+ with different ink: hoanne duns] ante dicto in studio Parisius anno domini $M^{o}CCC^{o}$ IIJ.' See Pelster, ibid., *IIJ* excepted, for Pelster read: *I q^{o}*.

[109] See Balic, *Les commentaires de Jean Duns Scot*, 127–133. See *Codex 205*, ff. 187r–287r, of Balliol College and *Codex 61*, ff. 115r–222v, of Merton College.

[110] *Codex 206*, ff. 105r–151v, of Balliol College and *Codex 62*, ff. 229r–260r, of Merton College.

As to *Reportatio Parisiensis* IV (1303) yet a further different story has to be told. We stick to the same family of manuscripts. However, because *Reportata Parisiensia* IV (Wadding XI and Vivès XXIII 531–XXIV) is not a reliable edition, we have to fall back on the Oxford and Worcester codices and on *Codex* 105, ff. 38ra–148v, of the Library of Utrecht University.[111]

3.6.12 *Lectura Oxoniensis* III

Opera Omnia XX–XXI: *Lectura* III 1–40

One of the challenges of Scotist scholarship is having to account for the puzzling fact that two Oxonian *Reportatio Parisiensis* III–IV codices and a Polish manuscript have a double *Sententiae* III text which differs both from *Reportatio Parisiensis* III and from *Ordinatio* III (see §2.3.1). The second *Sententiae* III text is found in the beautiful manuscript *Codex* 206, ff. 1r–104v, of the Library of Balliol College, and *Codex* 62, ff. 124r–228v, of the Library of Merton College (both in Oxford). A third manuscript, *Codex latinus* 1408 of the Library of Cracow University, contains an incomplete text of *Lectura* III.[112] *Codex* 206 of Balliol College covers all the forty distinctions of *Sententiae* III. The manuscripts talk of a *lectura completa*, but in this case 'lectura' refers to a course, not to a text. The best way this *Sententiae* III text can be called is *Lectura* III: it is due to Oxford and Duns' exile. The critical edition of *Lectura* III 1–40 long awaited for appeared recently (2003). I do not think that there was ever an Oxonian *Lectura* IV.

3.6.13 *Lectura Cantabrigiensis* I

Lectura Cantabrigiensis I has been discovered in *Codex* 12, ff. 121ra–199vb, of the Public Library of Todi ((= Tudertum) Umbria, Italy). *Lectura Cantabrigiensis* I is identical with *Rep.* IC of the list of Duns' major texts on *Sententiae* I. The manuscripts *Vat. Borghese latinus* 50 and *Borgh. latinus* 89 of the Vatican Library in Rome are much shorter *reportatio* texts and do not contain *Lectura*

---

[111] For Duns Scotus' theology of sacrament and eschaton, see the reliable *Opus Oxoniense* (= *Ordinatio*) IV.

[112] On the manuscripts, see *Opera Omnia* I 148* and *Opera Omnia* XX xii. *Lectura* III 1–17 deals with christology.

Cantabrigiensis I.[113] I do not believe that it is a *reportatio*, but consider it to be a *lectura*, because, in Cambridge, in contradistinction to Paris, by that time Franciscan bachelors did not enjoy the company of a *socius* (see §2.3.2).

3.6.14   *Quaestiones Quodlibetales*

Wadding XII and Vivès XXV–XXVI

Duns Scotus' *Quodlibet* immediately became a popular text. It has survived in more than eighty manuscripts.[114] *Codex lat*. 26309 of the State Library in Munich has a colophon giving a completion date of 1311. Harvey of Nedellec had already discussed Duns Scotus' views, including views taken from his *Quodlibet* (1307), when he (d. 1323) became master in theology in Paris and conducted his first *quodlibet*, and afterwards. *Codex lat. Mon.* 8717 available in the same library contains substantially the same version, but also shows traces of the original *reportatio* of the quodlibetal disputation itself.[115] According to the *Commissio Scotistica*, an adequate revision of the text of the Wadding/Vivès editions can be arrived at on the basis of both Munich manuscripts and *Codex F*. 60 of the Cathedral Library of Worcester.[116]

We have a semi-critical edition and some good modern translations. There is the Latin edition provided for by the team of the editors of the review *Verdad y Vida*: Celestino Solaguren, Bernardo Aperribay and Antonio Eguiluz, cooperating under the direction of Alluntis, published in Madrid by the *Biblioteca de Autores Cristianos*.[117] Besides this bilingual edition, we have the fine translation into English by Wolter and Alluntis, based on the same edition with some corrections and improvements.[118] Here Duns Scotus offers precise, compact and well-organized teaching. When we compare

---

[113]   See *Opera Omnia* I 145* and ibid., s.v. *Rep. ID*.

[114]   *Opera Omnia* I 150* f. Cf. Pelster, 'Eine Handschrift des vierzehnten Jahrhunderts – *Codex lat. Mon.* 8717,' *FS* 17 (1930) 271 f.; cf. idem, 'Handschriftliches zu Skotus,' *FS* 10 (1923) 16–21.

[115]   Wolter and Alluntis, *God and Creatures*, xxxiii: 'Question 21 ends abruptly with the words: "Tertium membrum" [. . .] with the marginal note: Finis. Quodlibet repertum in suis quaternis. Quod sequitur est de *Reportatione*.'

[116]   See Wolter and Alluntis, *God and Creatures*, xxxii f.

[117]   *Obras del Doctor Sutil Juan Duns Escoto. Cuestiones cuodlibetales*, XVIII. The excellent introduction, translation and notes are by Felix Alluntis.

[118]   Wolter and Alluntis, *God and Creatures. The Quodlibetal Questions*, XXXI–XXXIV, likewise with an excellent introduction, helpful notes and a fine glossary (493–540).

Clm 8717 with the prefinal text of the modern editions, we still have a sense of how Duns made an effort to be clear and complete.

3.6.15 *De primo principio*

Wadding III 208–259 and Vivès IV 721–789

With *De primo principio* we have suddenly reached the final stage of Duns' life. Tradition, including the manuscript tradition, is unanimous in ascribing the authorship of this fascinating booklet to Duns Scotus. The available text form is good, and although the definitive critical edition is still missing there is a series of semi-critical editions. The first edition of the *Tractatus De primo principio* was intended to be a perfect critical edition; in fact, it was the first critical edition of any work of Duns Scotus. However, the very difficult circumstances under which Müller had to work in the second year of World War II, affected the quality of his edition, although he did make use of the known manuscripts. Müller's work is now difficult to come by. After the war Evan Roche emended this edition by collating again seven manuscripts, but not all changes were improvements.[119] The third semi-critical edition is Wolter's, accompanied by a translation into English (1966). Kluxen improved on some weak spots in Wolter's edition using the previous editions in his translation and commentary. Wolter also published a revised edition of the text and translation, adding an excellent commentary.[120] The bilingual edition (Spanish–Latin) by Felix Alluntis also has to be mentioned.[121] We even have numerous good translations, for example, in Italian and Dutch.[122]

In *De primo principio* the monographic tendency culminates. From the very start we meet excursions in Duns' writings. In *Lectura* I–II excursions on central issues already develop into little monographs,

---

[119] Müller, *Joannis Duns Scoti Tractatus de Primo Principio*, and Roche, *The De Primo Principio of John Duns Scotus*. See Kluxen, *Johannes Duns Scotus. Abhandlung über das Erste Prinzip*, XVII f. For the list of manuscripts, see *Opera Omnia* I 154* and Wolter, *Scotus. A Treatise on God as First Principle*, XXII. For a description of the manuscripts, see Müller's and Roche's editions. Wolter's and Kluxen's editions serve systematic purposes in an excellent manner.

[120] *A Treatise on God as First Principle*, 157–373. Allan Wolter is unique as a translator of Duns, although Italy also has a special tradition of translating Scotus (Scaramuzzi).

[121] *Dios uno y trino*, 593–710, which also appeared in the *Biblioteca de Autores Cristianos*, volume 193.

[122] Scapin, *Il primo principio degli esseri* (1968), and Peters, *Duns Scotus. Het eerste beginsel* (1985).

thus the monographic tendency was born. The first working out of Duns' philosophical theory of divine attributes is also found in the *Lectura*: *Lectura* I 2. I derive from this literary characteristic that *De primo principio* belongs to the last stage of Duns Scotus' life and work.

3.6.16   *Theoremata*

Wadding III 260–338 and Vivès V 2–125

The authenticity of the *Theoremata* was fiercely doubted when Déodat Marie de Basly contested it in 1918.[123] He carefully argued for the thesis that it has to be rejected as a spurious work, both from external evidence because he was not able to find an old manuscript containing the *Theoremata*, and from internal evidence. Wadding had assured his readers that *Theoremata* was an authentic work which testified to the ingenuity of Duns Scotus and was accepted by the great Scotists of previous generations.[124] In fact, Wadding simply harkened back to the research of his predecessor Maurice O'Fihely (1463–1513). In a few old copies, O'Fihely found a text difficult to read and open to question through the unmistakable errors of copyists. The order of the propositions was quite different in different manuscripts and there was clearly a problem of marginal notes and additions. To the best of his ability, he tried to master all these difficulties. We have to conclude that the outcome was an independent reissue of *Theoremata*.[125] It was clear to de Basly that O'Fihely was unable to cope with this daunting task, although he realized that there seemed to be serious divergences between the *Theoremata* and other authentic works of Duns, but, to O'Fihely's mind, the *Theoremata* was also an authentic work and so he tried make the reconciliation. However, in opposition to the trio of O'Fihely, Cavell (1571–1626) and Wadding, Sbaralea detected here two independent works: *De theorematibus* and *De creditis* (= *Theoremata* XIV–XVI).

In *La philosophie du B. Duns Scot*, Longpré did not deliver an evenly distributed treatment of the critical textual problems of Duns' works. Instead, he mainly focused on three philosophical opuscles, because Landry's exposition of Duns' views had been mainly based on *De perfectione statuum*, *De rerum principio* and the *Theoremata*.

---

[123] Déodat Marie de Basly, 'Les *Theoremata* de Scot,' *AFH* 11 (1918) 3–31.
[124] For his view, see his *censura* of the textual problems in the preface to his edition: Vivès V 1.
[125] Vivès V 3 and de Basly's analysis of Wadding's research report, 'Les *Theoremata* de Scot,' *AFH* 11 (1918) 4–8.

Longpré agreed with de Basly's main point of external criticism. Appealing to the expertise available at Quaracchi, he stressed that nobody knew of any manuscript in a European library. He amply pointed out that the philosophical doctrine of God in the *Theoremata* is incompatible with *De primo principio*. *Theorema* XIV is certainly not by Scotus, Longpré believed, and the same result can be demonstrated with regard to *Theoremata* XV–XVII. Because many doctrines seem to be parallel to Ockhamism, Longpré dated the *Theoremata* after Ockham.[126]

Later on, Balic was able to decide the authenticity dilemma in favor of Duns Scotus.[127] Although the *Collegium Sancti Bonaventurae* (Quaracchi) did not know of any manuscript containing Duns Scotus' *Theoremata* in the mid-1920s, Balic described two manuscripts in 1933 and the *Commissio Scotistica* listed four manuscripts in 1950. The *Theoremata* has survived in three complete manuscripts and one incomplete: *Codex* 307 of the Library of the Augustinian Canons in Klosterneuburg; *Codex AF. X. 7* of the Biblioteca Nazionale Braidense in Milan; *Codex* 1439 (M. LXXXII) of the Library of the Metropolitan Chapter of Prague; and the incomplete *Codex* 13 of the Dominican Library Saint-Dominique in Dubrovnik (Dalmatia). Balic paid glorious attention to the Dubrovnik codex.[128] The *Explicit* of the Klosterneuburg *Codex* 307 explicitly ascribes the *Theoremata* to *Magister Iohannes Scotus*. We look forward to the fine critical edition to be published in *Opera Philosophica* II, edited by Mechtild Dreyer, Gerhard Krieger and Hannes Möhle, which will appear in the near future.

3.6.17   *Ordinatio* I–IV

Opera Omnia I–VIII: *Ordinatio* I–II

Duns Scotus' *Ordinatio* is no true *ordinatio* because it was never finished and published, and an *ordinatio* is an officially published book.

---

[126] Longpré, *La philosophie du B. Duns Scot*, 22–48.

[127] See also Gál, 'De I. Duns Scoti "Theorematum" authenticitate ex ultima parte confirmata,' *Collectanea Franciscana* 20 (1950) 5–50.

[128] Balic, 'Alte Handschriften der Dominikanerbibliothek in Dubrovnik (Ragusa),' *Aus der Geisteswelt des Mittelalters* III A, 5–7. Cf. idem, 'Bemerkungen zur Verwendung mathemathischer Beweise und zu den scholastischen Schriftstellern,' *Wissenschaft und Weisheit* 3 (1936) 191–217. His descriptions of the Milanese and the Klosterneuburg manuscript (fourteenth century) are found in *Theologiae Marianae Elementa*, XXXIV–XXXVI. Cf. *Opera Omnia* I 154*.

What we call the *Ordinatio* is the enormous set of prepared drafts for the intended *Ordinatio* on *Sententiae* I–IV. *Ordinatio Prologus* – *Ordinatio* II 3 appeared between 1950 and 1973. The *Commissio Scotistica* was already in possession of proofs of *Ordinatio* II 4–44 in 1993, but the definitive edition only appeared in 2003. The internal critical textual problems are daunting, because the strategy applicable to *Book* I fails with respect to *Book* II.[129] *Opus Oxoniense* III–IV are in fact workable texts for *Ordinatio* III–IV. Because of the immense interest in Duns Scotus in the late Middle Ages, a bewildering number of manuscripts are still available: as to *Ordinatio* I, *Opera Omnia* I 9*–12* lists 103 manuscripts.[130]

3.6.18 *Opus Oxoniense* I–IV

Wadding V–IX and Vivès IX–XXI

The *Opus Oxoniense* is not a work (*opus*) written by Duns Scotus.[131]

> After Scotus' death in 1308, he (= Alnwick) oversaw the definite edition of the *Opus Oxoniense* and the *Opus Parisiense*. By 1314 he had given his own lectures on the *Sentences*, possibly at Paris, and around 1316 he became the Franciscan *magister regens* at Oxford.[132]

Although textual evidence originates from the South of England, my present proposal would be that Alnwick and his colleagues did this daunting job in the Franciscan *studium* in Oxford, where they had collected Scotus' autographs. So, the *Opus Oxoniense* is indeed an Oxonian work, composed by Alnwick and his friends to save Duns'

---

[129] Cf. Wolter, 'Reflections about Scotus's Early Works,' in Honnefelder et al. (eds), *Metaphysics and Ethics*, 42 ff. The *Ordinatio* was indeed a work *in statu nascendi*, but Wolter underestimates the value of *Ordinatio* I of the Vatican edition. The distinction between a rather immature Oxonian Duns and a mature Parisian Scotus is not a viable one. There is a valid point in Richter's criticisms: the old *Opus Oxoniense* edition was not as bad as Balic suggested, but Richter is overcritical as to the Vatican *Ordinatio*.

[130] See the impressive description of the 103 listed codices (*Opera Omnia* I 12*–126*). Cf. the list of thirty-one *Opus Oxoniense* editions before 1800 (I 128*–130*). Pay special attention to the incunables: 1472–1497 (*Opera Omnia* I 131*–137*). A great many manuscripts have *Ordinatio* II–IV texts. Balic had already described numerous *Ordinatio* manuscripts in *Les commentaires de Jean Duns Scot* (1927) and many other manuscripts in *Theologiae Marianae Elementa* (1933) XXIV–XLIV.

[131] See *Opera omnia Ioannis Duns Scoti* V–IX, Lyons 1639 (in twelve volumes, reprint Hildesheim 1968), and Vivès VIII–XXI.

[132] Courtenay, *Adam of Wodeham*, 58 (57 f.: William of Alnwick).

heritage, for they managed to complete this massive commentary before 1313. By 1316 Alnwick had already returned to Paris and Harvey Nedellec does not refer to the *Opus Oxoniense*, although he refers to the *Quodlibet*, the *Quaestiones Metaphysicae* and *De Anima*. I grant Pelster that the *Opus Oxoniense* is doctrinally reliable.[133] However, the true *opus Oxoniense* is the *Lectura*, not published during the Middle Ages. It was soon forgotten. Deeply felt friendship preserved an unfinished agenda for centuries to come.

3.7 THE MORAL

Whoever is able to find a path through the labyrinth of editions and manuscripts is able to study almost the whole of Duns Scotus' theology, logic and philosophy based on reliable texts, although this is not possible for every stage of Duns Scotus' output. There is a striking continuity since the middle of the 1290s. In particular, the *Lectura* I–II, *Ordinatio* I–II and *Ordinatio* III–IV (= Wadding, *Opus Oxoniense* III–IV) offer, together with the *Quodlibet* and *De primo principio*, a universe of thought

> Of realty the rarest veinèd unraveller; a not
> Rivalled insight, be rival Italy or Greece . . .[134]

When the storm was over and the new strategy established, the new *Commissio Scotistica* relieved the old team of Quaracchi College. Balic moved into the *Antonianum* with an impressive team in 1938 but it was not until 1950 that the first beautiful volumes of the *Editio Vaticana* appeared. During the 1950s, the output was much more promising: five volumes of *Ordinatio* (*Prologus – Ordinatio* I 25). From 1960 onwards, five further volumes appeared up to 1982. Eventually, the 1990s saw new triumphs: the completion of *Lectura* I–II in 1993 when *Lectura* II 7–44 was published at Rome, the crowning glory to the beatification of John Duns by Pope John Paul II in March 1993, and the splendid critical edition of the blue volumes of Duns Scotus' *Quaestiones super libros Metaphysicorum Aristotelis* I–II (1997) and his *quaestiones* on Porphyry's *Isagoge* and Aristotle's

---

[133] Pelster, 'Review of C. Balic, "Die Frage der Authentizität und Ausgabe der Werke des I. Duns Skotus," *Wissenschaft und Weisheit* 2 (1935),' *Scholastik* 11 (1936) 133. See also *Opera Omnia* XVII 1*–4*. For the original format of the *Opus Oxoniense*, see the early fourteenth-century English manuscripts *Codex lat.* 15360 and *Codex* 15361 *lat.* of the Parisian Bibliothèque Nationale.

[134] Gardener (ed.), *Poems of Gerard Manley Hopkins*, 84 – sonnet 44: 'Duns Scotus's Oxford.'

Categoriae. In addition, *Ordinatio* II 4–44 and *Lectura* III 1–40 appeared very recently.

In order to understand the blue volumes edition of Duns Scotus' *Opera Philosophica* we have to go back to the mid-1980s when the team assembled by Gedeon Gál – Girard Etzkorn, Francis Kelley and Rega Wood – foresaw that the critical edition of Ochkam's theological and philosophical works would soon be completed.[135] Prior to the completion of the Ockham edition, it was decided that Gedeon Gál and Rega Wood would work on the edition of Wodeham's *Lectura Secunda*, while it would be crucial for promoting the *causa Scoti* that Etzkorn, the successor of Gál, Kelley, Romuald Green and George Marcil should undertake the edition of Duns Scotus' philosophical works, because the Scotist Commission was completely engrossed in editing *Lectura* II and the *Ordinatio*. John Vaughn, the then Minister General of the Franciscan Order, granted this permission. The only thing the St Bonaventure team, Girard J. Etzkorn being the general editor, could do was to find its own way. After the untimely death of Francis Kelley (October 1988), Robert Andrews, trained in Copenhagen, came on board as his replacement. In the ensuing years, Timothy Noone, later to be Wolter's successor at the Catholic University of America in Washington, and Roberto Plevano were added to the team. By the time of Etzkorn's retirement (1995), three volumes were ready to be sent to the publisher: *Opera Philosophica* I and III–IV, while, in the meantime, the Bonn team had finished the edition of the *Theoremata*. However, problems regarding the *Quaestiones in librum Elenchorum Aristotelis* and printing problems regarding the *Theoremata* of the Bonn team delayed the publication of Duns Scotus' *Opera Philosophica* II: *Quaestiones super libros Perihermenias, Quaestiones super librum Perihermenias. Opus alterum, Quaestiones super librum Elenchorum Aristotelis* and the *Theoremata*. The team of editors of Duns Scotus' *Opera Philosophica*, namely Tim Noone, Carlos Bazan, Kent Emory and Roberto Plevano, relocated to the Catholic University of America in Washington, and is now working on the edition of Duns' *Quaestiones de Anima* which will be printed in the not too distant future.[136]

---

[135] This edition was funded by the National Endowment for the Humanities from 1973 to 1985.

[136] The valuable information in this section is derived from Girard Etzkorn's communication, dated 5 April 2002. Etzkorn is the former general editor of Duns Scotus' *Opera Philosophica* edition. Cf. Tim Noone, 'Appreciation of Girard J. Etzkorn,' *Franciscan Studies* 56 (1998) IX f.

More than eighty years after Pelster's and Pelzer's admonitions (1923), we note that the critical edition will still take much time. In terms of the present speed, the *Commissio Scotistica* will need a century to complete the *Ordinatio*.

> What the *Ordinatio* to Bks. III and IV will reveal is another matter, but a critical edition by the Vatican press is not something most of us can reasonably hope to see in our lifetime.[137]

The revolution in textual criticism during the 1920s yielded universal disturbance. Many works did not survive textual criticism. Moreover, the unexpected and discouraging impression provided by the new publications was that the texts of both the *Opus Oxoniense* and the *Opus Parisiense* – the fundamental theological works – were not reliable. It was already clear that the old editions of the *Quaestiones super libros Metaphysicorum Aristotelis* and the *Quaestiones de Anima* were problematic. The negative results of the 1920s caused an overreaction of prudence in the 1940s and the second half of the twentieth century. Duns' scientific popularity during the fourteenth century had given rise to scores of important codices. Balic and the *Commissio Scotistica* decided to utilize almost all the available manuscripts instead of collating only the essential group of the most important and best codices. The unintended effect was that the speed of editing the Ordinatio slowed down dramatically. In the meantime the Balic generation of editors has passed on. All this has resulted in discontinuity in Scotist scholarship. However, the foundations for restoring the whole of Duns Scotus' thought and reconstructing its implications have been laid.

---

[137] Wolter, 'Reflections about Scotus's Early Works,' in Honnefelder et al. (eds), *Metaphysics and Ethics*, 42.

Part II

The philosophy of John Duns Scotus

CHAPTER 4

Logic matters

4.1 INTRODUCTION

The *Lectura* and the *Ordinatio* contain many analytical and conceptual *praenotanda* or introductions which serve as preliminary analyses. The requirements of a theological revolution permanently press in the direction of new logical, semantic and ontological investigations. Important parts are theological parallels to Wittgenstein's philosophical investigations. The ordinary language of common life and common sense is the source of logical-philosophical creativity for the latter, the ordinary language of faith is so for the former, within the context of a powerful tradition of systematic theology. However, if we had the impression that Duns was driven by some religious wishful thinking we would easily mislead ourselves. Nothing is further from his mind. Apart from general human understanding and an open philosophical mind, the only ingredients required for studying Duns Scotus' philosophy are knowledge of medieval Christianity, its Latin and its Bible, and logical canons of consistency.

Attention must be paid to a series of topics important for understanding Scotus' way of analyzing systematic issues once we have cleared the way with some introductory remarks on the significance of his logical writings (§4.2): the subject matter of logic (§4.3), meaning (§4.4) and the problem of meaning and the problem of knowledge (§4.5), concept (§4.6), proposition (§4.7), negation (§4.8), truth (§4.9), logical impossibility and logical possibility (§4.10), elements of the theory of relation (§4.11) and a concluding section summing up John Duns' early development and its impact (§4.12).

4.2 THE SIGNIFICANCE OF JOHN DUNS' LOGICAL WRITINGS

Duns' first surname was *magister rationum* (*master of the argument*) and he is still called the *subtle doctor*, but Bocheñski only mentions

Duns Scotus in the bibliography of his mighty *Formale Logik*.[1] We also learn that 'perhaps the systems of St. Thomas Aquinas and John Duns the Scot deserve only the reluctant admiration we give to the pyramids of Egypt and the palace of Versailles.'[2] According to William Kneale, there were great logicians in the Middle Ages but, apart from Abelard and Adam of Balsham (*Parvipontanus*), they originated from the fourteenth century. Kneale also mentioned an interesting spurious work of Scotus, *In Universam Logicam Quaestiones*, to be found in Wadding's edition of Scotus' *Opera Omnia* I and to be ascribed to a Pseudo-Scot, a series of discussions on questions suggested by Porphyry's *Isagoge* and Aristotle's *Organon*. It is difficult to understand what this may mean. Wadding simply calls the whole of the logical writings of Scotus, authentic and spurious, *In Universam Logicam Quaestiones*. There is no spurious work called *In Universam Logicam Quaestiones*. The questions on *Isagoge*, *Categoriae*, *De Interpretatione* and *De Sophisticis Elenchis* are by Duns Scotus, the questions on the *logica nova* by others,[3] but, within the much later context of the formal developments after Frege, Duns Scotus is praised because $p \rightarrow (-p \rightarrow q)$ is considered to be a reformulation of the paradoxical theses, formerly attributed to Duns Scotus: any proposition may be derived from a self-contradictory conjunction.

Moody praises only the ideas of the *logica moderna* in his fine survey of medieval logic, almost forty years ago.

> Among the inauthentic writings included in the old edition of Scotus' *Opera Omnia* are some treatises on formal logic in which the ideas of the *logica moderna* are developed with the highest skill; these works, now attributed to an unknown author designated the pseudo-Scotus, were probably written in the fourteenth century and may well have been influenced by the work of William of Ockham (c.1285–1349), whose *Summa Logicae*, composed around 1326, inaugurated the period of maturity of medieval logic.[4]

Duns' absence is even more conspicuous in the impressive trilogy on the history of the theory of proposition by Gabriël Nuchelmans,[5] but since 1981 the tables have been turned regarding modal

---

[1] Bocheñski, *Formale Logik*, 169 ff.

[2] William and Martha Kneale, *The Development of Logic*, 226.

[3] Kneale, *The Development of Logic*, 242 f., cf. 525. Pseudo-Scotus is praised very much – see *The Development of Logic*, 242 f. and 277–288 (on *consequentiae*).

[4] Moody, 'Medieval Logic,' in *History of Logic*, EP IV 530 (528–534).

[5] Nuchelmans, *Theories of the Proposition* (1973), *Late Scholastic and Humanist Theories of the Proposition* (1980) and *Judgment and Proposition* (1983).

logic,[6] although, apart from modal logic and Duns' idea of *contingency*, even the *Cambridge History of Later Medieval Philosophy* does not pay much attention to Duns Scotus' logic. Attempts have been made to account for such omissions by doubting Duns Scotus' logical influence and significance. According to Balic, 'Duns Scotus' *Logicalia* did not exert a great influence upon the history of Scotism. The fact that they came down to us only in a few fourteenth-century codices seems to support this view.'[7] This view has been ably refuted by Bert Bos by showing that

> the number of manuscripts containing Duns Scotus' two commentaries on Aristotle's *Perihermeneias* can compete with the number of manuscripts, in which the commentaries on the same work by other logicians have been handed down, logicians who are generally recognized to have been influential.[8]

Jan Pinborg's judgement is even more striking.

> Even if Scotus had a tremendous impact on other aspects of English theology and philosophy in the 14th century, I find his importance for the specific change in conceptual languages here studied negligible.[9]

However, Pinborg put Duns Scotus rather massively in the Parisian *modistae* tradition, ignoring his English and Franciscan background.[10]

There are differences between the early books of *Quaestiones super libros Metaphysicorum Aristotelis* and the *Lectura*, but there are even more striking differences between the logical writings and *Lectura* I–II. So there is a riddle, but the right way to solve this riddle is by taking account of Duns' linguistic turn: a logical and semantic turn which took place between the early logical writings and Duns preparing the *Lectura* course. This miracle is the key to understanding both Duns and his methodological and logical influence. The logical writings enjoy special importance, positively and negatively: they play a double role, showing transition and containing preparatory ideas and theories, while they also show discontinuity (see §1.4 and §4.12). At any rate,

6 See Knuuttila, 'Time and Modality in Scholasticism,' in Knuuttila (ed.), *Reforging the Great Chain of Being*, 228–230, and *KN* (1981) 81–87 and 269–275. Cf. *CF* 1–3.

7 Balic, 'The Life and Works of John Duns Scotus,' in Ryan and Bonansea (eds), *Studies in Philosophy and the History of Philosophy* I, 22–23.

8 Bos, 'The Theory of the Proposition According to John Duns Scotus,' in De Rijk and Braakhuis (eds), *Logos and Pragma*, 122.

9 Pinborg, 'The English Contribution to Logic before Ockham,' *Synthese* 40 (1974) 32. Duns is also conspicuous by his absence in Pinborg's *Logik und Semantik im Mittelalter*.

10 See Pinborg, 'Die Logik der Modistae' (1975), in Ebbesen (ed.), *Jan Pinborg. Medieval Semantics*, V 41.

they are not a felicitous starting point for diagnosing Duns Scotus' logical influence. John Duns' Oxonian theological writings are the point of departure to discover the paradigm shift in English thought in the beginning of the fourteenth century (see §1.8).

4.3   THE SUBJECT MATTER OF LOGIC

One of the central problems of the medieval academic enterprise is the absence of a clear-cut notion of *subjects* or *fields* ('compartments of learning') to be taught at the university. In fact, an *auctoritates* culture is alien to a clear classification of academic subjects. The *quaestio* literature is in itself already a phenomenon of powerful emancipation from the principles of an *auctoritates* culture, although one still adheres to the techniques of such a culture. However, questions as to whether certain issues are covered by logic or metaphysics point to a growing consciousness of something like an internal classification of subjects. Logic matters, but why? Aristotle would answer that logic matters because matter does not matter, but to the medieval mind questions like what is logic and what is the 'subject matter' of logic are quite different questions. The modern mind likes saying 'the best way to discover what logic is about is simply by doing logic.' The common medieval answer is that the particular topic of logic is *argumentation*. Abelard had already taught that logic is about *arguments*, and that is also Duns' initial intuition for, according to Duns' traditional view in his *Super primum librum Perihermenias Quaestiones*, logic does not deal with words as such. Linguistic investigations are delegated to grammar (*grammatica*) and, according to William of Sherwood and Peter of Spain, the first object of logic is a sentence signifying the true and the false.[11] The formal object (*subiectum*) of logic is the *enuntiatio*, seen as something in the mind. In terms of this formal object, logic deals with the parts, the kinds and the properties of the *enuntiatio* or proposition and the broader category it falls under (the *genus*), namely the *oratio* (the locutionary act). The aspect of logic highlighted in *Super primum librum Perihermenias Quaestiones* 1 is entailed by the definition of *Quaestiones in librum Porphyrii Isagoge* 1–3. The elements of a demonstration are treated in the whole of logic, just as the components of a proposition are treated in the analytical part of logic. So logic is

---

[11] *Super primum librum Perihermenias Quaestiones* 1.1: 'Cum nulla pars logicae sit de voce, ut de subiecto, [. . .] quia omnes passiones subiectorum in logica eis aequaliter inessent, nulla etiam voce existente.'

no *scientia sermocinalis*, a science about linguistic entities as it was commonly held until Albert the Great (d.1280).

> The attempt to establish logic as a science of linguistic entities only may be called sermocinalism. During the years 1150 to 1250, when medieval logic was acquiring its distinctive character, sermocinalism held undisputed sway as the philosophy of logic, but it did so in the refined and strengthened form given it in the writings of Peter Abelard.[12]

A *science* proceeds from its necessary principles as does *logic* in so far as it instructs,[13] but Duns does not follow the traditional approach shared by Porphyry and followed by Albert the Great which looks on the *Organon* as

> a systematic course of logic, moving from simple expressions in the *Categories* to compound expressions (propositions) in *De Interpretatione* and to compounds of propositions (syllogisms) in the *Prior Analytics*, and thence to the several kinds of syllogisms in the *Posterior Analytics*, the *Topics* and the *Elenchi*.[14]

Duns is one of those who leave behind this sermocinalism and move on in the direction of Avicenna's approach which views logic in terms of *second intentions*. However, language analysis remains integrated into the new approach. Although the young John Duns feels critical of the views that logic is a *scientia sermocinalis* or a *scientia realis*, he will pull out all the stops of language analysis and dialogical expertise. Duns had an accumulative view of the tasks of logic. The argumentative dimension is vital to his approach. Logic is a science which primarily focuses on the nature of demonstration (see §§9.2–9.3). Several other aspects flow from this primary dimension. The validity of strict argumentation requires that the terms are used in a univocal manner and the issue of provability also requires much attention.[15]

---

[12] Kretzmann, 'History of Semantics,' *EP* VII 370.

[13] *Quaestiones in librum Porphyrii Isagoge* 1.6: 'Logica est scientia, quia quae docentur in ea demonstratione concluduntur, sicut in aliis scientiis.' Cf. §1.7: 'In quantum est docens, et sic ex necessariis ex propriis principiis ad necessarias conclusiones, et est scientia.'

[14] Ebbesen, 'Ancient Scholastic Logic as the Source of Medieval Scholastic Logic,' *CHLMP* 119. On Porphyry, see *CHLMP* 118 ff., and Henry, 'Predicables and Categories,' *CHLMP* 128–142. Views of Albert the Great are regularly discussed in the *Quaestiones in librum Porphyrii Isagoge*.

[15] The relationship between philosophy and theology comes to the fore, based on strict notions of *proof* and *demonstration* (see Chapter 9), not within a modern context of not being dependent on revelation.

Duns formulated a basic demarcation of logic in his *quaestio* whether the notion of *true being* has to be studied by a metaphysician. Factual questions concerning acts of knowledge have to be studied in connection with the book *De Anima* and so, we might say, they belong to psychology. They are properties of the mind but, from the formal point of view, they have to be studied by the logician. They are *formally* the logician's business, because the logician presupposes an analysis of the acts of knowledge by which the *second intentions* are formed. The level of logical studies is a *second order* level. It is also the level of modalities of propositions, like *possible* and *impossible*.[16]

However, Scotus' personal practice teaches us more on his conception of *logic* than the abstract demarcations of the very young Duns. The roots of his approach to logic are to be located in his ideas on concept formation. He starts with concept formation and he expands this type of analysis into a propositional analysis on the basis of the subject-predicate structure of a proposition (§4.7). Propositional analysis is enlarged into argumentational analysis. The dynamics of this approach turned on the distinction between essentiality and contingency and on the distinctions between derivability, validity, and self-evidence.[17] This way of thought is in line with mainstream thirteenth-century thought and its *logica modernorum*, but it differs considerably from Thomist thought and its terminology. In general, neoscholastic research neglected the specific nature of Scotian terminology. A new language has to be learnt and Chapters 4–6 serve this purpose.

4.4 MEANING

Duns treats of a great many issues in his theological works – *Lectura, Ordinatio, Reportatio* and *Quodlibet* – which have no parallel in his early philosophical writings. Duns' semantics is among the areas which show an interesting but also discontinuous development. Duns deals with the issue of the signification of a word in several places, namely: *Super primum librum Perihermenias Quaestiones, quaestio 2,*

---

[16] *Quaestiones Metaphysicae* VI 3.70: 'Formaliter pertinet [namely, truth known in an act of knowledge] ad considerationem logici, sicut et *"possible"* et *"impossibile"* et modi compositionum omnes. Praesupponit tamen logicus considerationem de actibus intelligendi quibus secundae intentiones formantur.'

[17] Duns' theories of concepts (§4.5), proposition (§4.5) and negation (§4.7), and of *natural law* (§12.4), love of God and of one's neighbor (§12.5) and predestination are just cases in point. See Vos et al., *Duns Scotus on Divine Love*, chapters 2–4.

Super duos libros Perihermenias Quaestiones. Opus secundum,
quaestio 1, *Lectura* I 27 and *Ordinatio* I 27.[18]

4.4.1 Meaning and 'vox' according to Duns' 'commentaries' on *De Interpretatione*

Aristotle's view on words is well-known: written terms are conventional signs (*sumbola*) of affections of the soul. The spoken sounds express directly the affections of the soul, which signify things or facts of the external world.[19] The level of *direct* contact with the external world is the level of mental phenomena where we speak the language of the human mind: 'mentalish.'[20] We observe here too that *thought* and *being* are parallel, not in the sense of a picture model, but in an absolute sense: the power of what is actual makes itself known in the receiving mind. The analogy of *reason* (*logos*) and *being* (*kosmos*) enjoys priority.

4.4.2 *Super primum librum Perihermenias Quaestiones,* quaestio 2

Duns' first treatment of *meaningful words* starts with posing the problem, followed by piling up pros and cons: does a noun, like *man* (*homo*), signify (*human*) *nature* or the *species?* He makes it quite clear in a preliminary note that the *species* of what is knowable is a knowable likeness (*similitudo*) and the intellect is the subject of that likeness, just as the senses are the subject of the *species sensibilis*.[21] We have to know that the following terms parallel each other, without being synonymous, in *Super primum librum Perihermenias Quaestiones, quaestio* 2 and in *Super duos libros Perihermenias Quaestiones. Opus*

---

[18] The W/V editions contain two writings, covering three texts, on Aristotle's *De Interpretatione*: *Super primum librum Perihermenias Quaestiones* (*Opera Omnia* (ed. L. Wadding) 186–203), *Super secundum librum Perihermenias Quaestiones* (203–210), constituting one work, and *Super duos libros Perihermenias Quaestiones. Opus secundum* (211–223). Present text criticism lists two writings: *Quaestiones super libros Perihermenias* and *Quaestiones super librum Perihermenias. Opus alterum,* cf. *Opera Omnia* I 153*. I quote from the old edition under their traditional titles. See §1.5 and §3.6.4.

[19] See Nuchelmans, *Theories of the Proposition,* 23–44, and also Marmo, 'Ontology and Semantics in the Logic of Duns Scotus,' in Eco and Marmo (eds), *On the medieval theory of signs,* 143–193.

[20] See Nuchelmans, *Wijsbegeerte en Taal,* chapter 11.

[21] *Super primum librum Perihermenias Quaestiones* §2.1: 'Dico autem *speciem* intelligibilium similitudinem intelligibilem quae est in intellectu ut in subiecto, sicut *species sensibilis* est similitudo rei sensibilis quae est in sensu ut in subiecto.'

secundum, quaestio 1: on the one hand, *passio (pathèma) animae, species animae, species (intelligibilis), conceptio intellectus* and, on the other hand, *res (ut concipitur), natura, ratio, (vera) essentia rei, substantia, quod quid est.*[22] In terms of this terminology, Duns discusses two theories. The first answer states that a word signifies the *species intelligibilis* in the intellect. Aristotle seems to subscribe to this view in *De Interpretatione*, chapter 1. Truth and falsity are in speech as in a sign. The pronounced 'proposition' signifies that which is true or false. Truth and falsity are therein and the bearer of truth and falsity is a composition of the intellect.

The second answer does *not* look for the meaning of a word in the mind but in outside reality: hearing a meaningful word constitutes understanding something real. 'The structure which a noun signifies is the definition, but a definition presents the true essence of a thing. Therefore, that essence is signified by a noun.'[23] A noun cannot signify the epistemic concept because, in that case, every proposition of the form *Socrates is* would be true.

After the introductory survey, the young Duns tries to integrate both points of view. The epistemic concept (*species intelligibilis*) is immediately signified by a word in the sense that

> every sign as far as it is a sign is a sign of what is signified. Therefore, a word which signifies a likeness as far as it is the sign of something real (*res*), *indirectly* signifies what is real (*res*), since it *directly* signifies that which is the sign for what is real insofar it is a sign.[24]

This approach integrates the *res* theory of meaning into the *species* theory of meaning and, in this way, Duns is able to grant all arguments which prove that the *essence* or nature of something is signified. *Homo est animal* is true in terms of the ultimate significates, but not as signs. 'Concepts are united as far as they are signs of what is real' – signs of *the reality* of a thing, that is its essence or nature, 'and that they are not the *real* things themselves.'[25] In the light of this position, Duns can

---

[22] For a later list of epistemological synonyms, see Nuchelmans on Holkot, *Theories of the Proposition*, 203 note 6.

[23] *Super primum librum Perihermenias Quaestiones* §2.2 (187b): 'Ratio quam significat nomen, est definitio, sed definitio indicat *veram essentiam rei*. Ergo, illa essentia per nomen significatur.'

[24] Ibid., §2.3 (187b): 'Cum enim omne signum, inquantum signum, sit signum signati, sequitur quod *vox* significans similitudinem inquantum signum rei, significat ipsam rem, sed mediate, quia *scilicet* immediate significat id quod est signum ei inquantum est signum.'

[25] Ibid., §2.5 (188a): 'Concesso, quod species uniantur inquantum sunt signa rerum et quod non sunt eaedem, non sequitur propositionem esse falsam.'

state: 'I grant that the concept is something else than that which is known by it, *i.e.*, the first object, since it is the concept of that object.'[26] All this is based on the thesis: '*Signifying* presupposes *knowing* as a necessary condition.'[27] Non-existence does not impair this view.[28]

4.4.3 *Super duos libros Perihermenias Quaestiones. Opus secundum, quaestio* 1

In *Super duos libros Perihermenias Quaestiones. Opus secundum, quaestio* 1, Duns first mentions Aristotle's answer to the question of the meaning of a *noun*, whether a *res* or a *passio* is signified: 'A noun first signifies affections of the soul, that is, concepts of the intellect.'[29] For a clear understanding of his own answer, Duns introduces a threefold distinction: three kinds of entities display their own ordering: (a) the epistemic concept (*species intelligibilis*); (b) the *essence* of something real (*ratio rei*) – the *quod quid est* which is presented to the intellect; and (c) something real, a thing which exists as a particular.

Duns discusses two views on the meaning of a *vox* which he rebuts: the *species intelligibilis* theory of meaning and the *individual referent* theory of meaning.

The species theory of meaning

The first item in the list – the *epistemic concept* (the *species* which is to be known) – cannot account for the meaning of a word (*vox*).[30] A *species* is a concept of a knower and precisely as an epistemic concept it does not belong to the realm of external reality. So, it cannot be meant primarily by our words, because *meaning* is based on *knowledge* and the essence of something real is what is primarily known. This approach rejects the view: the *meaning* of a word is the epistemic concept or *species* (*intelligibilis*).

---

[26] Ibid., §2.7 (188b): 'Concedo speciem aliud esse ab illo quod cognoscitur per illam, *id est*, a primo obiecto, quia illius est species, sed cum hoc stat, ipsam speciem esse aliquod intelligibile aliud a primo obiecto.'

[27] Ibid., §2.9 (189a): '*Significare* praesupponit *intelligere*, sicut illud sine quo non.'

[28] Ibid., §3.3 (189b): 'Sive sit, sive non sit, cum tam res, ut intelligitur, quam species maneant in transmutatae facta transmutatione in re, ut existit, quia per eandem speciem cognoscimus essentiam, et eandem scientiam habemus de ea, quando existit et quando non existit.'

[29] Ibid., §1.4 (212b): 'Nomen primo significat passiones animae, *id est*, conceptiones intellectus.'

[30] Ibid., §1.5 (212b): 'Primum [= *species intelligibilis*] non significatur primo per *vocem*, quia *quod quid est* prius intelligitur quam species rei intelligatur, et quod primo intelligitur, primo significatur.'

The individual referent theory of meaning

The *meaning* of a word is not the existing individual either. The intellect does not know primarily singular reality. A singular individual is not the primary object of the intellect, since the intellect can know its primary object – the essence of something real – while the individual thing does not exist in reality.[31]

The real essence (ratio rei) *theory of meaning*

The underlying semantic approach rebuts the *species* and the *individual referent* theories of meaning and considers meaning from an epistemological point of view. We *understand* what we *know*. *Meaning* derives from truth and leans on *truth*. This epistemological point of view leads to pointing out what the *meaning* of a word is. The order of *meaning* is based on the order of *knowing* and the *essence* of something is known in the first place. The *meaning* of a word is what is primarily *understood* and the *essence* of something is what is primarily *known*. In sum, this theory focuses on *words* and takes the *nature* or *essence* – as a universal referent – to be the meaning of the word. This theory is compared on the one hand with another rival theory which takes the individual thing – as the individual referent – to be the meaning of the word, and on the other hand with the *species* model of meaning. However, the story told so far is not the whole story. After Duns has doggedly defended the *real essence* theory of meaning, he returns to the *species* theory he had just passed by.

Again, the species intelligibilis *theory of meaning*

'According to the second solution, the *vox* primarily signifies the *species* in the soul, which is the means by which it, secondarily, signifies the thing outside (that is: the essence).'[32] In the second place, Duns returns to the older solution of *Super primum librum Perihermenias Quaestiones, quaestio* 2 and seems now to prefer to attain the *res* of something through the *species* instead of just the other way around. The *meaning* of a word is the *species* as the sign of the *essence*

---

[31] Ibid., §1.5 (213a): 'Tertium vero, *scilicet*, res existentes individualiter per suam rationem propriam non possunt primo significare, quis intellectus est in actu primo per suum obiectum proprium, quod est *quod quid est* rei. Intellectus non intelligit primo singulare, sed *quod quid est* sine conditionibus materialibus. Cum non existit, potest tamen considerare sine istis, et sicut intelligitur, imponitur rei nomen.'

[32] Bos, 'The Theory of the Proposition,' in De Rijk and Braakhuis (eds), *Logos and Pragma*, 127. Bos distinguishes two views: the *essence* theory and the *species* theory.

and precisely as the *essence* as conceived by the human mind. Consequently, the individual referent theory is rejected and the universal reference theory is absorbed. Aristotle's words are borrowed to frame a compromise.

We meet well-known traditional elements: the individuality of a singular thing lies in its materiality and the intellect has its own non-singular object, but Duns also deviates from the answer given in *Super primum librum Perihermenias Quaestiones*. First, he rejects the theory defended in the first writing (§§1.5–1.6); then, his argumentation makes a new start in §1.7:

> If anybody wants to maintain the thesis that nouns signify by virtue of a likeness of real things and that they signify what exists in the intellect, we have to say that the noun first signifies the concept in the soul and second signifies the real thing (*res* = essence) through the mediation of the concept.

Although he now slightly prefers the *species* theory, being more in harmony with Aristotle (§1.4 and §1.14), in fact he arrives at an *undecided*, for his final remark is: 'Neither way is cogent.' At any rate, he rejects the idea that only one component can account for the meaning of a word, but the order between them is a matter of balance. Both of them can be said to be signified in the first place and to be signified in the second place.

4.4.4 *Verbum* according to *Lectura* I 27

Duns returns to the issue of meaning within the quite different trinitarian context of *Lectura* I 27 which starts with the general semantic question whether the inner word be an act of knowledge. We are creatures and creatures are as such created. If man is created, his intellect is created too and our words are created as well, but what is to be said of the nature of a – created – *word*? The debate shows two levels: the level of counter-arguments and the level of alternative theories. The first level is always represented in the *obiecta* (§§1–3) and the second level in the part of the *opiniones aliorum* (§§10–11 and 14–19). The opposite view is the traditional view and states that a word does not mean an *act* of knowledge. A word means a mental idea (*phantasma, species*) and an *idea* of the mind is not an *act* of knowledge; so, a word is not an act of knowledge.

Now, the problem is stated in a manner rather different from the way Duns dealt with it in his early *Quaestiones* on Aristotle's *De*

Interpretatione. The traditional theory taken from Aristotle had been his starting point some years ago, but is now his target. The position he wants to defend in *Lectura* I 27 is derived from Henry of Ghent who sees *word formation* as the outcome of four acts: a simple act of understanding, a reflexive act, an act of saying (= expressing), and an element of declaring knowledge.[33] Duns tries to remove epistemic acts of understanding from the dilemma of either being *something active* or *something passive.* An act of understanding is an act of an agent, not a passive event, nor like something like a bodily action, just as *being white* is neither an activity nor a state something is subjected to passively. Actuality of understanding is in itself a *form,* just as *being white* is a form.[34] A *word* is not a material thing. A word is actually knowable, but it is not as such an object.

Again and again, Duns rejects the view that the intellect is purely passive and that the idea or impression is only received in the mind (*Lectura* I 27.1, 10 and 14). The opposite theory identifies the *species* of the external thing and the mental concept – quite the essence of the Aristotelian approach. With Duns, the natural place where *auctoritates* are to be found is the initial series of the *obiecta* and the *sed contra.* In *Lectura* I 27, the remarkable thing is that Duns' own reply runs in terms of *auctoritates,* stemming from Augustine (§§28–30). The gist to be derived from these *auctoritates* is that although *knowledge* is properly mental, a *word* is not. A *word* is accompanied by a thought and *saying* something is built on actual thinking, but is not to be reduced to an abstraction of the mind (§28 and §30). Having denied a host of alternative views (§§31–41), Duns presents his personal answer:

> In fact, a *word* is actually understanding. It is the term of an activity which belongs to the category of activities, for it is the term of an act of saying (*dicere*). *Saying* is an activity which belongs to the category of activities, while the actuality of understanding is not.[35]

The link between a word and a speech act is tight. We have to realize that *verba* are words in use. The problem of meaning is linked up with

---

[33] *Lectura* I 27.11: 'Ante formationem *verbi* sunt duo actus, primus *scilicet*, notitia simplex, et illa conversio, et sequitur, tertio, actio de genere actionis quae est *dicere* (quod est *exprimere*), et, quarto, est notitia declarativa in tali intelligentia, quam dicit esse *verbum*.' See Henry of Ghent, *Summa* 54.9 and 58.5 in the body of the articles.

[34] See *Lectura* I 27.40: 'Immo est forma absoluta, [. . .] unde licet gignet habitum, hoc non ut actio, sed ut forma.' Cf. §37. Identity depends on a form (*Lectura* I 3.404 ff.). Cf. the German word *Handlung* (= action). An epistemic act is not a sort of *Handlung*, nor something passive.

[35] *Lectura* I 27.42: 'Verbum est intellectio actualis, qui est terminus actionis de genere actionis quia est terminus actus dicendi, et *dicere* est actus de genere actionis et non intellectio.'

actual uses, not with potential uses. *Verba* are words as they are pronounced in sayings. *Words* (*verba*) are said (*dicuntur*).[36] We are in
possession of an intellect and there is an object of understanding
which is actually knowable. Such an object is present to the intellect
and this presence is an item of insightful understanding. The fitting
metaphor is *proles*, namely child or son, for the nature of a word
includes the idea of being brought forth. This is still not the whole
story. In *Lectura* I 27.2, an *auctoritas* of Augustine is commented on
as follows: 'An external word signifies something real (*res*), and not
a concept, neither an epistemic act. Otherwise, a proposition would
be false where a *genus* is predicated of a *species*.' This point recurs in
Duns' reply in *Lectura* I 27.51:

> When it is argued that an external *word* is a sign of something real
> (*res*), and not of an internal concept, I say that it is immediately a sign
> of each of the two, although the one meaning is signified *before* the
> other one is.[37]

The first immediate meaning of a meaningful word (*verbum, vox*) is
what in external reality is spoken about (*res*) and the second immediate meaning is the inner concept (*conceptus interior*). Although Duns
states that both relations are significative in §51, in §50 the relation
between the *idea* (*phantasma*) and the word is considered to be causal,
in the sense that 'an *idea* is required in order to cause a *word*.'[38] An
epistemic act gives rise to a word as the effect of an enquiry (*Lectura* I
27.47). A word (*verbum*) is a mental and meaningful act of saying.[39]

4.4.5 *Verbum/vox* according to *Ordinatio* I 27

Duns focuses on *verba* and *voces* as spoken terms and he states in
Ordinatio I 27.19 that what is meant by the spoken sound is some-
thing real rather than a concept. By the time of the Parisian *Ordinatio*
I 27, the ecumenism of *Super duos libros Perihermenias Quaestiones.*

---

[36] See Searle, *Speech Acts*, chapter 3. We have to approach the problem of meaning on the level
of illocutionary speech acts (Austin, Alston).

[37] *Lectura* I 27.51: 'Quando arguitur quod *verbum exterius* est signum *rei*, et non conceptus
interioris, dico quod est signum utriusque immediate: unum tamen signatum est prius signatum alio.' Cf. §2: '*Verbum extra sonans* significat rem, et non conceptum aliquem vel
aliquam intellectionem.'

[38] *Lectura* I 27.50: 'Ideo intelligendum est quod illa phantasia Carthaginis verbum est
causaliter, quia *species* requiritur ad causandum *verbum*.'

[39] *Lectura* I 27.52: 'Verbum [. . .] est proles et terminus actionis de genere actionis; et iste terminus est intellectio actualis quae dicta est, quae est vera qualitas mentis.'

Opus secundum 1 and *Lectura* I 27 has changed into a war report: we are told of a big clash concerning the theory of meaning. What does a *word* (*vox*) mean? Duns briefly indicates that a *word* properly means *something real* (*res*): several different kinds of *signs* may have the same significate without any hierarchy of meanings in just the same way so that a second sign does not mediate for the first sign, instead of a hierarchy wherein a second sign mediates for the first sign as *Lectura* I 27.51 will have it.[40] Here, Duns not only mentions words and concepts, but also written expressions. Here, Duns Scotus puts a written expression (*littera*), a spoken meaningful word (*vox*), and a concept (*conceptus*) on a par. All three enjoy a direct significative relation to signified reality. In addition to this main structure, Duns still maintains some ordering,[41] and he denies the productive nature of the act of understanding. A *word* is semantic knowledge.

We meet in Duns Scotus' theory of meaning the very unusual phenomenon of a chain of differing views, running from the orientation on Aristotle in his early *Super primum librum Perihermenias Quaestiones* to his final view in *Ordinatio* I 27 where both the theory that a word signifies a mental idea or *species intelligibilis* and the idea signifies what is real, and the theory that a spoken word signifies only what is real and not an inner concept, are rejected. The general background is formed by the Aristotelian model, supported by Boethius.[42] 'Is it so that the spoken word "tree" immediately signifies the concept *tree*, and that only the concept or mental language-sign "tree" signifies immediately the things which are trees? This question was, as it seems, unanimously affirmed, at least by the great Scholastics before Scotus,'[43] although we have to make an exception for Henry of Ghent. The *Ordinatio* I 27 view is characterized by Nuchelmans as saying that what is signified by the spoken sound is a thing rather than a concept. Bos added to this tantalizingly brief exposition a remarkable consideration.

---

[40] *Ordinatio* I 27.83: 'Licet *magna altercatio* fiat de *voce*, utrum sit signum rei vel conceptus, tamen breviter concedo quod illud quod signatur per vocem *proprie*, est res. Sunt tamen signa ordinata eiusdem signati *littera, vox et conceptus*, sicut sunt multi effectus ordinati eiusdem causae, quorum nullus est causa alterius.'

[41] Ibid.: 'Potest concedi de multis signis eiusdem signati ordinatis, quod unum aliquo modo est signum alterius, quia dat intelligere ipsum, quia remotius non signaret nisi prius aliquo modo immediatius signaret – et tamen, propter hoc, unum *proprie* non est signum alterius, sicut ex alia parte de causa et causatis.'

[42] See Aristotle, *De Interpretatione* 1, and both editions of Boethius' *De Interpretatione*, Book 1.

[43] Buytaert (ed.), *Boehner. Collected Articles on Ockham*, 218.

From all this it can be concluded that in his earlier period Duns Scotus considers it more probable that what is primarily signified by a *vox* is the concept as the means of signification, not the essence of the thing. Later, in his *Ordinatio*, as Nuchelmans indicates, Duns opines that the primary significate of a *vox* is a thing, and not a concept.[44]

Nuchelmans only signaled Duns' *Ordinatio* I 27 point of view, the developmental depth is Bos's point.[45] So, let us list the differences of the four main models in operation:

I *The Aristotelian Model*

spoken word
↓
passio animae
↓
something real

II *The Challenger Model*

spoken word . . .. passio animae
↓
something real

III Duns' *Lectura* I 27

spoken word

↙   ↘

something real   concept

---

[44] Bos, 'The Theory of the Proposition,' in De Rijk and Braakhuis (eds), *Logos and Pragma*, 127.

[45] Cf. Nuchelmans, *Theories of the Proposition*, 196, and Vos, 'On the Philosophy of the Young Duns Scotus,' in Bos (ed.), *Mediaeval Semantics and Metaphysics*, 199–201. This discovery was anticipated by Boehner's St Bonaventure team, for John B. Vogel 'discovered a considerable discrepancy between the treatment of this problem in the *Oxoniense* and the *Quaestiones in Perihermenias opus primum* and *secundum*' – see Boehner's 'Ockham's Theory of Signification,' in Buytaert (ed.), *Boehner. Collected Articles on Ockham*, 219 note 29. I do not know of a thesis published by Vogel Boehner promised in his contribution.

IV Duns' *Ordinatio* I 27

littera	*verbum exterius*	*conceptus*
written expression	*spoken word*	*concept*
↓	↓	↓
res	*res*	*res*

These models deserve some comments, as follows.

Model II

Model II challenges the basic model I inherited from ancient philosophy. Model II is the basically Christian challenger which achieves a radical breakthrough, but even when Duns had said goodbye to the ancient model, model III and model IV are evidence that he is too prudent to accept model II simply as it stands, just as model III of *Lectura* I 27 and model IV of *Ordinatio* I 27 show. Duns also rejected the early nominalist stance. The unique series of drafts show how much effort all these attempts cost.

Model III

The two key concepts of this model are: *immediacy* and *priority*. In this model, the direct semantic relation between a *word* and *something real*, between language and reality, is accepted, but is not cut off from the dimension of the concept. On the contrary, the same relation is now applied both to what is real and to the concept. However, the first semantic relation of *word-reality* enjoys *priority*.

Model IV

The key viewpoints of this model are: *immediately* and *properly*. In this model alone, all three – *the written sign, the spoken sign,* and *the mental sign* – signify *immediately* what is in reality, but only *a spoken word* signifies *properly* what is in reality. Nuchelmans stressed the evident differences between Aristotle and Scotus/ Ockham, but he continues by describing Ockham's theory, for Ockham assumes that

> there is a direct relation between written or spoken terms and things as well as between mental terms and things, one difference being that

in the first case the relation is that of conventional signification and in the second case that of natural signification.[46]

The second point Duns Scotus does not deal with, but the first point is precisely his view. I can only admire the precision of Boehner (1946):

> Scotus already broke with this interpretation of Aristotle's text, maintaining that the significate of the word, generally speaking, is not the concept but the thing, and that both word and concept immediately, though in subordination, signify the same significate or thing. In this the Doctor Subtilis was followed by Ockham, although not in every detail, at least in so far as the general idea of direct signification of words is concerned.[47]

The differences and agreements both with respect to Thomas Aquinas and to William of Ockham are quite interesting. The way Duns Scotus differs from Thomas Aquinas' view is clear. Aquinas states that a word does not signify actuality of understanding (*intelligere*), defended by Duns both in *Lectura* I 27 and in *Ordinatio* I 27. On the contrary, a spoken word signifies *the final product* of an act of understanding wherein the activity of the mind comes to an end. Nuchelmans observed that, in contrast with Thomas Aquinas:

> For Ockham the mental word or term is an act of apprehending which, together with the act of judging, belongs to the main operations of the human mind. This rejection of any intermediate entity between the act of understanding and the things to which it is related is one of the most characteristic features of Ockham's doctrine.[48]

The comparison with Ockham is rather challenging, for Ockham assumed that there is a direct relation between spoken terms and things as well as between mental terms and things. The rejection of any intermediate entity between the act of epistemic understanding of meaning and the thing to which it is related is just what Duns Scotus grants in *Ordinatio* I 27.83. So, the claim that this rejection is one of the most characteristic features of Ockham's doctrine is premature. On the contrary, the main structure simply originates from Duns,

---

[46] Nuchelmans, *Theories of the Proposition*, 196 (195–202: 'William of Ockham'). See Boehner (ed.), *William of Ockham. Summa totius logicae* I 12.39.

[47] Boehner, 'Ockham's Theory of Signification,' in *Collected Articles*, 219. Cf. Eco, also referring to Boehner and Vogel, 'Denotation,' in Eco and Marmo, (eds), *On the Medieval Theory of Signs*, 62 f.: 'Duns Scotus and the Modistae.' Eco's main tool is the dualism of intensionalism and extensionalism.

[48] Nuchelmans, *Theories of the Proposition*, 197; on Thomas Aquinas, cf. pp. 193 f. See also Thomas Aquinas, *De Veritate* IV 2 and *Summa Theologiae* I 34.1.

himself reconstructing Henry of Ghent's approach. Against this background, we may particularly appreciate the view developed by Irène Rosier that, in *Ordinatio* I 22.4, Duns Scotus himself signaled the *rupture* between the view of the majority of the thirteenth-century thinkers, based on the parallelism between *meaning* and *conceptual knowledge*, and his own stance, influenced and stimulated by Henry of Ghent's theory of meaning, particularly inspired by Augustine's *De Dialectica* and put forward in *Summa quaestionum ordinariarum* 73.[49] However, were we to conclude with Irène Rosier that Henry's splendid contribution constituted Duns Scotus' point of departure, we would be going too far. Duns' true starting point consisted of the requirements of the web of his own ideas and dilemmas. In Oxford, *Summa* 73 did not yet play any role in *Lectura* I–II, but in Paris he made a creative and grateful use of it in *Ordinatio* I 22 and 27. There was not only a *rupture* with regard to tradition, but Duns also distanced himself from what he had brought forward in his own logical writings, and he distanced himself from tradition in order to save tradition and his own position – by making them coherent.

Thomas Aquinas took a different road by rejecting the approach of seeing a *vox/verbum* as actually expressing a *meaning*. Maurer succinctly filled in a wider context:

> St. Thomas claims that a general word like 'man' directly signifies a concept, and not a reality, for it designates human nature in abstraction from individual men. Scotus, on the contrary, argues that general words can directly signify realities, for in his view there are real common natures. In this dispute Ockham agrees with Scotus, that words like 'man' are first of all signs of things and not of concepts; but he insists that the things they signify are only individuals. General words are not signs of general objects, for there are no general objects or universal things.[50]

We may add that Ockham took his lead from Duns, although he exclusively linked meaning and denotation. Thus Ockham radicalized mentalism, and Duns overcame it and joined Augustine and Henry of Ghent.

---

[49] See Rosier, 'Henri de Gand, le *De Dialectica* d'Augustin, et l'institution des noms divins,' *Documenti e studi sulla tradizione filosofica medievale* 6 (1995) 176–1991. Cf. Boulnois, 'Représentation et noms divins selon Duns Scot,' Ibid., 255–280, and idem, *Etre et représentation*.

[50] Maurer, 'William of Ockham on language and reality,' in Zimmermann (ed.), *Sprache und Erkenntnis im Mittelalter*, 797–798.

4.5 THE PROBLEM OF MEANING AND THE PROBLEM OF KNOWLEDGE

We met a series of views including some reist, mentalist and mixed positions:

1. The view put forward in *Lectura* I 24.2 and 51 and in *Ordinatio* I 27. 2 and 83, but not espoused by Duns, states clearly that a spoken word (*verbum exterius*) is the sign of something real (*signum rei*), and not of an inner concept. This kind of reist view is not to be confused with another kind of reist position Duns discussed in *Super primum librum Perihermenias Quaestiones* 2.2, but also considered more seriously in *Super duos libros Perihermenias Quaestiones. Opus secundum* 1.5.

2. This latter view, put forward in *Super duos libros Perihermenias Quaestiones. Opus secundum* 1.5, states that a spoken word (*vox*) signifies a *res* in the sense of the *essence* (*ratio, essentia rei*) of a thing.

3. A word directly signifies the epistemic concept (*species intelligibilis*) and, therefore, a word which signifies a likeness or a concept as far as it is the sign of something real (*res*) *indirectly* signifies what is real (*res*). This approach integrates the *res* theory of meaning into the *species* theory of meaning.

4. A new viewpoint is met in *Super duos libros Perihermenias Quaestiones* where the rivals of the reist and mentalist positions are not integrated but simply balanced.

5. The *Lectura* I 27 and *Ordinatio* I 27 stages are most fascinating. The ecumenism of balancing views is dropped and a *direct signification* not epistemologically based of what is real is introduced,[51] while the direct signification of the epistemic concept is maintained.

6. *Ordinatio* I 27.83 asserts that the direct semantic relationship between *word* and *reality* is the only proper type of signification.

4.5.1 Meaning and knowledge

A good vantage point for understanding Duns is to look at his refutation of the theory that we cannot refer to things more adequately than we can *know* them,[52] as expressed in the maxim: 'Just as it is understood, so it is also named' (see also *Ordinatio* I 22.4). Duns' criticisms

---

51 See *Lectura* I 22 and *Ordinatio* I 22, and the first half of §4.4.

52 *Lectura* I 22.2: 'Ut mihi videtur, haec propositio falsa est quod "nihil potest nominari a nobis magis proprie quam intelligatur." ' This thesis is the foundation of the *real essence* theory in *Super duos libros Perihermenias Quaestiones, quaestio* 1.

of this semantic maxim entail the rejection of any epistemology-based
theory of meaning, for this semantic maxim has far-reaching repercus-
sions for a theory of theological language as Duns is quick to consider
both in *Lectura* I 22 and in *Ordinatio* I 22. Again, he makes his substantial semantic point in general terms in *Lectura* I 22.2–3:

> I see whiteness in a wall and I see that whiteness changes while the
> size of the wall remains the same and is to be experienced in itself.
> I also see that a wall can be whitewashed at another occasion and that
> the size can change from one shape to another while it still remains
> to be white. From this I conclude that there is a third element, under-
> lying each of both, different from both: I give that element the name
> *a* by just naming the body in the category of substance. I only know
> it under a common *concept*, namely *this being* and in no way do
> I have a proper *idea* (*image*) of it – just as anybody can experience for
> himself. Therefore, I can name that element more adequately than
> I can know it.[53]

Duns makes his point quite well. A wall can be experienced in itself.
It need not be white, but if it is white, it is white to be experienced. It
is white, although its being white at this moment is different from its
whiteness some time before. When I take 'white' to mean the empirical whiteness of the wall some time before, my proposition *At this
moment the wall is white* is false and the same holds the other way
around. The same point can be made in terms of a wall. So, in order
to be able to say veritably of *both* 'whitical' or 'wallic' entities that
they are white or a wall, I need a third meaning which I impose on to
cover 'whate' and 'whute' and 'wull' and 'woll.'

What I am saying is perfectly meaningful and true, but still
absolutely annoying to the semantic empiricist of the thirteenth or the
twentieth century, because there is no picture or image (*species*) of the
white and *wall* unseeable any more, although the language involved is
perfectly meaningful. If you disagree, you must accept that you are
telling a falsehood when you say of yourself and your child: *We are
white*. There is no exhaustive understanding in terms of sense images
and our talk in terms of symbols and nouns is yet perfectly meaningful.

Duns does not cut off the sensible and 'abstract' dimension of our
language, but he removes it from its priority and puts meaning of

[53] *Lectura* I 22.3: 'Ex hoc ego concludo quod est aliud tertium, substratum utrique, alterum ab
eis: illi nomen impono *a*, vocando ipsum corpus in genere substantiae – quod tamen intelligo tantum sub intentione communi quod sit *hoc ens* et nullo modo propriam speciem eius
habeo – sicut quilibet potest experiri in se ipso – et ideo verius possum illud nominare quam
intelligere.'

language on its own footing. Even the meaningfulness of the famous expression 'golden mountain' cannot be accounted for according to abstractionist lines, because we cannot abstract the image or a picture of such a golden mountain from a golden mountain, for there are nowhere golden mountains. So, if we can only think and know of what we receive by our senses, we are unable to think of golden mountains, although we can think of golden rings. The expression 'golden mountain' is even meaningless.

However, we can expand the area of meanings of our language by analyzing and combining and thus we are able to construe meaningful talk of golden mountains and of God. Duns is quick to point out that an empiricist approach to meaning and language leaves us with a religious language which does not make any sense of God talk. If we should assume that we can only understand what we are saying because we know from experience, then all our talk not based on the outer senses would become meaningless. Duns is convinced that the pattern of *analogy* cannot save us. In *Lectura* I 22 Duns is only anxious to point out that the involved maxim endangers theological language and, for this reason, he only tries to refute what Thomas Aquinas put forward in *Summa Theologiae* I 13.1 c.a.[54] For Duns, *naming* and *denoting* are broader than *knowing*. The area of *saying* is not enclosed by the limits of our knowledge. *Meaning* does neither presuppose *truth* nor *empirical experience, pace* Aristotle. The profound difference between the young theological philosopher John Duns in about 1297 and Aristotle concerns the nature of the human intellect. For Duns, the human intellect is as such the intellect of an individual which is an individual and active intellect so that such an intellect cannot be accounted for in terms of Aristotelian passivism.

Likewise, God talk is not dependent on adequate knowledge of God's individual essence. We are not familiar with *haec essentia,* if this essence (*haec essentia*) is God's essence, 'but I only know by a common concept that He is *this infinite being who does not depend on anything,* and I give Him a name by calling Him *God* or *Qui est* or *Adonai*. For this reason, I believe that we have many names for God which properly signify the divine nature, although we do not know his nature.'[55] All this sounds

---

[54] Since this principle results in the thesis: *If we cannot experience something then it must be impossible,* an empiricist theory of knowledge entails that everything is necessary.

[55] *Lectura* I 22.4: 'Sed tantum (intelligo) sub intentione communi quod sit *hoc ens infinitum a nullo dependens,* et illi impono nomen vocando ipsum *Deum* vel *Qui est* vel *Adonai*. Unde credo quod multa nomina habemus de Deo quae proprie significant naturam divinam quam tamen non intelligimus.'

rather reasonable, for, although I am not acquainted with the haecceity of Francis of Assisi, I can talk in a meaningful way about him in terms of individual descriptions which entail his individual nature, for example the person portrayed in a fascinating way in *Respectfully Yours, Signed and Sealed, Francis of Assisi.*

4.6 CONCEPT

The theory of concepts, logic, and epistemology are tightly intertwined. According to Duns Scotus, there are two kinds of concepts: *simple concepts* and *concepts which are not simple.*[56] For *a concept which is not simple*, I use the term *a compound concept.*

A *simple concept* is a concept which is grasped just by one insightful act of understanding the content of the concept. We know the involved term by one act of understanding (*intellectio* or *actus intelligendi*).

A *compound concept* requires more cognitive acts of understanding, as is the case when an accidental predicate is ascribed to, like the expression *a pale man (homo albus)* does.[57] A *compound concept* can be analyzed, but if we rephrase it by a parallel proposition, then the truth of this proposition cannot be found by way of analysis. In order to understand such a concept, we need several acts of understanding in order to grasp the components which do not depend on each other. A *compound concept* does not entail a necessary truth which props up its conceptual content. A *complexum* is a compound *concept*, not a compound *proposition.*[58] A *simple concept* entails the necessary truth which grants its conceptual content. The distinctive contrast is seen in

> *man*
> and
> *a pale man.*

---

[56] For *simple concepts* and *concepts which are not simple*, compare *Lectura* I 3.68 and I 39.20 – cf. CF 74–77 – and, for *concepts which are not simple*, see also *Ordinatio* I 3.71.

[57] *Lectura* I 3.68: '*Conceptus simplex* qui concipitur una intellectione et uno actu intelligendi, est duplex: scilicet *conceptus simpliciter simplex* et *conceptus non simpliciter simplex.* [. . .] Et similiter definitio sic est *conceptus non simpliciter simplex*, licet simplici actu intelligendi concipiatur. Unde ille conceptus dicitur *non simplex* qui pluribus actibus concipitur, sicut ens per accidens, ut *homo albus*, et etiam alia complexa.'

[58] In contrast with the term *complexum*, a *complexio* is a proposition which can also be a necessary proposition. However, a *complexum* is as such an accidental unit.

Fortunately, *man* does not entail *being pale*, but, in terms of this standard example, *man* not only entails *sense-gifted being*, but also *being rational*.

This first distinction between *simple* and *compound* concepts turns on the difference between *one* act of understanding or one act of knowing what the involved term(s) mean(s), and a *plurality* of mental acts. This difference between *one* act or *more* acts turns on the *necessity-contingency* distinction. The fact that only *one* act of knowing the involved concept suffices, depends on its essential application or implicational connection. In the case of *simple concepts*, Duns explains their simple nature with the help of the feature of *essentiality*: the essentiality of a transcendent term or of individuality or the essentiality of other concepts which are essentially included in the concepts to be analyzed.

This last element indicates the key of Duns' second distinction. The class of simple concepts is twofold again (*Lectura* I 3.68):

> *Simple concepts* being grasped by one act of knowing are twofold, namely, concepts *which are irreducibly simple* and concepts *which are not irreducibly simple*.[59]

We have to stress that both kinds of concepts are grasped by a single act of knowing and Duns' standard examples pave the way for understanding the nature of this single act of knowing a simple concept:

1. *being (ens)* or the *individuality* of, for example, John, and
2. *man*.[60]

So (2) represents the level of analysis, but are there restrictions to be set on this level of analysis? Is an analysis still going on an analysis at all? Shall we ever get marks for an analysis without end? For Duns, (1) represents the level of the stopping points.

> Such a process of analysis, however, must eventually end up with irreducibly simple notions which are known *in toto* if they are known at all. Such, Scotus claims, are the concepts of *being* and its ultimate differences.[61]

---

[59] Ibid.: '*Conceptus* autem *simpliciter simplex* est ille conceptus qui non est resolubilis in alios conceptus priores. *Conceptus* autem *non simpliciter simplex* est ille qui est resolubilis in conceptus priores, ut conceptus *hominis* resolvitur in conceptum *generis* et *differentiae*.'

[60] *Ordinatio* I 3.71: 'Conceptus "*simpliciter simplex*" est qui non est resolubilis in plures conceptus, ut conceptus *entis* vel *ultimae differentiae*. Conceptum vero *simplicem*, sed "*non-simpliciter simplicem*" voco, quicumque potest concipi ab intellectu actu simplicis intelligentiae, licet posset resolvi in plures conceptus, seorsum conceptibiles.'

[61] Wolter, 'Glossary,' in Alluntis and Wolter, *God and Creatures*, 534 (493–540).

On the one hand, we have at our disposal notions which are so general that it is impossible to be more general. The transcendent terms represent what is the most universal possible. What can as such be said of what is a *being (ens)* can be said of everything and such propositions must be true, since there is no room left for falsifiability. Thus transcendent concepts belong to the group of irreducibly simple concepts. We cannot go on any more. On the other hand, the same is the case at the other end of the spectrum. We meet the individual and there is nothing more to think of. The whole range of reality to be thought of lies between *John* and *being*.

The distinction between two kinds of 'simplicity' points at a universal element which is also an essential feature or at different elements in a certain concept, and not at a series of mental acts understanding such a concept. This way of distinguishing concerns the internal analysis of the objects of thought, and an empirical or phenomenological analysis of thinking itself. Thus the series of (a) *simple concepts* I, (b) *simple concepts* II, and (c) *non-simple concepts* shows a range of concepts in terms of the internal structure of concepts. The standard examples already show the manner of complexity:

1. *being (ens)* or the *individuality* of a *being*;
2. *man*;
3. *a pale man*.

These clear examples enable us to yield clear definitions and, commenting on Duns' way of defining kinds of concepts, we are able to see the distinctive feature of a *single act of knowing* and *different acts of knowing*.

We present the set of definitions belonging to the three classes of concepts:

1. A concept which is *irreducibly simple* is a concept which is not analyzable into other more elementary concepts.
2. A concept which is *not irreducibly simple* is a concept which is analyzable into other more elementary concepts which it entails.
3. A concept which is *not simple* is a concept which is grasped by different acts, because the compounding element (*pale*) is not entailed by the component to be determined (*man*).

4.7 PROPOSITION

4.7.1 Introduction

The historical background of the exposition of any theory of the proposition is to be found in the monumental studies on ancient, medieval, and modern conceptions of the bearers of truth and falsity by Nuchelmans (1922–99).[62] Although Duns Scotus' contribution to the theory of meaning and proposition is quite remarkable, Nuchelmans's map of this area hardly mentions Duns Scotus at all.

> A discussion of the medieval philosopher John Duns Scotus' theory of the proposition is missing. This John [. . .], who, in my view, is one of the greatest thinkers of the Middle Ages, especially in theological matters, is mentioned only once in Nuchelmans' volume I, thrice in volume II and once in volume III without much discussion.[63]

Duns' theory of the proposition turns around the idea of *composition*, since he puts the analysis of the terms of the proposition in the center. He stresses the decisive point in his first elaborate treatment of the *possibile logicum* to be found in *Lectura* I 7.32–33. *Logical possibility* is a possible property of a proposition, for a proposition is possible or impossible. It is a modality of a combination of terms, anchored in the relationship of the terms.[64] Terms are connected in a proposition. They can only be connected or united if they are not incompatible with each other.[65] Repugnancy or incompatibility is a symmetrical property. If term *a* excludes term *b*, then term *b* excludes term *a*. If mutual exclusion between terms is at play, they cannot be united or combined in a coherent way.

The two possibilities of a combination or composition is the starting point of dealing with propositions. The notion of *possibility* or *compossibility* and the notion of *impossibility* or *incompossibility*

---

[62] Nuchelmans's *Festschrift Logos and Pragma* (1987), edited by De Rijk and Braakhuis, contains helpful contributions to the history of proposition theory by Abraham, Kretzmann, De Rijk, Braakhuis, Bos, Stump, Tachau, and Ashworth. On fourteenth-century analyses of modal propositions, see Lagerlund, *Modal Syllogistics in the Middle Ages*.

[63] Bos, 'The Theory of the Proposition,' *Logos and Pragma*, 121.

[64] See §4.5 and especially *Lectura* I 7.32: '*Potentia* autem *logica* ostendit modum *compositionis* factae ab intellectu cuius extrema non repugnant, et ista potentia nullam realitatem requirit nisi quod extrema non repugnent – quod autem sit potentia realis in uno extremo vel in alio, hoc accidit, nec hoc requiritur ad istam potentiam. Unde tantum requirit quod *termini compositionis* non repugnent.' Compare §4.6 and §4.10.

[65] *Lectura* I 39.49: 'Potentia logica non est aliqua nisi quando extrema sic sunt possibilia quod non sibi invicem repugnant, sed *uniri* possunt.' Cf. *CF* 116–117.

presuppose the act of *combining* or *compounding*.[66] The same structure governs Duns' theory of negation. The possible composition of
terms is just the necessary condition of *logical* possibility.

4.7.2   Contingent and necessary truths

The term *contingens* hardly occurs in Duns' logical writings, but he still
pays attention to what can be called a contingent proposition. Just as a
necessary proposition, a contingent proposition is a true proposition. So
a contingent proposition is in fact a contingent truth, for instance
Socrates is pale. In such cases, the predicate expresses an accidental property, namely *being pale*, which is asserted of someone and obtains in
reality. Contingent truths entail the existence of the involved individuals
or substances.[67] 'Socrates' is an exemplary name, like 'Smith' in modern
philosophical literature, for *Socrates is pale* is considered to be true and
Cesar is pale is considered to be false. So 'Caesar' functions as a historical name for, to Duns' mind, *Cesar is pale* (*Caesar est albus*) is a false
proposition, because Cesar does not exist any more at the present time.

4.7.3   Necessary truths

Here, the exemplary proposition is: *a man is a sense-gifted being*
(*homo est animal*). The combination of *species* in *A man is a sense-
gifted being* is true, but not because the one intelligible *species* would
be identical with the other intelligible *species*. This assumption would
be false. The proposition *A man is a sense-gifted being* is only true
with reference to the significates of its terms. If there be a man, then
that man is really a sense-gifted being.

   However, the truth of a necessary proposition does not entail that
its subject *exists*. We need not verify its truth from experience.
Significatio does not boil down to *verificatio*. So, meaning does not
boil down to truth. In John Duns' *Super duos libros Perihermenias
Quaestiones. Opus secundum* the levels of *meaning* (*significatio*) and
of *verification* (*verificatio*) are clearly distinguished.[68]

---

[66] *Lectura* I 7.33: 'Et quando est talis compossibilitas, tunc est veritas in propositione modali,
et quando non est talis non-repugnantia (= compossibilitas) terminorum, tunc est falsitas in
propositione modali.' See §4.8.

[67] *Super primum librum Perihermenias Quaestiones* I 8: '*Caesar est albus*, quia accidens reale,
sive per accidens cuiusmodi est album, nulli subiecto inest nisi existenti.'

[68] *Super duos libros Perihermenias Quaestiones. Opus secundum*, quaestio 1: 'Ad aliud dico
quod primo enuntiatur de re sensibili, ut illa res significatur, hoc est accipiendo nomen
absolute. Verificatur tamen primo per singularia.'

When the intellect has abstracted its first object, that is: the essence of a material thing, it can know all other things without a proper species corresponding to the truths deduced. Apparently, Duns Scotus means that from the knowledge of e.g. *man*, all other intelligible species can be deduced, e.g. *animal, organic being, substance.*[69]

So, a true proposition is a *compositio rerum*, combining realities as they are signified, not as *existing*.[70] *True* and *false* are said of affirmative and negative assertions to be made thoughtfully by a knower.[71]

Is (*est*) has a predicative function, for it has a function with respect to the predicate. *Est* is not a subject term or a predicate term, neither a part of the subject or the predicate. The specificity of *is* (*est*) lies in making intelligible the modality of actuality when something is predicated. The predicate is thought to belong actually to the subject, both when the referent exists in factual reality and when the referent does not exist so (*Super primum librum Perihermenias Quaestiones* 8 and *Super duos libros Perihermenias Quaestiones* 6).

> The implication of existence, *e.g.* in '*a man is white*' is a secondary function of '*est*.' The primary function of '*est*' is merely to denote the act of predication. This is in accordance with the general lines of Duns Scotus' semantical theory.[72]

This view of the necessary truth of propositions like *Caesar est Caesar* (*Caesare non existente*) is a major sign of the ongoing emancipation from the *plenitudo* principles of Greek and Hellenistic philosophy which entail that a true proposition entails the factual existence of the subject. There are no empty classes in Aristotelian syllogistics and, likewise, there are no possible truths on what there is not.

---

[69] Bos, 'The Theory of the Proposition,' in De Rijk and Braakhuis (eds), *Logos and Pragma*, 128, referring to *Super duos libros Perihermenias Quaestiones*.

[70] *Super duos libros Perihermenias Quaestiones* 2: 'Ad aliud de compositione et divisione intellectus, dico quod compositio est illarum rerum, non tamen *ut existentium*, sed ut *intelliguntur* [. . .] et in illo modo sunt res in intellectu, non species solae.' See Bos, 'The Theory of the Proposition,' in De Rijk and Braakhuis (eds), *Logos and Pragma*, 128–129.

[71] *Super duos libros Perihermenias Quaestiones* 3: 'Et per hoc dico quod *verum* et *falsum* sunt in intellectu componente vel dividente, sicut in cognoscente.'

[72] Bos, 'The Theory of the Proposition,' in De Rijk and Braakhuis (eds), *Logos and Pragma*, 130. Bos also points out that Duns agrees with, among others, Albert the Great. However, this agreement does not imply that he compiled these commentaries in Paris – cf. ibid., 131. These 'commentaries' are Oxonian – see §1.4: 'A senior theological student': The early logical writings.

4.7.4   *Propositio per se nota*

Lectura I 3.173 offers a marvellous explanation of what a *self-evident proposition* (*propositio per se nota*) is:

> We acquire the truth of *principles* as follows: When *a proposition* is *self-evident*, it can only be formed by our intellect, if our intellect knows its *terms*. The *terms* are as such [*naturaliter*] known just to the intellect: precisely the *terms* include a relation in which *terms are analytically united to other terms*. Therefore, they include the truth of such a union. Therefore, because the intellect can have certain knowledge [*notitia*] of *terms*, then it can also have certain truth about the *principle* of such *terms*.[73]

In the first part of *Lectura* I 2 Duns elucidates the nature of a self-evident proposition.[74] The self-evident character of such a proposition depends on knowing the terms used. The truth of a self-evident proposition is evident on the basis of the knowledge of the terms and the involved certainty is based only on something in the proposition itself.[75] Therefore, the idea is that the concept of the predicate is immediately entailed by the term in subject position.[76]

A *self-evident proposition* is certified from two sides: from itself, for the knower is certain of it on account of the contents of its terms, and from the side of *other* terms, because a proposition cannot be refuted on account of other terms if it must be true on account of itself. A self-evident proposition warrants its own truth on the basis of the contents or the meanings of its *terms*.[77]

---

[73] See §8.4: 'Deductive knowledge,' and for the Latin text, see note 17.

[74] See also §8.3. For an introduction to a terminological exposition typical for Duns, see *Lectura* I 2.13: 'Ad cuius solutionem primo videndum est quae est ratio *propositionis per se notae*; et, secundo, erit manifestum si ista *Deus est* sit per se nota, vel alia in qua enuntiatur *esse* de eo quod convenit Deo, ut *ens infinitum est*.' §§14–20 deal with Duns' elucidation of the term *propositio per se nota*.

[75] See *Lectura* I 2.14: 'Ad intellectum primi [namely, the *ratio propositionis per se notae*] est sciendum quod dicitur propositio per se nota, per ly *"per se"* non excluditur quaecumque causa, quia non notitia terminorum, quia nulla propositio est per se nota nisi habeatur notitia terminorum; sed excluditur quaecumque causa et ratio quae est extra per se conceptus terminorum propositionis per se notae. Et ideo illa propositio est per se nota quae non habet notitiam aliunde mendicatam, sed illa quae ex terminis cognitis habet veritatem evidentem et quae non habet certitudinem nisi ex aliquo in se.'

[76] See *Lectura* I 2.15–19. §19 yields a fine summary: 'Illa igitur *propositio est per se nota* quae ex sola notitia terminorum habet evidentiam et non mendicatam ex evidentia aliorum conceptuum.'

[77] For the theme of self-evident propositions, see Schmücker, *Propositio per se nota*, and Webering, *Theory of Demonstration According to William Ockham*, 51–53: 'Historical development,' and, in particular, the fine treatment in Vier, *Evidence and Its Function According to John Duns Scotus*, part two: 'Evidence of principles and conclusions' (66–116).

4.8 Negation

In Duns' theory of the proposition, the notions of *affirmation* and *negation* are interconnected. Just as an affirmative proposition or affirmation is specific, a negation is specific too.[78] *Truth* entails *meaning*, but does *truth* also entail *existence* and is *factual existence* a necessary condition for both affirmative propositions and denials to be meaningful? *Being P* or *being not-P* entails that there is a subject *a* which is *P* or is *not-P*, but what does the necessary falsity of a contradiction of the form *p and not-p* presuppose on the level of factual existence? We read in *Quaestiones super Praedicamenta Aristotelis* 42:

> Whether the subject exists or does not exist in contradictory propositions, it is always the case that one proposition is true of the subject and the other is false, since always the proposition *Socrates is ill* is true or the proposition *Socrates is not ill* is true, whether Socrates exists or not.[79]

What is to be said about the referential function in disjunctive pairs of contradictory propositions about what does not exist? Do terms in denials refer?

In *Quaestiones super Praedicamenta Aristotelis* 42 Duns asks whether in negative propositions the existence of the subject is irrelevant. Duns' treatment is most interesting. We have already observed now and again that there are substantial divergences between the early writings and the great theological works on the *Sententiae*, but the logical writings themselves already differ on the issue of *propositions* (*whether true or false*) and *factual reference*. In *Quaestiones super Praedicamenta Aristotelis* 42, Duns discusses the question whether *referring* presupposes existence or not, or whether it is irrelevant (*indifferenter*) that, in a negative proposition, a *being* (*ens*) or a *non-being* (*non-ens*) is involved. Duns plays with an interesting exchange of supportive arguments and counter-arguments: if Socrates does not exist, then in *Socrates is not ill* 'Socrates' must refer to a non-being (*non-ens*), since, otherwise, *Socrates is not ill* would mean: *Socrates who exists, is not ill*. Therefore, if *Socrates is not ill* is true,

---

Ockham distinguishes between *propositio per se nota* and *propositio primo vera*: a *propositio per se nota* is evidently known by its terms and in a *propositio primo vera* the subject entails the predicate – see Webering, *Theory of Demonstration*, 43–47 and 53–57.

[78] If *p* is an individual proposition, then *not-p* is also a proposition. A negation has only its proper *truth* value in virtue of an affirmation: if *p* is false, then *not-p* is true. It is a presupposition of Duns' theory of the proposition that the negation sign 'non' functions as a logical constant.

[79] *Quaestiones super Praedicamenta* 42 *introductio*, in *Opera Philosophica* I 546. See §4.2.

both *Socrates does not exist* and *Socrates exists* are false. The suggestion that in the case of a definite term reference to a non-being is possible, but not in the case of universal terms, is criticized by saying that *Everyman is ill* is false, if no man exists.[80] Duns does not round off this exchange of arguments, but by observing that, in such cases, we have to know what the *meaning* of the involved term is and what its *referents* are, Duns' main thesis is that a term both in an affirmative proposition and in a denial refers to its referent.[81]

In *Quaestiones super Praedicamenta Aristotelis* 42, Duns concludes that asserting, including denying, presupposes *referring* and *referring* entails a referent and a referent entails factual existence. However, the possibility of meaning and truth of what there is and of what there is not were hotly debated during the thirteenth century.[82] The young John Duns would soon take a rather different path. Bos discusses two kinds of propositions which are true, although no referent exists.[83] The following examples suffice to explain Duns' view with the help of the underlying rule interpreting them. This rule states that the intellect grasps a nature either as general or as belonging to an individual. Neither case entails the factual existence of that nature in an individual:

1   *Cesar is a man* (*Caesar est homo*) is true, although Cesar does not exist any more.

Being a man is predicable of many and Cesar is an individual who is essentially a man. The truth of *Cesar is a man* does not depend on the existence of Cesar, but on the essential nature of anybody who is a man, and once Cesar was a man. Existence and non-existence do not make the property of *being a man* equivocal. *There is no man older than I am in the family I am from* does not use a concept of *man* different from the concept of *man* in *I am the only man in the family I am from*, if I am the only man in the family.

In contrast with Duns' univocity thesis, Roger Bacon, among others, defends the equivocity of 'man' in *Cesar is a man* and

[80] *Quaestiones super Praedicamenta* 42.1–3: 'Subiectum stat pro ente et pro non-ente indifferenter?'
[81] *Quaestiones super Praedicamenta* 42.4: 'In omni enim propositione affirmativa sive negativa, supponit pro eius per se suppositis,' accompanied by an indirect reference to the future *Super duos libros Perihermenias Quaestiones*.
[82] See Braakhuis, 'Kilwardby versus Bacon,' in Bos (ed.), *Medieval Semantics and Metaphysics*, 111.
[83] Bos, 'The Theory of the Proposition,' in De Rijk and Braakhuis (eds), *Logos and Pragma*, 129 f.

Clinton is a man, because there is no human person Ceasar any more and there is still the human person Clinton.[84] According to Bacon and, in general, Parisian logic before 1250, there is nothing in common to being and non-being, to what there is and what there is not. With Duns, identity statements deliver the second kind of examples:

2 *A man is a man (homo est homo)* and *Socrates is Socrates (Socrates est Socrates)* are true even though no man exists and even though Socrates does not exist any more.

Such propositions are identity statements: the predicate repeats the subject. So, it is impossible that they are not true, without regard to the existence of people or of Socrates (*Super duos libros Perihermenias Quaestiones* I 8).

Still more is to be said on *negations* and it is said in an excursus on the theory of negation in the much later *Lectura Oxoniensis* III (1303). A negation is as such universal and communicable.[85] A property is incommunicable if no other individual can possess it, like traditional dogmatics tells us about God's omnipresence, omniscience and being incarnate. Thus a property is communicable if it is to be shared by others and if it is possibly common. In this sense a negation is as such common and communicable because, for example:

> *This is not pink*

does not only apply to my copy of *Lectura* II, but also to dictionaries and shoes.

There are three kinds of *negations*. The first group of denials is characterized by a self-contraditory force. What is white is not black and because *being white* entails *not being black*, affirming *black* of something white is incompatible.

The second group of denials depends for its truth value on a historical event. *White black* is a necessary falsehood, but *My pencil is white* is false because it is not made white, but this falsehood is not necessarily so, for my pencil could have been white. In this last case, there are two subgroups: a typical example of the first subgroup is

---

[84] See *Super duos libros Perihemenias Quaestiones* I 8. Cf. Alain de Libera, 'The Oxford and Paris traditions in logic,' *CHLMP* 180–185.

[85] *Lectura* III 1.42: 'Unde *negatio* non est de se incommunicabilis. Unde ergo est quod haec negatio dependentiae [that is, human nature being dependent on the Word (*Verbum, Logos*)] est propria et incommunicabilis, cum omnis negatio de se sit communis.'

dirty snow, a typical example of the second subgroup the hairs of my black cat: they can be colored pink, as some ladies do.[86]

This classification highlights Duns' two areas of attention: first, the main division hinges on the basic distinction between *necessity* and *contingency* which turns around the principle of consistency, and, secondly, the second division takes into account the natural aspects of our contingent world with its propensities and accidental events.

4.9   TRUTH

Duns deals with *truth* in *Quaestiones super Libros Metaphysicorum Aristotelis* VI 3 and this *quaestio* again shows the pattern often to be discerned in this remarkable book: an original layer (§§1–39 and §§65–73), and a long addition (§§40–64).[87] We pay attention to Duns' original argumentation. His primary distinction concerns the difference between *reality-related truth* (*in re*) and *mind-related truth* (*in intellectu*).[88]

4.9.1   Reality-related truth

There are two categories of *reality-related truth*: with respect to bringing forth or producing something and with respect to knowing.[89] With respect to knowledge, there are three kinds of *true reality* (*res vera*): the created intellect, reality in the intellect just as the known is in the knower, and the element of manifestation common to both. The relation of knowledge is a rational relation, founded on the known object.

4.9.2   Mind-related truth

Mind-related truth is twofold according to a twofold activity of the intellect. The first activity concerns concepts which are irreducibly

---

[86] *Lectura* III 1.45: 'Et haec negatio duplex est, quia aut agens non agit ad quod passum natum est inclinari naturaliter et tunc in illo passo est negatio alicuius quod aptum natum est esse in eo ut si esset ignis et non haberet calorem quem natus est habere, quia agens hoc non causavit in eo. Aut quia agens non agit, non causat in eo passo illud ad quod passum non naturaliter inclinatur, sibi tamen non repugnat illud, et tunc in passo est negatio alicuius ad quod est in potentia neutra, quia nec naturaliter, nec violenter inclinatur ad illud, sicut forte naturalia se habent ad formas artificiales.'

[87] *Quaestiones Metaphysicae* VI 3.22 ff. Cf. the exposition by Boehner, 'Ockham's Theory of Truth,' in Buytaert (ed.), *Boehner. Collected Articles on Ockham*, 195–200.

[88] See §§23–30 and §§31–39, respectively.

[89] The first category numbers three kinds: the Truth (*Veritas*) God the Son is, the truth of the imitating creature, and the equivocal truth common to both (§§24–25).

simple and the second activity concerns propositions. As to the first kind of activity of the mind, Duns' point is that what is irreducibly simple cannot be understood mistakenly, if it be understood at all. We may be ignorant of simple terms, but if we are familiar with any term of this type, we cannot be mistaken that it is applicable to anything. There is a basic intellectual trust on the level of the irreducibly simple concepts, just parallel to the basic trust in our senses. In the case of the non-irreducibly simple concepts, we might be mistaken, because an entailment is involved which might be overlooked.[90]

In the case of *simple concepts*, we may be ignorant, but we cannot be mistaken, if we understand them and adequately know their contents. Our mind may also form a proposition, seeing that the issue of truth or falsity is not decoded by the relationship of its terms. As to this second kind of activity of the mind, we frame contingent propositions, while we might be mistaken because what we believe can be false, 'namely when concepts are united which are not united in reality.'[91] By *formal truth* Duns means that we know that a proposition has a truth value. The proposition

Antonius Andreas introduced the ontological notion of possible being

is true or false in itself. In factual reality, Antonius Andreas was the first philosopher to build his ontology on a logic-based *onto*logical notion of *possible being*, or he was not. Perhaps, Duns Scotus himself was not, because, to his mind, *possible being* was only acceptable as a logical concept. According to this terminology, every proposition is as such *formally (formaliter)* true or false.[92] Adam Wodeham confirms that Scotus subscribed to the formal truth value of every proposition,[93] but we also frame and apprehend propositions without knowing whether they are true or false. If we consider the proposition

---

[90] *Quaestiones Metaphysicae* VI 3.31–33. For kinds of *simple concepts*, see §4.5.

[91] *Quaestiones Metaphysicae* VI 335: 'Secundae autem veritati opponitur ignorantia privative et falsitas contrarie, quando *scilicet* uniuntur quae in re non sunt unita.'

[92] *Quaestiones Metaphysicae* VI 3.37: 'Intellectus multas propositiones format et apprehendit actu secundo, quae tamen sunt sibi neutrae [= without any truth value]. [. . .] Licet ergo sit in illo actu *formaliter* veritas vel falsitas – aut quia est conformis rei extra aut non – tamen non est ibi *obiective*, quia non apprehenditur ista conformitas.'

[93] Wood and Gál (eds), *Adam Wodeham. Lectura Secunda* I 1.1 §4: 'Scotus [. . .] vult quod in propositione semper est *formaliter* veritas vel falsitas, quia propositio semper est conformis vel difformis rei extra, id est rei significatae sive intra sive extra.'

Antonius Andreas introduced the ontological notion of possible being

we know what we are saying, but we are not confirming or denying what we are saying, because it is not true or false *to our mind*. We leave the matter open. According to Scotian terminology, *objectively* (*obiective*) there is no truth or falsity, because we do not claim to know that

Antonius Andreas introduced the ontological notion of possible being

is true, nor that it is false.[94] There is no truth or falsity *objectively* (*obiective*). *Objectively* is here not used in the modern sense, but it means literally: *with respect to the object*, namely the contents of the proposition one assents to.[95] If the intellect reflects on its own acts of asserting or denying, it may state that the assertion or denial fits reality (*est conformis rei extra*) or does not fit reality. If the next step affirms truth or falsity, then truth or falsity is said to be there in an objective sense (*obiective*).[96] So, *truth* is *conformitas*. The two decisive aspects of truth as *conformitas* are as follows. A proposition assented to is only *true* if it is guaranteed by itself or by external reality. The distinction between *formaliter* and *obiective* truth value is not applicable to *principles*, for principles are built on *simple concepts* and the relationship between the concepts of a principle is self-evident. The intellect sees the internal connection at the same time, 'but in other propositions, for example, theses (*conclusiones*), a different temporal aspect matters.'[97] Duns' analysis of *truth* typically exemplifies his logic-based approach.

---

[94] *Quaestiones Metaphysicae* VI 3.36: 'Neutra veritas [namely, *formaliter* and *obiective*] est in intellectu *obiective* nisi reflectente se super actum suum, comparando illum ad obiectum, quae reflexio in cognoscendo, *scilicet* quod actus talis est similis vel dissimilis, non est sine compositione et divisione.'

[95] The same is to be noticed with regard to *subjectively* (*subiective*) = with respect to the subject.

[96] *Quaestiones Metaphysicae* VI 3.37: 'Licet ergo sit in illo actu *formaliter* veritas vel falsitas – aut quia est *conformis* rei extra, aut non – tamen non est ibi *obiective*, quia non apprehenditur ista conformitas.' See also Ibid., VI 3.66 and 68.

[97] *Quaestiones Metaphysicae* VI 3.38: 'Posset ergo dici quod ibi est alius actus, et reflexus sed imperceptus, quia *simul tempore*. In aliis, ut in conclusionibus, differunt *tempore*.' This combination of *derivability* and *time* is repudiated in *Lectura* I 3.166 and in *Ordinatio* I 3.233. See §8.3. So, while *Quaestiones Metaphysicae* VII 12 must be later than 1301, the original layer of *Quaestiones Metaphysicae* VI 3 must be pre-*Lectura*.

4.10   LOGICAL IMPOSSIBILITY AND LOGICAL POSSIBILITY

4.10.1   Impossibility

Logical *inconsistency* and *consistency* are a noteworthy area of attention in the whole of Duns' works. Although it is not true that the *logicum possibile* for the first time occurred in his writings, it is a central concept for him. His logical acumen earned him the name of *magister rationum* and he is still called *the Subtle Doctor*. The *quaestio* and the *disputatio* marked his academic milieu.

According to Gilbert of Poitiers, it is not just any problem that can be counted as a *quaestio*. Whether John Duns was born in 1265 or in 1266 does not constitute a *quaestio*. A *quaestio* requires a far more serious divergency. In the case of a *quaestio*, the answer is *p* or *not-p*, of course, but there is an additional requirement at stake. If *p* constitutes the answer, then *not-p* must be impossible, and if *not-p* is the answer, then it must be impossible that *p* is true.[98] This facet is in profound harmony with great questions of medieval theology and philosophy. The driving force is the consistency and thinkability of the Christian faith. It is a paradoxical and inspiring feature that here questions of *truth* and questions of *consistency* seem to coincide.

4.10.2   Contradiction

The contradiction is a logical phenomenon which is of great significance for Duns Scotus' argumentations. *Being contradictory* can be applied both to terms and to propositions. In straightforward oppositions between terms (*a and not-a*) and between propositions (*p and not-p*) we meet contradictions in a univocal way.[99] So, contradictions cannot be true and if a proposition of the form *p and not-p* is necessarily false, then a proposition of the form *p or not-p* is necessarily true.

> Whether the subject exists or does not exist in contradictory propositions, it is always the case that one proposition is true of the subject and the other is false, since always the proposition *Socrates is ill* is

[98] On the history of the meaning of '*quaestio*,' see PMA §4.5.

[99] *Quaestiones super Praedicamenta Aristotelis* 42 *Introductio* (*Opera Philosophica* I 545): 'Contradictio de qua hic loquitur, non tantum sit in incomplexis, quamvis hic loquatur principaliter de oppositione incomplexorum, quia contradictio forte univoce invenitur in propositionibus et in terminis.'

true or the proposition *Socrates is not ill* is true, whether Socrates exists or not.[100]

Duns Scotus' decisive arguments often take off from a basic contradiction. If *p or not-p* is necessarily true, then either *not-p* is inconsistent if *p* is necessarily true and vice versa, or *not-p* is possibly true if *p* is contingently true and vice versa. In this latter case, we have to be able to explain both possible aspects of reality. A contradiction means the end of all dispute or opposition. The *reductio ad contradictionem* is the omnipresent pattern of the arguments of the *magister rationum*, for contradictory propositions are simply impermissible. The range of *truth* and *falsity* is universal and the range of *truth* and *falsity* can only be operational if they are univocal.[101] There is no doubt on the part of the intellect that contradictories cannot be true.[102] The theological application is clear too:

> It is said that the term of a first principle is a *being*, to be classified in terms of the ten categories, and that this does not hold good for a theological subject. It is not worthwhile to say so. We no more doubt that contradictories are not true about God at the same time (e.g. *God is blessed and not-blessed*, and the like) than we do about something white.[103]

Duns not only rejects the possible acceptance of contradictions wholeheartedly, but it is also perfectly clear to him what the consequences are if we would accept an impossible predicate. 'The subject collapses, if the opposite of the predicate is given.'[104] The parallel formulation of *Ordinatio* I 2.11 is even more simple: 'The opposite of such a predicate is incompatible with the subject.' Impossible predicates are predicates of the form $P \& -P$ and they destroy the subject

---

[100] *Quaestiones super Praedicamenta Aristotelis* 42 *Introductio* (*Opera Philosophica* I 546): 'In contradictoriis, sive subiectum sit sive non sit, semper alterum est verum de subiecto et alterum falsum, quia sive Socrates sit sive non, semper haec est vera *Socrates languet* vel haec *Socrates non languet*.' Cf. Aristotle, *Categoriae*, 10.

[101] *Ordinatio Prologus* 84: 'Certum est intellectui ista prima principia vera non tantum in sensibilibus, sed etiam in insensibilibus.'

[102] *Ibid.*: 'Non enim dubitat magis intellectus quod contraditoria non sunt simul vera de immateriali quam de materiali.'

[103] Ibid.: 'Quod dicitur quod terminus primi principii est ens quod dividitur in decem genera, et illud non extendit se ad obiectum theologicum, hoc non valet. Non enim magis dubitamus quod contradictoria non sunt simul vera de Deo (ut quod – *Deus est beatus et non-beatus*, et huiusmodi) quam de albo.' Other manuscripts offer variants like *bonus et non-bonus* and *verus et non-verus*. Duns' statement that contradictory propositions cannot be true is easily to be seen to be true, when we assess $p \& -p$ in terms of its truth table.

[104] *Lectura* I 2.9: 'Si detur oppositum praedicati, destruetur subiectum.'

to be considered.[105] The weight of the logical phenomena of contradictory propositions and contradictory predicates is patently clear to the young Duns.

There is a paradoxical flavor to Duns' numerous examinations of types of possibility and potentiality. He offers his analyses of kinds of *possibility* within the context of the doctrine of God, specifically trinitarian theology. Duns needs a concept of *possibility* which enables him to assert consistently *It is possible that God exists*. The problem is as simple as that, since the Aristotelian notions of *potency* implying non-actuality cannot be applied to what is essential for God. The explanation of *logical possibility* is clear, being parasitic on *logical impossibility*. When we connect a predicate with a subject, the upshot can be unacceptable or acceptable. When we consider the proposition

The Son or the Holy Spirit can beget (generare)

then the upshot is unacceptable, for we have to conclude that this proposition is necessarily false. Its terms are incompossible, for it is impossible that the Son begets, and it is impossible that the Holy Spirit begets.[106]

The second possibility is that connecting a subject and a predicate is acceptable, when we may conclude that the involved terms are compatible or compossible. 'When there is such compossibility, then a modal proposition is true, and when there is no such compatibility (*non-repugnantia*) of the terms, then a modal proposition is false' (*Lectura* I 7.33). The analysis departs from the components of a proposition, namely the subject and the predicate, and their relationship. So, forming the concept of *logical possibility* rests on a propositional type of analysis which departs from the subject and predicate terms of the proposition. The only condition for *logical possibility* is that subject and predicate can be linked, and they can be linked if they are possibly true. Whether the subject refers to something existing in reality is not considered. Likewise, the propositions *God exists* (*Deum esse*) and *God the Father begets* are impossible in terms of Aristotelian *potency*. Duns' idea of *logical possibility* will do, as it does when we have to account for the validity of the principle *If p is true, then it is possible that p* (*ab esse ad posse valet illatio*). The inherited logical and philosophical tools spoil the coherence of the

---

[105] Just as the proof of a possible property of *a* demonstrates the possible existence of *a*, the proof of an impossible property of *a* refutes the possible existence of *a*. That is why both *a*theology and Duns' method matter.

[106] See *Lectura* I 7.31 ff. and *Ordinatio* I 20.11 f.

Christian faith. If these tools were adequate, the *fides* is impossible and there is no chance to steer to a *fides quaerens intellectum*.

The point of departure is spelling out what *logical possibility* is up to. What is at stake is the nature of necessary falsehood. In *Quaestiones Metaphysicae* IX 1–2.21 we meet a typically Scotian pattern. Falsity as such is accounted for by a contradictory pair, but not by a contradictory pair of *propositions*, rather by a contradictory pair of predicates or properties. On this fundamental level of possibility, the Scotian analysis is dominated by the *subject-predicate* structure.[107]

4.10.3 Logical possibility

Again and again, Duns piles up the meanings of *possibilitas* and *potentia*. Let us, first, survey these expositions and, then, consider their context and impact. One of the earliest expositions of the notion of *possibilitas logica* is found in *Lectura* I 2.188, where Duns lists several kinds of *possibility*. On the one hand, *possible* signifies *logical possibility* and, on the other hand, it signifies *real possibility*. Moreover, he adds to this pair of *logical* and *real possibility* so-called *metaphorical possibility*, which is found in geometry. Duns bypasses this kind of possibility since it is not to the point.[108] *Logical possibility* is at stake in possible *propositions* and *possible* propositions are propositions which contain the elements *possible* or *can*. Duns presents a concise definition of *logical possibility*:

> *Logical possibility* is found in propositions when the terms are not incompatible, and in this way the proposition: '*It is possible that the Father begets*' and the like are said to be true.[109]

Duns offers also a short definition of *real possibility*. In the parallel text of *Ordinatio* I 2.262 Duns gives an alternative definition of *possibile*

---

[107] Ibid.: 'Et sic *possibile* convertitur cum toto ente, nam nihil est *ens* cuius ratio contradictionem includit.'

[108] *Lectura* I 2.188: '*Possibile* uno modo significat *possibilitatem logicam*, qua utitur in propositionibus de possibili, et alio modo significat *possibilitatem realem*. Haec distinctio habetur ex V *Metaphysicae*, cap. "De potentia," ubi etiam ponit alium modum possibilitatis, qui invenitur in *geometricis*, qui non est ad propositum.' For the name of *metaphorical possibility* which does not occur here, see *Lectura* I 20.10; cf. *Ordinatio* I 20.11 and *Quaestiones Metaphysicae* IX 1–2.16–17: 'potentia metaphorica, "quae est in mathematicis,"' while 'potentia mathematica' occurs in *Lectura* I 20.10.

[109] *Lectura* I 2.188: '*Possibilitas* autem *logica* est in propositionibus quando termini non repugnant, et sic dicitur haec vera *Possibile est Patrem generare* et huiusmodi.'

logicum and drops *metaphorical* possibility. A similar definition of *logical possibility* is found in *Lectura* I 5.118:

> by speaking of *logical possibility*, namely where there is neither contradiction, nor incompatibility of terms.[110]

In *Lectura* I 7.31–43, *logical possibility* is contrasted with *potentia activa* and *passiva*. Neither are essentially in God. This last view is amended in *Ordinatio* I 20.13 ff. where, with a reference to *Ordinatio* I 2.43–58, Duns stresses that in contrast with passive potency God evidently enjoys active potency, but then *active potentiality* in an alternative sense.

4.11 ELEMENTS OF THE THEORY OF RELATION

Present logic of *relation* has no true counterpart in ancient Greek, medieval and early modern philosophy before Frege and Russell.[111] The predominance of Aristotelian syllogistics and theories of substance and accident do not seem to be profitable for the development of a theory of relation, but several central parts of Christian theology need an articulate theory of relation. Duns' theory of *relation, distinction* and *identity* is marked by a special historical importance. We may discern a widespread search of it in Scotus' thought.

However, we meet again the traditional obstacle that, on the one hand, many technical terms of medieval philosophy seem to be overspecialized, while, on the other hand, prima facie they do not provide the shades of meaning the modern mind is looking for. So, we have to pay close attention to the meanings of the key terms of the theory. Duns' difficult technical terminology is notorious and, against different semantic backgrounds, his theories patently sound absurd. The theory of relation is also the context of the famous *formalis distinctio a parte rei* (see §§6.6–6.7 and §7.6).

Terms like *relatio, relativum, extremum, fundamentum, terminus, realis,* and *relatio rationis* look rather general, but in fact they are specific and we can even get the impression that they are too specific to handle the theory in a natural way. This feature is the more demanding because these terms play an important part in quite different contexts: the ontology of properties and of creatures, the theology of

---

[110] *Lectura* I 5.118: 'loquendo de *potentia logica*, scilicet ubi non est contradictio nec repugnantia terminorum.'

[111] On the logic of relations, see Lemmon, *Beginning Logic*, 179–188, and Copi, *Symbolic Logic* ([5]1979), 116–156. Cf. Weinberg, *Abstraction, Relation and Induction*, 61 ff.

creation because of the relationship between God and his creation and the doctrine of the Trinity. Thus the theory of relation has to cope with complex challenges.

Time and again, Scotus' thought transcends the boundaries of the theories of the *Categoriae*. In Duns' *theory of relation* we meet a definite set of technical terms. Let us introduce some elements of his theory of *relation*: *relatio* (relation), *referri* (have a relation to), *extremum* (term), *fundamentum* (foundation) and *terminus* (end term). In terms of the formal pattern of a particular relation *aRb* we elucidate these expressions and their translations. In *aRb*, *R* is the relation as it runs from *a* to *b*. Duns has a lot to say on the different properties of the relationship running from *a* to *b* and the relationship as it runs from *b* to *a*.[112] The *extremes* (*extrema*) are the *terms* of a relation, just as the *extrema* are the *terms* of a proposition – e.g. in a proposition of the form *aRb* the components *a* and *b* are the terms (*extrema*) of relation *R*. The relation *R* is anchored in the *fundamentum* of the relation *R*. The *fundamentum* of *R* is the nature of *a* which entails *a*, *R* and *b* (see §7.6).

Simple examples of *relatives* (*relativa*) are *similar* and *dissimilar*, *equal* and *unequal*.[113] When *a* and *b* are relatives, because they are similar then a symmetrical relation obtains of both *a* and *b*: if *a* is like *b* then *b* is like *a*, and if *a* is unequal to *b* then *b* is unequal to *a*. The same is required of both terms of the relation in the same way.

In God *relativa* are different. Again and again, theology asks more than the old doctrine of the categories can give. For this reason even the characterization 'categorial relation' can be misleading. Such relations seem to have walked away from Aristotle's theory of categories; however, we have to dig out the presuppositions of understanding *e mente auctoris*, the *auctor* being the medieval thinker in question and primarily not Aristotle. This is true of Duns in a very specific way.

The usage of *relatio* and *relativum* are examples in case. Let us assume that we dispose of two pairs of *relativa*: *a* and *b* are *relatives* (*relativa*) and *c* and *d* are *relatives*. Then the following law holds: if the first term of the first relation is the same as the first term of the second relation, then the second term of the second relation is the

---

112 Duns does not possess an analytical tool in terms of sets and properties of reflexivity, transitivity, and symmetry. I propose to use these tools in order to clarify Duns Scotus' lines of argumentation, including the term 'argument,' indicating the members of a relation: in *aRbc* *a*, *b*, and *c* are the *arguments* of relation.

113 See *Lectura* I 5.3: '*Communicare* et *communicari* sunt relativa in divinis; sed non sunt relativa sicut sunt relativa communia, ut *simile* et *dissimile*, et aequale, etc., quia huiusmodi requirunt aliquod unum in utroque extremo.'

same as the second term of the second relation – if *a* is *c* then *b* is *d*.[114] The point is that one *relatio* (= *correlation*) has only two terms. In this respect the theory of *relation* is not a logical study of general features of relations in the modern sense, but in fact deals with concrete relations between particular individuals or entities. Why has it to be so? Because otherwise, the same would be (cor)related to different things in the same way. A (cor)relation between different entities is a different (cor)relation. Thus the individual character of the correlates (*relativa*) is taken to be the point of departure of a certain (cor)relation.

In addition to the specific character of relations, we have to pay attention to the way symmetry plays a part in the case of (cor)relations. Two different aspects deserve attention in particular. First, a relation is often characterized by the symmetry of that relation: if *a* bears relation *R* to *b*, then *b* bears relation *R* to *a*. Second, the fact that a connection is called a *relation* is often based on a logical feature, for example:

a is the father of (son) *b*
entails
b is the son of *a*.

Since, in fact, a specific *father–son* relationship is at stake, the reverse entailment holds too:

b is the son of *a*
entails
a is the father of (son) *b*.

Father and *son* are called *relatives* (*relativa*). In this case, *being relative* is not to be accounted for in terms of the symmetry of *being the father of* and *being the son of*, for these relations themselves are clearly asymmetrical. The reason for *being relative* is that, within the specific semantic web of the meanings of the Latin words involved, the indicated inferences are logically equivalent. In short, in the case of 'relatives' (*relativa*) there is a mutual derivation to be discerned.[115]

---

[114] See *Lectura* I 5.4: 'Quando sunt duo paria correlativorum, si extremum unius correlationis sit idem extremo alterius, et alterum extremum correlationis erit idem alteri alterius correlationis, – ut si *a* et *b* sint relativa et *c* et *d* similiter, si *a* et *c* sint idem, *b* et *d* erunt idem –, quia unius correlationis tantum sunt duo extrema.'

[115] *Lectura* I 5.9: 'In relativis est consequentia mutua: ut, si *hic* pater est *huius*, e converso, *illud* est filius *illius*.'

In comparison with the modern concept of *relation*, the awkwardness of the traditional term *relatio* is obvious. This phenomenon of *relation* language shows itself in the pattern of the specialized meanings of philosophical key terms, rooted in the Latin idiom itself. Scholasticism involves the transformation of Latin into a semi-artificial language, born of the pressures of philosophical and theological dilemmas which could not be solved on the basis of classic Latin. Originally, a *relatio* is a *correlatio* and thus a *relatio* is rooted in symmetry and analogy. Duns discusses this datum mainly in terms of Aristotle's threefold distinction of relations (*Metaphysics* 1020 b 26–32).

Relativa are of three kinds and in particular the third kind attracts the attention of Duns: the so-called relation of the mensurate to the measure is not mutual. Such a relation runs formally from the one to the other, but not vice versa, and it is neither a real relation nor a rational relation. Then there are three kinds of *relative entities (relativa)* which figure in relations. The classification rests on the nature of the foundation of the relationship.

The first kind concerns number or quantity, for example double to a half, triple to a third, that which exceeds to what is exceeded. What is equal, like or the same belong to this kind too.

The second kind is based on the distinction between acting and being acted upon, for example heating to what is heated, and what is active to what is passive. The point which is stressed by Duns is that such relations are mutual.

However, regarding the third kind of relative things, the analogous point stresses that these relations are not mutual. What matters here is more specific than symmetry. The Aristotelian mutuality seems to boil down to symmetry and this is indeed so in the case of equality, likeness and sameness. If *a* is equal to, like or the same as *b*, then *b* is equal to, like or the same as *a*, but this is not he case with double and a half, treble and a third, a property as *exceeding* and active and passive. The structures of the involved relations are different. In different ways relatives or relative entities form a specific couple. In the case of the relations of number and potency there is a reciprocity which promotes the end term into being a relative.[116]

This calls to mind another affiliated point that, originally, *relative* does not refer to *any* argument of a relation, but it refers to a specific

---

[116] *Lectura* I 30.36: 'Unde in aliis modis relationem, quia *relativa sunt aliorum et e contra*; secundum illud quod sunt, est *mutua habitudo*.' What is said to be a relative in virtue of number or potency is a relative because its essence is *ad aliquid*. Cf. *Metaphysics* 1021 a 26–28.

entity, namely the first entity of a dyadic relation, and thus to another entity which enjoys the relation together with the first entity – a very specific intrinsic combination indeed.

In terms of this overspecialized terminology we have to unravel and to assess what Duns is saying. In concentrating on the third kind of relatives like knowledge and the knowable or sensation and the sensible, Duns stresses that what can be known and knowledge are not the same or identical, nor are they equal items or to be compared to the potential in relation to the actual.[117] He unambiguously states the vital point of non-symmetry:

> *a knows that p* entails *p is knowable for a*, but
> *p is knowable for a* does not entail *a knows that p*.

Duns denies the necessity of the consequence between the epistemically weak *knowable* and the epistemically strong *knowing*. Of course, the notion of knowability depends on that of knowledge, but this insight does not imply that the state of affairs or fact which is knowable is as such the end term of a knowledge relation.[118] It is not true that all relatives are convertible. The focus of Duns Scotus' theory of relation is the separation of the notions of *identity* and *equivalence* from the notion of *relation*. The yeast in this operation is the idea of synchronic contingency. When we drop necessitarianism, such crucial relations have to be defined independently and they cannot be reduced to each other any more in virtue of identity. The idea of *synchronic* contingency, again, is firmly rooted in Duns' theory of will.[119] We see the beginnings of a new analysis of relation in his theory of will and *imago Dei*.[120] The breakthrough of the model of necessitarianism means that the restyled theory of *relation* rests on *necessity-contingency*-based distinctions, just as the the parallelism model of *reality* is wedded to the necessity model.

---

[117] *Lectura* I 30.36: 'Relationes tertii modi sunt non-mutuae, [. . .] nam alterum extremum refertur ad aliud, et e contra non refertur reliquum ad ipsum (nec realiter, nec secundum rationem). [. . .] Nulla enim est divisio relationis in extremo terminante relationem ad ipsum, secundum quod terminans est illam relationem.'

[118] *Lectura* I 30.39: 'Scientia enim dicitur ad scibile, sed non e contra: non enim si est scibile, necesse est scientiam esse.'

[119] It is interesting that, in the same vein, Duns Scotus deals with the relation between *act* and *potency*, while Aristotle counts these relatives with the mutual kinds.

[120] See *Lectura* I 3.216, 221–222 and 314–315. Cf. *Quaestiones Quodlibetales* XIII.

4.12   THE IMPACT OF JOHN DUNS' EARLY DEVELOPMENT

As to the theory of *meaning*, the young John Duns started with rejecting a reist position. The next step we have already met: *Super duos
libros Perihermenias Quaestiones. Opus secundum* 1 constructed a
kind of balance between the mentalist and the reist approaches and
this ecumenical attitude was systematically transformed into a theory
of a double direct signification of both words and concepts in *Lectura*
I 27.51. By the time of the Parisian *Ordinatio* I 27, the ecumenism of
Super duos libros Perihermenias Quaestiones. Opus secundum 1 has
changed into a war report which tells of a big clash. Now, there is a
definite priority of what is real and factual over the mental or conceptual dimension and Duns abandoned the preference for the mentalist structure of *meaning* and *reference*. We have observed the
medieval tendency towards emancipation from mentalist views, a tendency which Duns radicalized. The hypothesis of a Parisian origin of
the logical writings, as even Wolter accepts, destroys the intelligibility
of Duns' personal development. The logical and semantic details are
the checkpoints of a theological revolution, just as the *Oxonian
Articles* (1284) are the semantic and logical checkpoints of the
Parisian Articles (1277).

Scotus' semantic moves are saying goodbye to logical abstractionism and the abstractionist worldview. We are far away from the
logophoric semantics of ancient philosophy. The contemporary
problem of meaning lies in the far distance too. This type of Christian
philosophy of language passionately focuses on actual reality, the
created world. What in fact is the case, is thought of and is said is analyzed. It is the way of ideas of an open actualism. The whole of Duns'
analysis of *truth* is a typical example of his logic-based approach,
dominated by the fundamental distinction between *necessity* and *contingency*. Both Duns' analysis of *concepts* and of *truth* and his treatment of *negation* are structured by *necessity-contingency*-based
distinctions, turning on his personal notion of *synchronic contingency*
(see §4.10).

The early writings offer precious information to get acquainted
with the young John Duns, but, again and again, we meet newly styled
theories in the *Lectura* stage of his development, elicited by theological challenges. The whole of Duns Scotus' logical approach is embedded in a working unit of conceptual analysis, propositional analysis,
and the analysis and assessment of arguments. We observe a turn
to reality and reality turns out to be profoundly contingent. Both

ontology and the doctrine of God are dealt with in terms of *necessity-contingency*-based distinctions. In particular, we have seen that the inner dynamics of Duns' analyses is based on the initial function of the types of *concepts* which can be discerned. Just as the analysis of types of *concepts* is *necessity-contingency* (*essentiality-accidentality*) based (§4.6), so is the analysis of types of *propositions* also *necessity-contingency* based (§§4.7–4.10), as well as the theory of relation (§4.11).

Although we have to bear in mind the historical dimension, Duns Scotus' innovations can be easily restated in modern terms because, since the 1960s, the theory of contingency can be worked out impeccably. Thanks to their emancipatory tendency, Scotus' contributions can be amplified and extrapolated, for they are laden with creative perspectives in an ongoing liberation from archaic and ancient patterns of thinking.[121]

---

[121] See Chapters 14 and 15. Chapter 16 indicates how this scope can be broadened and Duns Scotus' theories can be repaired, renovated, and extended.

CHAPTER 5

Ars obligatoria

5.1 INTRODUCTION

In *Lectura* I 39.56 and 59 we notice quite an interesting feature: in reply to an objection to his theory of *synchronic contingency* (§§38–54) the young John Duns rejects a certain rule of logic. He also mentions the *ars* the rule under consideration belongs to:

> Concerning the next objection: we deny that rule. Nevertheless, the *disputational art of obligations* is handed down very well by that master without this rule.[1]

We observe that Duns is generous in his praise regarding the master who evidently was an expert in the field: a certain *magister* handed down the *ars obligatoria* very well. Apart from the term 'magister' in the expression 'Magister Sententiarum,' 'magister' refers to a *philosopher*, 'philosopher' taken in the modern sense of the word. With Duns, 'magister' refers to a philosopher and 'doctor' refers to a theologian. So the master referred to taught the *ars obligatoria*, but what does the *ars obligatoria* consist of?

The development of the *ars obligatoria* presupposes an ongoing development of the academic practice of *debate* and *rational refutation*. Theory sponges on reality. In matters theoretical, theory is parasitic on the practice of the theory. Subjects of theoretical reflection presuppose the inner dynamics of a practice wherein the art of debate, disputation, and refutation developed itself. The reality of an academic debate culture has to be considered the *habitat* of a growing *ars obligatoria*. Academic teaching enjoyed the activities of questioning (*interrogatio*), rebutting, refuting, and solving dilemma's. The *ars obligatoria* did not arise from the impulse of a few Aristotelian parallels but from a fruitful academic practice. *Quaestio* teaching and

---

[1] *CF* 136 (136–139). *Lectura* I 39.59 reads: 'Ad aliud: negatur illa regula. Verumtamen *ars obligatoria* bene traditur ab *illo magistro* sine hac regula; unde non dependet ex veritate huius regulae.' See also *CF* 94–129 and cf. 23–33.

disputatio teaching constituted the background to the analysis of logical aspects and other aspects of teaching.

The *ars obligatoria* presupposes the development of an academic culture which was fond of cheerful debate and rebuttal, and the development of the genres *quaestio, collatio, quaestio disputata*, and *quaestio quodlibetalis*, and the like. Fine examples of early traces of the coming *ars obligatoria* are to be found in the *Ars Emmerana*, the *Ars Burana*, together with the *Excerpta Norimbergensia Introductionum*. An obligation treatise does not present a kind of narrative of a moot question or disputation, but the core of such treatises consists of a set of rules and a string of paradoxes. There are no extant records of factual disputations, although the *ars obligatoria* treatises themselves and the early Oxonian works of Duns and Burley give us a clear indication of what was going on. The basic rules of obligations and the requirement that the respondent's original position be false suggest that scholastic interest in obligations focuses on a new way of dialectical disputation where formal requirements and dialogical insights meet.

About halfway through the fourteenth century, Robert Fland distinguished two traditions in the theory of dialogue and disputation (*obligationes*):[2] the old and the new logic of *obligations* are called the *antiqua* and *nova responsio*.[3] The new line of the theory of disputation and argumentation appears to have originated with Roger Swineshead,[4] who 'certainly appears to have been part of the intellectual circle with which Kilvington and Bradwardine were associated, and he may well have studied with them. Probably sometime after 1330 and before 1335, Swineshead wrote his pair of treatises on obligations and insolubles.'[5] The theory of obligations entered a new phase in the 1330s and has to be associated with the innovative scholars of Merton College, the so-called *Calculatores*. The old tradition, according to Spade, 'conforms to the views of Burley, to those of the treatise attributed to William of Sherwood, and to those found in most if not all the other early treatises' (ibid.).

---

[2] Fland wrote between 1335 and 1370, probably associated with the University of Oxford. See Spade (ed.), 'Robert Fland's *Insolubilia*,' *Mediaeval Studies* 40 (1978) 56–80.

[3] See sections 14 and 20 of Spade (ed.), 'Robert Fland's *Obligationes*. An edition,' *Mediaeval Studies* 42 (1980) 41–60; idem, 'Obligations: B. Developments in the fourteenth century,' *CHLMP* 335–341, cf. E. Stump, 'Obligations: A. From the beginning to the early fourteenth century,' *CHLMP* 315–334.

[4] Swineshead died about 1365, a Benedictine monk of Glastonbury and master of theology. See Weisheipl, 'Roger Swyneshed O.S.B. Logician, natural philosopher, and theologian,' in *Oxford Studies presented to Daniel Callus*.

[5] Spade, 'Obligations: B. Developments in the fourteenth century,' *CHLMP* 335.

In Paris, we meet a remarkable collection of three works on *obli-gationes* in the second quarter of the thirteenth century: *Tractatus Emmeranus de falsi positione* (together with the twin treatise *Tracta-tus Emmeranus de impossibili positione*), *Obligationes Parisienses*.[6] The most important *ars obligatoria* is the *Obligationes* of Nicholas of Paris.[7] We have these treatises from the thirteenth century and we have a *Tractatus de Obligationibus*, attributed to William of Sherwood (Oxford, *c.*1200/1210–*c.*1270) and Walter Burley's *Tractatus de Obligationibus* from 1302 (Oxford). Because of the intimate theoret-ical relationship between the treatise attributed to Sherwood and Burley's tract we can discern two puzzles: the systematics of both groups of treatises and the problem of the historical phases of the different contributions to the theory of *obligationes*. The treatises edited by De Rijk are much less advanced than the *Obligationes* of Nicholas of Paris and the putative *Tractatus de Obligationibus* of Sherwood.

Eleonore Stump surveys Sherwood's view on the disputation pro-cedure of obligations as follows:

> An obligations disputation proceeds in this way. [. . .] An interlocu-tor or opponent begins the disputation by putting forward a propos-ition which the respondent obligates himself to defend as true if the proposition is false (*positio*), or as false if the proposition is true (*depositio*), or as of uncertain truth-value (*dubitatio*).[8]

Stump identifies the *positum* as the position of the opponent or inter-locutor. The *defendens* or *respondens* and the *opponens* take oppo-site positions.

> After positing his original position, which the respondent grants (*con-cedit*) as true, the opponent successively proposes a number of propositions, each of which the respondent must grant or deny or maintain as doubtful [. . .], according to three basic rules. (ibid.)

---

6 These tracts were edited by De Rijk: 'Some thirteenth century tracts on the game of obliga-tion. I: Two separate tracts on *falsi positio* and *impossibilis positio*,' *Vivarium* 12 (1974) 94–123. The *Tractatus Emmeranus de falsi positione* is found, ibid., 103–117, and the *Tractatus Emmeranus de impossibili positione*, ibid., 117–123; idem, 'Some thirteenth century tracts on the game of obligation. II: The *Obligationes Parisienses* found in Oxford, *Canon. misc.* 281,' *Vivarium* 13 (1975) 22–54. For Yrjönsuuri's English translations of the Emmeran treatises on *falsi positio* and *impossibilis positio*, see Yrjönsuuri (ed.), *Medieval Formal Logic*, 199–215.

7 Braakhuis, 'Obligations in Early Thirteenth Century Paris: The *Obligationes* of Nicholas of Paris (?),' *Vivarium* 36 (1998) 152–233.

8 Stump, 'William of Sherwood's Treatise on *Obligations*,' in Koerner et al., (eds), *Sudies in Medieval Linguistic Thought*, 251.

It is the task of the opponent to trap the respondent into a pair of contradictory propositions. When the opponent has achieved this aim, he concludes 'Cedat tempus' and the debate is over.

There are specific differences to be observed between the Parisian origins of the *ars obligatoria*, the *antiqua responsio*, and the *nova responsio*. Duns highlights the *antiqua responsio*. The role the *ars obligatoria* played in his way of doing philosophy and theology is a rather unexplored area, but we may say that the basic patterns of this part of logic were constitutive by delivering a model Duns needed for constructing a new logic and a new ontology. Because we have also to answer some traditional historical questions, we focus on a series of issues popping up with regard to the *ars obligatoria* in Duns' books: the identity of the textbook on the *ars obligatoria* referred to by Duns, *Lectura* I 39.59 (§5.2), the identity of the *magister artis obligatoriae* (§5.3), William of Sherwood's *Obligationes* and Duns' *Lectura* I (§5.4), the *positio impossibilis* (§5.5), and the *consequentia naturalis* (§5.6), while §5.7 rounds off: 'Perspectives.'

5.2 THE IDENTITY OF THE TEXTBOOK ON THE *ARS OBLIGATORIA* REFERRED TO BY DUNS

The form of Duns' reference in *Lectura* I 39.59 is unique. This unique form disappears in *Ordinatio* I 39. Fortunately, the rule to be considered is quoted and even an elaborate defense is found in *Lectura* I 39.56. The rule runs as follows:

> (1) When a false contingent proposition is posited for the present moment, then it has to be denied that this present moment exists.[9]

The curious thing is that the authorship of the *ars obligatoria* quoted by Duns has been much debated during the last twenty years. The question raised in this debate is whether the treatise on obligations referred to is a work of William of Sherwood or not. Thus Simo Knuuttila leaves the authorship of the so-called putative Sherwood undecided:

> The first [i.e. of the two obligations treatises edited by Romuald Green in his unpublished dissertation] is putatively attributed to William of Sherwood and the other to Walter Burley; the latter was written about 1302. It may be that William of Sherwood is not the

---

[9] *Lectura* I 39.56: 'Posito falso contingenti de praesenti instanti, negandum est praesens instans esse.'

author of the first treatise [. . .]; however, both of the tracts can be considered as representative of the thirteenth-century tradition of obligational tractates.[10]

5.2.1   Some hypotheses

Let us have a brief glance at some hypotheses which have been put forward. Then we shall proceed by asking ourselves: is there a quotation at stake or can we only observe a reference to some genre of logical literature without being able to identify a definite quotation from a certain source? If so, the next question to be asked is: who is *the author* and what can be said about the relation between the young John Duns and this philosopher?

The *diachrony rule* Duns referred to and its treatment are found in the *Obligationes* treatise of the Parisian Codex *Bibliothèque Nationale Lat.* 16.617. The *Commissio Scotistica*, which discovered both the reference and the rule, not only ascribes the treatise to William of Sherwood, but also takes Duns to be consciously referring to this work by Sherwood. We find the ascription of this *ars obligatoria* to Sherwood as early as 1963 in *Opera Omnia* VI, Appendix A (393–445), where the *Commissio Scotistica* presents a text on the second part of *Sententiae* I 38 and on I 39 which is missing in the critical edition of *Ordinatio* I. The authenticity of this text is a vexing problem. The *Commissio* is convinced that it is not from Duns' hand, but a reliable text form composed by early pupils of his. Just this text enjoyed an enormous *Wirkungsgeschichte*, because it passed on in *Opus Oxoniense* I.[11] We now know on the basis of research done by Timothy Noone that the Appendix text is *Ordinatio* I 39.[12]

The *Commissio* not only identified the rule seeing the wording of the rule as a quotation,[13] but they also presented the text of Sherwood's defense of the rule.[14] From the quotation marks used, we

---

[10]   Simo Knuuttila, *Modalities in Medieval Philosophy*, 124; compare 127. Knuuttila now accepts Sherwood's authorship.

[11]   On the relationship between the *Ordinatio* and the *Opus Oxoniense*, see §§3.6.16–3.6.17 and Chapter 4. Cf. *DS* 59 f. Because of the importance of the text of *Opus Oxoniense* I 39, the *Commissio Scotistica* offered a critical edition in Volume VI.

[12]   See the introduction in the forthcoming edition of William of Alnwick's *Determinationes* by G. Gál, A. B. Wolter and Tim. B. Noone (Catholic University of America).

[13]   Duns has the rule in the form we meet in *Codex Lat.* 16.617 (Paris). This type of formula is also found in *Obligationes Parisienses*, but not in Nicholas of Paris's *Obligationes*, edited by Braakhuis.

[14]   Duns' description of the rule and the defense of the rule are found in *Opera Omnia* VI 421, Duns' personal critique of it on VI 423. The *Commissio* already provided the quotation from

have to conclude that accordingly Duns *quotes* a rule from a certain *ars obligatoria* and its specific defense as an objection against his theory of *synchronic contingency*. In the meantime, Green had given an edition: *An Introduction to the Logical Treatise 'De Obligationibus', with critical texts of William of Sherwood (?) and Walter Burley I–II*.[15] In spite of his reservations, he argued that this *ars obligatoria*, the first of his edited texts, should be attributed to Sherwood. I propose to call this work for the moment W.[16]

5.2.2   Did Duns quote the *Obligationes* of Paris' *Bibilothèque Nationale Lat. 16.617*?

The first thing to do is to present the text of the book *Obligationes, Paris B.N. Lat. 16.617*. Next, this will be compared to *Lectura* I 39.56 by italicizing in W that which exactly agrees with Duns' text in order to assess whether Duns' text of *Lectura* I 39.56 can be partially seen as a quotation:

> Item. *Posito falso contingenti de praesenti instanti, negandum est* ipsum[a] *esse.*
> Quod sic probatur.
> Sit *A* nomen praesentis instantis. Nomen, dico, discretum et non commune.[b]
> Cum igitur
> *te esse Romae*
> sit modo *falsum*, impossibile est quod modo, sive in *A*, sit verum.[c]
> *Verificari enim non potest nisi per motum aut mutationem. Per motum non potest*
> verificari in *A* quia *motus non est in instanti. Nec per mutationem quia si esset mutatio* ad veritatem in *A*, tunc esset veritas in *A*. *Quia quando est mutatio, est terminus mutationis.*
> Sic, *ergo*, impossibile est hoc falsum verificari in *A*.
> Si – *ergo* – est verum, *A* non est.[d]
> *ERGO – Si ponatur hoc falsum, oportet negare A esse*, et haec dicit regula.

Sherwood in notes 4 and 5 of VI 421, with a reference to *Lectura* I 39.56 (volume XVII, published in 1966). See *Opera Omnia* XVII 498. Compare *CF* 130–132.

[15] Louvain: Catholic University 1963. There was only a very limited number of copies.

[16] There is no reference to Green's edition in the *Editio Vaticana*. To my knowledge, this finding by the *Commissio Scotistica* had not been made use of till Knuuttila and Vos did so in 1981. Eleonore Stump refers to chapter V of the introductory part of the revised version of Green's dissertation, still not yet published as far as I know (*CHLMP* 316).

5.2.3   Comments

When we assess the hypothesis that Duns *quoted* the book under consideration from a purely quantitative point of view there might be some doubts. When we pay close attention to the relevant details, these doubts can be removed. The way *W* reads the rule is the same as in *Ordinatio* I 39.18.

Notes

a   Instead of 'ipsum' *Lectura* I 39.56 has 'praesens instans' which makes perfect sense and *B.N. Lat. 16.617* has 'praesens instans' in the margin.

b   This sentence yields additional didactic information which Duns takes for granted and he interprets the rule in accordance with these guidelines. The systematic context of his theory of contingency presupposes that the time under consideration is a singular and definite moment of time.

c   The exemplary statement *te esse Romae* occurs only in this treatise. Nicholas of Paris's *Obligationes* on which this treatise is dependent has different exemplary sentences.[17] Although Duns does not quote verbatim the remainder of this sentence, it is just this entailment he is opposed to. It is also precisely this theory which is replaced by Duns' theory of synchronic contingency. The psychologically interesting feature of *Lectura* I 39.56 is that Duns cannot wait to rebut the objection. His counterattack follows immediately on his statement of the objection which is contrary to common usage. So, he is extraordinarily keen to refute this objection.

d   The decisive element is present in the quoted sentence. The explicit conclusion of *Obligationes* is just the point Duns takes seriously.

5.2.4   Conclusions

Duns usually refers to an alternative *theory* (*opinio*) if he refers to a philosopher or a theologian from the thirteenth century. Most references are indirect. Although Duns discusses many theories of Henry of Ghent, even in this case his references are usually indirect for he

[17] See Braakhuis, 'The *Obligationes* of Nicholas of Paris (?),' *Vivarium* 36 (1998) 30–31. Consult the excellent introduction.

mentions Henry of Ghent only a few times by name. Moreover, such references are usually not verbatim quotations. Hence, references are not usually *quotations*, but here the relationship between two texts is much closer. Concerning the three decisive elements of the rule itself, its defense and the target of the conclusion we have to state that they are quotations. Therefore Duns *quotes* from this book on *obligationes W* in *Paris B.N. Lat.* 16.617.

5.3 THE IDENTITY OF THE *MAGISTER ARTIS OBLIGATORIAE* IN LECTURA I 39.59

We have established that it is indeed *W* Duns referred to. The next question to be raised is *who* is the author of that book. This is a fascinating ramified problem. The provisional edition of this *obligationes* treatise by Father Romuald Green has been a source of uncertainties. He was extremely cautious in attributing this work to William of Sherwood and put a question mark behind his name. In the middle of the 1970s, L. M. de Rijk was much engaged in rediscovering the early stages of the development of the *ars obligatoria*. De Rijk not only edited a thirteenth-century tract on logical puzzles, but he also developed criteria for handling *exemplary sentences* in order to extract biographical data. He demolished the view that Sherwood wrote his logical works in Paris, for example, by isolating exemplary sentences implying that the author did not work in Paris, but he also argued that Green had been overcautious:[18] 'Green's doubt as to Sherwood's authorship is (quite unfortunately) due to his ignorance of the medieval scribes' habit to underline an Explicit *by running through it*; words were suppressed by expunction or erasure.'[19] The occurrence of the name of William in the *Explicit* of *Lat.* 16.617 meant quite the contrary to what Green thought it to be.[20]

---

[18] De Rijk, 'Some thirteenth century tracts on the game of obligation. III: The tract *De petitionibus contrariorum*,' *Vivarium* 14 (1976) 26, 28, 37–38 (26–49). From the obligational context we are entitled to derive that both *tu es Romae* and *te esse Parisius* are false.

[19] 'The tract *De petitionibus contrariorum*,' *Vivarium* 14 (1976) 28 note 11. For a detailed description of the manuscript *Lat.* 16.617 of the *Bibliothèque Nationale* at Paris, see De Rijk, *Die mittelalterlichen Traktate De modo opponendi et respondendi*, 89–95.

[20] See Vos, 'Moments of the *ars obligatoria* according to John Duns,' *Franciscan Studies* 56 (1998) 394 f.

5.3.1   The evidence

1. The *Explicit* of manuscript *Paris B.N. Lat.* 16.617, the best manuscript of *W*, tells us: '*Expliciunt obligationes Magistri W.*'[21] We ask: *who* is this 'Master *W*'?
2. Another copy of these *Obligationes* is found in the Venetian codex (*Bibliotheca Marciana*) X 204 and its *Incipit* added later gives a different spelling of the name of the master, using its English form *Waltery Burley*,[22] but its *Explicit* runs as follows: '*Expliciunt obligationes magistri W. de syrewode.*' According to Green, the added specification 'de syrewode' had been deleted, but De Rijk effectively corrected this opinion by pointing out that *running through it* does not mean that it was deleted, but that the ascription is underlined and stressed.
3. According to De Rijk, both the Erfurt codex *Amploniana* Q 259 (1340) and the Parisian codex *Bibliothèque Nationale Lat.* 16.130 provide wrong additional information by ascribing the work to *Magister* G(u)alterus *Burley*.[23]

5.3.2   Conclusion

The first known Oxonian *Obligationes* treatise must have been earlier than the last stage of John Duns' theological studies. So, from the historical viewpoint the author cannot have been Burley. There is no good reason to doubt the results of analyzing the evidence from the manuscript tradition which boil down to the same conclusion: Sherwood is the author of the authoritative obligational work.

5.4   SHERWOOD'S *OBLIGATIONES* AND DUNS' *LECTURA*

5.4.1   Sherwood and the *ars obligatoria*

We have identified the book and its author which Duns refers to in *Lectura* I 39.56 and 59, but are there more points of contact between Sherwood's *Obligationes* and Scotus' *Lectura*? There are. There is the usage of '*incompossibilis*' which is quite revealing in

---

[21] Sherwood, *Obligationes* (ed. Green), 33b. For the manuscripts, see Green, op. cit., IV.

[22] Sherwood, *Obligationes*, 1a: 'Incipiunt obligationes magistri Waltery Burley.'

[23] Sherwoord, *Obligationes*, 33a: 'Expliciunt obligationes datae a Magistro Gualtero (Galtero) Burley. Amen.' For a more elaborate treatment, see Vos, 'Moments,' *Franciscan Studies* 56 (1998) 394 ff.

terms of Duns' use of it. In particular, *Obligationes* actually makes quite clear what is especially revealing in the *Lectura* in comparison with alternative treatments of the notion of synchronic contingency in parallel texts of Duns. In contrast to other texts, the exposition of *Lectura* I 39.47–51 stands out by distinguishing between *synchronic* and *diachronic contingency*. Already in *Lectura* I 39.49, Duns embarked on elucidating his alternative notions of *possibility* and *contingency* with the help of the logical sense of the *possibile logicum*: 'A possibility is only logical, when the terms are possible in such a way that they are not repugnant to each other, but can be united.'[24]

5.4.2.   Diachrony in Sherwood's logic

Interesting parts of Sherwood's *Obligationes* are two sections *De diversis opinionibus* in which he comments on the nature of the new field. By far the longest section is found in the first chapter, *De positione possibili*, of the first part, *De positione*. The first part of this discussion in section *A* 1 b delivers remarkable evidence.[25] Here, we meet a clear analysis of the *diachronic* notion of *possibility*. A specific function is ascribed to the so-called *divided sense* (*sensus divisionis*). The exemplary proposition is:

> (2) *Album esse nigrum est possibile.*

(2) is called a *modal* proposition, and not a *categorical* proposition. So, if there is a *modal* element in a proposition, Sherwood calls such a proposition a *propositio modalis*, whether this modal element be a predicate or an adverb.[26] The objection states that (2) must be false, because the proposition *Something white is black* (*album esse nigrum*) cannot be true, and if a proposition is not possibly true, then it is false that it is possible.

The *Sed contra* puts forward Sherwood's personal view. He rebuts the conviction that (2) must be false by introducing the famous distinction involved in the notion of *the divided sense* (*sensus divisionis*).

---

[24] See CF 114–117, and §4.9, §6.2, and §7.3.

[25] Sherwood, *Obligationes*, 5 (5–11). For the text, see Vos, 'Moments,' *Franciscan Studies* 56 (1998) 400.

[26] Sherwood's usage matches the definitions of the *Logica 'Cum sit nostra'* – see *Logica Modernorum* II B 428: 'Propositionum alia *modalis*, alia *de inesse*. [. . .] *Propositio modalis* est illa in qua predicatum inest subiecto cum modo, ut *possibile est hominem esse animal*. In hac propositione dico quod *animal* intelligitur in *homine* possibiliter.' Cf. CF 48–51 and 64–69 and §6.2.

In the *divided sense*, (2) is true. In (2) it is said of a proposition that it is *possible*. In terms of the proposition *Something white is black* (*Album esse nigrum*), this possibility is then to be asserted, but how can that be?

A fine specimen of the *ars obligatoria* is delivered here. Assume that (2) is given and 'affirmed' (posited). However, the truth of (2) depends on the truth value of *Album esse nigrum*, but which alternatives are now open to the *respondens* to respond? Let us assume that he grants (*concedit*): *Album esse nigrum*, but *Album esse nigrum* cannot be true, because the involved predicates exclude each other – on the basis of a *positio possibilis*. If he, on the contrary, denies *Album esse nigrum* – as possibly true – then he gets into conflict with the *positum*, and then the game is over again.

Sherwood elaborates on the interpretation of *secundum divisionem* in terms of which (2) can be said to be true: *possibile* is looked upon as a *diachronic operator* and its function is to broaden the scope of *being black* towards the future. What is white now can be black at a time in the future. For that future time *Album esse nigrum* is true, for what is white *now* can be black *in the future*. So, it *can* be true. *Possibility* is said of something that is not true for the present time and, therefore, it is a property of what is *not* the case. From the logical point of view it is the traditional meaning of *can*, meaning *being different at a later time*.

5.4.3   Conclusion

There is not only a positive impact of Sherwood's *Obligationes* on the thought of the young John Duns at the levels of terminology and theory formation, but it is also the central notion which is Duns' target and which is clearly explained by Sherwood. In *Lectura* I 39.48–59, Duns is precisely dependent on this field of logical forces. This relationship eloquently illustrates Duns Scotus' place in the development of Western thought. It is *tradition* and *renewal*. Duns Scotus' corrections and innovations are crucial, but they are parasitic on the legacy of a great tradition. The notion of *Scotism* is not of any help in order to understand this balance. When we read in *Lectura* I 39.59: 'The disputational art of *obligations* is handed down well by the master we have referred to – without this rule,' we would be very mistaken, if we were to think of an alternative *ars obligatoria* missing that rule to be looked for in the thirteenth century. In spite of the rule, Sherwood's *ars obligatoria* is good, very good indeed, for this approach is not built on that rule.

So, the mistaken rule does not destroy the system. 'This art does not depend on the truth of this rule' (*Lectura* I 39.59). Here, we sharply see the significance of Duns Scotus' innovations as in a mirror. Duns sees that they do not damage the tradition, but improve on and complete it. It is the interaction of *tradition* and *renewal* that matters.

5.5 Impossibilis positio

Important information concerning the *ars obligatoria* is to be gained from *Lectura* I 11 as we learn about the intricacies of Duns Scotus' theoretical language. In the analytical part on the nature of the problem: *De quaestione* (*Lectura* I 11.23–31), Duns reports that a certain solution appeals to the *ars obligatoria* in order to solve the problem under consideration. The problem is the Trinitarian question whether the Son and the Holy Spirit can be distinguished from one another, if the Holy Spirit does not proceed from the Son.[27] A preliminary solution discussed by Duns answers the question by immediately appealing to the *ars obligatoria*. The adherents of this solution cherish a specific view on the *ars obligatoria* which also brings in the *impossibilis positio*. Their view runs against the *impossibilis positio*. Their answer to the proposed question is: *no problem*.[28] According to them, there is no problem, since the proposition *The Holy Spirit does not proceed from the Son* cannot be true, but why does this stance run counter to the *positio impossibilis*?

According to the generally accepted view of the *ars obligatoria*, any possible truth can be stated – within the context of the *positio*, but with regard to the *impossibilis positio* there is no general acceptance. In one respect, the *impossibilis positio* is accepted, but in another respect it is not. If an impossible proposition does not include contradictory propositions, such an impossible proposition can be assumed, but if an impossible truth does include such opposite or contradictory elements, then such an impossible proposition cannot be asserted.[29]

As far as an impossible truth is concerned which entails a pair of opposite propositions, it is not allowed to assume such an impossible truth. In no art can such impossible truths be accepted. This view is accompanied by a specific defense. If one admits that such impossibile

---

[27] *Lectura* I 11.20: 'Utrum si Spiritus Sanctus non procederet a Filio, non distingueretur ab eo.'

[28] *Lectura* I 11.23: 'Ad quaestionem istam dicunt quidam quod quaestio nulla est.'

[29] Ibid.: 'Licet secundum artem obligatoriam posset poni quodcumque possibile, et etiam *impossibile non includens opposita*, tamen in nulla arte potest poni *impossibile includens opposita*.'

truths are stated, then the whole duty of observing the rules of the disputational art of obligation collapses. An articulated interpretation of the *ars obligatoria* is at stake. This criticism is based on the explicit rules of the *ars obligatoria*.[30] The way Duns describes this position makes it clear that the *ars obligatoria* contains the fundamental rules of disputation and debate. Duns elaborates on the possible collapse of the *ars obligatoria* in a sophisticated way: let us assume that a certain impossible proposition entails opposite propositions. When are two propositions opposite? Two propositions are opposite only if one proposition entails the denial of the other. In such cases, we cannot restrict ourselves to only one impossible truth, because 'other opposite propositions flow from an impossible proposition which includes opposite predicates.'[31] Then, Duns sets out an argument which consists of several steps:

> (3) It is *either* the case that we ought to grant contradictory propositions (if we were to assume an impossible proposition which includes opposite predicates), *or* it is the case that we *ought* to deny what is entailed by the assumption, [(if we were to assume an impossible proposition which includes opposite predicates)]. So, both disjuncts are incompatible with the entire *ars disputandi*.[32]

Consider the first disjunct which is in itself an entailment. In this disjunct:

> (4) *If* we assume an impossible proposition which includes contradictory predicates

is the antecedent and the consequent clearly follows:

> (5) *then* we ought to grant other contradictory propositions.

The entailment relation between (4) and (5) is taken to be valid, but in that case the game of obligation is violated. 'Then there would be no end to disputing' (*Lectura* I 11.23), for if contradictions are permitted, then there is no way of trapping the defendant and, so, the game cannot be finished. However, the point of this *genre* of disputation is that it is over when the defendant is trapped into a proposition which is incompatible with the *positum* or what has already been granted by the defendant. So, if a contradiction were harmless, we

---

[30] Ibid.: 'Nullum impossibile potest poni, quo posito, non salvantur regulae observandae in disputatione et arte obligatoria.'

[31] Ibid.: 'Nunc autem ex impossibili includente opposita sequuntur opposita.'

[32] Ibid.: '*Vel* igitur oporteret concedere opposita (si poneretur impossibile includens opposita), *vel* negare sequens ex posito; et utrumque est contra omnem artem disputandi.'

would gamble away our means of winning the game. Therefore, on the basis of the first disjunct the game of obligation cannot be played any more, but what is the outcome of the second disjunct?[33]

The second disjunct enjoys the same antecedent as the first one and thus we again assume (4). Now, the consequent is:

(6) *then we ought to deny what follows from the positum.*

Again a sin against the rule of the game of obligation is committed, because one of the basic rules is that in every case what follows from the *positum* has to be granted. The view considered by Duns holds that if one violates this rule by denying the implications from the premisses, then there is nothing to be derived from the premisses. If what follows from the *positum*, looked upon as a premiss, is denied, nothing has to be accepted and if nothing has to be accepted, nothing can be proven.[34] Therefore there is a dead end in both cases and so intrinsically inconsistent propositions ought not to be permitted into a chain of arguments.

We find this view on the *ars obligatoria* discussed within a theological context and thus it is applied to the already mentioned trinitarian problem. The proposition to be considered is:

(7) the Holy Spirit does not proceed from the Son.[35]

(7) is considered to be inconsistent because a necessary truth about God cannot be more necessary than it is and so the denial is impossible in the highest way.

Such a theological dilemma can only be solved with the help of an elaborate logical and proof theoretical apparatus. Surely, according to John Duns, *The Holy Spirit does not proceed from the Son* is necessarily false. Thus, from the point of view of the *ars obligatoria*, the significance of the *positio impossibilis* is at stake. We may only go on debating this impossibility if there is room for framing proofs. However, there can only be room for framing proofs if there is a vital distinction between *being self-evident* and *being derivable*. Logic and ontology cannot be reduced to epistemology. Reality is complicated

---

[33] Ibid.: 'Secundum *primum* [that is, the first disjunct of the disjunction quoted in the preceding note] non esset meta [= end, finish, cf. Dutch 'meet'] in disputando.' Again, we meet here a point of contact with Sherwood's *Obligationes*.

[34] Ibid.: 'Secundum *secundum* [that is, the second disjunct of the disjunction quoted in note 32] nihil posset probari, quia nihil sequitur.'

[35] Ibid.: 'Nunc autem – ut dicunt – ista includit opposita quod "Spiritus Sanctus non procedat a Filio". Igitur, suum oppositum est summe impossibile, sed tale includit opposita, ergo, etc.'

and, so, we need a wealth of distinctions and theories. Fruitful the-ological debate on the *processio* of the Holy Spirit is only possible if *proceeding from the Son* does not belong to the *definiendum*: *being the Son*. The meaning of fruitful theological research is served by a rich semantics and a rich logic, a rich *ars obligatoria* and a rich theory of dialogue. We continue to investigate the development of these riches.

5.5.1   The principle of negation

This quite interesting digression entails the main principle of the *ars obligatoria*:

>   (8) *Anything can be assumed.*[36]

It reports on the ways some problems can be tackled in terms of the argumentation within the *ars* itself. *Observing rules* is at the heart of the matter. The first argument considers the case that a hypothesis is assumed which includes contradictory elements. Then it is pointed out that this is at variance with the *ars obligatoria* itself. Allowing for incon-sistencies is at variance with the game, for in this case the game would have to go on forever. I propose to call this *the principle of negation*.

The *principle of negation* is clearly evidenced in the older literature on the subject. In the first chapter, *Regulae*, of the first part of his *Obligationes*, Sherwood offers a coherent set of basic rules based on the distinction between *pertinent propositions* and *impertinent propositions*:

>   A *pertinent* proposition is either an entailed proposition or a propos-ition incompatible with the *positum* and an *impertinent* proposition is neither.

Within this context, we meet the *basic rule of negation*. Sherwood defines his *principle of negation*:

>   (9) Every statement must be denied within the time of the dispute, if it is known that it is incompatible with what is posited or granted, or with statements which have been granted on the basis of the *positum*, or with a statement or statements which are opposite to what has been well denied or to statements which have been well denied on the basis of the *positum*.[37]

---

[36] This idea is in perfect harmony with the so-called *hypothesis rule* of modern logic.
[37] Sherwood, *Obligationes* (ed. Green), 3.28–31: 'Omne repugnans posito vel concesso vel con-cessis cum posito vel opposito vel oppositis bene negati vel bene negatorum cum posito, scitum esse tale in tempore positionis est negandum.'

By the way, the degree of agreement with the *principle of negation* in the *Obligationes* of Nicholas of Paris is quite astonishing. The only systematically relevant difference is that *verum* (omne *verum* repugnans posito) is added to the rule by Nicholas of Paris. Such features mirror the fact that Nicholas of Paris is preoccupied with the problem of the truth value in factual reality of the *positum* and what follows from it or is excluded by it. Therefore, what is incompatible with the *positum* (*repugnans posito*) is in fact a truth (*verum*), although such a truth has to be denied within the game of the dispute, because its denial is assumed in the game. The rule of negation is governed partly by the internal rules of the game of obligation and partly by the external requirements of truth and falsehood in reality. The same is the case with the parallel *rule of affirmation*. Either what is true is excluded by the *positum* and then the rules of the game of obligation dominate, or the alternative possibility is that what is true is not incompatible with the *positum* or what has already been granted. In this case the truth to be considered has to be granted. All this does no longer bother Sherwood.

The setting of *Obligationes Parisienses* differs from the setting of the *Tractatus Emmeranus de falsi positione* which offers a list of rules which even now is not arranged in a definite way. In *Obligationes Parisienses* the distinction between rules concerning *ponere* and rules concerning *respondere* has been abandoned and one integral set is presented. Two fundamental rules dominate the scene: the first rule concerns *entailment* and the second concerns *inconsistency* and reformulates our rule. The main point is that anything that contradicts the *positum* has to be denied and therefore every truth which is incompatible with the *positum* has to be denied. Moreover, there is an additional fascinating feature to be noticed, because the *rule of negation* is expanded upon in such a way that a falsehood which is not entailed by the *positum*, or anything else that has already been granted, or anything else that is incompatible with what has been denied correctly, has to be denied. In sum, this rule governs the wide range of proposals which have to be rejected.

The *principle of negation* already occurs in the *Tractatus Emmeranus de falsi positione*: everything which is incompatible with the *positum* has to be denied if it can be denied. In the general introductory exposition on what *positio* is up to, the foundation of the *ars obligatoria* is clearly expressed, including the ambiguity Duns is still discussing at the end of the 1290s. There are propositions which can be assumed and there are other propositions which cannot be assumed hypothetically. The dividing line is marked by *the principle of non-contradiction*. If there is a hypothesis from which no contradiction follows, then it can be assumed; but if there is a hypothesis on the basis of which a contradiction follows, then this hypothesis cannot be defended. So far, we have considered the rules which are implicitly appealed to in arguing against the possibility of assuming an impossibility including two opposite elements. This argument in itself has its roots in the tradition of the *ars obligatoria*. The kernel of the argumentation is an interesting view on the *impossibilis positio* and, in a rather strict sense, the *impossibilis positio* is left to one side.[38] On this score, Duns not only disagrees, but in discussing the difference of opinion he also introduces another approach to the *positio impossibilis* which substantially affects his *ars obligatoria*.

5.6 CONSEQUENTIA NATURALIS AND CONSEQUENTIA INNATURALIS

In her fine contribution to the history of the vicissitudes of the rule *Ex impossibili sequitur quidlibet*, Joke Spruyt pays attention to different kinds of *consequences (consequentiae)* in thirteenth-century treatises of logic.[39] In particular Nicholas of Paris's distinction between the *consequentia naturalis* and the *consequentia innaturalis* is an important one. Two *genres* of logical treatises are quite helpful in shedding more light on such terms: *syncategorematic treatises* and *obligationes treatises*, for different kinds of *consequentiae* are dealt with in treatises on the syncategorematic terms and in treatises belonging to the *ars obligatoria*. Specific ways of distinguishing between types of *consequentiae* are found with the proponents in favor of the rule *Ex impossibili sequitur quidlibet*, for example John le Page, Nicholas of Paris, and Matthew of Orleans.[40] John le Page discusses several arguments both in favor of and against the *Ex impossibili* rule.[41]

> Like Nicholas of Paris, John le Page goes along with the claim that from the impossible anything follows, without, however, restricting the application domain of this rule to one particular type of consequence,

---

[38] See also Vos, 'Moments,' *Franciscan Studies* 56 (1998) 405–408. The *Impossibilis positio* already occurs in *Tractatus Emmeranus de impossibili positione* and in *Sophistaria wrongly attributed to Burley*. See Joke Spruyt, 'Thirteenth-century positions on the rule "Ex impossibili sequitur quidlibet"', in Jacobi (ed.), *Argumentationstheorie*, 183.2–5.

[39] Spruyt, 'Thirteenth-century positions,' in Jacobi (ed.), *Argumentationstheorie*, 176–181 and 183–191.

[40] See Joke Spruyt, 'Thirteenth-century positions,' in *Argumenationstheorie*, 174–180.

[41] See her analysis in 'Thirteenth-century positions,' in Jacobi (ed.), *Argumentationstheorie*, 179–180, and her edition of the relevant text, ibid., 191–193: *Appendix* III.

for instance to what Nicholas would call 'non-natural consequences'. For John le Page the rule applies universally (in fact he does not even make a distinction at all between different types of consequences).[42]

Against this philosophical background, a different approach is to be observed when we pay attention to Nicholas of Paris.

[He] does not go into details as regards the different arguments in favor of or against the 'Ex impossibili'-rule. However, his own account on the matter does shed light on what he might have to say about them. According to Nicholas we must keep the distinction between two different types of consequence in mind, viz.

1. the consequentia naturalis: this type of consequence is such that the antecedent cannot be true without the consequent and, moreover, that the consequent is understood in the antecedent;
2. the consequentia innaturalis: this type is such that the 'Ex impossibili'-rule applies to it.[43]

What is at stake in the philosophical framework of John le Page and Matthew of Orleans is an operational distinction between the level of theoretical argumentation and the level of reality, and demonstration bound to reality. On the latter level, the rule Ex impossibili sequitur quidlibet does not apply. This is the level of Nicholas of Paris's consequentia/consecutio naturalis. In the case of a consequentia innaturalis we assume deductive necessity (necessitas positionis).[44] In terms of a consequentia naturalis, the consequent only follows from the antecedent because the consequent is included in the antecedent. What can be derived is limited. In the case of a consequentia innaturalis, there is no restriction to what can be derived.

5.6.1 On the early history of the consequentia naturalis

Research on early developments in the theory of consequences is still rather poor.

[42] Spruyt, 'Thirteenth-century positions,' in Jacobi (ed.), Argumentationstheorie, 180. For the Parisian developments, see Vos, 'Moments,' Franciscan Studies 56 (1998) 409 f.

[43] Joke Spruyt, 'Thirteenth-century positions,' in Jacobi (ed.), Argumentations theorie, 176–177.

[44] Nicholas of Paris, Syncategoreumata (ed. Braakhuis), 203: 'In consequentia innaturali nichil prohibet sequi quiclibet, quia illa non querit aliud nisi necessitatem positionis. Quia ergo posito impossibili ponitur equaliter quiclibet aliud, propterea ex impossibili posito sequitur quiclibet aliud.' This defense of the rule makes use of the ars obligatoria by taking into account the structure of a disputational match. If the starting point is not a self-evident proposition, the consequentia is not 'natural'. In the case of an impossibilis positio everything follows. Nicholas of Paris's Obligationes rejects the impossibilis positio.

In his work on the tradition of topics in the middle ages, Niels J. Green-Pedersen discusses the origins of the theories of consequences of the thirteenth century.[45] In his opinion the thirteenth-century treatises on Syncategorematic Words and *Sophismata* have at least contributed to the development of these theories. [. . .] Now apart from what Braakhuis mentions on the issue not much attention has been paid to the thirteenth-century conceptions of the validity of consequences.[46]

The origin of the notion of *consequentia naturalis* is also still shrouded in darkness[47] but an early occurrence is found in the *Dialectica* of Garland the Compotist.[48]

5.6.2   Garland the Compotist

In Garland's *Dialectica* we observe the specific state of advancement in reinterpreting traditional logic which the generation of Lanfranc had already achieved after the decisive new start by the generation of Abbo of Fleury (d.1004) and Gerbert of Aurillac (= Pope Sylvester II, d.1003). According to Garland the Compotist a *consequentia* is a kind of a *propositio coniuncta/connexa*.[49] The term *consequentia* is restricted to simple, incomposite *propositiones hypotheticae*. The basic distinction is between a *consequentia naturae* (a 'natural' conse-quence) and a *consequentia per accidens* (an accidental conse-quence).[50] A *consequentia per accidens* is a *temporal consequence*.

---

[45] Green-Pedersen, *The Tradition of Topics in the Middle Ages*, 265–295.

[46] Spruyt, 'Thirteenth-century positions,' in Jacobi (ed.), *Argumentationstheorie*, 161. See also Boh's observations on the early development of the theory of consequences in his survey 'Consequences,' *CHLMP* 301–306, where he pays attention to Boethius, Garland the Compotist, Abelard, William of Sherwood, Lambert of Auxerre, and Peter of Spain.

[47] See De Rijk (ed.), *Peter of Spain. Tractatus called afterwards Summulae Logicales*, 7: *Tractatus* I, section 13: *De triplici materia propositionum* on the *propositio naturalis* – the exemplary sentences are *homo est animal* and *homo est risibilis* – and ibid., 169–170: *Tractatus* VII, sections 150 and 154, on the *simplex consequentia* – the exemplary sentence is *si est homo, est animal*. See also De Rijk (ed.), *Peter of Spain. Syncategoreumata*, 224: *Tractatus* V, section 32, on the *naturalis consequentia*.

[48] De Rijk (ed.), *Garlandus Compotista. Dialectica*, XLV (IX–XLV): 'The master Gerland named in the title of the Fleurian manuscript, must be the eleventh century compotist Garlandus, who was *magister scholarum* at Besançon at the end of his life (c.1015–*before* 1102).' He originated from the south of Dutch Limburgia, in the neighborhood of the famous schools of Liège, and his logic might have been published about 1040 (ibid., XLIX).

[49] Garland, *Dialectica*, 141 ff. For *De hipotheticis compositis*, see pp. 145–189. A *propositio* is a predicative *oratio*, simple or composite, and an *oratio* is a spoken (and meaningful) sen-tence primarily consisting of spoken (and meaningful) words (= *nomina*). Boh in fact pre-sents a fine summary of Garland's logic of propositions ('Consequences,' *CHLMP* 303–305).

[50] Garland, *Dialectica*, 141: 'Unde hec divisio potest fieri: consequentia alia per accidens, idest temporalis, alia secundum consequentiam nature, idest naturaliter.' Cf. the later Scotian

The tension between the development of a new way of ideas and the heritage of ancient thought is keenly to be observed. Garland still follows the structure of *diachrony*: an ontological term like *accidentality* is defined with the help of the framework of temporal concepts. However, it has already been cut off from the conceptual structures of necessitarianism. Garland enjoys an open view of time and no longer equates *always* and *necessary*. The logician Garland does not expect ever to be a bishop, but if he never will be a bishop, it is not impossible that he becomes a bishop. *Never (numquam)* does not entail that it is impossible.[51]

The points of contact and the differences in comparison with Scotus' approach are remarkable. On the level of systematic comparison of conceptual structures the field of forces is to be compared with Anselm. From the very start of early scholasticism, we meet ever new stages of emancipation from the ancient way of ideas. Against a new background of *fides quaerens intellectum* old habits of thought make their power felt. The connection between *necessity* and *time* is one of the most difficult theoretical knots to be unraveled.

The second important distinction is between two kinds of *natural consequences*. The connective of a *consequentia* as a composite statement is either *si* or *cum*. This duality also demarcates subsets of *natural consequences*. The first subset concerns the natural, or structural, relation of entailment between *genus* (also called *causa*) and *species* or *causa* and *effectus* – a *genus/causa* 'follows' the *species/effectus*. The second subset concerns the causal relationship between *cause* and *effect*. Within the first subset the *consequentia necessaria* has its primary *locus* and again the exemplary sentence is *si homo est, animal est*.

usage of *consequentiae naturales* versus *consequentiae accidentales* and the usage of the *ars obligatoria* tradition from Paris: *consequentiae naturales* versus *consequentiae innaturales*. This distinction is akin to the distinctions between *necessarium per se/per accidens* and *impossibile per se/per accidens*. Garland characterizes an 'accidental consequence' in terms of time. Cf. also Boh, 'Consequences,' *CHLMP* 304: 'He even goes so far as to suggest a division of consequences based on this distinction (*viz.* the distinction between *cum* in the causal sense of *because* and in the temporal sense of *at a time when*), into consequences *per accidens* and natural consequences.'

51 Garland, *Dialectica*, 83–84: 'Potentia extra actum quam effectus consequitur, est cum possible est aliquem fieri album et fit albus vel aliquo casu vel aliqua dispositione; aliqua etiam necessitate sequitur effectus aliquando, sicuti *possibile est occidere solem*. Potentia vero extra actum quam effectus non consequitur, est illa cui nec natura repugnat nec tamen umquam erit, ut cum dico: *possibile est Iarlandum fieri episcopum*, numquam tamen episcopus erit.' He also distinguishes between *temporal necessity* and *absolute necessity* (ibid., 84). Cf. Anselm, *De Concordia* I.

The *consequentia naturalis* of the Parisian tradition is to be seen as a moment in a long-standing tradition with the use of *naturalis* originally having a cosmological background in a *phusis*-metaphysics. Nevertheless, a proper level of definition and argumentation is under way and makes itself felt in defining crucial terms like *ratio* and *consequentia*. The Parisian definition of *consequentia naturalis* is a fine example of a mixed approach:

> In a *consequentia naturalis* the antecedent cannot be true without the consequent being true and the consequent is understood in the antecedent.

So, in such a consequence the consequent must be true if the antecedent is true. Therefore, if the antecedent entails the truth of the consequent, the consequent is understood in the antecedent.

Here we still observe traces of the origin of the notions of *consequentia*, *antecedens* and *consequens* and of *understanding* in the *phusis*-(meta)physics of Aristotle. However, much has changed. The Aristotelian level of *substantia* is replaced by the propositional level of *definition* and is linked with the theoretical level of argumentation. The *ars obligatoria* creates a new dimension of alternative possibilities. We are now ready to compare this type of definition with John Duns'. The definition of Nicholas of Paris clearly consists of two main parts: the *validity* component – the antecedent cannot be *true* if the consequent is false – and the *epistemological* component – the antecedent cannot be known without the consequent.

We shall pay attention to Duns' two definitions of *consequentiae naturales* and *consequentiae accidentales* which will remind us of the two main ingredients of Nicholas of Paris's definition: in a *consequentia naturalis* the consequent is as such known in virtue of the antecedent, and in a *consequentia accidentalis* the antecedent cannot be true without the consequent being true because of their *loca extrinseca*. A paradoxical difference strikes the eye, for with Duns the two main elements of Nicholas of Paris's definition are distributed over the two definitions of *consequentia accidentalis* and *consequentia naturalis* respectively. The 'epistemological' component is the definition of *consequentia naturalis* and the 'validity' component is the definition of *consequentia accidentalis*. From the systematic point of view, we have to state that Duns disconnects the *logical* and *epistemological* dimensions which are found in the definition of Nicholas of Paris, but how is this to be explained historically?

5.6.3   William of Sherwood

William of Sherwood's *Obligationes* discusses the possibility of the *positio impossibilis*. His analysis is found in the second chapter of Part I, *De positione impossibili*, and in fact parallels John Duns' exposition in *Lectura* I 11.23–24.[52] In its turn, it explains the two kinds of *consequentiae*: there are *consequentiae finitae* and *consequentiae infinitae*. In terms of the *consequentiae infinitae* the rules *Necessarium sequitur ad quodlibet* and *Ex impossibili sequitur quodlibet* obtain.[53] Concerning the problem of the possibility of *positio impossibilis* consequences of the latter type do not matter. William of Sherwood also mentions two kinds of *consequentiae finitae*: in the first type the consequent is understood in the antecedent and here we meet Duns' definition of *consequentia naturalis*. In the second type we meet Duns' definition of *consequentia accidentalis*: the antecedent cannot be true without the consequent being true.[54]

The relationship between the theories of consequences of Nicholas of Paris and William of Sherwood is quite interesting. These theories are rather similar in the treatises on *Syncategoreumata* of both authors. In fact Nicholas's (and William's) *consequentiae innaturales* are called *consequentiae infinitae* in Sherwood's *Obligationes*. Moreover, Sherwood's short elucidation of what constitutes a *consequentia infinita* sheds light on what Nicholas might have meant by his *consequentia innaturalis*.

> From what we have seen above we may conclude that Nicholas accepts the rule 'From the impossible anything follows', however, only in non-natural consequences. Unfortunately he does not give a precise description of what he means by non-natural consequences: it seems that that he only wishes to indicate consequences containing an impossible premiss by that name.[55]

---

52 See Sherwood, *Obligationes* (ed. Green), 24–27.

53 Sherwood, *Obligationes*, 26.11–21: 'Quaeritur quae consequentia attendenda est in hac positione. Est enim *consequentia* duplex: aut finita, aut infinita. Infinita dupliciter: aut ex parte *ante*, qua dicitur quod necessarium sequitur ad quodlibet, aut ex parte *post*, qua dicitur quod ex impossibili sequitur quodlibet. Neutra istarum est hic attendenda, tum, quia infinita, et ob hoc, extra artem, cum, quia sic omnia essent sequentia, et sic non esset hic *meta*. *Finita* autem dupliciter est: quando *consequens intelligitur in antecedente*, et quando *antecedens non potest esse verum sine consequente*, cum non intelligitur in ipso.' See also note 33 on *meta*.

54 Cf. Duns' *Antecedens non potest verum sine consequente* from *Lectura* I 11.24 with Sherwood's *Consequens non potest esse verum sine antecedente*. For the involved text critical problem, see Vos, 'Moments,' *Franciscan Studies* 56 (1998) 416 f.

55 Spruyt, 'Thirteenth-century positions,' in Jacobi (ed.), *Argumentationstheorie*, 178. She goes on delivering a fine specimen of systematic extrapolation of what is entailed by what Nicholas

William of Sherwood does not restrict himself to the rule *Ex impos-sibili sequitur quodlibet*, but takes it together with the dual rule *Necessarium sequitur ad quodlibet*. He does not criticize or reject these rules from the logical points of view of deduction and validity, but however valid they may be, they are of no use in a contest, because along these lines valid consequences might be derived endlessly (*infinita*). In that case the contest can never be finished. It has to go on for ever. There can be no *finish*, in Sherwood's words *non meta*, because everything including all necessary truths are to be derived in a valid way, but an endless (*infinitus*) is no contest.

The basic distinction of Nicholas of Paris remains intact with William of Sherwood, although under a different heading. The two ele-ments of Nicholas's definition are used in order to distinguish between two kinds of *consequentiae finitae*. These kinds do not coincide with the traditional pattern *innaturalis/per accidens* versus *naturalis/per se*. Sherwood's new distinction within the realm of *consequentiae finitae* enjoys a different aim by remaining within the boundaries of what is necessarily true or necessarily false. This move creates room for tack-ling another aspect which makes room in its turn for debating impos-sible propositions. This level is indicated by Sherwood's remark that *believing that a man is not a sense-gifted being* is not the same as *believ-ing that a sense-gifted being is not sense-gifted*.

5.6.4   Duns Scotus

Duns' distinction between *consequentiae naturales* and *consequen-tiae accidentales* is not immediately built on the Parisian distinction between *consequentiae naturales* and *consequentiae innaturales*, but on Sherwood's two kinds of *consequentiae finitae* which are liable of an epistemological and proof theoretical specification. Unfortunately, the exemplary sentence of a *consequentia naturalis* is missing, but with Sherwood it is still 'Si homo est, animal est' and with both of them the exemplary sentence of the set of *consequen-tiae accidentales* – as Duns calls them – is 'Si homo est, risibile est.'[56] All this remarkably fits in with the hypothesis that with Duns *con-sequentiae naturales* are self-evident consequences. Self-evident con-sequences are of a very specific type: if they are entailments, their

---

only vaguely indicated in terms of the modern theory of logical connectives (= 'propositional logic'). William's elucidation is in terms of the contemporary game of obligations.

[56] See Sherwood, *Obligationes*, 26.22–24 and *Lectura* I 11.24.

antecedents are necessarily true and their logical relationship is strictly necessary; if they are inferences, their premises are necessary and their inferential relationship is valid.

However, all these requirements are not sufficient: the antecedents and their premises must also be *self-evidently* true. The same move is to be observed when Duns distinguishes between *rationes necessariae* and *rationes naturales*. Therefore Duns gives a particular twist to the traditional notion of *consequentia naturalis*: a *consequentia naturalis* is not only necessarily true if it is an entailment or valid if it is an inference, and does not only consist of necessary propositions, but it also has a *self-evident* antecedent or *self-evident* premises, while a *consequentia accidentalis* does not. In this precisely defined aspect, it does make sense to discuss impossible propositions, because it is not in every case clear from the start what constitutes an impossible proposition. In this way Duns broadens the scope of (8) *Anything can be assumed*, even including impossible propositions. This fruitful use of the *ars obligatoria* is not limited to formal rules of validity. The *ars obligatoria* itself had already embraced dialogical rules governing the contest. Here Duns also adds the dimension of epistemic assessment to this academic enterprise and all these ingredients are put into the service of sound theology and philosophy.

5.7 PERSPECTIVE

Why is the *doctor subtilis* so subtle? Could his contribution to Western thought not have been more accessible? We may ask for the historical place in academic life his works once enjoyed.[57] In the logical works of Duns' tradition we find the theoretical key to his complex practice of doing philosophy and theology. In the *Lectura* we meet the intensely dialogical atmosphere of discussion and debate that we may also discern in his early logical works and the *Collationes Oxonienses*. Here the rules of the *obligationes* are at work within the spheres of philosophical logic and theology, the atmosphere of *ponere*, *opponere*, *proponere*, *improbare*, and *concedere*. The disputational color is often intense. A definitely new stage of the tradition of *lectio*, *quaestio*, and

---

[57] Compare the early Oxonian tradition: *Ut dixit* and *Cum sit nostra*, to be found in *Logica Modernorum* IIA 375–451. It is advisable to study the fruitful interplay between the *ars obligatoria* and the works of the young Duns within the context of the Oxonian logical and semantic traditions of William of Sherwood and the young Burley.

meditatio is inaugurated. From this world Duns also derives his main model in reconstructing theology. The basic idea is that of *one and the same time – in eodem instanti/tempore*. It is elaborated in the light of the analysis of the *positio* and its time (*retorquere ad unum tempus*). William of Sherwood's crucial qualifications *discrete* and *instans indivisibile* originate from Nicholas of Paris who adds the viewpoint of *tempus incorruptibile/corruptibile*, and they pass on to Duns Scotus. However, Duns drops the *non-synchrony* rule and reconstructs the ordering of *ponibile* and *possibile*. What is possible can be stated and what can be affirmed consistently, whether it be true or false, is possible. So, Duns has not only mastered the model and the tools, including the language of the *ars obligatoria*, but he also uses the tools in order to frame a new ontological model: just as we can state and discuss what is in fact not true, what is true is possibly not true at the same time.

There is an inherent linkage between Duns' reference to the *ars obligatoria* and the way he expounds his personal theory. In fact, the *ars obligatoria* invites just this type of ontology while concentrating on discussing what is not true. We also see that Nicholas of Paris endorsing a quite different ontology has great difficulties with the items of the *positum* and the *falsum positum*. He solves the problem by piling up many different kinds of *tempora* which widen the universe of discourse with the help of 'moments' related to what we may *think*. The way out of ontological alternatives is not rejected; it is not in the picture. The Parisian tradition prepared the way for a methodology of thought which eventually ended in early modern and modern forms of *philosophical idealism*. Modern philosophical idealism simply ignores ontological alternatives.[58]

Duns Scotus opted for a completely different direction. With Duns the dialogically tuned theory of the *ars obligatoria* is linked up with ontology and the theory of contingency. On the level of debate and dialogue he made the most of the opportunities of *dialogical synchrony*. What is discussed and argued for is *in eodem tempore/at the same time different* from what is the case. Duns transposed the *dialogical contingency* into a conceptual and theoretical framework which admirably fits in with the requirements of the theory of divine activity and creativity. According to Duns' theological view, God's activity and creation are not necessary in strict and radical senses of

---

[58] Even early modern Scotist alternatives are simply ignored, not refuted. See Vos, 'Ab uno disce omnes,' *Bijdragen* 60 (1999) 173–204.

'not' and 'necessary.' The theoretical articulation of this radical sense constituted a major scientific problem. Now we are able to solve this dilemma in terms of modern Fregean logic and semantics, Cantorian infinite sets and their alternativity and mutual accessibility, quantifier theory and ontology of possible worlds. All these essential phenomena are modern phenomena and Duns did not have them at his disposal. So he created means on his own. *Logica modernorum* and semantics were already in the center. The *ars obligatoria* played a decisive role. Within this framework the notions of *synchronic possibility* and *synchronic contingency* are tightly interwoven.[59]

It was not only this fundamental model which Duns partly derived from the *ars obligatoria*, but we also find that its technical terminology, dialogical structure, and formal methodology are omnipresent in his systematic language and argumentation. His critical way of doing systematic theology is itself a positive and constructive mirror image of the *ars obligatoria*. The whole of his heavy apparatus is put into the service of truth. The impact of huge discussions about what is *not* true (*ponitur*) is built into his careful investigations of the counterarguments of alternative theories.

In *Ordinatio* I 11.27, Duns Scotus points at the basic rule of the *ars obligatoria*. The *ars obligatoria* can only be salvaged and the fairness of debate and disputation can only be maintained if we stick to what we say and defend it by granting what follows from what we have accepted (*concedendo sequens*) and by denying what is incompatible with what we have asserted and granted (*negando repugnans*). Strict reliability asks for consistency. Integrity must also rest on proofs. The ethics of belief requires a strict practice of thinking, and thinking and arguing in all seriousness are the fruit of the will to do justice to other persons.

Duns learnt a lot from the *ars obligatoria*. It was just to his taste, but there is also a gap between the Parisian origins of the *ars obligatoria* and its Scotian version in Oxford. However, there is also a gap to be discerned between the Scotian theory of obligations and his fourteenth-century successors. In the fourteenth-century history of the theory of *obligationes* we are struck by the collapse of the *positio impossibilis*, rather dear to Duns Scotus' mind.[60] Deep structures of

---

[59] Yrjönsuuri, *Obligationes. 14th Century Logic of Disputational Duties*, chapter 2, neatly summarizes the history of pre-Scotian obligational theory. In fact, his own historical point of departure is Walter Burley's theory (*Obligationes*, chapter 3).

[60] See Yrjönsuuri, *Obligationes*, chapter 4.

language and logic and the strict requirement of consistency are crucial to understand Duns Scotus' methods of analysis and way of thinking. Both the Parisian origins and the fourteenth-century Oxonian aftermath give way to doxastic alternatives where, in spite of his actualism, Duns Scotus utilizes logical tools in order to widen out the ontological spectrum.

CHAPTER 6

Conceptual devices

6.1 INTRODUCTION

Contingency thought presupposes that reality is complicated. Because our reality is complicated, a simple set of parallel distinctions does not satisfy if we have to cope with true, and sometimes harsh, reality. There is no simple *one-dimension* reality. Since there is only multidimensional reality, we need logical complexity and more devices to do justice to reality. Contingency thought derives its inspiration from the positive drive of biblical revelation that reality has to be better than it usually is. The logic of conversion does not square with the idea of the only one best possible world *Actua* is. Scholasticism is often ridiculed for piling up unnecessary distinctions, but what is *scholasticism*?

> *Scholasticism* is a method applied in philosophy and theology which uses an ever and ever recurring system of concepts, distinctions, definitions, propositional analyses, argumentation techniques and disputational methods, as terminist logic already shows.[1]

Apart from the over-technicalities of some authors, the gist of this approach is to the point. Reality is not simple, let alone simplistic, and it is of no help to dream away in the presumption that we can start with clarity and simplicity. If we recognize that reality is complicated and that this complexity has to be acknowledged, there has to be a search for tools which are able to do justice to this complex reality. This is the *Sitz im Leben* of Scotus' ramified logic and analytical method. *Scholastic* method is to be explained as *analytical* method *avant la lettre*.

As to the technicalities of Duns Scotus' method, we have to survey a host of devices. §6.2 deals with the famous distinction *in sensu composito* and *in sensu diviso* and its early history. In terms of Duns' new way of handling this distinction, his way of distinguishing *ante* from *post* can be clarified (§6.3), just as can the nature of 'nature': *prioritas*

---

[1] See *PMA* 85 ff., and §15.4.

naturâ (structural priority) (§6.4). Likewise, there is a need of the *structural moments* to do justice to complicated reality (§6.5). However, not only is the layer of acts multidimensional, but the layer of entities and their properties is multidimensional too and here Duns' theory of the formal distinction fits in. The *formal* distinction belongs to a family of distinctions, like the *real* and the *rational* distinction do and, thus, the theory of the *formal distinction* presupposes the theory of the *real* and the *rational relation* on the one hand (§6.6.1), and the concept of *identity* (§6.6.2) on the other. In the end we arrive at the famous formal distinction (§6.7). A little epilogue completes this story in §6.8.

6.2   IN SENSU COMPOSITO AND IN SENSU DIVISO

6.2.1   Abelard

Abelard applies the distinction between *per compositionem* and *per divisionem* to modal propositions. Suppose that

> It is possible that one who is standing is sitting

is interpreted *per compositionem* or *de sensu*. This move means that possible truth is ascribed to the proposition *One who is standing is sitting*. However, this is not a very attractive result, since *One who is standing is sitting* cannot be true, but this is not the only possibility in which we can read *It is possible that one who is standing is sitting*. We may analyze this proposition by disconnecting *is standing* and *is sitting*. Then we start with someone who is standing and we ascribe to this person that it is possible to be sitting. Now we have arrived at the sense of *per divisionem* in contradistinction to *per compositionem*.

Nevertheless, this cannot be the whole story, for we have still to ask in what sense it is precisely said *per divisionem* that it is *possible* for *a* to sit, if *a* is standing. Simo Knuuttila addressed this question in a careful and prudent interpretation of Abelardian modalities in *Time and Modality in Scholasticism*, based on the main idea of diachronic alternatives.[2] Weidemann offered a bold analysis arguing that a theory of counterfactual alternatives is found in Abelard's *Super Periermenias*. Apart from improbable details in Weidemann's exposition, we have to be aware that modern formalizations can easily mislead us by ascribing much later precisions to a semi-artificial Latin

---

[2] See Knuuttila, 'Time and Modality in Scholasticism,' in idem (ed.), *Reforging the Great Chain of Being*, 178–187, cf. 166–169. For an excellent treatment of Abelardian modalities, see also his *Modalities in Medieval Philosophy*, 82–96. Cf. §7.10.

still containing the rather vague uses typical of a natural language. When we realize what enormous efforts the young John Duns had to invest in order to clarify the idea of *synchronic contingency* – his discoveries were wasted on the logical acumen of an Ockham – it is evident that explicit and decisive evidence is needed to prove the presence of a theoretical translation of the vision of an open reality in terms of counterfactual alternatives or synchronic contingency before Richard Rufus, Henry of Ghent, or Scotus.[3]

6.2.2   From Abelard to William of Sherwood

Subtle observations are found in the *Glose in Aristotilis Sophisticos Elencos*, one of the earliest extant sets of notes on Aristotle's *De Sophisticis Elenchis*. The author realizes that the inference 'Socrates can write. Therefore, *Socrates is writing*' is a fallacy. *Divisio (division, analysis)* is seen as a device: when it is applied, a statement sentence is made false – *divisim* – while it is true *coniunctim*:[4]

> *Two and three is five*

is true *in the composite sense (coniunctim)*, but it is false *in the divided sense (divisim)*:

> *Two, and three is five*.[5]

The same work offers an early diachronic application of the distinction between *secundum compositionem* and *divisim*.[6] The terminology is fluent and the use of examples not systematic, but the tendency is clear, to be explained by means of the example *Socrates is reading*. The

---

[3] In sharp contrast to modern logic and modern logic-based contributions to the history of medieval modal logic, most philosophers and theologians are still afraid of the notion of *synchronic contingency*. We have to distinguish ideas which require *synchronic contingency* for a consistent interpretation from the objective presence of this notion. The presence of this type of consistency has to be proved explicitly, not assumed.

[4] *Divisim* means: separately, e.g. used when things are classified. Cf. the range of meanings of *divisio*: separation, division (mathematics), distribution (logic), classification.

[5] *Logica Modernorum* I 210: '*Divisio est proprietas orationis secundum quam oratio divisim est falsa, coniunctim vera*, ut *"quinque sunt duo et tria"* coniunctim est verum, et divisim est falsum.' These *Glosses* (*Logica Modernorum* I 186–255) date from the middle of the twelfth century (*Logica Modernorum* I 82–88).

[6] Ibid., lines 10–17: '*Secundum compositionem* autem huiusmodi, ut *posse sedentem anbulare, idest* possibile est quod *sedens simul anbulet*, vel possibile est quod *sedens alio tempore anbulet. Si quis didicit litteras, possibile est nunc discere litteras quas scit*. Hec oratio significat aliquem didicisse litteras et eum nunc posse illas litteras discere, que *coniunctim* sunt falsa, quia aliquis non potest didicisse litteras et *simul* discere; sed *divisim* potest aliquis didicisse et discere. Sicut si Deus providit Socratem legere, possibile est Socratem [non legere].'

predicates *reading* and *not reading* are mutually exclusive, like *sitting*
and *walking*. In the composite sense (*secundum compositionem*), it is
false that Socrates can read and not read at the same time (*simul*). He
who is reading (or *sitting*) cannot *not-read* (*walk*). However, in the
divided sense (*divisim*), it is possible that Socrates who is reading at the
moment does not read *at another time* (*alio tempore*). The *Summa
sophisticorum elencorum*, originating from the 1150s, deals with a
sitting-walking type example: *It is possible that a healthy person is ill.*
If this proposition is understood as a composite one, it is false; however,
if it is understood as a divided proposition, it can be true, because he
who is healthy may be ill *at another time* (*alias*).[7]

The generations of Peter Abelard and Adam of Balsham, Robert of
Melun and Peter Helyas contributed enormously to the flourishing of
Western thought. The way of thinking was transformed by the development of the *logica modernorum*. De Rijk discovered that the
origins of the *logica modernorum* dated back to the second quarter
of the twelfth century.[8] The new logical and semantical approach
invaded the Parisian theological schools in the 1160s, as the
Sententiae of Peter of Poitiers (d.1205) and the works of Robert of
Melun testify.[9] The *Sententiae* of Peter of Poitiers offer a marvellous
illustration of the logic of *diachrony*.[10]

6.2.3 William of Sherwood

An interesting feature of Sherwood's *Obligationes* are two sections *De
diversis opinionibus* in which he comments on the nature of the new
field. By far the longest section is in chapter *De positione possibili* of
the first part *De positione*, where alternative views are discussed,

[7] *Logica Modernorum* I 316.4–7: 'Sophisma est *compositionis*, quia prima propositio potest
intelligi *composita* et *divisa*. Si intelligitur *composita*, idest quod possibile sit sanum et egrum
esse *simul*, falsum est. Si vero intelligatur *divisa*, scilicet quod possibile sit id quod est sanum,
esse egrum *alias*, verum est.' See *Logica Modernorum* I 88 f. Compare the pioneering observations of Knuuttila, 'Time and Modality in Scholasticism,' in idem (ed.), *Reforging the
Great Chain of Being*, 188–191.

[8] See *PMA* 4.2. Cf. §4.2, §§15.5–15.6 and Chapter 16. For a fascinating chapter of the history
of scholarship discussing the origins of the *logica modernorum*, see *Logica Modernorum*
I 13 ff.

[9] *Logica Modernorum* I 153–178: 'On the use of the doctrine of fallacy in twelfth century
theology.'

[10] *Logica Modernorum* I 175, citing *Sententiae* II 17: 'Sicut dicitur quod *nigredo erit in albo*,
idest in eo quod erit album, non in albo quod simul sit album et nigrum. Ponatur quod iste
vivet usque ad A, et tunc morietur: post A vero sequetur B et C, que erunt duo momenta. Iste
potest esse victurus in B, quia licet sit moriturus in A, tamen posset vita eius protelari usque
in B vel C. Sicut, ergo, iste potest esse victurus in B, et ita iste potest esse peniturus in B.'

including a clear analysis of the diachronic notion of *possibility*.[11] A specific function is ascribed to the *divided sense*. The exemplary proposition is:

(1) *Album esse nigrum est possibile.*

(1) is called a *modal* proposition, not a *categorical* one. So if there is a *modal* element in a proposition, Sherwood calls such a proposition a *propositio modalis*, whether this modal element be a predicate or an adverb.[12] The objection states that (1) must be false, because the proposition *Something white is black* (*album esse nigrum*) cannot be true, and if a proposition is not possibly true, then the assertion that it is possible must be false.

The *Sed contra* puts forward Sherwood's personal view. He rebuts the conviction that (1) must be false by introducing the famous distinction involved in the notion of *the divided sense* (*sensus divisionis*). In the *divided sense*, (1) is true. In (1) it is said of a proposition that it is *possible*. In terms of the proposition *Album esse nigrum* this possibility is then to be asserted, but how can that be?[13] Sherwood

---

[11] Sherwood's text is offered here because the critical edition is not easy to come by: Green (ed.), *An Introduction to the Logical Treatise 'De Obligationibus,' with critical texts of William of Sherwood* (?) *and Walter Burley* II, 5: 'His habitis, videndum est de diversis opinionibus circumstantibus hanc artem. Dicunt ergo quidam quod licet possum dicere *Album esse nigrum est possibile*, tamen non potest poni, et hoc hac ratione, quia haec possibilitas non est ipsum dici, et propterea non sequitur quod ipsum possit poni quia possibilitas et positio non cadunt super idem. *Sed contra. Album esse nigrum est possibile.* Haec est vera *in sensu divisionis.* Sic autem est modalis, ergo ly *possibile* dicit possibilitatem alicuius compositionis, ergo ratione illius compositionis potest poni. Sed dubitatur nunc, facta positione, qualiter sit ad hanc respondendum *Album esse nigrum*, quia si concedat, concedit impossibile, possibili facta positione. Si neget, negat positum. Et possumus dicere quod in hac *Album esse nigrum est possibile*, ly *possibile* ampliat ly *esse nigrum* ad aliquod tempus futurum, et ly *album* stat pro eo quo nunc est album, quod quidem *in futuro tempore* potest esse nigrum. Unde si illud futurum accipiamus tamquam *praesens*, erit ly *album* respectu huius ut praeteritum; sic autem accipitur cum ponimus. Ponitur enim pro tempore pro quo est possibile et propterea per haec verba ponimus *esse nigrum* in esse praeterito albo, et est ipsum positum non: *Album esse nigrum*, sed *Quod fuit album esse nigrum.*'

[12] Sherwood's usage matches the definitions of the *Logica 'Cum sit nostra'* in *Logica Modernorum* II B 428: 'Propositionum alia *modalis*, alia *de inesse.* [...] *Propositio modalis* est illa in qua predicatum inest subiecto cum modo, ut *'possibile est hominem esse animal'*. In hac propositione dico quod *animal* intelligitur in *homine* possibiliter.' Cf. CF 48–51 and 64–69.

[13] In the meantime, a fine specimen of the *ars obligatoria* is delivered. Assume that (2) is given and 'affirmed' (posited). However, the truth of (2) depends on the truth value of *Album esse nigrum*, but which alternatives are now open to the *respondens* to respond? Let us assume that he grants (*concedit*) *Album esse nigrum*. Then the ax will fall, for *Album esse nigrum* cannot be true because the involved predicates exclude each other – on the basis of a *positio possibilis.* If he, on the contrary, denies *Album esse nigrum* – as possibly true – then he gets into conflict with the *positum*, and then the ax falls again.

elaborates the interpretation *secundum divisionem* in terms of which (1) can be said to be true: *possibile* is looked upon as a *diachronic operator* and its function is to broaden the scope of *being black* towards the future. What is white *now* can be black at a time *in the future*. For that future time *Album esse nigrum* is true; so, it can be true. *Possibility* is said of something which is not true for the present time and therefore it is a property of what is *not* the case. From the logical point of view it is the traditional meaning of *can* which means *will* within the diachronic framework of 'contingent' meaning *being different at a later time*.

Conclusion

There is a positive impact of Sherwood's *Obligationes* on the thought of Duns as to terminology and theory formation, but here we find the central notions of *diachronic* possibility and contingency clearly explained by Sherwood. In *Lectura* I 39.48 Duns is dependent on this exposition (see §4.9 and §7.3).

6.2.4   John Duns Scotus

The exposition of *Lectura* I 39.47–51 stands out by distinguishing clearly between *diachronic* and *synchronic* contingency. Understanding this distinction requires an alternative notion of *possibility*, a notion Duns elucidates in *Lectura* I 39.49:

> From that freedom of the will still another potency results, a logical one (to which a real potency also corresponds). A potency is only logical, when the terms are possible in such a way that they are not repugnant to each other, but can be united.[14]

So far, so good. The elucidation of the crucial notions of *diachronic possibility* and *diachronic contingency* is found in *Lectura* I 39.48, a section worth quoting in full:

> One kind of *contingency* and *possibility* is that the will is *successively* related to opposite objects, and this *possibility* and *contingency* follow from its mutability. And according to this possibility a distinction is made regarding *possible propositions* which are composed of contrary and opposite terms, such as *Something white can be black*. And according to *the divided sense* the proposition is true, as far as the terms are understood to have a possibility *at different times*, such as

---

[14] CF 116 and §49: 'Extrema sic sunt possibilia quod non sibi invicem repugnant.' See §4.9.

> *Something white at a can be black at b.*
> Hence, this possibility results from succession. In this way, the
> proposition
> *The will loving him, can hate him*
> is also true *in the divided sense.*[15]

Here, we meet the old concepts of *possibility* and *contingency*, being of the same type, indicating change and mutability. So, the alternative type of *possibility* and *contingency* must essentially differ from the first type. The first kind of *possibility* and the first kind of *contingency* Duns expounds are successive or diachronic. The first kind of *possibility* we already met with Sherwood. In *Lectura* I 39.48 Duns explains *diachronic possibility* and mentions *diachronic contingency*,[16] for *contingency*$_1$ is simply the time logical mirror image of *possibility*$_1$:

> (2) p *is possible*$_1$ = $_{def}$ *not-p* is true *at the very present time* t_k and p will be *true at a future time* t_1

and:

> (3) p *is contingent*$_1$ = $_{def}$ p is *true at the very present time* t_k and *not p* will be true *at a future time* t_1.

The 'swing'

The concepts of *possibility*$_1$ and *contingency*$_1$ are based on differences of temporal indexation. Time indexes are connected with *terms*: *something white at a* and *something black at b*, but the main idea behind *logical* possibility is *consistency* (see §4.9). The definition of *logical* possibility is linked with the definitions of *possibility*$_1$ and *contingency*$_1$: 'This logical possibility does not obtain as far as the will has acts *successively*, but as far as it has them *at the same moment*' (§50). This move meshes well with the way *diachrony* is replaced by *synchrony*. *Diachronic priority* (*precedence*) is transformed into *synchronic priority*. The secret of consistent Western thought lies in the transformation of its concepts.

---

[15] CF 114 and §48: 'Secundum *sensum divisionis* est propositio vera, prout intelliguntur extrema habere possibilitatem *pro diversis temporibus*, ut "album in *a* potest esse nigrum in *b*". Unde ista possibilitas consequitur successionem. Et sic etiam haec vera *in sensu divisionis* "voluntas amans illum, potest odire illum".'

[16] *Lectura* I 39.48: 'Et secundum *hanc possibilitatem* distinguuntur propositiones de possibili quae fiunt de extremis contrariis et oppositis.' The diachronic analysis follows. See CF 114–115.

The newly styled divided sense

In terms of the transformation of the *diachronic* way of thought into a *synchronic* – and *structural* – way of thought, the new Scotian idea of *the divided sense* is easy to expound: the newly styled *sensus divisionis* is related to the old *sensus divisionis* in just the same way as the old concept of *possibility*₁ is related to its *synchronic* counterpart *possibility*₂ and the old concept of *contingency*₁ is related to its *synchronic* counterpart *contingency*₂. Duns explains the old distinction between the *composite* and the *divided sense* in terms of understanding the *divided sense* in a new way, applied to the proposition *A will willing something can not-will it*, in *Lectura* I 39.51:

> We must distinguish between the *composite* and the *divided sense*. [...] The proposition is true, however, *in the divided sense*, not because we understand the terms *for different times* [...], but it is true *in the divided sense*, for there are two propositions, because it implicitly includes two propositions. In one proposition the will is said to have the act of willing, and in the other one the will is said to have the opposite act taken on its own with the possibility operator, and then the meaning is: *The will is willing at a* and *The will can be not-willing at a*. This is true, for the will willing at *a*, freely elicits an act of willing, which is not its attribute.[17]

The essential comment is that the proposition *A will willing something can not-will it* is true *in the analytical sense*, but not *in the old sense of discerning different moments of time*, for the terms are not understood *for different times*. That old sense matters, for we successively will different things. *The old sense of dividing* is explicitly acknowledged, but Duns points out that he does not mean this.

The proposition *A will willing something can not-will it* is true in terms of an alternative *analytical sense*, since this proposition is analyzed. The upshot of the analysis consists in two propositions: this proposition implicitly includes two propositions, namely:

1. the categorical proposition *The will is willing that p at a*;

---

[17] *Lectura* I 39.51: 'Est distinguenda [namely, 'volens in *a*, potest nolle in *a*'] secundum *compositionem et divisionem*: [...] *in sensu* autem *divisionis* est propositio vera, non quia extrema intelliguntur *pro diversis temporibus* (ille enim sensus habet locum, quia est *successio* in actibus), sed est vera *in sensu divisionis* quia sunt ibi duae propositiones, quia implicite includit duas propositiones: enuntiatur enim actus volendi de voluntate in una propositione, et oppositus actus de voluntate *absolute accepta cum nota possibilitatis* enuntiatur in alia propositione, et est sensus "voluntas est volens in *a*" et "voluntas potest esse nolens in *a*" – et hoc verum est, quia voluntas volens in *a*, libere elicit actum volendi, nec est eius passio.'

and:

2. the modal proposition *The will can be not-willing that p at a.*

Thus:

> The first application of *the divided sense*, in §48, was along tradi-
> tional lines: the division ('divisio') is related to *different, successive*
> moments of time. Now, *the divided sense* is applied to propositions
> of *synchronic* possibility. [...] The possibility operator now only refers
> to the second of these conjuncts. *In this divided sense* the proposition
> is true and states that at the moment at which the will factually has
> an act of willing something, there is the *possibility* (not the factual-
> ity!) of not-willing it.[18]

The paradoxical effect of this innovation is that the new analytical
function of the *divided sense* is in line with the traditional composite
sense. What does the traditional composite sense consist of?

> We must distinguish between the *composite* and the *divided sense*. It
> (namely, the proposition *A will willing something can not-will it*) is
> false *in the composite sense*, as we understand the predicate to be
> attributed to this whole: *the will willing at a*, together with the pos-
> sibility operator.[19]
>
> If we read this sentence (namely, *A will willing something can not-
> will it*) in the *composite* sense, we see a false proposition, Scotus says.
> For in that case, we consider the first part ('John wills something') as
> the subject to which we ascribe the last part ('he does not will it at
> the same moment') as a predicate, together composing *one* proposi-
> tion. Then the possibility operator ('nota possibilitatis') concerns
> this single proposition as a whole and the result is the following
> proposition:
> *It is possible that: John who wills something does not-will it at the
> same moment.*
>
> This proposition is false, for it states the possibility of a contradic-
> tion. This application of the composite sense concerns the logic of *one*
> proposition, in which a subject, a predicate incompatible with it and
> a modal operator are combined.[20]

---

[18] *CF* 121 and 123. For §48, see *CF* 114 f. and for §§51 f., see *CF* 118–125.
[19] *Lectura* I 39.51: 'Est distinguenda [namely: 'volens in *a*, potest nolle in *a*'] secundum *compositionem et divisionem*: et *in sensu compositionis* falsa, prout intelligitur praedicatum cum
nota possibilitatis attribui huic toti "voluntas volens in *a*".'
[20] *CF* 121. So, $M (aWp_{t1}$ & $a - Wp_{t1})$ is false. See also Knuuttila, 'Time and Modality,' in idem,
Reforging the Great Chain of Being, 227; idem, 'Modal Logic,' *CHLMP* 354, and Alanen
and Knuuttila, 'The Foundations of Modality and Conceivability in Descartes and his
Predecessors,' in Knuuttila (ed.), *Modern Modalities*, 35.

Let us reformulate such a proposition as a conjunctive proposition. Why is such a proposition, preceded by the modal operator *possible*, untenable? It is untenable, since the conjuncts in M $(p_t \& -p_t)$ are taken to hold for the same time t. If one were to state M $(p_{tk} \& -p_{tl})$, considering p and $-p$ for different moments of time, just as is done in the case of the old *divided sense*, then there is nothing faulty. The remarkable thing is that the traditional *composite sense* intuitively added *the same time index* to both propositions, while according to the traditional *divided sense* the terms of the proposition or the propositions are understood to have a possibility *at different times* (*Lectura* I 39.48). In Duns' new *divided sense*, the *same time index* is added to the terms or propositions to be considered in a democratic manner. In one case, synchrony leads to a contradiction, in the other it does not.[21]

In sum, in the light of his new theory of *synchronic contingency*, Duns Scotus revises the old diachrony type of the *composite/divided sense* distinction into a new one. The meaning of the proposition

Something white can be black

is no longer salvaged by reading it diachronically as

Something white at a can be black at b

but by reading it according to *synchronic* lines as:

Something is white at a and it is possible that it is black at a.[22]

6.3   ANTE AND POST

Let us look at the diachronic interpretation of *before* (*ante*), when we try to diagnose the meaning of *ante* in Duns Scotus' philosophical language. In the logic and ontology of *diachrony* wherein *time* determines the structure of *being*, the cause temporally precedes the effect. In diachronic models, *before* (*ante*) and *after* (*post*) can only be used temporally, because the diachronic order of succession structures

---

[21] A contradictory proposition – a conjunctive proposition of the form $p \& -p$ – cannot be true, since a conjunction can only be true if at least both conjuncts are true, as the truth table method easily shows.

[22] Compare $p_{tk} \& M - p_{tl}$ and $F_{tk}a \& - F_{tl}a$ with $p_t \& M - p_t$ and $F_t a \& M - F_t a$.

reality. *Everything has its time* (Ecclesiastes). It is as the objection Duns himself brings forward in *Lectura* I 36.57 says:

> If the will willing something at *a*, can not-will it at *a*, then either this potency is with the act or it is *before* the act. Not with the act, because then there would be opposites at the same time. Therefore, it is a potency *before* the act. (CF 132)

Several steps have to be noticed here. The opponent does not primarily intend to defend his own view but to refute Duns' approach, but in trying to refute Duns he reveals where he stands himself. We assume:

> *a* wills at time *t* that *p* and it is possible that *a* does not will at time *t* that *p*.[23]

Then, in terms of the opponent, either this possibility is accompanied by an act or it is *before* the act. The conceptual web of this opposition excludes Duns' approach in two ways, boiling down to the same assumptions. According to the opposition, *possibility* and *act* cannot go together, accompanying each other, since this connection leads to a contradiction. *Simul* refers to the combination of opposites in a contradiction wherein *p* and *not-p* go together (*simul*). They are linked for the same moment of time, for if different times are concerned, then there is not a contradiction at stake. There is no simultaneous conjunction of this kind of an *opposite possibility* and *act* possible. Therefore, the *potency* or *possibility* of something or of a state of affairs *precedes* its act, but in order to elicit a contradiction, it is necessary that *possibility* entails *act*. 'Then there would be opposites at the same time' (§57).

These assumptions are coherent within their own context, for in rebutting Duns' view the possibility of *synchronic contingency* has to be eliminated and, therefore, *synchronic necessity* has to be embraced. So, in terms of the dilemma of (*together*) *with* and *before*, the opposite possibility has to be construed as *preceding* the act, but, within the context of Duns' proposal, it has to be assumed for the same indivisible time, 'but this is false, since no potency can be at *a* preceding its act: then *a* would be divisible and would not be an indivisible moment, the opposite of which is assumed.'[24] Duns' view can

---

23 *Lectura* I 39.57: 'Si voluntas volens aliquid in *a*, potest non velle illud in *a* – aut igitur ista potentia est *cum* actu, aut *ante* actum. Non *cum* actu, quia tunc opposita essent simul. Ergo, est potentia *ante* actum.' The Latin syntax makes it clear that the temporal index *a* has to be linked with *willing*, and not with the 'operator' *potest*.

24 Ibid.: 'Sed hoc falsum est, cum nulla potentia potest esse in *a*, praecedens actum suum: tunc enim *a* esset divisibile et non instans indivisibile, cuius oppositum supponitur.' $p \& M - p$

only be refuted if the whole texture of his concepts is rejected, for the contradiction is only elicited if the possibility and the act are enclosed in one time frame. Of course, we may refuse to accept Duns' web of concepts. However, *saying* that they are impossible is one thing, *proving* that they are impossible is quite another.

Duns feels himself challenged by this criticism. He has to widen the scope of the available concepts, for 'the potency is not *temporally before* the act, neither is the potency together *with* the act, but the potency is *prior by nature* in regard to the act.'[25] Duns is not happy with indicating only two alternatives. He widens the scope of the alternatives by introducing the new notion of *natural/structural priority*, in contradistinction to *temporal* or *diachronic priority* which presupposes precedence and succession.

Lectura I 39.60 starts with a critical note: 'One argues in terms of the *fallacy of insufficiency*.' The opponent's argument does not satisfy, for he reasons *ab insufficienti*.

> This means, that one tries to reach a valid conclusion ('*consequens*') on the ground of too few premisses. In this paragraph Scotus points to the fact that the opponent draws a conclusion on the ground of merely two possibilities. As Scotus demonstrates, there is a third possibility, however, which renders the opponent's conclusion invalid.[26]

The opponent's argument is logically invalid and ontologically wrong, for 'a cause *structurally* (*naturâ*) *pre*cedes its effect, when its cause, causing freely and contingently, is causing' (ibid.).

Duns ignores the temporal precedence and priority of *possibly willing* over the *actual* will, since this notion of possibility cannot help us out. If this kind of potency entails its actuality, and if *it is possible that p* and *it is possible that not-p* are democratically treated as equals, then the upshot is a contradiction, just as the opponent noticed in §57. We need an alternative notion of *possibility*. The *temporal before* (*ante tempore*), which is also called *ante duratione* (*before of duration*) in *Ordinatio* I 39.19, cannot play this role. The pattern of *temporal precedence* or *priority* cannot be of any use within a theoretical framework

---

only generates a contradiction if $Mp \rightarrow p$. If we replace p by $-p$ in $Mp \rightarrow p$ and add this to $p \& M - p$, we have: $p \& M - p \& (M - p \rightarrow - p)$, which entails: $p \& -p$.

[25] *Lectura* I 39.60: 'Non potentia *ante* actum *tempore*, nec potentia *cum* actu, sed potentia *ante* actum *naturâ*.' For the crucial notion of *naturâ*, see §6.4.

[26] CF 139, note 72. Peter of Spain utilizes this fallacy *ab insufficienti* in *Tractatus* XII §13 of his *Summule Logicales*. See De Rijk (ed.), *Peter of Spain. Tractatus, called afterwards Summule Logicales*, 281 ll. 25 and 29. The critic assessing a line of argumentation is not satisfied. The conclusion is not backed by enough information.

of one indivisible moment of time. It is just the *diachronic model* which has to be dropped, because it cannot account for the nature of reality, neither for the nature of *contingency*, nor even for the nature of *necessity*. If we drop the model of several *different* times *before* or *after*, we are left with the model of *one and the same time*. The temporal *before* or *after* cannot help out, for faith and common sense need a structural, synchronic approach to reality and its logic.

We listen again to the opponent. The starting point is something that is actually true – *a* wills that *p* at *t*. The opponent, of course, believes that the *possibility* of *willing that p* exists *before t*. Of course, if *willing that p* is at any time impossible, then it cannot be willed at all, but this is impossible, for *a* wills that *p* at *t*. Now, we look at the second possibility of *a not willing that p*. The opponent also grants that the *possibility* of *not-willing that p* exists *before t*. Of course, if *willing that not-p* is at any time impossible, then it cannot be willed at all, but this is also unacceptable for the opponent himself, for he tries to account for the contingency of willing and acting in terms of differences of *before* and *after*. So, if we lose the possibility of *diachronic* differences, we all lose the possibility of contingent willing and acting. So, the opponent grants both possibilities of *willing that p* and of *not-willing that p* in a diachronic framework. We have seen Duns arguing that just this *diachronic* and *temporal* sense cannot help us out. This line of argumentation also teaches the meaning of *post*. Both *before* (*ante*) and *after* (*post*) are used in a temporal sense. From the logical point of view, this usage implies that the structure of causality – the nature of the *cause-effect* relation – has to be formalized with the help of the strict implication.

Now, both diachronic possibilities of *willing that p* and of *not-willing that p* are, as it were, swing over and are transformed in a *synchronic* manner. 'A possibility "by nature", or structurally, "*precedes*" the actuality of the opposite at the *same* moment. Put otherwise: every contingent act presupposes the potency (and the possibility) of its opposite act at the same instant,'[27] precisely as the possibility of an actual act *by nature*, or *structurally*, *precedes* the actuality of the same act at the *same* time and every contingent act presupposes the possibility of its own act at the same time.

---

[27] CF 139. The rule $N (aWp_{t1} - MaW - p_{t1})$ governs contingent proposition *p*. For the transformation or 'swing' of diachronic possibility and contingency in the Sherwoodian sense into *synchronic possibility* and *synchronic contingency*, see *Lectura* I 39.47–48 and CF 112–117. On the terms and concepts of *synchronic possibility* and *synchronic contingency*, see §4.9, §5.4 and §7.4, and cf. §6.2.

The terminology of *Reportatio Parisiensis* I 39 clearly expresses this point: *praecedere duratione* (*durationally preceding*) goes with *ordine durationis*, in contradistinction to *prior naturaliter* (*by structural priority*). The terminology of *Ordinatio* I 39.19 is even more specific: '*ante* pro prioritate *durationis*' is used in contradistinction to '*ante* pro prioritate *naturae.*'[28] The *diachronic priority* (*precedence*) is not only replaced by a *synchronic priority* (*precedence*), but *diachronic priority* (*precedence*) is also transformed into *synchronic priority* (*precedence*) which in fact boils down to *structural* priority (see §6.4). *Prior* and *prae* get entirely new meanings. The secret of Western thought lies in concept transformation. The semantic contents of *before* (*ante, prae*) and *after* (*post*) and of *prior* and *posterior* are synchronically transformed, in precisely the same way as the concepts $possible_1$ and $contingent_1$ are simply transformed *synchronically* into the new concepts *possible* and *contingent*, and just like *natura* which originally meant *nature, phusis, growth*, became the kernel of a new language, both in logic and in theology, as, for example, the expression *natura Dei*, the 'nature' of God, shows. Christianization of thought boils down to double thinking, to creating a new level of concept formation as we can already observe in the works of Anselm: $necessity_2$ (*necessitas sequens*) is added to $necessity_1$, $goodness_2$ (*bonum iustitiae*) is added to $goodness_1$ (*bonum commodi*) and $velle_2$ (*to will*) is added to $velle_1$ (*to be inclined to, to wish*). New theological contents cannot be accounted for in old thought patterns inherited from ancient philosophy. New wine cannot be put into old wineskins. What matters is double concept formation.

As to the usage of the structural *prior/prius* Stephen Dumont made a splendid discovery by pointing out that Peter Olivi utilized the concept *prius naturaliter* in his *Summa quaestionum in libros Sententiarum* II 42 and the same concept, worded *prius naturâ* and *prioritas naturalis*, based on synchronic conceptual structures, in *Summa quaestionum* II 57.[29]

---

[28] See Wolter, 'God's Knowledge of Future Events,' in *The Philosophical Theology of Scotus*, 306 note 56, and *Opera Omnia* VI 423.

[29] Dumont, 'The Origin of Scotus's Theory of Synchronic Contingency,' *The Modern Schoolman* 72 (1995) 164 f. Although we know that Duns had already consulted Olivi's *Summa* when preparing his Oxonian *Sententiae* course in 1297–98, I do not think that Olivi's discoveries played a major role in constructing his own synchronic web of concepts, although it was a helpful background. Cf. §1.6 and §7.10.

6.4   THE NATURE OF 'NATURE': *PRIORITAS NATURÂ* (STRUCTURAL PRIORITY)

We have already met *naturâ* (by nature, structurally) and *naturaliter* (in a natural way, structurally). The new *ante/prae* (*before*) and *post* (*after*) usage is a specific illustration of the general conceptual break, visible in the semantic history of *natura/phusis/nature*. Broadly stated, most great thinkers of the Western tradition *say*, on a locutionary level, the same things. Nevertheless, if we interpret what they *say* in terms of their personal philosophical language and conceptual and theoretical structures, then worlds of differences show up.

For this reason, the key terms of Western philosophy have a complicated biography and the most complicated biography is the semantic and conceptual biography of *natura/nature*. The complex thing is that we cannot investigate a priori and directly a certain *concept c* in someone's philosophy. We *see* where certain *words* and expressions are found, but where are the *concepts*? Under which coverage are they hidden? If the word *praedestinatio* is missing, it is not allowed to infer that a *doctrine* of predestination is missing too.

Fortunately, we have in Duns' works almost monographic discussions of the theoretical framework of *synchronic contingency*, but if such an analysis was missing, it would be tremendously difficult to discover Duns Scotus' conceptual structures, although his thought would be exactly the same. When we compare *nature* in biblical language, Aristotle, Thomas Aquinas, and Duns Scotus, we see that 'nature' is almost conspicuous by its absence in biblical language, while the Aristotelian, Thomist, and Scotist usages are very different, in spite of the fact that the literature says again and again that Thomas Aquinas and Duns Scotus are Aristotelians. Even Thomas Aquinas differs much more from Aristotle than from Duns Scotus whose thought is just the opposite of Aristotle's, although he admired Aristotle immensely. When we put a host of questions to Thomas Aquinas and Duns Scotus, allowing them only to answer *yes* or *no* on the basis of their shared *patrimonium fidei*, then they would almost invariably give the same answer. Nevertheless, in spite of the prima facie agreement on the *fides* level, their philosophical language and philosophy are rather different on a deeper level of concept and theory formation.

At this point, Duns introduces the alternative of the *structural before* or the *before by nature* (*ante naturâ*) which is also called *ante naturaliter.*[30] No series of successive acts helps us to determine *what* the act means, but only the structure of this act. The logic of time maintains itself, just as a successive series of temporal acts does not become superfluous when we have discovered the *nature* of that act. It is precisely the temporal and historical act and event which have to be accounted for *structurally*, but, moreover, the terminology of the old order and of the old model is still used in order to find words and expressions and to develop concepts needed to build up the new way of thinking. This new way of systematic thinking reveals the way we act and will, for

> a cause *structurally* (*naturâ*) precedes its effect, when its cause, causing freely and contingently, is causing. At that moment at which it causes, it causes contingently, for, if it would not cause contingently for that moment, it would not cause contingently, because in that case it does not cause for another moment either.[31]

If *a* works, *a* works either *necessarily* or *contingently*. If *a* only works *necessarily*, *a* cannot be free, for there is only *one* way possible for *a*, and, so, there are no alternatives and there are no alternatives possible which may give content and substance to the freedom of *a*. Either freedom is impossible, or it is possible that *a* being *free* works *contingently*. Here, Duns does not try to prove that *freedom* cannot be eliminated and that *contingency* cannot be destroyed. He simply assumes the possibility and the actuality of *freedom* and he simply tries to elaborate what *freely acting* is all about. One can only act freely, if one can *will* freely, for if it is impossible *to will freely*, then it is impossible *to will tout court*, and the impossibility of the will makes *acting freely* impossible.

Duns argues the other way around. He starts with the *free cause* the will is, and makes the point that it is necessary that *at the very moment of time* the will works, it works *contingently* for that very moment of time. This simple move is often overlooked. Why has this to be so and *why* can a diachronic model of freedom and contingency not help us out? The diachronic model operates with several different times $t_{1,\dots,n}$, but the will does not act *contingently*, if it does not act contingently *at*

---

[30] *Ordinatio* I 39.19 (*Opera Omnia* VI 423): 'Ad tertium dico quod est potentia *ante* actum: non "*ante*" *duratione*, sed "*ante*" *ordine naturae*, quia illud quo *praecedit naturaliter*, ut *praecedit* actum *naturaliter*, posset esse cum opposito illius actus.'

[31] Ibid.: 'Quando causa causans libere et contingenter causat, *praecedit natura* suum effectum. Et in illo instanti in quo causat, contingenter causat, quia si non pro illo instanti contingenter causaret, non causaret contingenter, quia tunc contingenter non causat pro alio instanti.'

the very time it *acts*.[32] So, it is necessary that the will or an agent works *contingently*, when it works, if there is the slightest possibility to act *contingently* and not necessarily. If it does not work *contingently* for that time, it works *necessarily*, for *not-contingently* means *necessarily*.[33] Against this background, Duns Scotus is transforming *natura/naturaliter* into a key concept. If the concept of *time* is systematically banished from determining the nature of reality, contingency, and necessity, there is a vacancy to be filled. Duns replaces the diachronic framework by a synchronic framework of *one and the same time* (*in eodem tempore*),[34] but the moral of this move is the introduction of a new and strict concept of *the nature of x*. If we abstract from the history and dynamics over time and focus on *one and the same time*, *synchronic contingency* turns out to be *structural* contingency. This kind of *contingency* and of *necessity* rests on the inner nature of the proposition. We move on to modal logic and ontology. In the Aristotelian model, physics does the job. According to the modern nineteenth-century historicism, history does the job. If necessitarianism would do, the philosopher may resign, but if it is wrong, there is work to be done.[35]

6.4.1 A law of modal distribution $(M p \,\&\, M q) \rightarrow M (p \,\&\, q)$?

What *structural priority* means is aptly illustrated by the issue of modal distribution and the conjunctive *et* (&). We have seen that the whole battle boils down to the difference between rejecting or accepting $p \,\&\, M -p$ in the case of p being contingent.[36] At the close of *Lectura* I 39, a kind of appendix is found where Duns discusses three

---

[32] Likewise, the will – or whichever agent – does not act *necessarily* if it does not act necessarily *at the very time* it acts. The diachronic model teaches us that *necessary* means *always*, just as *contingent* means *not-always*. This would imply that the nature of *tomorrow* – continuous, or not – would define the status of *necessary*. However, when I would act necessarily, then I act necessarily precisely when I act, and not tomorrow.

[33] Within the diachronic framework, the will acts *necessarily* as such and never acts contingently, for *contingently* and *necessarily* are no variable concepts. If one acts necessarily, it is necessary that one acts necessarily and if one acts contingently, then it is necessary too that one acts contingently.

[34] *Ordinatio* I 39.17: 'Et istae duae propositiones verificantur, quia significantur attribuere praedicata sua subiecto *pro eodem instanti*; et hoc quidem verum est, nam voluntati isti *in eodem instanti* convenit *non velle a* cum possibilitate ad oppositum pro *a*, sicut significatur inesse cum illa de possibili.'

[35] Where Scotus uses *naturâ* language, the theory of modalities comes to the fore.

[36] In this light, the impact of necessitarianism is easily detected, for $p \,\&\, M -p$ does not hold in the case of p being necessary. If necessary propositions are the only ones, we must reject $p \,\&\, M -p$.

objections (§§88–90). §88 raises the matter of a supposedly contingent will of God, §90 utilizes the idea of *structural moments* (see §6.5), but §89 introduces a logical puzzle, while these objections are responded to in the concluding §§91–93. The counterargument of §89 discusses the central Scotian thesis that

> *A will, willing something, can consistently not-will the same thing.*

This thesis is objected to, for if

> the fact that the will wills something at *a* and the fact that it could still *not-will* it at *a*, are compatible at the same time, then the fact that the will can *will* something at *a* and the fact that it can *not-will* that same thing at *a*, are compatible at the same time; and so, it can *not-will* and *will* at the same time.[37]

The opponent is convinced that this proposal is logically absurd, since it ends up in a blatant contradiction and his criticism starts with a generally accepted rule: *factuality* entails *possibility* (*ab esse ad posse valet consequentia*). Because Duns had already stated that the opposite possibility is also acceptable, the opponent asserts the possible simultaneity of two opposite possibilities. He straightforwardly derives a contradiction:

> It is possible that (*a wills* at *t* that *p* and that *a* does *not will* at *t* that *p*).

Duns criticizes this move in *Lectura* I 39.92 which appeals to the method of making a distinction in terms of *in sensu composito* and *in sensu diviso*. His reply is without embellishment:

> We can concede 'The will can will something at *a* and The will can not-will that same thing at *a*' according to the divided sense. Yet, it does not follow that it can *not-will and will* at the same time, just as
>> *This body can be in that place at a*
>> *and another body can be in the same place at a.*
>> *Therefore: two bodies can be at the same time in that place*
> is not valid, and neither is
>> *I can bear this weight at a*
>> *and I can bear that weight at a.*
>> *Therefore: I can bear this and that weight at once at a.*[38]

---

[37] Ibid.: 'Si igitur stant simul quod voluntas *velit* aliquid in *a*, et tamen quod posset *nolle* illud in *a*, stabunt simul quod voluntas potest *velle* aliquid in *a* et potest *nolle* illud idem in *a*, et sic simul potest *nolle* et *velle*.'

[38] *CF* 186, and §92: 'Ad aliud dicendum quod *divisim* est concedendum quod "voluntas potest *velle* in *a* aliquid" et quod "voluntas potest illud idem *nolle* in *a*"; non tamen sequitur quod simul potest *nolle* et *velle*.'

Duns Scotus parries this objection by formulating two possible propositions:

> The will can will something at a

and:

> The will can not-will that same thing at a.

The conjunction of these propositions does not yield the contradictory conjunction

> The will wills something at a and the will does not will that same thing at a

which, of course, is impossible. Here, the systematic reply is extraordinarily brief and crisp, even for Duns: 'We have to grant according to the divided sense that "the will can will something at a" and "the will can not-will that same thing at a",' but why does the challenged consequent not follow? Here, we have to remind ourselves of the new Scotian sense of the divided, or analytical, sense (see §6.3). The essence of this new divided sense consists of two elements: (1) the proposition to be considered according to this divided sense has to be analyzed into a conjunction of two or more propositions, and (2) one of these propositions or each of them has to be qualified by a modal operator (nota). In this way, opposite predicates can also be ascribed for one and the same time, for example:

> Something white can be black reads in the divided sense: a is white and it is possible that a is black (Lectura I 39.48); a white man is necessarily a sense-gifted being reads in the divided sense: a is white and it is necessary if a is a man, then a is a sense-gifted being; he who can will something can not-will it reads in this sense: it is possible that a wills that p and it is possible that a does not will that p.[39]

The first step consists of dividing, that is analyzing, a complex proposition into two or more propositions to make clear the inner structure. The second step consists of elucidating the relationship between the main components with the help of the new notions of synchronic possibility or synchronic necessity once the different components have been separated. This method has matured in Ordinatio I 39 and potentia in the sense of potentia ad opposita boils down to

---

[39] The interpretations according to the composite sense are, respectively: it is possible that a white thing is black; a white man is a necessary white and sense-gifted being; and it is possible that a wills something and does not will it.

the modern modal operator *possible* (M).[40] However, Duns is wrong only if the suppressed presupposition used by the opponent in order to derive his contradiction is right. The opponent proposes the following deduction:

> If it is possible that *a wills* at *t* that *p* and it is possible that *a* does *not will* at *t* that *p*, *then* it is possible that (*a wills* at *t* that *p* and that *a* does *not will* at *t* that *p*).

This move is a bit more complicated than the analysis of the arguments in *Lectura* I 38.55–57 and their replies – and in *Ordinatio* I 39.18–19 – show, because there the opponent implicitly made use of *If it is possible that not-p, then not-p*. Here, use is made of

> If it is possible that *p* and if it is possible that *q*, then it is possible that (*p* and *q*).

Both parties accept:

> If it is possible that *p* and *q*, then it is possible that *p* and it is possible that *q*.

So, the difference between the two rival approaches seems to be a tiny one: Duns Scotus rejects

> If it is *possible that p* and if it is *possible that q*, then it is *possible* that (*p* and *q*)

while the opposition still accepts it.[41]

According to Wolter, Duns Scotus only counters 'to the specific objection unique to the *Reportatio*,' but both the objection and the reply are also found in *Lectura* I 39 and in *Ordinatio* I 39.[42] The second-last objection of *Lectura* I 39.89 is presented and discussed as

---

[40] We may say, as Duns does not, that the opponent commits the logical mistake of considering the conjunction M *a*W*p* & M *a*–W*p* equivalent to M (*a*W*p* & *a*–W*p*) which implies that an explicit contradiction is possibly true. If an explicit contradiction can be derived from what is stated, then what is stated is proved to be wrong by *modus tollens*.

[41] The difference consists in either accepting or rejecting the following law of distribution: (M *p* & M *q*) → M (*p* & *q*). Notice that *Lectura* I 39.89 repeats *potest* in the consequent of the challenged counter-argument: *potest* nolle et velle (= *potest* (nolle et velle)) (// M (*p* & *q*)). See the ample assessment in §16.8.

[42] See *Lectura* I 39.89 and 92 and *Ordinatio* I 39.20, respectively. Cf. CV (1992) 194–197 and 200–203 and CF 187 note 110: 'He [= Wolter] overlooked the fact that they also occur at this place, the end of *Lectura* I 39. as a kind of appendix. In the *Reportatio* they take their more logical place, as they do in what Wolter calls the *Apograh* [= *Appendix A* of the *Ordinatio*].' See Wolter, 'God's Knowledge of Future Events,' *The Philosophical Theology of Scotus*, 306–308. Wolter also signals differences between *Lectura* and *Reportatio* which are non-existent.

the fourth objection in addition to the series of three objections from *Lectura* I 39.55–57.[43] *Reportatio* I 39 and *Lectura* I 39 offer the same kind of rebuttal by indicating a general point of view and by presenting concrete examples to give the natural impression that the view of the opponent must be false. The terminology is similar, both in *Reportatio Parisiensis* I 39 and in *Ordinatio* I 39, but the reply in *Ordinatio* I 39.20 goes further and tries to point out explicitly the logical blunder of the criticism:

> I reply to this point according to the Philosopher in *Metaphysica* IX: he who has a potency for opposites acts just as he has that potency to act, but he does not have the possibility to act so that its modality concerns the end term of what is possible, nor the possibility itself, since I simultaneously possess the possibility of opposites, but not a possibility of simultaneous opposites.[44]

Here, Duns Scotus points out that the synchronic contingency of opposites functions in precisely the same way as someone has possibilities to act in the real world. Of course, the possibility of opposites is not to be understood in a self-contradictory manner. The different possible end terms ought not to be conjoined. The modality of *possibility* does not elicit the end term of what can be done. The possibility of opposites does not consist of opposites going possibly together, but it means that alternative 1 of a set of possible alternatives is possible and that the opposite alternative 2 is possible too. I possibly actualize p at t and at t I possibly actualize *not-p*, but the opponent takes it also to be – Duns suggests – that I possibly actualize p *and not-p*. However, this is completely excluded. There is no possibility of opposites which go together for me (non habeo *potentiam ad opposita simul*). I simultaneously enjoy opposite alternatives, but the opposite alternatives are not conjoined together for one and the same time.[45]

Seventeenth-century thought distinguished *simultas potentiae* ($M\ p\ \&\ M\ -p$) from *potentia simultatis* ($M\ (p_t\ \&\ -p_t)$) – the first

---

[43] The parallel text is found in *Ordinatio* I 39.18, where the replies occur in §19.

[44] *Ordinatio* I 39.20 (*Opera Omnia* VI 424): 'Ad istud respondeo – secundum Philosophum IX *Metaphysicae* – quod habens *potentiam ad opposita* sic faciet ut faciendi habet potentiam: non autem ut potentiam habet faciendi ita quod modus referatur *ad terminum potentiae*, non ad ipsam potentiam, quia simul habeo *potentiam ad opposita*, sed non *ad opposita simul*.'

[45] The maximalist modal distribution law of the opposition which reads ($M\ aWp\ \&\ M\ a–Wp$) $\leftrightarrow M\ (aWp\ \&\ a–Wp)$ is untenable. It is not accepted in any system of modern modal logic – see Hughes and Cresswell, *A New Introduction to Modal Logic*, chapters 2 and 3. The issue of modal distribution is one of the logical roads along which the dilemmas between contingency thought and necessitarianism are decidable. See §§16.4 and 16.8.

concept is perfectly acceptable, but the second is impossible.[46] This terminology is derived from Duns Scotus' mature terminology, for example in *Ordinatio* I 39.21, while the particular passage has no parallel, either in *Lectura* I 39 or in *Reportatio Parisiensis* I 39.[47]

6.4.2 *Ante/ordine naturae*

The debate regarding modal distribution which Duns deals with in terms of his new tool of the *divided sense* finely illustrates what he means by *structural priority* (*prioritas naturae*). The attack of the opponent is blocked by granting $p \to Mp$ and the implication

$$M (aWp \& aWq) \to (M aWp \& M aWq)$$

and by denying the converses $Mp \to p$ and

$$(M aWp \& M aWq) \to M (aWp \& aWq)$$

If Duns Scotus stresses the *ante naturâ* character of q with respect to p (*Lectura* I 39.60) or the '*ante*' *ordine naturae* character or the *prioritas naturae* (*Ordinatio* I 39.19) of q, he indicates that q is a *strictly necessary condition* of p. If p entails q, although q does not entail p, then q enjoys structural priority over p.

The enormous difference in comparison with the old model consists in the treatment a *potency* enjoys there: according to the old model, it is something which already exists in the factual world in order to explain a later event, while, in Duns Scotus' worldview, a possibility is not a causal item at all. In sum, disconnecting *nature* and *time* already decides the match of the conceptual structures. *Nature* (*structure*) is essentially distinguished from *time* and the *only possible world* model is dropped. The targeted model treats accidental and essential properties and contingent and necessary propositions in the same way and if we leave this model, contingent propositions are distinguished from necessary ones by seeing that temporally indexing does not change the logical-ontological status of a proposition. Therefore, the point of all this is that we have to address the issue of the *nature* of anything in its own right. *Nature* has been emancipated itself from itself, for *logic* has been emancipated itself from itself.

---

[46] See Vos, 'Ab uno disce omnes,' *Bijdragen* 60 (1999) 198–201, and Beck, 'Gisbertus Voetius (1589–1676): Basic Features of His Doctrine of God,' in Van Asselt and Dekker (eds), *Reformation and Scholasticism*, 215–217.

[47] The chronological order is: *Lectura* I 39 (1298), *Reportatio Parisiensis* I 39 (autumn semester 1302 and Christmas Holiday 1302–03), and *Ordinatio* I 39 (after 1304).

6.5 *INSTANTIA* (STRUCTURAL MOMENTS)

Duns Scotus needed a new model in the process of reconstructing theology, but he was also able to derive such a model from his own academic world. The techniques and theory of disputational dialogue (*ars obligatoria*) shows up the same terminology Duns utilized in trying to make clear what he meant (Chapter 5). The basic idea of the *ars obligatoria* is that of *one and the same time*: *in eodem instanti/tempore*, for it is not allowed to change one's view in the course of the exchange of thoughts. The dialogue between the opponent and the defendant is supposed to take place *at one and the same time*. This is elaborated in an analysis of the *positio* with the help of the idea of *one time* (*retorquere ad unum tempus*). Sherwood's crucial qualifications *discrete* and *instans indivisibile* originated from Nicholas of Paris, who had already added the point of view of *tempus incorruptibile/corruptibile*, and this Oxonian tradition was passed on to Duns, but he also dropped the *non-synchrony* rule.[48] The alternatives which are discussed are assumed to hold *for one and the same time*. The model of the *ars obligatoria* is applied to logical and ontological dilemmas and the harvest of solving these puzzles yields innovations which govern Duns Scotus' reconstruction of theology. The pattern of *diachrony* is transformed into the model of *synchrony* (§6.3), but the bare notion of *structure* is rather simple. The next step is transforming basic temporal distinctions, like *ante* and *post*, and *prior* and *posterior*, into systematic and structural ones so that the bare outlines of a new approach which rests on depth analysis are introduced (§§6.4–6.5). However, such a basic duality of *priority* and *non-priority* is still simple and not very complex, how fundamental it may be. The device of *structural moments* (*instantia*) tries to fill in this gap.

In fifteenth-century philosophy, the formal distinctions (§6.7) and the analytical tool of *instantia* (*structural moments*) were considered to be distinctive of the *via* of the *scotistae*. Scotists were often called *formalistae* and many Scotist experts fabricated treatises on *formalitates* in the course of six centuries, thus we find a tradition of famous names such as Francis Mayronis, Antonio Trombeta and Maurice O'Fihely among them.[49]

The *instantia* device is already present in the *Lectura*. We distinguish between the theory and its thrilling complications. The *instantia* device

---

[48] See *Lectura* I 39.56 and 59, CF 130–133 and 136–139, and §§5.3 ff.
[49] See Grajewski, *The Formal Distinction of Duns Scotus*, XII–XIV.

is internally linked with the basic ambiguity of understanding Duns
Scotus' ontology. Thus first we explain the device, and, second, we deal
with the complication.

6.5.1   The *instantia* device

A dense formulation is found in the last section of *Lectura* I 39:

> The intellect of God, seeing his essence *at the first moment*, sees all
> things according to their knowable being, since in terms of that
> moment they are constituted into their knowable being, but still they
> have no being in producible being *before* they have voluntative being
> by the will. Therefore, when a thing has that voluntative status, the
> intellect of God sees it in seeing his own essence.[50]

The tool of the different *structural moments* is applied to the relation
between divine knowledge and divine will and the distinction
between the first and second moments is connected with the concept
of *before*, taken in its new structural meaning. Thus the starting point
is the theory of divine knowledge.

> God can know whatever is knowable. He can only know what He
> actually knows, since there is no potency in Him. Therefore, He has
> everything knowable in his mind and, so, everything knowable is eter-
> nally known.[51]

The pattern of *omni*science is connected with the idea of *knowability*. God does not only know everything that is in fact the case, but
also everything knowable. However, what there is cannot be derived
from the whole of what is knowable. Knowledge of factual events is
not entailed by knowledge of what is knowable, just as what is factual
is not entailed by what is possible, although what is possible is
entailed by what is factual, and what is factual is comprised of what
is possible. The logic of *structural priority* is at work. What enjoys the
priority of the *first moment* is seen under the aspect of what is essential without any specifying qualification and, at the same time, most
universal. From the ontological point of view, all possible reality is

---

[50] *Lectura* I 39.93: 'Intellectus divinus *in instanti primo* videns essentiam suam, videt omnes
res secundum earum *esse intelligibile*, quia tunc constituuntur in *esse intelligibili*, sed adhuc
non habent esse in esse producibili *antequam* habeant *esse volitum* a voluntate; et ideo
quando habet res illam rationem, eam videt in videndo essentiam suam.'

[51] *Lectura* I 35.15: 'Deus potest intelligere quodcumque intelligibile, non autem potest intelligere nisi quod actu intelligit, quia in ipso non est potentia. Igitur, habet omne intelligibile
in intellectu suo aeternaliter cognitum.'

what comes first. From the theological point of view, the essential property of God which is most universal comes first. Within the Scotian framework, essentiality and universality do not coincide, since necessity and essentiality do not coincide any more. God has this first-rate knowledge and, so, from the epistemic point of view, God's self-knowledge is primary. God has this knowledge since He is God. From this knowledge flows what is the best possible knowledge of everything else, for there is a point of contact between God's properties and what comes ontologically first.

In this way, Duns' terminology is to be explained: the intellect of God sees his essence *at the first moment*. In the light of this self-knowledge, God sees all things as far as they are knowable. Duns says: they are known by God according to their knowable being. So, this divine knowledge constitutes them in terms of that moment into their knowable being. Nevertheless, factual reality cannot be explained on the basis of these structural moments.[52] Since the contingent states of affairs cannot be eliminated, we need a further moment to explain the complete ontological status of what there is, including its contingency.

At this point, Duns introduces the divine will.[53] As Duns says in his terminology of *Lectura* I 39.93, it still has no producible being *before* it is willed and has voluntative being by God's will. The role of the voluntative structural moment is to lend status to an open, undetermined situation. Its role is crucial. It completes the ontological status of what was still only knowable. So, it also completes the epistemic status, for, of course, God knows what He wills. In fact, this structural moment itself consists of several moments. Every structural moment is essential, but not deducible from what enjoys priority. These moves are a reply to the objection worded in §90. The stance of the objector is quite helpful in showing how Duns' ontology has to be interpreted.[54]

---

[52] Knowledge of *Actua* is included in knowledge of all possible worlds, but all possible knowledge does not specifically entail which possible world is *Actua*. If knowledge of *Actua* could be derived from the knowledge of all possible worlds, *Actua* would be the only possible world. However, it is impossible that there is only one possible world. Systematically, it is clarifying to expound Duns' theory of divine knowledge and will in terms of the ontology of possible worlds, but, historically it is not correct, because medieval thought has no theory of possible worlds. The systematic tendency of Knuuttila's interpretation is correct, but it is no exegesis of what Duns actually writes. Where the concept of *possible world* can play its role, is the *neutral proposition* is redundant. See §16.5.

[53] See *Lectura* I 39.53 f. and 62 ff., and CF 104 ff., 124–129 and 141 ff.

[54] It delivers the evidence to decide the differences between Knuuttila and Normore.

6.5.2   A complicated objection

The theological objector of *Lectura* I 39.90 is a Christian theologian. He shares many theological notions with Duns. He not only accepts a doctrine of God's essence and existence, intellect and omniscience, but also a doctrine of God's creativity and creation and will. Neither does he identify all these aspects. He starts from Duns' own proposals and he also uses the idea of different moments, but the way he handles them is rather different from Duns. His thesis is something Duns himself has put forward in *Lectura* I 35.13–15: the divine essence represents something real (*res*) according to all its aspects, and, according to the objector, these aspects are all in line. What is to be derived from this complaint?

In fact, Duns' device of *structural moments* is objected to by criticizing his theory of the neutral proposition (§§62–66). There is a paradoxical ring in stating the difficulty: the divine intellect *first* grasps what is to be done, but not as something which must be done. The opponent spots that, according to Duns, *what is to be done* (*operandum, faciendum*) has to be linked with the divine will. It is the divine will which constitutes something into *producible being* so that it is to be done. The primary aspect of what there is, is *knowability*. The criticism of the opponent is very instructive. He derives from Duns' theory that the divine intellect knowing everything follows from the divine essence, considered in itself, but the divine intellect knows everything so that it lacks every aspect which might determine the divine essence.[55] The objector is convinced that this is sheer incoherence, since the divine essence represents something real (*res*) according to *every* aspect. Therefore, at the first structural moment (*in primo instanti naturae*), the divine essence represents just what is to be made, to the divine intellect. The paradoxical ring of the formulation originates from the objector's way of putting his logical complaint. According to him, Duns states that what is to be done is grasped as what is *not* to be done. Duns simply contradicts himself.

Therefore, Duns' main moves have to be denied. What is to happen follows from the divine essence and the divine intellect so that it is possibly promulgated by the divine will. *Operandum, fiendum, producibile* do not depend on the divine will as predicates, but these aspects are given in the divine essence, representing them to the divine

---

[55] Compare *Lectura* I 39.90 and *Lectura* I 35.14.

will by the divine intellect. This viewpoint distinguishes moments of reality, but here all moments are in line.[56] This debate clarifies two issues: the historical issue of the tendency of Duns' ontology: does the domain of knowability coincide with creation, or not? As to the historical issue, according to Duns, there is a moment of choice and decision between the *knowable being* and the *voluntative being*.

As to the systematic issue, the line of the objector is untenable, for its consequences are that what is knowable, what is to be done and producible, and what is willed by God are strictly equivalent. So, if anything, an entity or a proposition, is selected, it does not only belong to what is knowable, but what falls under what is knowable is also selected. So, there is nothing that is not selected. However, if there is nothing that is not selected, all selected beings are necessary beings and all selected propositions are necessary ones. Is this possible? Is it possible that the domain of knowability coincides with the domain of voluntative being? It is possible that it coincides, but it is impossible that it necessarily coincides.[57]

Is this all to be said on *making distinctions*? A simple set of parallel distinctions is not sufficient to cope with reality. Since there is only multidimensional reality, we need the device of *structural moments* to do justice to complicated reality. There are many kinds of entities and many kinds of properties. Here Duns' theory of the formal distinction fits in. The *formal* distinction belongs to a family of distinctions, as do the *real* and the *rational* distinction, and this theory presupposes the theory of the *real* and the *rational relation* on the one hand (§6.6.1), and the concept of *identity* (§6.6.2) on the other.

6.6 REAL AND RATIONAL RELATIONS AND IDENTITY

6.6.1 Real and rational relations

A text from *Lectura* I 31 is the starting point. The context is definitely theological, for the initial question of *Lectura* I 31 runs as follows: 'Are *equality*, *similitude* and *identity* real relations in God?' First, we ask what are *real relations* (*relationes reales*)? Likewise, we shall ask: what is *identity*? In his personal response to the question Duns starts

---

[56] In modern terms: all ontological alternatives coincide with the epistemic alternatives, and all epistemic alternatives coincide with the voluntative ones. See also §7.10 on Normore versus Knuuttila.

[57] On ontological dilemmas, see §16.4.

with an analytical preamble as he is accustomed to. The vital text runs as follows:

> There are only three elements to be required for a *real relation*: first, it is required that the *foundation* is real and that the end term is real too; second, it is required that the foundation really differs from the end term and the one term from the other, and, third, it is required that the relation follows on the foundation and the end term on the basis of the nature of the first term.[58]

Moreover, Duns informs us in *Quaestio Quodlibetalis* VI 82 that this definition is the common one.[59] Now we are able to extract explicitly a definition of 'real relation' (*relatio realis*) from Duns' list of conditions:

> *aRb* is given and *R* is a *real relation* only if,
> (1) both the foundation of *R* and the end term *b* really exist,
> (2) *a* and *b* are real without being identical

and

> (3) *R* and *a* and *b* are entailed by the existence of *R*'s foundation.

The adjective 'real' in the expression 'real relation' returns in every condition of Duns' threefold definition. In such a relation three factors are involved. If the relation is a binary one, the terms of the relation and the relation itself require that there have to be at least two individuals which are definitely distinct from each other. On the basis of this ontological difference of being two distinct entities, they enjoy a relation.[60] On the one hand, the qualification 'real' amounts to saying that in fact, this is about a relation between truly existing entities. So, the relation itself is factually existing too. On the other

---

[58] *Lectura* I 31.6: 'Respondeo quod sunt *relationes reales*, nam ad *relationem realem* non requiruntur nisi tria: requiritur enim *primo* quod fundamentum sit reale et terminus realis, et *secundo* quod fundamentum realiter differat a termino et extremum a extremo, et *tertio* requiritur quod fundamentum et terminum consequatur relatio ex natura rei.' *Ordinatio* I 31.6 repeats this definition. The second condition is now worded as follows: 'Quod extremorum sit *distinctio realis*.' The same definition is used in Alluntis (ed.), *Juan Duns Escoto. Cuestiones cuodlibetales*, VI 5 and 82.

[59] Alluntis, *Cuestiones cuodlibetales* VI 82: *Conclusio generalis*. Ex his tribus articulis concluditur solutio quaestionis: 'Si enim – secundum *communem sententiam* – nisi ista tria: primum, fundamentum reale quod scilicet sit in re et ex natura rei; secundum, et extrema realia et realiter distincta; tertium, et quod ipsa ex natura rei insit extremis, absque scilicet omni consideratione intellectus, vel absque operatione potentiae extrinsecae, [...] sequitur quod haec *aequalitas* erit *relatio realis*.'

[60] According to this crucial condition of the definition, the *identity relation* between the Morning Star and the Evening Star is not a 'real' one, because they are the same star.

hand, in the case of *aRb*, *R* being a *real relation*, both *R* and *b* are entailed by the nature of *a* which exists in reality.

Let us assume that *a* exists. In virtue of (3), we conclude that *a* enjoys *R*, for *R* is *essential* to *a*. Otherwise, it would not be entailed by *a*'s existence, because a property is only essential to *a* if *a* cannot lack it. Therefore, if *a* exists, then *a* enjoys *R*, but because *R* entails *being R to b*, *b*'s existence is entailed too. We conclude that the notion of a *real relation* is a very specialized notion which differs considerably from the modern notion of *being real*. What matters is the role of the *foundation*. A relation *R* is only real if *R* enjoys a *fundamentum* and the *foundation* of *R* is a specific feature of *a*: the nature of *a* which has to entail *R* and its end term. When we follow what characterizes *a* essentially, we get the relation to be considered. This is precisely what the term *realis* tells us, since a *res* is something according to its essential aspects (see §6.7). In sum, a *real relation* depends on its *foundation* (*fundamentum*) – see §4.11.

Rational relation

Now we can easily understand what a *rational* relation means.

> A *rational relation* is a relation where at least one condition is missing.

If at least one of the considered conditions for being a *real relation* is missing, then *R* and *b* are possibly absent, although *a* is given. In such cases, the relation is called *rational* (*relatio rationis*), although the involved relation might be quite *real* in the modern sense as we can observe when Duns continues his discussion:

> For those things which are *rationally* (*secundum rationem*) related because any of these conditions are missing, are related by a *rational relation*.[61]

In the case of a *rational relation*, at least one condition is missing: contradictory properties are a helpful example. We have *Pa* & *Qb*, while *Pa* entails *b* possessing *–Q*. Therefore, in virtue of the contradiction which entails the exclusion of *b*, the other component of the contradictory pair *a* and *b* does not exist, for if (*Q* & *–Q*)*b*, then it is impossible that *b* exists. There is no end term (*terminus*) and, so, condition (1) is violated. The other way around, the end term may exclude the

---

[61] *Lectura* I 31.6: 'Nam illa quae referuntur *secundum rationem* (propter defectum alicuius istorum), referuntur *relatione secundum rationem*.'

foundation of the relation and, therefore, we have to conclude that a *contradiction* constitutes a *rational relation*. So, in the case of a *rational relation* R, the relation R does not entail its end term, since its foundation does not entail its end term.

6.6.2   Identity

The meanings of *identitas*, *simplicitas*, and *actus purus* are often difficult to come by. These terms have caused much theoretical confusion. They are not only stumbling blocks in interpreting medieval thought, but 'neoscholastics,' both on the Catholic and the Protestant side, have also derived ideas from them which definitely run against the flow of medieval scholasticism. The term 'real relation' and the medieval denial of a real relation between God and his creation gave rise to the conclusion that the faith behind such an unbiblical relation must have been utterly unrealistic and far from a Christian sense of reality. Moreover, the identity and simplicity sentences occasioned the view that monism must be at hand. So, let us explain Duns' definitions of *identitas* and his theory of identity. There are two concepts of *identity*. Both are applicable in the doctrine of God.

*Identity*₁

The first concept of identity – *identity*₁ – is the identity of *a*, being identical with *a* itself, being the same as *a* itself.[62] Duns' example is a theological one, that of a divine Person, for the Father is identical with the Father and the Son is identical with the Son. Of course, this notion of *identity*₁ can also be applied to orchids and books, but we immediately realize too how much modern intuition fails in understanding this identity language when we see Duns stating in *Lectura* I 31.6 that, in the cases of $a = a$ and $a = b$, the identity relation is a *rational* relation.

   In terms of Duns' definitions of 'real relation' and of 'rational relation,' it is clear why this must be so. This concept of *identity*₁ does not satisfy the condition that the terms of a real relation must be different. *Identity* in the sense of *a's being identical with oneself* is a relation in Duns' terms, but not a real one. It is a rational relation. In his terminology, it cannot be a 'real' one, but it is perfectly clear too that

[62] *Lectura* I 31.23: 'In divinis duplex est *identitas*: una qua persona est eadem sibi, et alia qua una persona habet identitatem cum alia.' Cf. *Lectura* I 31.6: *Identitas eiusdem ad se* non est relatio realis, quia non est distinctio relatorum. See also §4.10, §6.6, and §7.5.

it is *real* in the modern sense of 'real.' From the modern point of view, we easily recognize *identity*₁ as the Leibnizian notion of *identity*.[63]

Identity₂

The second concept of identity – *identity*₂ – is quite a different matter. Again the example is a theological one: the one Person of God Triune *enjoys identity with* (*habet identitatem cum*) another Person. *Identity*₂ constitutes a real relation, because all three conditions are met: there is a real foundation, namely the nature of God, and the relational terms – the divine Persons – are really and truly distinct. A *real* identity follows from the divine nature, existing in two Persons. The foundation of a *real relation* does not only entail the relation, but also the terms of the relations, including the end term.

According to Duns, this divine *being identical* is perfect identity, not found in creation. Only in God do we see identity in diversity. In the world of creation we also observe entities belonging together, but this unity of belonging together does not derive from their nature, let alone that only the foundation of one nature accounts for their unity. Their unity is contingent, so the one term may lack the other term. The real identity of God is the identity of the divine nature constituting itself in three Persons. Creation lacks such a unity in order to found *identity*₂. It is clear what Duns intends to say. *Identity*₂ is a theological application of a kind of identity we often meet in the old theory of matter and individuals which may be called *material identity*. The point is not that *a* and *b* are identical themselves, but that they are present in one and the same individual.

6.7 THE FORMAL DISTINCTION

The doctrine of the *formal distinction* is considered to be a distinctive part of Duns Scotus' philosophy and Scotism in general. Its importance is seen in resolving dilemmas in the theories of divine attributes and of universality and individuality. In explaining the formal distinction, one traditionally starts with the difference between the so-called *real* and *rational distinctions*.

---

[63] We have to be aware that, in general, the term *idem* often means something quite different from 'the same' according to Leibnizian or Fregean terminology. On the logic and philosophy of relation, see Lemmon, *Beginning Logic*, 159–168, Copi, *Symbolic Logic*, 158–169, and Ishiguro, *Leibniz's Philosophy of Logic and Language*, 17–34, cf. 60–65.

6.7.1   The real distinction

If a *real distinction* is at stake, then some things *really* differ from others. Two books and two orchids, two stones and two apples are numerically different and they are really (*realiter*) different. Two golden delicious apples may be in my basket and three books on my desk at the same time, but *De primo principio* and *Reading Latin* may share each other's company, or not. The one may be there and the other only in the Late Latin Library. This way of defining the *real distinction* is at home in Thomist thinking.

> Whenever two entities are found to exist separately and apart from each other in time and space, one can immediately and validly conclude to a real distinction between them. Thus two individuals like Peter and Paul are really distinct. [...] Since composition implies parts, real composition implies real parts which by their very nature are distinct.[64]

We see that concept formation rests on the notion of matter. Wolter's formulation is straightforward too: a real physical distinction 'exists between two or more physical entities (*inter rem et rem*).'[65] Because matter matters, the notion of *matter* reigns over the theory of distinction: material separability defines real distinctness and difference. So, inseparability defines identity. Even the Thomasian doctrine of divine simplicity is rooted in the idea that materiality is the key to making distinctions. Thus the *real* distinction is defined by a criterion which may be aptly labeled the *separability criterion*. Real separability is a necessary and sufficient condition of a real distinction. Two objects x and y are separable if and only if at least x or y can exist without the other. Such *real distinctions* and differences are also acknowledged by Duns Scotus. If such a *real distinction* obtains, then there is one thing (*res*) and another thing (*res*) so that there are two, or more, material things, and not one real thing. A difference is made so that this is one thing and that is another thing.[66] The world of creation shows evident differences. 'Reality shows an evident distinction

---

[64] Grajewski, *The Formal Distinction of Duns Scotus*, 57. On the *real distinction*, see pp. 55–62, Roth, *Franz von Mayronist*, 283 ff. Cf. Weinberg, *A Short History of Medieval Philosophy*, 226, and, in particular, McCord Adams, *William Ockham* I, 16–29: 'Real distinction, distinction of reason, and formal distinction.' Cf. Wolter, 'The Formal Distinction' (1965), in *The Philosophical Theology of Scotus*, 27–41.

[65] Wolter, *The Transcendentals in the Metaphysics of Duns Scotus*, 21.

[66] *Ordinatio* I 2.402: 'Illud quod habet talem distinctionem in se non habet *rem et rem*, sed est *una res*, [...], et illa non distinguit, sicut si illa una res et ista alia.'

of real things and this distinction is twofold, namely the distinction of individuals and of natures.'[67] However, we shall see that this usage dominated by the *separability criterion* does not determine exhaustively Duns Scotus' terminology which also considers the formal distinction to be a kind of *real* distinction.[68]

6.7.2 The rational distinction

A *real* distinction clearly differs from a so-called *rational distinction*. I have an apple in my hand and I can image four parts of the apple, one for every child, but it is still one and the same apple. We may distinguish the form from the volume of a sphere and the form of the vase from its content. Along these lines, the *real distinction* and the *rational distinction* are traditionally distinguished. The one distinction concerns reality and the other distinction is a matter of the mind, without any corresponding difference in the external world.[69] Because Duns Scotus' concept formation follows different lines, this notion of *rational distinction* does not play any role of importance with him.

6.7.3 The formal distinction: a theological riddle

The literature does not deliver a simple picture at all. Let us ask what Duns may mean by *formal difference* or *formal distinction*. Dealing with the vexed problem of the relationship between the divine nature and the three Trinitarian Persons, Duns sighs that 'a great difficulty' lurks here.[70] What does the difficulty consist of? The way the 'great difficulty' arises reminds us of Ockham's complaint about the formal distinction. In terms of his semantics it is difficult to explain why

> *The divine nature is the Father,*
> *the divine nature is the Son,*
> therefore: *the Father is the Son*

is not valid. In this case, Ockham swallowed the formal distinction, but he was not prepared to admit this distinction elsewhere. The

---

[67] *Ordinatio* I 2.396: 'In re autem manifesta est *distinctio rerum*, et hoc duplex, suppositorum, *scilicet*, et naturarum.'

[68] See §6.7.6.

[69] See Weinberg, *A Short History of Medieval Philosophy*, 226, cf. *Quaestiones Metaphysicae* VII 9.4.

[70] *Lectura* I 2.258: 'Adhuc remanet magna difficultas.' Cf. 'ulterior difficultas' in *Ordinatio* I 2.388.

formal distinction was as mysterious as the Trinity itself was. Indeed, what matters in *Lectura* I 2 part 2 is the relation between the *nature* of God and the Persons, the individual subjects (*supposita*), of the Trinity. The one nature of God and the three individual subjects are *really* (*realiter*) identical, but they have also to differ from one another, since the divine nature is communicable – all three *Persons* share in the one *nature* of God. A moment of individual subjectivity (*suppositum*) in God is incommunicable. There is a difference (distinction) to be discovered. They cannot be 'indistinct.' Apart from elaborating on the trinitarian difference, Duns also deals with the issue of *differences* in itself.

6.7.4 Terminological preliminaries

For the modern mind, the usage of *res* and *realis* is difficult to grasp. We have already felt this in trying to understand what a *real relation* might be (§6.6.1). The medieval formulation that there is no *real* relation between God and his creation has caused much scandal in the literature. However, this statement can be accounted for by the combination of the meaning of *realis* (*real*) and Christian contingency thought. There is only a *real* relation *aRb* if the nature of *a* entails both the existence of *a*, the relation *R*, and the end term *b*, but creation is not entailed by the nature of God. So, there is no real relation between God and creation, although there is a real relation between creation and God. This meaning of *realis* (*real*) originates from the basic meaning of *res*. Here, the 'thing' and 'matter' of school dictionaries are not quite helpful, although a *res* is something real that matters. On the contrary, the old translation of the Greek *onta* by *res* is quite helpful. A *res* is something real in concrete reality, but it is there because of its own essence.[71] The complicating element of essentiality is given in the original meanings of *res*, *ousia*, and *substantia*, in Latin and Greek. A *res* is a thing, something real, considered from the viewpoint which accounts for its reality, namely the viewpoint of

---

[71] The same phenomenon is met in *ousia*: an *ousia* is an individual substance in virtue of its own being. Its essence is also called 'sub-stance' which literally means 'under-standing.' The idea is that the essence is standing under an individual substance in order to support and buttress it – its eternal 'withstand' (in Dutch we have: *be-stand*, cf. *bestand zijn tegen* = to withstand) in virtue of which it is existence-proof. In virtue of its eternal *ousia*, the temporal *ousia* can 'withstand' the vicissitudes of the *kosmos*. The roots of the Aristotelian *proote ousia – deutera ousia* distinction lie in this ancient sense of a material thing as a bond of time and eternity, for they are two aspects of one and the same sub-stance, *ousia*.

its essence.[72] Against this background, attention has to be paid to the semantic information Duns himself provides. *Real* is what is mind-independent. This statement is enigmatic in terms of ancient thought, because ancient thought does not know of the concept of *individual mind*, but medieval thought had familiarized itself with the notions of the *individual* mind of an individual person whose individuality is essential (Chapter 11). It follows neither the footsteps of British empiricism, nor those of German idealism. Duns states:

> I mean by *really* what exists, but in no way by an epistemic act. Nay, it would be such an entity, if there were no intellect to consider it at all. By '*existing before* every mental act' I mean: it is there and it is so.[73]

6.7.5 Formal non-identity

The distinction Duns wants to develop is called a *distinctio a parte rei* (§260) and *differentia virtualis* (§271). If a *formal* distinction obtains, a certain feature of *non-identity* has to be pointed out. '*Formal* identity is not necessarily to be deduced from *real* identity' (*Ordinatio* I 2.408). All this talk of *real* and *rational* presupposes that we understand the terms *realis* and *secundum rationem*.[74] For Duns, the most natural designation is *formal distinction*. Within the framework of his own terminology and concept formation, the formal distinction is a *real* distinction, not to be confused with the *real distinction* of the Aristotelian traditions. The term *distinctio virtualis* is acceptable too and this term means *implicative distinction* (*Ordinatio* I 2.402). Even if an entailment or an equivalence holds, there is a difference to be pointed out. In virtue of the authority of Bonaventure, Duns also accepts *differentia rationis*, but he adds an important note on *ratio*, for the terminology of *differentia rationis* is only acceptable if one understands by *ratio* an aspect of what really exists.[75]

The issue of the *formal* difference is linked with definitions: *animal* and *rationale* are not formally identical. 'In the case of what is formally identical, both definitions coincide.'[76] Duns' comment is

---

[72] See Wippel, *Metaphysical Themes in Thomas Aquinas*, 120–122.

[73] *Ordinatio* I 2.390: 'Intelligo sic *"realiter,"* quod nullo modo per actum intellectus considerantis, immo quod talis entitas esset ibi, si nullus intellectus esset considerans; et sic esse ibi, si nullus intellectus consideraret, dico *"esse ante* omnem actum intellectus." '

[74] On *realis*, see this section, §6.6.1 and §4.9. On *ratio*, cf. §9.2.

[75] *Ordinatio* I 2.401: 'Non quod *"ratio"* accipiatur pro differentia formata ab intellectu, sed ut *"ratio"* accipitur pro *quiditate rei* secundum quod quiditas est obiectum intellectus.' Cf. §9.2.

[76] *Lectura* I 2.275: 'Idem *formaliter* sunt quae sic se habent quod in definitione unius cadit alterum. Nunc autem si *genus* et *differentia* definirentur, in definitione unius non caderet aliud.'

clear: although, within this framework, *being a rational person* entails *being sense-gifted*, *being sense-gifted* does not entail *being rational*. On the other hand, the divine nature is communicable and a divine Person is *in*communicable. So, *real identity* cannot be the only kind of identity (*Ordinatio* I 2.397–398). Identity, in the sense of *identity*₂, is a real relation (§6.7.1). One can be led astray, because this kind of identity is said of *distinct* entities. '*Formal* identity is not necessarily to be deduced from *real* identity' (*Ordinatio* I 2.408) seems an impossible statement, but what does it mean for Duns? Real identity, in the sense of *identity*₂, and the conditions of a real relation are met in this case. The terms of a real identity are distinct, although they are necessarily connected. It must be possible to point out differences. If not, there cannot be a real relation or a real identity.

Not every kind of identity is real, but it is also true that 'not every kind of identity is formal.'[77] The formal identity of *a* does not only comprise what is essential to *a*, but this formal identity is also expressed in the definition of the essence or nature of *a*. It is essential *per se primo modo*. Different 'formalities' can entail other formalities or they can entail each other, although they are not identical and belong to the same real thing or person. If two entities are *really* identical – in the sense of *identity*₂ – the difference between them must be a *formal* difference. So, *formalities* (*formalitates*) or 'realities' (*realitates*) are not property-bearers, although they imply different properties. Of course, there are also formal differences between entities which are not really identical. If there is a formal distinction at work, there are at least two formal objects. Either two different real essences correspond to these two formal objects, as in the case of understanding what *a man* is and what *a horse* is, or only one external real thing corresponds with the two formal objects, as in the case of knowing a specific *color* and what *a* color (*disgregativum*) is. Against this background, Duns states that the formal essence of God's nature does not include the characteristic property of a divine person, nor conversely. The *realitas* of God's essence and the different *realitas* of a divine Person have to be granted. They are not formally identical.[78]

---

[77] *Ordinatio* I 2.403: 'Non omnis identitas est formalis. Voco autem *identitatem formalem*, ubi illud quod dicitur sic *idem* includit illud cui sic est idem, in ratione sua formali quiditativa et per se primo modo.'

[78] If, according to the modern meaning of *strict equivalence*, properties are strictly equivalent, as in the case of *being divine* and *being the Father*, the definitions do not coincide. So, a formal distinction is at stake. Grajewski surveys the ontological applications of the formal distinction in chapter 7, the psychological ones in chapter 8 and, finally, the theological applications in chapter 9.

Thus the crucial thing is to locate the *formal distinction* in the whole of the family of kindred distinctions and relations. In terms of the Aristotelian tradition, also followed by Thomas Aquinas, Duns Scotus' *formal* distinction is not a *real* distinction. However, in terms of Scotian terminology, a *formal* distinction is *real*, since it constitutes a *real relation*, even if it is grounded in *real unity*. Duns utilizes a scale of *unity* concepts. *Aggregate unity* is found at one end of the spectrum and *formal unity* at the other (see §10.3). The point of Duns Scotus' *formal* distinction does not concern kinds of unity where it is evident that *formal differences* are also at stake. Of course, they are at stake if *aggregate* unity, *accidental* unity, and *substantial* unity are concerned (§10.3).

The best thing to do in explaining the specific role of Duns Scotus' *formal distinction* is to pay attention to his theory of *unity*. 'Perhaps the most suggestive and fruitful aspect of Scotus's thought which we shall encounter here, [...], is one which should properly be classified as a part of metaphysics: Scotus's nuanced account of the different sorts of *unity* which can be exhibited by different sorts of composite object.'[79] At the one end of the *unity* spectrum, we meet *aggregate unity* where unity is as loose as possible – as in the case of heaps and piles – and, of course, formal differences are at stake here. At the other end of the spectrum, we meet *formal unity* (*unitas formalis*, *identitas formalis*) where any distinction has been eliminated so that no *formal* distinctness can have any application. So, we have to go on with enclosing the non-trivial space still left for the *formal* distinction. The formal differences of accidental and composite units are also obvious and, thus, only *real unity* is left. In addition to the theological applications, the master examples of the *formal disctinction* are to be found in the formal differences between a category and a specifying difference, like *being sense-gifted* and *being rational*, and *enjoying individuality* and *enjoying its nature*. Such *formal* distinctions and differences must be to the point, if there obtains a formal difference between a wallaby and a ladybird.

6.7.6 Epilogue

The bottleneck of some pervasive misunderstandings consists of the old meanings of *realis* and *idem* which Duns uses, and which

---

[79] Cross, *The Physics of Duns Scotus*, 2; see also p. 7 and chapters 4–5. Cf. §10.3. Cross mainly distinguishes five sorts of *unity*: *aggregate*, *accidental*, *substantial*, *real*, and *formal unity*.

markedly differ from Thomist terminology. The traditional view
states that

> Scotus's criterion for real identity is real inseparability. In fact, real
> inseparability (such that the real separation of two or more realities
> is *logically impossible*) is *necessary and sufficient* for real identity.
> Conversely, real separability is necessary and sufficient for real dis-
> tinction. More precisely, two objects x and y are inseparable if and
> only if, both, it is not possible for x to exist without y, and it is not
> possible for y to exist without x; conversely, two objects x and y are
> separable if and only if at least one of x and y can exist without the
> other. I shall label this the 'separability criterion'.[80]

However, the separability criterion of what is to be a *real distinction*
holds for the Aristotelian way of defining a real distinction, because
the fundamental distinction between form and matter dominates the
theory of distinction. With Duns, the separability criterion does not
dominate the whole of the concept of the *real* distinction. We have to
keep in mind that he can also say that distinguishing the one divine
Person from the other is a *real* distinction. The meaning of *realis* is
partially determined from other backgrounds. The old dilemmas
still confuse recent research. Even the intelligent investigations of
Grajewski are compromised by not separating clearly the Aristotelian
logic of the *real distinction* from the Scotian language of *realis* and
formalis, where the *formal* distinction is a kind of a *real* distinction,
but according to quite different definitions of *realis* and *res*. With
Duns, the notions of *real identity*, *real distinction*, and *formal distinction* may go hand in hand. When we overlook this, the whole
theory becomes a mess. If the formal distinction is banished, these
properties are really identical – as Duns grants – but they are also formally identical. Duns rebuts this consequence, because it entails identifying all essential and equivalent properties.[81] The famous formal
distinction is primarily clarified in the light of a feature all parties
accept, namely the formal differences between a category and a specifying difference, like *being sense-gifted* and *being rational*, and
between quite different categories, like *being a man* and *being a horse*.

---

[80] Cross, *The Physics of Duns Scotus*, 8.

[81] Ibid.: 'Sic etiam si definiretur deitas, in eius definitione non caderet paternitas. Igitur, *post*
unitatem realem est unitas formalis, qua aliqua sunt idem formaliter, et non solum realiter.
Licet igitur aliqua sunt idem realiter, tamen possunt differre secundum *rationes formales*,
fundatas et ortas in re, et non per operationem intellectus.' Cf. *Ordinatio* I 2.403, and Cross,
The Physics of Duns Scotus, 7 f.

If we do not master the details of this philosophical language, the terminology gives cause to a very paradoxical ring. If two entities are said to be *identical*, they have to be *distinct* – according to the first condition of *identity*₂ (§6.6.2). Thus, here, the language of *identity* and simplicity expresses quite the reverse of what the modern mind expects. If it is said that a real distinction holds, it may be that all involved propositions are necessarily true and strictly equivalent. At any rate, the formal distinction does the job, done by *strict entailment* and *strict equivalence* in modern analytical thinking. Here, the language of *distinctness* expresses quite the reverse of what the modern mind hopes to learn. Nevertheless, all that is said here can be translated and extrapolated into modern terminology and conceptual structures so that a coherent overall philosophy arises, and it may be asked whether any alternative is able to survive the same strict surgery.

6.7.7 A personal note

Duns' practice of making distinctions and his handling of the *formal distinction* turned out to be influential, but in *Ordinatio* I 2, *pars* 2, Duns is still on his guard. The whole of his brilliant excursus on the non-identity character of the *formal distinction* (§§388–410) is introduced in a prudent way: 'I do not say this positively and I am open to any better theory.'[82] However, from *Lectura* I 2.275, it is clear that he was subjectively sure of his ground: 'He who can get it, may get it: there is no doubt in *my* mind that it is so.'[83]

6.8 A BRIEF EPILOGUE

When Duns Scotus suddenly died in Cologne in November 1308, he was in the midst of composing an astonishing oeuvre, but he was also constructing a new ramified network of concepts, partially worded in a rather specific, sometimes idiosyncratic, but still not yet stabilized, texture of terms. In understanding Duns Scotus it is crucial to master this network of terms and concepts. 'A notoriously difficult and highly original thinker, Scotus was referred to as "the subtle doctor"

---

[82] *Ordinatio* I 2.389: 'Et dico *sine assertione* et praeiudicio melioris sententiae.' This qualification expresses that the teacher does not take public responsibility for what he expounds. We would say that it is presented as a hypothesis in the privately academic sense of the word. With Duns, it only occurs a few times.

[83] *Lectura* I 2.275: 'Qui igitur potest capere, capiat quia sic esse intellectus meus non dubitat.'

because of his extremely nuanced and technical reasoning.'[84] Of course, these subtle technicalities are rooted in the tradition of the scholastic method itself. Scholastic method and training themselves are subtle and technical. Duns Scotus is no exception to the rule: he is at the summit of a scholarly landscape. He did not simply invent his many typical terms and concepts – there is a broad historical background to them. Nevertheless, intriguing as it is to explore the historical development of the key terms and the key concepts at the turn of the century, e.g. the background of the formal distinction, it usually does not offer much help for improving understanding of Duns Scotus, interesting as it certainly is.[85] First and foremost, we have to understand how his devices are woven together. Already profoundly familiar with Aristotle, John Duns discovered, again and again, that the theological dilemmas he was researching, collided both with the logical and philosophical tools he had mastered himself (see §1.4 and Chapter 4) and with many theories he had already studied. In particular, the old-fashioned modal complexes were unfit and confusing. Logic steeped in diachrony was not apt to solve the omnipresent puzzles and dilemmas of systematics.

In *Lectura* I 39.45 ff., the pattern of the old pair of *possibility* and *contingency* is maintained and their diachronic pattern is simply swung over synchronically. As to the new pair of *concepts*, still named *potency* or *possibility* and *contingency*, *diachronic* alternativity is replaced by *synchronic* alternativity. The upshot is that we not only have to study the historical series of events, but also the *nature* of a proposition. *Synchronic* alternativity is *structural* alternativity. In matters logical and philosophical, the *ordo durationis* is replaced by the *ordo naturae*. Duns' paying attention to what a term or proposition means *naturaliter/naturâ* is a natural consequence of the *synchronic contingency* revolution. If time is not the key to unveil the *nature* of concepts, we have to discover a new concept of *natura/nature*. The notions *ante* (*prae*)/*post* undergo the same process. Their *diachronic* function is *synchronically* transformed, just as the word *priority* expresses. The *prioritas de tempore* is replaced and succeeded by a *prioritas naturae*. The comic effect of these moves is that *natura* originally belonged to the

---

[84] Dumont, 'John Duns Scotus (*c*.1266–1308),' *REP* III 153 f.

[85] See Jansen, 'Beiträge zur geschichtlichen Entwicklung der *Distinctio formalis*,' *Zeitschrift für Katholische Theologie* 53 (1929) 317–344 and 517–544, Kraml, 'Beobachtungen zum Ursprung der "*distinctio formalis*",' *Via Scoti* I 305–318, and Huning, 'Petrus de Trabibus: ein Vorläufer des Johannes Duns Scotus,' *De doctrina Ioannis Duns Scoti* I 285–295. Cf. Grajewski, *The Formal Distinction of Duns Scotus*, 102–123.

same family as *time* and *duration*. When we are in possession of the new *ante* and *post* we have the beginnings of a new plural structure. If something enjoys *priority*, there is something which does not. The formal distinction feels at home in this panorama of ideas (§6.7). What if the formal distinction is rejected? We assume that *a* possesses the essential property *P* and the essential property *Q*. So, they are really identical, but there is no formal non-identity available to nuance *P* and *Q*. *P* and *Q* cannot be different. If anything inseparable from anything must be identical with anything, then all essential properties must be identical. It is necessary that everything has only *one essential* property. The principle of *simplicity* rules ontology. So, if there is any common essential property, everything there is has only one essential property and there can be only one essential property. Likewise, some theologians asserted that God can only have one attribute. Both statements are impossible.

CHAPTER 7

Ontology

7.1 INTRODUCTION

Duns Scotus' philosophy has many ontological solutions which arise from theological dilemmas and the tension originates from the familiar modal limitations of conceptual structures at home in traditional thought. At the end of the thirteenth century, there is an innovative mixture of *logica modernorum* and *theologia antiqua*. John Duns' faith, the follower of the *poverello* from Italy, cannot be accounted for in terms of semantic, logical, and ontological presuppositions which are basic to any form of necessitarianism. When one sticks to such a type of logic, semantics, or ontology, the theory of divine properties and the doctrine of the incarnation become involved in glaring inconsistencies. The language games of Christian faith, philosophical theology, and church dogmatics are utterly incoherent if Aristotelian logics and ontologies were right. This is the general background of many philosophical digressions Scotus wove into his theological expositions. His theory of *transcendent terms* (*transcendentia*) is a major illustration.

Scotus' ontology, or metaphysics, is multifaceted. §7.2 discusses the subject matter of ontology. A host of themes are then reviewed separately: the main lines of his ontology of contingency (§7.3), the neutral proposition (§7.4), essence and existence (§7.5), real, rational, ideal and eternal relations (§7.6), universals (§7.7), conceptual univocity (§7.8), transcendent terms (§7.9), and, finally, the dilemma of rival interpretations of *potentia* (§7.10).

7.2 THE SUBJECT MATTER OF ONTOLOGY

The motto of the *Prologue* in Duns' *Quaestiones super libros Metaphysicae Aristotelis* (*Quaestiones Metaphysicae*) is: *All people desire knowledge by nature*.[1] The *Prologue* itself illustrates the central

---

[1] *Opera Philosophica* III–IV: *Quaestiones super libros Metaphysicae Aristotelis* (1997).

problem of the *Quaestiones Metaphysicae*, for it consists of two layers. The basic text comprises the first eighteen sections, while a later addition is introduced by the critical note 'This proof does not seem to be definitive' (§§19–31). The discussion is rounded off in §32, dealing with the material cause of metaphysics. The original answer is offered in §16: *We all desire knowledge by nature*, because the most knowable is also what is most desirable.

7.2.1 Metaphysical knowledge

The most knowable is what is self-evident. So, we are here concerned with the most knowable knowledge, because the self-evident governs the science of metaphysics in two ways:

> But there are two senses in which things are said to be *maximally knowable*: *either* [1] because they are the first of all things known and without them nothing else can be known; *or* [2] because they are what are known most certainly. In either way, however, this science is about *the most knowable*. Therefore, this most of all is a science and, consequently, most desirable.[2]

This answer is first confirmed with the help of authoritative texts taken from Avicenna's *Metaphysica* I 5 and Aristotle's *Metaphysica* IV (§17), followed by §18 where the thesis is proved to be true.

> The need for this science can be shown in this way. From the fact that the most common things are understood first, it follows – as Avicenna proves – that the other more particular things cannot be known, unless these more common things are first known. And the knowledge of these more common things cannot be treated in some more particular science. For the same reason that one particular science could treat them, allows all the others to do so as well, since *being* and *one* are predicated equally of all, according to *Metaphysica* X, chapter 3. And thus we would have many useless repetitions. Therefore, it is necessary that some general science exists that considers *transcendent terms* as such. This science we call '*metaphysics*', which is from '*meta*' which means 'transcends' and '*ykos*' which means 'science'. It is, as it were, *transcending science*, because it is concerned with the transcendent terms.[3]

---

[2] *Questions on the Metaphysics of Aristotle by John Duns Scotus, Prologus* 16: translated by Wolter and Etzkorn (1997).

[3] *Quaestiones Metaphysicae Prologus* 18 where the conclusion reads: 'Igitur, necesse est esse aliquam scientiam universalem quae per se consideret illa transcendentia. Et hanc scientiam vocamus metaphysicam, quae dicitur a "meta," quod est trans, et "ycos" "scientia," quasi transcendens scientia, quia est de transcendentibus.'

7.2.2   The subject of metaphysical knowledge

What does the term 'transcendent' mean at this stage of Duns' personal philosophical development? In *Quaestiones Metaphysicae* I 1, the *subject* of the science *metaphysics* is discussed. The logical writings already make clear that Duns started with a concept of *being* which departs from created reality, not from a kind of a priori concept of *being*. *Being* (*ens*) implies *factuality* (*actualitas*). The *Quaestiones Metaphysicae* continue this line of thought, but in what way is it linked with the issue of the *subject* of metaphysics? Duns joins Aristotle in accepting that this science concerns all beings, but he still uses the idea of *dependence* in order to define what *metaphysics* is about.

> Not only is substance the *first subject*, but also the common attributes considered here are in it primarily, and through its nature are attributed to other posterior things. Also things other than *substance* are not only treated here as attributes demonstrable of substance, but also insofar as they are certain beings having in their own right proper attributes. Consequently, also these properties can be demonstrated of them in this science. [. . .] For *accidents* are considered in this science under a twofold aspect. Hence, all the arguments marshalled for both sides lead to this one truth. Those of the first [i.e. the view of Avicenna] show it has to do with *all beings*; those of the other side [i.e. that it is substance], that it is not about all of these about one [being], nor is it about something they all have in common; it is about a first being to which other things are attributed.[4]

7.2.3   *Quaestiones Metaphysicae* I 1.1–163

The *quaestio* 'The *subject* of metaphysical science' shows the composite nature of this work in an even more striking manner than the *Prologue* had already done. Although there are additions in the first part of this *quaestio*, the typical phenomenon that the *quaestio* consists of two parts is also met: the basic layer (the *Grundstock* of §§1–96)

---

[4] *Quaestiones Metaphysicae* I 1.96: 'Non solum autem est substantia primum, sed et passiones hic consideratae communes primo ei insunt, et per naturam attribuuntur aliis posterioribus. Alia etiam a substantia non solum hic considerantur tanquam passiones demonstrabiles de substantia, sed etiam in quantum quaedam entia in se habentia passiones. [. . .] Duplici enim ratione considerantur accidentia in ista quaestione in ista scientia. Unde omnes rationes ad utramque partem adductae concludunt unam veritatem. Primae quod haec est de omnibus entibus. Aliae quod non de omnibus istis tanquam de uno, nec de aliquo communi omnibus istis, sed de aliquo primo ad quod alia attribuuntur.'

and the added second part (§§97–163), but this added part does not expound the view on *metaphysics* which is found in the *Prologue* of the *Lectura*. In this second part, Duns indicates in which way we can say how God is both *subject* in metaphysics and likewise in theology (§103). Both the oldest and the later layer have to be dated *before* the *Lectura* text.

Duns' solution is found only at the end of the original *quaestio* – in §96 – because he paid a lot of attention to the positions of Avicenna and Averroes. Both views are rejected. Duns does not accept that the subject of metaphysics is *being as being*, nor that the *substantiae separatae* are the subject of metaphysics, but the way he argues for this rejection is surprising, for he tries to integrate both views. In the future he will refute a rival theory in terms of his own alternative. The key to his answer is that his concept of *substantia*, the subject of metaphysics, comprises both *being* and *God*. This solution, understandable from the linguistic point of view, is inspired by Henry of Ghent, but does not excel in systematic clarity.

The idiosyncratic beginning on Duns' part affects the way the definition of *metaphysica* in the *Prologue* of the *Quaestiones Metaphysicae* is dealt with. This definition takes the pride of place in the expositions of Weinberg, Kluxen, and Honnefelder. Kluxen, and Honnefelder launched the fascinating thesis of *the second beginning of metaphysics (der zweite Anfang der Metaphysik)*. This early definition is interpreted in the light of Duns' later concept of *transcendens* in the *Sententiae* books, but the *Prologue* of the *Quaestiones Metaphysicae* uses the term 'transcendent' in a way as ambiguous as *Quaestiones Metaphysicae* I 1 uses the term *substantia*.

7.2.4 *Lectura* I–II

God is not the first subject of ontology and Averroes is refuted because he teaches that the subject in metaphysics is the separated substance.[5] The subject of a higher science cannot be proved by a more restricted science. Physics cannot present the subject of metaphysics, but metaphysics is able to prove that God exists in a way much better than

---

[5] *Lectura Prologus* 97: 'Ad aliud dicitur quod Deus non est subiectum primum in metaphysica. Et falsum dicit Commentator quod subiectum in metaphysica est substantia separata, quod probatur in scientia naturali, nec potest alibi probari esse, quia non potest probari esse nisi per motum. Primo, enim falsum dicit quod naturalis probat subiectum metaphysicae esse: numquam enim scientia inferior probat subiectum scientiae superioris, unde secundum hoc metaphysica dependeret a physica.'

physics can achieve.[6] In the *Prologue* of *Lectura* I–II, the idea of *substance* does not play any role in defining what metaphysics or what ontology is all about. It is said very clearly that the subject of theology is God, just as infinite being. What then is the *first subject* of ontology? A *first subject* is a primary subject of a disposition directed towards its object.[7] In the case of ontology, the first subject contains by implication the epistemic disposition and what is required for this disposition. Discussing why *substance* has to be skipped as a candidate for being the ontological subject, Duns states that *ens* is the subject: 'which is the first subject which virtually contains everything which belongs to having ontological knowledge [= *habitus metaphysicae*].[8]

So, *being* (*ens*) is not allowed to be the ontological subject by being entailed by another notion: it has to be the basic subject of ontological propositions, but the way Duns unfolds this abstract program is full of surprises. Thus we turn to the main structures of his ontology.

7.3   THE ONTOLOGY OF CONTINGENCY

God is supremely good, just the best possible person. He deserves all possible affection and love and is the only possible source of an ocean of being from his necessary abundance. However, if God himself is absolute *necessary-being* (*necesse-esse*) and everything else depends on his activity, what do we have to say of the ontological status of everything else? Can it be otherwise than necessary? In the ontology of the young John Duns, the dilemma of divine causality towers over the crucial dilemmas which beset him. What is the logic of God at work? What are the modalities of his knowledge and will? The contention that if God wills and acts as the First Cause, then He has to will and to act necessarily and every effect is necessary is vital to the motives of Duns' thought. In defense of his attack on the necessary activity of the First Cause, the distinction between modes of necessity and of contingency are central moves (cf. §§14.3–14.4).

---

[6] Ibid.: 'Secundo, falsum dicit quantum ad secundum [as to the *substantia separata*], nam alio modo, et veriore, potest probari Deum esse, et ipsum esse necesse esse, et esse unum, quam per motum, nam hoc potest probari per actum et potentiam, quae pertinent ad considerationem metaphysici. Semper enim potentia praesupponit actum, et possibile-esse necesse-esse, et multa praesupponunt unum.'

[7] See *Lectura Prologus* 65 f.; cf. *Ordinatio Prologus* 140 f.

[8] *Lectura Prologus* 66: 'Dicitur "primo virtualiter continere," quia si non primo continet, non propter hoc dicitur obiectum habitus, quia sic ratio substantiae continet totum habitum metaphysicae, quia includit ens quod est primum subiectum quod continet virtualiter omnia quae pertinent ad habitum metaphysicae.' Cf. §88.

7.3.1 What is meant by 'synchronically contingent'?

Although Duns' theoretical framework is quite clear, nevertheless, his terminology is rather vexing. He distinguishes between *contingency* and *possibility*.

The first kind of possibility and contingency which Duns expounds is the successive or diachronic possibility and contingency. The first concept of *possibility (possibilitas)* can be perfectly recognized: it is the concept of temporal or *diachronic possibility* we have already met with Sherwood, while Duns only updates the analysis of Sherwood's *Obligationes*. In *Lectura* I 39.48 Duns precisely elucidates *diachronic possibility*, but he only mentions temporal or diachronic *contingency*.[9] Where is diachronic *contingency* found in this framework? Duns does not explicitly recur to the announced first kind of *contingency*, but it is not difficult to describe the meaning of this term, for this concept of *contingency* is the time logical mirror image of *possibility*: p *is possible*$_1$ $=_{def}$ *not-p is true* at the very present time t_k and p will be *true at a future time* t_1, and p *is contingent*$_1$ $=_{def}$ p is *true at the very present time* t_k and *not-p* will be true *at a future time* t_1.

The next move of Duns is surprising. The type of *possibility* now following is an old friend, named *logical potency (potentia logica)*. This kind of *possibility* is the key to the *synchrony* model. In §49 we meet a variant of the famous definition of the *possibile logicum*: *Logical possibility* only obtains

> when the terms are possible in such a way that they are not repugnant to each other, but can be united, although there is no possibility in reality.[10]

The old-fashioned concepts of *possibility* and *contingency* are based on differences of time indexation. These temporal indices are still connected with *terms*: *something white at a* and *something black at b*. The main idea behind *logical possibility* is *consistency, compatibility*: this possibility concerns nothing but the crucial fact that possibility propositions are true if they are composed of non-contradictory terms. The possibility of the *possibile logicum* is a kind of analytical possibility constituted by the interrelationship of the involved terms. The definition of *logical* possibility and Duns' analysis of the diachronic concepts

---

[9] *Lectura* I 39.48: 'Una contingentia et possibilitas, ut voluntas successive feratur in obiecta opposita et haec possibilitas et contingentia consequitur eius mutabilitatem. Et secundum hanc possibilitatem distinguuntur propositiones de possibili quae fiunt de extremis contrariis et oppositis.' Then, the diachronic analysis follows. Cf. *CF* 114–115. See also §5.4.

[10] *CF* 116. See *CF* 116–119. Cf. §4.9 and §5.4.

of *possibility* and *contingency* are connected in the next section: 'This logical possibility does not obtain as far as the will has acts *successively*, but as far as it has them *at the same moment*.' This move meshes well with the approach evidenced by the interpretation of the original concepts of *possibility* and *contingency*: the structural moment of *diachrony* is replaced by the structural moment of *synchrony* derived from the internal structure of *logical possibility* (see §4.9).

However, the structural moment of *synchrony* is still related to *terms*. The basic definition of *logical possibility* says: 'This logical possibility obtains with respect to *terms* which are not incompatible' (§50). The application of the idea of *logical possibility* to the phenomenon of *willing* is still based on *terms*. The properties *willing that p at this time* and *willing that not-p at this same time* can be ascribed to the will in such a way that the conjunction of the factual actuality of the first property and the synchronic or simultaneous possibility of the second property is perfectly sound (§50). The factual occurrence of a property and the possibility of the negation of the same property can go hand in hand if that property is an accidental, non-essential property.

Only in the next section (§51) is the new term *potentia realis (real possibility)* introduced. What does *real possibility* consist of? At this stage, the term-oriented approach is replaced by a *proposition*-oriented approach. 'The *proposition* is true [. . .] in the divided sense, not because we understand the *terms* for different times [. . .], but it is true in the divided sense because there are two *propositions*, because it implicitly includes two *propositions*.'[11] In contrast with the *possibile logicum, real possibility* is clarified in terms of an analysis of *propositions*. Duns had already said that *real possibility* corresponds with *logical possibility* (§49). The logical possibility of a combination of terms does not require that the predicate is factually true of the subject. The realm of logical possibilities is disconnected from the realm of factual reality. How is this idea of *real possibility* applied by Duns? Supposing that there is an act of will – *a*'s willing that *p* at *t* – we may add to this fact that it is possible that *a* wills that *not-p* at *t*. So, the alternative possibility is a willing that *not* is the case at the very present time but obtains in an alternative situation. This alternative situation is not some future but a synchronic alternative to the present situation.

In sum, what Duns calls *real possibility* is the synchronic counterpart of *diachronic possibility*. *Real possibility* is the *synchronic*

[11] *CF* 118. Cf. §§5.2–5.4 and §6.2.

mirror image of *diachronic possibility* and *real contingency* is the *synchronic* mirror image of *diachronic contingency*₁:

> *p is possible* =$_{def}$ *not-p* is true *at the very present time t* and *p* is true as *a synchronic (structural) alternative* at *t*.

Therefore:

> *p is contingent* =$_{def}$ *p* is true *at the very present time t* and *not-p* is true as *a synchronic alternative* at *t*.

'Possibility' is again linked with what is *not* the case, varied by what *is so* in an alternative way, and 'contingency' is linked with factual actuality, varied by what *is so* in an alternative way. However, the main idea of basic ontological alternativity is not connected with a theory of possible worlds for the simple reason that the basics of set theory were conspicuous by their absence. This place is taken by the theory of the *neutral proposition*.

7.4 THE NEUTRAL PROPOSITION

The theory of the *neutral proposition* is a crucial part of Duns Scotus' ontology. This theory is rooted in the doctrine of *divine knowledge*:

> The intellect of God, seeing his essence *at the first moment*, sees all things according to their *being knowable*, since in terms of that moment they are constituted into their knowable being. [. . .] Therefore, when a thing has that status, the intellect of God sees it in seeing his own essence.[12]

Omniscience is explained in terms of *knowability*. God being omniscient knows everything that is now the case, but that is not enough: He must also know all that is knowable, but what is the status of what is knowable? The logic of *structural priority* is at work. What enjoys the priority of the *first moment* is seen under the aspects of what is essential without any specifying qualification and, so, most universal. The theory of the *neutral proposition* replaces a possible theory of *possible worlds*:

> The divine intellect, understanding a proposition not as true or false, presents it to the will as *a neutral one* (just as when I apprehend: *Stars are even in number*). Suppose I can make a proposition true by my

---

[12] *Lectura* I 39.93. Cf. §6.5 and *CF* 188 f.

will (for instance, *I sit*), then at first it is understood by me *in a neutral sense*, but only as something theoretical; and when it is actualized and effected by the will determined to one component, then it is understood as true, and *before* it was only presented to the will as *neutral*.[13]

This new theory of the *neutral proposition* is also dealt with in *Lectura* I 39.44:

When the divine intellect understands *This is to be done* before an act of the will, it understands it as *neutral*, just as when it understands *Stars are even in number*.[14]

God knows the possible events as *neutral* and 'neutral' means: *without any truth-value*. Duns elucidates his point by comparing it with our epistemic attitude towards the proposition *Stars are even in number*. Apart from the fact that this proposition is true or false, we do not have any idea whether it be true or false. For us, it is a neutral proposition, without any truth-value. It has still to be decided. Literally, all propositions of the type *This can be done* have to be decided at the second moment of divine epistemic activity. They are still empty, just as, for us, the place of the truth-value of *Stars are even in number* is empty.

We have to remind ourselves, that, in Duns' mind, the matter of the truth-value of a proposition is decided by the divine will, since the choice and actualization of *contingent* facts is made by the divine will. We have also to keep in mind that, for Duns, *contingency* implies *truth*. So, apart from this role of God's will, a proposition has no truth-value, and *neutral* propositions are propositions without any truth-value. 'Obviously, we are moving on the level of *pure possibility*. It is the will which leads this possibility to factual being or not being and the corresponding truth-value.'[15] In *Lectura* I 39.62 Duns makes the same point in terms of the human action *I am sitting*.

Although this proposition will be true in the next future, I have still not decided to sit at that future moment. So, I myself understand it *as*

---

[13] *Lectura* I 39.62: 'Intellectus divinus offert voluntati suae aliquam complexionem ut neutram, non apprehendens ut veram vel falsam (sicut cum apprehendo "astra esse paria"); et si ponatur quod per voluntatem meam possim verificare aliquam complexionem (ut "me sedere"), [. . .] et [. . .] in effectu per voluntatem determinatam ad unam partem, tunc apprehenditur ut vera, et prius tantum offerebatur voluntati ut neutra.'

[14] *Lectura* I 39.44: 'Quando intellectus divinus apprehendit "hoc esse faciendum" ante voluntatis actum, apprehendit ut neutram, sicut cum apprehendo "astra esse paria".'

[15] *CF* 107. Cf. *CF* 104–109 and 142–147. It has to be stressed that this Scotian sense of possibility cannot be explained in terms of possible worlds, for a possible worlds approach handles the issue of truth-value in an alternative way by distinguishing between being true in a possible world and being true in *Actua*. See also §13.3.

> *open, as neutral.* From the viewpoint of my will it is not yet decided whether I shall sit or not, and that is why my intellect understands it neither as true, nor as false. But let us suppose that I choose to sit and decide to make it true that *I sit*. Then I make *I sit* true. (*CF* 143)

With the help of his notion of *neutral proposition* Duns Scotus makes his point, rooted in a factuality-based concept of *contingency*. So, the upshot of the basics of his ontology is that the notions of *essence* and *existence* are very close.

7.5 ESSENCE AND EXISTENCE

The issue of distinguishing *essence* from *being* or *existence* largely arose from the efforts of Christian medieval thinkers to account for the contingent and caused character of creation and challenged them to elaborate on alternative conceptions of *essence*. Rather divergent thinkers like Thomas Aquinas, Siger of Brabant, and James of Viterbo saw in Avicenna a philosopher making extreme distinctions between *essence* and *existence* in creatures by looking on *existence* as a kind of accident superadded to *essence*. In contradistinction to Avicenna, Averroes was seen as rejecting any such real distinction.[16] Many scholars accept that Thomas Aquinas preferred some kind of real distinction between essence and existence. In the case of immaterial personal beings, Thomas also sees *essence* being related to *being (existence)* as *potency* to *act*. This perfectly un-Aristotelian distinction embraces the whole of his quasi-Aristotelian conceptual framework. Thomas defends in *De ente et essentia* that essence and existence are really not identical, with one notable exception, since they are identical in God. Apart from God, the distinction is universal, while the *form-matter* distinction is not. Separate substances obey to the act-potency distinction, but not to the form-matter distinction. 'The impossibility of there being more than one being in which essence and existence are identical is sufficient ground for him to conclude to their real and factual otherness in all else.'[17]

---

[16] For the early origins of this doctrine, see Van Steenberghen, *Maître Siger de Brabant*, 280–282, and 286 f.: on Aquinas. Cf. Paulus, *Henri de Gand. Essai sur les tendances de sa métaphysique*, 260–291; Maurer, 'Esse and Essentia in the Metaphysics of Siger of Brabant,' *Mediaeval Studies* 8 (1946) 68–86; Cunningham, 'The "Real Distinction" in John Quidort,' *Journal of the History of Philosophy* 8 (1970) 9–28; and HCPMA 420–427.

[17] Wippel, 'Essence and Existence in the De ente,' *Metaphysical Themes in Thomas Aquinas*, 120. For the teaching of the later Thomas Aquinas, see idem, 'Essence and Existence in Other Writings,' *Metaphysical Themes*, 133–161.

Various thinkers such as Siger of Brabant, Godfrey of Fontaines, and Scotus rejected the real distinction between essence and existence.[18] Godfrey also rejects the intentional distinction between *essence* and *existence*, but agrees with Henry of Ghent, in common opposition to Giles of Rome, that the distinction is not real. For Godfrey, *essence* and *existence* are really identical.[19] Henry is critical of both sides. He was opposed to Giles of Rome's defense between the real distinction of essence and existence, but he was also opposed to the alternative of only acknowledging a functional distinction between them. He was eager to account for the possibility of meaningful knowledge of non-existent possibles.

> Possible essences, prior to their realization in individual existents, enjoy essential being from all eternity insofar as they are objects of God's knowledge. This essential being provides them with sufficient ontological consistency in themselves for them to be objects of knowledge prior to their realization as individual existents in time.[20]

Creation of individuals requires the decision of the divine will to create, but if we state that God acting as efficient cause bestows existence (*esse existentiae*) on certain essences in time, we frame a quasi-historical reformulation of Henry's views. His point is that temporal individuals – or history – depend on God's will. However, the concept of a radically contingent divine will is an impossible one for Plato and Aristotle, Plotinus and Avicenna, neither does it play a role in quite different ontologies of thinkers such as Godfrey of Fontaines and Eckhart. So, Henry of Ghent's device is precisely the opposite of Platonism and in such cases such labeling is not helpful at all.

7.5.1   Duns Scotus

Much research gets entangled in trying to define the nature of the distinction Duns draws between *essence* and *existence*. According to Wippel, it should be noted that the real distinction will not do, because the Scotian *real* distinction implies separability too. This is not true. Although the real distinction has to be applied to separable entities, it

---

[18] However, in his Commentary on the *Liber de causis*, Siger approaches Thomas Aquinas' theory of real composition of *essence* and *esse* in creatures. See Wippel, 'Essence and Existence,' *CHLMP* 399. On Giles of Rome, see Wippel, *Metaphysical Themes*, 396–398 and 401 f.
[19] See Wippel, *The Metaphysical Thought of Godfrey of Fontaines*, 39–53.
[20] Wippel, 'Essence and Existence,' *CHLMP* 403.

does not follow that distinctness is not real in the case of unseparable realities. For example, the Trinitarian Persons are unseparable, nevertheless distinguishing between Father, Son and Holy Spirit is real. As often is the case in Scotist studies, Aristotelian terminology is projected onto Scotus' systematic language. Moreover, 'a number of modern commentators have stated that Scotus here applies the intermediate kind of distinction that is so often associated with his name, the "formal distinction".'[21] At any rate, Duns' ontology has no room for independent essences. Only what exists has essences.

Henry of Ghent's defense of an intentional distinction between *essential* and *existential being* does not seem to have gained wide acceptance. Duns submitted Henry's notion of *essential being* (*esse essentiae*) to sharp criticism, but he did not fall back on either a Thomas Aquinas type of approach or on a Godfrey of Fontaines type of ontology. We easily misinterpret the tenor of Duns' criticism by looking on it as an attempt to refute Henry of Ghent's ontology instead of as an attempt to save its deeper implications. 'Despite the fact that Duns Scotus criticized Henry's ontology of essence as unworkable and implausible, it provided a major inspiration for his own innovative ideas about modality, which were formally quite similar to those Henry had laid down.'[22]

The situation is somewhat paradoxical. Duns' formal distinction tries to specify and to salvage Henry's intentional distinction. Henry's typical example of an intentional distinction is his *essence-existence* distinction, but the way this distinction is drawn differs thoroughly from the Scotian formal distinction. Duns is utterly critical in *Lectura* I 36.13–22 and his rejection is based on the theology of creation. According to Duns, Henry's *essential being* approach is incompatible with the doctrine of a *creatio ex nihilo* (*Lectura* I 36.16). What possesses quiditative being (= essential being), is not nothing. 'Created' (*creatum*) and 'creatable' (*creabile*) have to be distinguished sharply. 'If a thing has *essential being* from eternity and only by creation acquires *existential being* which expresses a certain relation, then *creating* is nothing else than effecting a relation. In this way it is less creating than changing.'[23] A creature is not formally necessary in itself according to its essential being, as is, Duns notes, granted by all. So, it

<hr />

21 Wippel, 'Essence and Existence,' *CHLMP* 406. Wippel leaves the issue undecided.
22 Marrone, 'Henry of Ghent,' *REP* IV 357. Essences constitute all simple possibles.
23 *Lectura* I 36.16: 'Ergo, creare nihil aliud erit quam facere unum respectum, et sic minus est creare quam alterare.'

has to be produced into its essential being. 'Then, I ask whether stone precedes just its production according to some true being' (*Lectura* I 36.17). This is impossible, since in that case it would not be nothing before it was.

> Therefore, this production by which stone is produced into *essential being* is a production of something, namely purely out of nothing; so, it is a creation. Therefore, there was creation from eternity, because something was produced out of nothing. This runs counter to what they say themselves and to truth. They say that a contradiction is involved in stating that something is created from eternity.[24]

At this stage of Duns Scotus' development, he establishes a rather tight terminological connection between the elements *true being, producing into being, essential being, absolutely nothing*, and *creation*. On account of this equation, any acknowledgement of an ontological aspect results in denying the idea of a creation out of nothing. If God knows some true being or an essence, then God also knows its actual existence. So, if God's knowledge actualizes *essential being*, it also actualizes eternal *existential being*. Put otherwise, 'I ask then whether God produced some thing into essential being by knowing it.' If He did so, He knew it before producing it into essential being. Then it does not make any sense to say that some thing has such essential being on account of God's knowledge, but if his *knowledge* does not produce it into essential being, then it is *necessarily* produced. This kind of linking divine knowledge and essential being entails necessary emanation and eternal creation.

Duns rejects the *essence-existence* model of Henry of Ghent, because he concludes that it results in a theory of eternal creation. On the part of Duns, this line of argumentation implies that Duns does not only link *essence* and *existence* very tightly, but also *essence* and *(f)actuality*. *Ordinatio* I 36, written about four years later (Paris), presents the same approach. However, *Ordinatio* II 1.82 ff. offers a different picture, stipulating new terminology:

> Something can be *produced* (not *created*, though) absolutely out of nothing, that is, not out of anything according to *essential being*, neither according to *existential being*, nor according to some *being in a certain respect*. A creature is produced in *being knowable*, but not

---

[24] *Lectura* I 36.17: 'Igitur, ista productio qua sic producitur lapis in esse essentiae, est alicuius, et de pure nihilo, igitur est creatio. Igitur, ab aeterno fuit creatio, quia alicuius et de nihilo – quod est contra eos et contra veritatem: dicunt quod contradictionem includit quod aliquid creetur ab aeterno.'

out of any *being* – neither in an absolute sense nor in a certain respect, nor from its own possibility. Nevertheless, this sense of *to be produced* is not *to be created*, because something is not created into *being* without ado, but is produced into *being* in a certain respect.[25]

The first line of argumentation held that acknowledging any ontological aspect preceding creation denies creation out of nothing. Now Duns drops this strategy of linking immediately any ontological aspect with the idea of a creation out of nothing. The idea of *merely nothing* is connected with the second moment of God's knowledge by which He knows all that is knowable, and not with the act of creation as such:

> Nevertheless, something cannot be *created*, that is, produced into being *absolutely* out of nothing, which is in no way – neither absolutely nor in a certain respect. Nothing is created which has not *being known* and *being willed* before, and it was formally possible in *being known*.[26]

Now, a new clear conclusion can be drawn:

> I say that God can create out of nothing (that is, not out of anything) according to *essential being*, and, consequently, He can create out of nothing (that is, not out of anything) according to *existential being*, for *essential being* is never separated really from *existential being*.[27]

With respect to God's being, a series of compositions is denied by Duns Scotus, namely the compositions of matter and form (the so-called essential composition), of quantitative parts and of (potential) subject and accidents (*Lectura* I 8.8–27). In this list the distinction between *subject* and *predicate* is missing. This distinction is not a 'composition,' neither is the distinction between *existence* and *essence*. Only what

---

[25] *Ordinatio* II 1.84: 'Potest aliquid produci (licet non creari) de simpliciter nihilo, id est, non de aliquo secundum esse essentiae nec esse exsistentiae, nec secundum aliquod esse secundum quid. Quia creatura producitur in esse intelligibili non de aliquo esse, nec simpliciter, nec secundum quid, nec possibili ex parte sui in isto esse. Istud tamen "produci" non est creari, quia non creatur aliquid in esse simpliciter, sed producitur ad esse secundum quid.'

[26] *Ordinatio* II 1.83: 'Tamen non potest aliquid creari, id est, *produci ad esse* simpliciter de nihilo, id est, nullo modo ente (nec simpliciter, nec secundum quid). Nihil enim creatur quod non prius habuit esse intellectum et volitum, et in esse intellecto fuit possibile formaliter.'

[27] *Ordinatio* II 1.82: 'Dico quod de nihilo (id est, non de aliquo) secundum esse essentiae potest Deus creare, et per consequens de nihilo (id est, non de aliquo) secundum esse essentiae, quia [. . .] numquam esse essentiae realiter separatur ab esse exsistentiae.' Cf. *Ordinatio* I 36.26–29, 48–49 and 53. This view was criticized by Ockham who denied that possibility is dependent on God. See Lagerlund, *Modal Syllogistics in the Middle Ages*, 91–98. Cf. Alanen and Knuuttila, 'The Foundations of Modality and Conceivability in Descartes and his Predecessors,' in Knuuttila (ed.), *Modern Modalities*, 1–69.

exists, can have an essence. Because matter is dropped as the principle of individuation, individuality itself appears on the scene as something that truly and fully exists. The logical subject-predicate structure is no longer seen as a universality relationship on the level of *essences* (*genera-species*); the inner structure of the subject-predicate relationship shows now an *individual* as subject of which *properties* are said.[28] So, the *subject-predicate* distinction is irremovable, nor can the distinction between *existence* and *essence* be cancelled out. Only what exists individually can have properties and only what exists can have an essence, and an essence is a property.

According to Duns Scotus, it is not true that every creature is composed of different realities, although every creature can be put together with something else in order to be a compound with something else. The same is true of incorporeal substances like angels, for an angelic act of knowing is an accidental property. An angel does acquire knowledge. So, the *existence-essence* relation is no real distinction and it is no composition, for neither the matter-form composition, nor the quantitative composition, nor the subject-accident composition are applicable. What kind of distinction is it? Is it a formal distinction? In the strict sense, a formal distinction applies to formalities, definable aspects of what is. In that strict sense, *existence* is no form or formality, for only in the case of what enjoys existence is distinguishing between forms or formalities possible. That is just what the term 'formal' tells us. However, this aspect of a *formal* distinction is incidental to what is intended by Duns, occasioned only by the semantic implications of the term *forma*. Duns also uses the synonymous expression *non-identitatis distinctio* (*non-identity distinction*). Although *existence* and *essence* themselves are essentially linked, they are not identical. In this enlarged sense, the *existence-essence* distinction is a formal distinction. 'It has also been suggested that Scotus appeals to another kind of distinction, a modal distinction which obtains here between a given essence and its intrinsic mode, existence,'[29] for the term *modal* distinction is not beset by semantic restrictions which obtain for a *formal* distinction.[30] Duns applies this distinction to creatures: only creatures are said to have (*eternal*) *ideas*. The *idea* is the eternity aspect of a creature. What

---

[28] The Aristotelian *SP*-structure has been replaced by a Fregean *Fa*-structure. *S* and *P* are located on the same level, *a* and *F* have logically and ontologically different functions.

[29] Wippel, 'Essence and Existence,' *CHLMP* 406 (405–407).

[30] Duns can also apply 'formaliter' to modal notions – see *Ordinatio* II 1.83.

never exists, though possible, has no ideas. Scotus' *existence-essence* distinction is only applicable on the level of creation, and not to the *being knowable/known* of God's a priori knowledge by which He knows all that is knowable. Granted, in terms of God's knowledge the creature's *existence* and *essence* are known by God, but the ontic actuality (*being*) aspect of *existence, being known* eternally, is not called *existence* by Scotus.

7.6 REAL AND RATIONAL RELATIONS

The Fathers loved to speak of the creatures existing in God's mind as *ideas*. It is a characteristic of Duns' terminology that an *idea* is not a divine concept in general, but a concept of a creature. For Harnack, the doctrine of the ideas in the divine mind meant a betrayal of the Christian faith, but it is a splendid piece of the christianization of philosophy. For the Platonists, ideas are above the gods, structuring reality. For the Christian thinkers, ideas belong to God's mind, not being above God, but being dependent on Him as models. The Creator is free to use them. There are no absolute *kosmos noètos* and *kosmos horatos*. A philosophical revolution had already taken place in patristic thought before such ideas reached the medieval West. Peter Lombard was aware that *idea* could be understood wrongly and Ockham supported his warning.

The medieval language of *real relations* and *rational relations* has caused a lot of misunderstandings in modern interpretations. Of course, such misunderstandings are not necessary if we pay close attention to the medieval definitions. Duns' definition is found in *Lectura* I 31.6. In addition to the definition, we have theories which amply illustrate this idiom. A fine example of this is provided for by Duns' theology of creation colliding with the view of the 'philosophers'. Our starting point is a clear text, taken from *Lectura* I 31.6. The context is theological, for the question of *Lectura* I 31 runs as follows: Are *equality, similitude* and *identity* real relations in God? We ask what *real relations* are. Duns starts with an analytical preamble, a practice which is one of the features of his methodological revolution in philosophy. The vital text reads as follows:

> I reply that they (*equality, similitude* and *identity*) are *real relations*. There are only three elements to be required for a *real relation*: first, it is required that the *foundation* is real and that the end term is real too; second, it is required that the foundation really differs from the end term and the one term from the other, and, third, it is required

that the relation follows on the foundation and the end term on the basis of its own nature [see §6.6.1].

Far-reaching judgements rest on this reportive definition. Many thirteenth-century authors state that God does not enjoy a *real relation* to creation. This view scandalized many modern readers, but the point is a trivial one, because if there were a *real* relation, God would have enjoyed an *essential* relation to his creation so that creation would be necessary reality. Now we are able to extract an explicit definition of 'real relation' (*relatio realis*) from Duns' list of conditions: aRb is given and R is a *real relation* only if: (1) both the foundation of R and the end term b really exist; (2) a and b are real and not identical; and (3) R and a and b are entailed by the existence of R's foundation in a. So, what does a's foundation (*fundamentum*) mean? The foundation of R is the nature of a which entails a, R, and b.[31]

The definition of 'real relation' is also the key to what a *rational relation* (*relatio rationis*) is:

> A *rational relation* (*relatio rationis*) is a relation where one of the three mentioned conditions of the definition of 'real relation' is missing.

Now we easily understand different kinds of *rational* relations: If one or more of the considered conditions is missing, then b and R are possibly absent, although a is given. In such cases, the relation is called *rational*, although the involved relation might be quite *real* in the modern sense as we can observe when Duns continues his discussion: 'For those things which are *rationally* (*secundum rationem*) related because of any of these (conditions) are missing are related by a *rational relation*.'

In the case of a *rational relation*, something is missing and Duns presents three helpful examples.[32] Example 2 concerns identity as *being identical with oneself*: this type of *identity* is a *rational relation*, because the second condition is violated (see §6.6.2). Example 3 deals with the relationship between the Creator and his creation which is not a *real* one, because the property of *creating* (*creans*) is not essential to God, although *creative* (*creativus*) is. On the other hand, *being created* is a real relation of a creature a, for if a exists, then a is a creature,

---

[31] Cf. Etzkorn, Review: 'L. M. de Rijk, *Nicholas of Autrecourt*,' *Franciscan Studies* 56 (1998) 369 (369 f.): '*Fundamentum* is the basis in reality for making relationships between the *termini*.'

[32] For the first example, namely that of the contradiction, see §6.6.1.

because *being created* is essential to *a*. The other relatum exists too, for God cannot fail to exist. This case is particularly important, because Duns has often been scoffed at on account of this theorem, as if he were trying to say that what is going on between God and his creation is simply unreal and a matter of idle speculation. Duns' point is that it is not a relation as such given the basis of the reality of God himself. 'Because the third condition is missing, it is stated that the relation between the Creator and his creation is rational, since that relation is discovered by the intellect paying attention to it.'[33] The point of this thesis is not that this relation is only mental, intellectual, or unreal. Duns' point of departure is the contingent reality of the created world, but the reality of this created world can only be discovered by the intellect paying attention to it.

7.6.1   A clarifying example: the view of the philosophers

'The philosophers state that something different from God is necessary: something other than God is necessarily produced by God so that the fecundity of divine nature includes that the creation is brought forth,'[34] because infinite perfection entails necessary creation.

Two striking features of this view and its description have to be observed. Duns keenly distinguishes between the Christian and non-Christian worldview. The 'philosophers' derive the necessity of the world from the necessity of God, since, according to them, God *works* just as He *is*. Therefore, God *necessarily* works. In terms of theological idiom, the philosophers defend a kind of necessary creation. Duns claims that the philosophers do not conclude that there is a real relation between God and the world in spite of the world being necessary. This thesis illustrates the *real/rational relation* language. Even the necessity criterion does not suffice to qualify for a *real* relation. Something different from God though necessary itself, but ranking below God because it is not absolutely perfect and simple, cannot qualify for being the intentional term of God's activity. There is no real relation between God and the world (*Lectura* I 30.61).

---

[33] *Lectura* I 31.6: 'Propter defectum tertii, ponitur quod relatio creatoris ad creaturam est rationis, quia est facta per intellectum considerantem.'

[34] See *Lectura* I 30.60: 'Philosophi ponunt aliud a Deo esse necessarium, quia a Deo necessario produci aliud, ita quod fecunditas naturae divinae includit creaturam produci, unde secundum eos non potest esse Deus seccundum infinitam perfectionem suam nisi sit aliquid necessario creatum ab eo. Et tamen philosophi non posuerunt relationem realem Dei ad creaturam. Igitur, non sequitur in Deo esse relationem realem si coexigat aliud necessario secum.' Cf. *Ordinatio* I 30.54.

Five final comments are still to be added. First, we might discern here the priority of the dimensions of divine mind and will. The life of the mind depends on the life of the Mind. In defiance of Plato and Plotinus, Aristotle and Averroes, the life of the cosmos is not as such given with the life of the Mind.

Second, according to Duns, logic is a second-order undertaking. Logical terms order the ways our words and language are working. Thus 'real (relation)' and 'rational (relation)' are second-order qualifications in order to characterize and to classify the language instruments we use in talking about reality.

Third, the distinction between *real* and *rational* relation molded in an important way Duns' handling of philosophical and theological issues. In particular, early Thomism at Paris was already sensitive to this point. Duns' precise handling of real and formal distinctions is tightly linked up with the theory of the *distinctio formalis a parte rei*. The theory of the *distinctio formalis a parte rei* is parasitic on Duns' theory of relations.

Fourth, the interpretation that Duns' theory of relations is strongly realist is unwarranted, for all these occurrences of *realis* are a matter of *definition* and not of *theory*. Duns calls a relation *not real*, while it is certainly *real* in the modern sense of this word.[35]

Fifth, Duns Scotus' theories on *essence/existence* and *relations*, based on his contingency ontology, are the key to his approach to what *universals* are.

7.7 Universals

'The vigorous early-fourteenth-century debate about universals was based on a rejection of Platonism, the theory that universal natures really exist independently of the particulars whose natures they are and independently of every mind.'[36] It is characteristic of medieval thought that it rejected separated Platonic forms almost generally, but we have to be aware that from the historical viewpoint medieval moderate realism is also incompatible with the Aristotelian solution, because Platonic forms and Aristotelian *eidè* are necessary entities

---

[35] Cf. Henry of Harcley's criticisms, based on the same misunderstanding – see Henninger, *Relations*, 98 ff. (98–118).

[36] McCord Adams, 'Universals in the Early Fourteenth Century,' *CHLMP* 411. For an introduction to the problem, see her *William Ockham* I 3–12: 'The Problem of Universals.' Cf. Dahlstrom, 'Signification and Logic: Scotus on Universals from a Logical Point of View,' *Vivarium* 18 (1980) 81–111.

alike, which function as the 'creative' forces of the cosmos. Such ontologies were considered inconsistent with Christian creation theology, just as the Greek Fathers thought.[37] The moderate realists' predilection for a reconstructed Aristotelian approach to an immanent connection between individual and essence was precisely anchored in their theology of creation. Duns Scotus regularly repudiates the Platonic viewpoint,[38] although he mildly observes in *Quaestiones Metaphysicae* VII 18.14 that Aristotle

> does not argue that the Ideas are impossible, but only that they are unnecessary. For because what is not obvious ought not to be postulated by those philosophizing without necessity, he argued against the Ideas that they were not necessary for the reasons given and hence they simply should not be postulated.

Duns Scotus himself is more strict. If an *idea* which is formally a universal is predicated of a particular thing by an identity predication, 'we immediately are faced, it seems, with this contradiction, *viz.* the same numerical thing is the quiddity of a multitude of diverse things, and at the same time exists outside them, for otherwise it would not be imperishable.'[39] Although the nominalist contributions of Henry of Harcley and Ockham unleashed a vigorous debate,[40] nominalism is much older than the time of Duns Scotus and Ockham and elaborate discussions of the nominalist position are found in Duns' works.[41]

Medieval Christian philosophy emphasizes that in the world there are only individuals. Again, conceptual structures are at stake, for, depending on the conceptual structure, this thesis has to be interpreted quite differently. As to Duns Scotus, the interaction of the concepts of *common nature* and *individuality* defines his position. On the level of entities, there *are* only individuals, but individuals of a kind

---

[37] See Sheldon-Williams, 'The Greek Christian Platonist Tradition from the Cappadocians to Maximus and Eriugena,' in Armstrong (ed.), *The Cambridge History of Later Greek and Early Medieval Philosophy*, 425–431, 447–451, 477 ff. and 497 ff. Cf. De Vogel, *Wijsgerige aspecten van het vroeg-christelijk denken*, 36–47. 'Creative' in the expression 'creative forces' is used in a metaphorical way, because ancient Greek metaphysics simply excludes creation belief. According to this worldview, the idea of a personal Creator is inconsistent: see Guthrie, *A History of Greek Philosophy* VI. *Aristotle*, 252–263.

[38] *Quaestiones Metaphysicae* VII 18.13–15, and *Lectura* I 3.114 and 153–171, I 8.220 f., I 17.178 and II 3.38 and 157, and parallel texts.

[39] *Quaestiones Metaphysicae* VII 18.15: 'Si autem ulterius ponat quis quod dicta idea est formaliter universale [. . .], statim videtur includere contradictionem quod idem numero sit quiditas multorum diversorum, et tamen extra ipsa – aliter non esset incorruptibilis.'

[40] On Ockham, see McCord Adams, 'Universals,' *CHLMP* 417–422, 424–429 and 432–439.

[41] See *Quaestiones Metaphysicae* VII 18, *Lectura* and *Ordinatio* II 3 *quaestio* 1.

are essentially like each other. There are three horses near the river, but there are not as many kinds of equine animals as there are horses. Bucephalus is a horse, but this does not imply that Aristotle's horse is not a horse, but a 'harse'. In general, an individual *a* has both *a*-individuality and a common nature. The common nature of *a* is not a countable property, for there are no more natures if there are more individuals, neither is a nature a special sort of individual – it is not a universal or general individual. A nature is indifferent to being in one individual or more individuals – in contradistinction to the haecceity or individual identity of *a*. Duns Scotus also accepts that there are universal concepts, but he does not look upon such concepts as 'figments' of the mind. A universal actually exists in a mind as a concept applicable to many things, but it is also guaranteed by a common nature existing in individuals of external reality.

This view has been admirably summarized in six theses by Marilyn McCord Adams:

    (1) A nature is common of itself and is common in reality.
    (2) Individuality is numerically one and particular of itself.
    (3) The common nature of *a* and the haecceity of *a* exist in reality as constituents of *a*.
    (4) The nature is numerically one denominatively and is numerically many in numerically distinct particulars.
    (5) The nature is completely universal only insofar as it exists in the intellect.
    (6) The nature of *a* and the haecceity of *a* are not formally identical.[42]

Ockham is convinced that (1)–(6) are an inconsistent set of propositions. In spite of a philosophically successful defense of Duns, McCord Adams's eventual assessment is that there is an argument of Ockham showing that Scotus' theory of universals is unacceptable.

> If humanity in Socrates is formally but not really distinct from Socrateity, it follows that it is not logically possible for the former to exist in a thing without the latter existing in the same thing, as it *is* logically possible for Socrates to exist without whiteness inhering in him and to have blackness inhering in him instead.[43]

Ockham treats Scotian common natures as if they were accidental properties, but this argument is flawed, because, accepting for the sake

[42] McCord Adams, 'Universals,' *CHLMP* 414. Her *William Ockham* I 3–167 offers a monograph on universals. Cf. §6.7 and §10.3.
[43] McCord Adams, 'Universals,' *CHLMP* 422. Cf. her *William Ockham* I 13 ff.

of argument Scotus distinguishing between the *real* and the *formal distinction*, Ockham interprets the nature of the *real* distinction along the lines of the separability criterion as modern literature on the subject usually does likewise. Duns Scotus does not accept a dualism between the concepts *being real* and *being formal*. Neither 'real' nor 'rational' nor 'formal' mean what they mean in modern usage.

7.8 CONCEPTUAL UNIVOCITY

Variability asks for univocity. 'The doctrine of univocation runs through the whole theory of the transcendentals,'[44] but what did Duns mean by *univocity* originally? The theory of *univocity* depends on the theory of *definition*. A *definition* deals as such with *genus* and *species* relationships. The definition of a *genus* first posits the *genus* and, second, the *differentia specifica* (see §4.4 on *definitio*). In general, a definition runs in terms of *genus* and the *specifying difference*.[45] A definition runs in terms of specific essential components, departing from the *genus*, the most general element which has to be 'specified' further. A definition has to be as economic as possible.[46] A definition demarcates the range of univocity, indicating an essence of whatsoever. What can be defined is knowable. A universal is as such knowable (*Quaestiones in librum Porphyrii Isagoge* 6.6). The five predicables are said to be universal in a univocal way. Duns' early use of 'univocal' is instructive. A *genus* is univocally predicated of its *species*,[47] but when Duns offers a definition of *x* in our modern sense of the word, he can simply say: there are two kinds of *x*. However, *being (ens)* is used equivocally with respect to *substance* and *accident*, since both are meaningful under an essential aspect of their own, and is equivocal with respect to the categories (*Quaestiones super Praedicamenta Aristotelis* 4.36–38).

---

[44] Wolter, *The Transcendentals and Their Function*, 12.

[45] *Quaestiones in librum Porphyrii Isagoge* 15.9: 'Cum igitur in definitione generis ponatur "praedicari de pluribus," ponitur genus eius. Postea ponitur "differentibus specie" et "in quid" quae sunt per se differentiae generis.' Cf. §15.34 and §15.35: 'Patet per dicta in solutione (§15.19), quia definitio generis ponitur pro genere et cum illa differentia per se.'

[46] *Quaestiones in librum Porphyrii Isagoge* 25.9: 'Species abundat a genere in differentia, quia definitio exprimit totum per se intellectum definiti; et non amplius, quia aliter non conveniret primo definito. Sed definitio constat ex genere et differentia. Igitur, differentia est aliquid de per se intellectu speciei, et non de intellectu generis.'

[47] See *Quaestiones in librum Porphyrii Isagoge* 7–8.12: 'Logicus ponit genus univocum propter unitatem rationis, sicut in principio Praedicamentorum animal univocum est homini et bovi.'

'Universal' is used univocally, for

> a *conceptual* univocal can be applied to realities of all categories, since any difference in realities of first intention does not prohibit them from being conceived by the intellect in the same conceptual modality. *Concepts* of the same *species* can be ascribed to different realities, because *concepts* are ascribed to these realities as far as they are conceived by the intellect.[48]

However, even according to the early *Quaestiones super Praedicamenta Aristotelis*, univocity is not limited to the area of definition. If so, only *species* would be univocal and there would be a strict parallelism between ontological and conceptual univocity. However, at an early stage, univocity is freed from such categorical fetters and made to be a universal tool, but in a rather specific manner.

> Now although *being (ens)* is predicated analogously or equivocally when it is taken as a perfect and proper concept, *being (ens)* as an imperfect and common concept is univocal to God and creatures and to substance and accident, etc. Scotus insists that *being* is one of many concepts which must be unequivocal because otherwise we could not reason at all, because otherwise we could not (at least in our present state) have any idea of substance, and because otherwise, in the present state, we could not reason at all about God.[49]

The proper context where Duns raises the question of *being univocal*, is given by the challenges of theological language. The large *quaestio 3* of *Lectura* I starts with a first part on *the knowability of God*.[50] Duns is not happy with the theory that there are no concepts common to theological language and our talk on creation, because the individuality of the divine nature would forbid doing so. He rejects an approach which only runs by analogy and degrees of knowing (*Lectura* I 3.10–13). To his mind, the theoretical situation is rather simple. If there are no common and unambiguous concepts, knowledge of God is quite impossible (*Lectura* I 3.25). Such skepticism is untenable. Duns intends

---

[48] *Quaestiones super Praedicamenta Aristotelis* III 8: 'Aliquod intentionale univocum potest applicari rebus omnium generum, quia omnis diversitas in rebus primae intentionis inter se non impedit ipsas posse concipi ab intellectu per eundem modum concipiendi. Intentiones autem eis attribuuntur in quantum ab intellectu concipiuntur, et ideo intentiones eaedem specie possunt diversis rebus attribui.' See Marrone, 'The Notion of Univocity in Duns Scotus's Early Works,' *Franciscan Studies* 43 (1983) 390 ff.

[49] Weinberg, *A Short History of Medieval Philosophy*, 217. This view is basically Wolter's – see *The Transcendentals*, part 1. Generally, Weinberg follows Wolter.

[50] *Lectura* I 3.18 ff.: 'Deus concipitur in conceptu communi univoco sibi et creaturae.'

to make a consistent whole of this theological approach. God is perfectly good, true, and wise, but we humans simply do not enjoy this perfect and infinite goodness and wisdom. If, in terms of our knowledge, wisdom can only be an accidental property, we cannot know that God is necessarily wise. So, Duns states that *being, good,* and *wise* are common concepts which are univocally used in our talk about God and creation. When we characterize God as *being* and when we characterize Duns as *being*, we do not use two concepts of *being*.[51] Duns makes use of the terms *conceptus communis* and *conceptus univocus*. If a *common concept* (*conceptus communis*) is applicable to *a*, then there must be a *b* to which it is applicable too, but what does Duns mean by *conceptus univocus*?

> A *univocal concept* [*conceptus univocus*] is a concept which forms a unit in such a way that its unity safeguards a contradiction by affirming and denying it about the same.[52]

Duns is not interested in caviling about words (*Ordinatio* I 3.26). According to his conception, *univocity* is simply required in order to formulate a decent contradiction and a decent inference. 'Univocity has to be understood in this sense' (ibid.). Otherwise, *God is good* and *God is not good* are both acceptable and an inference like *God is my rock* and *my rock is my property* – therefore *God is my property* – could be valid. Either all kinds of contradictions flow from the rejected view, or contradictions are simply impossible. In all cases of doubt or difference of opinion, I am certain and uncertain about the same. The philosophers disagreed on the issue of the first principle, but all looked on their own first principle as *being*. Only the absence of semantic ambiguity makes rival theories debatable. Only conceptual univocity makes it possible to argue for certain views and to refute or to confirm certain solutions.

  Duns' crucial point of theological methodology is that

> all the masters and theologians seem to use a concept common to God and creation, although they deny this literally, for all of them agree in this respect that they accept metaphysical concepts and they ascribe to God what is perfect by denying creaturely imperfection. (*Lectura* I 3.29)

---

[51] In fact, we should not even be able to frame the concept of divine being.

[52] The *adnotatio interpolata* added to *Lectura* I 3.22: 'Conceptus univocus est qui ita est unus quod eius unitas sufficit ad contradictionem, affirmando et negando de eodem.' This text will be incorporated in *Ordinatio* I 3.26. The fallacy of equivocity can only be avoided with the help of such concepts.

His basic position rests on a philosophical generalization of this point, or the other way around, because our communication, exchange of ideas, and debate need semantic univocity, theological univocity is compelling too. 'If a concept said of God and of creation is analogous if they are really two concepts, we would know absolutely nothing about God' (*Lectura* I 3.25). The consequent is false, so is the antecedent. In order to discuss the difference between the goodness of God and the goodness of a creature, and between God's and the creature's being, we need more common concepts.[53] So, deriving from Duns Scotus' theory of univocity that God and creature are *beings* in just the same way is just the opposite of what he claims. It is in fact a semantic theory, enriched by important ontological consequences.[54]

7.9 TRANSCENDENT TERMS

7.9.1 Definition and denotation

What is usually named 'transcendental' by modern historians of medieval logic and ontology – in harmony with modern philosophical terminology in a Kantian vein[55] – is called a *transcendens* (pl. *transcendentia*) in medieval texts. A *transcendens* is a term of a specific kind which has to perform a specific function. The definiton elucidates this function: a *transcendens* or *transcendent* (*term*) does not have a higher or more general category above itself.[56] It has no *genus*. What has to be said of God ontologically can be semantically said of the Scotian *transcendens*: *non in genere*. The denotation of *transcendens* presents an easy introduction to this term: the clear key text is found in *Lectura* I 8.109:

> There are some attributes, understood in an absolute way, which are coextensive with *being* (*ens*), for instance, *true*, *good*, and the like. Some attributes are attributes construed as disjunctions, which describe an attribute which is coextensive with *being*: a common

---

[53] See *Lectura* I 3.22: 'Ens et bonum secundum se important alium conceptum a conceptu boni et entis in Deo et in creatura.'

[54] See Cross's excellent exposition of Duns' account of the univocity of being in his '"Where angels fear to tread",' *Antonianum* 76 (2001) 11–24 (7–41), accompanied by some devastating criticisms of interpretations of Scotian ideas by some modern theologians. Cf. Wolter, *The Transcendentals*, chapter 3 (31–57): 'Univocation and Transcendentality.'

[55] Compare the title of Wolter's *The Transcendentals*, a pioneering work and still a principal study.

[56] *Lectura* I 8.109: 'Passiones quae convertuntur cum ente, consequuntur ipsum ens prius quam dividatur in decem genera et dicuntur transcendentia.' These *transcendentia* transcend the general categories of what there is.

attribute, like *necessary or contingent, reality or possibility*, and the like.[57]

This passage teaches us that Duns Scotus distinguishes between three kinds of transcendent terms. This threefold structure of universal transcendent terms is lucid. We see *ens* playing the fundamental role and is Duns' theoretical starting point.

The first remarkable group of transcendent terms only enjoys one member, namely *ens*:

1. *Being (ens)*, which Duns calls 'the *first transcendent term*.'[58]

This unique transcendent term *ens* is followed by two groups of transcendent terms: (a) the *simple* transcendent terms; (b) the *compound* transcendent terms. Both groups are groups of convertibles. Thus a *convertible transcendent attribute* is as such convertible with *being*. Of course, convertible attributes, then, are also convertible with one another – *ens, verum* et *bonum* convertuntur – but they are convertible with one another, because they are convertible with *being*. Their form is either *not compound* or simple – *unum, verum* and *bonum* – or *compound*, according to the structure of a *disjunction* – *necessarium vel possibile, actus vel potentia*.

2. Attributes which are coextensive with *being* in the simple way of expressions which are not compound, for instance *one* (in the sense of *unity*), *true* and *good*.[59]
3. Attributes which are coextensive with *being* in a compound way are, for example, *necessary or contingent, real or possible, infinite or finite* and *substantial or accidental*.

Such disjunctive attributes are transcendent because they are not confined or determined (*determinari*) to a definite category but classified under a more general category.[60] A typical feature of the theory

---

[57] *Lectura* I 8.109: 'Sic etiam sunt aliquae passiones absolute acceptae quae convertuntur cum ente (ut verum, bonum et huiusmodi). Et aliquae sunt passiones acceptae sub disiunctione quae circumloquuntur unum convertibile cum ente: passionem communem, ut necessarium vel possibile, actus vel potentia et huiusmodi.' *Ordinatio* I 8.115 defines disjunctive transcendents as follows: '[Ens] habet aliquas passiones ubi opposita distinguuntur contra se,' that is, (being) has some attributes where the opposites are distinguished from each other.'

[58] *Ordinatio* I 8.115: 'Non oportet autem transcendens, ut transcendens, dici de quocumque ente nisi sit convertibile cum primo transcendente, scilicet ente.'

[59] *Ordinatio* I 8.115 calls them *passiones simplices convertibiles*. *Lectura* I 8.109 only mentions *verum* and *bonum*. *Ordinatio* I 8.115 adds *unum* to them.

[60] Cf. *Ordinatio* I 8.115: 'Sicut autem passiones convertibiles sunt transcendentes quia consequuntur ens in quantum non determinatur ad aliquod genus, ita passiones disiunctae sunt transcendentes.'

consists in the detail that not only the disjunctive property of *being necessary or contingent* is called a *transcendens*, but that both disjuncts – *necessary* and *contingent* – are also called transcendent terms. Only God is necessary and although *necessary* characterizes only one being, nevertheless *necessary* is a transcendent term.[61] All convertible transcendent attributes are said of everything there is. Of course, *being* is said of everything there *is* and every predicate which is equivalent to *being* (*convertibilis*), is said of everything. Like *idem*, *convertibilis* is by Duns considered to be an irreflexive characteristic. According to his terminology, a convertible is not convertible with itself; *ens* is a convertible, but *ens* is not a convertible *transcendens* which is convertible with itself and *ens* is in the company of two sets of convertible transcendent terms, namely the simple and the compound. However, Duns' use of 'general' is rather subtle. Let us consider a category *c*. This category *c* has no members belonging to different kinds under itself. So there are no kinds of *c*: *c* cannot be more specific than it is. It is a *species specialissima*.[62] On the one hand, *c* does not have specifying kinds; on the other hand, *c* itself is not a kind (*species*) either. So it does not belong to a broader category *b* to be classified into $c_{1,\ldots,n}$. So, there is no fabric of more general kinds *c* belongs to: *c* cannot be more general than it is. It is a *genus generalissimum*.[63] In this special case, the most general kind and the most specific kind coincide. Can this special case be identified?

In answering this question we touch one of the most characteristic features of Duns' philosophy. The simple (convertible) *transcendentia* are convertible with the compound (convertible) *transcendentia*, but according to Duns, some so-called noble terms (like *necessarium*, *infinitum*, and *actus*) of the disjunctive transcendent properties refer to an absolutely unique individual: *God*. Only God is necessary and only God is infinite. Moreover, God is not only unique, but there can only be one God. If a set can only have one member, the most specific set of members of this set and the most general set of all members of this set coincide. Duns' exposition of *genus generalissimum* and

---

[61] See *Lectura* I 8.110: 'Immo potest convenire (*sc.* transcendens) uni soli, sicut: necessarium.'

[62] *Lectura* I 8.110: 'Sicut aliquid dicitur esse genus generalissimum, et tamen forte non est nisi species specialissima eo quod non habet plures species sub se.'

[63] *Lectura* I 8.110: 'Dicitur esse genus generalissimum quia non habet aliquod genus superveniens. Sic dicitur aliquis conceptus transcendens quia non habet supervenientem conceptum quam determinat: ideo est transcendens. Et sic est sapientia transcendens, quae formaliter de Deo dicitur et sapientia increata.'

species specialissima coinciding obtains concerning a category enjoying only one member.

Here, Scotus' theory of *transcendent terms* comes in. The most general term is *ens* (*being*). It is an irreducibly simple notion of anything which implies no contradiction. *Ens* does not entail *not-being* and is incompatible with impossibility. *Being one* (*unique*), *true* (*verum*), and *bonum* (*good*) are strictly equivalent to *ens* (*being*).[64] The primary division of *being* results in *finite being* versus *infinite being*. What can said on this primary logical level has priority over what can be said of beings, once this basic distinction has been made. On the basis of the distinction between finite and infinite being, we can go on with the classification into a certain number of categories. This move sets the theory of the categories apart and construes a broader semantic dimension. In fact, it demolishes the semantic monopoly of the framework of the *Categoriae*. On the semantic level of *being*, we are not restricted to concepts which are not entailed by *being* at all.[65] When we use *being*, then there is common space for using 'being' and for what fits *being* in general, being finite or not. The 'categorical' classification is neither inevitable nor necessary, but only applies to a part of what we can talk about, namely material objects.[66] Duns refrains from the restrictions of such 'categories.' Hence what we can say is not essentially restrained by these differences. What is common to God and his finite creation is 'indifferent' to arbitrary restrictions.[67]

This initial demarcation of the *transcendentia* is only the starting point of a broader development of the theory of transcendent terms. In sum, the basic transcendent term is *ens*. The content of it is as broad as possible. It only excludes that of which it is not true that it possibly exists. Only the impossibility of existence is excluded. The next step is that of the disjunctive transcendent terms. So far two elements are at

---

[64] In terms of an ontology of possible worlds 'ens' means: existent in a possible world. Although Duns' ontology differs from Plantinga's actualism, his concept *ens* is still near to the *actual* of the latter. See Plantinga, *The Nature of Necessity*, chapters 4 and 7–8.

[65] *Lectura* I 8.107: 'Sicut ens sic primo dividitur, ita illa quae consequuntur ens absolute per prius conveniunt sibi quam dividatur in decem genera.' 'Genera' often means: *predicamenta, categoriae*, categories.

[66] Grammar and mathematics would also be destroyed by a semantic monopoly of the *Categoriae*.

[67] Ibid.: 'Sed omnia quae consequuntur ens ut commune est Deo et creaturae, consequuntur ens secundum suam indifferentiam et ideo consequuntur ens per prius quam determinetur ad genera. Huiusmodi autem quae sic consequuntur ens, sunt transcendentia, et ideo non erunt in genere.'

work in defining *transcendents*: first, the element of surpassing the categorical classification in the Aristotelian sense; second, the factor of
being common to everything. What dominates Scotus' theory? He
drops consciously the condition that a transcendent term has to apply
to everything and retains the element of crossing the narrow boundaries of the category formation of Aristotelian empiricism. Then, it
will suffice that it is said of something which is not limited to finite
being. This is true of the most general terms and, thus, this constituent
is picked up in order to clarify the term *transcendens*.

Duns puts in the center that transcendence overcomes conceptual
isolationism. The difference with Aquinas' approach leaps into view. It
is even possible that the transcendent character only applies to one
thing as *necessary* does. Then *transcendens* is not taken to be coextensive with *being* (*Lectura* I 8.110). The sufficient condition is dropping
the limitation that only material things are semantically acceptable.

7.10   THE DILEMMA OF RIVAL INTERPRETATIONS OF *POTENTIA*

Is Scotian *contingency* well known? Steven Marrone once launched
the paradoxical remark that it is quite evident now *that* Scotus played
a decisive part in the development of modal thinking, but not *what*
this part consists of.

> That Duns Scotus's thought marks a turning point in the under-
> standing of modality has ensconced itself among the commonplaces
> of the history of medieval philosophy, a fact almost due to the efforts
> of Simo Knuuttila. But if debate over *whether* Duns altered the course
> of thought on this critical area of philosophy has virtually disap-
> peared, confusion seems still to reign about exactly *what sort of
> change* he wrought.[68]

Emancipation from inherited ways of thought is one thing, but consistent alternative theory formation is quite another, and creating a
new and lucid terminology is something different again.

Contrary to claims like Scotus introducing the idea that opposites
are possible at the same time, or the suggestion that he fathered the
idea of *possible worlds*, or the view that semantic relations among
concepts and propositions are independent of God's power, Calvin
Normore offers an alternative picture of the meaning of Scotus'
philosophy of modality. Duns Scotus entertains one fundamental

---

[68] Marrone, 'Duns Scotus on Metaphysical Potency and Possibility,' *Franciscan Studies* 56
(1998) 265.

notion of *possibility* which is a metaphysical notion, in terms of which he defines other modal concepts. A possibility rests on a power to something. It is not true that the possible is prior to the actual. The two notions of *non-repugnancy of terms* and of *power to bring things about* are completely coordinate, although the consistency of terms is there in virtue of themselves, and not because this consistency would have been caused by God's power. 'Thus I claim that, for Scotus, God gives to the constituents of natures the ontological status required of possibilities.'[69] This very view is shared by Allan Wolter and Ansgar Santogrossi, and Normore wants to elaborate just on this view.[70] Scotus never severed the link between actuality and possibility. In some sense, actual existence is prior to and foundational for possibility. Scotus' tool for rejecting the necessity of the present does not consist of establishing possibility on the logical and semantic analysis of alternatives, but of dividing the present into moments of nature.[71]

Normore's analyses of the relationship between the (in)consistency of *notae* and terms and God's power run parallel to Knuuttila's, apart from the fine point of difference that, for Normore, the production of beings into *esse intelligibile* and *esse possibile* is also a production. *Producing* involves dependence, since the *esse intelligibile* as an instant of nature enjoys priority over the *esse possibile* as an instant of nature.[72] Marrone rightly recognizes the strength of Normore's admonitions with a view to a possibilist interpretation of Duns Scotus' ontology.

7.10.1   Simo Knuuttila

Duns Scotus criticized Aristotelian cosmology dealing with the contingency of causally determined effects in terms of the so-called 'statistical' interpretation of modality.

> Defining necessity and possibility in temporal terms, [. . .] would have meant for Aristotle to base his modal notions entirely on what might be called a *statistical* model of modality: something's being possible must be shown by its *sometimes* happening, and what is

---

69 See Normore, 'Scotus, Modality,' in Honnefelder et al., *Metaphysics and Ethics*, 162.
70 See Normore, 'Scotus, Modality,' in Honnefelder et al., *Metaphysics and Ethics*, 161 f., 166 f. and 169.
71 See also Marrone, 'Metaphysical potency and possibility,' *Franciscan Studies* 56 (1998) 266 ff.
72 See Normore, 'Scotus, Modality,' in Honnefelder et. al., *Metaphysics and Ethics*, 168. Consult also *Ordinatio* I 43.14.

always must be by necessity. Applications of modal notions reduce in effect to comparisons of what happens at different moments of time. [. . .] The whole statistical model can be said to have been one of the conceptual paradigms of Aristotle's modality. It was not the only one, however, and hence did not quite yield to him *definitions* of the different modal notions.[73]

For Knuuttila, Hintikka's investigations of Aristotle's conceptual structures are the point of departure. The 'statistical' model of modal notions applied to temporally indefinite propositions entails the principle of plenitude:

(P) No genuine possibility can remain unrealized.

According to Knuuttila, this principle was disseminated in many ways in medieval thought. The importance of this way of thought for medieval philosophy is pointed out in reference to conceptual patterns found in the traditional line of Boethius and Thomas Aquinas.[74] The thirteenth-century theory of causality shows off the necessitarian principle of causality: *The effect is entailed by its cause*, but the Christian thinkers avoided a deterministic theory of nature and

> the 'statistical' theory of modality was not accepted by most schoolmen without qualification, because it was thought to restrict God's freedom. In the twelfth century one made usually a distinction between natural possibilities and God's possibilities.[75]

Knuuttila varies this assessment in *Time and Modality in Scholasticism* by concluding that the *principium plenitudinis* was usually not

---

[73] Hintikka, *Time and Necessity*, 102–103. Pay attention also to the words of thanks to Knuuttila and Remes, *Time and Necessity*, VIII (V–VIII: 'Preface'). Cf. J. Hintikka, in collaboration with Remes and Knuuttila, 'Aristotle on Modality and Determinism,' *Acta Philosophica Fennica* 29, 13–58, and Hintikka's contributions, digested in 'Realizations of Possibilities in Time,' in *Time and Necessity*, chapter V: 'Necessity, universality, and time in Aristotle,' *Ajatus* 20 (1957) 65–90, and Hintikka, 'A. O. Lovejoy on Plenitude in Aristotle,' *Ajatus* 29 (1967) 5–11.

[74] See Knuuttila's fine summary of the Aristotelian point of view in his 'Time and Modality in Scholasticism,' in Knuuttila, (ed.), *Reforging the Great Chain of Being*, 166–170, and his illuminating expositions on Boethius, Abelard, and Thomas Aquinas, *Reforging the Great Chain*, 170–187, 197 f. and 208–217. For Averroes, see idem, 'The Statistical Interpretation of Modality in Averroes and Thomas Aquinas,' *Ajatus* 37 (1978) 79–98.

[75] Knuuttila, 'Scotus' Criticism of the " 'Statistical" Interpretation of Modality,' *Sprache und Erkenntnis im Mittelalter*, 443. Cf. idem, 'Time and Modality in Scholasticism,' *Reforging*, 198–207: 'God's possibilities in early scholasticism.' *Time and Modality in Scholasticism* is based on *Aika ja modaliteetti aristotelisessa skolastiikassa*: the turning point!

accepted for the same reasons. The 'statistical theory of modality' (Hintikka, Knuuttila) and the principle of plenitude are connected logically, but the Christian thinkers of the twelfth and thirteenth centuries were more on their guard with respect to the *principium plenitudinis* than with respect to the logic of diachrony.[76] The evidence for the widespread presence of the 'logic of diachrony' does not signal a hidden necessitarianism – the presence of contingency thought being strongly felt in many quarters of theology intuitively – but it simply signals a lack of theoretical power to offer a consistent alternative. This is a fact known from the history of the sciences. The scientific revolution of the seventeenth century did not touch all sectors of physics at the same time. Likewise, the philosophical revolution of the thirteenth century did not touch all sectors of theology and philosophy at the same time. What Newton did for the natural sciences at the end of the seventeenth century, John Duns did for theology and philosophy at the end of the thirteenth century.

Within this context, Knuuttila's general observation holds: 'One should always bear in mind the possibility of the statistical interpretation of modality in discussing medieval texts containing modal concepts.' Knuuttila then continues his breathtaking story of Duns Scotus' alternative:

> I will put forth a definite limit after which a scholar also has to consider the possibility that the model in question had been rejected on the basis of an entirely different understanding of modality. I mean John Duns Scotus' criticism of the statistical interpretation and his own theory of modality which is based on a distinction between logical and real possibilities, on an extension of the focus of attention to alternative states of affairs with respect to the same moment of time, and on the essential function of the concept of compossibility.[77]

The first part of Knuuttila's exposition is mainly based on *De Primo Principio*, Duns Scotus' ontological monograph, dating from the last phase of his career.

I agree with many elements of Knuuttila's admirable contributions. There are also some tensions. The fact that a scientific revolution does

---

76 The same phenomenon can still be observed in theology: most modern theologians reject the principle of plenitude, still succumbing to the logic of diachrony, and being afraid of the logic of synchrony.

77 Knuuttila, 'Time and Modality in Scholasticism,' in Knuuttila (ed.), *Reforging*, 217 f. Cf. 165 f. *KN* (1981) sees Duns' logical revolution as the cornerstone of a broader theological and philosophical revolution – in the sense of Thomas Kuhn's paradigm shift. Cf. *PMA* §§2.6–2.8. Knuuttila's pages 226–233 contain one of the very first expositions on *Lectura* I 39.

not touch all sectors of science at the same time is applicable to philosophical revolutions too and, in particular, to that of the thirteenth
century. This pattern also holds for the explosive series of Scotian
innovations. Knuuttila investigates them in terms of the modern
notion of *possible worlds*.

> In this model possibilities are classified into equivalence classes on the
> basis of relations of compossibility. One of the classes into which
> logical possibilities are partitioned is the actual world. Because these
> classes contain only mutually consistent propositions, it is impossible
> according to Scotus that the actual world would contain all possibil-
> ities as actual. The relationships between possible states of affairs
> always exclude part of them from any joint world. This is the back-
> ground of Scotus' treatment of the claim that if God knows that *p and*
> *M–p*, it follows that God is liable to err. Scotus states that nothing
> impossible follows if it holds that *p* while it is possible that – *p* and
> the possibility is thought to be actual.[78]

This is perfectly sound doctrine, but was it taught by Duns Scotus?
It was not, because Duns Scotus does not have a theory of equivalence classes. Such an ontology of possible worlds can be validly
derived from Duns Scotus' innovation of *synchronic alternatives*,
but, from the purely historical point of view, there are some obsta-
cles. Duns Scotus' notion of *synchronic contingency* entails *factual
actuality*. For this reason, *contingency* is not a necessary feature of
the whole of possible reality. *Contingency* is will-dependent, for it is
constituted by a decision of the divine will. Since the status of what
is contingent differs from our approach to *contingency* – *if* we
acknowledge *true contingency* – the status of what is possible also
differs from what is now understood by *possibility*. These notions of
Duns Scotus are *Actua*-based, as it is the case in the ontological
drafts of Kripke and Plantinga. Duns Scotus was an 'actualist', just
as Alvin Plantinga and Bob Adams are, but an actualist without possible worlds. There is still another difference in comparison with
Plantinga. Duns Scotus is not a Platonic actualist. He does not accept
states of affairs and propositions and so on as necessary entities. The
Scotian counterpart of Plantinga's necessary entities and Knuuttila's
equivalence classes is *the knowable being (esse intelligibile)*.
However, the knowability sphere of the *esse intelligibile* does not
house states of affairs or propositions which are true or false, but

[78] Knuuttila, 'Time and Modality in Scholasticism,' *Reforging*, 232. We have to distinguish historical from systematic questions.

neutral propositions. Their truth value of a *possibility which is opposed to factuality* is empty.[79] The status of what is possible in this sense is the *nihil* of the *creatio ex nihilo*. Scotus' ontology is anchored in theology of creation. It is an ontology of an open creation and the basic openness of God. However, the important tool of alternative maximal sets is missing, although the notion of ontological alternativity is basic to his thought.

The most pressing problem of Duns Scotus' ontology is the status of the *possible*. In general, there are astonishing disagreements in Scotist studies, running from one end of the ontological spectrum to the other. Nevertheless, in many cases we may readily discern what goes wrong in reading Scotus, but in the case of the essential of Duns Scotus' ontology things are different. We are not allowed to say that the interpretations of John Boler and Simo Knuuttila, Calvin Normore and Stephen Marrone are simply misreadings of Scotus' texts. The tenor of Duns Scotus' ontological innovations is clear, but the detailed contents of the whole of his ontological moves are often enigmatic. What was his ontological stance when his development suddenly stopped and what were the contours of his personal kind of actualism? In the Middle Ages, all shades of Christian ontological options were actualist, but the concrete 'applications' were rather different.

On the one hand, we meet the view that Duns Scotus' ontology itself eventually collapses into a kind of necessitarianism (Schwamm, Pannenberg).[80] On the other hand, Duns Scotus' ontology is considered to be a kind of 'possibilism': he should reason from possibility to actuality and it is sometimes said that, in comparison with Aquinas, this is his gross error. The consequence of this interpretation is that Duns Scotus must mean by *being* (*ens*) something *possible*.

> We can explain 'being' (*ens*) only by saying that it applies to that 'to which it is not repugnant to be.' I take this to mean that the concept 'being' refers to what can exist, i.e., it applies to anything, the assumption of whose existence contains no contradiction.[81]

---

[79] The crucial possibility is a type of possibility which is not dealt with by Hughes and Cresswell. Cf. §7.4.

[80] Cf. Wycliffe's condemnation at the Council of Constance (1415). The ontology of the Reformed tradition, based on Scotian contingency, is rather generally considered to be a kind of determinism.

[81] Weinberg, *A Short History of Medieval Philosophy*, 217 (216–220). This approach is still reflected in CF 96–102. See *Ordinatio* I 2.262 and *Quaestiones Metaphysicae* IV 1.40.

The first line of interpretation simply ignores Scotian contingency and the specific connection between *will* and *contingency*. As to the second line of interpretation, it is not true that, according to Duns Scotus, *being (ens)* and *possibility* coincide:

> *Possible* is more common than *being in actuality* or *being* in the sense of *essential being*. For this reason, we have to be aware that what follows is not valid: *impossible* and *possible* are contradictory and *not-being* and *being* are contradictory. Therefore, the fourth concept does not follow from the second one (namely: if it is *possible* (2), then it is *being* (4)), although the third concept follows from the first one (if it is *impossible* (1), then it is *not-being* (3)), but rather conversely, the second concept follows from the fourth, namely, if it is *being*, then it is *possible*.[82]

This is confirmed by a conclusion written down about four years later in *Ordinatio* I 36: 'The point of the present discussion is that just as every being is possible, everything that is *impossible* is *not-being*,'[83] but Duns Scotus passes. For him, the predicate *being possible* is entailed by the predicates *known* or *being intelligible (esse cognitum)*. However, this *esse cognitum (being known)* shares in the *esse volitum*, by God, from eternity.[84]

7.10.2   The dilemma and perspective of ontology

What subject are we studying, when we concentrate on medieval philosophy? Jan Aertsen once wondered in a mild mood of despair whether there be medieval philosophy at all. It surely is an aesthetic asset to be a professor of medieval philosophy, but you still find yourself permanently reading theologians. The Parisian tradition of studies in medieval philosophy from Cousin to Bréhier denied that there was medieval philosophy at all. A likewise famous Christian response to his courageous view on medieval thought acknowledged that there was some medieval philosophy, but denied that doing philosophy existed within the religious order John Duns adhered

---

[82] *Lectura* I 36.36: '*Possibile* est communius quam ens in actu vel ens secundum esse essentiae. Ideo, non sequitur: Impossibile et possibile contradicunt, et non-ens et ens contradicunt. Igitur, licet sequitur ad primum tertium ("si est impossibile, est non-ens"), non tamen ad secundum sequitur quartum ("quod si est possibile, quod sit ens"), sed potius e contra.'

[83] *Ordinatio* I 36.57: 'Ita in proposito: sicut omne ens est possibile, ita omne impossibile est non-ens.'

[84] A Plantingian type of ontology, Platonist ingredients being stripped off, is to be derived from the main lines of Scotian ontology.

to: Bonaventure was a mystic and Duns Scotus a theologian at best (Mandonnet, De Wulf, Van Steenberghen).

Another view stresses that the knowledge about God we might acquire outside revelation is stored in the philosophical discipline labeled metaphysics. The philosophical coherence of Scotus' theological claims is always of extreme importance to him.

> Scotus never relies merely on theological arguments when ex professo discussing philosophical matters. Scotus is thus interested in giving a coherent account of the world independently of revelation. Scotus should therefore be counted as a philosopher with a philosophical agenda.[85]

This is the reverse of what Cousin and Hauréau thought. At any rate, it is an impressive rehabilitation. Duns Scotus started as a non-philosopher in the cradle of medieval studies in philosophy and now he is acknowledged to be a great philosopher.

The range of such interpretations of Duns' thought is remarkable. Richard Cross senses the mystery in all this when he remarks: 'The correct way of trying to understand revealed truth, for Scotus, necessarily involves a defense of what we could call the philosophical coherence of such truth. Theology, for Scotus, is a deeply rational exercise' (ibid.). My question would be whether it be even possible for us to characterize adequately the nature of Duns' thought and what his thought means to us, in terms of our concepts of philosophy and theology. In a sense, the predominance of faith and theology in medieval thought was a relief to scholars like Cousin and Hauréau, Renan and Bréhier. During the age of faith, people were unable to think.

'A distinction between the realms of philosophy and theology, of reason and faith, was as foreign to the eleventh century as it had been to St Augustine in the fourth,'[86] although there was some debate about the place of logic in theology. Even the 'rationalists' supported the ideal of *fides quaerens intellectum* and the so-called anti-dialecticians were also sophisticated in interpreting matters of faith. The breach between faith and reason so dear to old-fashioned historical literature on eleventh-century thought is itself a myth. In contrast with patristic thought, there was no philosophy as an independent power. When it is said that even Anselm did not have an adequate idea of what

---

[85] Cross, *Duns Scotus*, 13.
[86] Sidwell, *Reading Medieval Latin*, 230.

philosophy was, then this appraisal might be true, but is as irrelevant as the trivial truth that he did not have any idea of soccer or a handkerchief.

Our sense of mystery deepens when we ask ourselves in what way Bonaventure and Thomas Aquinas, Henry of Ghent and Duns Scotus would answer our questions. According to Hauréau, the situation was easy. Although the medievals were unable to produce a distinct philosophy, they knew what philosophy was. Again and again, they appeal to the Philosopher and *Philosophus* was not a Christian. The contribution of the medievals was important, because they kept the philosophical legacy alive and were mediators of real philosophy to later generations.

There is some grain of truth in this remarkable theory. Apart from the extreme variety of the history of the word *philosophia*, it is clear what the Christian thinkers thought of the *philosophia* of the *philosophi* after the clash during the second quarter of the thirteenth century. By and large, philosophy is wrong.[87] *Philosophia* did not connote the intellectual discipline of an academic subject, but a way of thought, a way of ideas characterized by a specific set of conceptual structures. Here, modern terminology is quite different. Duns is convinced that we can demonstrate certain truths about God and he does so in metaphysics, an important philosophical discipline, affiliated with modern natural theology. Surely, Duns distinguishes between theology and metaphysics. They have different first objects: the first object of theology is God as He is infinite, and the first object of metaphysics is *ens*. We find the first view expressed by Duns. We might expect that he also says that metaphysics belongs to philosophy and that natural theology is a part of metaphysics. Nevertheless, he does not do so and that is precisely what we expect when we realize that, to his mind, *philosophia* is impressive untruth.[88]

Apart from the point of medieval terminology, Abelardo Lobato is quite right in spotting the presence of a Christian metaphysics in Duns Scotus' thought. In order to elaborate on it we have to be aware of the ontology of contingency and will and of creation theology.[89] Lobato

---

[87] On Scotus' assessment of 'pagan philosophy,' see Lobato, 'La metafísica cristiana de Duns Escoto,' *De doctrina Ioannis Duns Scoti* II 76–80. Cf. González, *Historia de la filosofía* II, Madrid 1886, 328: Scotus is the Kant of the thirteenth century.

[88] See Chapter 14. Cf. the desideratum of Honnefelder in *Ens inquantum ens* (1979) 3: a monograph on the place of philosophy within Duns' theology has long been missing.

[89] See Solaguren's excellent contribution 'Contingencia y creación en la filosofía de Duns Escoto,' *De doctrina Ioannis Duns Scoti* II 297–348.

talks of it in terms of a *new Christian metaphysics*. The main ingredients are theories by which it can be proved that the Lord our God is as perfect as possible. Such an ontology focuses on the clarification of the infinite being, of freedom and love and the knowledge of the mystery of Christ.[90]

---

[90] See Lobato, 'La metafísica cristiana de Duns Escoto,' *De doctrina Ioannis Duns Scoti* II 80–85.

CHAPTER 8

Epistemology

8.1 INTRODUCTION

The originality of medieval philosophy and the creativity of its logic and theory of knowledge speak very much in its favor. Medieval philosophy may have been considered uninteresting because of its alleged lack of originality. However, its contributions are actually of tremendous cultural importance and they are theoretically interesting for modern philosophy and systematic theology. The reason is that many of its innovations do not have parallel theories in ancient philosophy. Medieval thought yields plenty of evidence refuting the popular view that systematic thought during these dark centuries was unilluminating, but the legacy of medieval theories is fresh and particularly conspicuous in logic and semantics, theology and philosophy. L. M. de Rijk brilliantly pointed out how creative medieval thought has been.[1] In his important introduction to medieval philosophy, De Rijk lists four examples of original contributions that excel the inventions of ancient Greek, Hellenistic and Latin philosophy: terminist logic, which is in fact a part of the much wider phenomenon of the *logica modernorum*, the metaphysics of Thomas Aquinas, the critical theory of knowledge of the fourteenth and fifteenth centuries, and a way of thought which differs markedly from necessitarian Greek philosophy.[2] Duns Scotus' contributions to a critical theory of knowledge are the main theme of this chapter.

The union of existential and intellectual forces in the thirteenth and fourteenth centuries created many theoretical innovations. Revelation influenced philosophy in terms of a specific *theological* model of thought. Ontology approached being *as being* and its essential structures.[3] The secret weapon of the new way of doing philosophy is the

---

[1] Compare Chapter 14, especially §1 and §10. Cf. Chapters 15 and 16.

[2] See *PMA* 69–71, and *PMA* §§3.2–3.4 and 4.4–4.7. Consult *Logica Modernorum* I–II.

[3] See *PMA* 214–215. Compare Vos, 'Middeleeuwse Wijsbegeerte,' *Nederlands Theologisch Tijdschrift* 34 (1980) 72, and Bettoni, *Duns Scotus*, 15–21.

semantics and ontology of necessity and contingency. Gilson, Boehner, and De Rijk speak of *radical contingency* as the peculiar trait of Franciscan-Augustinian thought,[4] but what is *radical contingency* up to? My answer reads: *radical* contingency is *synchronic* contingency.[5] The young Duns built this concept into the whole of his systematic theology, the historical and systematic context of his theory of knowledge. Now, it is to be pointed out how this radical approach to contingency touches the theory of knowledge, against the background of an absolute approach to knowledge and science.

If the epistemic principle of certainty: 'If *a* knows that *p*, then *a* knows that *a* knows that *p* (*C.KK*),' and the epistemic principle of necessity: 'If *a* knows that *p*,' then it is necessary that *p* (*C.KN*)' dominate a philosophical system, then the consequences are far-reaching, for they entail the epistemic principle: 'If *a* knows that *p*, then it is necessary that *a* knows that *p*,' to be labeled as (*C.K,NK*). This outcome is important, for (*C.K,NK*) entails the decisive principle of necessitarianism:

(N) All states of affairs are necessary

and vice versa. The strict equivalence of (N) and (*C.K,NK*) formally reflects the fundamental structure of ancient Greek epistemology and *philosophia*, characterized by the parallelism of *thought* and *being*.[6] In contrast to ancient and modern philosophy, medieval theology and philosophy show a wealth of exceptions to these principles. For Christian thought, the cause was the more pressing, because the certainty rule cannot be dropped in the theory of divine knowledge. So, (N) was under enormous pressure. The way Duns Scotus transformed the epistemic rules in the whole of the web of his concepts and theories constituted an epistemological revolution.[7] His epistemology eminently illustrates this philosophical emancipation on many scores.

Ockham's razor is still one of the famous tools of doing philosophy. However, Ockham's razor is, in fact, the *razor Scoti*: the basic epistemological and methodological principle of *parsimony* (§8.2). We also consult Duns' splendid epistemological excursus in *Lectura* I 3.172–181 and look at its systematic background (§8.3). The three

---

[4] See *PMA* 71 ff., 80 ff. and 216–218.
[5] See *CF* 4–5 and 23–37: 'Scotus' Theory of Contingency.'
[6] See *PMA* §§7.21–7.22 and *KN* I–III and VII. The parallel principle of plenitude plays the role of (N) and (*C.K,NK*) in the Helsinki School of Hintikka and Knuuttila.
[7] See also §§1.4–1.6 and chapters 9 and 14. Cf. *DS* 27–45 and 60–63.

kinds of certain knowledge Duns considers in due course are dealt with, while the parallel text in *Ordinatio* I 3.229–245 is also considered: knowledge of self-evident principles (§8.4), experiential and inductive knowledge (§8.5), and self-evident knowledge of human acts (§8.6). §8.7 treats of intuitive knowledge and §8.8 deals with memory. §8.9 rounds off with an evaluation in terms of the history of the main epistemological concepts.

8.2   METHODOLOGICAL PARSIMONY: THE *RAZOR SCOTI*

Essentialist and modist interpretations of Scotus' thought depict the subtle master as a mind, fond of inventing freely shadowy entities. However, his philosophical style of careful analysis and argumentation does not create any room for such theoretical frivolity. The principle of ontological parsimony, or economy, is usually formulated as follows:

> Entities are not to be multiplied beyond necessity (entia non sunt multiplicanda praeter necessitatem).

This formulation is not precisely found in the works of Ockham (±1285–1349), but the thought itself occurs again and again with him. Its frequent use by him gained it the name of *Ockham's razor*. This principle of parsimonious explanation is frequently worded as follows:

> Plurality is not to be assumed without necessity.

Moody believed that

> Entities are not to be multiplied without necessity

is absent in the works of Ockham. He is also very generous in pointing out the meaning of the use made of the principle by Ockham,[8] but let us now have a look at some of Duns' formulations of this razor. The oldest formula pops up in early occurrences in *Quaestiones super libros Metaphysicorum Aristotelis* (*Quaestiones Metaphysicae*) I 4.41 where we read:

> *Numquam est ponenda pluralitas sine necessitate*

and in *Quaestiones Metaphysicae* IV 2.136 where we find this wording:

> *Pluralitas numquam ponenda est sine necessitate.*

---

[8] See Moody, 'William of Ockham,' *EP* VIII 307 (= idem, 'William of Ockham,' in White (ed.), *Ernest A. Moody. Collected Papers 1933–1969*, 413 f.).

This formula can be compared with a variant we find in *Quaestiones Metaphysicae* VII 12.30:

> *Numquam ponenda sunt plura sine necessitate.*[9]

Duns' proposal to solve the main problem in this same *quaestio* uses just this maxim as its basis:

> *Pluralitas non est ponenda sine necessitate.*

This *quaestio* of the *Quaestiones Metaphysicae* also has much in common with *Lectura* II 18. In the later text of *Quaestiones Metaphysicae* VII 18.14 we read:

> *Nihil non manifestum ponendum est a philosophantibus sine necessitate.*

Scotus' razor is also found in *Lectura* II 2.99:

> *Non est ponenda pluralitas entium sine ratione* (A plurality of entities has only to be assumed if it can be defended well).

The parallel text of *Ordinatio* II 2.130 uses this formula in characterizing a theory defended by Henry of Ghent. Duns' criticism concludes:

> *Sed haec positio ponere videtur pluralitatem sine necessitate* (However, this position seems to assume some plurality without any necessity).

A later occurrence is found in *Ordinatio* III 34:

> *Pluralitas specierum non videtur ponenda sine necessitate manifesta.*[10]

Now we understand the weight of Moody's observation that Ockham 'seems not to have used the formulation "Entities are not to be multiplied without necessity",'[11] for the ingredients *entities* (*entia*) and *without necessity* occur with Duns Scotus, while *multiplied* is elicited by *plurality*. Duns did not only father the principle, but his texts also seem to be the main source of its traditional formulation, and in addition Ockham's expressions are also found with Duns.

Duns' ontology makes it also clear in what direction we have to look for the impact of *the principle of parsimony* in its Scotian sense.

---

[9] The formula is paralleled in *Lectura* II 14.4: 'Plura non sunt ponenda sine necessitate.'

[10] See also *Lectura* I 2.202 and *Ordinatio* IV 11.3 and IV 11.14. For the *razor Scoti*, see *DS* 92 and 222, cf. Vos, 'De ethische optie van Duns Scotus,' *Kerk en Theologie* 44 (1993) 29, and idem, 'Hauptlinien der Scotischen Ethik,' in Schneider (ed.), *Johannes Duns Scotus. Seine Spiritualität und Ethik*, 21.

[11] Moody, 'William of Ockham,' *EP* VIII 307.

Duns does not frame entities in order to make coherent a speculative picture. The existential status of the entities criticized much by Ockham and modern thinkers is argued for by him on the level of ontological necessity. Of course, one may deny this level outright, but it is not fair to adorn a priori the alternative type of ontology with the epithets *sober* and *empirical*, and Duns' type of ontology with the epithets *speculative* and *abstract*. Here, we have only to observe the secret of Duns' use of the principle: Duns only assumes the existence of *a* if it is impossible that *a* is not.

This situation contrasts with Moody's view on the meaning of the principle:

> The principal use made by Ockham of the principle of parsimony was in the elimination of pseudo-explanatory entities, according to a criterion he expresses in the statement that nothing is to be assumed as necessary in accounting for any fact, unless it is established by evident experience or evident reasoning, or is required by the articles of faith. (Ibid.)

Ockham precisely drops Duns' *Lectura* notions of *possibile logicum* and *synchronic contingency* and the *Ordinatio* notion of *potentia ad opposita*. What is the *possibile logicum* for Duns is the theory of *suppositio* for Ockham. With him the downfall of the *possibile logicum* and *synchronic contingency* in the Scotian sense is accompanied by the downfall of the notions of *structural moments* and *the formal objective distinction*, but these kinds of differences are not to be seen as reasons for charging Duns Scotus with speculative and pseudo-explanatory reasoning. Duns simply tries to defend every argumentative step – against the background of the principle of parsimony. If the realm of *synchronic contingency* is dropped, one drops also the realm where necessary patterns may obtain.

8.3   THE THEORETICAL BACKGROUND OF *LECTURA* I 3.172–181

The theme of *Lectura* I 3.144 ff. belongs to the theological theory of knowledge. The question under consideration is whether a believer (*viator*) needs a specific revelation in order to have certain knowledge. The answer of Henry of Ghent is a positive one and it is built on his exemplarism. There have been many points of debate and disagreement between Henry of Ghent (±1235–93) and Duns Scotus (b.1265/1266), but it is always important to ask what is precisely at stake between them. They defend the same type of philosophical position. The main position they agree on is to be summarized as follows: there exists the possibility of certain knowledge of the *deductive* form of argumentation (*Lectura* I 3.165–166), of certain knowledge of *experience*, and of certain knowledge of *personal human acts* (*Lectura* I 3.167).

John Duns does not attack *what* Henry of Ghent defends, but *the way in which* he defends his position. He contests that the epistemological argumentations of Henry of Ghent can give sufficient support to his own conclusions. According to Duns, his line of argument leads to the skepticism of the ancient *Academy* (*Lectura* I 3.162 and 167) and does not lead to the view of Augustine.[12] Duns follows a fixed pattern in criticizing Henry of Ghent whose basic intentions and views he does not attack. The point at issue is that the direction which is philosophically and theologically at stake cannot be effectively defended in the way Henry of Ghent has worked it out. In this particular case things are even worse: 'His arguments destroy this view completely.'[13] *Lectura* I 30 and 35–36 show fine examples of this pattern. Of course, Duns does not believe that one of the contributors to the condemned *Parisian Articles* (1277) embraces a necessitarian point of view. On the contrary, just that point of view is his personal target and Duns joins forces, but, unfortunately, *in concreto*, Henry's arguments lead to that unfavorable position as Duns interprets it. Duns develops his own fundamental point of view in order to make sure his defense. The weak spot of the skeptical opposition is the conviction that corrections and amendments are impossible. Duns combats the impossibility of correcting.[14] Within the context of faith and a rational inquiry for decisive arguments, Duns points out three kinds of certain knowledge. Knowing *certain truth* (*certa veritas*) is possible in three ways: (a) certain knowledge of *principles* on account of the terms used in such propositions (*Lectura* I 3.173–176); (b) certain experiential knowledge (*Lectura* I 3.177–180); (c) certain

---

[12] *Lectura* I 3.162: 'Sed contra hanc opinionem sic procedo. Primo ostendo quod auctoritates Augustini non sint allegatae secundum mentem suam, sed magis secundum mentem academicorum dicentium omnia esse dubia, et quod omni homini falsum concludant.' See *Lectura* I 3.162 ff., 168 and 171.

[13] *Lectura* I 3.168: 'Rationes suae hoc totum destruunt.' These arguments of Henry are summarized in *Lectura* I 3.157–159, and the point of view they tend to destroy is found in *Lectura* I 3.162–167.

[14] *Lectura* I 3.169: 'Si anima sit passiva erroris [. . .] et ideo per nihil in ea potest rectificari, nec veritas haberi, cum actus intelligendi sit mutabilior anima in qua est, sequitur quod ipse actus intelligendi non erit verus nec veritatem continebit.'

knowledge of human acts (*Lectura* I 3.181).[15] §§8.4–8.6 deal with these kinds of certain knowledge, and likewise with the parallel analysis of *Ordinatio* I 3.

8.4   DEDUCTIVE KNOWLEDGE

The first type of *certain knowledge* is *knowledge of principles*. The subject of this branch of epistemology consists of *knowable propositions which are known on account of their terms*.[16] How does Duns approach this kind of certain knowledge of principles (*principia*)? In a deductive argumentation we distinguish between *premisses* and *conclusions*, the former being the propositions from which we derive conclusions. In *Lectura* I 3.173–176 Duns focuses on knowledge on the logical level of *premisses*, and not knowledge on the logical level of *conclusions*. On this level, a more precise specification has still to be added: the so-called *principles* (*principia*) are as such *first* principles and these first principles are propositions which can function as premisses and are *self-evident*. *Lectura* I 3.173 contains a marvellous statement of this epistemic aspect:

> We acquire the truth of *principles* as follows: when a *proposition* is *self-evident*, it can only be formed by our intellect, if our intellect knows its *terms*. The *terms* are as such (*naturaliter*) known just to the intellect: precisely the *terms* include a relation in which *terms are analytically related to other terms*. Therefore, they include the truth of such a union. Therefore, because the intellect can have certain knowledge (*notitia*) of *terms*, then it can also have certain truth about the *principle* of such *terms*.[17]

In the next section Duns presents as a standard example:

> *Every whole is larger than any of its parts.*

The key terms in Duns' theory of analytical propositions are *conformitas* and *deformitas*. In an affirmative proposition *terms* are united

---

[15] For an English translation of *Lectura* I 3.172–181 and commentary, see Frank and Wolter, *Duns Scotus, Metaphysician*, 124–133 and 164–183.

[16] *Lectura* I 3.172: 'Scibilia [. . .] ex terminis cognoscuntur.'

[17] Ibid.: 'Veritas principiorum sic acquiritur in nobis: quando enim propositio est per se nota, intellectus noster non potest eam componere nisi cognoscat terminos, termini autem sunt noti ipsi intellectui naturaliter; sed ipsi termini includunt conformitatem unionis terminorum ad ipsos terminos, igitur includunt veritatem talis unionis; cum igitur intellectus possit habere certam notitiam de terminis, igitur et certam veritatem de principio talium terminorum.'

or combined. So, a *proposition* can also be called a *composition* (*compositio*) because of the *union of terms*. The terms of the proposition

> *Omne totum est maius sua parte*

are: *totum, maius,* and *pars*. When these terms are united, the analytical structure of *whole* and . . . *being larger than* . . . must be able to bear the truth of the proposition. The *conformitas* of a proposition is the *analytical coherence* of the relationship between subject and predicate. The *deformitas* is not the simple absence of this kind of analyticality, but the inconsistent relationship between subject and predicate.[18] Understanding terms involves seeing that these terms include each other or exclude each other.

8.4.1 *Ordinatio* I 3.229–245

In *Ordinatio* I 3 *pars* 1 *quaestio* 4, Duns covers the same ground, but the theory of deductive argumentation shows a coherent expansion. In this way the relationship between *Lectura* I–II and *Ordinatio* I–II can be commented on. *Lectura* I 3.181 claims that there is certain knowledge of self-evident and axiomatic principles. *Ordinatio* I 3.229 is concerned with certain knowledge of *principles* and *theses* (*conclusiones*). First, there is a clear exposition of the status of self-evident principles (*Ordinatio* I 3.230–232) and, second, the status of derivable *conclusiones* is dealt with (*Ordinatio* I 3.233–234).

Why can we be certain of *principles*? *Principles* are *self-evident* (*per se nota*), and they are self-evident since the *terms of a principle* stand in a specific logical relation to each other: the one term of a principle necessarily *includes* the other term in an evident way.[19] The intellect puts these terms together and provided it understands them, it grasps them in their logical relationship. If that logical relationship is *analytical coherence* (*conformitas*), then we necessarily grasp the conceptual basis of this kind of *analyticality* in composing the terms under consideration (*actus componendi*) while such a self-evident proposition is

---

[18] *Lectura* I 3.174: 'Si igitur cum apprehensione terminorum stet deformitas unionis, tunc in eodem intellectu erunt contrariae opiniones, una tamen formaliter et alia causaliter – quod est inconveniens.'

[19] *Ordinatio* I 3.230: 'Termini principiorum per se notorum talem habent identitatem ut alter evidenter necessario alterum includat.' Here, *includere* means more than *to entail*: P includes Q only if, semantically, the meaning of Q is a part of the definition of P. Cf. *KN* 73 f. On Duns Scotus' theory of knowledge of first principles in *Ordinatio* I 3, see Effler, 'Duns Scotus and the Necessity of First Principles of the Knowledge,' *De doctrina Ioannis Duns Scoti* II 3–20.

the result of the *composition* (*compositio*) or combination of these terms.[20] If there is a *composition* of such terms, then such a *compositio* must be true.[21] Given the logical relation of *inclusion* of the terms of a proposition, the proposition must be true and we see that it is necessarily true. If we have the one component without the other in such a way that the other term is excluded, then a contradiction is involved (*Ordinatio* I 3.232). The method of proving a necessary truth consists of the denial of such a proposition while this negation turns out to be impossibly true. Against this logical background Duns expounds the epistemic status of a thesis (*conclusio*):

> Once we are certain of *first principles*, it is clear how we are also certain of *theorems* which are derived [*illatis*] from them – on the basis of the formal demonstrative force of the sound syllogism – because the *certainty of a thesis* [*theorem*] depends only on the *certainty of the principles* and the *demonstrative force of the inference* [*illatio*].[22]

Why is the possibility of error excluded in such cases? We might suppose that erring senses endanger even the conviction that such propositions are true. However, our sense experience constitutes only the occasion of such certain knowledge, because it gives occasion to understanding the involved terms.[23] The intellect uses the terms in its own way. Such truth claims are themselves independent of sense experience.[24]

---

[20] Ibid.: 'Intellectus, componens illos terminos ex quo apprehendit eos, habet apud se necessariam causam conformitatis illius actus componendi ad ipsos terminos quorum est compositio, et etiam causam evidentem talis conformitatis; et ideo necessario patet illa conformitas cuius causam evidentem apprehendit in terminis.'

[21] Ibid.: 'Haec autem *conformitas compositionis ad terminos* est *veritas compositionis*, ergo non potest stare compositio terminorum quin sit vera, et ita non potest stare perceptio illius compositionis et perceptio terminorum quin stet perceptio conformitatis compositionis ad terminos, et ita perceptio veritatis, quia prima percepta evidenter includunt perceptionem istius veritatis.'

[22] *Ordinatio* I 3.233: 'Habita certitudine de principiis primis, patet quomodo habebitur de conclusionibus illatis ex eis, propter evidentiam formae syllogismi perfecti, cum certitudo conclusionis tantummodo dependeat ex certitudine principiorum et ex evidentia illationis.' The same consideration is already found in *Lectura* I 3.166 – without integration into Duns' total view of knowledge. Cf. *KN* 73 f. There it functions as an independent note regarding the *auctoritates*: Duns claims the tradition, including Augustine – against Henry – for, according to Duns, his own view *follows from* what the tradition says.

[23] *Ordinatio* I 3.234: 'Respondeo [. . .] quod intellectus non habet sensus pro causa, sed tantum pro occasione, quia intellectus non potest habere notitiam simplicium nisi acceptam a sensibus.'

[24] Ibid.: 'Illa tamen accepta, virtute sua potest simul componere simplicia – et si ex ratione talium simplicium sit complexio evidenter vera, intellectus virtute propria et terminorum assentiet illi complexioni, non virtute sensus a quo accipit terminos exterius.'

There are propositions which are necessarily true in virtue of the meanings of their terms. If this deductive relationship is not immediately seen, we need a deductive argument in order to derive theses from self-evidently known premises. Duns stresses that the certainty of a thesis or a theorem exclusively depends on the certainty of self-evident premises and the demonstrative force of an inference. In such an inference, we deductively derive the thesis to be concluded, step by step. According to Thomas Aquinas, a conclusion loses some degree of certainty by doing so, because the argument, going forward step by step, takes some time.[25] Duns Scotus rejects this loss of certainty, since the degree of reasonableness of a necessary conclusion is not diminished by the process of deductive reasoning. Duns constructs an alternative epistemic framework by replacing *time* with *structure*. The nature of *validity* decides the issue of certainty, not the fact that the argument is construed in time, within some historical context. Scotus abandons the parallelism of *thought* and *being* and uncouples *deductive reasonableness* and *time*. This last point had already been put forward clearly in *Lectura Prologus* 109:

> For the transition from principles to conclusion it is not required that such a transition takes place in diverse moments of time, but that it takes place simultaneously; our intellect also knows principles and the deduction of a conclusion from them. Therefore, for a deduction it is required only that something is known structurally ealier, and something else structurally later, and that the intellect can deduce, temporally simultaneously, what is known structurally later from what is known structurally earlier.[26]

8.5 EXPERIENTIAL AND INDUCTIVE KNOWLEDGE

The second type of *certain knowledge*, to be dealt with in *Lectura* I 3.177–180, is *certain experiential knowledge* (*cognitio certa veritatis per experientiam*). What does this kind of certain knowledge look like? This second kind of certain knowledge (*certitudo cognitionis*) is come by from experience (*per experientiam*).[27] However, Duns' first treatment of inductive generalization is an earlier one, to be found in *Quaestiones super libros Metaphysicae Aristotelis* I 4.

---

[25] Thomas Aquinas, *Expositio in libros Posteriorum Analyticorum*, Book II *lectio* 20.4.

[26] Vos et al., *Duns Scotus on Divine Love*, 15 (14 ff.) and 24 ff. Compare also §9.7.

[27] See Crombie, *Robert Grosseteste and the Origins of Experimental Science 1100–1700*, 169, Weinberg, *Abstraction, Relation, and Induction*, 139–141 (133–150), and Losee, *A Historical Introduction to the Philosophy of Science*, 32–34 and 38–40.

The *Quaestiones Metaphysicae* are unique among Duns' works. There are still many doctrinal differences in comparison with *Lectura* I–II, just as is the case in the early logical writings, but the arguments from recent great theologians are prominently present, while they do not play any substantial role in the logical writings.[28] Let us consider how these patterns behave regarding inductive generalization in *Quaestiones Metaphysicae* I 4.

8.5.1   *Quaestiones super libros Metaphysicorum Aristotelis* I 4

This substantial chapter deals with Heraclitus and Plato, Aristotle and Avicenna, Averroes and Thomas Aquinas, Augustine and Henry of Ghent. Julius Weinberg reports that Duns Scotus here holds 'that no experimental inference can yield a conclusion free from all doubt.'[29] Sense experience provides occasions for concept formation. Despite the fact that a sense experience itself may be mistaken, the analysis in terms of the acquired concepts is reliable. By experience (*experimentum*) we know *that* something occurs frequently. So, there is an occasion to set up an inquiry and to find out its cause. Duns accepts this proposal, formulated in *Quaestiones Metaphysicae* I 4.69, but his critical question runs as follows: how do we arrive at true knowledge of the cause? He gives the answer himself:

> *Reply* – by the following analysis: *b, c* and *d* are present in *a*. If you wish to know whether the cause be *d, b* or *c*, make an analysis of the involved factors. Suppose, you find *b* without *c*, if *d* follows on *b*, and not on *c*. Therefore, *b* is the cause of *d*, in *a*. This is the process of knowing a cause, if there is a connection of more factors.[30]

This analysis may be reconstructed as follows:

Instance	Hypothesis	Effect
*a*1	BCD	*e*
*a*2	BD	*e*
*a*3	B → D	*e*

[28] See §1.4 and §§3.6.2–3.6.6.

[29] Weinberg, *Abstraction, Relation, and Induction*, 139. *Quaestiones Metaphysicae* I 4.24: 'Experimento cognoscenti *quia* est, datur occasio *inquirendi* causam, et sic inveniendi *propter quid*, et per consequens sic esse in omnibus singularibus.' Cf. §69.

[30] *Quaestiones Metaphysicae* I 4.70: '*Responsio*, dividendo sic: in *a* sunt *b c d*. Si vis scire quid est causa *d, b* an *c*, separa haec. Ubi invenis *b* sine *c*, si ibi *d* consequitur *b*, et non *c*. Ergo, in *a, b* fuit causa *d*. Sic contingit causam cognoscere, si plura essent coniuncta.'

*a*4	D → B	*e*
*a*5	C	*non-e*[31]

A series of counterarguments is brought forward in §71, §72, and §75. Such a test is not entirely conclusive, for it may be that the fallacy of the consequent is at stake. *b* may be the cause of *d*, but *d* may also be the cause of *b*, or *bd* may be the effect of another common cause. So, although we have some good reasons to believe so, we still do not know the cause. Weinberg builds his description on these counter-arguments, but Duns is not impressed. Although we are unable to demonstrate the crucial premiss, we possess certain knowledge removing all doubt. In scientific knowledge, there is still the point in assessing a proof that we have some basic premisses which cannot be demonstrated any more since they are immediately certain (*Quaestiones Metaphysicae* I 4.77 and 79). Here, Duns simply makes his point, but in *Lectura* I 3 and *Ordinatio* I 3 he paid thorough attention to this delicate matter. In sum, *pace* Weinberg, Duns did not defend that 'experimental' inferences cannot be free from all doubt. He defends just the opposite stance more fully in *Lectura* I 3.[32]

8.5.2   *Lectura* I 3.177–180

In §8.4, we have seen that the Scotian theory of self-evident and deductive knowledge is basically structured according to the duality of (*first*) *principles* and *theses* (*theorems*). This is the first type of scientific generalizations which deliver necessary truths. However, Duns Scotus acknowledged two types of scientific generalizations resulting in necessary truths about unions of phenomena. In the case of experiential knowledge we meet again the duality of *principle* and *thesis*. By experience we acquire both certain knowledge of the truth of a proposition to be stated and certain knowledge of the principle that fixes the status of that proposition. Certain knowledge of experiential truths concerns events that regularly occur: they are seen as effects, but to which type of effects do they belong?[33]

---

[31] The last crucial line has no counterpart in Duns' analysis. The medieval methods of agreement and of difference relate to factual occurrences and the method of difference is not applied to *non*-occurrences.

[32] 'Experimentum' and 'experientia' mean *experience,* and 'experimento' = *to learn/to know by experience.* The modern ring of 'experimental' is rather misleading.

[33] *Lectura* I 3.177: 'Nam primo habetur cognitio *quia est* de conclusione ex hoc quod (homo) videt frequenter talem effectum provenire, ut quando videt lunam eclipsari aut aliquam herbam frequenter sanare a tali infirmitate.'

According to Duns Scotus, the underlying principle of experiential knowledge which governs this kind of certain knowledge boils down to the following self-evident proposition:

> What regularly occurs is a natural effect which has a cause and that cause is related to such an effect in a natural way.

In *Lectura* I 3.177, Duns defines, as it were, a *natural effect* just on the basis of *regularity* with which events of a certain kind occur. A *natural effect* is ordered towards a *natural cause* and *Ordinatio* I 3.235 makes explicit that, in these cases, what regularly occurs is caused by a non-free cause, for, of course, free agents are also able to perform acts in a regular way. Clearly, Duns considers this kind of experiential knowledge in the context of natural agency.

The cause of a natural effect is, of course, a natural cause and a natural cause is a non-free cause, 'the only instance of a free cause being human or supra-human volition. This proposition Scotus regards as self-evident: a natural cause by its very definition is a cause that has only one sort of effect,'[34] so that if cause *c* naturally causes effect *e*, then *not-e* cannot be an effect of cause *c*. Natural causality is *one-way* causality, personal causality is *two-way* causality. This is the main line of the thirteenth- and fourteenth-century discussions which infer the causal connection from the regularity with which events of certain kinds occurred. These discussions depend on the influx of ideas from Avicenna, although their background, of course, is to be found in the works of Aristotle. The channel was mainly Robert Grosseteste's *Commentary on the Posterior Analytics*.

Duns departs from the *principle-thesis* relation at work in experiential knowledge. Certain factual knowledge is acquired, if it is to be concluded that somebody sees a specific effect frequently occurring. Typical examples of such experiential truths are:

> Someone sees that the moon eclipses

and

> Someone sees that a particular herb frequently cures a certain illness.[35]

---

[34] Weinberg, *Abstraction, Relation, and Induction*, 140.

[35] *Lectura* I 3.177: 'Videt [. . .] aliquam herbam frequenter sanare a tali infirmitate,' which leads to the generalization: 'Omnis herba talis speciei sanat a tali infirmitate.' Cf. §179 and *Ordinatio* I 3.235. Duns universalizes this almost omnipresent example, derived from Avicenna, that administration of scammony is followed by the purging of bile, so that scammony must by its nature be purgative of bile. See Weinberg, *Abstraction, Relation, and Induction*, 124 f.

This experience of a regular event is accompanied by grasping a self-evident proposition:

> Whatever frequently occurs is a natural effect which has a cause which is ordered to such an effect in a natural way.[36]

This self-evident proposition gives rise to a definite thesis. 'From this principle the intellect concludes that such an effect likewise obtains in all singular cases.'[37] The intellect connects a self-evident proposition with such an experience (*experimentum*) and these conditions suffice for acquiring certain *factual* knowledge *that* it is the case.

8.5.3 The method of difference and the method of agreement

The experience that an event occurs in many cases and the presence of a self-evident proposition that underscores it, suffice to make sure *that* something is the case. We still do not know *why* it happens. In what way is this *why?* question to be answered? The *why* is discovered *per modum divisionis*. In *Lectura* I 3.178, Duns offers a version of the *method of difference* and in *Ordinatio* I 3.235, he again applies the *method of agreement*. When we certainly know of a natural cause, we are probably unable to explain *why* it happens in this way. The thing to be observed here is that medieval scholars became more and more interested in outlining inductive techniques for discovering explanatory principles.

Suppose, that we know that such and such regularly happens. So, the considered effect must have a certain natural cause, but which cause is the cause of effect *e*? The only thing we can do, Duns states, is to *inquire* why it is so. We need *r*esearch and our research needs a method. Duns' favorite example both in *Lectura* I 3 and in *Ordinatio* I 3 is the example of a lunar eclipse. The point of an *inquiry* is made in a straightforward way: if we face a certain phenomenon and we *see* the cause, then there is no need to *inquire* it. Suppose, for example, that we are placed above the moon and that we *see* the earth placed between the moon and the sun, then there is no need to inquire *why* there is a lunar eclipse. However, if we do *not see* how things are, we have to arrange an inquiry and the inquiry requires a *method*.

---

[36] *Lectura* I 3.177: 'Cum isto autem experimento habet intellectus propositionem per se notam, istam scilicet quod "quidquid evenit in pluribus, est effectus naturalis et habet causam naturaliter ordinatam ad talem effectum".'

[37] Ibid.: 'Ex hoc concludit intellectus quod similiter est in omnibus singularibus talis effectus.'

The method is *per modum divisionis*. First, we do know *that* something occurs regularly, but we do not know *why* it is the case or *why* it works. So, we have to eliminate the candidate causes which fail and drop out, because, apparently, they do not explain the nature of the considered cause and it is even the case that they cannot explain the causal connection of the lunar eclipse. We frame possible explanations:

1. Is the moon a body which is defective in such a way that an eclipse occurs?
2. Is the moon a variable object in itself?
3. Does the moon take its light from another object, etc.?

Duns suggests a structural investigation:

Instance	Hypothesis	Effect
1	A	*non-e*
2	B	*non-e*
3	C	*e*

This method rests on a qualitative assessment of the proposed hypothesis. In terms of its consequences and test implications, the analysis 'infers the true cause of the eclipse by eliminating the possible explanations which apparently cannot be the cause' (*Lectura* I 3.178).[38] This kind of the method *per modum divisionis* is not a direct forerunner of what we may call Ockham's *method of difference*, for the method of difference frames more instances in order to discover which combination of circumstances leads to *e* and which does not.

In the case of *Lectura* I 3, the method does not aim at finding the cause, but at explaining *why* the considered cause works. The reason is that we may believe that we *sense* and *see* the cause of an effect, but that we are mistaken nevertheless. Two persons may see the same object and judge differently how large it is because of differences in distance from the object. In such a case, a structural analysis has to contribute to the right solution, as in the case of the bent or broken stick in the water. On the one hand, according to one outer sense, we *see* that the stick is bent in the water, but, on the other hand, according to another sense, we *feel* that it is a straight stick. A structural

---

[38] *Lectura* I 3.178: 'Ultra, intellectus habens cognitionem *quia est* de conclusione, et sciens quod eius est *causa naturalis*, inquirit tamen *per modum divisionis* et, removens illa quae non sunt causae nec esse possunt, concludit hanc esse determinatam causam illius: et sic habetur scientia et cognitio *propter quid*.'

analysis has to solve the dilemma. The tactile sense is judged to be right and the visual sight to be wrong on the basis of the self-evident truth that soft and moist stuff cannot bend or break a hard object. Moreover, the analysis tries to explain *why* the stick *seems* to be bent, namely because of a certain kind of transparency.

Ordinatio I 3.235 elaborates on the method *per modum divisionis* in a different way, indicating aspects of the method of agreement. The factors *ABCDE* play a role in the case of a particular phenomenon. We are able to vary these factors and circumstances:

Instance	*Circumstances*	*Effect*
1	ABC	*e*
2	ABD	*e*
3	ACD	*e*
4	ADE	*e*

By this method of variation, we get the following result: only *A* maintains itself as a candidate in explaining the phenomenon under consideration when we have investigated various circumstances under which that phenomenon occurs. The human intellect concludes:

Cause A is the definite cause of that phenomenon.

John Losee only considers the aspect of Duns Scotus' method of agreement in his expositions on the *modus divisionis*, but he leaves aside *Quaestiones Metaphysicae* I 4 and *Lectura* I 3.177–180.

> Duns Scotus' claims for his Method of Agreement were quite modest. He held that the most that can be established by an application of the method is an '*aptitudinal union*' between an effect and an accompanying circumstance. [. . .] But application of the schema alone can establish neither that the moon necessarily must be eclipsed, nor that every sample of the herb necessarily is bitter.[39]

Losee ascribes to Duns a rather paradoxical position which undermined confidence in inductively established correlations, although Scotus also augmented the method of resolution. Losee's exposition is rather paradoxical, since he also states that 'sense experience provides occasions for recognizing the truth of a first principle, but sense experience is not evidence for its truth. Rather, a first principle is true in

---

[39] Losee, *A Historical Introduction to the Philosophy of Science*, 33 (33–34: 'Duns Scotus' Method of Agreement'). This is also the method in geometry and astronomy.

virtue of the meanings of its constituent terms.'[40] Losee realizes that, according to Duns, first principles support statements of aptitudinal unions of phenomena, and that, therefore, such statements formulate necessary truths. 'By contrast, he held that empirical generalizations are contingent truths. For example, it is necessarily true that all ravens *can* be black, but it is only a matter of contingent fact that all ravens examined have been black' (ibid.). The first point is perfectly true, in spite of what Losee expounded in 'Duns Scotus' Method of Agreement,' for statements of experiential knowledge express necessary truths. Scotus held that it is necessarily true that all ravens *can* be black, but this is certainly no item of experiential knowledge. Duns does not treat this topic in this context at all. Nor are contingent universalizations are instances of experiential knowledge.

Losee added a comment to his analysis on the basis of the principle that denying a necessary truth is formulating a self-contradiction: 'Duns Scotus held that even God could cause a self-contradiction to be implemented in the world' (ibid.). However, Duns Scotus did not say this. He held that self-contradictions as such cannot be implemented in the world at all. That is the way *self-contradictions* are. Only contingent states of affairs can be implemented in the world. The proposition that God can implement self-contradictions is false, *pace* René Descartes. When we say that *even* God cannot do so, it is simply misleading, for it suggests a restriction, but a restriction which does not exist cannot be validated. So, it is senseless rhetoric to assert that *even* God cannot do so if it simply cannot be done. Only if something can be done and if it agrees with divine nature, it *can* be done by God.

Losee's analysis presents a picture which is not coherent, but this incoherence is not due to Duns' texts. For this reason, we have to ask which half of the description is to be dropped. The second half of the description found in 'Duns Scotus on the "Aptitudinal Union" of Phenomena' is correct. The excursus on *certain experiential knowledge* does not deal with the phenomenon of *aptitudinal unions*, because experiential knowledge concerns causal connections which are necessary connections. Duns deals with it at the end of his excursion in *Ordinatio* I 3: there are cases where we do not know an actual union of terms, but an aptitudinal one, because the property to be considered is not entailed by the subject and can be separated

---

[40] Losee, *A Historical Introduction to the Philosophy of Science*, 39 (39: 'Duns Scotus on the "Aptitudinal Union" of Phenomena').

from it.[41] The interpretations of Weinberg and Losee do not fit the facts, for they imply that *experiential knowledge* does not fall under certainly known necessary truths. For better or for worse, the historical Scotus thinks that experiential knowledge does not cover knowledge of *aptitudinal* unions, because *aptitudinal* unions are not necessary connections between cause and effect (*Ordinatio* I 3.237).[42] The specific merit of the argument in *Lectura* I 3 is that we profit from its didactic fluency. More attention is paid to the method of division, but *Ordinatio* I 3 plainly confirms the picture known from *Lectura* I 3.

When we combine the areas of *experiential* knowledge in its Scotian sense and *aptitudinal* knowledge, we move on the boundary between knowledge of what is necessary and knowledge of what is contingent. Duns Scotus does not exclude certainty from the dimension of contingency. In both areas, certainty can be arrived at. Thus, with Duns, *induction* has a different setting. His type of *induction* differs both from *Aristotelian induction* and *enumerative induction* in a marked way. *Aristotelian induction* lays the intuitive foundation of deductive certainty: *induction* is grasping the necessary truths which eventually function as the axiomatic premisses of a valid deduction. *Enumerative induction* uses the stable property P of a limited number of a set of individuals in order to conclude that *all* such individuals enjoy having P. In terms of this induction we infer from *some* (*ravens*) to *all* (*ravens*).

8.6 KNOWLEDGE OF PERSONAL ACTS

In the fascinating section *Lectura* I 3.181, Duns raises the question 'how we can have certain knowledge of our acts, for example how we can know that we think, feel, sleep or are awake, and so on.'[43] In *Lectura* I 3.177–180 Duns had left a side the ontological status of a natural cause and a natural effect. When the epistemic status of

---

[41] See *Ordinatio* I 3.237: 'Et forte ibi non habetur cognitio actualis unionis extremorum, sed *aptitudinalis*. Si enim passio est alia res, absoluta, a subiecto, posset sine contradictione separari a subiecto, et expertus non haberet cognitionem quia ita est, sed quia ita aptum natum est esse.'

[42] Their formalization does not utilize the strict or necessary implication, as experiential knowledge does: if cause c causes effect e, then it is necessary that cause c causes effect e. Cf. Bos, 'A Contribution to the History of Theories of Induction in the Middle Ages,' in Jacobi (ed.), *Argumentationstheorie*, 570–572.

[43] *Lectura* I 3.181: 'De tertio est considerandum quomodo potest haberi certa cognitio de actibus nostris, puta quomodo possumus scire nos intelligere, sentire, aut dormire, aut vigilare etc.'

thinking, *feeling*, and *being awake* is taken into consideration, the problem of the ontological status is pointed out immediately. Duns stresses that here contingent propositions are involved: the category of contingent propositions also possesses propositions which are direct (*immediatae*) and self-evident (*per se notae*).[44] Propositions concerning human acts like *thinking* and *being awake* are also propositions which are both contingent and self-evident:

> It is not possible that propositions about our personal acts are clear on account of something prior, because the fact that somebody is awake is more known to us than the fact that he reflects on his own acts, and in the same way the fact that somebody is asleep is more known to us than the fact that he cannot reflect on his own acts,[45]

for it is bad reasoning to defend the experience that I reflected on an act of mine in my dreams with the statement: I have dreamt that I dreamt. We are certain about personal acts which are within our power, because they are not hidden to us. On the contrary, we can be deceived and we can be mistaken concerning acts of ours which are activities of the vegetative life, because they are not in our power. Short-term memories of seeing are reliable too.

Duns shows how *certain knowledge* and *contingency* can be linked up. Both the realm of necessary propositions and the realm of contingent propositions are consistent with the phenomenon of *being self-evident*. Moreover, in *Ordinatio* I 3.238 Duns is considering the range of what is self-evident in a more extended way. The original context of the predicate *being self-evident* seems to be the theory of necessary propositions. A necessary principle is self-evident because it is irrational to ask for a proof of it. Presenting proofs must be a demonstration of rationality; trying to prove the unprovable is a demonstration of irrationality. Within new epistemic structures, something contingent can also be self-evident:

> *We are awake*
> is as self-evident as the principle of a demonstration and the fact that it is contingent is no obstacle, because contingent propositions are

---

[44] Ibid.: 'Dico quod, sicut supra dictum est in isto primo libro, in genere propositionum contingentium sunt aliquae propositiones immediatae (alioquin in contingentibus esset procedere in infinitum, vel aliquod contingens verum immediate esset ab aliqua causa necessaria), sicut in genere propositionum necessariarum et per se notae.' Here, Duns refers to *Lectura Prologus* 114–118.

[45] *Lectura* I 3.181: 'Nec possunt nobis manifestari a priore, nam magis notum est nobis aliquem vigilare quam se reflectere supra actus suos, et similiter nobis magis notum est aliquem dormire quam se non posse reflecti supra actus suos.'

ordered too as we have said elsewhere: *One or another contingent proposition is a primary and direct one.* (If this assumption were not to hold), either there would be a *regressus ad infinitum* regarding contingent propositions or a contingent proposition would follow from a necessary premiss. Both alternatives are impossible.[46]

The point of the appeal to the *regressus ad infinitum* is clear. We look at a demonstrative argument, a proof wherein we derive theorems from theorems. If we accept a *regressus ad infinitum* in the case of necessary arguments, then we could never finish a proof. We could never present a *proof* because it would be impossible to finish it off. Acceptance of the pattern of the *regressus ad infinitum* in the case of necessary arguments would endanger the possibility of *proving* at all. So, demonstrative knowledge of what is necessary would be impossible.

The same line of argument excludes the reasonableness of accepting the pattern of the *regressus ad infinitum* regarding *contingent propositions*. Given the possibility of knowledge of contingent propositions there have to be contingent propositions which are immediate or direct. If there are no propositions which are contingent *and* self-evident, then we have to give account of every contingent proposition. This pattern would entail that there are no contingent propositions to be accepted without any doubt. So, when I am awake somebody might try to prove that I am asleep convinced that he will not lose his reasonableness. However, Duns insists, he will certainly lose his 'status' as a reasonable person when he tries to disprove what is self-evident to someone else. If there is nothing to be self-evident, no proof is possible and if something is self-evident, there is no need to prove it. If somebody asks for a demonstrative account (*ratio*) of a contingent and self-evident act, then lack of rationality is on his side and not on the side of the challenged person.[47] *Contingency* is basic and Duns drops the 'eternal' bond between *knowledge* and *necessity*. This fundamental move constitutes a 'scientific revolution' in the development of epistemology.[48]

---

[46] *Ordinatio* I 3.238: '"*Nos vigilare*" est per se notum sicut principium demonstrationis; nec obstat quod est contingens, quia, sicut dictum est alias, ordo est in contingentibus, quod aliqua est prima et immediata – vel esset processus in infinitum in contingentibus, vel aliquod contingens sequeretur ex causa necessaria, quorum utrumque est impossibile.' Here, Duns is referring to *Ordinatio Prologus* 169.

[47] Ibid.: 'Nec possunt nobis manifestari a priore, nam magis notum est nobis aliquem vigilare quam se reflectere supra actus suos.'

[48] See Krop, *De status van de theologie volgens Johannes Duns Scotus*, 211–213.

8.7   INTUITIVE KNOWLEDGE

> Scotus differs from Aristotle by recognizing the great importance of
> the mind's ability to know and to remember both its own acts and
> those of the senses. Even our knowledge of logical and mathematical
> truths or of truths beyond our own experience has a history, since
> there was a moment when we acquired that knowledge – a moment
> we may even remember. Scotus' discussion of memory and intuition
> involves a reconsideration of personal individuality and identity
> which, alone, is enough to suggest that Scotus' celebrated 'subtlety' is
> not a euphemism for triviality or muddle-headedness.[49]

Henry of Ghent and Duns Scotus were clearly dissatisfied with the
Aristotelian views of knowledge and science, as, in general, the
Augustinians were, but even the so-called 'Aristotelians', like Thomas
Aquinas and Godfrey of Fontaines, were far away from Aristotle's
epistemology and much more akin to the 'Augustinians.' The theories
of all these great theologians present, in a striking way, an important
feature of much later medieval philosophy: its contents are shaped by
theological concerns, although their philosophy is definitely not a
kind of 'theologism' and their theology is certainly not fideistic. In the
last third of the thirteenth century, many outstanding epistemologists
tried to do full justice to the human mind and its specific worth.[50]
Henry of Ghent and Godfrey of Fontaines were eager to show that
the dignity of the cognitive mind entails that the intellect functions in
itself. Both try to dispense with an independent role for the *epistemic
concepts (species intelligibiles)*. Duns Scotus takes an independent
stance. Let us start with his theory of *intuitive knowledge*.

8.7.1   Intuitive knowledge

'Perhaps Scotus' most important contribution to medieval epistemology was his theory of intellectual cognition.'[51] It was clear to
him that his approach deviated from Aristotle, who 'seems to have
said nothing on intellectual vision.'[52] The term *intuitio* seems to
have been introduced by Franciscan thinkers in the last quarter of

---

[49] Marenbon, *Later Medieval Philosophy (1150–1350)*, 169.
[50] Consult the excellent expositions of Marenbon, *Later Medieval Philosophy*, 116–160, in
   particular 155 f.
[51] Wolter, 'Duns Scotus on Intuition, Memory, and Our Knowledge of Individuals,' *The
   Philosophical Theology of Scotus*, 98.
[52] *Quaestiones Metaphysicae* VII 15.36: 'De *visione intellectuali* nihil videtur locutus.'

the thirteenth century[53] and when in the fourteenth century William
of Ockham and Peter Aureoli explain their own theories, they start
by discussing Duns Scotus' contribution, a contribution which was
not ignored for the next five centuries. But what does *intuitive
knowledge* consist in?[54]

The distinction between *intuitive* and *non-intuitive* knowledge is
at home both in the theory of perceptual or sensory knowledge and
in the theory of intellectual knowledge. Duns introduces some helpful
distinctions with respect to *intuitive knowledge of the senses* (*cognitio intuitiva in sensu*) in the early text *Quaestiones Metaphysicae* II
2–3. There is a sixfold distinction to be made where, especially, the
structuring distinction between *intuitive knowledge* and *non-intuitive
knowledge* has to be observed. So, there are two series of *intuitive* and
non-intuitive knowledge connected with the senses:

Intuitive knowledge:	*Non-intuitive knowledge*:
(1) *seeing* a certain color	(2) *imagining* the same color
(3) *seeing* no color	(4) *imagining* that the color is not seen
(because of darkness)	(5) imagining *a golden mountain*
	(6) *imagining* an absent person.[55]

Duns resumes this line of argument in §109. The basic distinction
holds between (1) and (2): the object *a* is present in the case of *knowledge* properly called *intuitive* and the very nature of *a*, knowable for
sure, is intuitively known in virtue of *a*'s proper concept. Intuitive
knowledge is integral knowledge. Intuitive knowledge considers both
the particular *a* and its universal aspects. In the case of *non-intuitive*
knowledge, we have the same knowledge as in the case of (1), from
the purely cognitive point of view, but now the object is not *seen* any
more: I '*see*' (Duns: *imaginor*) my mother who died years ago or my
boy's pink bike years ago in my 'mind's eye.' In Duns' terminology, (1),
(2), and (5) are cases of conceptual knowledge, but (1) exemplifies

---

[53] Foreruners of the theory are Matthew of Acquasparta and Vital of Furno.
[54] See, for example, Torrance, 'Intuitive and Abstractive Knowledge from Duns Scotus to John
Calvin,' *De doctrina Ioannis Duns Scoti* IV 291–305.
[55] *Quaestiones Metaphysicae* II 2–3,80. The example in (1) – 'propria cognitio intuitiva' – is:
'visus *videt* colorem'; the example in (2), the *non-intuitive* variant of (1), is: 'phantasia *imaginatur* colorem'; the example in (3), *accidental* in relation to (1), is: 'visus *videt* tenebram';
the example in (4), the *non-intuitive* variant of (3), is: 'phantasia *imaginatur* tenebram'; the
example in (5), constructing sense images which are not experienced together, is: '*imagin-
ando* montem aureum'. See also *Lectura* II 3.290.

both *intuitive* and *conceptual* knowledge. So, in terms of the theory of perceptual knowledge, the distinction between *intuitive* and *non-intuitive* knowledge is clearly established. The type of perceptual knowledge which is not intuitive is simply called *non-intuitive* in *Quaestiones Metaphysicae* II 2–3, but it is called *abstractive* knowledge in *Lectura* II 3.

> According to the first one of these kinds of knowledge, the intellect knows something real by not considering any aspect of existence and this kind is called *abstractive knowledge*. According to the second kind, the intellect sees something real in its existence and this kind is called *intuitive knowledge*, as it is distinguished from abstractive knowledge by which something is known in itself through its *species*.[56]

In contrast with *abstractive* which refers to what is essential (*Ordinatio* II 3.321), *exsistentia* and *praesentia* make a couple. *Exsistentia* not only indicates pure existence, but has also an existential and cognitive component, as the original meaning of *ex* expresses: something existent comes out and shows up. Precisely this element is put between brackets as far as *abstractive knowledge* is concerned.

The distinction between *intuitive* and *non-intuitive* knowledge structures the theory of intellectual knowledge. Duns defends this structure as follows: the eyesight or power of vision is a complete, or 'perfect,' kind of knowledge, for it can know something real according to its true existence. Of course, it can know the same thing in its imaginary state. So, on the level of the senses, there are both *abstractive* (non-intuitive) knowledge and *intuitive* knowledge to be discerned. Consequently, on the level of the intellect where we certainly have abstractive knowledge, we also enjoy intuitive knowledge.[57]

If there were only abstractive intellectual knowledge, we could not have knowledge of what exists if that knowledge is not accompanied

---

[56] *Lectura* II 3.288: 'Prima istarum cognitionum secundum quam intellectus intelligit rem abstrahendo ab omni exsistentia, dicitur esse *cognitio abstractiva*, et alia secundum quam videt rem in exsistentia sua dicitur esse *cognitio intuitiva* [. . .], prout distinguitur contra abstractivam qua per speciem cognoscitur res in se.' Cf. *Lectura* II 3.285: 'Alia intellectio potest esse rei secundum quod praesens est in exsistentia sua.' Duns notices that 'intuitive' means also *non-discursive*, but this is not intended here – see *Lectura* II 3.288. Cf. Wolter, 'Duns Scotus on Intuition,' *The Philosophical Theology of Scotus*, 107.

[57] *Lectura* II 3.287: 'Quod sit ponenda secunda cognitio [namely, intuitive] patet: quod est perfectionis in potentia inferiore, est in superiore. Sed hoc est perfectionis in potentia inferiore (ut in visu) quod potest cognoscere rem secundum suum verum esse existentiae. Igitur, similiter in intellectu hoc ponendum est, quod ipse potest cognoscere rem in exsistentia sua.'

by perceptual evidence. The implication would be that I impossibly know that my dear boy exists if he is playing upstairs while I am enjoying Duns' company and not his. 'Such knowledge which is called *intuitive* can be intellectual. Otherwise, the intellect would not be certain of any existing object.'[58] Conversely, if there were no abstractive knowledge, knowledge of what exists would melt into non-knowledge, where the known is not any more perceived to exist. It would even be impossible to know of anything if it does not exist any more, neither could we write about Scotus. The theological point of this approach is that Christians do not expect the knowledge of the blessed to be of the *abstractive* type. What matters is real and true knowledge of God. So, He must be known intuitively, but He cannot be known intuitively if there is no intuitive knowledge possible. We expect God to know intuitively *in patria* (*Lectura* II 3.289).

Duns does not use this idea of *species intelligibilis* in his theory of intuitive knowledge and abstract knowledge, but what does he mean by *intuitive knowledge* (*cognitio intuitiva*)? *Intuitive knowledge* is the awareness that something exists here and now. There is knowledge which abstracts from factual existence and from not-existing. There is knowledge of something which exists and knowledge which exists in the present, privileged as it is by factual existence in the present. The use of *intellectio intuitiva* and *cognitio intuitiva* follows the logic of *visio*.[59] The definition of *Quaestiones Quodlibetales* VI 8 is clear:

> The other type of knowledge is the act of knowledge which we do not experience in ourselves by the same certainty. Nevertheless, such knowledge is possible so that it is related to a present object as it is present and to an existing object as it exists.[60]

This kind of act of knowledge is contrasted with the act of abstract knowledge in §7.[61]

---

[58] *Ordinatio* IV 45 *quaestio* 2 (Wolter, 'Duns Scotus on Intuition,' *The Philosophical Theology of Scotus*, 118 note 55, citing *Codex A*): 'Talis cognitio quae dicitur intuitiva, potest esse intellectiva. Alioquin intellectus non esset certus de aliqua existentia alicuius obiecti.' On *aliquis*, see De Rijk, 'Glossary,' in *Nicholas of Autrecourt*, 39, cf. 121 f.

[59] *Ordinatio* II 23: '*Visio* est exsistentis ut exsistens est, et ut praesens est videnti secundum exsistentiam, et secundum hoc distinguitur *visio* ab *intellectione abstractiva* quae potest esse *non-existentis* – non in quantum in se praesens est.' Cf. *Quaestiones Quodlibetales* VI 7 and 8, VII 8 and XIII 8 and 13.

[60] *Quaestiones Quodlibetales* VI 8: 'Alius autem *actus intelligendi* est quem tamen non ita certitudinaliter experimur in nobis – possibilis tamen est talis qui, scilicet, praecise sit objecti praesentis ut praesentis et exsistentis ut exsistentis.'

[61] *Quaestiones quodlibetales* VI 7: 'Iste *actus intelligendi* [. . .] potest satis proprie dici *abstractivus*, quia *abstrahit* obiectum ab existentia et non existentia, praesentia et absentia.'

We have still to explain what is meant by *abstrahere*. *Abstrahere* means: not taking into account, not considering something. So, the point of *abstraction* is not taking away something or pulling something from something,[62] but leaving aside something. Different aspects of one and the same are involved. Intuitive knowledge and abstract knowledge regard the same object. The distinction concerns *knowledge* itself, and not objects of knowledge. The existence of something can also be known abstractively.[63]

The presence of existential qualification in the sense of a property – and not only in the sense of existential quantification – distinguishes intuitive knowledge from abstract knowledge. Both kinds of knowledge are located on the level of non-discursive knowledge. Both are immediate and are to be characterized as *apprehensio simplex*. Both can be *distincta*. Both may concern a common nature or an independent individual (*singulare ut hoc*). When we have to analyze what is *evident*, we need the notion of *intuitive knowledge*.

An Aristotelian epistemology rests on abstractionism: it is assumed that *concept formation* requires abstraction and *forms* or *essences* are the heart of epistemological matter. Duns leaves aside abstractionism. Thus, Day is able to summarize:

> 1.   Scotus shows clearly that an exclusively abstractionist explanation of intellection is false and impossible. He does this by proving:
> (a)   that the theory of abstraction does not and cannot guarantee the certitude of knowledge of existents and of voluntary activity;
> (b)   that the theory of abstraction, if considered as the sole explanation of intellectual activity, ignores the primitive and evident *fact* of intuitive cognition.
> 2.   He establishes that fact of intuitive cognition or proves that we do have intuitive cognition as well as abstractive cognition.[64]

The notion of *abstract knowledge* can be elucidated on the basis of the meaning of *cognitio intuitiva*. The range of *intuitive knowledge* is wider than the range of sensible knowledge. Moreover, intuitive knowledge is wedded to certainty. This approach entails that *knowing* as such does not depend on abstract concepts. Duns says goodbye to abstractionism.

---

[62] *Reportatio Parisiensis* III 14.4 n. 12: '*Abstrahere* non est decipere.'

[63] *Quaestiones quodlibetales* XIII 10: 'Etiam ipsa existentia potest cognosci cognitione abstractiva.'

[64] Day, *Intuitive Cognition. A Key to the Significance of the Later Scholastics*, 137.

8.7.2 An interpretative complication

Many authors are aware of and worried about the impression that Duns Scotus intended to limit the enjoyment of intuitive knowledge of the intellect to immaterial persons. The fact is pointed at that he regularly stressed that intuitive knowledge lacks the same certainty abstractive knowledge of the intellect has. However, the point of this thesis is a logical one, for in the case of intuitive knowledge more epistemic risks have to be coped with. I know that I am called *Antoon* and I know that $1 + 1 = 2$, but in the case of *I know that I am called Antoon* more epistemic risks have to be overcome. *If* they are overcome, everything will be all right, although, from the viewpoint of epistemic appraisal, the credentials of $1 + 1 = 2$ are better than *I know that I am called Antoon*. *I know that Duns was called John* is more complicated. The point of this epistemic appraisal is not a degrading of *intuitive knowledge*. Perhaps I am most certain that God exists; nevertheless, the proof is most complicated too. The concept of *intuitive knowledge* is a cornerstone of the whole of Duns' theory of knowledge.

Indeed, the evidence used to show that the intellect can know intuitively is often not related to humans in this life, for on one occasion it refers to angels, on another to beatification. 'Intuitive intellectual knowledge is usually discussed in an overall context which is not that of human life on earth: the beatific vision (*Quaestiones Quodlibetales* VI), angelic cognition (*Ordinatio* II 3), Christ's knowledge (*Ordinatio* III 3), knowledge and memory in disembodied souls (*Ordinatio* IV 45).'[65] However, most books of Duns Scotus belong to the genre of the *quaestiones* literature which focuses on systematic puzzles and does not aim at didactic completeness. Therefore, the context of immaterial personhood is linked to the issue of *intuitive knowledge*, since immaterial or disembodied persons cannot have abstractive knowledge. If there is no intuitive knowledge, they have no knowledge at all.

> The intellect does not only know universals [. . .], but it is also able to know intuitively what a sense knows, for a more complete and higher power of the same subject knows what the subordinate power knows and it can also know of sensations. Both theses are proved from the fact that the intellect knows contingently true propositions. [. . .] The truth of these propositions concerns objects known intuitively,

---

[65] Marenbon, *Later Medieval Philosophy*, 159 (154–169: 'Duns Scotus on Intuition and Memory').

i.e, under their existential aspect, which is also something known by sense.[66]

Duns Scotus' purely theological example is eloquent. God knows only intuitively. In contrast with intuitive knowledge, non-intuitive, abstractive knowledge is somehow incomplete and dependent upon *sense*-based knowledge. *Intuitive knowledge* is knowledge of an epistemic object as it exists actually, namely either in itself or in something else which eminently contains the whole of its being.[67] Divine completeness requires intuitive knowledge and again we are reminded that the *Sitz im Leben* of most issues Duns is interested in is theological, while philosophical interests only focus on one vein of his universe of thought. *Intuitive knowledge* is knowledge as complete as it can be. It immediately grasps the whole of the reality of the known object.

The intimate connection between abstractive and intuitive knowledge in the case of sensorial knowledge reminds us that, to Scotus' mind, the role of *intuitive knowledge* is truly vital in the life of the human mind. Nevertheless, the role of intuitive knowledge is not exclusively correlated with sensorial knowledge. It has a much wider scope and certainty of personal acts is the key to discover what intuitive knowledge means. Bérubé's interpretation rests on the pattern that every time a sense perceives something which presently exists, the intellect intuitively knows it too. What we sense, we intuitively know in our intellect. This type of interpretation was ably refuted by John Marenbon.[68] The role of intuitive knowledge in remembering and recollecting things is much broader (see §8.8).

Intuitive knowledge does not share a humble corner in Duns Scotus' theory of knowledge. This concept is crucial and vital to the whole of his epistemological fabric. The theory of intuitive knowledge perfectly meshes with his new theory of meaning (see §4.5 on *Model* IV). The rejection of any intermediate entity between the act of knowing reality and the things to which it is related is one of the most characteristic features of Duns Scotus' theory of knowledge. This is just the point of contact with the epistemology of Ockham,

---

[66] *Ordinatio* IV 45 *quaestio* 3. Cf. Wolter, 'Duns Scotus on Intuition,' *The Philosophical Theology of Scotus*, 119.

[67] See *Ordinatio* I 2.394: '*Cognitio* autem *intuitiva* est obiecti ut obiectum est praesens in exsistentia actuali, et hoc in se vel in alio continente eminenter totam entitatem ipsius.'

[68] Marenbon, *Later Medieval Philosophy*, 164 f. See Bérubé, *La connaissance de l'individuel au moyen âge*, 134–224.

although Ockham dropped other distinctively Scotian conceptions. True knowledge is possible and vital, but it is not the outcome of the omnipotent impact of 'formal' activity on the passive soul – knowledge is as such knowledge of somebody; it is person related.

8.7.3 Did Duns' theory of intuitive knowledge significantly develop?

Wolter distinguished an incipient state of development (*Lectura* I) from a second stage, documented by *Lectura* II. Is this hypothesis a substantial one? Duns prepared the lectures of his first *Sententiae* course at the same time in one and the same year. From the beginning of the *Lectura* we observe that Duns is referring forward. In comparison with the early logical and philosophical writings, we are struck by an incisive breach of philosophical development, but there are no signs of this turn in *Lectura* I–II itself. We meet a stabilized and homogeneous position. So, a hypothesis of two stages of development *within Lectura* I–II does not fit the facts. Of course, many facets of Duns' new start are incipient in *Lectura* I–II, but, in fact, the wealth of revolutionary innovations, all in line with the theory of *synchronic contingency*, in *one* text is almost beyond imagination. It is a fact and this fact is to be discovered, but if it were no fact, we should not have thought of it.

Another element of Wolter's sketch of the development of Duns Scotus' theory of intuitive knowledge is more far-reaching. After having expounded his view on the incipient state and the second stage of the development of the theory, Wolter pays attention to *Quaestiones Metaphysicae* II 3.

> What is interesting about the present question, so far as intuition is concerned, is his admission: 'As for the first degree, namely intuitive cognition, it is *doubtful* whether it is in the intellect in our present life. It seems however that it is'. Here, for the first time, if our dating is correct, Scotus recognizes the fact that we may have intuitive cognition in this life.[69]

However, the dating is not correct. At any rate, this part of Duns' *Quaestiones Metaphysicae* antedates *Lectura* I–II (§1.4). Moreover, if Duns notices that there is a *dubium*, he does not express personal

---

[69] Wolter, 'Intuition, Memory, and Knowledge of Individuals,' *The Philosophical Theology of Scotus*, 109 f.

doubt: 'it is *doubtful* to me,' but this comment only indicates that there is an objective academic problem. What this text shows us precisely is that in this case the element of development is weaker than in many other cases. There is real development to be discerned between the young John Duns of his *quaestiones* on Aristotle's logical and philosophical works and the likewise young Duns of *Lectura* I–II. Nevertheless, it is perfectly correct that *Ordinatio* III and IV offer substantial extensions of Duns Scotus' contribution to philosophy (see §§8.7–8.8 and §12.6).[70]

8.8 MEMORY

Duns Scotus discusses *memory* in *Ordinatio* IV 45 *quaestio* 3, a text from the last stage of his life. We are familiar with knowing the past as an object of knowledge. We call this *remembering*. However, a past event is not directly known, for the remembering subject remembers a personal act of his own, the remembered event being absent. Duns makes clear that he focuses on personal acts (see §8.5)

> for I only remember that you were sitting down, because I remember that I saw or knew that you were sitting down[71]

although we say that we remember that he was there. Duns stresses his point, since knowledge that a friend was there is based on the fact that we have seen him there. If my wife told me that he was there, then I know that he was there, but I do not remember that he was there, for I had not seen him. I also know that I was born, but *I* do not remember that either. Duns defines someone's *remembering* as knowing a personal act where the act as an act of his own is recognized as a past act. Duns makes four points:

1. The act of remembering something takes place after a lapse of time.
2. That lapse of time is perceived by the remembering subject, for we say that we saw him there a fortnight ago.
3. If we remember that we have seen him, we do not see him for the moment, for if we see him now, we do not say that we are remembering doing so.
4. Conceptual knowledge is involved in memory and remembering.

[70] See Wolter, 'Intuition, Memory, and Knowledge of Individuals,' *The Philosophical Theology of Scotus*, 114–122.
[71] *Ordinatio* IV 45.3: 'Recordor me vidisse vel nosse te sedisse.'

These four points are tightly connected with Duns' definition of *remembering*, but there is still more to be said. If we now remember a past event there are two linked objets to be discerned: what Duns Scotus calls a *remote* object – the person having been seen – and the proximate 'object' – the personal act of having seen that person. The present act of remembering him is due to the 'proximate object' and not to the 'remote object.' Perhaps the latter no longer lives here, but in a quite different place. In sum:

> Only what concerns one's own act – where this is human – is subject to remembrance, for it is only through knowing one's own act as proximate object that we know its object *qua* remote object. Hence, a person cannot remember the same sort of act in another as he can in himself.[72]

The whole range of acts of memory is covered by intuitive knowledge. Here, the superior exposition is Marenbon's. Sensible knowledge can be remembered, but

> it can also remember many proximate objects which the sensible memory cannot – every past wish and thought (*intellectio*). Scotus goes on to comment that some memories are proper to the intellect, not only by virtue of their proximate object (as in the case of wishes and thoughts in general), but by virtue of their remote object too, when this is a fact of the sort expressed by a necessary proposition (for instance, 'I remember my past learning that a triangle has three sides').[73]

Scotus also deals with *recollection* (*reminiscentia*).

> When I remember something, I bring it back into my mind without effort; recollection for Scotus, is remembering which requires mental discourse or some external stimulus before the thing remembered can be successfully brought to mind. For example, I may have forgotten what someone looks like, but recognize him when I see him again; or I might be able to recollect what a particular painting looks like by picturing where it hangs in a gallery, or remember a particular argument by recalling those which I read in the same book.[74]

---

[72] Ibid., *et* is Wolter's translation in 'Intuition, Memory, and Knowledge of Individuals,' *The Philosophical Theology of Scotus*, 119 (118–122: 'Duns Scotus on *Memory*'). Cf. *Ordinatio* III 28.1 in the body of the article, in Wolter, *Duns Scotus on the Will and Morality*, 450–453.

[73] Marenbon, *Later Medieval Philosophy*, 164 f. Cf. the excellent summary and table 6 on 166 and 167, respectively.

[74] Marenbon, *Later Medieval Philosophy*, 163 f. (160–169: 'Aristotle, Aquinas and Scotus on Memory'). See *Ordinatio* IV 45 *quaestio* 3, 13 f. and 18.

In the case of *recollection*, the combination of discontinuity and continuity is typical. I may think that I have forgotten something, but an effort provides help and it brings to mind what I thought to have lost on the basis of continuity to which recovery of what I had known is due. What I possibly remember, I can also recollect.

Duns Scotus stresses the vitality of the mind to know and to remember its personal acts, its sensible cognitions and even knowing mathematical and necessary truths. The differences in comparison with Aristotle's 'cosmological' epistemology are at hand.

> Duns Scotus' theory of memory and intuitive knowledge presents, in a particularly striking way, an important feature of much later medieval philosophy: it cannot be understood apart from the specifically theological questions which it is designed to tackle, yet it also analyses concepts which modern philosophers will recognize as important and difficult. Scotus' dissatisfaction with the Aristotelian view of intellectual knowledge is provoked both by problems (of concern only to a theologian) about memory in disembodied souls, and the problems about cognition and memory in humans in this life.[75]

8.9   The perspective of an epistemological revolution

Duns Scotus drops the epistemic rules of certainty (*C.KK*) and necessity (*C.KN*) as a general foundation of the whole of epistemology and he opens up a new epistemic continent. Within the new field of forces of British logic, philosophy, and theology at the close of the thirteenth century, Duns started along rather traditional lines: true rational knowledge is knowledge of what is universal, for what is material and individual cannot be *known*, but God, the best possible Knower, is not subjected to the severe limits of necessitarian epistemology. So, the old type of epistemology cannot be true.

God perfectly knows contingent reality and the pattern *knowledge entails necessity* is abolished. The contingent is to be known too and human knowledge also numbers several kinds of perfectly viable knowledge of what is contingent. The blockade between *knowledge* (*epistème*, *scientia*) and *contingency* is raised and the bond between *certainty* and *necessity* is uncoupled too. This move is the more surprising when we realize that this bond still figures in Roderick Chisholm's theory of knowledge.[76] Duns Scotus opens up new areas of

---

[75] Marenbon, *Later Medieval Philosophy*, 169.
[76] See Chisholm, *Theory of Knowledge*, 9 f. and 40 ff.

epistemic analysis. The interrelationships of many kinds of knowledge and belief can be investigated, if the core concepts are no longer seen as related by means of absolute inclusions and exclusions.

Ancient epistemology rests on the internal connection between *knowledge* and *necessity* and the connection between *knowledge* and *time*. Scotus uncouples both connections: what is contingent is knowable with certainty and a new deductive step does not diminish the degree of reasonableness, again *pace* Chisholm (see §8.4).[77] In the whole of Duns Scotus' thought, the parallelism of *knowledge/thinking* and (*necessary*) *being* systematically disappears. The young John Duns elaborates a full-fledged theory of synchronic contingency and draws the epistemological consequences from it by laying the foundations of an alternative theory of knowledge.

---

[77] On the status of what is known a priori, see Chisholm, *Theory of Knowledge*, 42–45.

CHAPTER 9

Argument, proof, and science

9.1 INTRODUCTION

In many respects, modern philosophy profoundly differs from medieval thought. In a sense, this truth is a trivial one, for medieval thought also differed from ancient philosophy, just as archaic, pre-philosophical thought profoundly differed from ancient Greek, Hellenistic and Roman *philosophia*. Still, there is a secret to be uncovered. Sixteenth- and seventeenth-century thought, both in its philosophical and its theological sources, is much more alike medieval thought than is usually considered. Just as, in important respects, the fourteenth and fifteenth centuries might be reckoned among the early modern centuries, so the sixteenth and seventeenth centuries might also be reckoned among the Middle Ages. The academic continuity was still immense.[1]

Nevertheless, in terms of the influence of the great individual early modern thinkers – single, usually writing in a modern language, outside the university – the Cartesian and Lockean revolution in the theories of knowledge and science delivers a different picture. In philosophy, epistemology became the heart of the matter, although this was only fully effectuated in the nineteenth century. However, medieval thought did not know of the dictatorship of epistemology, which was only broken by, for example, Wittgenstein halfway through the twentieth century. In the Middle Ages, epistemology and the theory of proof and demonstration were not a central concern, although they were dealt with skillfully. There was no epistemic anxiety, a phenomenon which arose mainly in the nineteenth century. The nineteenth century was the century of epistemological and methodological supremacy.

---

[1] See Richard Muller, 'The Problem of Protestant Scholasticism – A Review and Definition,' Willem van 't Spijker, 'Reformation and Scholasticism,' Vos, 'Scholasticism and Reformation,' and Beck, 'Gisbertus Voetius (1589–1676): Basic Features of His Doctrine of God,' in Van Asselt and Dekker (eds), *Reformation and Scholasticism*, 45–64, 79–98, 99–119, and 205–226, respectively.

In medieval thought, the philosophy of language and logic, theology and anthropology were central concerns. Scotus' conceptual and methodological precision and perfection did not spring from uncertainty in matters religious, but from *faith* searching for philosophical truth and understanding.

If Duns Scotus were to apply his distinction between *necessary theology* and *contingent theology* to philosophy, he would call that which we call philosophy 'necessary philosophy'. In theology, things are distinct, for in theology contingency is decisive and the theoretical framework of contingency results in an alternative methodology. In terms of the basic phenomenon of contingent propositions the important role of necessary propositions in theology is discovered. The meanings of some terms, including key terms, have to be clarified, for example *ratio naturalis* and *ratio necessaria*. These terms belong to an analytical family of terms and we need an introduction to some of its other members. In order to explain the notion of *ratio naturalis*, we need to explain the notions of *ratio*, *ratio recta/erronea*, *ratio demonstrativa*, *ratio necessaria*, *argumentum* and *propositio per se nota* as well.

Viewed in this light, Duns Scotus' notion of *argument* is dealt with and the area of kinds of arguments surveyed in (§9.2), and his notion of *proof* is dealt with and the area of kinds of proofs surveyed in (§9.3).[2] §9.4 discusses Duns Scotus' theory of science and affiliated concepts, like the *subject* and the *object* of a science. In terms of the modern primacy of stating philosophical problems in a proof theoretical way, the omnipresence of arguments and Duns' way of using proofs do not only have a paradoxical ring, but also constitute something of a dilemma (§9.5). For this reason, Gilson's views on Duns Scotus' theory of proof and demonstration are briefly assessed (§9.6). §9.7 rounds off with a short comparative appraisal.

9.2 KINDS OF ARGUMENTS

9.2.1 *Ratio*

'Ratio' enjoyed an impressive career in philosophical and theological Latin during the Middle Ages. A wide spectrum of meanings is found in the literature:

---

[2] 'Proof' is here taken in a broad sense, also covering its meanings in ordinary academic language. For such an epistemological proof theory, see Mavrodes, *Belief in God*, 22–35, and *KN* 23–24, 60–62, and 381–384. Cf. Chisholm, *Theory of Knowledge* ([2]1977), 34 ff., 67 ff., and 114 ff., and Quine, *Philosophy of Logic*, 54–58.

computation, calculation, account; reason, account (to render account for, to give reason for); amount; proportion, proportionate sum; underlying principle, definition; aspect, characteristic; manner, arrangement, method; argument, theory; motto.

Moreover, '*ratio*' relates to other impressive families of words, terms like 'idea,'[3] 'forma,' 'conceptus,' 'intentio,' 'notio,' and 'species.'[4] With regard to philosophical usage, De Rijk's summary of important uses of 'ratio' is quite helpful. Since the times of Boethius, *ratio* was used to indicate one specific characteristic, be it essential or accidental, that a thing has in common with another thing. Moreover, *ratio* may signify the complete nature of a thing. 'Distinguishing several *rationes* in one and the same thing is a procedure which is typical of man's intellectual capability. This procedure forms the backbone of many philosophical and theological arguments concerning God and the entities occurring in the outside world.'[5]

Viewed in this light, translations to be preferred are *aspect* or *characteristic* or *feature*. These aspects are especially relevant to Scotus' philosophical usage. For him, two aspects of *ratio* are particularly intertwined: the argument line, based on the line of the logical aspect, in conjunction with the ontological aspect. The argumentational dimension of *ratio* shines out in combination with essential aspects of what there is and what can be known.

The habitat of this family of *ratio* is the range of the analytical meanings of *ratio*:

1. *Ratio* means: (a) argumentation, argument; (b) analysis; (c) structure (nature); (d) concept; and (e) reason, account; ground.

A critical remark fits in here. In the expression *ratio Anselmi*, *ratio* does not mean *reason*; in general, *reason* is not adequate for translating *ratio*.[6] It is misleading to translate the terms *ratio naturalis* and *ratio necessaria* with *natural reason* and *necessary reason*, respectively. *Ratio* is primarily *a* 'ratio' and *a* 'ratio' is *an* argument or *an* analysis provided by somebody, just as *ratio Anselmi* refers to an argument provided by Anselm and *ratio Richardi* refers to an argument

---

[3] See De Rijk, 'Un tournant important dans l'usage du mot *idea* chez Henri de Gand,' in *Idea*. VI Colloquio Internazionale, 89–98.

[4] See *Idea* (note 3), and *Ratio*. VII Colloquio Internazionale.

[5] De Rijk, 'A Special Use of *ratio* in 13th and 14th Century Metaphysics,' *Ratio*, 218.

[6] An exception is the case of *ratio* occurring in the expression *reddere rationem* which means *to account for*.

elaborated by Richard of Saint Victor. On this fundamental level, the meanings (a) and (b) are applicable.[7]

9.2.2 *Ratio recta* and *ratio necessaria*

Ratio recta *and* ratio erronea

Ratio recta and *ratio erronea* are prominent members of the *ratio* family:

2. A *ratio recta* is a correct argumentation or correct analysis.

When we act in such and such a way, there are many factors to be reckoned with. When we account for a specific act, we take into account: the possibility and the object of the act, the time and the place of the act.[8] A necessary condition for the moral goodness of an act is the requirement that an agent can elucidate its goodness.[9] The argumentation can go right or go wrong. *Ratio recta* and *ratio erronea* make a couple and thus we can go right in the first case and we can go wrong in the second case:

3. A *ratio erronea* is a wrong argument, a wrong argumentation or a wrong analysis.[10]

Ratio necessaria

Our next step is to contrast the term *ratio naturalis* with *ratio necessaria* against the background of the meanings of *ratio*. The term *ratio*

---

[7] Examples of Duns' use of *ratio Anselmi* are found in *Lectura* I 2.9 and 35, and in *Ordinatio* I 2.11 and 35, and examples of *ratio Richardi* are found in *Lectura* I 2.41 and 123 and in *Ordinatio* I 2.180.

[8] *Ordinatio* I 17.62: 'Bonitas moralis actus est [. . .] includens aggregationem debitae proportionis ad omnia ad quae habet proportionari (puta ad potentiam, ad obiectum, ad finem, ad tempus, ad locum et ad modum), et hoc specialiter ut ista dictantur a ratione recta debere convenire actui: ita quod pro omnibus possumus docere quod convenientia actus ad rationem rectam est qua posita actus est bonus, et qua non posita – quibuscumque aliis conveniat – non est bonus.'

[9] Ibid.: 'Quantumcumque actus sit circa obiectum qualecumque, si non sit secundum rationem rectam in operante (puta si ille non habeat rationem rectam in operando), actus non est bonus. Principaliter ergo conformitas actus ad rationem rectam – plene dictantem de circumstantiis omnibus debitis istius actus – est bonitas moralis actus.' Cf. *Ordinatio* I 17.64: 'Ex hoc – ex consequente – inclinat ad actum qui sit conformis rectae rationi, si recta ratio insit operanti.'

[10] See *Ordinatio* I 17.65: 'Idem enim habitus in natura, qui generaretur ex actibus abstinentiae elicitis *cum ratione erronea* in eliciente, manens post cum ratione recta, esset post virtus abstinentiae et prius non habitus vitutis, quamdiu non fuit ratio recta abstinendi.'

naturalis is extensively used by the young Duns in *Lectura* I 42, treat-ing the question whether divine omnipotence can be demonstrated with the help of *a* 'natural argument' (*ratio naturalis*).[11]

Duns simply states that *necessary arguments* and *natural argu-ments* differ, since necessary arguments are more simple than natural arguments. We approach the difference between them by first paying attention to necessary arguments. Duns acknowledges necessary arguments without any blemish concerning validity, but according to his terminology they are not *proofs* in the sense of *demonstrations*:

> Many arguments are made about the Trinity which are necessary and completely valid argumentatively, and yet they are not demonstra-tions [*demonstrationes*] which lead to certain and evident knowledge of the conclusion, because the propositions which function as pre-misses and on which they depend are not evidently known.[12]

Duns makes the same argumentation theoretical move in *Ordinatio* I 42.16: there are arguments in the doctrine of the Trinity which are necessary and have sufficient argumentative force in order to *prove* something (*ad probandum*), but not sufficient argumentative force in order to *demonstrate* something, for although they are necessary, yet they are not *evidently* true. Duns makes the crucial point that *neces-sity* does not entail *being self-evidently true*. In *Lectura* I 42.19 a similar distinction is made:

> Concerning the first *argument* we have to say that having *a necessary argument* and having *a demonstrative argument* which leads to an evident conclusion do not amount to the same thing. The reason is that a derived [*mediata*] proposition is only evident in the way that it leads to a proof [*ad probandum*] [. . .], if the direct [*immediata*] proposition on which it [namely the derived proposition] depends, were evident.[13]

Duns Scotus clearly explains the meanings of the expressions *immedi-ata propositio* and *mediata propositio*. The first kind of proposition

---

[11] *Lectura* I 42 has *ratio naturalis* in §§1, 4, 7, 10, 12, 13, 14, 15, 18, and 19. In *Ordinatio* I 42 *ratio naturalis* occurs in §§1, 6, 9, 11, 14, 17, 20, 21, and 22.

[12] *Lectura* I 42.19: 'Unde multa argumenta fiunt circa Trinitatem, quae sunt *necessaria* et non est defectus in arguendo, et *tamen non sunt demonstrationes* facientes certam evidentiam de conclusione, quia propositiones immediatae a quibus dependent, non sunt evidenter notae.'

[13] *Lectura* I 42.19: 'Ad primam rationem dicendum quod non est idem habere *rationem neces-sariam* et *rationem demonstrativam* evidenter concludentem, nam propositio mediata [. . .] non est evidens ad probandum, nisi propositio immediata – a qua dependet – esset evidens. Compare *Ordinatio* I 42.15.

functions as premisses and the second does not. Such necessary arguments are characterized by the double requirement of the necessity of the premisses and of the logical necessity of validity, for the theory of the immanent Trinity belongs to necessary theology (*theologia necessaria*) and, moreover, the point of validity has been explicitly stated. So, necessary arguments (*rationes necessariae*) are to be defined as follows:

4. A *ratio necessaria* is a valid argument in which necessary conclusions are deduced from necessary premisses.

Regarding necessary arguments, two requirements are at stake: first, the necessity of the logical connection between the premisses and the conclusion and, second, the necessity of the involved premisses. If these two requirements are fulfilled, the conclusion must be necessary too. The first requirement is of a logical nature – to be combined with ontological implications – and the second requirement is an ontological one. The premisses have to state an ontological necessity and they entail the conclusion in virtue of logical necessity. The fundamental ontological feature is necessity and the fundamental logical feature which governs a necessary argument, is *validity* (deductively logical necessity).

In sum, there are necessary arguments which can 'prove' something, although their premisses are not necessary *and* 'evidently' true, because they are only necessary (*Ordinatio* I 42.21).

Ratio naturalis

Moving on to the meaning of *ratio naturalis*, we see that Scotus adds the *condition of evident knowledge* to the concept of a necessary argument. So, an *epistemological* feature still to be defined has to be added to the *logical* feature of validity and the *ontological* feature of the necessary truth of the premisses.

Propositio per se nota

In order to see the specific difference between necessary and natural arguments we have to explain another important epistemological term: *propositio per se nota*. The self-evident character of such a proposition depends on being acquainted with the terms used. The truth of a self-evident proposition is evident on the basis of knowledge of the terms. The involved certainty is only based on something of the proposition itself. It cannot be falsified from the outside.

The main idea is that the predicate is immediately entailed by the subject term:

5. A *propositio per se nota* warrants its own truth on the basis of the meanings of its *terms*.[14]

Persuasio

In this light, we have also to translate *persuasio* with *proof* in the modern sense of the word (see *Lectura* I 42.19). It is crucial in studying Duns' epistemological evaluations to realize that *valid arguments based on provable premisses* are not called 'demonstrations'.

Fallacy

We can also approach the phenomenon of a natural argument from the opposite direction: a *fallacy* is an argument which shows something impossible and, so, a fallacy cannot be true. It is impossible to deliver a 'natural argument' in order to substantiate it. Suppose there is a proposition which is argumentatively unfalsifiable (*Ordinatio* I 42.21). Such a proposition is either immediately true as the analysis of its terms can show, or it turns out to be a conclusion from terms which eventually are immediately evident.

Conclusion

The element of Scotian, and medieval, 'evidence' (*evidentia*) makes up the difference between a necessary and a natural argument. The feature of the self-evidence of the necessary premisses accounts for the distinctive character of a natural argument to be added to an argument which is a necessary argument. So, the definition of 'natural argument' (*ratio naturalis*) is provided for:

6. A *ratio naturalis* is a *necessary* and *logically valid* argument in which the necessary conclusion is derived from premisses which are eventually both necessary and self-evident.

Duns Scotus was fascinated by the phenomenon of *deductivity*, as the great ancients were too. When he probes into the profound insights to be taken from this phenomenon, Scotus' analytical way of doing

---

[14] See *Lectura* I 2.15–19, containing a fine summary in *Lectura* I 2.19: 'Illa igitur *propositio est per se nota* quae ex sola notitia terminorum habet evidentiam et non mendicatam ex evidentia aliorum conceptuum.' Consult also §4.6: 'Proposition'. Cf. §8.4.

philosophy and theology finds its center in the notions of *argument* (*ratio*) and *concept* (*conceptus*). He frames a network of terms of epistemic appraisal, turning around the question of how to arrive at validity and truth. The relation between *axioms* or axiomatic propositions (*principia*) and *theses* (*conclusiones*) yields the basic structure which delivers two overarching distinctions embodying two crucial dualities. The first distinction starts from the first essential point of *deductivity*, namely *being derivable from necessary propositions* and its complement *not being derivable from necessary propositions*. Contingent propositions are not derivable from necessary ones. So, the first characteristic of deductivity entails the basic duality of *necessity–contingency*. The second distinction starts from the second essential point of *deducing*: *being deducible* and its complement *not being deducible*. In order to finish a complete deduction, we have to have conclusions and propositions which do not function as conclusions, since they are only derivable from themselves. So, the second characteristic of deductivity delivers the basic duality of *being deducible* (*not being self-evident*) and *being self-evident*. Duns Scotus' theoretical framework is built on these two basic dualities governing the systematic behavior both of concepts (§4.6) and of arguments. For these reasons, §§9.2 and 4.6 are fundamental in Chapters 9 and 4 respectively.

9.3 KINDS OF PROOFS

We cannot conclude that natural arguments form the only kind of certain arguments. Necessary arguments, based on proved premisses, and contingency arguments provide us often with certainty. Indeed, Duns would not like to deny this. Many arguments from Scotus' theology of the Trinity are in fact proofs viewed according to modern terminology, although they are not 'demonstrations' according to Scotian terminology. According to this terminology, such arguments are only arguments which 'prove' (= *probare* or *ostendere*). So, on the one hand, *probare* (*to prove*) is specifically related to *demonstrare*; on the other hand, we also observe the basic distinction between *authoritative proofs* and *argumentative proofs*. Something may be *proved authoritatively* (*auctoritate*) or may be *proved argumentatively* (*ratione*). A *demonstration* is a distinct kind of argument (*ratio*), but *proofs* (*probationes*) can be delivered both in virtue of *authoritative texts* (*auctoritates*) and in virtue of *arguments* (*rationes*).

As regards a certain inference, Duns Scotus notices in *Quaestiones Quodlibetales* II: 'The first inference is proved in virtue of an *authoritative text* and *argumentatively*.'[15] First, the proof from tradition is offered and the next section yields the argumentative proof. This strategy deserves two comments. First, the modern verdict that the first kind of 'proof' is no proof is an *a*historical statement, nor is it to the point from a systematic point of view. It is an *a*historical statement because we have simply to realize that within Duns Scotus' university culture such authoritative texts are read and seen as proofs. That simple fact has only to be understood by us, not judged. An authoritative text (*auctoritas*) is not something like a modern authoritarian gesture or command. The modern type of authority hardly existed in the Middle Ages. Medieval culture was not an authoritarian culture. An authoritarian culture is a modern phenomenon.

An *auctoritas* was not read as an 'authority' but as a text revealing truth. This truth claim cannot be discovered by researching historically the source under consideration but by studying the mind of the medieval author as he expresses himself in his writings according to the rules of historical method. An *auctoritas* truth is her or his truth. Moreover, in the adduced example Augustine is in fact referred to, but it is crucial to see that the distinction between 'authoritatively' and 'argumentatively' does not run analogous to the distinctions between *faith* and *reason*, or between *theology* and *philosophy*. The *auctoritate* proof can also be based on Aristotle. In *Lectura Prologus* 116–117 it is read: 'This is proved *argumentatively* and *by an authoritative text*. [. . .] This is also proved by an authoritative text of the Philosopher.'[16] Proving in virtue of authoritative texts (*auctoritates*) and in virtue of arguments (*rationes*) is a distinction internal to reading texts in medieval culture, and not a symptom of the modern faith–reason dualism. The first step of an *auctoritas* concerns discovering truth; the second step of offering *rationes* makes this truth intelligible. Duns Scotus mainly relates this last step to his necessary theology – and to his (necessary) philosophy.[17]

---

[15] *Quaestiones Quodlibetales* II 48: 'Probatio primae consequentiae *auctoritate* et *ratione*.' Cf. §49: 'Probatur eadem consequentia *per rationem* sic.' On the phenomenon of an *auctoritates* culture, see §§14.7–14.9.

[16] See Vos et al., *Duns Scotus on Divine Love*, chapter 1.

[17] Authoritative texts possess, to the medieval mind, probative force, but there is also the liberating modern discovery that many medieval proofs and demonstrations can be read and reformulated as valid proofs.

9.3.1 *Ratio demonstrativa*

In *Lectura* I 42 Duns draws the distinction between *rationes necessariae* and *rationes demonstrativae*:

> We have to say that having *a necessary argument* and having *a demonstrative argument* [. . .] do not amount to the same thing. (*Lectura* I 42.19)

Two kinds of comments have to be made: terminological comments and comments on the level of argumentation theory. We present some terminological comments. Within the context of the theory of argumentation, the terms *ratio naturalis* and *ratio demonstrativa* are synonymous. In *Lectura* I 42 the expressions *per rationem naturalem cognosci* and *naturaliter cognosci* are used synonymously.[18] If Duns states that something cannot be demonstrated by *a natural argument* (*Lectura* I 42.18), then he can conclude in a parallel way that in such cases the arguments are not *demonstrationes* (*Lectura* I 42.19). In sum:

7. A *demonstratio* is a *ratio demonstrativa*.

In the same section he elucidates the distinction between a *ratio necessaria* and a *ratio demonstrativa*, introducing the answer to the question: 'Can divine omnipotence be *demonstrated* by a *natural argument*?' The answer seems to be affirmative, for there are necessary arguments of Anselm and Richard of Saint Victor to be cited in its favor (*Lectura* I 42.1–2). Duns, however, does not appeal to these arguments for a very specific reason: necessary arguments do not suffice to build up demonstrations. Duns' denial basically consists of the distinction between a *necessary argument* and a *demonstrative argument* as it is called this time (*Lectura* I 42.1–2 and 19). We conclude:

8. A *demonstrative argument* (*ratio demonstrativa*) is the same as a *natural argument* (*ratio naturalis*).

On the basis of (7) and (8), together with

6. A *ratio naturalis* is a *necessary* and *logically valid argument* in which the necessary conclusion is derived from premises which are necessary and self-evident propositions

---

[18] Compare, for example, *Lectura* I 42.1, 4, 7, 10, 12, 13, 14, and 15–16. In *Ordinatio* I 42 expressions as *naturaliter cognosci/probari/ostendi* and *per rationem naturalem cognosci/demonstrari* are interchangeably used even more frequently. In *Ordinatio* I 42.4, we meet the expression *ex puris naturalibus* which is well known from Renaissance philosophy. However, with Duns it means *ex puris naturalibus*, namely *rationibus*.

the definition of demonstration, which also functions as an important hermeneutical principle, can be derived:

9. A demonstration (*demonstratio*) is a *necessary* and *logically valid argument* where the thesis is eventually derived from premisses which are necessary and self-evident propositions.

9.3.2   Demonstrability and underivability

In the idea of demonstration (*ratio naturalis* or *ratio demonstrativa*) self-evidence and derivability are specifically contrasted: if there is any proof of a particular proposition possible, then that proposition cannot be a self-evident one.[19]

Thus we see that the Scotian notion of *self-evidence* is very strict and in fact boils down to *underivability*:

10. A *self-evident proposition* is an *underivable proposition*.

With the help of the terms presented so far, it is easy to define *ratio naturalis* in an alternative way: a *ratio naturalis* is *per definitionem* a necessary argument, but at the same time something has to be added to it in order to make it up to a *natural argument*. The component to be added to it is what I would like to call *absolute derivability*: absolute derivability includes the *provability of a conclusion*, while the *premisses* are eventually *underivable*.

According to this line of argument, (6) can be specified in terms of (10):

11. A *ratio naturalis* is a *necessary argument* in which the *necessary conclusion* is eventually *derived* from *necessary and underivable premisses*.

9.3.3   *Demonstratio propter quid* and *demonstratio quia*

This distinction derives from Aristotle's *Posterior Analytics* I 13–14. This is a fact on the level of an authoritative text, but Duns also

---

[19] *Lectura* I 2.20: 'Non dicitur propositio per se nota quia est nota cuicumque intellectui, sed [. . .] termini nati sunt facere per se evidentem notitiam intellectui concipienti terminos per se notos; et ideo nulla est per se nota quae alicui intellectui potest demonstrari. Verumtamen in *propositionibus per se notis* sunt gradus secundum dignitatem et ignobilitatem. Unde dignior est ista *impossibile est idem esse et non esse* quam ista *omne totum est maius sua parte*.' Cf. *Lectura* I 2.12: 'Per se notum negari non potest a mente alicuius' (= *Ordinatio* I 2.14) and *Ordinatio* I 2.22–24.

believes that the distinction is worthwhile, because we not only have necessary truths which are self-evident, but also other necessary truths which can be deduced from them. So, what is at stake here is that we have both necessary truths which are 'evident' in virtue of their own terms, and necessary truths which are not immediately evident in virtue of their own terms. The *non-evident* necessary truths Duns is concerned with are not simply 'non-evident,' but although they are not evident in virtue of their terms, they still enjoy a necessary and evident relation with necessary truths which are necessary and self-evident. In deductive concatenations we argue from premisses to conclusions – and principles are basic premisses – and from conclusions to their premisses.

The literature often offers rather vague explanations of these terms, but two elementary elements support the whole of the argumentational fabric: self-evident premisses and logically valid deducibility. When Duns says that a demonstration *propter quid* is valid in terms of its *causa/cause*, then 'causa/cause' refers to the premiss(es) the demonstration is eventually founded on. The end of a demonstration *propter quid* is the starting point in a demonstration *quia*. Here, *effectus/effect* refers to the level of the conclusion. Both kinds of proofs are each other's counterpart and enjoy the same demonstrative value and all this is anchored in one and the same structure of the deduction.[20] 'Truths on the level of premisses can neither obtain without certain truths on the level of conclusions, not conversely' (ibid.).[21]

Viewed in this light, it is clear that Duns concludes that principles cannot be demonstrated by a demonstration *quia*, since a basic self-evident premiss cannot function as the conclusion of a demonstrative argument – it is the foundation of a demonstrative proof.

The importance of this set of definitions is easily to be pointed out by discussing Anthony Quinton's allegation:

> What is clear is that although animated by the same kind of general rationalistic intent as Aquinas, Scotus took the first effective steps

---

[20] *Quaestiones Quodlibetales* VII 7: 'Prima distinctio est nota ex I *Posteriorum*, quae est quod demonstrationum alia est *propter quid* sive per causam, alia *quia* sive per effectum. Probatur ista distinctio per rationem: quia omne necessarium verum, non evidens ex terminis, habens tamen connexionem necessariam et evidentiam ad aliud ut necessarium evidens ex terminis, potest *demonstrari* per illud verum evidens. Nunc autem, aliquod *verum necessarium non evidens ex terminis* habet connexionem necessariam ad aliquod verum *acceptum a causa*, et aliquod ad verum *acceptum ab effectu*.'

[21] On demonstrations *quia* and *propter quid*, see Wolter, 'The "Theologism" of Scotus' (1947), in *The Philosophical Theology of Scotus*, 215–224: 'On the Nature of Demonstration.'

toward that firm demarcation between the domains of revealed faith and philosophical reason that was the fundamental principle of Ockham's philosophy and that tended to eliminate rational discussion of religious truth altogether.[22]

In fact, just the opposite is true. The young John Duns enlarged the range of debatable and provable truths within theology.[23] The decisive point is not a mental or psychological feature, but one of a logical and epistemological nature. A *self-evident* proposition is an *underivable* proposition, for, according to Duns Scotus, self-evidence and provability exclude each other. So, underivability need not elicit a complaint. Instead, it can signal some compliments. Along these lines, we have to interpret the expressions *holding (only) by faith ((de) (sola) fide tenere)* and *assenting by faith (assentire per fidem)*.[24] If Duns' thesis is that some theological point cannot be demonstrated or proven (*demonstrare*, not *probare*),[25] then this fact has often been taken to mean that Duns subscribes to fideism (Gilson). However, again and again, the systematic point of such statements is to be taken from the theory of argumentation: if something cannot be demonstrated then it may be self-evident, and if it is neither demonstrable nor self-evident – in the specialized senses which Duns imposes on these terms – then it might be held (only) by faith,[26] although it is still possible that it can be proven, both in the sense of Scotian *probatio* and the modern sense of *proof*.

Therefore the point is a classificatory one, taken from epistemology and the theory of argumentation, and it is no evidence for any fideism or irrationalism on Duns' part. A score of such theological

---

[22] Quinton, 'British Philosophy,' *EP* I 372.

[23] In *DS*, Chapter 11: 'God Drieënig,' I defend that a great part of Duns' Trinitarian theology also belongs to the philosophical theory of God.

[24] See, for example, *Lectura* I 42.17: 'Ideo dico quod *sola fide tenendum* est Deum sic esse omnipotentem,' and *Lectura* I 2.23: 'Omnis assentiens per fidem vel credulitatem aut demonstrationem alicui complexioni, habet apprehensionem terminorum.'

[25] See *Lectura* I 42.19 and *Ordinatio* I 2.242.

[26] *Lectura* I 2.23: 'Quaelibet propositio per se nota, est nota ex terminis cuilibet intellectui concipienti terminos; sed haec *Deus est* – intelligendo per Deum non hanc essentiam quam nos concipimus, sed intelligendo conceptum aliquem nos de hac essentia concipimus – vel etiam *Deus est infinitus*, vel ens infinitum est, non est nota ex terminis cuilibet concipienti terminos; igitur non est per se nota. Maior patet. Minor ostenditur: omnis assentiens per fidem vel credulitatem aut demonstrationem alicui complexioni, habet apprehensionem terminorum; sed nos assentimus huic *Deus est* vel ex fide vel ex demonstratione; igitur prius termini apprehenduntur, ante fidem et demonstrationem; sed ex apprehensione terminorum non assentimus, quia tunc non tantum per fidem aut demonstrationem. Cf. the helpful excursion on simple concepts in *Lectura* I 2.24–31. Cf. §4.6.

points can be proved, if we take *proving* in its modern sense. The modern issue of (im)provability is here not at stake. We have to grant that, in terms of the modern meaning of 'proof,' many arguments of Duns' salvationary historical theology have to be assessed as *proofs*, although Duns says that they cannot be *demonstrated*.

9.4 THEORY OF SCIENCE

The *Prologue* of the *Lectura* deals with a few crucial issues in a short and forceful way. The first question of the third part introduces the perennial question whether theology is a science. This *quaestio* is roughly to be divided into three parts. The first introductory part presents the Aristotelian definition of *scientia* and is linked with an analysis which contrasts the epistemic status of *knowing* itself with the modal status of the epistemic object (*Prologus* 107–110). Here, a terminological comment is in place: strictly, *scientia* does not mean *science* but, basically, *scientia* is *an act* or *a disposition of knowing* related to a specific proposition as its epistemic object. An intrinsically organized set of such epistemic dispositions can form what may be rather similar to what might be called a *science*.

Words like *scientia* and *geometria*, *theologia* and *metaphysica* signify *epistemic acts* or *dispositions* – for the moment, we leave aside the aspect of being an *act* and concentrate on dispositions. An epistemic disposition like *scientia* is a relation and, so, it has an object. For Duns Scotus, the nature of this relation between the disposition and the object defines what *scientia* as such (*simpliciter*) is supposed to be: *scientia* as such is knowledge which does justice entirely to the involved epistemic object.[27]

Geometria, *metaphysica* or *theologia* is knowledge which does justice to the involved geometrical, metaphysical or theological object, and the *primary object* of the disposition is identical with the *primary subject* of the propositions to be known.[28] There is much

---

[27] *Lectura Prologus* 65: 'Unde cognitio quae est proportionata obiecto secundum se, est simpliciter *scientia*. Et sic cognitio de obiecto theologiae quae nata est haberi secundum se, est *theologia* simpliciter.'

[28] The *scientia* structure can be formalized as follows: there is a primary subject s, s entails its primary truth p_s, constituting what the essence of s basically includes. p_s entails the principles $p_1, p_2, \ldots$ of the *scientia* under consideration and the principles $p_1, p_2, \ldots$ entail its theses $r_1, r_2, \ldots, r_n$ (*conclusiones*). The concept of knowledge of such *scientia* is governed by a dual epistemic condition: $(C.K_{h1})$ $(p_s \rightarrow p_1) \leftrightarrow (_aKp_s \rightarrow {_a}Kp_1)$ and $(C.K_{h2})$ $((p_1 \,\&\, p_2) \rightarrow r_1) \leftrightarrow ((_aKp_1 \,\&\, {_a}Kp_2) \rightarrow {_a}Kr_1)$.

confusion about Duns' use of the terms *subiectum* and *obiectum*: *subiectum* is used in connection with a proposition – the primary subject is a subject of a proposition – and *obiectum* is used when the object of a relation is meant, e.g. the disposition of *knowing*, as Richter has also seen.[29]

The second part puts forward an objection to be expected: if theology largely is about contingent propositions, how can theology be a science if science is intrinsically connected with necessity (*Prologus* 111–113)? The third and largest part of the first *quaestio* of the third *pars* of the *Prologue* (§§114–118) deals with the challenge that the largest part of theology is about contingent propositions and, so, theology largely consists of contingent theology. Instead of adhering to a concept of *science* which excludes the contingency realm of theology, Duns drops the condition of necessity. This move creates a problem. In contrast to Aristotle's approach, the idea of the subject of a science plays a major role in Duns' methodology of science. The Scotian idea of the *subject* of a branch of knowledge is connected with a necessary basis and a deductively organized elaboration of its contents.[30] We meet a well-known challenge: how is it possible that there is a *subject* of contingent propositions scientifically known?

9.4.1   The literary structure of *Lectura Prologus pars* 3 – a unique *quaestio*

These preliminary problems arise from the definition Duns had already offered in the introductory part. The stand taken by him is clear: *theology in itself* is *scientia* as far as *scientia* itself is spotless. Then he offers the Aristotelian definition of *scientia/epistèmè* and goes on comparing two of his three types of theology with this conception of science. The first remarkable phenomenon in the third part of the *Prologue* of the *Lectura* is that the questions center around semi-Aristotelian notions: *science* and *being subordinate* (*subalternare*), and not around concepts Duns Scotus himself subscribes to. The effect is that *Lectura Prologus pars* 3 is quite exceptional from the literary point of view.

---

[29] See O'Connor, 'The Scientific Character of Theology According to Scotus,' *De doctrina Ioannis Duns Scoti*, 5–17.

[30] On *Lectura Prologus pars* 3 (text, translation and commentary), see Vos et al., *Duns Scotus on Divine Love*, Chapter 1. For an early treatment of the conditions of a science, see *Quaestiones in librum Porphyrii Isagoge* III 13.

The standard pattern of a distinction or a part of a distinction turning around a *quaestio* is characterized by three main parts: *counter-arguments – personal theory – refutations*. In the third part of this *Prologue* the situation is quite different. There are (two) questions at stake: is theology *scientia* (§107) and is theology *subordinate* or *subordinating*? Because of the striking trait that there are no counter-arguments, no *Sed contra* and no refutations, the question is to be raised: what about the main part of the body of the *quaestio* itself, offering the personal theory? As is to be expected, the body of the *quaestio* where the author usually develops his own theory is missing too.

What does he offer instead? Duns offers instead a threefold treatment: (1) a comparison of two kinds of *theology* (divine knowledge and the theology of the blessed) with the Aristotelian conception of *science*; (2) an analysis of the problem of *contingent theology*; and (3) an analysis of the problem of *the primary subject* of contingent theology. First, a comparison is offered. It has often been said that Duns transformed Augustinian theology by applying Aristotle's theory of science. It is not easy to substantiate this claim.

§107 has to be divided into five parts:

107(a) According to this approach, it is obvious that other questions can be solved and one of them is whether *theology* [namely divine knowledge] be *science*.

107(b) As to this question we have to say that *theology* is science as far as *science* is perfectly right.

107(c) Just as it is obvious from the definition of *science*, *science* is *certain knowledge* of *necesary propositions*, acquired in virtue of a *premiss* and *the evident nature of the object* and in virtue of *a conclusion accounted for from its premiss*.

107(d) The next step points out that *science*, *discursive* and *deductive* as it is, is not perfectly right and that *science* being *based on a premiss* is not perfectly right either, since, in this way, it depends on preceding knowledge.

107(e) *Therefore theology in itself* is *science* as far as the other conditions which are perfectly right are concerned, namely *theology* is *knowledge* which is *certain, necessary* and *self-evident* in virtue of its object.[31]

---

[31] *Lectura Prologus* 107: 'Iuxta hoc patet solutio aliarum quaestionum, quarum una est, an *theologia* sit *scientia*. Ad quam dicendum est quod est *scientia* quantum ad id quod perfectionis est in scientia. Nam sicut patet ex definitione *scientiae*, *scientia* est *cognitio certa* de *necessariis*, habita per *causam* et *evidentiam obiecti* et per *applicationem causae ad effectum*. Sed quod scientia sit per *discursum et applicationem*, hoc est imperfectionis; et etiam quod

Comments

1. §107(a) introduces the problem at stake, following on the previ-ous part – *pars 2* of the *Prologue* – on *the subject of theology*.
2. §107(b) delivers the straightforward answer: *theology is science* as far as it is absolutely valuable.
3. §107(c) offers the Aristotelian definition of *science* listing five con-ditions:
   - C1 – *scientia (epistèmè, science)* is *certain knowledge*;
   - C2 – it is certain knowledge of *necessary propositions*;
   - C3 – it is knowledge which is *based on a premiss*;
   - C4 – it is knowledge in virtue of *the evident nature of the epistemic object*;
   - C5 – it is acquired by *deriving a conclusion from a premiss*.
4. §107(d) lists the components being epistemically not perfectly right.
5. §107(e) applies the epistemological analysis §107(d) to the case of the scientific character of *theology* in the light of the definition of *science* (§107(c)), thereby substantiating the thesis of §107(b) and answering the question of §107(a).

The five conditions of §107(c) are weighed with the help of the litmus test of *being perfectly right* from the epistemic point of view: is this condition perfectly right as an epistemic value? In fact, the verdict is devastating. Two out of the five conditions are rejected as being not right, and a third condition is repaired: C3 is not faultless (§107(d)), since it formulates that the scientific knowledge under consideration is based on a premiss (= *causa*). Such knowledge depends on preced-ing knowledge and, for this reason, it is not independent and complete in itself. It is dependent upon and has to be supported by preceding knowledge. So, Duns says that there is some imperfection at play not being perfectly right by itself. There is something wrong in terms of the idea of complete and independent knowledge. C5 is not faultless either, for the dependence of the considered knowledge entails that it must be deductively acquired (§107(d)). We have to go on discursively by seeing a conclusion in the light of its premises and by discovering that it follows from them. Such knowledge is not complete in itself and not perfectly right (*perfectus*), for it has to be conquered.

sit habita per *causam*, imperfectionis est, quia sic dependet ex cognitione praecedente. *Theologia, ergo, in se* quantum ad alias condiciones quae sunt perfectionis (quod sit *cogni-tio certa* et *necessaria* et *per obiectum per se evidens*, non per causam efficientem in intel-lectu), est *scientia.*'

Therefore *theology in itself* which is all in knowledge as had already been expounded in the decisive §104 – and, so, knowledge God personally possesses – is not embarrassed by conditions *C3* and *C5*. Nevertheless, it enjoys the conditions *C1*, *C2*, and *C4*, although §112 repairs the necessity condition *C2* by transforming its *necessitas consequentis* into a *necessitas consequentiae*. Moreover, §§112 and 118 show that just divine knowledge takes the pride of place, because it is perfectly right and evident knowledge of what is contingent.

Conclusion

Only two out of the five conditions of *scientia* survive the litmus test of true epistemic perfection which is entailed by divine perfection. The theory of divine knowledge explodes the preconceived Aristotelian conception of *epistèmè* and delivers the foundation of an alternative epistemological and proof theoretical approach. The secret of Duns' flourishing philosophical originality is to be diagnosed as genial theological enthusiasm. His epistemology centers around *certainty* (the theme of *Lectura* I 3 and I 39) and the clarity and evident nature of the epistemic object (the theme of Duns' theory of the subject of a science in the *prologues* of the *Lectura* and the *Ordinatio*). It is the radically theological dimensions which press medieval thought, and Duns in particular, to trod unknown paths. Again and again, it is theological dilemmas which crack the conceptual structures of Greek *philosophia*.

9.4.2 *Scientia* and science

In the second part of the *Prologue* of the *Lectura* Duns discusses an objection to be expected: if theology largely is about contingent propositions, how can theology be a science if science is intrinsically connected with necessity (*Prologus* 111–113)? The drive of Duns' argumentation is quite clear. The *object* of real knowledge does not intrinsically constitute the *nature* of genuine knowledge. When reasonable *knowledge* (*epistèmè, scientia*) and *necessity* are disconnected, there is a shift from the modal status of the epistemic object to the epistemic quality of the act or disposition of *knowing*.

The most decisive Knower is God who is omniscient. By disconnecting the object and act of knowing, the parallelism of thought and being, so characteristic for Greek and Hellenistic philosophy, is dropped. Theological strains force Duns to revolutionize epistemology and philosophy of science. Because God knows contingent truths by heart, his knowledge must be splendid knowledge and radiant wisdom and if it cannot be accounted for according to Aristotle's canons of scientific knowledge, we have to concede that this is the worse for these canons, not for divine knowledge.

Duns Scotus' thought is profoundly revisionary. His orientation settles on a new universe of thought. It is even misleading to say that he is busy revising the theories of Aristotle. Edward O'Connor noticed that 'it is not always easy, in analyzing the philosophical views of Scotus, to draw an exact line between what he took from Aristotle, and what he added personally.'[32] It is just questionable as to whether the *addition* model fits the situation. Unfortunately, O'Connor adds to his observation 'but there is no need to be nice about that question here; it is enough to note exactly those features of his theory of science which significantly affect his idea of theology.' Although this phenomenon occurs rather generally in the literature on the subject, it is to be regretted, for if we compare the historical Aristotle – not the disguised semi-Christian Aristotle of medieval texts, an Aristotle who never existed as a person of flesh and blood in history – and the historical John Duns Scotus, we find that they are worlds apart, including their philosophies of science.

Our picture of Duns' theory of science seems to be rather different from O'Connor's.[33] For O'Connor, the *Prologue* of the *Ordinatio* represents the last stage of Duns' theoretical development. However, we have seen that it was still at Oxford that Duns invested much in revising the *Prologue* of the *Lectura*. There are only two or three years between writing the first prologue and rewriting the second, while the Parisian *Prologue* dates from the autumn of 1302. In fact, we read in the *Ordinatio*: 'From the definition of *science*, it is quite clear that it does not seem possible that *science* is about what is contingent.'[34] O'Connor sounds quite convinced. 'Because our theology lacks that insight into the nature of its subject which is the indispensable root principle of science, it follows inevitably that our theology is not a science. Scotus takes this famous position in conscious opposition to St. Thomas.'[35] O'Connor attacks the interpretation of Minges that

---

[32] O'Connor, 'The Scientific Character of Theology,' *De doctrina Ioannis Duns Scoti* III, 4.

[33] See also §10.7. Cf. *DS* chapter III: 'Geloof, existentie en theologie.'

[34] *Ordinatio Prologus* 210. Even Krop reads this as if it is Duns' personal view, but only the problem (*dubium* = preliminary problem) to be considered is formulated in §210.

[35] O'Connor, 'The Scientific Character of Theology,' *De doctrina Ioannis Duns Scoti* III, 39, where also the views of Minges and Magrini are discussed.

Scotus looks upon theology as science in the broad sense, as well as Magrini's interpretation that, according to Scotus, theology is science in the general sense of the word. However:

> The fact is that Scotus never taught this, and I think it is very questionable that he would have admitted it in any sense of the term *science* recognized by him. Whenever the question of the scientific character of 'theologia nostra' arose in his commentaries either on the prologue or on book III d. 24 of the *Sentences*, Scotus always took an unqualifiedly negative position' (ibid.).

This assessment is followed by a statement, almost perfectly true. 'Scotus recognized, as we have seen, that theology in the mind of God, and in the case of contingent truths, cannot be called a science according to the strict definition of Aristotle, but only with a certain qualification.'

The first observations are perfectly true, but, on Duns' side, there is not a qualified 'yes' to the thesis that the theology of the Church is a science in its Aristotelian sense. O'Connor thinks that, from the point of view of Duns Scotus' notions of *science* and the *subject of a science*, Scotus feels uneasy when confronted with the splendor and contingency of divine knowledge and the *theologia contingens*. Duns' rebound does not consist in a qualification of affirmative answers, but in the revision of the involved concepts. If Aristotelian conditions do not satisfy the nature of God's knowledge, exemplifying what *theology* as such is, then Duns simply drops the condition of deductively discovering and deriving conclusions and theses from premises. Already in *Lectura Prologus* 107, Duns' first statement was: as far as perfection is at stake, *theology in itself* is *scientia*. 'Theology in itself' is certain knowledge in virtue of the epistemic object which is evident in itself.

God's perfect knowledge is, again and again, called (*divina*) *scientia*. If a concept of *scientia* excludes contingent propositions, then we see Duns pointing out, in a parallel way, that the condition of necessity has to be dropped, since it concerns the epistemic object, and not the status of *knowing* itself. Duns does not say that the whole of theology, including contingent theology, excludes the element of *scientia*, but that it *seems* to be so and this '*videtur/it* seems to be so' belongs to the language of the *obiecta*. His straightforward alternative is that '*scientia* is best seen as *certain and evident knowledge*.'[36] For humans, even

---

[36] *Ordinatio Prologus* 211: 'Hic dico quod in scientia illud perfectionis est, quod sit cognitio certa et evidens.' Discussing this in *Lectura Prologus* 110 Duns disconnects the elements of time and deducibility.

knowing necessary propositions is itself contingent. Duns' move is to distinguish between the necessity of the act or disposition of *knowing* and the necessity of the epistemic object. In *Lectura Prologus* 112 he still accepts that the concept of our *scientia* requires the necessity of the epistemic object, but, later on, he simply drops the necessity condition.

9.4.3   Subject and object of a science

In the last short chapter of the third *pars* (§§119–121), Duns skips the whole idea of *subordinating* and *subordinated sciences* in matters theological. Will the idea of a *scientific subject* which seems to be so dear to Duns suffer from the same experience in matters theological, and, by the way, what is the *primary subject* of a *science*? A given science may deal with various particular subjects, but, notwithstanding, there is only one *subject* which is *primary* (*primum subiectum*).

A *subject* includes by definition essential characteristics which constitute its essential identity (*passiones*).[37] However, a *primary subject* is at stake. A *primary subject* includes both essential attributes (*passiones*) and *principles* and, so, the axiomatic basis of a science seems to be included in the notion of *primary subject* itself. Let us frame a metaphysical example: we have an item of metaphysical knowledge, stored in an epistemic disposition:

> A *contingent proposition is itself necessary* (*necessarily contingent*).

Contingent being is a subject of metaphysics, but it is not the *primary* subject of metaphysics. The theory of basic contingency belongs to the broader theory of transcendent terms and within the theory of transcendent terms the most basic item is to be discerned, namely *being* (*ens*) itself. So, *being* (*ens*) is the primary subject in doing metaphysics.[38]

In general, the basic notion of a science entails the whole of the body of knowledge to be considered. Thus Duns says: the *primary subject* is that subject which, in the first place, entails having this virtually and what is required for having this.[39] It is easily seen that such

---

[37] Compare the use of *passio* in Duns' theory of *passiones entis*. See CF 96–99.

[38] *Lectura Prologus* 66: 'Sic ratio *entis* continet totum habitum metaphysicae, quia includit *ens* quod est *primum subiectum* quod continet virtualiter omnia quae pertinent ad habitum metaphysicae.'

[39] Ibid.: '*Primum subiectum* cuiuscumque habitus est illud quod primo continet virtualiter illum habitum et quae requiruntur ad illum habitum.' *Continere* means to entail, *virtualiter* indicates that the deductive relation is implicit, and *primo* (= immediately) indicates that the involved entailment is the first and basic entailment.

a conception of *primary subject* fits quite well a type of philosophy according to which reality is necessary, but how is such a notion of primary subject to be reconciled with contingency thought? What does Duns Scotus make of it?

We see Duns commenting on his definition and its consequences: this approach of what it is to be a primary subject of a science excludes contingent properties and if God is the primary subject of theology, how can theology be a science? If actuality is mainly contingent, then we have to point out that there are also two layers to be discerned in the notion of primary subject. The logic of true necessary propositions hinges on the idea of self-evident necessary propositions. There must be a self-evident starting-point (*immediatum*). Does the realm of contingency have self-evident points of contact? The Aristotelian philosophy of science excludes a positive answer. Duns' hypothesis runs as follows: indirect contingent propositions have a recourse to self-evident contingent propositions (*propositiones contingentes immediatae*).

True contingent propositions have a primary subject on their own. Duns keeps the same basic idiom: just as a triangle contains its principles and theses, so Socrates contains his contingent truths. The analysis is elementary: it moves on the level of *saying of* – in both cases truths are *said of* someone or something and the most elementary truth grants *evidentia*. Socrates is the primary subject of *Socrates is sitting* and God in his individual nature is the primary subject of the contingent truths in theology. With the help of his new notion of *subject* (*of a* science) Duns rearranges available scientific knowledge, integrating both the necessary and contingent part of it by the interplay of necessary and contingent truths, while the necessary truths demarcate the space of the contingent ones.

9.5 THE DILEMMA OF PROVABILITY

The proof theoretical dilemma consists in the possibility that a theological argument may enjoy cogency and probative value while, nevertheless, it is not a demonstration for the philosopher. Such statements on the part of Duns have again and again been used as evidence for concluding that Duns accepts a fundamental chasm between theology and philosophy, and between faith and reason. However, the awkward thing is that some interpreters looked upon him as a rationalist and others as a fideist.

One easily forgets that it is Duns Scotus who claims that a sound argument need not be a demonstration for Aristotle, and that it is not Aristotle who refuses to be convinced. Thus we have to explain why Duns takes the philosophers under his wing when he concludes that a certain theological proposition cannot be demonstrated. In such cases, even Gilson claims that it is not scientific knowledge in the strict sense of the word, but only belief. If Scotus' profound insights eventually rest on revelation, is it not clear that all proofs derive their cogency from faith? However, when we take into account that Duns Scotus does not concede that the issue of provability is not decided for himself, it may dawn upon us that a different problem is at issue. If a certain proposition p is provable for a, it may still be not-provable for b. In that case, p is not demonstrable, but if proposition p is provable for any b, p is demonstrable. What kind of epistemic property is (un)demonstrability then?

In *Quaestiones Quodlibetales* VII Duns again discusses the provability of omnipotence. In *Quaestiones Quodlibetales* VII 53 he presents an argument on behalf of its provability. Its demonstrability is at stake. His assessment of the argument under consideration runs as follows: 'Although this argument enjoys probative value (*probabilis*), it is not a *demonstration* for the philosopher.'

This assessment is executed in terms of the theory of proof and has as such nothing to do with the perennial dilemma of faith and reason. Although it may sound differently to modern ears, in fact Duns does not say that his theological issue is not a philosophical one and cannot be accounted for rationally. On the contrary, he is presenting an epistemological analysis, far away from the battle between theology and philosophy. For Duns, what the philosophers present is not what *we* mean by philosophy, but a specific ideological stance. Even in the case of an argument being a straightforward proof, Duns realizes that someone embracing a different basic view may not be convinced. The point is not that Duns Scotus is not rational or that Aristotle is not rational, but there is a theoretical shift somewhere:

> If there is a debate concerning p between a and b and a is able to deliver an excellent defense of p, while b simply denies one of the grounds supporting p, then a's defense cannot count as a *demonstration* for b. If there be a basic difference between a and b and if a's defense is related to that basic difference, then a's defense cannot constitute a *demonstration* for b. So, the epistemological point – and here epistemology boils down to theory proof – is that for Duns epistemic appraisal is person relativized.

There is even more to be said about the proof theoretical framework:

1. Let us accept that Duns admires the probative value of a certain argument and realizes that it cannot constitute a *demonstration* for Aristotle or Avicenna (or Freud or Flew). This fact does not exclude that Duns may be convinced himself that he is able to frame an alternative knockdown argument. His works deliver many instances of this type of epistemic appraisal.

2. It is also possible that in a particular situation Duns realizes that he too is unable to deliver a stronger alternative. According to Duns, there is no need to conclude now that the involved assertion *p* is absolutely undemonstrable. Perhaps his philosophical grand-son can do the job. Still, either *p* is true or *p* is false.

3. Historically, the most interesting challenge is the possibility exem-plified by Thomas' view that the non-eternity of creation cannot be demonstrated. Both Thomas Aquinas and Duns Scotus believe for themselves that they are unable to demonstrate that the created world is not eternal.[40] Both believe that it is not true that the world is eternal, but Thomas Aquinas is also convinced that the non-eternity of the world is undemonstrable at all. It is just this proof theoretical appraisal Duns diverges from. In the case of Thomas Aquinas and Duns Scotus, it is not so that Thomas Aquinas believes that the non-eternity of the world is undemonstrable and that Duns believes that he is able to deliver the knockdown argument. Nevertheless, according to Scotian epistemic principles there must be something wrong when Thomas Aquinas and others state that something *true* is undemonstrable. If we were able to demonstrate that *p* cannot be demonstrated, then it is possible that we are able to demonstrate *non-p*. However, if it is possible that we are able to demonstrate *non-p*, then *p* cannot be an article of faith which is true as such, but the non-eternity is an article of faith. If *p* is true, then it is epistemically impossible that *p* is absolutely undemonstrable.[41]

9.6 GILSON ON DUNS SCOTUS' THEORY OF PROOF

Gilson observes an overemphasis of the role of theology in Scotus' philosophy. Duns Scotus and Gilson obliged themselves to rather

---

[40] See *DS* 163 f. and Vos, 'Almacht volgens Thomas van Aquino en Duns Scotus,' *Thomas-Jaarboek 1984*, 61–64.

[41] *Quaestiones Quodlibetales* VII 63. We are also able to demonstrate that, in the epistemically relevant possible worlds, it is impossible that we know that *not-p*, if *p* is true.

different concepts of what philosophy and theology are. The critical thing with Duns is that he is analytically aware of the specific nature of this dilemma, though he was unable to solve all of the difficulties involved in it. Gilson's analysis of Scotus' theory of proof and demonstration is difficult to understand. First, Gilson took for granted that for Duns it is possible that a *demonstratio quia* is not a demonstration. In fact, his hypothesis was that, according to Scotus, a *demonstratio quia* is not a kind of demonstrative proof, but an *opinio*, only a belief and a matter of doubt. However, even quite the reverse is possible for Duns Scotus: it is possible that we discover a *demonstratio propter quid*, while the parallel *demonstratio quia* fails.

Second, Gilson in fact confused the concepts of *demonstratio quia* and of *ratio necessaria*, because he did not pay attention to the difference between a *ratio necessaria* and a *ratio naturalis*. The nature of Duns Scotus' proof and demonstration language escaped Gilson. The results of this present chapter shed a different light on the problem of whether specific propositions from the philosophy of religion and the philosophical theory of divine properties can be demonstrated or proved. In many cases, Duns remarks that such propositions cannot be demonstrated, although they certainly can be proven or shown to be true. If we overlook the differences between *demonstrare* and *probare/persuadere/ostendere* (see §9.3), the statement that certain theological truths cannot be *demonstrated* or *proven* makes a rather different impression from what Duns in fact says. Such talk seems to be open to fideism and authoritarianism, but Duns certainly does not. Duns only scores a specialized point in terms of the theory of argumentation. Such arguments do not belong to the specific set of *rationes naturales* or *demonstrationes*. This position also solves the debate between Gilson and Wolter regarding the so-called 'theologism' of Duns Scotus.[42]

In several respects, modern historical research would greatly have helped Duns Scotus, but it is not historical to require such an achievement from him. It is even more problematical when a modern historian does not translate the old dilemmas into their modern counterparts. We cannot handle the difference between ancient philosophy and Christian medieval philosophy within a *duplex ordo* way of thought, either on the level of proof theory and epistemology or on the level of worldviews and theology. The Christian tradition of

---

[42] See Wolter, 'The "Theologism" of Duns Scotus' (1947), in *The Philosophical Theology of Scotus*, 209–253.

medieval thought does not presuppose a unity of experience, although one is much interested in creating a unity of experience. A new way of thinking is developed. We have seen that Henry of Ghent tried to refute directly Aristotle and Avicenna on the basis of an ontology of contingency. Although Duns Scotus delivers subtle epistemological criticisms, he strengthens the confrontation with the weapon of contingency theory. The modal fallacy of a potency ontology is the master mistake of philosophy. Building up new ways of thinking testifies to this spirit and rediscovering these great achievements of the classic European university between 1200 and 1800 contributes to our own cultural heritage and to the heritage of our world. First, we unearth the two philosophies of Athens and Jerusalem and, second, we handle and solve their discrepancies in terms of a new type of rationality. Duns was advocating that type of rationality.

9.7 CONCLUSION

The Christian intuition of a radically contingent reality cut off philosophy from determinism. From the technical point of view, the argumentational acumen of the *ars obligatoria* cut off the ideal of acquiring knowledge from the ancient conviction that necessary and self-evident knowledge has to be the starting point. *Certain knowledge* and *necessity* are disconnected by Duns and *certain knowledge* and *necessity* on the one hand and *deductive reasoning* and *truth* on the other hand have also to be unlinked.

That Roderick Chisholm, one of the greatest epistemologists of the twentieth century, did not promote the contingent to the epistemic degree of certainty, or even the directly evident nature of self-presenting propositions to the same epistemic degree of certainty (= *maximal reasonableness*) of axiomatic propositions, possibly changes this impression. The Chisholmian epistemic pattern entails that only necessary propositions which are self-evident can require the maximal degree of reasonableness. Duns disconnects the conceptual bond between *time* and *deductive knowledge*. By about 1300, Duns had already structurally broken away from the implicative connections between *necessity, self-evidence* and *certainty*.

Apart from clarity, it may help to see the power of Scotus' argumentation if we compare it with some outstanding epistemologists from different periods. The decisive point of his epistemological analysis is that the degree of reasonableness of a necessary proposition is not diminished if we derive it by one step of deduction or by a series of deductive steps. We may say that we know such a theorem a priori. However, regarding a priori propositions, even Thomas Aquinas saw things differently:

> Those who have knowledge of the principles have a more certain knowledge than the knowledge which is through demonstration.[43]

This philosophical style assumes an intrinsic connection between *time* and *being* and between *time* and *argument*, as a philosophy of *the parallelism* of *thought* and *being* is supposed to do. The same style of epistemology we meet with Locke. Roderick Chisholm is in deep sympathy with Locke and summarizes his point of view admirably:

> Complex proofs or demonstrations, as John Locke pointed out, have a certain limitation. They take time. The result is that the 'evident lustre' of the early steps may be lost by the time we reach the conclusion: 'In long deductions, and the use of many proofs, the memory does not always so readily retain.' Therefore, he said, demonstrative knowledge is more imperfect than intuitive knowledge.[44]

Descartes and Kant are on the same side. They follow the epistemic logic of *time* and time-bound *knowledge*. Duns follows a different track and develops a different type of epistemic logic which is controlled by structures: he does not work with *moments of time*, but with *structural moments* (*instantia naturae*) in a fundamental way. Here, we envisage an independent tradition of Western theory of knowledge saying goodbye to the 'eternal' tradition of *time and necessity*. If a type of thought is able to withstand such a tradition it must enjoy mighty resources in itself.

Scotus was fond of neither the participation model nor the abstraction model. The philosophy of Thomas Aquinas was hardly his target, but much of what we have to learn in interpreting Thomas' thinking adequately, we have to put aside in interpreting Scotus, who was opposed to the *act–potency* continuum, as it was practised by the Christian Aristotelians of the second half of the thirteenth century. In his conceptual framework, the place of the *act–potency* continuum is taken by the *necessity–contingency* duality. Duns Scotus draws the contents of his thought from the wells of faith, revelation and the theology of the Church, while his central method derives from the structure of

---

[43] *Expositio super Analytica Posteriora Aristotelis* II 20,4.
[44] Chisholm, *Theory of Knowledge* (²1977), 44. See John Locke, *Essay concerning Human Understanding* IV 2, section 7.

scientific deducibility. His analytical way of doing philosophy and theology turns on the dualities of *necessity–contingency* and *being self-evident* and *not being self-evident*. The latter distinction is again applied to the first one. Duns Scotus' theories of *proof* and *scientia* are vital both to the epistemological contents and to the methods of his thinking.

CHAPTER 10

Physics

10.1 INTRODUCTION

Absolute conceptions of knowledge and being are characteristic of all important positions of ancient philosophy. These conceptions molded the ideas of physical reality, but they are incompatible with physics as it was built up in the revolution of the natural sciences during the sixteenth and seventeenth centuries. The foundations of the scientific revolution were laid in earlier centuries. For Duns Scotus, physics was not a dominating interest as semantics and logic were, but it is still of interest to pay attention to a number of physical themes within a wider philosophical context. Moreover, in contrast to the other subjects (with the exception of ethics (Wolter) and ontology (Honnefelder)), we have a major and brilliant monograph on the subject, written by Richard Cross.[1]

We start with Duns Scotus' theory of matter (§10.2). Even in this day and age, matter is not a subject dear to modern theology, but long before Van Ruler stressed that both ends of the ontological spectrum – God and matter – share the common property of *impeccability*,[2] the medieval theory of matter had already moved with the times. Long before Duns Scotus, the pure potentiality theory of matter was a minority opinion in the West, but Duns not only dropped matter as the principle of individuation, he also elaborated on more complex theories of matter and individuality (see Chapter 11). Matter is not something negative, let alone something dirty, for it exists in its own right, not as a *non*-being facet of being. Scotus' theory of unity plays an overarching role (§10.3). The debate on the unicity or plurality of forms was a heated one in the thirteenth century (§10.4), and we also ask what accidents mean (§10.5). Astronomical themes are dealt with in §10.6.

---

[1] Cross, *The Physics of Duns Scotus* (1998).
[2] This thesis symbolizes a late rehabilitation of matter. For a theology of matter, see Van Ruler, *Theologisch Werk* V, 9–31.

Finally, §10.7 offers an afterthought: 'Theology and the scientific revolution.'

10.2 MATTER

Differences and similarities between Parmenides' and Aristotle's ontology are clear. The divine unmoved Mover shows the same distinctive features of unity and indivisibility, eternity and actuality, and necessity as *being*, with Parmenides. So, Aristotle's idea of *divine* being shows the same characteristics as the Eleatic idea of *being*, but in the theory of material reality Aristotle preserves diachronic change. In Aristotle's physics only synchronic contingency is excluded.

> Aristotle did not retain 'Parmenides' radical necessitarianism; he looked for an alternative ontology, which would leave room for change and contingency. [. . .] Aristotle agrees with Parmenides on the equivalence of necessity and immutability. Holding on to this equivalence, yet assuming that there are mutable states of affairs as well, Aristotle arrives at the equivalence of mutability and contingency. If we take a closer look at this Aristotelian theory of contingency, however, it turns out that a state of affairs p is contingent if $-p$ can be the case at a different moment. The possibility of the opposite obtains for a later moment, and does not obtain for the same moment at which p is the case.[3]

According to Aristotle, the absolute immutability of God does not explain away the temporal mutability of the world, but it is just the hook on which the finite and potential world of change and becoming hangs.

The immutable reality of divine thought is the force of attraction for the whole cosmos. Divine thought is the final cause of reality and all real change. *Nature* has to be explained. The key concepts are *tò energeíai ón – that which is actually –* and *tò dunámei ón – that which is potentially –* but potential being is as such the potentiality of something. There is no potentiality from no-thing. *Non-being* as a characteristic of the world is absolutely impossible.

The contrast with a *creatio ex nihilo* view is distinctive. In a monotheistic worldview *nihil* is possible, but *nihil* is absolutely impossible in Aristotle's view. For Aristotle, *potentiality* is a *kind of being*. What is potentially, is *not* the case, but it enjoys the potentiality of *being*. That which cannot exist, cannot *be* either. The universe is

[3] CF 24. See Guthrie, *A History of Greek Philosophy* II 1–121.

eternal and the universe is one. Things perish and come into existence, but the universe shares the old-fashioned features of space and time. There can only be *one* space and there can only be *one* time. So, there can only be *one* universe which is the only possible one. What Christians state only about God, Aristotle says about the universe, the invariable *cosmos* of change.

This worldview has vast consequences for Aristotle's fundamental theory of material substances being composed of form and matter.[4] On the one hand, Aristotle's philosophy is a philosophy of change; on the other hand, the decisive dimension of form must explain change. However, it cannot explain change, because forms are imperishable, eternal and necessary. They have to act in a necessary way. Apart from the question of how what is necessary and acts necessarily can account for change and development, this pattern also makes clear which role has to be ascribed to potentiality and matter. It is a kind of being which is not.

> Finding the putative distinction between *pure potentiality* and *non-being* unintelligible he [= Scotus] feels justified in identifying the former with the latter. Accordingly, he reasons that it is contradictory to say that prime matter is part of *a composite* and yet deny that it is a positive being on its own.[5]

In medieval traditions, we meet a Christian variant of the Aristotelian view of matter as pure potentiality. Thomas Aquinas clearly defines *matter* as pure potentiality in his early *Scriptum super Sententias* and *De ente et essentia*. For Aquinas, a definition is a real definition. A definition of a reality (*res*) offers the essence (*essentia*) and the essence of a natural substance comprises its form and matter. A being is a compound of form and matter, 'for matter is made actual being and this thing is by the form which makes up the actuality of matter.'[6] The form bestows being and actuality on an individual thing – it is the actuality moment of matter and in virtue of its form matter is, for qualified matter is the principle of individuality. 'It is not prime matter alone, nor dimensive quantity alone, but "matter signed by quantity" that is the principle of individuation.'[7]

---

[4] See *Metaphysics* VII 3 and *Physics* I 7.
[5] McCord Adams, *William Ockham* II 642.
[6] *De ente et essentia*, cap. 1, in Busa's *Opera Omnia* edition III 584a: 'Per formam enim, quae est actus materiae, materia efficitur ens actu et hoc aliquid.'
[7] McCord Adams, *William Ockham* II 676 (672–680: 'Aquinas on matter, quantity, and individuation').

We may say with Peter Geach, that 'in virtue of whichever form it has at the moment, the matter is made to be an actual thing (*fit ens actu*).'[8] This does not mean that the matter of this actual thing exists truly, for being actually is due only to form, imprisoned in a kind of non-being as it is. According to this type of approach, Socrates and Plato are individuals, but they are only material individuals, since they are the same essentially. There is only one type of *nature*, namely the universal nature. Of course, Aquinas can say that matter becomes being, for matter is a basic component of 'essence' and the principle of individuation, but these attributions do not promote matter itself to *actuality*. It represents still the potential dimension of what relatively is *not* and is educed from the glory of what is truly actual. The fact that matter accounts for *this* being (*ens et hoc aliquid*) underlines the problematical nature of this individual.

The theological translation of this viewpoint is illuminating. 'Matter apart from form is a contradiction in terms, unrealizable even by Divine power; so a given parcel of matter always has some actual attributes – only not always the same ones.'[9] Within Aristotle's conceptual framework, the material universe is the necessary complement of necessary divine noetic activity. However, the pure potentiality theory of matter in various forms was definitely a minority report in the thirteenth and fourteenth centuries (cf. §10.4 and §10.6). In Duns Scotus' physics, both form and matter enjoy quite a different status. Essences are only essences of existent things (see §7.7). So, essences are not uncreated. They are created just as matter is and matter is not the *non*-being aspect of creation, but it is itself a positive aspect of creation.

The causal powers God brings into action in bringing forth creation belong to all three divine persons. Only God Triune creates. Duns perfects the Augustinian line asserting that God's external activity is an undivided activity of God the Father, God the Son and God the Holy Spirit. The world of material things is created out of nothing (*Lectura* II 1), but, in *Ordinatio* II 1, the notion of *ex nihilo* is applied to producing from eternity the *being known* (*esse intelligibile*) objects of God's knowledge (§7.10). The substantial form unites with the material component to form a single complete substance and the 'substantial act' is the reality of such a substance being an individual

[8] Geach, 'Aquinas,' in Anscombe and Geach, *Three Philosophers*, 70.
[9] Geach, 'Aquinas,' in *Three Philosophers*, 71. We may ask why the reverse does not hold alike: *form* apart from *matter* is a contradiction in terms. Why is the notion of *an unmoved mover* not a contradiction in terms, if independent forms are impossible?

subject (*suppositum*). Plato and Socrates are 'numerically distinct.' The primary ontological position is assigned to such individuals. *Numerical unity* is exemplified in an individual (*suppositum*). O'Connor was mistaken when he stated that although 'in particular, the doctrines of the Incarnation of Christ and of transubstantiation depended for their rational justification upon a plausible theory of substance,' nevertheless, 'these theological outworks produced no new basic insights that can be regarded as an improvement on the work of Aristotle. They are variations upon Aristotelian themes.'[10] It is just the other way around, the nuisance value of the Christian doctrines of creation and incarnation elicited an enormous pressure on the old ways of thinking to give way to 'new basic insights.'

> When we turn to Scotus' theory of the material world, we encounter other doctrines which are of considerable interest. The first of these is that Scotus holds matter to be some positive entity really different from the reality of form; hence, [. . .] matter does not exist simply in virtue of some form which determines it. Matter must exist in its own right and distinct from form.[11]

Because there are things which come into being, generation occurs and because there are corruptible things, corruption exists. Because of the existence of generation and corruption, matter exists. In the case of accidental change something changes from one feature to an opposite one, but *what* changes remains the same under both opposites. However, the form of the thing does not change, for it is the same *horse* or the same *tree* which changes. So, change must take place on the level of matter, but what is *not* at the present cannot change by now. It is a contradiction to say that matter is an essential component of a compound and that it is not real in its own right. In terms of Aristotle's approach, the odd thing is that matter in the sense of *pure potentiality* is something belonging to the future. Something potential is not the case for this moment, but will be at some later time. The future is not yet, but just for this reason *present* matter cannot be matter, because matter is pure potentiality. So, according to Duns, the processes of accidental and substantial changes require presently existent matter which must be held to exist if such changes are to be accepted.

[10] D. J. O'Connor, 'Substance and Attribute,' *EP* VIII 37 f. (36–40). On medieval contributions relevant to the development of kinematics, cf. M. Jammer, 'Motion,' *EP* V 397 f. (396–399), and Stephen E. Toulmin, 'Matter,' *EP* V 213–218.

[11] Weinberg, *A Short History of Medieval Philosophy*, 225.

A compound is caused in virtue of all its necessary conditions and *being material* is such a necessary condition, 'but something is only a natural cause of something real if it has independent reality. Therefore, if matter is a condition different from form, it is necessary that it has reality.'[12] So what kind of being is matter? Duns answers this question as follows:

> I say that it has such *being* as the aspects which we know of it express. *Matter* is called as such a principle [see *Physics* I], and also as such a cause [see *Physics* II]. It is also called as such a component of what has become [see *Metaphysics* D, for it is something 'out of which something non-existent arises'] and it is also the subject of change [see *Physics* V]. [. . .] It is also something that remains under both terms of change and production and we add, according to the theologians, that it is a term of creation.[13]

The conclusion can only be that matter is something, something definite.

Because matter is a cause and a principle of what there is it can only be a subjective potency and a potency in a subject must be actual.[14] We may say that, apart from its own form, matter does not entail any other form. So, a contingent relationship holds between matter and form. Therefore, it is possible that matter exists without form and 'that matter is knowable apart from any form which informs it.'[15] Within the context of a purely potentiality theory of matter, the patterns of *form* and *matter* and of *act* and *potency* are not meant as compliments paid to the individual. Just the fact that a certain ontology needs a 'principle of individuation' shows how problematical the status of the individual is. The status of the form and the universal is given and sacrosanct – the universal forms are the starting point for a philosophical explanation of what there is. The individual only comes to the fore by a degradation, for an element of *non-being* comes in. An individual is a negative item. However, on the shoulders of biblical revelation and Patristic thought, medieval thought took a new line. Duns Scotus' philosophy of matter and individuality was the

---

12 *Lectura* II 12.24: 'Sed nihil est naturalis causa rei, nisi quod habet realitatem absolutam. Ergo, si materia sit alia causa a forma, oportet quod habet realitatem.'

13 *Lectura* II 12.29; cf. *Opus Oxoniense* II 12 *quaestio* 1 (*Wadding* VI 671). See *Lectura* II 12.36: 'Si sic esset *ens in potentia*, non posset esse "terminus creationis," quia quod terminat creationem, est realiter, et non in potentia.' Unfortunately, distinction 12 is missing in *Ordinatio* II.

14 See *Lectura* II 12.32; cf. *Lectura* II 12.37 f.

15 Weinberg, *A Short History of Medieval Philosophy*, 225.

culmination point of this development. Matter is something, something definite. Matter matters.

10.3 UNITY

The concept of *unity* is explained in the elaborate excursus on the *formal distinction*, found in *Lectura* I 2.258–277, in §275:

> There are many kinds of unity in reality. First, there is aggregate unity. Then, there is accidental unity, for instance the unity of *a pale man*. After this we have compound unity, and next simple unity.
>
> There can still be a *formal difference* in a simple unity in terms of what is real, for example the unity of a kind and its specific difference. Although they are really present in a simple item of reality, nevertheless, they are not formally identical. [. . .] Therefore, after *real unity* we have *formal unity*.[16]

We may formulate this list as follows:

	Latin name or synonym	*Typical example*
aggregate unity$_1$	*unitas aggregationis*	heap, pile
accidental unity$_2$	*unitas per accidens*	a pale man
substantial unity$_3$	*unitas compositi*	man
simple unity$_1$	*unitas simplicitatis*	
	unitas simplex	
real unity$_4$	*unitas realis*	formally distinct properties
simple unity$_2$		
formal unity$_5$	*unitas formalis*	formally identical properties
	identitas formalis	

This list is not an arbitrary enumeration, for the items follow a logical order in terms of complexity of structure. Duns' use of the structural *after* (*post* – §6.4) is indicative of a structural composition of the involved meanings of *unity*, and, moreover, he introduced his

---

[16] *Lectura* I 2.275: 'Multiplex est *unitas* in rebus. Primo est *unitas aggregationis*, post quam est *unitas unius per accidens*, ut "hominis albi," post quam est *unitas compositi*, post quam est unitas simplicitatis. Et in *unitate simplici* secundum rem adhuc potest esse *differentia formalis*: sicut unitas generis et differentiae, licet sit secundum rem in re simplici, tamen non sunt formaliter idem. [. . .] Igitur, post *unitatem realem* est *unitas formalis*.' See Cross's pioneering explorations in his *The Physics of Duns Scotus*, 7, 88–92, 98–107, and 139–156. Compare also §6.7.

exposition with the remark that there are *degrees* of unity in the things which exist. The easiest way to understand the different senses of *unity* Duns discerns here is to start where there is always a problem in Scotist studies: the formal distinction. Duns' series of types of *unity* leads to an exposition which turns around the formal distinction: the crucial difference between *real unity$_4$* and *formal unity$_5$* is that the formal distinction is not applicable any more to *unity$_5$* which is formal unity.

10.3.1 Formal unity = unity$_5$

Strict identity is the ultimate degree of unity, since, in this highest kind of unity, no stronger unity can be thought of, for no sort of distinction applies any longer. If all sorts of distinction are eliminated, there are no means left to strengthen the bond of unity. If we know that a list is a systematizing enumeration, then the most simple final point is the most profitable point of reference. From the point of view of *formal unity/identity*, in its quality as point of reference, the enumeration must show degrees of tightness of structure.

10.3.2 Real unity = unity$_4$

We continue with explaining what *real unity* consists in. From the viewpoint of *real unity*, the enumeration must again show determinable degrees of structural tightness and we continue by looking at the other end of the spectrum. *Accidental unity$_2$* and *real unity$_4$* are linked with an important principle: Duns makes a distinction between *simple* and *compound* concepts (see §4.5). This main distinction runs parallel to *unity$_2$* and *unity$_4$*. The series of the kinds of unity involved and the kinds of concepts involved are inversely proportional:

accidental unity$_2$	compound concept
real unity$_4$	reducibly simple concept
formal unity$_5$	irreducibly simple concept

10.3.3 Aggregate unity = unity$_1$

This is clearly seen when we start with the other end of the spectrum. The first kind of unity is found in exemplifications of *aggregate unity* as heaps and piles are, where the structure is as loose as possible. This end of the spectrum knows of no intrinsic connection at all. There is no bond of unity – everything sticks together as do grains of sand. There is no pattern or structure to be formalized. The elements of $unity_1$ have no intrinsic connection with the unity they are members of. Whether a grain of corn belongs to this or that heap changes neither the nature of the heap nor of the grain. The last kind of unity – *formal unity$_5$* – concerns the most strict kind of unity, since now even the formal distinction is not applicable any more. When *formal unity$_5$* obtains, we surpass the relation of strict equivalence and, therefore, we arrive at identity.

When we apply these extremes to the history of ontology, we meet the extremes to be found in ontological classification. If everything were to center around *formal unity$_5$* (formal identity), we share the company of Parmenides and Zeno. At the other end of the spectrum, we meet extreme nominalism: there are no necessary entities and no essential links between what is there.

10.3.4   Accidental unity = unity$_2$

The immediate neighbors of *unity$_1$* and of *unity$_5$–unity$_4$* fit in close with the structuring device. If we tighten the coherence a bit, we arrive at the phenomenon of *accidental unity$_2$*, the unity of accidental properties: we may miss a factual accidental property, for instance *being pale*, without loosing our identity, but accidental properties still fill and color our identity, in contradistinction to *unity$_1$*. Each category is self-contained, but in the case of accidental *unity$_2$* it is not the case that *a* is essentially *F*, if *a* is *F*. This is crucial to Duns Scotus' theory of accidental units.[17]

Cross made a successful effort to identify how Duns Scotus distinguishes *accidental unity$_2$* from *aggregate unity$_1$*.

> He suggests that 'accident' and 'inherence' are synonyms, from which, I take it, we can infer that a necessary condition for unity$_3$ (= *DPhil*'s *unity$_2$*) is that one part of the whole *inheres in* another. This criterion would be sufficient to distinguish a unity$_3$ from a *unity$_1$*, since I take it that the parts of a *unity$_1$* do not inhere in each other.[18]

The components of an accidental unity do not have to go together. It is not necessary that a man is pale. 'Something man-pale' is more

---

[17] Mind that, in a way analogous to Duns' concept of *contingent*, *accidental* combines the modern notion of *accidental* with the notion of *being true in the actual world*. For an alternative view, see Cross, *The Physics of Duns Scotus*, 98–100.

[18] Cross, *The Physics of Duns Scotus*, 103.

a unit than when *man* and *something pale* are separated so that the human person to be considered is not pale. 'The fact that the inherence of *being pale* affects a man is not to be looked upon as an addition to reality. Nevertheless, when *being pale* is in a man, 'something man-pale' is a unit, and they are not when they are separated.'[19] However, on the level of *simple unity*: *real unity*$_4$ and *formal unity*$_5$ separation is impossible. So, the principle worded in *Lectura* I 17.339 makes possible both distinguishing *accidental unity*$_2$ from *aggregate unity*$_1$ and *accidental unity*$_2$ from *simple unity*$_{4+5}$.[20] Only *substantial unity*$_3$ is left to be discussed.

10.3.5   Substantial (composite) unity = unity$_3$

According to Duns Scotus, the essential constituents (*partes essentiales*) of a material *substance* are prime matter and usually several substantial forms. A heap or a pile is a unit displaying unity$_1$: the parts of a heap or a pile are not essentially related to each other. If there is a heap of sand behind our house for the children to play on, my neighbor may take some sand to repair the wall of her barn and I may add some sand later on, but we do not say that we now have another heap of sand behind our house. Some changes have taken place and our heap of sand now differs from the heap a week ago, but it is not a new heap now. Here, the notion of an accidental change is indeed applicable, for in the case of an accidental change there is a difference, but this difference does not entail that another subject is involved. A unit of the type of unity$_1$ is not identical with its parts; it is simply an aggregation of parts. However, a *material substance* is neither identical with its parts, nor is it simply an aggregation of its parts.[21]

Copleston wondered whether Scotus taught the doctrine of universal hylomorphism which, in its various monotheistic forms, states that all creatures are compounds of matter and form. 'If the *De rerum principio* were authentic, there could be no doubt as to Scotus's acceptance of the Bonaventurian view, but the *De rerum principio* is not the work

---

[19] *Lectura* I 17.239: 'Quod enim facit inhaerentia albedinis ad hominem, non est aliqua realitas addita – tamen quando albedo est in homine, tunc est *homo-album* "unum," et non quando sunt separatae.'

[20] See Cross, *The Physics of Duns Scotus*, 100–107: 'Non-relational accidents and accidental unity.'

[21] See Marmo, 'Ontology and Semantics in the Logic of Duns Scotus,' in Eco and Marmo (eds), *On the Medieval Theory of Signs*, 156–158, Stella, 'L'Ilemorfismo di G. Duns Scoto,' in *Testi e studi sul pensiero medioevale* II, 147–163, and especially Cross, *The Physics of Duns Scotus*, chapter 5: 'Composite Substance.'

of Scotus, and in his authentic writings the latter nowhere expressly states the Bonaventurian doctrine.'[22] That debate was still marked by the textual revolutions of the first half of the twentieth century. Moreover, Copleston followed the Aristotelian approach in defining hylomorphism and 'St. Thomas is thus quite clear on the fact that only concrete substances, individual compositions of matter and form, actually exist in the material world.'[23] On the surface level of sentences there is an enormous agreement among all kinds of Christian thinkers of the thirteenth century and in an *auctoritates* culture the agreement could be expanded naturally to thinkers who were rather different religiously. However, what is at stake is revising the concept of *matter* and such a revision is much more important than the question whether angels are also compounds of matter and form.

10.4 THE PLURALITY OF FORMS

During the last quarter of the thirteenth century, the unicity versus plurality of forms issue was heatedly debated. In any matter and form compound is there only one substantial form or there are more than one. If one opts for a plurality of forms in material substances, will such be true in all kinds of them, or only in certain kinds, for instance humans? Adherents of the unicity of forms thesis insist that the existential unity of a given substance implies that there is only one substantial *form*. Among many theological complications linked with this disagreement in physics and ontology, the issue of Christ's human nature occupies a prominent position. The unicity thesis, for instance, has far-reaching consequences for how to look on a dead body, for according to this view a dead body cannot be identical with the person who is dead. The form, in contradistinction to matter, gives existence and life to something. Duns Scotus, a radical adherent of the plurality thesis, was committed to the continuity of bodies through death.

> Given this, Scotus could have argued (though he did not) for the continuity of a body through death on the basis of its capacity for supporting the *same* qualities. The redness of my rose is thus a good reason for supposing that its body is numerically the same as the rose-body that was in my garden this morning.[24]

---

[22] Copleston, *A History of Philosophy* II 513.
[23] Copleston, *A History of Philosophy* II 327. The reconstruction of doing philosophy is the crucial interest which developments in thirteenth-century thought have for us now.
[24] Cross, *The Physics of Duns Scotus*, 102, cf. 223 f.

At the beginning of the 1270s, the plurality view was widely held in various ways. Stout defenders of the unicity view were Thomas Aquinas, Giles of Lessines, Giles of Rome, and Godfrey of Fontaines. Thomas Aquinas rejects universal hylomorphism which states that the distinction of matter and form obtains for the whole of created being. *Essence* and *existence* are only identical in God and the existence of spiritual creatures depends on God. So, he need not postulate spiritual matter for spiritual and incorporeal creatures, for it is enough to apply the essence–existence distinction to explain their dependence on God.

The kernel of Thomas Aquinas' approach can be summarized as follows:

(1) A material substance can only have one substantial form

because:

(2) A material substance has only one substantial existence.

Thomas presupposed that there is a necessary one-to-one correspondence between the evident fact that this individual rose is only one existent thing and the form which gives existence to this material individual. A particular has many accidental forms, but only one substantial form. In terms of Aquinas' distinction of *essence* (on the level of *potentiality*) and *existence/being* (on the level of *actuality*), 'the recipient of a substantial form is something which is pure potentiality, whereas the recipient of an accidental form is something which is itself an actual existent.'[25] This way of thought is also applied to *humanity*.

> On Aquinas's account of the human soul, the soul is created both directly and in the form of the body. This entails that a human body is a very different sort of thing from any non-human animal body: its form is something created directly by God, not something produced naturally, which is an extremely counter-intuitive thesis (although not one which, it seems, troubled Aquinas).[26]

It is even more complicated to identify Henry of Ghent's standpoint. Henry evidently cherished sympathy for the unicity theory about 1277,

---

[25] Cross, *The Physics of Duns Scotus*, 48 (47–49: 'Thomas Aquinas'). For an excellent historical exposition, see Zavalloni, *Richard de Mediavilla et la controverse sur la pluralité des formes*, and for an excellent philosophical analysis, see McCord Adams, *William Ockham* II 647–669.

[26] Cross, *The Physics of Duns Scotus*, 54–55.

but became convinced that the Parisian theological faculty had condemned this stance. He accepted that there is just one substantial form in all material substances, with the exception of humans, for a human being has two distinct substantial forms. In general, Henry rejected the plurality theory as being inconsistent, because he accepted the Aristotelian view that distinction of acts is a sufficient condition for the distinction of potentialities. 'Thus, inanimate objects, plants, and non-human animals all satisfy the unitarian thesis.'[27]

Godfrey of Fontaines devoted a long philosophical discussion to the issue of unicity versus plurality of forms in *Quodlibet* II *quaestio* 7 (1286). He subscribed to the tenet that two entities cannot unite to constitute the unicity of a being. If we accept the substantial actuality of something, the other properties can only be accidental. *Form* and *matter*, *act* and *potency* run strictly parallel to each other. 'Godfrey's metaphysics might well be described as one that ultimately rests on the act–potency theory.'[28] The role of prime matter as pure potentiality is crucial. Assigning any distinctive actuality to matter compromises the essential unity of the composite. Prime matter is pure potency, neither absolute non-being nor actuality in itself.

Godfrey argued in precisely the same way for the relative non-being of matter as he argued for the absolute unicity of forms. If one rejects the purely potential character of matter possessing some actuality in itself, then we cannot explain the unity of a material substance. Moreover, Godfrey identified *essence* and *existence* in all beings. The peculiar effect of these moves is that *essence* has to be identified with form, since essence cannot be a mixture of being and *non*-being.[29] Against the background of his own stance, Godfrey discussed three types of plurality theories in *Quodlibet* II 7. The first type acknowledges different substantial forms corresponding to the *genus* and the specific difference of a certain kind. The second type claims that several substantial forms are needed to explain that mixtures are constituted by their elements. Thirdly, Godfrey's regular target is Henry of Ghent which is confirmed by Godfrey's sustained attempts

---

[27] Cross, *The Physics of Duns Scotus*, 53 (49–55: 'Henry of Ghent,' namely on the plurality of forms). Henry blends the amended unicity view with creationism: God is directly responsible for creating the human soul.

[28] Wippel, *The Metaphysical Thought of Godfrey of Fontaines*, 379; cf. 371 f. For Duns Scotus' criticism of Godfrey's act–potency axiom, see Effler, *John Duns Scotus and the Principle 'Omne quod movetur ab alio movetur'*, 92–97 and 149–155.

[29] See Wippel, *The Metaphysical Thought of Godfrey of Fontaines*, 39–99: 'The relationship between essence and existence,' cf. 268–270.

to refute Henry's approach implying that the combination of cor-
ruptibility and incorruptibility in man requires different substantial
forms.

According to Godfrey, the first theory implies that the *species* is
treated as an accident. Godfrey not only defended that two ontological factors cannot constitute unity of being, but also that essential
components are impossible. In a strict sense, *distinguishing logically*
and *separating physically* coincide, just as *form* and *actuality, matter*
and *potentiality* do. Striking consequences may be drawn from the
essentials of Godfrey's ontology, for material reality as far as it is *material* is a kind of relative non-being. This holds for individuality too.
Godfrey's criticisms of the second type followed the same strategy. In
criticizing the theory of Henry of Ghent, Godfrey again applied his
principle that two substantial forms cannot combine to guarantee the
substantial unity of a being. This claim implies that man can also have
only one substantial form. Nevertheless, Godfrey was very cautious
and scarcely gave unqualified support to the unicity version of anthropology. Likewise, he did not defend that there cannot be many immaterial beings which differ only numerically rather than specifically, but
it certainly follows from his premises, and at the end of the 1290s,
'Godfrey obviously views the position which rejects the possibility of
numerical multiplication of angels within *species* as theologically
defensible in itself.'[30]

Godfrey's approach to the principle of individuation followed the
same path. Numerical identity is only met in material substances,
insofar as they are quantified. He rejects the view that quantity itself
is the individuating principle. Godfrey arrived at the assertion that the
substantial form of a material thing is its nature and the formal principle of individuation, but 'quantity's causality is mediate rather than
immediate. And it apparently is of the material dispositive order, for
it enters into individuation as such only by enabling matter to serve
as the material cause of the same.'[31] It will be difficult to find a purer
form of Christian 'Aristotelianism' in the second half of the thirteenth
century. We shall see that Godfrey's younger Parisian *confrère* Duns
Scotus is just at the other extreme of the philosophical spectrum,
within the ambit of Christian thought.

[30] Wippel, *The Metaphysical Thought*, 369 (364–369: 'Individuation, Separated Souls, and
Angels').
[31] Wippel, *The Metaphysical Thought*, 362 (359–364: 'The Role of Quantity in
Individuation').

10.4.1   John Duns Scotus

Duns Scotus' approach to the unicity–plurality of forms issue is rather different from the positions taken by Thomas Aquinas, Henry of Ghent, and Godfrey of Fontaines. In opposition to Thomas Aquinas and Godfrey of Fontaines, he agrees with Henry that more than one form should be posited in a human being, but he also holds that, in general, plants and animals have several substantial forms. So, it is clear that Duns rejects

(1) A material substance can have only one substantial form.

Both Henry of Ghent and Duns Scotus distinguish between the form of the body and the animating soul, but Duns generalizes this distinction: it is true of any living body so that all animate substances, including humans, have at least two substantial forms: the bodily form and the 'soul', so that non-personal animate beings also have two substantial forms, subject to different mutations:

> It can be posited, with respect to any animate thing, that it has two agents, or *quasi* two. Although any living form is simply more excellent than any mixed form (and thus, whatever produces a living form must be more perfect than itself (or than some other [agent]) precisely as it produces the mixed form), and although the mixed form in a plant or brute [animal] is generated by the same [agent] as that by which the soul is produced, nevertheless there the [agent] is like two agents, since [it is an] agent containing in itself the *ratio* of a more perfect [agent] and of a less perfect agent.[32]

There is an order of perfection and, in general, the organs of animate beings have different substantial forms. In the case of human beings, Duns Scotus' position runs parallel to Henry's, for the form of the body is the end term of human generation and the soul is the end term of a divine act of creation.

Duns Scotus applies his principle of parsimony to the contemporary issue both of the separate vegetative, sensory and intellectual souls of human beings and of the vegetative and sensory souls of animals.

> In a pluriformed composite, Scotus thus holds that we will find, in addition to matter, a bodily form, an animating soul, and the forms of the various organs. Matter, bodily form and animating soul are arranged hierarchically, such that bodily form, and animating soul

---

[32] *Ordinatio* IV,11 *quaestio* 3.41 – ET by Cross, *The Physics of Duns Scotus*, 65.

actualize just one potentiality in matter. The forms of the different organs actualize different potentialities in matter, and they occupy the lowliest place in the hierarchy of substantial forms.[33]

10.5 ACCIDENTS

Individuals play a decisive role, not only in Duns Scotus' ontology, but also in his physics. According to act–potency physics, matter and accidents determine what is individual. Duns Scotus' points of reference are clear:

> Socrates and Plato differ. Therefore, we have to get some factor by which they differ, in view of which their difference ultimately maintains itself. However, the nature, present in this and in that person, cannot primarily explain their difference, but only their agreement. Therefore, there must be something else by which they differ. This factor is not quantity, not existence, nor negation.[34]

Socrates and Plato cannot differ in terms of their sortal kind or common nature. We have to look for a different factor to explain their individuality. Duns analyzes and refutes a series of five theories which tried to explain the individual nature of material things and persons in *Lectura* II 3.1–229. Successively, he discusses the theory that there are only individual natures (*quaestio* 1, §§1–38), the double negation (*quaestio* 2, §§39–53) and existence theories (*quaestio* 3, §§54–60), and the quantity (*quaestio* 4, §§61–124) and matter theories (*quaestio* 5, §§125–138 and 189–195).[35] Eventually, Duns explains his own haecceity theory (*quaestio* 6),[36] applying it to the issue of the individuality of angels (*quaestio* 7 (§§196–229). The quantity theory is the fifth theory: *quantity* is the positive element by which a material substance is this individual entity. Here, Duns makes clear what he thinks of the nature of accidents, for quantity is an accident. The exposition of this theory is followed by its fourfold refutation. The three first of these refutations have in common that

---

[33] Cross, *The Physics of Duns Scotus*, 71. Cf. his excellent expositions on pp. 55–71.

[34] *Lectura* II 3.167: 'Socrates et Plato differunt. Ergo, oportet advenire aliqua quibus differunt, ad quae ultimo stat eorum differentia. Sed natura in hoc et in illo non est causa differentiae primo, sed convenientiae. [. . .] Ergo, oportet dare aliud quo differunt. Hoc non est *quantitas*, nec *exsistentia*, nec *negatio*, sicut ostensum est in quaestionibus praecedentibus.' On negation, see §§45–52, on existence §§56–58, and on quantity §§72–107.

[35] Wolter deals with these theories in his 'Scotus' Individuation Theory' (1990), in *The Philosophical Theology of Scotus*, 74–83, 84, 84 f., 85–88, and 88 f., resp. (68–97).

[36] See Wolter, 'Scotus' Individuation Theory,' *The Philosophical Theology of Scotus*, 89–97.

they prove with respect to every accident, without any exception, that no accident can explain why a material substance enjoys *this* individuality.[37]

The challenging interpretation of Duns' approach to accidents is by Cross. He states that it is clear that accidents are individual things, reading this interpretation into a rather complicated text in *Ordinatio* II 3.90 and seeing this confirmed by *Quodlibet* III §2. According to Cross, the basic position accepted by Scotus is:

(3) An accident is an individual item.

> Scotus holds [. . .] that
>> (4) An item belonging to a category is individuated without reference to any other category.
>
> As he puts it: 'In every categorical hierarchy the singular or individual is not established through anything belonging to any other hierarchy.'[38]

This interpretation is mainly based on *Ordinatio* II 3.90:

> In one important passage he makes the point explicitly: in every categorical hierarchy there can be found something intrinsically individual and singular of which the *species* is predicated – or at least there can be found something not predicable of many.[39]

(3) An accident is an individual item

is based on this quotation. Cross takes *categorical hierarchy* (*coordinatio praedicamentalis*) just to mean *category*, and the quotation from *Ordinatio* II 3.90 is read as an assertion on *categories* in general. So, *in* every category something individual is to be found. This is understood to mean that something intrinsically belonging to every category makes a category individual. However, most categories are categories of accidents. Apparently, we arrive at the inferential chain: every category is individual, every accidental category is individual, and an accidental category can be individual only if its accidents are individual themselves. Substances being individual can also be derived from this interpretation. Of course, according to Duns, properties are usually properties *of individuals*, and if this is what is meant by *individual*, there is no problem.

---

[37] *Lectura* II 3.72: 'Ostendunt universaliter de omni accidente quod nullum accidens potest esse causa quare substantia materialis est *haec* [namely, *natura*].'

[38] Cross, *The Physics of Duns Scotus*, 97; cf §6.1: 'The Individuation of Accidents' (95–100).

[39] Cross, *The Physics of Duns Scotus*, 95. For an alternative interpretation, see below.

Cross's approach starts from the thesis that an accident is an individual item and finds evidence for this thesis in some cryptic texts. Let us have a look at *Ordinatio* II 3:

> In whatever coordination (namely, of *genus* and *species*) there can be found something that is intrinsically individual and singular of which a kind (*species*) is predicated, or at least there can be found something that is not *predicable of many*. Otherwise, there is nothing of a most specific kind to be found at all in this coordination, if nothing of the kind can function as subject. *Being predicable* just depends on the phenomenon of the individual.[40]

What is Duns talking about? In *quaestio* 4 of part 1 of *Ordinatio* II 3, the theory that quantity accounts for the individuality of a material thing is at issue. Duns offers four refutations of this approach and the third refutation rests on the idea of categorical coordination. The subject of this chapter is individuality and the argument is that individuality cannot be accounted for in terms of quantity. Duns' point is that predication cannot be dealt with satisfactorily, if individuality is not taken into account. However, the *Commissio Scotistica* suggests that the sentence 'at least there can be found something that is not *predicable of many*' has to be completed with 'but of one thing,' while the editors allude to the heavenly spheres where a *kind* numbers only one *individual*.[41] For Spade, the clause 'at least there can be found something that is not *predicable of many*' is unclear too, but his comment that the suggestion of the *Commissio* is hardly relevant is to the point.[42]

Here, Cross scents danger. 'Perhaps Scotus is unhappy with an unqualified identification of accidents as *subjects* of predication, and wants to argue that even an individualized accident is (standardly) in some sense not an ultimate subject of predication' (ibid.). This sounds reasonable enough, but does Duns consider accidents as first-order *subjects* of predication? Is 'accident' the grammatical subject in the sentences quoted from *Ordinatio* II 3.90? The whole of the argumentation Duns sets up in this chapter is based on the logic of predication.

---

[40] *Ordinatio* II 3.90: 'In qualibet coordinatione potest inveniri aliquid intrinsice individuum et singulare, de quo species praedicatur aut saltem potest inveniri aliquid non *de multis praedicabile*. Alioquin non erit in hac coordinatione aliquid specialissima species, de cuius ratione est esse praedicabile, si nihil sit huiusmodi subicibile.'

[41] See note 2 of *Ordinatio* II 3.90.

[42] Paul Vincent Spade, *Five Texts on the Mediaeval Problem of Universals: Porphyry, Boethius, Abelard, Duns Scotus, Ockham*, 80 §90 note 27.

In §90 he focuses on the structure of categorical predication. He concludes that categorical predication eventually requires an individual: there can be found something (*Fido*) of which a *kind* is predicated: Fido is a *dog*. Duns also rounds off his conclusion with his major point: '*Being predicable* just depends on the phenomenon of the individual.' In between, we encounter a remark and an implicit *reductio ad absurdum*. He stresses that predication does not require that there are *many* individuals a sortal property is predicated of. There are dying kinds of animals and plants, but although there are only a few animals or plants of these kinds left, there are still more than one of them. At least, there has to be one exemplar a sortal property can be predicated of.

Let us have a look at some parallel texts in *Lectura* II 3, starting with the end of *Lectura* II 3.91:

> When we have put in brackets whatever of the other category, then there is something ultimate in the category of substance – that category taken intrinsically – and this is an individual of that category.[43]

In this way, we come straight to the point, for this thesis is the conclusion of an argument, but what is argued about? The third method to refute the idea that quantity can explain individuality appeals to the concept of *categorical coordination*:

> Everything belonging to that coordination is found in every coordination, exclusively looked at.[44]

What do we expect from a categorical coordination of *substance*? The answer is:

> Whatever is relevant for the category of *substance* is present in a categorical coordination of that category.[45]

The final solution is found in *Lectura* II 3.91:

> The essence of categorical order requires a term which is more restricted and, hence, it requires an ultimate end term, just as it requires a higher, more general term.[46]

---

[43] *Lectura* II 3.91: 'Circumscripto quocumque alterius generis, erit aliquid ultimum in genere substantiae – de illo genere intrinsice – et hoc est singulare illius generis.'

[44] *Lectura* II 3.91: 'In omni coordinatione praecise accepta inveniuntur omnia illius coordinationis.'

[45] Ibid.: 'In coordinatione praedicamentali *substantiae* est quidlibet illius.'

[46] *Lectura* II 3.91: 'Sicut ordo praedicamentalis requirit *terminum in sursum*, ita etiam essentialiter requirit *terminum in deorsum*, unde requirit *ultimum*.'

This teaching is confirmed in *Lectura* II 3.93:

> A kind in whatever category is a kind according to the essential pattern of that category, but it is typical of a kind that it is predicable of more things, or at least of one thing. Therefore, the kind still has something of which it is predicable, when we have put in brackets whatever of the other category, and this factor is the *individual*. So, the individual is in the category of substance, when we have put in brackets every accident.[47]

Duns' line of argumentation rests on the structure of a categorical coordination. We may consider the category of *substance* in relation to another category, e.g. the category of *time*, or whatever accidental category. Duns focuses on the relationship between *genus* and *species*. If we put in brackets every 'generic' factor, we arrive at a *species* which is not itself again the *genus* of an even more limited *species*. Let us illustrate this abstract story a bit. Duns asks himself what is that kind predicated of when we arrive at a most limited kind of which no further sortal predication can be found? The answer is: the singular, the individual – this *this*. If we did have to tell the whole story of the structure of a categorical coordination, we should have the transcendent terms at one extreme of the spectrum, and, at the other extreme of the spectrum, we have the individual.

So, predication is impossible without individuality. Such a categorical coordination shows this basic structure:

——.——.——. sortal property S_3
——.——. sortal property S_2
——. sortal property S_1
. individual a bearing S_1

If I say that a sheepdog is a dog, my sentence has a subject, but there is still no real animal at hand I am saying something of. If the series S_3, S_2, S_1 does not end in an individual, then no individual can be found and no subject can be found. The context is one of the proofs (§§91–94) Duns brings forward to refute the thesis that the individuality and numerical identity of a material substance can be explained in terms of quantity (§§73–106). More than that, accidents cannot explain individuality at all,

[47] *Lectura* II 3.93: '*Species* in quocumque *genere* est species secundum rationem illius generis. Sed de ratione speciei est quod sit praedicabilis de pluribus, vel saltem de uno. Ergo, circumscripto quocumque alterius generis, adhuc species habet aliquid de quo est praedicabilis, et hoc est *singulare*. Ergo, est singulare in genere substantiae, circumscripto omni accidente.'

> for the three preceding theories run counter to every accident, without exception, while no accident can explain individuality, but the fourth theory, in particular, runs counter to quantity.[48]

Quantitative predication is related to what is individual. Quantity does not make something individual. It is not the case that a drop of water is no water, and that only much water is water. Only if we have *this* water, for instance this glass of water, may we ask: how much water? With Duns, and in much modern ontological literature, *individuum/singulare* and *individual* have a different meaning: *not shared by another individual*. In that case, it is not probable that accidents are individual, for *I may be pale*, but, in some areas, *being pale* is not an individual property, although in some villages or areas *being pale* may be an encaptic property, following Plantingian ontological language.

Quantity is an accidental property. An accident cannot explain individuality, for individuality is an essential feature, but an accidental trait is a property which an individual may lack without loosing its individual identity, because it is a property it can be without – it has it contingently. An accidental property may be lacking, but an individual cannot be without its essential features. Therefore, an accidental property cannot explain an essential feature.[49] Whatever essentially individuating principle there may be,

> William of Champeaux's position that accidental properties individuate was denied by virtually everyone on the Aristotelian ground that substance is naturally prior to accidents but particular substances are not naturally prior to what individuates them. Thomas Aquinas held that prime matter, the ultimate property-bearer in composite substances, combines with quantitative dimensions to individuate. But Duns Scotus found this tantamount to conceding that accidents individuate after all.[50]

10.6   Astronomical themes

10.6.1   The number of heavens

The question whether there be only one heaven is dependent on the hypothesis that the motions of the stars are not to be explained in

---

[48] *Lectura* II 3.95: 'Nam tres praecedentes universaliter sunt contra omne accidens, quod nullum potest causa singularitatis, ista autem quarta via specialiter est contra quantitatem.'

[49] See §76 and the end of §79.

[50] McCord Adams, 'Universals in the early fourteenth century,' *CHLMP* 411.

terms of forces or properties of their own, but in virtue of the sphere (*orbis*) they are fixed on.

> Every star which is fixed on a sphere is always equidistant from any other star fixed on the same sphere, because it could only be at a shorter distance one time and at a greater distance another time, if it would move by its own motion.[51]

Otherwise, all stars were 'erratic stars' (*stellae erraticae*) or planets (*planetae*). Because there are seven planets, there are at least eight spheres (*Lectura* II 14.6 and 9). The astronomers also assume a ninth 'heaven' and Avicenna said that Ptolemy was the first one to assume a ninth heaven. Alpetragius tried to restrict the number of spheres as much as possible, but, according to Duns, the elevation and depression of planets occasion a problem, for these heavenly bodies are not always in an equal angle with the horizontal.[52] 'For this reason, we assume more other deferent and revolving heavens in order to save that difference.'[53] All heavens move from east to west in a circular motion. The higher heavens move faster than the lower ones, for a lower heaven has a shortened orbit and is assumed to have less force (*virtus*), 'just as there seem to be opposite motions if two things move according to the same circle, but at different speeds, when they arrive at the same point where they started to move.'[54] The different distances of heavenly bodies require more heavens. Their motions cannot be explained in terms of the natural motion of falling. However, the philosophical and theological approaches are rather different, because the philosophers believe that everything happens necessarily, for 'it follows from the fullness of his perfection that God acts necessarily, although He acts by his intellect and will.'[55]

---

[51] *Lectura* II 14.8: 'Omnis stella quae est fixa in orbe aliquo, est semper aequaliter distans a stella fixa in orbe eodem, quia non posset aliquando magis distare, aliquando minus, nisi moveretur motu proprio.' Cf. *Ordinatio* II 14.32.

[52] *Lectura* II 14.12: 'Motus planetarum apparet in triplici differentia, scilicet latitudinis, longitudinis, et elevationis et depressionis, quia non semper sunt in aequali elevatione a terra.' See *Ordinatio* II 14.38–46.

[53] *Ibid.*: 'Ideo, propter illam differentiam salvandam ponuntur plures alii caeli, deferentes et revolventes.' Cf. Alpetragius, *De motibus caelorum*, chapter 6 (see note 61).

[54] *Lectura* II 14.15: 'Sicut si duo moverentur super eodem circulo, unum tardius et aliud velocius, quando venient ad idem punctum in quo incepiebant moveri, videntur moveri contrario motu.'

[55] *Lectura* II 14.25: 'Ex perfectione sua plenaria consequitur quod Deus necessario agat, licet agat intellectu et voluntate.' See §10.7 and cf. §§14.4–14.6. *Lectura* II 14 *quaestiones* 2 and 3 (§§18–36) have no parallel text in *Ordinatio* II 14.

10.6.2 Heavenly matter?

Medieval scholars were no flat-earthers, but the question whether there is heavenly matter – still a popular issue during the Renaissance – was answered in different ways. Aristotle had held the view that there is no familiar matter in heaven. The fifth element ether (*aithèr*) (*quinta essentia*, hence 'quintessence'), enjoys its own eternal circular motion. Everything in the world is trying to realize its own form. The activity of the ether is perfect and eternal physical activity, most near to God's eternal mental activity. So, we have two different physical realities: the sublunary one and the heavenly one.

Thomas Aquinas held that the matter of a heavenly body is of a kind different from the matter of the four known elements, but Giles of Rome rejected this dualist astronomy. Duns' pertinent question reads whether a heavenly body is simple by nature. Duns observes that, according to ancient astronomers, a heavenly body does not have any potentiality, for Aristotle and Averroes

> assert that the heaven is formally necessary of itself and that it is impossible that it is not. If it did have matter, it would follow that it is not necessary, but I see no necessity to assume two kinds of prime matter of a different type.[56]

So, Duns denies that a heavenly body is not a compound of form and matter and the first argument he refers to is his principle of parsimony (cf. §8.2). This application of his principle of parsimony also occurs in *Ordinatio* II 14.10. Moreover, Duns Scotus stresses in *Ordinatio* II 14.12–14 that theologinas have to disagree with the philosophers stating that heaven is necessary and incorruptible. His basic counter-argument is that sublunary matter and heavenly matter are of the one and the same kind of matter.

10.6.3 Celestial influence

Duns acknowledges influence from celestial bodies on our earthly world, as the influence of the sun shows. 'It is clear that by virtue of the sun plants are brought forth and quickened and that they shrivel

---

[56] *Lectura* II 14.39: 'Ponunt quod caelum sit ex se formaliter necessarium nec potest non esse, quod tamen sequeretur si materiam haberet. Nec video necessitatem ponendi duas materias primas alterius rationis.' Duns deals with this issue in *quaestio* 4 – §§37–52.

up and die without the sun.'[57] The example of ebb tide and high tide makes the same point. 'As to water in motion, it is clear that the moon has its influence in this case, for high tide follows the motion of the moon, followed by high water and low water.'[58] However, the judgement of the astronomers (*iudicium astrologorum*) is still ambivalent. The example of high tide and ebb tide illustrates that their judgement may be certain, but as to rain and the weather we do not have enough experience to have a firm judgement. The judgement may also be audacious and dangerous, for 'it is entirely false that the heavenly bodies immediately act upon intellect and will.'[59]

Resolved though Duns might have felt as to the question whether a celestial body be a compound of matter and form, he left open the issue whether it can be decided that a certain heaven be animated or not. 'Hence, I do not see whether God can animate such a perfect body,'[60] because there are no decisive arguments, neither does Scripture tell us what to think of this matter.

A special feature of *Lectura* II 14 are the references to Alpetragius. They concern a work *De motibus caelorum*, but who was Alpetragius?[61] Alpetragius is *Abu'l-Barakât al Bagdâdî*, an inhabitant of Iraq and the last outstanding Jewish philosopher of the Islamic East (d.1164). 'His philosophy appears to have had a very strong impact on Islamic thought, whereas its influence upon Jewish philosophy and theology is very hard to pin down and may be practically non-existent.'[62] His main work is *Kitâb al-Mu'tabar* (= The Book of that which has been Established by Personal Reflection). In a personal way he develops Avicenna's doctrine of the soul. Being an old man, he was converted to Islam and his biographers explain this decision in terms of expediency. From the physical viewpoint, Duns' 'Alpetragius' is very interesting, because he stood at the cradle of the *impetus* theory of throwing projectiles.[63]

---

[57] *Lectura* II 14.35: 'Hoc patet de sole quod ipso accedente plantae generantur et vivificantur, ipso recedente arescunt et moriuntur.'

[58] *Lectura* II 14.33: 'Hoc patet quantum ad motum aquae, quod luna habet ibi efficaciam, nam tumor aquae – ad quem sequitur fluxus et refluxus maris – sequitur motum lunae.'

[59] *Lectura* II 14.36: 'Quod habeant [namely, corpora caelestia] actionem immediate circa intellectum et voluntatem, est omnino falsum.' 'Astrologus' can simply mean *astronomer* (= *astronomus*), but it may also have the designation of *astrologer*.

[60] *Lectura* II 14.45: 'Unde non video quin Deus potest animare illud corpus perfectum.'

[61] See Carmody (ed.), *De motibus caelorum* (1952).

[62] Shlomo Pines, 'Jewish Philosophy,' *EP* IV 267 (261–277).

[63] See Clagett, 'Some General Aspects of Physics in the Middle Ages' (1948), in *Studies in Medieval Physics and Mathematics*, chapter I 39–42.

10.6.4   The alternative of 'theologia'

From Augustine to the Scotists of the fifteenth and sixteenth centuries, theology is the cradle of a new philosophy. The prologues of the *Lectura*, the *Ordinatio* and the *Reportatio* open with this fundamental issue and Duns elaborately comments on the relationship between theology and the philosophers. This theme recurs in Duns' astronomy. Discussing the question whether the heaven is effectively moved by an intelligence, he notes in *Lectura* II 14.27:

> What might we say according to theological truth [on the issue of the effectivity of astronomical intelligences]? I say that we ought not to share their conclusions, because we do not share their principles. Hence, we do not agree with them that an intelligence acts necessarily and, for this reason, it does not follow from the fullness of his perfection that He necessarily moves the heaven.[64]

God can immediately move the heaven, but Duns believes that an angel does so following Augustine. In contradistinction to the philosophers, theology embraces the view that the heaven is a compound of matter and form, *pace* Thomas Aquinas. Duns cites Bonaventure, but this view is confirmed by Augustine and Bede, Peter Lombard, Richard of Middleton, and Giles of Rome. Duns believes with Bonaventure that in Genesis 1:1: 'In the beginning God created heaven and earth,' 'heaven' refers to the empyrean, created on the first day, and 'earth' to the matter of all other creatures.

> The firmament being in between the waters – that is, the whole of the heaven where the planets and the fixed stars are – is made from that same matter. For this reason, matter is in heaven of the same type as the matter of the four elements and, consequently, it is as such possible that it is not yet preserved in being by the divine will.[65]

In spite of the fact that Duns Scotus was not involved in a program of reconstructing the philosophy of nature as he was engaged in rebuilding semantics and logic, theory of knowledge and proof, anthropology

---

[64] *Ibid.*: 'Quid dicemus secundum veritatem theologiae? Dico quod ex quo non communicamus cum eis in principiis eorum, ideo nec oportet quod in conclusione. Unde non concordamus cum eis quod intelligentia necessario agat. Et ideo non est ex plenitudine perfectionis suae quod necessario moveat caelum.'

[65] *Lectura* II 14.44: '*Firmamentum* quod est *in medio aquarum* – quod est totum caelum in quo sunt planetae et stellae fixae – fuit factum de illa materia. Et ideo in caelo est materia eiusdem rationis cum materia istorum inferiorum, et per consequens ex se *possibile non esse*, conservatum tamen in esse voluntate divina.'

and ethics, ontology and philosophy of religion, there are striking illustrations of the process of emancipation from ancient physical patterns. Modern physics is rooted in creation thought (Foster) and this new foundation underwent a new conceptual revision: the contingency of creation is synchronic contingency. The theoretical center is constituted by the theory of *synchronic contingency*. This tendency and this center are the hermeneutical key to this way of thinking. Whoever grasps this dynamics, is able to master the details of Scotus' thought.

10.7 THEOLOGY AND THE SCIENTIFIC REVOLUTION

Even in the history of medieval physics the historical facts deviate a great deal from the general picture of medieval thought as a mixture of Aristotelism and Thomism. We often find sentences like 'such and such a view is all the more striking and remarkable when contrasted with that of Thomas Aquinas,' but, in the present chapter, we observe that Christian variants of an Aristotelian position often are minority reports. However, it seems odd to characterize the thought of a period in terms of its minority opinions. The upshot of doing so is that a whole world of thought is seen though the lenses of a mere handful of thinkers.

We take our systematic starting point from Eleatism. Here the propositions *Reality is* and *Reality is one* are axiomatic. They represent the basic structure of ancient Greek religion. Ancient Greek philosophy is a kind of rationalization of old Greek religion.[66] The common ground of Greek and Hellenistic philosophies is all the more striking than the differences. Even far-reaching disagreements are a key to their basic common ground. Heraclitus and Parmenides advance towards fatefully dividing reason from the senses.[67] Everlasting is the logos, which is the rational principle ruling the universe, either constituting the law of changeless reality or the law of cyclic change. Parmenides is the philosopher of absolute immutability. Every kind of change and physical motion is excluded. The change of our experience only appears to be. Eleatic philosophy denies the very possibility of

---

[66] Cf. Verdenius, 'Hylozoism in Early Greek Thought,' *Symposium. Hooykaas and the History of Science* (Utrecht), *Janus* 64 (1977) 25–40.

[67] On Heraclitus, see Guthrie, *A History of Greek Philosophy* I 403–492: 'Heraclitus,' Mansfeld, *Fragmenten*, and chapters VIII and IX of Mansfeld, *Studies in Later Greek Philosophy and Gnosticism*. On Parmenides, see Guthrie, *A History of Greek Philosophy* II 1–80.

motion and change. They do not take place. Necessity and immutability coincide.[68]

10.7.1   Aristotle (384–322 BC)

The relation of the divine world to the physical world held the attention of Aristotle during the whole of his philosophical career.[69] The idea of an unmoved mover is not excluded in *On philosophy* and *On the Heavens*, but it is not explicitly present either. The last two books of the *Physics* show ample evidence that Aristotle now believed in the necessity of an unmoved mover and *Metaphysics L*, chapter 8, fully develops the theory of *actuality* and *potentiality*. The potential is only actualized by an actually existing cause. The prime mover exists because it actualizes potential change throughout the universe. In *Metaphysics L*, Aristotle presents his theology. His theories of substance and accident, actuality and potentiality, form, privation and matter support his theology. Change is eternal and necessary, because the nature of time entails the necessity of time and the necessity of time entails the necessity of change. The *First Mover* is eternal, immutable and necessary. Form and actuality without matter must be equated with thought and, so, the unmoved mover is divine mind.

However, Aristotle is considered to be the philosopher of change. How is divine immutability seen here? Aristotle reduces all movement, change and becoming to one principle: God.

> On such an archè depends the universe and nature. His life is like the best which we can enjoy for a brief spell. He is always in that state (which for us is impossible), for his activity is also pleasure. [. . .] Thought in itself is of what is in itself best, and the purer the thought the more truly best its object. Now mind thinks itself by sharing the nature of its object: it becomes object of thought by contact and the act of thought, so that mind and object of thought are the same. That which is capable of receiving the object of thought, is mind, and it is active when it possesses it. This activity therefore rather than the capability appears as the divine element in mind, and contemplation the pleasantest and best activity. If then God is forever in that good state which we reach occasionally it is a wonderful thing – if in a better state, more wonderful still. Yet it is so. Life too he has, for the activity of the mind is life, and he has that activity. His essential activity is

---

[68] Guthrie, *A History of Greek Philosophy* II 80–101: 'Zeno'; cf. *KN* 1–13, 254–258, and *CF* 23 f.

[69] See Guthrie, *A History of Greek Philosophy* VI: 'Aristotle: An Encounter.'

his life, the best life and eternal. We say then that God is an eternal living being, the best of all, attributing to him continuous and eternal life. That is God.[70]

God is unmoved and unchangeable. So, the object of God's thought and knowledge has to be without change. According to Greek philosophy, thought is an assimilation of the mind to the object.[71] Change in the object of knowledge entails change in thinking and knowing and in the thinker and the knower. If change is absolutely excluded in thought and knowledge and knowledge and knower are identical, then the absolute knowing subject is immutable and, therefore, the object of knowledge is immutable too. A further example of this way of thought is the conviction of the primacy and perfection of circular shape and motion which affected astronomy until the time of Kepler. All of them culminate in the presumption of *the parallelism of thought and being* (De Rijk).

10.7.2 The historical background of the scientific revolution

In order to understand the scientific revolution of the sixteenth and seventeenth centuries, we have recourse to the Middle Ages, just as we have to in order to understand the architecture of a magnificent sixteenth-century church, for it makes no sense to assume that we can explain the architecture of the Dordt *New Church* by means of the style of a Roman basilica. The secular Enlightenment understanding of the history of the sciences ignores more than a millennium of the history of Western ideas before Renaissance and Humanism (see Chapter 15). It also offers a distinct explanation of the enormous delay the development of the natural sciences since Aristotle and Archimedes suffered from. Why did the sciences not arise in antiquity? This delay is said to be mainly due to the unfortunate influence

---

[70] *Metaphysics* 1072 b 13–20 (*ET* according to Guthrie, *Aristotle*, 260). For Aristotle's theology, compare Guthrie, *A History of Greek Philosophy* VI 243–276; for the historical development of Aristotle's theology, see Guthrie, 'The Development of Aristotle's Theology,' *Classical Quarterly* 27 (1933) 162–171, and 28 (1934) 90–99.

[71] Guthrie, *The History of Greek Philosophy* I 2–3: 'Without belittling the magnificent achievements of the Greeks in natural philosophy, metaphysics, psychology, epistomology, ethics and politics, we shall find that because they were pioneers, and therefore much nearer than ourselves to the mythical, magical or proverbial origins of some of the principles which they accepted without question, we can see these origins clearly; and this in turn throws light on the dubious credentials of some of the principles which gain a similarly unquestioned acceptance among many today.'

of the Hellenistic religions and, in particular, to a sort of detrimental obstructionism in church and theology. The irrational forces of faith and church always tried to block the victory of rationality. Only when this obstruction was overcome in the Renaissance can we cheer at the rise of the sciences.

However, physical reality is quite different from what it was considered to be by the Greeks. In spite of the Enlightenment view, a fresh start was inevitable. A detour of centuries was needed in order to make a new start. New foundations had to be laid after the fiasco of the Greek philosophy of nature. The road of the 'philosophical' understanding of *phusis* was a dead end. Old conceptual structures had to be pulled down in the new academic education. Patristic theology absorbed the biblical creation belief in order to crack cosmological necessitarianism. The creativity of creation belief is the cradle of modern science.

Before the Renaissance there was not only an ontological and philosophical revolution revealing itself in contingency thought and creation and incarnation theology, but this new way of thinking also paved the way to the new sciences. This process started with discovery of new types of experiments in the thirteenth century and the beginning of mathematization of physics in the fourteenth century (the Mertonians of Oxford). The critical tendencies of the fourteenth century demolished Aristotle's physicist approach to nature, which was a specific approach in terms of his own notion of *phusis*, and the sixteenth century saw a continuous renewal of theology and philosophy. During the seventeenth and eighteenth centuries great Christian thinkers built the new sciences of astronomy, physics, and chemistry, and modern science is a harvest of Christian thought. The critical attitude of the exact sciences could not have been the fruit of ancient Greek and Hellenistic philosophy, the reason being quite simple: the nature and structure of modern science are excluded by the type of thought embodied in the Greek way of doing philosophy – *philosophia*. One had still to wait for the true *scientific* spirit for centuries because it took an enormous effort to demolish all kinds of fundamental errors of ancient philosophy and to construct a totally new way of thought. Contingent reality has to be approached in terms of contingency. The hypothetical-deductive structure of scientific explanations asks for the acknowledgement of contingency and not an absolutely closed system of physicist phenomena.[72]

---

[72] See Hempel, *Philosophy of Natural Science*, chapter 3.

The Christian intermezzo for more than fifteen centuries before 1800 enjoys a definite meaning. The *due nuove scienze* (Galilei) had to be prepared. The medieval phase had an articulated function, even in the development of the physicist method. The modern scientific revolution (Thomas Kuhn) is no fruit of ancient thought, it is the harvest of medieval thought. The exact sciences are invented and developed by faithful scholars. After the first 'industrial' revolution of the twelfth century (the new mill using replaceable millstones being the medieval factory), technology and physics received new impulses in the thirteenth and fourteenth centuries. The rise of a new technology of glass and screw, crankshaft and clockwork is to be observed and the experiment itself is 'invented' and developed.

> The same period sees the idea of a progress of mankind, to be acquired by technology. There was the anthropology of man as image of God, commissioned to subdue the earth. We have already mentioned the connection between this anthropology and the use of technical means to be used for a new goal. Christian theology of creation sees earthly existence as a purposeful present of God, a present of time to be used for fulfilling God given tasks. Such creation thought changes human experience of the world and creates a new attitude toward nature. An alternative cultural self-understanding arises. The sources of the development of the modern sciences are to be looked for in this new self-understanding in connection with technological progress.[73]

10.7.3 New practices and new vistas

In the course of new processes, nature is de-deified and de-mythologized. If the cosmic process is divine, mother Earth has to be respected and spared, but, now, a new understanding of nature makes room for a new agriculture of plow and plowshare, and a new system of leaving fallow and manuring (Brabantia and Flanders). If the cosmic process is necessary, it does not make sense to ask *why*. Things cannot be different and the only logically possible answers must fit reality. Asking *why* is asking what one already knows. Reality is its own answer, but a new understanding of reality makes room for a new *why*-question. If reality can be different, the big question is *why* what happened in fact happened. A new *why*-question is born – the *why* of Anselm's *Cur Deus homo?*

---

[73] De Knijff, *Tussen woning en woestijn* (*On environmental ethics*), 52 (42–56).

New ideas and techniques are developed, new institutions built. Institutional revolutions had given rise to university education and research and this type of medieval university was the scene of a fundamental *paradigm change of thought*. The theoretical ways of thought practised in analysis and argumentation themselves changed. At the thirteenth-century universities, the battle between Christian thought and ancient Aristotelian philosophy was fought out and decided.[74] Christian contingency thought replaced ancient necessitarian thought. New modalities of thought, like Scotism and Nominalism, did not have a counterpart in ancient philosophy and medieval Jewish and Islamic thought.

Many new developments came to be integrated more than a millennium and a half after Aristotle's contributions to physics, astronomy, and biology. The alternative view to the Enlightenment reconstruction simply departs from the observation that Aristotelian physics and the physics and astronomy as they were developed by Galileo and Kepler, Boyle and Newton are incompatible. In a necessitarian view of reality no scientific explanation is needed. Reality is just as it is. There is no room for alternatives and alternative events, not for the hypothetical–deductive model, so characteristic of modern scientific explanation, but the hypothetical–deductive model of understanding modern scientific thought presupposes that things can be different. We cannot a priori calculate how nature must be.[75] It is not true that there is only one possible logic, physics, ontology and philosophy (Avicenna, Spinoza, Scholten). The ancient *philosophia* model of reality and of explaining reality has collapsed.

10.7.4   The modest place of Duns Scotus

The scientific revolution of the sixteenth and seventeenth centuries is rooted in the Middle Ages. Duns Scotus is not one of the masterminds of the biography of the natural sciences. However, the broader context of physicist developments illustrates the crucial point: the whole of the development of Western thought moved into a new type of scientific thought, just as, before, the whole of the development of Western thought had moved into a new type of philosophy and theology. This background was the breeding ground for new scientific

---

[74] See *DS* 9–14, and Chapters 4, 9 and 14–16.
[75] On the view of Newton who also upheld the contingency of natural laws, see C. de Pater, 'Petrus van Musschenbroek (1692–1761). A Dutch Newtonian,' *Symposium Hooykaas, Janus* 64 (1977) 77–87.

revolutions. The history of the Condemnations of 1277 is also instructive as far as the development of physics is concerned.

> Of course, what really mattered to Tempier was only the full recognition of the sovereignty and freedom of God, but in rejecting any limits to these, he unintentionally took away limitations to scientific theorizing as well. Not only the theology of necessity was at stake, but also the natural science of necessity. Among the theses he condemned were those that suggested that God could not make an empty space; that He could not create new species; that He could not make more than one planetary system; and that He could not give other than circular motions to the heavenly bodies. All these prohibitions hampered the freedom of scientific research; all of them in the long run turned out to be false.[76]

The fourteenth century showed many a new theory (Bradwardine and the Mertonians, Buridan and Oresme).[77]

However, Scotus' contributions were striking, in spite of being relatively modest. His articulation of 'radical contingency' gave rise to the view that natural laws are contingent.[78] The chasm dividing the Christian approach to nature from the ancient idea of *phusis* was worded in much the same way as the ontological disagreements (§10.6). The material things of the world shine in a new manner, promoted from a kind of *non*-being to contingent individuals, enjoying individuality in their own right (§10.2; cf. Chapter 11). On many points, the thirteenth-century Aristotelian options in physics were minority reports and, again and again, Duns Scotus sided with the majority views and continually tried to improve on them: the specifically formal identity of matter and the homogeneity of matter throughout the universe (§10.2), the plurality thesis of forms (§10.4),

---

[76] Reijer Hooykaas (1906–1994), *Religion and the Rise of Modern Science*, 32. Cf. MacKay, 'Religion and the New Mechanics,' *Hooykaas Symposium, Janus* 64 (1977) 119–129. On Hooykaas, see Cohen, 'Editors' Foreword,' in Boudri, Cohen, and MacKay (eds), *Hooykaas. Fact, Faith and Fiction in the Development of Science*, X–XIII, and Luis de Albuquerque, 'History of Sciences in Portugal,' *Hooykaas Symposium*, 1–13. Hooykaas's introduction to the history of the natural sciences, *Geschiedenis der Natuurwetenschappen. Van Babel tot Bohr*, Utrecht ⁴1983, is second to none. See also his *G.J. Rheticus' Treatise on Holy Scripture and the Motion of the Earth* (1984) and *Robert Boyle* (1997). For a kindred climate of scientific thought, see Russell Stannard, *Grounds for Reasonable Belief*. Cf. Losee, *A Historical Introduction to the Philosophy of Science*, 29–95, and Grant, *Physical Science in the Middle Ages*, 20 ff.

[77] See Sylla, *The Oxford Calculators and the Mathematics of Motion 1320–1350*, and Thijssen and Zupko (eds), *The Metaphysics and Natural Philosophy of John Buridan*.

[78] See DS 237–245 and Veldhuis, 'Ordained and Absolute Power in Scotus' *Ordinatio* I 44,' *Vivarium* 38 (2000) 226 (222–230).

and the new approach of accidental properties (§10.5). Scotus' position 'explains better than Henry's theory the persistence of plant and non-human animal bodies through death.'[79]

The intension and remission of qualities was a fundamental problem of scholastic natural philosophy. The issue originated from Peter Lombard's *Sentences* I 17, dealing with the way love increases or decreases. The addition theory, advocated, for example, by Duns Scotus, John Dumbleton, and Ockham, is to be contrasted with the succession theory which holds that varying forms succeeded each other (Walter Burley). A specific theory was proposed by Oresme.[80]

> Scotus's quantitative account of qualities had a fair amount of historical significance. The Mertonian mathematicians of the first half of the fourteenth century regarded velocity as the *quality* of a motion. Seeing degrees of qualities in quantitative terms allowed them to quantify velocity, and thence to formulate the famous proof that 'the space traversed in a given time by a body moving with uniformly accelerated velocity [is] equal to [. . .] the total time of moving multiplied by the mean of the initial and final velocities', first found sometime before 1335 in the works of William Heytesbury, Richard Swineshead, and John Dumbleton.[81]

10.7.5   Perspective

The data mentioned so far and comparable evidence fit in with a fresh approach to the history of Aristotelian natural philosophy during the late medieval and early modern centuries proposed by the Center for Medieval and Renaissance Natural Philosophy (University of Nijmegen, The Netherlands). This approach drops the idea of a clear essence of the term 'Aristotelianism.'[82] Many results of this research

---

[79] Cross, *The Physics of Duns Scotus*, 75. See section 'The alternative of *theologia*' in §10.6, §§14.4–14.5 and also Chapter 11.

[80] See Kirschner, 'Oresme on Intension and Remission of Qualities in His Commentary on Aristotle's *Physics*,' *Vivarium* 38 (2000) 255–274.

[81] Cross, *The Physics of Duns Scotus*, 191 (186–192). On John Dumbleton, see Sylla, *The Oxford Calculators and the Mathematics of Motion 1320–1350*, 207–211, and on Swineshead, see Clagett, 'Richard Swineshead and Late Medieval Physics. The Intension and Remission of Qualities' (1950), in *Studies in Medieval Physics and Mathematics*, chapter 3. On Duns Scotus, see Anneliese Maier, *Zwei Grundprobleme der scholastischen Naturphilosophie*, 50–74. For relevant texts, see Clagett, *The Science of Mechanics in the Middle Ages*, 255–329.

[82] See Lüthy, Leijenhorst, and Thijssen, 'The Tradition of Aristotelian Natural Philosophy. Two Theses and Seventeen Answers,' in Leijenhorst, Lüthy and Thijssen (eds), *The Dynamics of Aristotelian Natural Philosophy*, 1–29. See also the new series: Thijssen and Lüthy (eds), *Medieval and Early Modern Science*, Leiden: Brill, 2001–.

group are revisionist in a fascinating way and they are achieved by interpreting physicist texts from within, and not as if their authors were as such true Aristotelians in a historical sense. The new sciences grew in a new world of a new way of ideas expressing the openness and contingency approach to reality.

A fresh approach also asks for philosophical adjustments. If the leading ideas of the Nijmegen School are correct, the designation 'the dynamics of . . .' is no longer applicable to *Aristotelian natural philosophy* in the strict sense of 'the dynamics of . . .' If new wine is poured into old wine skins, then the age of the skins does not make the wine modernized old wine. When Charles Lohr observes that the impressive increase in the number of 'commentaries' on Aristotle's writings on natural philosophy is especially due to the efforts of the Jesuit Order, it is not helpful to call the natural philosophy of the Jesuits *Aristotelian*.[83] Lohr reminds us that the *Constitutiones* of the Jesuit Order prescribe that Aristotle was to be followed in philosophy and Thomas Aquinas in theology, but what can such a strategy mean? When a thesis is said to be true *secundum Aristotelem et veram philosophiam*, we have to explain *Aristoteles* on the basis of *vera philosophia*, and not the other way around. The impact of the qualification *Aristotelian* has to expounded as follows: philosophically true/sound/solid. Likewise, in the seventeenth-century Dutch Republic, 'Cartesian' does not mean strictly following Descartes, but *new, progressive*.[84] One of Lohr's examples is the thesis of the immortality of the individual thinking mind, a thesis which was not defended by the historical Aristotle at all. On the contrary, his system excludes this thesis. During the early modern centuries, the *auctoritates* were mainly studied as sources of truth and not in any historical way. Suárez was the representative thinker of the Jesuit Order, but if we remind ourselves that his theory of individuals is rather Scotist and his theory of universals enjoys a strong Nominalist flavour, it is clear that it is not of any help to call his thinking Thomist in any modern sense of this characterization. Nineteenth-century qualifications have little use in the centuries before the historical revolution.

It is clear that there is no coherent philosophy of nature to be derived from Scotus' *Ordinatio*, but 'this is not to say that there is

---

[83] See Lohr, 'The Social Situation of the Study of Aristotelian Natural Philosophy,' in Leijenhorst et al. (eds), *The Dynamics of Aristotelian Natural Philosophy*, 345 f.

[84] See Vos, 'Voetius als reformatorisch wijsgeer,' in Van Oort et al. (eds), *De onbekende Voetius* (1989), 228 f.

nothing in the *Opera* of Scotus which is utilizable in the realm of a philosophy of natural science, for the case of C. S. Peirce shows clearly
that Scotism and a sophisticated and creative philosophy of science are
not necessarily incompatible.'[85] During the following centuries
Scotists tried to offer a philosophy of nature alternative to the logic
and natural philosophy of Nifo, Zimara, Picolomini, and Jacopo
Zabarella.[86]

Many creative lines in Duns Scotus' thought can be extended and
extrapolated, but several of these options need to be completed by
modern developments which do not have a true counterpart in
medieval thought. In order to see the power of Duns Scotus' logical
insights, they have to be wedded to Fregean logic, just as his ontology
and doctrine of God have to be wedded to Cantor's theory of infinite
sets, and to modal logic and an ontology of possible worlds. The great
scientific question is how true contingency can be recognized in modern
physics, if it is not excluded by laws of nature. Recently, Axel Schmidt
linked Duns Scotus' contingency ontology to quantum theory by
exploring the intimate connections between reality which is synchronically contingent and the ontological structures which quantum physics
is in need of. Schmidt's dauntless achievement not only adds an ontological account to modern physics, but also radicalizes, extends, and
improves on Scotian physics.[87]

---

[85] Schmitt, 'Filippo Fabri's *Philosophia naturalis Io. Duns Scoti,' Regnum Hominis and Regnum Dei* II 308. Cf. Wolter, 'The Realism of Scotus,' *The Philosophical Theology of Scotus*, 42–53, Boler, *Charles Peirce and Scholastic Realism*, chapter 1, and De Waal, 'Peirce's Nominalist–Realist Distinction, an Untenable Dualism,' *Transactions of the Charles S. Peirce Society* 34.1 (1998) 183–202.

[86] Probably, Filippo Fabri was the first to attempt to compose a full-fledged handbook of natural philosophy along Scotist lines.

[87] See Axel Schmidt's *Habilitationsschrift* (Paderborn): *Natur und Geheimnis. Kritik des Naturalismus durch moderne Physik und scotische Metaphysik*, 129 ff. and 358 ff.

CHAPTER 11

Individuality, individuals, will, and freedom

11.1 INTRODUCTION

At the close of the thirteenth century, there was no feeling of a *fin de siècle* in Oxford. The young university flourished and the expanding Franciscan movement led the way in the shadow and light of the weighty Parisian condemnations of 1277, and in the light of the Oxford condemnations of 1277 and 1284. Step by step, Duns Scotus pushed back the boundaries of semantics and logic. Massive theological problems lay ahead and the new lecturer of divinity tried to cast new light upon the dilemmas surrounding *individuality*. During these remarkable years of the mid-1290s everything changed. The theoretical center of the new way of thought was Duns' theory of *synchronic contingency*. His is an ontology of individuals, comprising the past, present, and future of the created universe. The theory of individuality is a fine example of how philosophy changed. 'Because of its theological implications, the problem of individuation in the latter portion of the thirteenth century became one of the more controversial and hotly discussed issues in university circles, especially at Paris and Oxford.'[1] Nevertheless, true individuality is still a rather neglected issue in philosophy. 'The purely and pre-eminently philosophical problem concerning the ultimate constitutive element of individual reality is either totally neglected or only partially treated by modern philosophers.'[2]

The principal ontological consequence of far-reaching conceptual shifts is discerned in the theory of individuals. Scientific revolutions are, for the most part, matters of major conceptual shifts, and at the end of the thirteenth century, one such shift took place. In ancient philosophy, the individual poses a problem. In the whole of the

---

[1] Wolter, 'Scotus' Individuation Theory,' in *The Philosophical Theology of Scotus*, 68.
[2] Tonna, 'The Problem of Individuation in Scotus and Other Franciscan Thinkers of Oxford in the 13th Century,' *De doctrina Ioannis Duns Scoti* I 257.

history of philosophy, the positive individual is a rare specimen. From the heaven of universals, it is a long way to the lowly individual in matter and quantity. The Bible has made us familiar with the idea of a fall from grace, but the stark view of Genesis is like a child's optimism in comparison with the ontological and eternal fall taught by Gnosticism and Manicheism. The portrayal of man in this main tradition of Western thought can be characterized as the view of *the unpleasant* or *disreputable individual*. One can sense the discomfort that certain medieval thinkers would have with this view when 'we listen to the Franciscan friar Roger Bacon saying – and it is an irritable remark: *One ought not to nag about universal being, for it is the individual and the concrete that matters.*'[3] De Rijk stresses that in the thirteenth century one was not satisfied to see reality through Aristotelian lenses:

> What do they not accept any more, you will ask. Let me try to state it sharply. In the garden of our new Philosophical Institute there are two individual maple trees. According to Aristotle, they differ from each other only in terms of their matter; so, not in an essential way. I understand that this assertion is not able to shock you and now I have to become really personal. According to Aristotle, you and I differ from one another and from all other human persons because one and the same essence of man is only realized in different pieces of matter. (Ibid.)

This implies that two individuals are not in any sense *essentially* different from one another. The personal vein of these remarks consists in the idea that were such a view plausible no reasonable complaint is possible if one realizes that there is an essential identity between some reader and an unpleasant criminal. When matter is understood to be, as it is within this context, an inferior principle and as far as individuality in itself is concerned, individuality boils down to more or less nothing.[4] Matter is not-being, absolutely indefinite in its basic structures.

Duns Scotus not only revolutionized the ontology of individuals, standing on the shoulders of his predecessors, but also the theory of

[3] L. M. de Rijk, *Het ongure individu. Uitdager èn spelbreker van het denken* (The disreputable individual. Challenger and spoilsport of philosophical thought), 11. Excellent expositions on aspects of the medieval philosophy of individuality are found in Gracia, *Introduction to the Problem of Individuation in the Early Middle Ages*, and idem (ed.), *Individuation in Scholasticism* (1994).

[4] See De Rijk, *Het ongure individu*, 6–13.

universal predication and predicate logic. Again, Duns Scotus sided with the majority report (twelfth-century thought, Thomas of York, Bonaventure, John Pecham, Roger Bacon, Richard of Middleton, Matthew of Acquasparta, Olivi). If the world of individuals is open and contingent, there is dynamics of change. It is only in terms of such an ontology that the individual becomes morally accountable. Hannah Arendt searched for a philosophy of will in the history of Western thought and the only philosophers of will she could find were Augustine and Duns Scotus. The true individual is even more rare,[5] so there is something at stake. The following topics will be discussed. The matter theory of individuals is dealt with in §11.2 and the early nominalist theory of individuality in §11.3. In §11.4 Duns Scotus' own personal theory of individuality (haecceity, *hecitas*) is expounded. On the personal level, individuality implies will, constituting what persons are (§11.5). The issue of whether Duns' teaching in Oxford differed from his Parisian doctrine is discussed in §11.6, while §11.7 treats the crucial links between *willing* and *freedom*. The chapter is rounded off in §11.8: 'Perspective.'

11.2   THE MATTER THEORY OF INDIVIDUALITY

11.2.1   Introductory remarks

Lectura I–II weaves a web of concepts of a special kind. At its center is a notion of critical contingency intended to cover the whole of reality. The importance of the theory of individuality in the first part of Lectura II 3 (§§1–229) cannot be easily overestimated. Here, we meet several important ontological boundaries against the background of doctrines about God's will and creation and theories of contingency and reality which have dominated the *Lectura* up to II 3. Duns Scotus' refutations of necessitarianism and of extreme realism and semi-mentalism (semi-ideationalism), his affirmations of the formal objective distinction and of a realism which includes views of counting and predicating, and his affirmation of the non-accidental character of individuality and the perspective of personal identity shine forth.

---

[5] Apart from many occasional references to his theory of individuality, we find extensive treatments in the following works: *Quaestiones supra libros Metaphysicorum Aristotelis* VII 13, *Lectura* II 3 (1298), *Ordinatio* II 3 (1302), *Reportatio Parisiensis* II 12 (1304), and William Godin's *Disputatio publica* (1306). Consult also Josef Estermann's fine dissertation on Leibniz, *Individualität und Kontingenz*.

Individuals play a decisive role in Scotus' ontology and physics. According to an *act–potency* physics, matter and accidents determine what is individual. Duns is not happy with this approach, nor with some alternatives, and he also states his own point of view:

> Socrates and Plato differ. Therefore, we have to get some factor by which they differ, in view of which their difference ultimately exists. However, the nature, present in this and in that person, cannot primarily explain their difference, but only their agreement. Therefore, there must be something else by which they differ. This factor is not quantity, nor existence, nor negation.[6]

Socrates and Plato cannot differ in terms of their sortal kind or common nature. So, we have to look for another factor to explain their individuality. Duns analyses and refutes a series of theories trying to explain the individual nature of material things and persons, in *Lectura* II 3.1–229. Successively, he discusses the theory that (1) there are only individual natures, (2) the double negation and (3) the existence theories, and (4) the quantity and (5) matter theories.[7] Eventually, Duns explains his own haecceity theory in *quaestio* 6, applying it to the individuality of angels in *quaestio* 7.[8]

The core issue is the possibility of *individual natures (haecceities)*. The nature of reality and the presence of an essentially individual layer of reality is what matters. This also points to the problem of whether we need a formal distinction between *nature* and *individuality* in terms of essentiality, because there is no way left to define individuality in terms of matter or quantitative aspects. The effect is that a quantitative plurality or number of angels or stones is impossible. We discern how interwoven Duns' ideas are: just the idea of a formal objective distinction is vital to the issue under consideration. Duns'

---

[6] *Lectura* II 3.167: 'Socrates et Plato differunt. Ergo, oportet advenire aliqua quibus differunt, ad quae ultimo stat eorum differentia. Sed natura in hoc et in illo non est causa differentiae primo, sed convenientiae. [. . .] Ergo, oportet dare aliud quo differunt. Hoc non est *quantitas*, nec *exsistentia*, nec *negatio*, sicut ostensum est in quaestionibus praecedentibus.'

[7] Wolter deals with these theories in his 'Scotus' Individuation Theory,' in *The Philosophical Theology of Scotus*, 74–83, 84, 84 f., 85–88, and 88 f., respectively (68–97).

[8] See, successively, in *Lectura* II 3 *quaestio* 1 – §§1–38 (*// Ordinatio* II 3.1–42), *quaestio* 2, §§39–53 (*// Ordinatio* II 3.43–58), *quaestio* 3 – §§54–60 (*// Ordinatio* II 3.59–65), *quaestio* 4 – §§61–124 (*// Ordinatio* II 3.66–128), *quaestio* 5 – §§125–138 (*// Ordinatio* II 3.129–141), *quaestio* 6 – §§139–195 (*// Ordinatio* II 3.142–211) and *quaestio* 7 – §§196–229 (*// Ordinatio* II 3.212–254). See Wolter, 'Scotus' Individuation Theory,' *The Philosophical Theology of Scotus*, 89–97.

theory of individuality and his theory of the formal distinction belong together.[9] Both are constitutive of Scotus' realism. *Being individual* and *being common* – in the sense of a nature *being common* – and *possibly being common* (*communicabilis*) are at home on the level of *being essential*. Duns' revolutionary move is admitting individuality to the degree of essentiality and saving it from the undervalued role of accidental factors. He is not only a *philosopher of will* (the phrase is Hannah Arendt's), freedom and contingency, but also the philosopher of individuality. It seems worthwhile to explore in further detail the theory as put forward for the first time in *Lectura* II 3 (1298), in comparison with his later treatments.

First, the so-called *matter* theory of individuality is discussed. Duns' refutation of the 'matter theory' of individuality is striking, but there is not only the theoretical Scylla of Aristotelianism, but also the Charybdis of an early form of ideational mentalism. The negative arguments are mainly found in *Lectura* II 3.1 through 6, but in *Lectura* II 3.1 the main target is not an Aristotelian but an early nominalist or, as I would like to call it, mentalist theory of individuals.[10] However, his refutation of the view that matter constitutes individuality is a striking move which reconstructs anthropology and, in general, the theory of reality. First, the so-called *matter* theory of individuality is dealt with, and, second, the early nominalist approach is analyzed.

11.2.2 The matter theory of individuality

In the medieval theory of individuals, the issue of individuality looks like a problem in angelology. For moderns, it may seem strange that angels have to indicate the direction in which to address the problem of individuals. It seems rather unlikely that philosophers like Ayer and Strawson would look to angels in their accounts of the nature of individuals, as both Aquinas and Scotus do. In Duns' *Lectura* and *Ordinatio* the theory of individuality is treated in Book II 3, one distinction among many others in a massive cluster of chapters on angelic theology or angelology. Let us take this angelological starting point for granted and listen to Duns answering the question, whether

---

[9] This connection was pointed out by Kraus, *Die Lehre des Johannes Duns Scotus von der natura communis*, 136–142. Cf. Wolter, *The Transcendentals*, 27–30 and 103–111.

[10] Unfortunately, Wolter and Sondag overlook this feature of Duns' argumentation, spotted by Tonna, 'The Problem of Individuation,' *De doctrina Ioannis Duns Scoti* I 265.

angels can be multiple and different personal individuals.[11] The counter-arguments answer negatively, Duns answers affirmatively.

The first observation reveals that the counter-arguments are pleading 'no,' with Duns saying 'yes.' Duns' answer runs this way: angels are of a single kind, not only two of a kind, but many of a kind. Angels are of the same *angelic* kind and enjoy the same personal nature (*Lectura* II 3.206).

The second comment runs as follows: one opposite view wants to have it true that *being individual* or *being an individual* is dependent on matter and quantity. Because angels are not supposed to be material, according to this view there cannot be a number of angels. There can only be one absolutely individual *bangel*, one *cangel*, one *gangel*, but it is impossible that there *angels*. ANGEL is not a countable or numerical term. There are only individual essences like bangelicity, cangelicity, gangelicity, and so on.

The third comment says that Duns does not solve the problem by conceding that there is angelic matter. In his view, angels are not material.

My fourth comment points to formulating the problem: we need a formal distinction between nature and individuality on the level of essentiality, because in this special case there is no way of defining individuality in terms of matter. The effect would be that a number of angels or stones is impossible.

A fifth comment stresses that just this idea of a formal objective distinction is vital to the issue under consideration. Duns' theory of individuality and his theory of the formal distinction belong tightly together. Both are constitutive of what Charles Sanders Peirce termed 'Scotus' realism.'[12] Being *individual*, being *common* and *possibly being common* are at home on the same ontological level, namely the level of essentiality. Duns Scotus allows individuality to the level of essentiality and he thereby saves it from the unpleasant and under-valued role of accidental factors. He is a *philosopher of will* (Hannah Arendt), a philosopher of freedom and contingency and also the philosopher of individuality.

The medieval tradition shows a Christian variant of the Aristotelian view that matter is pure potentiality. Thomas Aquinas, among others,

---

[11] *Lectura* II 3.194 ff., Wolter, 'Scotus' Individuation Theory,' in *The Philosophical Theology of Scotus*, 68–97, and Sondag, *Duns Scot. Le principe d'individuation*.

[12] Hartshorne and Weiss (eds), *The Collected Papers of Charles Sanders Peirce* I, section 29; cf. sections I 4 and IV 51.

defines *matter* as pure potentiality. The essence of a natural substance comprises its form and its matter. The form bestows actuality on an individual thing – in virtue of its form matter becomes a being, but quantified matter is the principle of individuality. Accordingly, John and Peter are individuals, but they are only material individuals, since essentially they are the same, because there is only one type of *nature*, namely the universal nature. In his debate with Godin (1306), Duns Scotus states his case in this way:

> Against this [that is, Godinus'] position: the singularity about which we are asking in this discussion is being a something per se one among other things (aliquid per se unum in entibus) to which it is repugnant to be divided into subjective parts; of this repugnance there can only be a single cause.[13]

The theological translation of this view is illuminating: matter apart from form is a contradiction in terms and a contradiction is unrealizable, even by God's power. We might ask why the reverse does not hold alike: why is *form* apart from *matter* not a contradiction in terms? Why is the notion of *actus purus* not a contradiction in terms within this conceptual framework? In a philosophy of creation, as Thomas' philosophy is, the denial of the basic intuition that form and matter cannot occur apart from each other and the acceptance of separated substances are still exceptions to a rule. Either the rule demolishes the exceptions or exceptions demolish the rule.

11.3 A NOMINALIST THEORY OF INDIVIDUALITY

Nineteenth-century studies on the history of medieval philosophy mainly looked upon medieval philosophy as a battleground for realists and nominalists fighting on the issue of universals. On this issue, Duns Scotus' stance is clear: 'A universal is not a substance (against Plato).'[14] What is universal belongs to many individuals. Therefore, a universal is not an individual substance. According to Plato, however, a universal is a substance and that numerically one and the same substance or essence is the quiddity of, for example, Socrates or Plato. A universal substance cannot belong to Socrates

---

[13] Noone, 'Individuation in Scotus,' *American Catholic Philosophical Quarterly* 64 (1995) 531. He especially deals with comparing the Scotian stance with the Thomist one. Cf. §11.4.

[14] *Lectura* II 3.2: 'Universale non est substantia (contra Platonem).'

properly. Possibly, it is only Socrates, but then it is impossible that Plato exists.[15]

Against this general ontological background, the first target of Duns Scotus' ontology of individuality which he deals with in *Lectura* II 3 and *Ordinatio* II 3 is the twofold theory that (1) there are only individuals, and (2) that there can only be individuals and individual essences. The nature of a thing consists in its singularity or individuality.[16] If we consider a thing in itself, then it has what it has in order to be individual and singular. Its singular individuality is its 'nature.' 'A nature is of itself single and singular.'[17] For quite simple reasons, Duns is convinced that this view is absurd. If the nature of a stone belongs to the stone, because it is this individual nature of itself, then it is impossible that there is more than one stone.[18] The other way around, a *kind* can number only one exemplar. There are as many kinds as there are individuals:

> If one of two opposite features belongs to anything essentially, then the opposite feature is incompatible with it. Therefore, if it belongs to the nature of a stone that it is singular of itself, then a multitude of stones in that same kind is incompatible with that stone.[19]

What does this pre-Ockhamist nominalism say of universals? A thing is only universal to the extent that an intellect apprehends it as such. Universality is an ascription of the intellect (*Lectura* II 3.6), and although this theory is diametrically opposed to Aristotelianism, Duns takes it under fire. According to this theory, 'being individual [*singulare*], which is simply being, belongs adequately to a thing on itself, from its own nature.'[20] However, 'because being universal is

---

[15] See *Lectura* II 3.38: 'Concludit tantum contra Platonem, qui ponit universale esse substantiam separatam, unam numero, et illam esse quiditatem huius et illius, ut Socratis et Platonis. [. . .] Sed tale universale non potest esse proprium Socrati [. . .] quin secundum se totum sit in Platone [. . .]. Et ideo sequitur quod nullum tale universale potest esse substantia.' No true universal can be an individual substance. In fact, this refutation not only hits Platonist, but also Aristotelian ontologies.

[16] See *Lectura* II 3.5. Cf. Alvin Plantinga's notion of *essence* in the sense of individual essence in *The Nature of Necessity*, chapter 4.

[17] *Lectura* II 3.7: 'Natura de se singularis est.'

[18] *Lectura* II 3.3: 'Si natura lapidis conveniat quod de se sit *haec*, igitur convenit ei in quocumque est, et per consequens non possunt plures lapides esse.'

[19] *Lectura* II 3.4: 'Cui convenit ex se unum oppositorum, ei repugnat oppositum. Si igitur naturae lapidis conveniat quod de se singularis sit, ergo ei repugnat multitudo in eadem specie.' For the extended refutation, see *Lectura* II 3.5–38.

[20] *Lectura* II 3.5: 'Esse autem singulare, quod est esse simpliciter, conveniet rei ex se, ex natura sua.'

being from a certain point of view [*secundum quid*], it belongs to a thing by way of the intellect.'[21]

Duns contests this view according to which universal being is only mental being (*Lectura* I 3.7), because *mental being*, in his view, is not *being* at all. Not only has mentalism to be completely discarded, but also semi-mentalism. For Duns Scotus, the object of the intellect enjoys priority over and against the intellect's act of knowing and, therefore, this object cannot be a mental entity. The intellect and 'Mentalish' do not create reality. In *Lectura* II 3 part 1 *quaestio* 1, Locke and Kant, Berkeley and Hegel have already been implicitly refuted. The stone enjoys priority over and against its being known and beyond its being known. Otherwise,

> knowing a stone under its aspect of universality is knowing it under an aspect which is objectively contrary to the proper structure of the object.[22]

Accordingly, such belief cannot be knowledge at all. Duns is adamant on this point in just the same way as he had refuted the Thomist view that God can know contingent reality in a necessary way in the *Prologue*. The statement 'Contingent reality can be necessarily known,' like the statement 'Individual reality can be known as universal reality,' is inconsistent. If there is only a universal and necessary mode of knowing, reality must be universal and necessary. If only these modes of knowing are to be joined with reality itself being only singular and contingent, radical skepticism is the only possible upshot. However, 'the stone enjoys priority over the act of knowing it.'[23] Essential unity is not numerical unity, essential unity is less than numerical unity. The theory under review discards essential unity. The Aristotelian alternative opts precisely for the other way round. It downgrades numerical unity by stating that essential unity is more

---

[21] Ibid.: 'Cum igitur esse universale sit esse secundum quid, conveniet rei ab intellectu.'

[22] Lectura II 3.8: 'Sed in illo priore, secundum hanc opinionem, lapis de se est singularis; ergo intellectio lapidis sub ratione universalis est intellectio eius sub opposita ratione obiective propriae rationi obiecti.' This place has to be amended with the help of the critical apparatus. The Committee reads: *sub opposita ratione obiectivae propriae et ratione obiecti*. This has to be replaced by *sub opposita ratione obiective propriae rationi obiecti*, correcting a sentence which is otherwise mysterious.

[23] *Lectura* II 3.8: 'Lapis ergo secundum quod primo obicitur intellectui, est prior sua intellectione.' The first part of this section runs as follows: 'Obiectum intellectus naturaliter est prius actu quo intelligitur, quia sicut dictum est in I, est causa actus, vel si non sit causa actus, oportet tamen quod praecedat propriam intellectionem (secundum omnes).' The reference to *Book* I concerns *Lectura* I 3.365.

than numerical unity. Duns points to the constructive way out: essential unity is something, it is real unity, but as such it is less than numerical unity on which counting individuals is based.

11.4   INDIVIDUALITY

11.4.1   Introduction

What is at issue is *why* any material thing is individual. Duns copes with this crucial matter in a tight sequence of analyses. The first target is the theory dealt with above answering the question as follows: *being individual (individuatio)* meets its ground *(causa)* in itself. There are only individual natures possible. If an individual nature is not the only positive element, then the common nature or universal must be something positive. So, the next question to be raised is: is a material substance individual in virtue of an element which is intrinsically positive (*Lectura* II 3.39 ff.)? Note that for a material thing *being multiplied (dividi in plura)* is incompatible *(repugnat)* with its individual nature. However, when an accidental property is denied – unfortunately, I become blind – the bearer of the accidental property does not disappear. Nor is it impossible that other people become blind too, when I become blind. Accidental changes do not touch something's individual nature, for accidental changes and properties can be multiplied (§10.5). Duns contrasts this phenomenon with the fact that an individual *qua* individual cannot be multiplied. We have Fido and two nice puppies Fides and Fidus, but neither Fides nor Fidus is identical to Fido. Apparently, an individual *a* cannot be absorbed by more individuals, because they cannot be identical with *a* one by one. Why not? A purely negative aspect cannot explain this fact. Duns underlines that something positive is at play.[24] If so, several alternatives pop up.

11.4.2   Double negation

The next target of Duns Scotus' list is a theory proposed by Henry of Ghent who claimed that a double negation is all that is needed to explain what individuality means. *Individuality* is not seen by Duns as a logical feat, structuring logical predicates (second intentions),

---

[24] *Lectura* II 3.45: 'Omne quod repugnat entitati alicuius, repugnat ei propter aliquid positivum in eo.'

but as a real property. For this reason, neither is the mathematical notion of *unity* at stake. The issue is ontological. A nature can be multiplied: there are many stones and there are many horses, but an individual *a* is unique.[25] The individuality of *a* cannot be multiplied. So, the second denial comes to the fore: the individual nature of *a* cannot be identical with the individual nature of *b*, for, Duns Scotus would say, the individual *a* cannot be identical with the individual *b*. Individuals are not identical and cannot be identical. So, self-identity must be an essential property.

The *double negation* view will not do, because if an individual *a* were of a kind, then its nature would not be multiplied either. However, in this case, the nature of *a* would still be incapable of accounting for the individuality of *a*, although it is instantiated in only one individual. A nature can be multiplied in most cases; so, the denial of factual plurality cannot explain that a denial is implied if individuality is at stake. Only a positive factor explains the involved inconsistency. That element also makes clear that a certain individuality cannot be multiplied. Duns Scotus makes a great deal of effort to show that an accidental feature cannot account for individuality, but quantity also obtains on the level of accidentality (see §10.4).

11.4.3 Actual existence

The next option reads that actual existence accounts for individuality. However, if factual existence is a necessary condition for being individual, then Anselm and Duns Scotus cannot be different individuals, because they do not exist any more. Existence is not restricted to only one ontological aspect, namely the aspect of the individual, for existence presupposes the whole of the essential order, comprising general types, intermediate kinds and individuals alike: '*this man* includes no more factual existence than *man* does' (*Ordinatio* II 3.62 f.).[26]

11.4.4 Quantity

The quantity theory is the fourth theory: *quantity* is the positive element by which a material substance is this individual entity. Duns

---

[25] This point was also stressed by Richard of Middleton – see Tonna, 'The Problem of Individuation,' *De doctrina Ioannis Duns Scoti* I 263 f. Middleton linked the elements of negation and existence.

[26] Note that, to Duns' mind, *existence* and *essence* are coordinated. See §7.5.

makes clear what he thinks of the nature of accidents, for quantity is
an accident. The exposition of this theory is followed by its fourfold
refutation. The three first of these refutations have in common that

> they prove with respect to every accident, without exception, that
> no accident can explain why a material substance enjoys *this* indi-
> viduality.'[27]

First, we paid attention to the matter theory of individuality in an
Aristotelian vein; second, we described the extremely Christian
alternative approach of early nominalism preceding Ockhamism,
which I characterized as semi-mentalism. In *Lectura* II 3 Duns
follows the reverse order. First of all he copes with the purely individuality approach of early nominalism and of Henry of Ghent
(*Lectura* II 3. part 1 questions 1–3), then secondly with the
universality approach (questions 4–6). Duns' criticisms of the universality approach were reviewed in comparison with those of the
nominalist approach. All that matters here is counting. In Duns'
devastating analysis the nominalist alternative entails that there
cannot be more or several stones. Plurality is impossible, not only in
heaven as far as the angels are concerned, but also on earth. There
is only one *stone* and one *stane* and one *stine*, and so on. Singularity
blocks the common nature in terms of which there may be a plurality of stones. The plurality approach makes counting even more difficult. Here the non-individual nature blocks the singularity. There
cannot be individual stones. From a logical point of view both Plato
and Aristotle and Aquinas have to face the same dilemma: if true
reality has to be what they decide it to be, a singular stone or tomato
or angel cannot be real and therefore not a real stone or a real
tomato or a real angel.

The nominalist has to say that there is only one stone. The upper
limit of counting is one. There is simply only individual life. In sharp
contrast to this view, the Aristotelian has to conclude: there *is* no stone
at all, for there are only universals. However, a universal is not a substance and therefore a universal stone is not a stone at all. The upper
limit is identical with the lower limit of counting and so it is zero.
Therefore, according to both views, counting things would simply be
impossible. On both of them we cannot count, because we cannot
count at all. In one view the individual is not virtuous at all; in the

---

[27] *Lectura* II 3.72: 'Ostendunt universaliter de omni accidente quod nullum accidens potest esse
causa quare substantia materialis est *haec* (*sc., natura*).'

alternative view it is too virtuous. The pure potentiality theory of matter in various forms was definitely a report of the views of the minority of thinkers in the thirteenth and fourteenth centuries (cf. §10.4 and §10.6). In Duns Scotus' physics, both form and matter enjoy quite a different status. Essences are only essences of existent things (see §7.7). So, essences are not uncreated. They are created just as matter is and matter is not the *non*-being aspect of creation, but it is itself a positive aspect of creation.

The causal powers God brings into creation belong to all three divine persons. Just God Triune creates and only God Triune creates. Duns Scotus perfects the Augustinian line asserting that God's external activity is an undivided activity of God the Father, God the Son and God the Holy Spirit. The world of material things is created out of nothing (*Lectura* II 1), but, according to *Ordinatio* II 1, the notion of *ex nihilo* is applied to producing from eternity the objects of God's knowledge of *being known* (*esse intelligibile*). Material or bodily substances are composed of matter and form. The substantial form unites with the material component to form a single complete substance and the 'substantial act' is the reality of such a substance and such a substance is an individual subject (*suppositum*). So, Plato and Socrates are 'numerically distinct' and the primary ontological position is assigned to such individuals. *Numerical unity* is exemplified in an individual (*suppositum*).

Duns Scotus pays tribute to both essential aspects of numerical and essential unity. The more common or more general something is, the less unity it has. Therefore, essential unity (unity of the *natura communis*) is less (*minor*) than numerical unity or numerical identity.

11.4.5   *Quaestiones Quodlibetales* II 49

In his *Quaestiones Quodlibetales* II, Duns Scotus discusses the crucial Trinitarian issue whether God can be considered as having an indeterminate number of intrinsic essential characteristics. If so, or not, whether something unique is at stake or a plurality, it must have *being* (*entitas*). Here, we meet the distinctive Scotian triadic pattern of *being – one – many* (*entitas, unitas, pluralitas*).[28] The distinctive terms of Duns Scotus' theory of individuality in *Lectura* II 3 and in *Ordinatio* II 3 are reviewed.

---

[28] *Quaestiones Quodlibetales* II 50: 'A posteriori nihil habet suam entitatem, ergo nec unitatem nec certam pluralitatem.'

> Any kind of thing that can be multiplied or is related to more indi-
> viduals of the same kind, is not of itself limited to a certain number.
> This proposition is evident, if you relate what is common to its
> individuals, or a cause to what is caused by it, or a principle to
> what proceeds therefrom. If what is common, can be multiplied into
> what is of the same kind, then it is not limited to a certain number
> of itself, neither is a cause limited of itself to a certain number of
> effects.[29]

Thus, when the issue of *one* and *many* is discussed, we meet the distinctive expressions *plurificare, plurificabile, ad plura,* and *pluralitas.*
Moreover, on the one hand, we have what is *common (natura
communis),* on the other hand, *individuals (singularia).* Even, the
Aristotelian notion of *matter* is expounded in terms of Scotus' own idea
of *individuality.*

> On the other hand, the quiddity is called form by him in many places;
> by contrast, whatever serves to restrict or to qualify the quiddity
> is called matter. Thus, the individual difference, whatever it may
> be, is called matter with respect to the specific quiddity. Therefore,
> sometimes matter is called that which receives the determining
> form; sometimes that which restricts or qualifies the indifferent quid-
> dity. However, such a restricting or qualifying factor can be under-
> stood in two ways: one, as intrinsic to the determinate member falling
> into such a common class. [. . .] For example, the individual differ-
> ence of Socrates restricts *being man* in the first way, for it is intrinsic
> to Socrates.[30]

It is to be concluded that the same model is operating in Duns
Scotus' *Quodlibet* as in *Lectura* II 3 and *Ordinatio* II 3. There are
different kinds of universal or common quiddities: generic types
and specific kinds. We arrive at a specific kind from a generic type

---

[29] *Quaestiones Quodlibetales* II 49: 'Quidquid est plurificabile eiusdem rationis vel ad plura
eiusdem rationis se habens non determinatur ex se ad certam pluralitatem. Haec propositio
patet, sive comparando commune ad sua singularia, sive causam ad sua causata, sive principium ad sua principiata. Commune enim plurificabile eiusdem rationis non determinatur ex
se ad certam pluralitatem inferiorum, causa etiam non determinatur ad certa causata ex se.'

[30] *Quaestiones Quodlibetales* II 59: 'Alio modo, forma dicitur quiditas secundum ipsum in
multis locis; et per oppositum *materia* dicitur quidquid habet rationem contrahentis vel
determinantis ipsam quidiatatem, et hoc modo *differentia individualis* quaecumque sit ipsa
dicitur materia respectu quiditatis specificae. Dicitur ergo materia quandoque illud quod
recipit formam informantem, quandoque illud quod contrahit vel determinat quiditatem
indifferentem. Sed tale contrahens vel determinans potest intelligi dupliciter: *uno modo,*
quasi intrinsecum inferiori vel determinato sub tali communi. [. . .] *Exemplum: differentia
individualis* Socratis contrahit hominem primo modo, quae est intrinseca Socrati.'

in virtue of a *specific difference*. Analogously, Duns Scotus arrives at the individual from a specific kind by virtue of the *individual difference*.

Why is Duns Scotus so sure of what he is doing, even though he squarely disagrees with all of the conceptual patterns regarding reality of the *philosophi*, including the Christian adaptations of Aristotelian philosophy? 'Because Aristotle's theory of individuation by matter was regarded by many medieval theologians as unacceptable for several reasons.'[31] Duns Scotus' views are in line with the majority of thinkers. Moreover, he lived in a huge spiritual community within a reform movement, bursting with optimistic self-confidence, to which all this was clear. The distinctive Scotian contributions belong to a much wider family of theories which dominated the scene. The impact of Duns Scotus' innovations was to strengthen the middle-of-the-road position. Moreover, the alternatives were not 'convenient.' *Conveniens* does not simply mean *absurd*, but that the view to be considered is incompatible and '*in-con*-sistent' with what is clear and widely endorsed. First, Duns Scotus indicates three main areas where evident issues are incompatible with the view he refutes.

If the individuality of something does not reside in its own inalienable individual nature, then individuality is to be looked for in the specific nature of something in itself, individualized as it is in a quantitative manner. If a nature of something, e.g. the nature of a stone, is in this stone and in that stone according to the same singularity, then there is no nature common to this stone and that stone. Analogously, without the notion of essential individuality it is not possible that the divine nature is typical of God the Father, God the Son and God the Holy Spirit, the three divine persons.[32] Moreover, this conception is incompatible with the doctrine of transubstantiation.

Likewise, the rejection of individuality is ontologically impossible. It is even more absurd than Platonic realism, because this piece of wood is identical to that piece of wood if individuality is rejected (*Lectura* II 3.157). It also leads to the inconsistency that a possible but not actual accidental property *P* of something is identical to

---

[31] Frank and Wolter, *Duns Scotus, Metaphysician*, 196 (196 f.: 'Individuation, Universals, and Common Nature'). *Duns Scotus, Metaphysician*, 184–187, also offers the English translation of crucial sections:*Ordinatio* II 3, 172, 175 and 187 f.

[32] Cf. *Ordinatio* II 3.158: 'In theologia quidem sequitur inconveniens hoc, quod non sit proprium essentiae divinae infinitae esse *haec*, scilicet quod ipsa exsistens una, in se indistincta, possit esse in pluribus suppositis distinctis.'

the factual accidental property *P*. This approach is even mathematic-
ally impossible, because two quantities of the same size have to be
identical. Natural philosophy also excludes leaving aside individuality, for the effect of the corruption of a piece of wood would be that
there is no wood any more. We count. We count stones, horses and
ladybirds: *a* is a ladybird, *b* is a ladybird, and *c* is a ladybird. The
remarkable thing is that traditional Greek philosophy attributed only
true *being* to what individuals have in common. The sortal property
of *being a ladybird* enjoys *being*, while Duns Scotus is defending the
ontological rights of the individual. Now, it is his point that if we can
talk of *one* item of something real, we have to accept that such a unity
enjoys *being* (*entitas*).[33] However, we exclusively meet *being one* in
an individual. An individual is as such individual, it is essentially
individual. It cannot be subdivided into more identical individuals.[34]
For Scotus, the notions of *being individual, numerical unity*, or
countability and *singularity* are equivalent. What does he mean by
them? Articulated unity (*unitas determinata*) is at stake. He calls it
by a fine metaphor: *signed unity. This* unity – the unity of being *this*
– is signed unity. *Being individual* and *being subdivided into more
subjects* are incompossible, but what accounts for this in(com)pos-
sibility? *This* thing cannot be *not-this* thing; it is *signed* (*signatum*)
by its singularity.[35] Duns Scotus' solution reads as a definition in his
answer to the seventh question in *Lectura* II 3.209:

> The essential aspect [*ratio*] of individualizing a specific nature is an
> entity which contracts such a nature and is outside the content [*extra
> rationem*] of quiddity and nature. Every nature is limited in such a
> way. Therefore, it is contractable and determinable and possible and
> just as it is not this nature [*haec*, that is *natura*] from itself, in such a
> way it can be contracted and determined by that formal entity which
> is found in every limited nature.[36]

---

[33] *Ordinatio* II 3.169: 'Sicut unitas in communi per se consequitur entitatem in communi, ita
quaecumque unitas per se consequitur aliquam entitatem.'

[34] Ibid.: 'unitas individui [. . .] cui repugnat *non esse hoc signatum*.' Cf. *Ordinatio* II 3,48, 76
and 165.

[35] *Ordinatio* II 3.76: 'Individuum incompossibile est non esse *hoc* signatum hac singularitate,
et quaeritur causa non singularitatis in communi, sed *huius* singularitatis in speciali signatae,
scilicet ut est *haec* determinate.'

[36] Ibid.: 'Ex quo per se *ratio individuandi naturam specificam* est aliqua entitas contrahens
naturam, quae est extra rationem quiditatis et naturae, ad quam natura est in potentia, et
omnis natura limitata est huiusmodi, quare ipsa est contrahibilis et determinabilis et in
potentia, et ideo sicut non est de se *haec*, ita potest per illam entitatem formalem contrahi et
determinari quae invenitur in omni natura limitata, ut praedictum est.'

What Duns calls *hecitas* (*haecceitas*, haecceity) in *Reportatio Parisiensis* II 12 is here described as *ratio individuandi naturam specificam* and *entitas contrahens naturam*. The typical logical relation between the haecceity of *a* and the nature of *a* makes it possible to count: *a* is an angel, *b* is an angel, *c* is an angel, and if you prefer horses you can do the same. Only if the nature of *a* is not in itself the individual nature can we speak about these individuals in the plural as angels and as horses. An adequate theory of counting is for Duns as basic to his view of individuals as his theology. At the one extreme of the ontological spectrum we have the *transcendentia*, the most general characteristics, and at the other one the haecceities, the most specific characteristics which are not general at all.

Ivo Tonna observed in his fine contribution to the history of the theory of the individual that 'Scotus's solution to the problem of individuation made it possible for the individual to regain that importance which it had completely lost in Greek philosophy.'[37] However, we are not even able to say that the inalienable dignity of the individual had been *lost* in Greek philosophy. It was never there, nor in other archaic and ancient cultures. It had to be discovered. In the wake of biblical revelation, philosophical theology designed a new approach to individuality culminating in Duns Scotus' contribution. 'Hence we can rightly deduce that the supreme and unique preeminence of individuality and personality which is a necessary postulate of every Christian philosophy cannot in any way be reconciled with these assertions of ancient Greek philosophy' (ibid.).

11.5 WILL

Between Anselm and Bonaventure the notion of *will* became a new focus in systematic thought, both in the doctrine of God and in anthropology. In the second half of the thirteenth century *will* 'came, saw and overcame' in theology and anthropology. From the middle of the 1290s, *will* was one of the central concepts of Duns' thought constructing new patterns in the theory of divine attributes, including the doctrine of the Trinity. Again and again, he dealt with its pivotal role in his lectures and seminars, and the writings which arose from them. At the same time, it is a rather sensitive theme.

---

[37] 'The Problem of Individuation,' *De doctrina Ioannis Duns Scoti* I 269.

Even Balic believed that problems emerged around Duns' theory of will, by his time in Oxford, and he tried to shed light on this issue in a careful and prudent manner. The old-fashioned idea that voluntarism was his shibboleth casts shadows even on the early history of Duns Scotus' development.[38] He was considered to be preoccupied with will.

In opposition to intellectualism – ascribed to Thomas Aquinas, for better or for worse – *voluntarism* was considered to adhere to the primacy of the will, culminating in the idea that if something is good, it is good, because God wills it so and because God does not will anything except what is good (see §§12.4–12.8). This theory of will is often directly linked with an extreme version of the theory of God's absolute power, putting God's agency outside and over against the law.[39] Balic saw immediately the importance of the texts on *willing*,[40] but the fact of the matter was only clarified in 1993 when the critical edition of *Lectura* II 7–44 appeared. Wolter has no texts on the will taken from Duns' *Lectura* I–II or *Reportatio Parisiensis* II in his splendid collection *Duns Scotus on the Will and Morality*,[41] while it was thought that '*Ordinatio* II 25' is missing. *Lectura* II 7–44 appeared only in 1993.[42]

11.5.1   The text: *Lectura* II 25

The main question of *Lectura* II 25 concentrates on the systematic problem as follows: 'Is an act of will caused in the will by the object which changes the will or by the will which changes itself?' The decisive sections (*Lectura* II 25.69–74) read as follows:

> (69) I answer to the question that the effective cause of the act of willing is not only the object or the image just as the first theory

---

[38] On this fictitious development of Duns Scotus' thought, consult C. Balic, 'Une question inédite de J. Duns Scot sur la volonté,' *Recherches de théologie ancienne et médiévale* 3 (1931) 191 f.

[39] Cf. William J. Courtenay, 'The Dialectic of Omnipotence,' in Rudavsky (ed.), *Divine omniscience and omnipotence in medieval philosophy*, 253 f. If we state that Duns Scotus acknowledges that any other action of God results in another order, for God never acts *inordinate*, then it is inconsistent to assert that God acts arbitrarily. Duns Scotus' view only acknowledges that God acts freely.

[40] See already Balic, *Les commentaires de Jean Duns Scot*, chapter 2 and Appendix II.

[41] Washington 1986. It contains some *Ordinatio* II texts on sin. Cf. Frank and Wolter, *Duns Scotus, Metaphysician*, 186–195: *Quaestiones Metaphysicae* IX 15 (partially) and 196–208: Commentary.

[42] See *Opera Omnia* XIX 71*. In *Ordinatio* II, distinctions 15–25 are thought to be missing.

states, because this point salvages freedom in no way.[43] However, the effective cause of the act of willing is neither only the will, as the second extreme theory states, because not all conditions of an act of willing can be satisfied, as we have shown.[44] For this reason, I steer a middle course: Both the will as the object go hand in hand in order to cause the act of willing so that the act of willing is caused by the will and the known object – both constitute the effective cause.

(70) However, how can this obtain for an object? An object has abstract being in the intellect and this something must also be an agent in reality. For this reason, I say that the intellect really knowing the object concurs with the will in order to cause the act of willing. In brief, a nature really knowing an object which is also free is the cause of willing and not-willing. The free judgement consists in this, whether in ourselves or in angels. Sometimes many factors concur in order to cause one effect so that one factor borrows the effective power of causing from the other one, just as a heavenly body and a particular agent (that is, an element or a mixture) with respect to causal acts. It is neither so as to the point to be discussed, because an object which is really known by the intellect does not have its causal power for a first act by the will, nor conversely.

(73) Third, sometimes more agents concur in causing so that their nature or structure is different (against the first option). Neither of them takes its active power from another, but both have their own causality, complete in their own category. Nevertheless, one agent is the main factor and the other is not the main factor, for instance, father and mother in order to beget offspring, a style and pen to write and a man and a wife to run the house. As to the point to be discussed, the will has the function of a cause with respect to the act of willing, namely a partial cause, and the nature which actually knows the object has the function of another partial cause. Both are simultaneously one total cause with respect to an act of willing. Nevertheless, the will is the superior cause and the knowing nature is not, because the will activates freely for whose activity the will activates something else. Hence it is for the will to decide that something else acts. However, a nature which knows the object is active in an essential manner, always active as far it is up to that nature.

---

[43] Dealing with this theory, Duns discusses, among others, the theory of Thomas Aquinas: *Lectura* II 25.22–53. Duns is convinced that this theory is incompatible with tradition (*Lectura* II 25.37). This thesis had been condemned in the 219 *Parisian Articles* of 1277 (article 194): 'Quod anima nihil vult nisi mota ab alio; unde illud est falsum: "anima se ipsa vult". *Error*, si intelligatur "mota ab alio" scilicet ab appetibili vel obiecto, ita quod appetibile vel obiectum sit tota ratio motus ipsius voluntatis.'

[44] The approach of Henry of Ghent is discussed in *Lectura* II 25.54–68.

This factor is never sufficient to elicit an act, unless the will concurs. Therefore, the will is the superior cause. This is also obvious from what has been said in the third distinction of *Book* I: with respect to the act of knowing, the intellect is a more important cause than the object is.

(74) Now it is obvious how there is freedom in the will, for I am said *to look freely*, because I can use freely my sight in order to look. This is the case as to the point to be discussed, as far as a cause is a one-way cause and always active in a uniform manner, as far as it is up to that cause. Nevertheless, this cause neither determines, nor necessitates the will in order to will, but the will can concur with it from its own freedom in order to will something or not to will it. In this way, the will can freely use it. Therefore, it is said that *freely willing* and *not-willing* are in our power.

11.5.2   *Lectura* II 25: the theory

This crystal-clear line of argumentation enables us to identify Duns' systematic position. What is at stake in this position is the interaction between *willing* and *knowing* in an agent. The theme assumes a reasonable agent who can give a good answer to the question *why* he acts and wills as he does. What are the general aspects of such an answer? According to Duns, such an answer has to satisfy some preconditions. A good answer has to humor the *freedom* of willing and, in general, it has to do justice to all kinds of conditions for acts of will. The alternative theories of, among others, Thomas Aquinas and Henry of Ghent do not do so (*Lectura* II 25.69). It is also crucial that *willing* is considered to be intentional and object-related. However, how can a voluntative object play a decisive role, if only knowledge of *willing* settles the issue? In that case, we only have a mental object, but can a mental object be a causal factor? Duns suggests not to make a fuss, but simply to take for granted a free personal subject who actually knows his voluntative object. Free judgement is also constituted by knowing what we can will and by the patterns of synchronic contingency which *willing* and *not-willing* have to follow (*Lectura* II 25.70).

Two concurring or cooperative factors can be structured according to three models. Interaction and concurrence can be purely accidental, as is the case when many people pull a cart. None of the factors – or pullers – is essential (§71). The second model implies that the one factor confers effective power or force on the other factor, as the sun causes processes on earth and ebb tide and high tide are dependent on the motion of the moon.[45] As to acts of will, the first model is rejected by Duns, because the constitutive elements of *willing* presuppose each other. The crucial components constitute an essential order (*per se ordo*). The second model does not satisfy, because the will and the object of knowledge do not confer causal power on each other. Intellect and will have each their own dynamics and their own causality.[46]

Having rejected the two first models Duns accepts the third model. An accidental connection is not sufficient. Nor does causal dependence delivers the solution. The third model stresses the interaction of two independent components which are essential in the act of willing and are ordered nevertheless. The will is the primary factor which guarantees the freedom of willing. Knowledge is related to reality in a different manner: it is bound to reality. *Knowing* is governed by the truth entailment.[47] This entailment of *knowing that* implies a *one-way* relation to actual reality, if the known reality is contingent. Although contingent reality is itself *two-way* ordered, knowledge of contingent reality is not – it is *one-way* ordered. This is what Duns means when he calls knowledge *naturalis* within the framework of the essential distinction between *natura/intellectus* and *voluntas*. The will is that faculty by which an agent acts freely, not *per modum naturae*.

Knowing that *p* entails the truth of *p*. However, *knowing that p* does not entail *willing that p*. John may be quite familiar with physics, but, nevertheless, he does not decide that he shall study physics. Moreover, he knows much more of Ann than he knows of Mary – and he thinks Ann is quite pretty – but he is in love with Mary. He who knows Oxford, its spires and meadows quite well, need not live there. According to Duns, the will is the main factor, just because *knowing* does not entail *willing*. Duns does not make the *will* operational – it is not the case that he is a practicing voluntarist while his opponents are not. Duns' theory of will is not only

---

[45] See *Lectura* II 14.33: 'Quantum ad motum localem, corpus caeleste habet influentiam super elementa, quia moventur ad motum corporis caelestis. [. . .] Et hoc patet de impressionibus, quae generantur in interstitio aeris, quod moventur circulariter. Similiter, hoc patet quantum ad motum aquae, quod luna habet ibi efficaciam, nam tumor aquae – ad quem sequitur fluxus et refluxus maris – sequitur motum lunae.' Cf. §10.6.

[46] *Lectura* II 25.73: 'Utrumque (*voluntas* and *natura actu cognoscens obiectum*) habet causalitatem propriam, perfectam in suo genere.'

[47] The formula of the truth entailment recognizable in all kinds of languages reads as follows: if *a* knows that *p*, then *p*. Cf. §8.3.

applicable to voluntarists, it is applicable to all men, even to deter-minists. Duns is not eager to invents facts; he only states them. Duns does not decree that the will must be operational in acts of willing and he does not reject the alternative theory asserting that the object of knowledge entails willing that object, for this excludes his own option. Duns simply acknowledges the operationality of acts of will, while knowledge does not activate as such, as all teachers are familiar with. *Knowing* does not entail *willing* as all preachers are familiar with. The will activates something else. This approach is at home in a wider web of Scotian preferences: in general, subjectivity enjoys preference. In epistemology, the epistemic subject enjoys prio-rity over the epistemic object.[48] As to *willing*, the subject has prece-dence over the object.

In terms of this model Duns Scotus defends the will as a rational faculty because it is able to act reasonably. The will can account for its choices in an argumentative manner (*ratione*). After deliberate consideration of what is better or worse, the agent freely elicits an act of will or a nolition.[49] The will is also a reasonable faculty, because it is able to appreciate a voluntative object for its own value. In that case, it focuses on the other from its affection for what is good and right. Anselm and Scotus call this the *affectio iustitiae*.[50]

11.5.3   Criticisms

All this indicates the distance between Duns Scotus' point of view and the Aristotelian approach in its broadest sense. In terms of such alter-native patterns, Duns believes, freedom of will, contingency of know-ledge, and personal subjectivity cannot be maintained. In *Summa Theologiae* I 82.4 in the body of the article Thomas Aquinas asserts that the good to be known is the object of the will which activates the will finally. Godfrey of Fontaines, Giles of Rome, and Thomas Sutton defended similar views. For them, the dilemma is: either the

---

[48] See *Lectura* I 3.365–368 and 379 f. Cf. *Lectura* I 3.380: 'Illud est causa perfectior quod primo agit et ad cuius actionem agit aliud; sed intellectus agit ad intellectionem et obiectum coagit, et non e converso, ut probatur; igitur anima sive intellectus erit perfectior causa intel-lectionis quam obiectum. Probatio minoris: intelligere est in potestate nostra, dicente Philosopho: "Intelligimus cum volumus"; sed intelligere non est in potestate nostra ex parte obiecti, quia quantum est ex parte obiecti, semper ageret et intelligeret.'

[49] A *nolition* is an act of willing that something is not the case.

[50] See Wolter, 'Native Freedom of the Will as a Key to the Ethics of Scotus,' in *The Philosophical Theology of Scotus*, 148–162. Cf. Frank's excellent contribution in his *John Duns Scotus' Quodlibetal Teaching on the Will*, chapter 5.

will is activated by something else, or it activates itself. The first element of the dilemma is as self-evident for them as the second one is absurd. We should not overlook the fact that Duns does not take the second horn of the dilemma. Duns realizes that the positions he is critical of do not make a united front (*Lectura* II 25.24 ff.). Duns rejects the fundamental passivity of our personal acts, because our acts of will would not be our own, if they were only passive (*Lectura* II 25.28). Duns also criticizes Godfrey of Fontaines and Thomas Sutton, but in this case the reader is struck by the fundamental criticisms of the views of Thomas Aquinas who, in general, is no special target in *Lectura* I–II.[51]

As to Thomas' theory, the main issue is, Duns believes, the freedom of the will,[52] and the issue of freedom is coming to a head when we realize that an agent who possesses sufficient preconditions of his own activity, owns an activity which does not lie within the range of what is passive. Natural factors precede every act of will and every act of knowledge. If an act of will strictly depends on the object, then the act of will is not within the power of the will and, so, it is no act of will. The horse ridden by the horseman cannot be the horseman. Therefore neither is he a person. Duns takes a step farther, for he links the act of knowledge with an act of will. In his *Quaestiones super libros Metaphysicorum Aristotelis* IX 15, he even portrays the will as the rational potency par excellence.[53]

Duns Scotus is not satisfied if a theory of will considers acts of will to be necessary or only grants acts of will the appearance of contingency (*Lectura* II 25.51 ff.). Neither does Duns favor the other extreme which states that only the will is the effective cause of willing. Henry of Ghent does not argue that the will keeps out of knowledge, but, according to him, only knowledge of the object of will is a necessary condition of willing (*Lectura* II 25.54). That is not enough for Duns. If a sense is a purely active potency, we shall always experience it. If the will is a purely active potency, nothing else need activate our will. Such a will would move on to action merely from itself, without any intentionality with respect to the object. 'If the will were an active potency in itself being sufficient to cause an act of will, [. . .] then it

---

[51] He only receives special attention in Duns Scotus' ethics (*Lectura Oxoniensis* III).

[52] *Lectura* II 25.29: 'propter [. . .] libertatem voluntatis salvandam.'

[53] See Wolter, 'Duns Sotus on the Will as Rational Potency,' in *The Philosophical Theology of Scotus*, 163–180, cf. 35, 37, and 144–173. Cf. *Lectura* I 25.30: 'Unde volitio quae est ab obiecto non est in potestate eius [namely, *voluntatis*]; in potestate tamen eius est quod voluntas faciat intelligere intellectam vel non intelligere, in operando.' See also *Lectura* I 25.36 f.

can move on to acting from itself.'[54] According to Duns, in terms of the first type of a theory of will the act of will is swallowed up by the reality of the objects; in terms of the second option it is the act of will which swallows up the object.

What matters is a delicate balance of subjectivity and objectivity. In the case of absolute voluntarism the potency of will becomes an infinite power and it is this complaint of Duns which returns in the seventeenth century when Revius criticizes Descartes.[55] Duns rejects both objectivism – and passivism – and subjectivism. In terms of 'passivism,' intentionality and object-relatedness are dropped.

> The act of willing is essentially related to an object as what is measured is related to a measure, and not *vice versa*. The fact that one wills a stone does not make the stone dependent on the will [. . .]. The act of will does not depend on knowing the object as something that was caused before. (*Lectura* II 25.66)

The upshot would be a miraculous life if the love of a believer is unfounded. Consequently, faith would be unreasonable.[56]

In spite of the criticisms of the great minds of previous generations, the result is remarkably constructive. Duns presents his own solution as a middle course, but not because he wants to run with the hare and to hunt with the hounds.[57] Neither is Duns interested in criticism as such. It is his method to take a crucial dilemma and to force a solution on the basis of a point the opponent shares with him. He incorporates the best sides of the alternative theories of predecessors like Thomas Aquinas and Henry of Ghent. From the start, he pays much attention to the most radical 'Aristotelian' of his day: Godfrey of Fontaines. In this case, his strategy is remarkable because he integrates the strong parts of Thomas Aquinas and his followers into the fundamental pattern put forward by Henry of Ghent, already foreshadowed in the theology of Augustine and Anselm. The *subject* dimension of willing, essentially connected with true freedom, is stressed by Henry of Ghent,

---

[54] *Lectura* II 25.55: 'Si voluntas esset potentia activa sufficiens ad causandum actum volendi, igitur esset in potentia accidentali ad volendum; sed quod est in potentia accidentali, ex se potest exire in actum. Igitur, voluntas semper de se potest velle.'

[55] *Lectura* II 25.65. Cf. Theo Verbeek, *Descartes and the Dutch*.

[56] *Lectura* II 25.67: 'Si dicatur quod Deus per miraculum potest causare dilectionem perfectiorem, saltem sequitur quod voluntas potest habere dilectionem aeque perfectam circa bonum delectabile absens sicut circa bonum delectabile praesens existens, si maiore conatu feratur in ipsum – quod falsum est, quia perfectius potest amari bonum delectabile quando est praesens quam quando est absens.'

[57] *Lectura* II 25.69: 'Teneo viam mediam.'

and the *objective* side of willing is highlighted by Aquinas. Both elements return in Duns' approach as pillars of his model. This constructive line is elicited by the relational character of *willing* and *knowing*.

11.6 PARIS VERSUS OXFORD?

For centuries Scotus' method earned a lot of admiration. However, after the decline of scholasticism in about 1800, the contingency dimension of Western thought disappears from the philosophical scene in the course of the first half of the nineteenth century. Carlo Balic, the discoverer of numerous Scotus manuscripts, went through a difficult period halfway the 1920s and his sense of danger is even mirrored in the fact that he assumed that Duns Scotus had to retract his views on the will at Oxford. Among the important appendixes of Balic's *Les commentaires de Jean Duns Scot* we find Appendix II which contains William of Alnwick's *Additiones magnae secundi libri* (II) 25, an important text on the will, commenting on *Sententiae* II 25, which was provisionally edited by Balic.[58] His interpretation of the information preserved in this chapter by William of Alnwick concludes that Duns had already corrected his doctrine of the will at Oxford. Balic's references mirror the battle which raged on Scotus' philosophy during the 1920s in France (Landry, Longpré):

> We know that Duns Scotus' voluntarism has been for centuries the center of lively controversies. Nowadays, the Scotists themselves do not agree whether, for instance, the intellect has to be considered as an effective partial cause of an act of will according to the doctrine of Scotus.[59]

Balic offered the text in order to foster research on this issue and promised to edit a second text in the near future. This promise was soon carried out for he edited *Lectura* II 25, which is now to be found in Scotus' *Opera Omnia* XIX, in 1931.[60]

---

[58] Balic, *Les commentaires de Jean Duns Scot*, 264–301: *Additiones Magnae* II 25. *Appendix* IV, containing texts taken from *Lectura completa* (= *Lectura Oxoniensis* III) is also particularly conspicuous.

[59] Balic, *Les commentaires de Jean Duns Scot*, 264. *Additiones Magnae* II 25 offers the same doctrine as *Lectura* II 25, but is quite differently arranged, especially focusing on theories put forward by Thomas Aquinas and Godfrey of Fontaines. Cf. §3.5.

[60] Balic, 'Une question inédite de J. Duns Scot sur la volonté,' *Recherches de théologie ancienne et médiévale* 3 (1931) 191–218. He did so on the basis of the Viennese manuscript *Codex Lat. 1449*. See §3.6.8.

The text of Alnwick caused a lot of confusion. First, it contests a Christian version of the Aristotelian theory of will, but Alnwick also continues immediately to discuss the opposite theory of Henry of Ghent, without indicating this explicitly, adding the interesting historical note: 'He [= Duns] refuted this theory, I say, many times in Oxford.'[61] The refutation of Henry of Ghent's view is rounded off as follows: 'Therefore, he discussed this problem in a *different* manner in Oxford.'[62] Balic concluded that Duns had put forward in Oxford views *different* from his Parisian lectures, but this 'different' refers to Henry of Ghent, and not to the Parisian Scotus himself. The true meaning of Alnwick's communication is that Duns had often refuted Henry's views in Oxford, not that he had been forced to retract his own view.[63] Alnwick's *Additiones Magnae secundi libri* was already playing a major part in Balic's principal work.[64] He also expounds that, according to Balic, Duns' theory of matter (*Lectura* II 15) and his theory of the will (*Lectura* II 25) differed from the insights launched in Paris, but any evidence of this is missing. Balic's hypothesis that Duns lectured twice at Paris on *Sententiae* II is likewise unfounded. Doctrinally, Alnwick is perfectly reliable.

The present chairman and former secretary of the *Commissio Scotistica*, B. Hechich, mainly edited *Lectura* II 7–44 and reported on the solution of the Oxford-Paris problem in a fascinating section, which also deals with other problems of textual criticism. The

---

[61] *Les commentaires de Jean Duns Scot*, 276 f.: 'Notandum quod secundun hanc opinionem, que ponit voluntatem esse totam causam activam voluntatis et obiectum non esse activum eius nec cognitio obiecti, sed quod obiectum requiritur sicut causa sine qua non, cognitio vero propter amotionem sive solutionem impedimenti, quia cognitio unius obiecti impedit ne aliud non cognitum possit appeti, et ideo voluntas removet impedimentum imperando intellectum ad cognoscendum sive considerandum aliud obiectum; *hanc inquam opinionem Oxonie multipliciter improbavit.*'

[62] Op. cit., 282: 'Ideo et aliter dixit Oxonie ad questionem, quod volitio est per se a voluntate, ut a causa activa et ab obiecto intellecto ut ab alia causa partiali, ita quod totalis causa volitionis includit intellectum in actu primo et secundo, voluntatem in actu primo et obiectum.' Cf. *Lectura* II 25.68–69. The continuation of Alnwick's argumentation runs parallel to *Lectura* II 25.70 ff.

[63] Cf. *Lectura* II 25.54: 'Alia opinio – Gandavi – extrema est, quod sola voluntas est causa effectiva respectu actus volendi, et obiectum cognitum est tantum causa "sine qua non".' Alnwick's description fits in with this section. So, Alnwick's communication concerns the contest of Henry of Ghent by Duns in Oxford.

[64] *Les commentaires de Jean Duns Scot*, 93–101. *Codex 208* (Balliol College) contains an excellent text of the *Additiones* which says that this summary is composed by William of Alnwick on the basis of the Parisian and Oxonian courses (folio 40v). Cf. Balic, op. cit., 103 f. and 107 f.

Committee made this discovery when preparing volume XIX of the *Opera Omnia* during the 1980s.[65] The present conclusion of the *Commissio Scotistica* is our final chord: Duns Scotus always subscribed to the same type of doctrine of will.[66]

11.7 FREEWILL AND FREEDOM

The existential center of Duns Scotus' thought is his attention to God in Christ within the whole of the reality of faith. It is crucial always to hold on to the will – contingency structure. The new conceptual contents also require language shifts and the history of the term *velle* illustrates this phenomenon. Wolter shed new light on the will tradition and at the same time always contested the arbitrariness interpretation. When Anthony Quinton summarized Duns Scotus' view in 1967 as follows: 'Things are good because God wills them,' Wolter refuted this interpretation elaborately.[67] In *Reportatio Parisiensis* III 17, the last chapter of Duns' Parisian course on *Sententiae* III, Duns indicates that *voluntas* (*will*) generally means 'striving/endeavor accompanied by reasoning' (*appetitus cum ratione*). *Appetitus* (striving, 'appetite') itself has two meanings: sensory (*sensitivus*) and rational (*rationalis*) – being active with the help of the senses and being active by thinking and reasoning.[68]

Wolter saw that Duns Scotus integrated the Anselmian revolution in the theory of will. 'Appealing to Anselm he argued that the will has a twofold attraction towards the good. One is the affection for what is to our advantage [*affectio commodi*]. [. . .] But there is a second and more noble tendency, an inclination or affection for justice [*affectio iustitiae*].'[69] The first sort of *willing* is derived from the original meaning of 'velle' in classical Latin. *Velle* means *to be*

---

[65] *Opera Omnia* XIX, Rome (March–June) 1993, 38*–41*. The former president Luka Modric had already indicated some new discoveries in 'Rapporto tra la *Lectura* II e la Metaphysica di G. Duns Scoto,' *Antonianum* 62 (1987) 504–509.

[66] *Opera Omnia* XIX 41*: 'Duns Scotus suam de actu volitionis doctrinam nec retractavit nec immutavit, sed eandem constanter docuit.' There is no problem at all, let alone a problem of heresy.

[67] 'British Philosophy,' *EP* I 373. See Wolter, 'Native Freedom of the Will as a Key to the Ethics of Scotus' (1972), *The Philosophical Theology of Scotus*, 148–162. Cf. idem, *Duns Scotus on the Will and Morality*, 3 ff.

[68] See *Reportatio Parisiensis* III 17 in: *Codex 206* (Balliol College), f. 141r. Cf. Wolter, *Duns Scotus on the Will and Morality*, 126–128, and idem, *The Philosophical Theology of Scotus*, 148 ff. and 163 ff.

[69] Wolter, *The Philosophical Theology of Scotus*, 151.

inclined. The second sort of *willing* is elicited by the semantic needs of the Christian faith and takes on a new meaning of active and resolute *willing*, just as in English *to will* in the sense of articulated *willing* (= *velle* II) expands on the semantic field of *to want* (*velle* I). To will, in the sense of *to wish* or *to want*, is much more akin to *velle* in classical Latin which is connected with what suits and is convenient for me and is convenient to me (*bonum commodi*), while the new Christian sense of *willing* is especially a matter of what we *ought to* do. Duns also refers himself to Anselm's *De casu diaboli* 14 and *De concordia* III 19.[70]

The precise definition of the nature of the will occurs in Duns Scotus' christology. He expounded *Sententiae* III 17 three times: *Lectura Oxoniensis* III 17 (1303), *Reportatio Parisiensis* III 17 (1305), and in about 1307: *Ordinatio* III 17. One might also account for two wills in Christ in Aristotelian terms. The opposition suggests that there is a natural will and a free will in Christ, a lower and a higher part in his soul.

11.7.1   *Lectura Oxoniensis* III 17

Lectura III 17 deals with the issue of Christ's two wills in an elaborate and theological way. The answer is given in terms of Christ's two natures, with a plea from John Damascene. The anthropological part has become a substantial one, while the fall is addressed in a rather intriguing section. It is obvious that the will and not desire is the key property.[71]

Duns observes that, in general, *voluntas* and *appetitus* may be used as synonyms. In this case, there have to be more wills in Christ, for, according to this usage, 'will' also refers to the sensory 'drive' and, so, there as many 'drives' as senses. Duns explicitly states that every sense has its own *appetitus*, for seeing or sight (*visus*) has a relation to what is visible different from the relation hearing or the sense of hearing (*auditus*) has with regard to what is audible. Duns eventually arrives at the *will* in its proper sense, which transcends *appetitus* (drive). The will is defined as *appetitus cum ratione liber* – a free striving which is argued and accounted for. The question to be considered is still: is the

---

[70] See *Ordinatio* III 26 and Wolter, *Duns Scotus on the Will and Morality*, 178 f.
[71] *Codex 206*, f. 55v: 'Proprietates naturales utriusque et per consequens potentie consequuntur naturas inter quas perfectior est voluntas. Ergo sicut in Christo sunt due nature, et due potentie.' Cf. §3.6.12.

natural will a potency different from the free will or not? Duns apprehends the will essentially as 'drive' and strive – a kind of orientation
which is proper to the will itself in order to serve its own completeness. What falling is for what is heavy, willing is for the free will. So,
the natural will and the free will are no different potencies.[72] The
will includes a natural inclination towards its own completeness.
Therefore, the natural inclination is no potency different from the will
itself and the natural will and the free will are not two potencies. The
interaction is also made explicit. The characterizations *naturalis* and
ex puris naturalibus are related to the essential structure of the will
so that freedom is entailed by the will's nature:

> In the third way, we talk of will, when the will elicits an act, which
> agrees with its natural inclination. In this way, the will is also free will,
> because the will elicits freely which is in agreement with its natural
> inclination, while he also elicits another act which runs counter to the
> natural inclination. In this way, it is obvious that the natural will is
> no other potency.[73]

In other words, assume that an ice cream entices me, just as *Lectura*
II 7–44 does, but, regardless of empirical sensitivity, it is the free act
of will, which takes along the empirical substratum, either through
affirming or ignoring it. It is one process of will, where freedom
absorbs what is purely psychological and molds it to its will.

11.7.2 *Reportatio Parisiensis* III 17

Duns holds on to the view that the will of Christ constitutes one
whole. The will as natural inclination is a 'drive' in the broad sense
of the word, wanting what is convenient and suitable for itself or for
its own good (*inclinatio ad commoda*):

> If we consider the will as eliciting natural acts, nevertheless, there is
> the one potency as it is inclined towards an act, being really identical
> with the free will.[74]

---

[72] *Codex 206* (Balliol College) f. 55v: 'Uno modo dicitur voluntas naturalis appetitus et inclinatio naturalis ipsius voluntatis ad perfectionem naturalem sibi propriam et sic in quolibet
ente est appetitus naturalis ad perfectionem propriam, sicut in gravi ad esse deorsum.'

[73] *Codex 206*, f. 56r: 'Tercio modo dicitur voluntas quando elicit actum conformem inclinationi naturali et sic etiam est voluntas libera, quia voluntas libere elicit actum conformem
inclinationi naturali et alium elicit actum contra inclinationem naturalem et sic manifestum
est quod voluntas naturalis non est alia potentia.'

[74] *Codex 206*, f. 141r. Cf. *Codex 206*, ff. 1–104: *Lectura Oxoniensis* III and ff. 105–142:
Reportatio Parisiensis III.

Both dimensions of the will are seen as tightly linked. A distinction may be made, but the will as inclination (*inclinatio*) is only a 'layer' in the whole of the one free will. The crucial point of view is that the will is as such *domina sui actus*. Assume that inclinations or 'instincts' show us the way so that we act accordingly, then such activity is exactly based on a decision of the free will. Here, the theory of the active free will itself absorbs natural 'behaviorism.'

11.7.3   *Ordinatio* III 17

What will Duns Scotus' next step be in *Ordinatio* III 17? We meet lines of argumentation we are already acquainted with, followed by a surprising move:

> I say that the will is in a different position: the natural will is no will, neither is natural willing *willing*, but 'natural' injures both. A natural will is nothing else than a relation, which follows from the potency in terms of its own completeness. Hence, the same potency is called a natural will having such a relation which follows necessarily its own completeness and it is called free according its own and intrinsic relation, which is the will in its specific sense.[75]

Here, the original main lines of *Lectura* III 17 and *Reportatio Parisiensis* III 17 get a specific new twist. A new clarity reigns and yields a new power to the text of *Ordinatio* III 17. The old notion of natural willing is no longer incorporated in Duns Scotus' theory of will. He now drops the two dimensions view, but the blunt wording is: 'natural will' and 'natural willing' are contradictory expressions *in adiecto*. 'Natural' is incompatible with *will*. *Willing* cannot be *one-way*. It is obvious that here *naturalis* means '*essential*.' If *a* wills that *p*, then *willing that p* cannot be essential for *a*.

The will is as such free and if what the will aims at, suits and pleases the will, then the will is called 'natural' in that respect, but from its own structure the will is a *two-way* and open potency. I will toast someone's health and quench my thirst while we drink together; nevertheless, drinking together is a free activity, because I need not do so. We like someone else and, at the same time, we quench our thirst.

---

[75] *Ordinatio* III 17 (Wolter, *Duns Scotus on the Will and Morality*, 182): 'Tunc dico quod sic est de voluntate, quia voluntas non est voluntas nec velle naturale est velle, sed ly naturalis distrahit ab utroque et nihil est nisi relatio consequens potentiam respectu propriae perfectionis. Unde eadem potentia dicitur naturalis voluntas cum respectu tali necessario consequente ipsam ad perfectionem, et dicitur libera secundum relationem propriam et intrinsecam, quae est voluntas specifice.'

Then, it is not the case that we will freely, because we quench our thirst spontaneously, but precisely because we can give preference to someone else or to something else. Along these lines, Duns can continue his line of argumentation with:

> I grant [. . .] that every will is queen over his own act. [. . .] I say that the natural will is to be characterized as follows: the will as far as it is *natural* does not function as a potency, but it only implies the inclination of a potency to tend towards its own completeness, not to acting as such. For this reason, the will is only complete if it possesses that completeness to which that tendency inclines that potency. Hence, a natural potency does not tend, but is the tendency by which the independent will tends, namely passively in order to receive something. However, there is another tendency in the same potency so that it tends freely and actively by eliciting an act so that one and the same potency is a twofold – namely an active and passive – tendency. Then, I say that the natural will is not a potency, namely *will*, as far as its formal aspect is entailed, but an inclination and tendency of the will by which it tends to receive passively which makes it complete.[76]

What the whole story in Aristotelian terms boils down to is a functional substratum for letting the true will work as complete as possible. The theory of will transforms the doctrine of God handed down through the ages as the new doctrine of the Trinity amply testifies to. Analogously, the theory of will transforms anthropology, and ethics as well. Duns does not indulge in 'wishful thinking.' The profile of his theory of will follows from the anatomy of willing as is demonstrated in reality. Analogously, the profile of his theory of freedom rests upon the anatomy of freedom in reality. We also need the profile of human freedom in order to understand divine will and freedom on the level of their similarities, in spite of all incisive differences. The profile of freedom of the human will is to be sketched as follows:

1. The human will is, primarily, free towards *opposite acts* (*acts of will*). I call this freedom *active freedom*. Within this context, Duns

[76] Ibid.: 'Concedo [. . .] quia omnis voluntas sit domina sui actus. [. . .] Dico quod voluntas naturalis sic, et ut naturalis non est voluntas ut potentia, sed tantum importat inclinationem potentiae ad tendendum in propriam perfectionem suam, non ad agendum ut sic. Et ideo, est imperfecta nisi sit sub illa perfectione ad quam illa tendentia inclinat illam potentiam. Unde naturalis potentia non tendit, sed est tendentia illa qua voluntas absoluta tendit, et hoc passive ad recipiendum. Sed est alia tendentia in potentia eadem ut libere et active tendat eliciendo actum, ita quod una potentia est duplex tendentia activa et passiva. Tunc, ad formam, dico quod voluntas naturalis, secundum quod formale importat, non est potentia, vel voluntas, sed inclinatio voluntatis et tendentia qua tendit in perfectione passive recipiendum.'

talks of first, second and third freedom several times.[77] The *active* freedom is the first freedom. Examples of opposite acts of will according to the first type of freedom are: *willing* changing to *willing that not, loving* changing to *hating*. This sort of freedom is somewhat contaminated, for freedom in this sense has something imperfect, because such freedom includes changeability and, for this reason, changeability for the worse. God does not have any imperfect freedom.[78]

2. The second freedom of the human will is related to *opposite objects*. I call this freedom *objective freedom*. This freedom is mediated by opposite acts of will. This sort of freedom is as such complete and perfect. Our will can address itself toward different things which are to be willed, in virtue of different acts of will. If one item of what is to be willed excludes that something opposite can be willed, incompleteness and imperfection would be unavoidable. Both God and man possess this type of perfect freedom.

3. The third freedom is *effective freedom.*The human will is free towards *opposite effects*. This kind of freedom as such is not imperfect, because the second objective freedom can be associated with this freedom. The third sort of freedom does not regard the characteristic difference between divine and human freedom, because this type of freedom can be had on the basis of the second type of freedom. On the contrary, the first kind of so-called active freedom is only applicable to humans, because it is impossible that God changes his will unfortunately.

So, the hinge everything is turning around is the second type of objective freedom. How does this freedom work in the case of men?

A human act of will is bound to its object. There is a definite restriction at work. If the will has an object of will, then it is not the case that the will does not have that object of will for the same time. In order to reach a different or another object the act of will has to change. Therefore in human affairs the fine second freedom implies the first. Writing a kind of Thomas' *Scriptum* or making an Ajax transfer cannot be the object of the same act of willing of a human person (*volitio, actus voluntatis*) when the same act of will is oriented towards writing a kind of Duns' *Lectura* or making a Manchester United transfer,

---

[77] See *Lectura* I 39.45–48 and 53. Cf. *Ordinatio* I 39.21 in *Opera Omnia* VI.
[78] See *Lectura* I 39.45 f. and 53.

> for there is no freedom in our will such that it simultaneously wills
> opposite objects, because they are not simultaneously the term of one
> potency. (*Lectura* I 39.47)

A human person can only reach different objects of will through the
mediation of different acts of will.[79] Divine and human freedom meet
each other as follows:

1. Although both enjoy the second – objective – freedom, the human
   will has this complete and perfect freedom in a diachronic sense:
   the human will does not reach out to opposite objects of will in a
   synchronic manner.
2. In the case of men, the first – active – freedom flows from the second,
   with God the second objective freedom excludes the first. In sum:

   God: freedom 2 and freedom 3, without freedom 1.
   Man: freedom 2 in a limited way and freedom 1 on the basis of freedom
   2, and freedom 3 on the basis of freedom 2 and freedom 1.

Freedom 2 and 3 imply two sorts of *contingency*: diachronic contingency, affiliated to real, radical contingency, and synchronic contingency. The Scotian concept of will is filled from the new theory of
contingency.

11.8 PERSPECTIVE

In Duns Scotus' thought, theology is the heart of the matter of
anthropology. To adapt a famous adage (Feuerbach): anthropology
is theology. This structure is based on the theocentric and christocentric character of all possible reality. Man is the image of God
(*imago Dei*) and this definition of being human touches humanity on
the level of man's nature, just as the later reformational theology
shall say, in its Augustinian vein: the image of God is 'naturalis'
(Maccovius), and not super-natural. The God-based necessary
propositions of necessary theology deliver the preconditions of the
whole of Duns Scotus' thought.

Duns Scotus not only defines the structure of anthropology in
terms of his concept of will, but also by constitutive cross connections
linking different parts of his thought. In particular, his theories of
individuality and contingency and his ethics have to be observed in

---

[79] See *Lectura* I 39.45: 'mediantibus actibus oppositis.'

this respect. The first thing to be done is to restore the coherence of all Duns Scotus' theories. Divine creativity and free will, human freedom and sinfulness, and so on, turn out to be logically connected.

> Thus the affection for justice provides the natural basis for a rational ethical philosophy. Both affections are essential to human nature, but they can be perfected supernaturally and directed to God as their object. Charity perfects the will's affection for justice, inclining it to love God for his own sake.[80]

Freedom of will and rationality are integrally linked. 'The will alone has the basic freedom, when it acts with reason, for alternate modes of acting'[81] Scotus promotes the philosophy of the early Franciscans into a consistent whole of thinking.

Duns' theory is excellent philosophical consolation. What counts is life considered to be good by the best possible Person, to be lived by the individual. The individual is good and precious. God is the most precious possible person. The will of the individual is the seat of virtue and God is the source of virtue. They are together in love. All this is a piece of necessary, philosophical, ethics. It was the dream, the theory, and the life of a young genius. Alasdair MacIntyre distinguished between tradition, encyclopaedia, and genealogy, but he neglected the best tradition.[82] Thus we lose the adequate alternative to 'encyclopedia' and 'genealogy.' In the light of the alternative Anselm-Scotus tradition we may conclude: the individual is precious, individual virtue is needed.

---

[80] Wolter, 'John Duns Scotus,' *ER* IV 515.
[81] Wolter, 'John Duns Scotus,' *ER* V 514. Wolter's hypothesis runs that Duns Scotus weaves the Augustinian line into the Aristotelian main tradition. However, these models are incompatible and the medieval model is a new achievement, illustrating the dynamics of the development of anthropology.
[82] See MacIntyre, *Three Rival Versions of Moral Enquiry*, chapters 7–9. Cf. Manzano, 'Das An-sich-Sein der Freiheit nach J. D. Scotus,' in Schneider (ed.), *Fons Salutis Trinitas – Quell des Heils Dreifaltigkeit*, 79–100.

CHAPTER 12

Ethical structures and issues

12.1 INTRODUCTION

In antiquity, ethical interests were different from what they are now in Western thought. In Greek *philosophia*, ethics is more something given than a set of problems and issues to be reflected on, because the connection between *nature* and customs, commands, precepts, or law is intrinsic. What is at stake here depends on the ontological impact of the ideas of *being essential* and *reality*. If natural law is invoked as a standard, what kind of rule is to be invoked? Does the validity of this rule consist in being invoked or is reality as such law-like and natural? The non-Christian type of *natural law* is clearly expressed by the Roman philosopher Cicero (106–43 BC): true law is right reason in agreement with nature. It is of universal application, unchangeable and everlasting; it summons to duty by its commands, and averts from wrongdoing by its prohibitions.[1] We may put the key notions of *law*, *reason*, *truth*, and *nature* within the contexts of Platonism, Aristotelianism, Stoic or Neoplatonist thought and we find that still the same pattern of absolute reality obtains, although the nature of this reality is interpreted in different ways.

The decisive point is whether *being natural* is seen as an ethical or political rule in its own right or *nature* itself is a kind of society and social reality truly natural.[2] According to ancient thought, everything is necessary, law-like and natural. This necessitarianism is the hard core of every important movement of ancient philosophy, apart from patristic thought, and even the philosophy of the church fathers only deviates from it on an intuitive level, although its rejection of the necessitarian view of reality is clear.

---

[1] See Marcus Tullius Cicero, *De re publica*. Cf. Sturm, 'Natural law,' *ER* X 318–324, and Finnis, 'Natural law,' *REP* VI 685–690.

[2] See Beth, 'Metafysica en wetenschap' en 'Algemene beschouwingen over causaliteit,' in *Door wetenschap tot wijsheid*, 28–36 and 74–81. Cf. Beth, *De wijsbegeerte der wiskunde van Parmenides tot Bolzano*, 5–92, and Finnis (ed.), *Natural Law* I–II.

It is a remarkable fact that the history of Western ethics possesses a
main alternative. It is even more remarkable that this alternative mainstream of thought in Augustine, Anselm, and Duns Scotus has largely
been forgotten.[3] Anselm and Scotus are conspicuous by their absence
in Alasdair MacIntyre's *A Short History of Ethics* (1966). Duns' theory
of virtues is missing in his *After Virtue*. Neither Anselm nor Duns
Scotus are mentioned in *After Virtue* at all, Augustine is mentioned
once and Thomas Aquinas is only marginally dealt with.[4] This situation drastically changed in *Whose Justice? Which Rationality?* (1988)
and in *Three Rival Versions of Moral Enquiry* (1990), where
Augustine and Aquinas keep Aristotle company.

> While scholastic writers other than Aquinas continue to receive
> comparatively little attention, Aquinas's own thought is discussed
> at considerable length. No more is MacIntyre's tragic hero the
> Aristotelian tradition; it is now the Thomistic tradition. The
> 'Thomistic dialectical synthesis', which reconciles the radical conflict
> between Aristotelianism and Augustinianism, yields to increasingly
> incoherent and indefensible rivals, until the West finally degener-
> ates into liberal individualism, the worst tradition of them all.[5]

MacIntyre is fair enough to make a disclaimer. 'My account of
Aquinas's work as the culmination and integration of the Augustinian
and Aristotelian traditions is not at all how Aquinas was understood
by much the greater part of both his contemporaries and his immediate successors.'[6] However, there is still a *bête noire*: Duns Scotus who
rejected Aristotle's psychology. The consequences of this rejection
were of primary importance for future history. MacIntyre sees Scotus'
ethics as a type of ethics founded on a command theory and 'if
the answer is that the command is God's and that God is wholly
good, then the questions arise as to whether, counterfactually, we
would still be morally obliged if God had not so commanded.'[7]

In their *History of Ethics*, Abelson and Nielsen signaled only
Scotus' 'voluntarism.'[8] Duns Scotus' ideas are not discussed in Gene

---

[3] The recent change of climate, however, is remarkable. See Wolter, *Scotus on the Will and Morality* (1986), Shannon, *The Ethical Theory of John Duns Scotus* (1995), Möhle, *Ethik als scientia practica nach Johann Duns Scotus* (1995), and Ingham, *The Harmony of Goodness* (1996).

[4] See MacIntyre, *After Virtue*, 165–168 and 186–189.

[5] Kent, *Virtues of the Will*, 20 (19–25). Cf. Vos, 'De ethische optie van Duns Scotus,' *Kerk en Theologie* 44 (1993) 17 f., 24–28 and 31 f., and *DS* 84 and 101 f.

[6] MacIntyre, *Three Rival Versions of Moral Enquiry*, 151.

[7] MacIntyre, *Three Rival Versions of Moral Enquiry*, 155 (154–157). Cf. §§12.3–12.6.

[8] See Abelson, 'History of Ethics,' *EP* III 90 (81–117).

Ouka's fine *Agape* (1972), although his ethics is an ethics of love (see §§12.4–12.5). The written history of Western thought shows a one-sided view, which is not matched by acknowledging the influence of Thomism in later European thought. Indeed:

> It was the achievement of St. Thomas Aquinas that he managed, within a certain framework of thought, to solve what might be called the 'selectivity' problem of natural-law theory by grafting on to the Stoic principle of 'Follow nature' the Aristotelian concept of nature as a teleological system. The general principles of the law of nature are, St. Thomas argued, known equally to all through their use of reason. [. . .] That phenomena are divided into natural kinds, that each natural kind is distinguished by the possession of an essence, that the essence stipulates an end, that virtue and goodness are necessarily linked with the fulfillment of these ends – these are some of the assumptions behind St. Thomas' *lex naturae*.[9]

Thomas Aquinas and Scotus shared substantial views of the *patrimonium fidei* on an intuitive level, but their theoretical outlook was quite different. Moreover, the sphere at Oxford at the close of the thirteenth century differed markedly from what was the case in Paris more than one generation before. Oxford was not battered by internal conflicts as Paris's university had been during the 1260s and the 1270s. Oxford followed its own semantic and logical tracks.

In the next section the bare challenge of Scotian ethical dilemmas is presented. §12.3 interprets the key words of Duns Scotus' ethical terminology with a view to his language of argumentation in ethics, for the technicalities of this language are the foundation stone in order to explain the natural law expressions *lex naturalis* (*natural law*), *lex naturae* (*law of nature*) and *recta ratio* (*right reason*).[10] In §12.4 the outlines of Scotian ethics are presented. The essentials of his philosophy of love are sketched in §12.5 and a theme, typical of Duns Scotus passionately rejecting slavery, is dealt with in §12.6. The *Quintonian* and *Harrisian fallacies* are solved in the next section (§12.7) and §12.8 treats of the Scotian solution of the problem of dispensation from law. §12.9 deals with the structure of virtue and §12.10 with the unity of virtue, before we conclude with 'Perspective' (§12.11).

---

[9] Wollheim, 'Natural law,' *EP* V 451–452.

[10] For *ratio, ratio recta* and *ratio erronea, ratio necessaria* and *ratio naturalis, propositio per se evidens* and *persuasio*, see §9.2.

12.2   Duns' ethical paradox

We read in many handbooks of church and dogma history that 'his criticism of Aristotle and Thomas Aquinas was utterly intelligent and he taught in Oxford, Cambridge, Paris and, at last, as *lector* at the *Studium* of his Order in Cologne.'[11] Traditional research found it difficult to discover the inner coherence of Scotus' thought. The reputable Gilson confesses in the introduction of his famous *Introduction* that the reader will fail to find the sketch of a 'system.' The simple reason, he wrote, is that he found none.[12] De Bruin's characterization sees Scotus' strength in his acute analysis and critical mind as his weakness. The same tone we also learn from Knowles's *The Religious Orders in England*: 'Unfortunately, he found it necessary to express himself in novel technical terms, and to create a forest of metaphysical forms which make it next to impossible for a reader to comprehend his thought unless he is willing to "bolte him to the bren".'[13]

In ethics, the central dilemma concerns the traditional complaint of Duns Scotus' alleged voluntarism. What is good is good because God has willed it so. God's will would have been subjected to God's intellect, if He would have willed it, because it is good. Historians and philosophers meet in this choir. A black–white contrast with Thomas Aquinas also belongs to this picture.

> Over and against Thomas Aquinas who adhered to the primacy of the intellect, Duns was a fiery protagonist of the priority of the will. This is especially crucial in the doctrine of God and in anthropology. The will enjoys primacy in God too. This divine will is the ultimate ground of all being and itself without any ground. Something is good, because God has willed so, and the reason that God has willed it, is not that it is good.[14]

Of course, divine will enjoys a key position in Duns Scotus' ontology, but, nevertheless, things are different (see §§12.3–12.5).

Understanding Scotus depends on accompanying him on his ways of terminological and systematic proposals. He explores his own ideas within his own personal framework of concepts and theories. Simple

---

[11] C. C. de Bruin, *Handboek der Kerkgeschiedenis* II, Franeker ⁵1981, 174.

[12] Gilson, *Jean Duns Scot. Introduction à ses positions fondamentales*, 7–10.

[13] Knowles, *The Religious Orders in England* I, 237.

[14] A. D. R. Polman, 'Johannes Duns Scotus,' *Christelijke Encyclopedie* II, Kampen ²1977 (first printing ²1957), 520.

summaries and easy catchwords are not of any help. In mapping his ethical viewpoints, we have to start where the medieval scholars started themselves, namely in the subjects of the *trivium* (see Chapters 4–6 and 9). There is also an ontological center – the *infinite being* who is identical with the theological center – *God* in his own identity, the historical center of his own salvation history. All this is common Christian heritage and there is the central theoretical tool in the concept of *logical possibility* and the theory of *synchronic contingency* which lends coherence and clarity to the whole of Scotus' systematic fabric. Reality is open whether it be open or closed according to experience. Individuals and institutions may feel that they are locked in, but we can only be locked in if there is open space. Freedom and contingency are essential characteristics of reality. There is no logical room to ignore them. The same holds good for God, his free will and love. Divine will is full of unselfish and abundant love in willing people who serve through free will.

12.3 SCOTIAN ETHICAL LANGUAGE

12.3.1 An analytical family of terms

In philosophy Duns Scotus mainly acknowledges as philosophy what we may call 'necessary philosophy.'[15] In theology things are different. In theology, contingency is decisive and the theoretical framework of contingency is used to build up an alternative methodology. In terms of the basic phenomenon of contingent propositions or states of affairs the important role of necessary propositions in theology is discovered. Here, we have to distinguish *necessary theology* from *contingent theology*. Likewise, we have to distinguish *necessary ethics* from *contingent ethics*. This role yields the solution to a fundamental problem in ethical theory, namely, that of key terms like *lex naturae*, *ius naturae*, and *ratio recta*.

The hypothesis I propose is that the semantic background of these terms is to be clarified with the help of the terms *ratio naturalis* and *ratio necessaria*. These terms belong to a family of analytical terms and we need an introduction of some other members. In order to explain the notion of *ratio naturalis*, we need to explain the family of *ratio*, but the modern notion of *the reason* (*Vernunft*) is not helpful.

---

[15] *Necessary philosophy* is that part of philosophy which consists of necessary propositions and what can be derived from them.

12.3.2 Natural and necessary

We observe the duality of necessity and contingency in ethics. The duality of *necessary ethics* and *contingent ethics* constitutes the methodological ellipse of Scotian ethics. It is the key to a proper understanding of Scotus' *natural reason* and *natural law* terminology and to solving the difficulty of Scotus' so-called 'voluntarism.' The viewpoint of *de lege naturae* is at the center of defining elementary terms of necessary ethics, but what does it mean that something is valid in terms of *natural reason* and *natural law* (*de lege naturae*)? The analytical and semantic expositions of §§9.2–9.3 function as an introduction to the line of reasoning in *Lectura* III 37, where the ethical question runs as follows:

Do all commands belong to the law of nature?

We read a short answer to this question about natural law:

> What is known on account of the terms used is structurally [*naturaliter*] known, before any act of will [volition].[16]

The context of this statement is Duns' refutation of the idea that the commands of the Decalogue as such embody the first principles of ethics. For the moment, I only select the elements which concern his technical terminology:

> We may say that some elements belong to *natural law* [*de lege naturae*] as they follow from its proper principles. In this way they belong to natural law even if there were no understanding or will. In this sense the Decalogue is not part and parcel of natural law. What is good in terms of a correct will does not belong to natural law, but other elements belong to natural law, because they can be derived from the first principles of practical thought.[17]

This definition is simple and basic. What belongs to natural law necessarily follows from the axioms of ethics. Such derivable propositions are necessarily true because they are deduced from necessary

---

[16] *Lectura* III 37.13: 'Item, que sunt nota ex terminis, sunt *naturaliter nota* ante omnem actum voluntatis.' On *Lectura* III, see §2.3.1.

[17] *Lectura* III 37.16: 'Potest autem dici quod aliqua sunt de lege nature ut sequentia ex propriis principiis, talia autem etsi nullus intellectus, nec voluntas esset, sunt de lege nature. Et sic non est Decalogus de lege nature. Que autem sunt ex voluntate recta, non de lege nature, sed alia sunt de lege nature, quia sunt bene consona cum lege nature, quia stant cum principiis primis practicis.' Cf. §8.4.

propositions. Of course, the ethically necessary principles are themselves also part of natural law, as Duns explicitly states when he refutes an alternative theory. In a typically Scotian way, necessary truth and will are connected.

What is necessarily true is true even if there were no will. Duns Scotus assigns a fundamental part to the will, in particular to God's will, but he does not do so in an arbitrary manner. He does not preach: everything is will. Duns is not a 'voluntarist.' He does not praise will to the skies; he only acknowledges the will, in particular the will of God, and spells out its functions. The starting point of this analysis is precisely to be found in necessary propositions. Why is talk of '*after* (*post*) an act of will' meaningful? Talk of '*after* an act of will' is meaningful, since talk of '*before* (*ante*) an act of will' is indispensable, for the truth-value of a necessary proposition is not will based:

> Their truth does not depend on that act of the will and they would have been known by God's intellect, if God were not to be a willing God – although that is impossible.[18]

There are propositions which are true *before an act of willing*, for if it is impossible that a certain proposition is false, there is no alternative possible to be willed. So, they cannot be will based and the point of view of *ante actum voluntatis* is indispensable. However, if it is impossible that necessary propositions are the only possible ones, since the truth value of many propositions is neither necessary nor impossible, the point of view of *post actum voluntatis* is indispensable too.

Goodness in terms of will or an act of willing (volition) does not belong to the goodness of 'the law of nature,' because the law of nature is true 'before any act of will' (*ante omnem actum voluntatis – Lectura* III 37.13). Its truth is 'naturally' known and this '*naturally (structurally)' known* is being known on account of the terms which the proposition under consideration consists of. So, the necessary truth of such basic propositions depends on the analysis of the involved terms. The necessity of such propositions is analytical. When we apply this pattern to the ethical content, the result is as follows:

> When we completely leave out the act of will and the intellect of God grasps the terms of those principles, then it grasps the power and correctness of those principles before an act of will.[19]

---

[18] *Ordinatio* I 39.23: 'Eorum veritas non dependet ab illo actu et essent cognita ab intellectu, si – *per impossibile* – non esset volens.'

[19] *Lectura* III 37.13: 'Igitur, circumscripto omni actu voluntatis, cum intellectus Dei apprehendit terminos illorum principiorum, apprehendit virtutem illorum et rectitudinem ante actum

Basically, a truth is naturally (*naturaliter*) true if it is true in terms of the intrinsic nature or structure of the proposition involved, and not in terms of an absolute concept of nature, derived from cosmology. Natural truths are truths which are true in terms of their own nature, for a *recta ratio* is a correct piece of reasoning from a correct basis.

12.3.3   Conclusions

Duns defines what he calls a truth *de lege naturae*. The analytical meaning of *ratio naturalis* is the key to explaining what is true *de lege naturae/naturaliter*. This key is not the absolute notion of natural law or of absolute reason. In this analytical vein, Duns strips off the old notion of natural law. If a correct reasoning is built upon a necessary basis which is also self-evident, then it constitutes a *ratio naturalis* (see §9.2.2). This self-evident basis is constituted by the specific identity or essence of God's personal character. Scotus' treatment presents an important chapter of the history of the concept of *natural law*, for he gets rid of the notion of *absolute law* of ancient Greek philosophy (see §12.4).

12.4   Ethical structures

It is a pity that Duns' ethics is not well known. Like other areas of his thought, his ethical thought never reached completion. Nevertheless, it is impressive. It is built on the distinction between *necessary theology* and *contingent theology*:

> Not only knowledge of necessary propositions belongs to this doctrine, but also knowledge of contingent propositions. Indeed, for the largest part of theology deals with contingent propositions.[20]

The divine essence is the first subject of the necessary and contingent truths of theology. One already finds the structure of necessary and contingent theology illustrated by an *ethical* example in the *Prologue* of Duns' *Lectura* I–II:

---

voluntatis.' The last part of this section runs as follows: 'Igitur, vel voluntas necessario vult hoc, si est recta, cum intellectus dicit illud esse rectum, vel erit nonrecta, si discordet.' On principles, see §8.4, and on the notion of *ratio naturalis*, see §9.2.

[20] *Lectura Prologus* 111: 'Ad istam doctrinam non tantum pertinet cognitio necessariorum, sed contingentium, immo maxima pars theologiae est de contingentibus.' Cf. *Lectura Prologus* 114 and 118. For the theme of *philosophy, theology,* and *scientia*, see Chapter 14 and §§16.2–16.3.

Therefore, I say that there are necessary truths about what is contingent:

A stone is falling down

is contingent and yet there are necessary truths about falling, for example, that it looks for the center and that it falls down according to a straight line. In the same way,

I love God

is contingent and yet there can be a necessary truth about it, for example, that I must love God above all. This thesis can be proved as follows:

God is the greatest one we can think of.

Therefore, He is most lovable and I ought to love Him most.

In this way I can have knowledge of contingent propositions. Then this knowledge really regards contingent contents in its first object, although it is not a content in the first sense. Yet, it concerns necessary truths which can be concluded about what is contingent.[21]

In terms of the basic distinction between *necessary theology* and *contingent theology*, it is to be seen that, with Duns, there are also two kinds of ethics: *necessary ethics* and *contingent ethics*. So, necessary ethics is a part of necessary theology and contingent ethics is a part of contingent theology. We may suggest that the incisive problems of the status of the commandments of the Decalogue and the nature of revocation of law will be treated in terms of this distinction.[22]

Besides Duns' renewal of ontology, the other main ingredient of Scotian ethics is the Anselmian revolution which turns around the distinction between the agreeable good (*bonum commodum*) and the good of justice (*bonum iustitiae*). The first kind of goodness is related to what we feel to be pleasant and agreeable to ourselves.

---

[21] *Prologus* 172: 'Ideo dico quod de contingentibus sunt veritates necessariae, quia contingens est *lapidem descendere*, et tamen de descensu eius veritates necessariae, ut quod appetit centrum et quod descendit secundum lineam rectam. Similiter, *me diligere Deum* est contingens, et tamen de hoc potest esse veritas necessaria, ut quod debeam Deum diligere super omnia. Et hoc demonstrative potest concludi sic: *Deus est quo maius cogitari non potest*; igitur est summe diligibilis; igitur summe debeo eum diligere. Et sic secundum hoc possum habere scientiam de contingentibus. Ista igitur scientia est vere circa contingens contentum in primo obiecto, quamvis non sit primo ibi contentum, et tamen est de veris necessariis quae possunt concludi de contingentibus.' Cf. the much later parallel text in *Ordinatio* III 27 (= *Opus Oxoniense* III 27): see Wolter, *Scotus on the Will and Morality*, 424 (Latin) and 425 (English).

[22] See Duns Scotus' *Opus Oxoniense* (= *Ordinatio*) III 37 and IV 17. For the philosophical ramifications of his ethical theory, see Ingham, *Ethics and Freedom*.

It presupposes the spontaneous and almost instinctive experience of *nice!* and is constitutive of the whole of ancient non-Christian ethics.

For Anselm, the second kind of goodness is decisive: just goodness is good, for the objective goodness of the other appeals to us and absorbs us in order to respect and to love it. In depth, its character is defined by being *in line with* divine goodness. Anselm interprets *iustus* as *rectus*: right, straight, not bent. He did not despise the first dimension, but concentrated on the second one. Duns took over this distinction and saw that the first kind of goodness is not moral at all, neither is it immoral. It is to be reckoned with as a real human phenomenon, but ethics can only be based on moral goodness. Such ethical goodness focuses on the other who is our neighbor, and the Other in a contingent world.

There is a double shift from the ego to orientation on the other and the neighbor and from natural inclination to an open-ended deed. *Being free* becomes a central notion of Scotian ethics and anthropology, but it is also a distinctively *new* concept. Freedom in this sense is not longer opposed to sin, but precisely *sinning* presupposes freedom and so *being free* is essential to a human person.[23] *Being free* is, of course, also essential to God, but He is also impeccable. How are the ethical dimensions related to his essence and will?

12.5   LOVE OF GOD AND LOVE OF NEIGHBOR

Duns Scotus' contingency thought has nothing to do with an unsound preference for arbitrariness or capriciousness. Reality is open reality and just as open reality it has to be ordered. Ordering reality is warranted from its center and its center is personal. The center of reality is God. This central focus points at ethical and anthropological meaning and consequences. God is not only the ontological but also the existential and ethical center. God is as good as possible and *not loving God* is deontically impossible.

It is also a natural perception that love is a basic category of Christian life. Duns Scotus expresses this in his medieval style by asserting that to love God is a theological virtue. 'The disposition by

---

[23] For an elaboration of this point, see Dekker and Veldhuis, 'Freedom and Sin. Some Systematic Observations,' *European Journal of Theology* 3 (1994) 153–161.

which God is loved is a theological disposition,'[24] and the word Duns uses to express this theological virtue is *caritas* ('charity'), for 'the disposition by which we hold God to be dear (*carus*) is called *caritas* (love).'[25] It is a present from God. It is primarily ordered towards God and we ought to love our neighbor as ourselves.

12.5.1   Love of God

Loving God is not only something we ought to do, but it also takes pride of place in Duns Scotus' necessary ethics.

> I say that to love God above all is an act which follows from a correct and a priori argument which prescribes that what is best must be loved most of all. Consequently, it is an act which is right of itself, nay, it is self-evident that it is right, just as a first principle of ethics is right. What ought to be loved most of all is nothing but the highest good, just as nothing but the highest good must intellectually be held to be true most of all.[26]

Just as is the case in his philosophical theory of what God is, Duns starts with an axiomatic basis in his necessary ethics and what is valid in his necessary ethics is either self-evident, or axiomatic, or a priori. There is always the duality of *ratio* – argumentation, analysis, and proof – and *auctoritas*. Philosophy and revelation, logic and faith are hand in glove. We have already met the proof, a revelation which coincides with Revelation:

> This is confirmed by the fact that moral commandments belong to the law of nature [*de lege naturae*], and, consequently, the commandment: *Love the Lord, your God*, and so on, belongs to the law of nature [*de lege naturae*]. Therefore, it is evident that this act is right. It follows from this that there can be a virtue which directs essentially towards this act, and this virtue is theological, for it concerns God

---

[24] *Ordinatio* III 28 *obiectum* 2 (Wolter, *Scotus on the Will and Morality*, 446): 'Ille habitus quo diligitur Deus est habitus theologicus.' On love of God, neighbor and self, see Wolter, ibid., 89–98.

[25] *Ordinatio* III 28 *articulus* 1 (Wolter, *Scotus on the Will and Morality*, 448): '*Caritas* dicitur habitus quo Deus habetur *carus*.'

[26] *Ordinatio* III 27 *articulus* 1 (Wolter, *Scotus on the Will and Morality*, 424): 'Dico quod diligere Deum super omnia est actus conformis rectae rationi naturali, quae dictat optimum esse summe diligendum, et, per consequens, est actus de se rectus. Immo, rectitudo eius est per se nota, sicut rectitudo primi principii in operabilibus. Aliquid enim summe diligendum est nihil aliud a summo bono est maxime tenendum tamquam verum apud intellectum.' Cf. §9.2.2 and §§12.3–12.4.

immediately. This is not all, since it is immediately based on the first
rule of human acts and has to be given by God. Such a virtue as such
aims at perfecting the highest part of the soul.[27]

There is still more to it. We ought to love God and this love is not
only a primary preference, theoretically to be proved, but also an
existential preference. We do not love God to satisfy ourselves and
to congratulate ourselves: how nice we are!

> This virtue of *love* is distinct from faith, for its act is one neither of
> knowing nor of believing. It is also distinct from hope, for its act is
> not one of desiring a good for the lover as far as it fits the lover
> himself, but it directs towards its object for its own sake and it would
> do so – to assume the impossible – even when its benefit for the lover
> were excluded. Therefore, I call this virtue which perfects the will as
> far as it appreciates justice: *love*.[28]

12.5.2   Love of neighbor

Loving God and *loving our neighbor* seem to be rather different realities. Duns deals with this issue economically according to the requirements of the principle of parsimony (see §8.2). Are *loving God* and
loving our neighbor dispositionally different realities or do they
concern one and the same attitude? The theology of love belongs to the
ethical theory of the virtues and the starting point is the disposition
love (*caritas*). The qualification *theological virtue* is strict and clear, for
loving *God* is at stake.

Loving someone can take place in two ways. It may be a personal
and private love which is built on jealousy. It may also be a love
which is not reserved for one lover or a happy few. The first love does

---

[27] Ibid. (Wolter, *Scotus on the Will and Morality*, 424 and 426): 'Confirmatur etiam istud quia
praecepta moralia sunt *de lege naturae*, et, per consequens, istud: *Diliges Dominum Deum
tuum*, etc., est de lege naturae, et ita notum est hunc actum esse rectum. Ex hoc sequitur
quod ad illum actum potest esse aliqua virtus naturaliter inclinans, et haec est theologica,
scilicet circa Deum immediate. Nec hoc solum, sed etiam innititur immediate primae regulae
humanorum actuum, et infundi habet a Deo. Huiusmodi enim natura est perficere supremam
portionem animae quae non est perfectissime perficitur nisi immediate a Deo.' 'Love the
Lord, your God' refers to Matthew 22: 37 and Luke 10: 27; cf. Deuteronomy 6: 5. For the
term *de lege naturae*, see §12.3.

[28] Ibid.: 'Haec virtus distincta est a fide, quia actus eius non est *intelligere* vel *credere*. Distincta
est etiam a spe, quia actus eius non est concupiscere amanti bonum inquantum est commodum
amantis, sed tendere in obiectum secundum se, etiamsi – *per impossibile* – circumscriberetur
commoditas eius ad amantem. Hanc itaque virtutem perficientem voluntatem inquantum
habet affectionem iustitiae voco: *caritatem*.'

not wish that there is any co-lover (*condiligens*). This love does not wish that the beloved is loved by anyone else. Duns Scotus addresses two aspects of such a love. Such a love is not orderly. This love is not only incorrect, but also not complete or perfect (*perfectus*). Such a love is not the love whereby God is loved, for God is not a private interest for us. He is a common good, a good for all (*bonum commune*).

> Since God is a common good, He does not will to be a good which is the property and the private good of someone, not is it rationally permissible that anyone appropriates a common good to himself. For this reason, a disposition, namely this love, would be a love which is not orderly, if it would direct towards that good as a good exclusive to himself, not to be loved by anyone else, not to be had by anybody else.[29]

It is not permissible to privatize God, because He is God in a universal way, because a common good is a universal good. Having a private God is logically faulty. A love of God which does not want any co-lovers (*condiligentes*), is not acceptable; it is a wrong love (*amor inordinatus*).

If anything is wrong qualitatively, it may also be wrong quantitatively. So, we have to ask, in the second place, *who* are to be loved, if this love is in order. Why ought I to love my neighbor? Duns Scotus' answer reads: I ought to will that the other wills to be just and righteous and that the other person wills on account of himself to perform righteous acts.

The first idea is that the other person ought to wish to be just and righteous, but which righteous act is involved? What is a righteous act? God is the center of possible reality. So, everything gets content and meaning in relationship with Him. A *righteous* act is an act which is aligned with God's character (*recte*). God defines *righteousness* and He is also the source of righteousness, for if He is the best possible, He ought to be treated in an optimal way. So, the act to be considered here is the act of love, for God is optimally good and lovable.[30]

---

29 *Ordinatio* III 28.7 *articulus* 1 (Wolter, *Scotus on the Will and Morality*, 448): 'Deus quia est bonum commune, non vult esse bonum proprium et privatum alicuius personae, nec secundum rectam rationem debet aliquis sibi appropriare bonum commune; et ideo habitus vel amor iste inclinans ad illum bonum, ut ad bonum proprium, non condiligendum, nec habendum ab aliquo, esset amor inordinatus.' Cf. Vos et al., *Duns Scotus on Divine Love*, chapter 2.

30 The saying *A good husband makes a good wife* reads in Dutch: *He who does well, encounters goodness.*Thus, in terms of Scotus' philosophy of *love*, we may say: *He who acts in a loving manner encounters love.*

Let us spell out the logic of love among human beings. *I* ought to will that *I* love God, but this love is no private matter. God is not only lovely and lovable for me, but also for anyone else. It is love which matters. So, the Beloved is the point of orientation and the criterion of love too. God's will and preferences are the moral and existential center, for God is the ontological center.

> Love wills that God be loved by anyone whose love is perfect, and directed to loving Him [*dilectio*] as He is in Himself. Loving Him is orderly and, by willing so, I love [*diligere*] both myself and my neighbor out of love [*caritas*], by willing that both of us love God for Himself. This act is simply good and a righteous act. The good object of love is only God in Himself.[31]

I ought to will that *you* acquire the good act of loving God, and, so, *I* ought to *will* that *you will* acquire this disposition of love as a source and principle of acts of love. However, if *I* ought to will that you are filled by this love, then *I* also ought to will that I love you. Then, you are what you ought to be in God's eyes and loving 'look.' Just as I ought to love Him above all, because He is above all, then it is true that *you* ought to love Him above all because it is his goodness to will so. You are also lovely and lovable and, of course, I ought to love you too. Then, you *are* what you deserve to be: somebody who loves God, you are what God appreciates you to be. This point of view again defines your goodness and worth and that valuable goodness can only be done justice by me, if I recognize this by loving you.

The conclusion that God and our neighbor ought to be loved through the one and the same disposition of love follows from this universalized attitude of love. The love of the neighbor works through the existential worth of divine love. The existence, character, and work of God are the cornerstone of a contingent and open reality. The priority of God places everything else in its own light.

Scotus' thinking is lucid. He faces the challenges and dilemmas of an open and risky reality from the axiomatic dimension of reality. God gives unity to open, contingent reality. It is faith which gives unity to human life. Christian thought and critical theology serve the elementary predicament of human life to reach out for 'the unity of

---

[31] *Ordinatio* III 28 *articulus* 1 (Wolter, *Scotus on the Will and Morality*, 450): 'Velle eum diligi a quocumque, si est perfecta dilectio eius, et velle eum haberi per dilectionem a quocumque, quantum est in se. Est ordinata dilectio eius et in hoc volendo, diligere me ipsum et proximum ex caritate, volendo mihi et sibi diligere Deum in se, quod est simpliciter bonum et actus iustitiae, ita quod bonum obiectum est solus in se.'

life' (Gunning). Human existence is the source for theoretical thinking and its secret is to be there in love with God and to be there for God and our fellow men. The way of God discloses the road to neighbors and to ourselves, for I am also my own neighbor. I am even my nearest neighbor.

> Most directly after loving God someone wills that by which he is stretching out to God or by which he wills that he loves God. He loves himself out of love in willing that he loves God, since he loves what is good for himself in a just way. Therefore, he loves himself out of love, immediately after loving God.[32]

Duns Scotus' theological view on *loving God* turns on the logic of *willing*, since *loving* is an act of will. Within this context, the concept of *being a neighbor* is defined. The neighbor is he who loves God as far as God appreciates his love. Love is not only something which can only be given freely, but is also something which can only be received freely and it is he who receives love who decides whether that love is desirable and adequate.

> I say that my neighbor is anyone whose friendship is pleasing to the Beloved so that He is loved by him. It is not reasonably permissible to will that the one loved above all by me is also to be loved [*condiligi*] by anyone else by whom He does not want to be loved or by anyone whose love does not please Him.[33]

Dictatorship is unwanted and a dictatorship of love is impossible. Everything turns on the Other and the understanding for the Other determines the relevant understanding of the others and of ourselves. It is one and the same disposition which matters

> for there is only one goodness which motivates to tend towards God for Himself and towards the neighbor as he is tending towards God.[34]

Duns Scotus again pays a great deal of attention to concept formation. If we misuse our tools, our activities may fail too. The main

---

[32] *Ordinatio* III 29, *c.a.*(Wolter, *Scotus on the Will and Morality*, 456): 'Post Deum immediatissime vult quis ex caritate se illud diligere quo tendit in Deum sive quo vult se diligere Deum. In volendo se diligere Deum, diligit se ex caritate, quia diligit sibi bonum iustitiae. Igitur, immediate ex caritate diligit se post dilectionem Dei.'

[33] *Ordinatio* III 28 *articulus* 2 (Wolter, *Scotus on the Will and Morality*, 452): 'Dico quod proximus est quilibet, cuius amicitia grata est dilecto, ut scilicet ab eo diligatur. Non autem debeo velle rationabiliter a me summe dilectum ab alio condiligi a quo non vult diligi vel cuius dilectio sit ei non grata.'

[34] *Ordinatio* III 28 resp. 3 (Wolter, *Scotus on the Will and Morality*, 454): 'Tantum est una bonitas quae est ratio tendendi in Deum in se et in proximum ut tendat in Deum.'

theme of *Lectura* I 17 is that God's eternal happiness is an answer to love, but the love Duns discusses is a certain kind of *disposition* (*habitus*), and not an act of love. Missing this point means losing the match. The same dilemma is at stake here. The issue Duns Scotus discusses is not that the acts of *loving God* and of *loving our neighbor* are the same acts; they certainly are not. These acts are different as to their object and their status, but they are anchored in the same soil, the *disposition* of love as such. The basis is the self-evident goodness of the act of *loving God* because of himself, without any concerns of utility and self-interest. This act has its own identity and its own character. This act is good without further ado. In Scotus' terminology, derived from Anselm, this act is essentially a righteous act (*actus iustitiae*). However, an act can be essentially good, only if the object, to which the act is related to is essentially good. God is the only one to fulfil this condition. The relation towards the object determines the status of a relational act. If an act is related to God, the act can only be good in an absolute sense. So, *hating God* can only be forbidden.

Duns Scotus does not place God in a higher structure of reality. God is relevant to all aspects of reality. So, he is not a *nature-supernature* thinker. Nothing is neutral. Everything is related to God. Nothing can be cut off from his friendly countenance. Grace is no encore. It is not secondary. Grace is crucial and decisive. The goodness of our neighbor is defined in terms of the relationship with God. There is neither identity, mysticism, nor monism. *Loving God* is not the same as *loving the neighbor*. Whether the source is the same does matter. The persons of God's loving attention are interwoven in the relationship with God and the goodness and the radiance of his countenance illuminate the whole of reality.

12.6   SLAVERY

When we survey Duns Scotus' inspired output during the last years of his life (1305–08), we discover a general trend already visible in comparing *Lectura* III with *Ordinatio* III (= *Opus Oxoniense* III): a spectacular increase of interest in ethical, social, and even economic issues. John the Scot delivered an elaborate course on *Book* IV for the first time in his life at Paris during the first half of 1303. Treating of a problem of the quality of the life of a slave, he simply sided with canon law in *Reportatio Parisiensis* IV 36.1. Apparently, he had seen no opportunity to go deeply into it, but *Ordinatio* IV 36.1 offers a totally different picture. In order to appreciate Duns Scotus' views properly, I select some elements from the history of slavery.

Slavery was a much respected social institution in antiquity which maintained itself for many centuries in some parts of the world. Slaves and the majority of women did not enjoy an enviable status in ancient society. Aristotle discussed various models of government (democracy, oligarchy, tyranny) and their existing varieties, and introduced fundamental questions of political theory in his pioneering *Politics*, which remained influential even in the thirteenth century: the nature and function of the state, the meaning of citizenship, what it is to be a good citizen, and elements of constitution. As to slavery, he held that the master can sell his slave like an animal, for a slave cannot exercise acts of manly excellence because he has to perform servile actions at the command of his master. Political philosophy looked on slavery as a natural phenomenon. Ancient culture could hardly imagine a world without slaves. In parts of Greece, about 90 per cent of the population might have been slaves, responsible particularly for manual labor.

The old Hebrew Law tells us not to 'covet' (the Hebrew term means to hook, to nab) our neighbor's house, our neighbor's wife, his slave, his slave-girl, his ox, his ass, or anything that belongs to him. What belongs to a possessor matters. Although the Law of the Old Testament shows interest and mercy concerning the situation of slaves,[35] yet, at the time of Jesus, the situation of the slave was not easy. Jesus' parable of the so-called 'unprofitable/unworthy servant' sketches all the hardships of these 'servants,' as the New English Bible still rather mildly translates.[36] There were two kinds of slaves in the Jewish countries: 'Canaanite' slaves who were foreigners, and *Israelite* slaves who were Jews themselves. 'There were relatively few slaves in the Land of Israel, but many people found a use for them. *Jewish* slaves were apt to be burdensome, and they were less popular.'[37]

In contrast with the 'Israelite' slaves, the 'Canaanite' slaves were not only excluded from the religious community, but also from all

---

[35] See Wright, *God's People*, chapter 8. Cf. Job 31: 15 with the Akkadian saying 'A man is the shadow of a god, a slave the shadow of a man.' Cf. Wright, *God's People*, 239 ff.

[36] 'Unprofitable' and 'unworthy,' let alone 'useless,' are also ill-chosen translations. *Achreios* is an expression of modesty and humility: 'We are poor/sorry figures.' Dennett's witty translation is 'profitable.'

[37] Derrett, 'The Parable of the Profitable Servant (Luke XVII.7–10),' *Studies in the New Testament* IV, 158.

the considerations to which a Jewish slave had to be entitled. A 'Canaanite' slave did not have the right to marry and did not belong to the formal context of the household as the parable shows. At any rate, there was food for him afterwards, but even this was not a right as the parable of the Prodigal Son proves. His was a duty-bound life, but there was more to the life of slavery for by serving in a friendly and attentive manner, the slave could win the affection of the foreign master. A harsh foreign master may also become grateful to his slave who did more than simply carry out his orders. There was already a synagogue, called the *Synagogue of the Freedmen* (*liberti*) in gratitude on the part of their masters (Acts 6: 9), during the 30s in Jerusalem, and

> Christian ethical attitudes and principles did something for the inter-
> ests of both (slaves and women) without, however, pressing for
> changes in their legal rights. The Church had enough trouble repelling
> the charge of sedition without giving the accusation this degree of
> plausibility. [. . .] St Paul expressly lays down that, while within the
> Christian family all are equal to their heavenly Father, the Church
> makes no change in the civil status of slaves (I Cor. 7: 21).[38]

However, this concession was not to the taste of Duns Scotus.[39]

Nevertheless, the Christian faith elicited a movement to improve on the position of the slaves, and in particular the Western Church was much more critical of the customs of lords and noblemen. Leo I (440–461) suggested that a true calling for the religious life was a proper reason to free a slave.[40] Reform movements of the eleventh, twelfth and thirteenth centuries confirmed this tendency. Duns Scotus eloquently defended the right of a slave to marry, even the right to marry a free woman.[41] Moreover, while it is true that the Church came into being in a world where slavery was universally accepted as a social and economic institution pertaining to the very structure of society, it is simply wrong to assert, as the general view does, that in Duns Scotus' days slavery was still a universal social fact. Even during the Dark Ages, slavery was scarcely found in Flanders, the

---

[38] Chadwick, 'Christian doctrine,' in Burns (ed.), *The Cambridge History of Medieval Political Thought c.350–c.1450*, 15 (11–20), cf. 21–47.

[39] See the last *responsum* of *Ordinatio* IV 36 *quaestio* 1 (Wolter, *Scotus on the Will and Morality*, 526 (Latin) and 527 (English)).

[40] See Robert Somerville, 'Leo I,' *ER* VIII 514 f.

[41] Cf. *Reportatio Parisiensis* IV 36, 1 in *Codex* 206 of *Balliol College* with *Ordinatio* IV 36, 1, found in Wolter, *Scotus on the Will and Morality*, 522–533, where a fine exposition is given on the issue whether slavery can or must obstruct marriage.

Brabantine Counties, Holland and Zealand (The Netherlands), and the Rhineland, and there was also a strong sense of liberty in John Duns' Scotland and England.[42]

12.6.1 Duns Scotus on slavery

After the introductory pros and cons, the fundamental question of the justice of slavery is dealt with within the contexts of the law of nature and positive law made by those entitled to govern (*Ordinatio* IV 36). All people are born free *de lege naturae* (see §12.4), but slavery is imposed by virtue of positive law. *De lege naturae, being free* is an essential property of men, to be derived from primary necessary truths regarding *being human*. It is asked in the light of what is essential to man whether slavery can be acceptable at all. Duns restricts slavery to two cases:

> I say that this worthless slavery can only be imposed in a just way in two cases: on the one hand, someone has voluntarily subjected [*subiecit*] himself to such slavery. However, such subjection is irresponsible. More than that, it runs counter to the law of nature that a man would give up his freedom. Nevertheless, once he has done so, it is necessary to keep it.[43]

This reluctant admission that slavery can be accepted in a couple of cases is quite different from a wholehearted defense of it. Scotus does not defend giving up our freedom, but *this* is just: keeping to our word. This side of slavery was a topical subject by then. Members of some new religious orders, for instance the Mercedarians (1218), 'not only specialized in working with the slaves, but added a fourth vow to the usual three of poverty, chastity, and obedience, the vow to act as captives themselves if necessary to free those Christian slaves of the Moors whose faith was in danger.'[44] It seems not to have been pleasant to Duns' ear, although he accepted drastic sacrifices on our part, but not as a rule.

---

[42] The semantic field of *servus* is rather broad (slave, serf, workman's mate, servant, tenant, officer, employee – compare 'being a servant, to serve' (*servire*)). The use of *servus* in a medieval text in itself does not tell us which kinds of people are dealt with.

[43] *Ordinatio* IV 36 *quaestio* 1 in the body of the article (Wolter, *Scotus on the Will and Morality*, 522): 'Dico quod ista vilis servitus non potest esse iuste inducta nisi dupliciter: uno modo, quia aliquis voluntate subiecit se tali servituti, sed talis subiectio est fatua. Immo, forte contra legem naturae est quod homo libertatem suam a se abdicaret. Postquam tamen facta est, necesse servare, quia *hoc* est iustum.'

[44] Wolter, *Scotus on the Will and Morality*, 116 (114–120).

The second case concerns freedom as a possible source of damage to the involved persons and the public good. The authorities can punish vicious people by slavery. The first case amounts to a very cautious acknowledgement of the right of self-determination to accept *freely* captivity and the second case is a counterpart of the prison of modern society. In this latter case, slavery is prevention by means of punishment. Ancient society did not have many means to prevent crimes, with the exception of slavery and the death penalty:

> On the other hand, if anyone rules justly over society and sees that some are so criminal that their freedom harms both themselves and the public, then he can justly punish them by slavery, just as he could justly execute them in certain cases for the welfare of the public.[45]

Duns also makes unambiguously clear what he thinks of the hard core of slavery: taking prisoners in war as a source for the slave trade. The text is too fascinating not to be quoted in full:

> If you say that there is a third good reason for slavery, for instance, if someone has been taken a prisoner of war and he, preserved from death as he is, becomes a slave, destined to serve, I doubt this, unless 'serf' [*servus*] is here taken to mean *preserved* [*servatus*]. Neither is this a clear case of justice. The captor might have killed his prisoner of war bravely, if he carried on a just war of self-defense, and not a war of aggression, and his adversary persevered in doing so. Nevertheless, it seems inhuman to inflict on a prisoner of war a punishment running counter to natural law inasmuch as he ceases to be an enemy, since he wills to be a captive. The third reason for slavery does not apply here, for in this second case he would neither abuse his freedom, since he does not continue to rebel strongly, but he would become obedient strongly, and use well the freedom given to him.[46]

---

[45] Wolter, *Scotus on the Will and Morality*, 524: 'Alio modo, si quis iuste dominans communitati, videns aliquos ita vitiosos, quod libertas eorum et nocet eis et rei publicae, potest iste punire eos poena servitutis, sicut et iuste posset eos occidere in ceteris casibus propter bonum rei publicae.'

[46] Ibid.: 'Si dicas quod est etiam tertia causa servitutis, utpote si captus in bello servetur et sic servatus a morte, fiat servus deputatus ad serviendum, de hoc dubito, nisi dicatur " servus " ibi "servatus". Nec apparet hic manifeste iustitia, quia etsi forte captor potuisset occidere captum, si habuit bellum iustum defendendo se, sed non invadendo, et hoc stante pertinacia ipsius contrabellantis, tamen ex quo desinit esse pertinax quia est in voluntate iam captus, inhumanum videtur sibi infligere poenam contra legem naturae. Non enim est haec ratio quia in isto secundo casu, quia forte non permanet iste rebellus, nec abuteretur sua libertate, sed forte fieret obediens, et libertate sibi donata bene uteretur.'

There is a great distance here from the views of Aristotle and Thomas Aquinas who offered a kind of Christian synthesis: Aquinas did not put the defense that slavery belongs to natural law (Aristotle), but that it is part and parcel of the *ius gentium* (Ulpianus). However, this *ius gentium* obtains universally among nations. So, the ethical profit is limited. In Duns' ethics, there is no room for a *ius gentium*.[47] Something running counter to the law of nature cannot be justified. Old customs cannot save something wrong; on the contrary, it is much more reasonable to stop old injustice. An appeal to the apostle Paul cannot mollify Duns. He not only offers a clear view, but his pathos is the more striking, because his objective mentality always shines out: slavery is inhuman, worthless, and something to be cursed.

12.7 THE QUINTONIAN AND HARRISIAN FALLACIES

The main structure of Scotus' ethics belongs to the most pressing problems of his ethics. In general, it has often been suggested that his theory of will and freedom is one of the most distinctive foundations of his ethics and this is patently true. However, in this light the paradoxes of contingency, will, and freedom are seen as the roots of his ethics, and many consider the priority of will over intellect to be the basic element. According to this view, the freedom of the act of creation runs parallel to the role of freedom in constituting what is good. During a century of neoscholastic revival, the charge that only the will constitutes moral truth has been repeated again and again.

> Perhaps the most persistently recurring objection to the moral philosophy of John Duns Scotus is voiced most succinctly by Anthony Quinton in his article in the new *Encyclopedia of Philosophy*: 'Things are good because God wills them and not vice versa, so moral truth is not accessible to the natural reason'.[48]

However, the conceptual structures, treated in §12.3, and the distinction between necessary and contingent ethics are the solution to those well-known puzzles of Scotian ethics, the *Quintonian* and *Harrisian fallacies*, and the notion of ethically neutral propositions.

---

[47] For Aristotle, see *Politics* I chapter 4, and for Thomas Aquinas, see *Summa Theologiae* I II 94, *Summa Theologiae* II II 57 *articulus* 3, and *Summa Theologiae* III 51 *articulus* 1. See Wolter, *Scotus on the Will and Morality*, 114–123.

[48] Wolter, 'Native Freedom of the Will,' in *The Philosophical Theology of Scotus*, 148, quoting Quinton, 'British philosophy,' *EP* I 373.

12.7.1 The nature of the Quintonian fallacy

Quinton's section 'Duns Scotus and Scotism' is part of an impressive overview of British philosophy full of remarkable insights and judgements and his general attitude is certainly not unfair to Duns.

> It was John Duns Scotus (*c*.1266–1308), the first major British philosopher since Erigena and perhaps the most powerful philosophical intellect of the Middle Ages, who initiated a new system of ideas which led English thought in a fresh direction, away from the conflict of Aristotle and Augustine.[49]

Quinton points to Scotus' fertile innovations of terminology. In spite of this prudent insightfulness, the complex terminology of Duns Scotus is not taken into account. Quinton hypostasizes natural reason. According to Quinton's analysis, Duns separates goodness from necessity. However, Duns does not link goodness and will from an extremely nominalistic bias. The allegation of an exclusive connection of will and goodness is an unwarranted claim which not only runs through the whole history of neothomistic thought, but also dominates nineteenth-century history of Western philosophy. Wolter notices that this claim has also been periodically refuted; he mentions Minges, Longpré, De Wulf, Copleston, and Hoeres. In fact, Wolter's 'Native Freedom of the Will as a Key to the Ethics of Scotus' (1972) is directed against Quinton's distortion.

Wolter followed two paths of argumentation. First, his opponents consulted rather unreliable texts.[50] Second, Scotus' basic distinction is the distinction between *natura* and *voluntas*.

> Natural agents [. . .] have their action specified by what they are in themselves, and given the same set of extrinsic conditions or circumstances, their action is uniform. Self-determination on the contrary presupposes two things: (a) logically alternative modes of behavior, specifically the possibility of acting or not-acting (liberty of contradiction) or acting now this way, now that (liberty of contrariety); (b) in freely determining itself to one or the other of these several alternatives, the free agent acts with, but is not determined by, knowledge.[51]

This basic distinction between 'nature' and will constitutes the systematic background of Scotus' use of the Anselmian distinction of the

---

[49] Quinton, 'British Philosophy,' *EP* I 372–373.
[50] See Wolter, *Scotus on the Will and Morality*, 2 ff.
[51] 'Native Freedom of the Will,' in *The Philosophical Theology of Scotus*, 149.

twofold inclination of the will: the *affectio commodi* and the *affectio iustitiae*.

> It is the *affectio iustitiae* that represents the ultimate specific difference, as it were, of the will as free. This native liberty or root freedom of the will, in short, is a positive bias or inclination to love things objectively.[52]

12.7.2 The solution of the fallacy

In spite of these important insights into Scotus' ethics Wolter is unable to solve the Quintonian fallacy. He touches on several aspects of goodness as will-dependent as Duns seemingly sees it, but although these remarks are helpful and true, they cannot solve the complaint of 'voluntarism' because they are restricted to the impact of the will.

The solution lies in the basic distinction between contingency and necessity and the concepts of contingent and necessary ethics. In terms of necessary ethics, goodness cannot be will-dependent. Contingent ethical propositions, for example:

a loves God

are based on a conjunction of necessary propositions, for example:

Necessarily, God has to be loved

and contingent truths, for example:

a exists and *a* knows God.

Necessary propositions are not will based (see §12.4). There are also ethically open propositions, belonging to contingent ethics, for they are will-dependent. Will and goodness are only linked if they can be linked and must be linked. They must be linked intrinsically

---

[52] Wolter, 'Native Freedom of the Will,' in *The Philosophical Theology of Scotus*, 152. 'Objectively' has to be taken in the medieval sense. Compare some recent restatements of Duns Scotus' 'voluntarism': Santogrossi, 'Scotus's Method in Ethics,' *Theological Studies* 55 (1994) 314–325, Williams, 'Reason, Morality, and Voluntarism in Duns Scotus,' *The Modern Schoolman* 74 (1997) 73–94, and idem, 'The Unmitigated Scotus,' *Archiv für Geschichte der Philosophie* 80 (1998) 162–181. If the structures expounded in §§12.1–12.5 hold, Williams's reconstruction of Scotian ethics is misguided. See Vos et al., *Duns Scotus on Divine Love*, 58–64.

if the situation is contingent and open and a certain solution must be found. The relevant decision must be made and accordingly is only made in agreement with the best possible will. This basic point can be appropriately illustrated with the Sabbath commandment. There is no intrinsic element of a particular day which entails the sanctification of that particular day. This particular choice must be made by divine revelation as, according to Duns Scotus, the Bible as document of revelation tells us. The Quintonian fallacy is an unwarranted allegation against Scotus' ethics. A systematic bias as supposed in the Quintonian fallacy is quite foreign to his mind. The refutation of the fallacy has two aspects: the necessary good cannot be willed contingently and the contingent good can only be constituted by God. So, the Quintonian complaint is unfounded. Duns' ethics is not based on 'voluntarism' in its simplistic sense.

12.7.3   The Harrisian fallacy

Quinton overlooked the pivotal role of necessary theology and necessary ethics within Scotian thought and thus the essential interaction between necessary and contingent propositions in Scotus' theories of intellect, will, and ethics. If we miss one of the two banks, we cannot build the bridge. In contrast to Quinton, Harris had fruitfully discerned the kernel of Scotus' ethical philosophy in his *Duns Scotus* II, while stressing the so-called Anselmian core of his ethics:

> His insistence on the distinction between will and desire enables him to grapple more adequately with the psychological analysis of ethical problems and lends his thinking a deeper insight into the facts of moral experience than was displayed by any Christian thinker since the days of Augustine.[53]

Harris sees the importance of the distinction between will and desire and the proper role of the will in the theory of action and in ethics, and he warns not to look at Duns as a simple voluntarist. Therefore, Harris judges the interpretation of Landry and Jourdain, Schwane and Werner to be mistaken. Moreover, he discerns the flip side: Scotus' statement that the goodness of an act depends on conformity with 'right reason.' So far, so good, but then Harris concludes that the

---

[53] Harris, *Duns Scotus* II, 303.

conjunction of both sides constitutes a contradiction. So, Harris replaces the dilemma of an arbitrary voluntarism with the complaint of inconsistency. 'It is only by a frank recognition of this antinomy that we can hope to avoid the one-sided interpretation in which his teaching has so often been distorted.'[54]

However, if the fault does not exist, there is no need of a one-sided interpretation to put it right. Duns does not work with an exclusive disjunction of intellect and will. The key lies in the distinctions between necessary and contingent propositions in ethics. There is a realm of necessary propositions which is not constituted by contingent acts of will. Both dimensions of necessity and contingency in ethics are themselves necessary. The systematic upshot is that there is no separate heaven of 'the right reason.' This heaven is demythologized and made empty, for 'natural reason' and 'right reason' are both adequately unpacked in terms of logical, ontological, and epistemological characteristics of propositions.

The ethical structures expounded in §§12.3–12.4 solve the Harrisian fallacy. It is a paradox that traditional interpretations of Duns' ethics and theory of will show so many deficiencies. There is no gulf between will and reason. There is only the indispensable distinction between necessary and contingent propositions and the right ways in which knowledge and will can be related to them. *Ratio necessaria, ratio naturalis* and, *ratio recta* are related to certain logical, ontological, and epistemological characteristics of arguments. The will fills in the realm of contingency, constituted by what is not necessary. Moreover, 'natural law' and 'natural reason' have completely different meanings with Duns in comparison with the Aristotelian and (neo)thomistic traditions.

12.8 ETHICAL REVOCATION

In 'Die Bestimmung der *ratio legis* bei Thomas von Aquin und Duns Scotus,' Berthold Wald sees the essential divergence between Thomas Aquinas and Duns Scotus in the perennial conflict between realism and idealism in philosophy.[55] In terms of idealism, the weakness of

---

[54] *Duns Scotus* II 335. For criticisms of 'voluntarist' interpretations, see Vos et al., *Duns Scotus on Divine Love*, chapter 2, part 2.

[55] Wald, 'Die Bestimmung der *ratio legis* bei Thomas von Aquin und Duns Scotus,' in Zimmermann and Speer (eds), *Miscellanea Mediaevalia 21/2. Mensch und Natur im Mittelalter*, 681.

realism is to be seen in claiming real insight into the true nature of things. Thus it is liable to skeptical criticisms. Here, the theological voluntarism of Scotus comes to the fore. Duns looks for freedom for theological propositions, but the choice of such a philosophical starting point cannot be decided in a philosophical way. In spite of this deep divergence the practical differences between Aquinas and Duns are seen to be very limited.

The remedy is found in a far-reaching reversal of viewpoints. If Scotus' logical and analytical approach is seen as an ontological demythologization – a demythologization of 'metaphysics' – the entire dilemma of idealism and realism disappears. Duns does not speak in a substantialist vein of *the natural law* as the law of *nature* (*Naturgesetz* and *Naturrecht*) and the natural reason altogether. In the same general sense, there is no rock-bottom philosophy. There are only sound and unsound arguments and there is necessary and contingent truth, both to be discovered in a contingent way. The ontological structure of Scotian thought is not to be neglected in reconstructing his ethics. The basic importance of a comparison between Aquinas and Duns is not to be looked for in practical differences, although, for instance, the differences in the theory of slavery must not be minimized. On the contrary, they are substantial ones.[56] In general, they share the same patrimony of faith, but the decisive point is whether their theoretical contributions explain or undermine what they both believe. The problem of ethical revocation is just one case of it.

Duns Scotus' criticism of Thomas Aquinas' theory is precisely that his ethics cannot explain the ethical character of the divine command in Genesis 22.[57] In this case, the problem does not arise from a specific theory of Thomas or Duns, but from biblical evidence. If the command of Genesis 22 rests on 'historical' and ethical revelation, the sixth commandment of the Decalogue must be contingent. Thomas Aquinas' theological explanation is not acceptable to Duns,[58] because according to Aquinas that commandment

---

[56] See Wolter, *Scotus on the Will and Morality*, 114–123 and 522–533, and DS 99–101.

[57] See Hedwig, 'Das Isaak-Opfer,' *Miscellanea Mediaevalia 21/2. Mensch und Natur im Mittelalter*, 647–651.

[58] The logical core of Thomas' argumentation has been adequately formulated by Hedwig: 'Die Kritik zielt auf den Begriff, um den es letzlich geht: die *dispensatio*, die – nach Thomas – die allgemeine Norm der Gerechtigkeit nicht verändert, während dagegen der Einzelfall dem Gesetz "entzogen" werden kann. Diese Konstruktion ist für Scotus nicht mehr annehmbar' ('Das Isaak-Opfer,' *Miscellanea Mediavalia 21/2. Mensch und Natur im Mittelalter*, 651). However, the point of Scotus' evaluation of the Thomasian argumentation is not a historical (*nicht mehr*), but a logical one: the involved derivation is invalid.

belongs to the natural law. So, Duns concludes that it must be a part of necessary ethics. However, a necessary truth of ethics cannot be revoked or dispensed with. When there is alternative biblical information, contingency seems the only logical way out and Duns utilizes it. In fact, it is not ethical *revocation* that matters, but *dispensation*.[59] In sum, their interrelations are contingent ones. It is the same logical relation which yields the answer to the question of the next distinction (*Lectura* III 37 and *Ordinatio* III 37): it is not true that all commandments of the Decalogue belong to natural law. For instance, the commandment of the Sabbath would belong to natural law, if sanctifying the Sabbath could be proven to be a necessary truth in terms of the meanings of 'Sabbath,' 'seven,' 'week,' 'rest,' 'sanctification,' 'God,' 'creation,' and so on. Then it would be derivable from the precious gift of regular rest. The commandment that only the seventh day of a week of seven days could give the opportunity of a day of rest for God, one another, and ourselves would be a piece of necessary ethics.

Modern systematic theology has alternative means of handling such a dilemma by dealing with it in a purely historical way, but the historical way of thought was not available in the Middle Ages, and not before Niebuhr and Ranke in the first half of the nineteenth century at all.[60]

12.9 THE STRUCTURE OF THE ETHICS OF VIRTUE

During the last years of his short life (1305–08), Duns Scotus paid a lot of attention to ethics and social and political theory. The central texts are to be found in the drafts of *Ordinatio* III–IV. If we concentrate on *virtue*, we have to realize that modern schemes are not simply applicable to Duns Scotus' thought. In particular, the modern dualism of philosophy and theology is not congenial to his mind. He would not have favored the distinction of modern Renaissance theology between nature and supernature. With Duns Scotus, the central logical-methodological distinction is that between necessary and contingent ethics. Duns' theory of

---

[59] *Lectura* III 37 (Balic, *Les commentaires de Jean Duns Scot*, 344): 'Si precepta omnia Decalogi illo modo haberent *bonitatem intrinsecam* talem essentialiter, non ut posset Deus contra ipsa dispensare, quia non subessent voluntati divine posita illa ratione, quinimmo actus contrarius esset de se malus essentialiter, sequeretur quod lex non esset in potestate divina, sed supra ipsam existens, et hoc saltem quoad decalogum.'

[60] Cf. Rodd, *Glimpses of a Strange Land: Studies in Old Testament Ethics*.

virtue also moves along the lines of his own conceptual and logical structures.[61]

We observe three dominant tendencies. The first tendency is the theocentric and christocentric character of Duns' thought. The second tendency is a tendency on the formal level, inspired by the central position of his contingency theory. The third tendency is the biblical outlook of his theory of virtue. Everything has a personal touch. We conclude with the personal note close to Duns' heart.

As to the second tendency, we ask what kind of structural inter-relationship demarcates the theory of virtue. We meet questions as whether the moral virtues are connected or whether natural law coincides with the Ten Commandments. Ancient tradition treated the virtues as an organic whole. Cicero and Seneca and many Fathers of the Church praised the interconnection and harmony of the virtues. Peter Lombard confirms that according to Jerome and Augustine all the virtues are somehow one. We read in the beginning of Jerome's Commentary on Isaiah: 'All the virtues hang together, so that if one is missing, all are. Hence, if somebody has one virtue, he has them all.'

Philip the Chancellor specified this type of solution by distinguishing between a broad and narrow sense of the cardinal virtues. In the broad sense every virtue is a necessary condition of any virtue, but, in the narrow sense, a cardinal virtue is defined by its specific object. The early Franciscan and Dominican masters of theology followed his lead.[62] After 1245, Aristotle's *Nicomachean Ethics* changed the ethical scene. The Aristotelian solution is that the four cardinal virtues are interconnected by the way prudence gives rise to the moral virtues. According to Thomas Aquinas, the cardinal virtues are tightly connected in their perfect state (*Summa Theologiae* I II 65).

Duns considers these questions in *Lectura* III 36 and in *Ordinatio* III 36. His answers are thoroughly determined by his views on contingency. First, the so-called theological virtues (faith, hope, and love)

---

[61] The best literature is found in Ingham, *Ethics and Freedom*, part II, and Kent, *The Virtues of the Will*, chapter 5, while Dumont correctly refuted Lottin's monolithic interpretation of Scotus' theory of the virtues in 'The Necessary Connection of Prudence to the Moral Virtues,' *Recherches de théologie ancienne et médiévale* 55 (1988) 184–206. Cf. McCord Adams, 'Scotus and Ockham on the Connection of the Virtues,' in Honnefelder et al. (eds), *Scotus. Metaphysics and Ethics*, 499–522.

[62] See Lottin, *Psychologie et morale aux XII et XIII siècles* IV, 551–742, and idem, 'L' "Ordinatio" de Jean Duns Scot sur le livre III des Sentences,' *Recherches de théologie ancienne et médiévale* 20 (1953) 102–119, and Wolter, *Scotus on the Will and Morality*, 78–89.

clearly do not entail the acquired virtues. They belong to the reality of conversion and the sacraments and these contingent phenomena have their own impact on the moral life. There is no imperialism of faith destroying all traces of prudence and justice, temperance and courage. 'The moral virtues do not require the theological virtues in order to be complete with respect to their own specific nature, though without them they do not have that further extrinsic perfection they could have.'[63]

So, there are no necessary entailments between the theological and the moral virtues, but nor are there necessary relations between the theological virtues themselves. The interplay between faith, hope, and love is vital to us, but in heaven we shall be filled by love and 'the dispositions and acts of love exist without the dispositions and acts of faith and hope.'[64] Our present life is contingent and nuanced and open too. There may be an accident in our history of love and grace, but still we can act in virtue of hope and faith. Duns sketches the Christian life as an open life and as a dynamic reality. In the same light he looks on human life in general.

Nor do the moral virtues form a monolithic block. Lottin had already pointed out that Duns had completely broken with the line of the Fathers and Philip the Chancellor, and Wolter correctly concurs with his analysis. Nevertheless, we have to nuance this picture somewhat. Indeed, all traces of necessitarianism have been wiped out. His ontological view of contingent dynamics opens up all the virtues. There is no single process of massive growth or decline. We grow and stumble on rather different paths. Nevertheless, Duns sticks to the perspective of one mature and harmonious growth. There is one open and vulnerable reality, which promises much, but there is no chaos or arbitrariness. According to the spirit, Duns keeps to the old wisdom; according to the ontological letter, he breaks new ground, summarizing it in *Ordinatio* III 36 in the body of the article:

> I grant there is no connection either of the categorically different moral virtues, commonly referred to as justice, courage and temperance. [. . .] This can be proved as follows: virtue is a perfection of man, which is not complete, because then one moral virtue would be sufficient.

[63] For this conclusion of article 3 in *Ordinatio* III 36, see Wolter, *Scotus on the Will and Morality*, 416.
[64] For the answer in Duns' article 4 in *Ordinatio* III 36, see Wolter, *Scotus on the Will and Morality*, 418.

When something has several partial perfections, it can of course be perfect according to one perfection and incomplete according to another, as is clear with a man who has many organic perfections and can have one perfection maximally, while having nothing of another one, for instance: he is maximally disposed as to sight or touch, although he cannot hear anything. Someone can have a maximal perfection as to temperance, without having any perfection which would be required regarding a different perfection and, consequently, he can be temperate, just like that, even as to every act of temperance, although he is not courageous. If he has none, he is not simply moral, as he is not simply sensory without any sense. [. . .] However, he is not less temperate, because he is morally weaker, just as he does not see less and not hear less, because his sensory power is weaker.[65]

At the end, Duns concludes that no virtues are specifically incompatible (*incompossibiles*) and the different kinds of moral and theological virtues are not necessarily connected. This insight also yields the answer to the question of the next distinction (*Lectura* III 37 and *Ordinatio* III 37): do all Ten Commandments belong to natural law? Duns' contingency model presents the key to his ethics too. He sees that no particular day embodies this splendid gift of rest of a certain pattern. Theological and ethical values are not exclusively and necessarily present in things or times, persons or structures.[66] This insight does not signal voluntarism, it only acknowledges a necessary trait of reality.

The opposition between *Something is good, because God wills it* and *God wills something, because it is good* rests upon misunderstanding these propositions. Duns does not defend that we do not need a Sabbath or a Sabbath commandment, but *Sabbath* is not derivable from the proper nature of any day. Because the will cannot

---

[65] Wolter, *Scotus on the Will and Morality*, 388: 'Concedo quod nec virtutes morales secundum genera sua, quae communiter assignantur iustitia, fortitudo et temperantia, [. . .], sunt necessario connexae. Ad quod est persuasio talis, quia virtus est perfectio aliqua hominis et non totalis, quia tunc sufficeret virtus una moralis. Quando autem sunt plures perfectiones partiales alicuius, illud potest esse perfectum simpliciter secundum unam perfectionem et imperfectum simpliciter secundum aliam, sicut apparet in homine, cuius est habere multas perfectiones organicas et potest habere unam perfectionem in summo, nihil habendo de alia, puta esse summe dispositus ad visum vel tactum, nihil habendo de auditu. Potest sibi aliquis habere perfectionem respectu materiae temperantiae in summo, non habendo de perfectione quae requireretur respectu materiae alterius perfectionis et per consequens potest esse simpliciter temperatus, etiam quantum ad quemcumque actum temperantiae, etsi non sit fortis. [. . .] Sed non est minus perfecte temperatus, licet sit minus perfecte moralis, sicut non est minus perfectus videns, nec est minus perfectus audiens, licet sit minus perfectus sentiens.'

[66] See *Ordinatio* III 37 in Wolter, *Scotus on the Will and Morality*, 278: Latin, and 279: English.

be excluded in constituting what is good, the will comes in. By stating the role of the will in ethics and anthropology we have reached the heart of the matter. If a necessitarian structure of ethical reality is rejected, new questions of structure arise. Broadly speaking, both Thomas Aquinas and John Duns move within the boundaries of teleological ethics, but the very different structures of their thought fill this teleological outlook in a rather different way. In the contingency model the act-potency structure is replaced by a theory of concrete action.

12.10 THE UNITY OF VIRTUE

How shall we give coherence and unity to our moral life, if contingency entrenches it? The second, formal, tendency points to the first theological tendency. Reality is God's reality. He is the necessary center of everything. In Duns' Christian view the doctrine of God is trinitarian theology (*Lectura* I). His doctrine of the Trinity is characterized by the theory of will and his theory of will dominates his anthropology too. The ethical link is put forward in *Lectura* III 34 and *Ordinatio* III 34: the will is the seat of moral virtues.

Scotus' argumentation can be easily followed, as long as we discern the Anselmian foundations of his ethics.[67] In ethics, Anselm had brought into prominence the basic distinction between something good which is pleasant for us (the *bonum commodi*) and something good which is good as such (the *bonum iustitiae*). As regards the *bonum commodi* we view what is agreeable to us and is doing us well. It serves the continuity of our existence and our well-being. We discern the interest of the other. What serves the good of our neighbor is here put central. A basic distinction between two kinds of *willing* runs exactly parallel to this distinction of two kinds of goodness. The first kind of will is seen in the classical meaning of *velle*: to be inclined to, to be disposed; compare 'to want' or 'to wish' in English as a translation of *velle*. The second kind of will is seen in the strong and specific meaning of *velle* and *voluntas*, presupposing a definite choice between alternatives on the basis of contingency.

The *bonum iustitiae* of Anselm and the Scotian *velle* make a couple and when we are familiar with the equivalence of *bonum iustitiae* and *bonum honestum* we understand Duns saying: 'Virtue has the *bonum*

---

[67] See Wolter 'Native Freedom of the Will' and 'Duns Scotus on the Will and Morality,' in *The Philosophical Theology of Scotus*, 148–162 and 181–206, respectively.

honestum = bonum iustitiae as its proper object. That (good) is the essential object of will' (*Ordinatio* III 33.8). The will is the proper rational faculty and endeavor and in deciding it enjoys a structural priority.[68] God's presence bestows inner coherence on this position. God is love, so the essential axiom reads:

God has to be loved above all.

Therefore, the virtue of love comes in as the virtue structuring and coloring the whole of Duns Scotus' ethics of virtue. This ethical overall structure of his thought is already clear from *Lectura Prologus* 172, 164, and 163. The theocentric structure also explains the Scotian conclusion that theology is a practical discipline. Basically, theology is a philosophical ethics of love.[69] The virtue of love is the center of the theological and moral virtues. Duns' theory of virtue is a phenomenology of existential functions, in terms of flourishing and maturity.

If we flourish in a rational way with a view to the other person, we possess prudence (*prudentia*). If we flourish rationally with a view to the Other, we have faith. If we flourish in our willing with a view to God because of Himself, we enjoy love. If we flourish in our willing with a view to our neighbor because of herself or himself, we possess justice. If we flourish in our willing with a view to our neighbor for our own good, we possess the virtue covering both temperance (*temperantia*) and courage (*fortitudo*). All these virtues are combined with the fruits of faith, the beatitudes, and the gifts of the Spirit. They are not ordered according to the pattern of nature and supernature, but in terms of simplification.[70]

12.11 PERSPECTIVE

The specialist literature on Duns Scotus' ethics has produced a rich harvest of paradoxes and antinomies for which Duns might be blamed. The general cause of such allegations consists in overlooking the logical and ontological center and structure of Scotus' thought. Exact exposition of Scotus' thought also shows that qualifications

---

[68] See the *responsio propria* of *Ordinatio* III 33, and consult Wolter, 'Duns Scotus on the Will as Rational Potency,' in *The Philosophical Theology of Scotus*, 163–180.

[69] The perfect summary is found in *Ordinatio* III 27 – see Wolter, *Scotus on the Will and Morality*, 424: Latin, and 423: English. Cf. §12.4.

[70] Cf. *DS* 92–97.

like 'voluntarism' and 'skepticism' easily miss the point. Mary Elizabeth Ingham's systematic approach of analyzing theories which Duns Scotus' ethics presupposes is preferable. She presented a fine survey of the basic parts of Duns Scotus' systematic thought wherein the whole of his ethical thought is rooted.[71] The historical context shows that these essentials closely fit in with the Condemnations of 1277 and its implications, although Scotus did not adhere to them because external authority had spoken. He was wholeheartedly convinced that this stance was true and that he was able to prove this. In fact, he saw it as his life-task to reveal the inherent reasonableness of all of the affiliated ideas and theories. Yet Ingham's final assessment is rather ambiguous. At the end of her fine exposition she concludes that 'Scotus corrects from a theological perspective certain philosophical errors; he does not appear to replace the Aristotelian tradition with something else.'[72] This was not Duns Scotus' conviction, not the view of the main tradition of thirteenth- and fourteenth-century thought he belonged to.

With John Duns, theory and life, head and heart point in the same direction. His scientific passion consists of truth and consistency. The whole of truth as he sees it is anchored in basic propositions about God and the essential propositions about God are necessary. If true, it is impossible that they are false. The fundamental truths of Duns' ethics are to be located on the same level, for faith and logic hold out a hand to each other. This basic dimension solves the allegations of paradox and antinomy. Ludger Honnefelder's thesis in *Scientia transcendens* characterizes Duns' ontology of contingency as the second start of the grand metaphysical tradition in the West.[73]

---

[71] Part I: 'The initial intuition' of Ingham, *Ethics and Freedom*, contains the following chapters: 1 – 'A philosophical context,' 2: 'The primacy of freedom,' 3: 'Divine freedom,' and 4: 'Freedom and the law.' An extrapolation of the Wolter and Ingham type of interpretation of Scotus' ethics is delivered by Shannon, linking Scotian ethics with the method of proportionalism: 'Method in Ethics,' *Theological Studies* 54 (1993) 272–293.

[72] Ingham, *Ethics and Freedom*, 143 (141–143). See §10.8 and Chapter 14.

[73] *Scientia transcendens. Die formale Bestimmung der Seiendheit und Realität in der Metaphysik des Mittelalters und der Neuzeit*, XI–XII: 'In zunehmendem Mass erwies sich vor allem seine Metaphysik als eine denkerische Leistung eigenen Ranges, die hinter der des Thomas nicht zurücksteht und die als der zweite grosse Entwurf bezeichnet werden muss, zu der die Auseinandersetzung mit der aristotelisch-arabischen Metaphysik im 13./14. Jahrhundert führte. Deutlicher als zuvor wurde damit auch die Voraussetzung sichtbar für das Übergewicht, dass im Spätmittelalter nicht die thomistische, sondern die scotische Schule gewann, sei es in Form der mit Antonius Andreas, Franz von Mayronis u.a. beginnenden – oft epigonalen – Fortführung, sei es in Form der mit Wilhelm von Ockham einsetzenden kritischen Transformation.'

John's personal spirituality shows the broad profile of an Augustinianism colored in a Franciscan way. For about thirty years, Duns lived and worked in Franciscan communities, in North England and Oxford, in Paris and Cologne. When he writes on hope, love, and faith, he almost unintentionally sketches his personal life of faith. The impersonal 'he' is changed into the personal 'ego' and this personal 'ego' is supported by his own desire that looks for God. The *summum bonum* or *bonum infinitum* deepens our desire for what is infinitely good. Hope is that desire, full of expectation, which is immediately directed towards God Himself for Himself. He gives Himself and Duns tells us: *I long for Him, I do not long for Him because of something else, but because of Himself.* 'I desire that this good (which is Himself) is mine' (*Lectura* III 26.19). He is my objective and 'I do not stop desiring it, desiring Him' (*Lectura* III 26.14). 'Non recedo.' It is the Augustinian sphere of *Cor nostrum est inquietum, donec requiescat in Te.* It is stable, dynamic, and very personal: 'I do not give up the act of desiring.' Duns' emotional life confirms the love structure of his theology, which is an expression of his life and experience. It is sensational to view reality through such eyes. We have to look after virtue. Reality is contingent and open.

CHAPTER 13

The philosophical theory of God

13.1 INTRODUCTION

The Christian faith confesses the openness of God and the openness of His reality. Classic Christian theology translates this openness into a structured concept of *God* by stating that the one divine nature (*una substantia*: Tertullian) knows of three divine Persons (*tres personae*: Tertullian). We see that a closed concept of God is rejected, since the concepts of *natura* and *persona* do not coincide. We may describe an absolutely closed concept of God as a concept where the notions of *natura* and *persona* coincide. The alternative form of monotheism knows of two processions (*processiones*) between the three Persons, which are generally acknowledged in thirteenth-century theology in terms of divine knowledge and will (Albert the Great and Thomas Aquinas, Bonaventure and Duns Scotus).

We focus on the first production or procession which is the generation of the Son by the Father: the Father brings forth the Son, the Father generates the Son. The generation is eternal reality: it is the eternal reality of an invariable act of God in God (*opus ad intra*) and this activity of generation presupposes the potency to generate:

1. If the Father generates the Son, then it is *possible* that the Father generates the Son.

However, the Aristotelian notion of *potency* (*possibility*) cannot elucidate this theological proposition. On the contrary, it makes it inconsistent. Aristotelian philosophy of nature and change is based on *potency* language, but if we apply this notion of *potency* to (1), the consequent

2. It is *possible* that the Father generates the Son

entails that by now there is no generation.[1] However, this consequence excludes the antecedent of (1). *Being possible to bring forth* and *being*

---

[1] For some aspects of notions of *possibility*, see §4.10, §7.3, and §10.2.

possible to be brought forth refer to the same reality (*Lectura* I 7.70–71). Nevertheless, the Father enjoys the very personal characteristic (*proprietas*) or profile (*notio*) in virtue of which He is God the Father (*genitor*). Pitfalls lurk on both sides of the doctrine of the Trinity: ancient philosophical concept formation makes the doctrine implausible and even incoherent and the mythological background of its terminology invites us to interpret it in a wrong way and to reject it too easily. Much modern theology asks for demythologization. The big surprise classic theology of the Trinity offers is the fact that theology already achieved demythologization in its own way. To my mind, Duns Scotus' doctrine of God is the culmination point of this ongoing process of demythologization – *pace* Harnack and Bultmann. However, such claims can only be substantiated if we accept an alternative treatment of *potency* and *possibility* because the reciprocal concepts of *passive potency* and *active potency* are not applicable. Such moments of the doctrine of God and the theology of the Trinity are at the heart of the matter of the scientific revolutions in logic and ontology Duns Scotus achieved. The new concepts of *logical possibility* and true (synchronic) *contingency* which were required, the new theories of will and of reality, all originate from the heart of the Christian notion of *God*. Duns Scotus' doctrine of God may be seen as the pinnacle and the crowning of the whole of his theology, but the underlying notion of God is the fruit of a way of thought that originates from the existential realities of repentance, spirituality, and the life of the sacrament. How is it possible that such specific sources make possible a universally applicable concept of God? In §13.2 we survey the issues regarding the existence and nature of God: some preliminary issues (§13.2.1), causation, finality and excellence (§13.2.2), infinity and unicity (§13.2.3), simplicity (§13.2.4), and several ontological aspects (§13.2.5). §13.3 expounds divine knowledge and §13.4 deals with several additional aspects of God's knowledge: the contingent nature of his immutable knowledge and the infallibility and eternity of divine knowledge. §13.5 clarifies the pivotal role of the divine will and the exposition is concluded in §13.6: 'Perspective.'

13.2   THE EXISTENCE OF GOD

13.2.1   Some preliminary issues

When we set out to study Duns Scotus' proofs for the existence of God, we may be surprised. The subtle doctor framed thousands of arguments, with a bewildering speed, and many of them are of a daunting complexity. Often Duns Scotus is not satisfied with the probative force of the arguments delivered by great predecessors nor by solutions proposed by famous older colleagues. Sometimes he is not even impressed by his own alternatives. Sometimes he thinks himself that the issue to be solved is very difficult: the nature of divine personhood, the possibility of an eternal world, and the doctrine of transubstantiation are examples in case. However, it is also evident that he does not think this as far as the existence of God is concerned. God is evidently not problematical for Duns, nor his existence – He is the source of an abundance of existential light and John Duns rejoiced in it for the whole of his life, especially in 1303, the year of personal distress. God incarnate is also the source of abundant certainty and joy. However, Duns does not think that christology is an easy affair. Not only is God not problematical, but showing that God exists is not thought to be problematical and, to Duns' mind, even demonstrating that God exists seems not to be a formidable task.

We do not observe any epistemological stress or a feel of incertitude. Nor do we find *one* complex, typically Scotian proof for God's existence, but the striking fact is that the harvest mainly consists of long series of small dense sketches of arguments and some elaborate digressions on preliminary issues.[2] It is evident that Duns is not prepared to reassure unquiet and uncertain minds. Nevertheless, he has a lot to offer and when revising his early *Lectura* I 2 notes he became so fascinated by the task that he only completed many an indicative argument. So, *Ordinatio* I 2 became a booklet on its own, but it is still not a sustained attempt to arrive eventually at the conclusion that God exists. That conclusion is reached at a rather early stage of the argumentation.

Duns' proof starts from the empirically evident claim that there exists something that is effected. The conclusion to be arrived at is that a first effective agent exists. Again and again, it is observed that no type of ontological argument starts from such an empirical premiss. Moreover, many philosophers have wondered why Duns assumed that the concept of a first effective agent is consistent, even if they lay stress

---

[2] See Van Breda, 'La preuve de l'existence de Dieu dans la *Lectura*,' *De doctrina Ioannis Duns Scoti* II 363–375. Cf. Wood, 'Scotus's Argument for the Existence of God,' *Franciscan Studies* 47 (1987) 257–277, and Craig, *The Cosmological Argument from Plato to Leibniz*, chapter 5.

on Duns' digressions on possibility which replace the contingent starting point with the idea of the possibility of a contingent proposition.
In particular, the premiss that it is possible that an agent is maximally
excellent is seen as the problematic cornerstone. How does Duns
know? When such questions beset us, we may appreciate Duns' point
of departure: *something is effected*. If we overlook this premiss, we
have a problem. Apparently, we have to believe alternatively that there
is nothing. If nothing *is* caused, there is only one thing, namely God. If
there is only a possible cause, then God exists, but the critic does not
look for this conclusion.

So, we may assume safely that something is caused. Then, we get
a complicated but not unacceptable theory of effective causation, for
if we reject all this material, we get into trouble when we try to
explain our actions, let alone divine existence. So, we accept some
effective causation and some causes and effects. If there is something
which is effected (*e*), then *e* is consistent and if there is *e* being consistent, then there is some effective agent which has to be a consistent
being, for an inconsistent being cannot exist and what does not exist
cannot be an effective agent. So, if the notion of *an effective agent* is
consistent, then the notion of *a first effective agent* is consistent too,
for a first effective agent is a kind of effective agent. Again, we are
struck by the fact that Duns does not make any fuss about it, but we
may appreciate this fact.

Essential (essentially ordered) and accidental causes

The crucial distinction holds between *essentially ordered causes* and
not essentially (accidentally) ordered causes. As to causes which are
not essentially ordered, one cause is not related to another cause in
order to cause together the effect. Grandfather and father are both
'causes' (*causae*) of *a* who is both the son of his father and the grand-
son of his grandfather, but father and grandfather are not coordinated
in order to bring forth *a*. However, *essentially* ordered causes require
such a coordination (*Lectura* I 2.45).

> Causalities of all essentially ordered causes concur at the same time
> in order to produce the effect, because the production of the effect
> requires that all its necessary causes concur. Moreover, all causes that
> are essentially ordered are necessary causes. Therefore, all causes that
> are essentially ordered actually concur in order to produce the effect,
> but this is not necessary in causes which are accidentally ordered,
> because every cause has its complete causality without any other

cause with respect to its effect. They are of the same status, immediately related to the effect.[3]

What is at stake in this argumentation is the notion of intermediate causes (*causae mediae*). All intermediate causes are caused themselves. So, the entire coordination of intermediate causes is caused. If there were no intermediate cause, then the effect would have to explain itself. If there was no first cause, then it is impossible that there is a first cause, but all causes are intermediate causes without a first cause. If there are no first causes and intermediate causes, it is impossible that there is any coordination of first and intermediate causes and, so, causes are not coordinated at all.

> Causalities of all essential causes concur at the same time in order to cause something that is caused. [. . .] But what is infinite cannot concur in one item. Therefore, there are no infinite causes. Therefore, it is the case that there exists a first cause.[4]

Causes that are essentially ordered are called *essential causes*. The coordination of essential causes is itself essential, for if such a coordination were not essential, the involved causes could have been missed. Then, the involved causes would have been accidental causes which would have been accidentally ordered. However, accidentally ordered causes cannot be essential causes. Just as the Scotian analysis of *contingency* is a structural matter, in the same way the analysis of *causality* is a structural matter. A structural analysis is related to one and the same indivisible moment of time. What matters is that it happens *at the same time* (*simul*). Structural moments are not chronologically ordered. If there are more effects successively, the involved causality of the first effect does not differ from the causality of other effects.

Duns appeals to a context within which these issues are explained: the essential order of essential causes. He presents a coherent frame which accounts for the overall validity of the whole argument. Let us

3 *Lectura* I 2.48: 'Causalitates omnium causarum essentialiter ordinatarum concurrunt simul ad productionem effectus, quia ad productionem effectus oportet quod omnes eius causae necessariae concurrant. Sed omnes causae essentialiter ordinatae sunt causae necessariae; igitur, omnes causae essentialiter ordinatae actu concurrunt ad productionem effectus. Sed hoc non oportet in causis accidentaliter ordinatis, quia quaelibet habet suam perfectam causalitatem sine alia respectu sui effectus, et sunt eiusdem rationis, immediate respicientes effectum.' On *essential causes*, see Brown, 'Infinite Causal Regression,' in Kenny (ed.), *Aquinas*, 214–236.
4 *Lectura* I 2.52: 'Causalitates omnium causarum essentialium simul concurrunt ad causandum aliquod causatum. [. . .] Infinita non possunt concurrere in unum, non igitur sunt infinitae. Est igitur dare primam.'

assume that such an essential order does not hold. Then the underlying entailment *If it possibly exists, then it actually exists* does not
hold water. Because such first effective agent possibly exists, it might
be not actual. If it is not actual, it is not an agent and if it is not an
actual agent, it is not a first being without further ado.[5]

Necessity and demonstration

We find one crucial string of argumentation added to the bare essentials of Duns' proof for the existence of God. He reformulates the
point of departure of his proof by installing alternative necessary premisses instead of a contingent premiss.

> I say: although beings different from God are actually contingent
> with respect to their factual existence, nevertheless, they are not
> with respect to their possible existence. Hence, those entities
> which are called contingent with respect to their factual existence
> are necessary with respect to their possible existence – for instance,
> although
>   *There exists a man*
> is contingent, nevertheless
>   *It is possible that he exists*
> is necessary, because his existence does not include any contradiction.
> Therefore
>   *Something – different from God – is possible*
> is necessary, because *being* is divided into the contingent and the
> necessary. Just as *necessity* belongs to a necessary being in virtue of
> its condition or its quiddity, so *possibility* belongs to a possible being
> in virtue of its quiddity. If the first argument is alternatively qualified
> with the notion of ontological possibility, then we have necessary
> propositions as follows:
> 'It is possible that there is something different from God – it is not
> of itself (because then it would not be the case that it were pos-
> sible), nor from nothing. Therefore, it is possible that it is from
> something else. Either it is possible that the other agent acts by
> virtue of itself – and not by virtue of something else, not
> being from something else – or it is not possible. If so, then it is
> possible that there is a first agent, and if it possible that it exists,
> then it exists, just as we have proved before.[6] If not and if there

---

[5] Wolter sees the theoretical relationship between *A first effective agent possibly exists* and *A
first effective agent actually exists* as an immediate one. See Frank and Wolter, *Duns Scotus.
Metaphysician*, 82, and cf. Wolter (ed.), *Scotus. A Treatise on God as First Principle* ([2]1983),
240 f.

[6] Consult *Lectura* I 2.41.

is no infinite regress, then the argument at once comes to a standstill.'[7]

The actualist start has still to be acknowledged. Duns does not argue from pure possibilities to the actual existence of God, but he starts with contingent reality and shows that the contingency of reality entails that this contingency itself is possible. In its turn, the possibility of contingent reality is necessary. So, there are moves from existence to possibility and from possibility to necessity, but then one crucial step is still to be made: the inference from necessity to God's actual existence.[8]

13.2.2 Causation, finality, and excellence

First of all, in *Lectura* I 2 *pars* 1 *quaestio* 2 the floor is open to Anselm. In *Lectura* I 2 the issue is whether the proposition that God exists is self-evident. A pro-argument is adduced on behalf of the affirmative answer:

> Furthermore, it is self-evident that that exists than which a greater cannot be thought.[9] The reason is that the subject collapses, if the opposite of the predicate is given. If this is not the case, then something greater can be thought, for *existence* that there is, is greater than

---

[7] *Lectura* I 2.57: 'Dico quod licet entia alia a Deo actualiter sint contingentia respectu esse actualis, non tamen respectu esse potentialis. Unde illa quae dicuntur contingentia respectu actualis exsistentiae, respectu potentialis sunt necessaria, ut licet *hominem esse* sit contingens, tamen *ipsum esse possibile esse* est necessarium, quia non includit contradictionem ad esse. Aliquid igitur *possibile esse* aliud a Deo est necessarium, quia *ens* dividitur in *possibile* et *necessarium*, et sicut enti necessario ex sua habitudine sive quiditate est necessitas, ita enti possibili ex sua quiditate est possibilitas. Fiat igitur ratio, quae prior, cum possibilitate essendi, et erunt propositiones necessariae sic: "Possibile est aliquid aliud a Deo esse, et non a se (quia tunc non esset possibile esse). Igitur, ab alio potest esse. Illud aliud aut potest agere in virtute sui, et non alterius, et esse non ab alio, aut non. Si sic, igitur potest esse primum; et si potest, igitur est, sicut prius probatur. Si non, et non est processus in infinitum, igitur aliquando stabitur".' Cf. *Lectura* I 30.59: 'Etsi aliud a Deo non sit necessarium ex se nec sit simpliciter necesse-esse, tamen aliud a Deo est necessario possibile-esse. [. . .] Licet non sit aliquid aliud a Deo simpliciter necessarium, est tamen aliquid simpliciter possibile.'

[8] See Frank and Wolter, *Duns Scotus. Metaphysician*, 80–85. Consult, in general, Cross's excellent expositions on the existence of God according to Scotus: *Duns Scotus*, 15–26. Cf. Gilson, *Jean Duns Scot*, 116–278, and *HCPMA* 454–461.

[9] There is the additional note *a*: 'Deus est huiusmodi, secundum Anselmum, *Proslogion*. Et ideo etiam non est finitum, igitur infinitum. Maior probatur.' This text tells us: 'This is the way God is, according to Anselm in the *Proslogion*. For this reason, He is not something finite; therefore, He is something infinite.' This addition is incorporated in *Ordinatio* I 2.11, which also makes explicit the *maior*. See Bonansea, 'Duns Scotus and St. Anselm's ontological Argument,' *De doctrina Ioannis Duns Scoti* II, 461–475.

non-existence.[10] This argument seems to be the argument of Anselm
in *Proslogion* 2.[11]

The defense of the self-evident nature of the proposition *God exists*
is dealt with as follows in *Lectura* I 2.35:

> When it is argued with respect to Anselm's argument that it is self-
> evident that that than which a greater cannot be thought exists, I say
> as to the second *obiectum* that this is not the case. It is not Anselm's
> intention to show that *God exists* is self-evident, but that it is true. He
> constructs two deductive arguments. The first of them runs as follows:
> *If there is anything that does not exist, then something is greater.*
>   *However*:   Nothing is greater than what is the highest.
>   *Therefore*:   What is the highest is not a non-being.
> The second deductive argument runs as follows:
>   What is not a non-being, exists.
>   *However*:   What is the highest is not a non-being.
>   *Therefore*:   What is the highest exists.[12]

It is evident that the young John Duns is quite familiar with Anselm's
thought. He agrees, but he also delivers a fruitful ontological translation by replacing the distinction between *in reality* and *in the mind*
(*in intellectu*) with the ontological opposition between *being* and *non-
being*. It is also evident that the framework is an actualist one.
Nevertheless, the *ratio Anselmi* is not the starting point of Duns' own
proof. That role is given to the *ratio Richardi*, although the point of
departure is a cogent explanation of the existence of created reality
with the help of the theory of transcendent terms.

In this light we look at Duns posing the problem. The second *quaestio* of *Lectura* I 2 asks whether the propositions *There is something
infinite* and *God exists* are self-evident. Duns sharply distinguishes

---

[10] Here note *b* is also to be considered: 'Quia si esset in re, maius esset quam si non esset in re
sed in intellectu.' Here, we meet Duns' actualist axiom: existence excels what does not exist
in reality. It does not exist in reality, if it is only in the mind. This addition is also incorporated in *Ordinatio* I 2.11.

[11] *Lectura* I 2.9: 'Praeterea, illud esse est per se notum quo maius cogitari non potest, quia detur
oppositum praedicati, destruetur subiectum. Si enim non sit, igitur aliquid maius cogitari
potest, quia *esse* quod est maius quam *non-esse*. Et haec videtur esse ratio Anselmi
Proslogion 2.'

[12] *Lectura* I 2.35: 'Ad aliud, quando arguitur de Anselmo: "Illud quo maius cogitari non potest
esse, est per se notum," dico quod non. Unde intentio Anselmi ibi non est ostendere quod
Deum esse sit per se notum, sed quod hoc sit verum. Et facit duos syllogismos quorum
primum est: Omni eo quod non est, aliquid est maius. *Sed*: Summo nihil est maius. *Igitur*:
Summum non est non-ens. Est alius syllogismus: Quod non est non-est, est; sed summum
non est non-ens. *Igitur*, summum est.'

between the epistemological level and the ontological level. He simply reformulates Anselm's proof in terms of this distinction. As far as the epistemological issue is concerned, if p is self-evident, then it is impossible to demonstrate that p is true. If we immediately know that p is true, we need not prove that p. Duns' proof theoretical stance is strict: if p is self-evident, then p is simply unprovable. If a strict proof can be framed on behalf of p, then it is not true that p is self-evident (see §9.3). However, the question whether *God exists* is true is asked in the first question: does the realm of what there is contain a being which is actually infinite? The idea that there is an actual infinite being is simply excluded by an Aristotelian philosophy of *actuality* and *potentiality*.[13]

In contrast with the famous five ways of Thomas Aquinas, Duns presents three theories: the *via efficientiae*, the *via eminentiae*, and the *via finalitatis*. The first *via* is the most important one and it is also the approach most attention has been paid to. The causal point of view is stressed, but the causal theory also has an enormous ontological impact. Moreover, the philosophical theory of God's existence is at home in church dogmatics. Duns' strategy is based upon his theory of transcendent terms. The key position is taken by what Duns calls God's *efficientia*. Nevertheless, the efficiency strategy has to be distinguished from physical proofs for the existence of God. Duns is not lenient towards to proof traditions like Aristotle's and Averroes' and particularly Averroes' view that metaphysics must be built on physics is criticized. The physical arguments are pushed out and the ontological line of Richard of St Victor is opted for.

In the first part of *Lectura* I 2 God's being and infinity are taken together. The question of divine existence immediately concerns *being* as it is infinite, although divine infinity shall be dealt with separately (*Lectura* I 2.64–95). The introductory question already demarcates the ontological context: on what there is. Everything that exists constitutes the domain to be considered. The question is: is there an actual infinite being (*ens infinitum*) among what there is (*in entibus*)? Duns introduces his exposition by pointing out that the infinite being has properties. These properties in particular are relational properties which are related to creation (*proprietates respectivae*). However, in itself, a relation presupposes something that has relations. Other being is to be derived from relational being and 'for this reason, properties of God which are related to creatures are the proper ways to

---

[13] In Aristotelian terms, only what is potential can be infinite. The notion of an *actual infinite* pops up only in Gregory of Nyssa's philosophy of religion.

know God's existence and his infinity and we have to prove such properties.'[14] This subtle strategy departs from an infinite being which possibly has some properties and, according to Duns, it has to be proved that this infinite being has some specific relational properties. For Duns, *per implicationem*, the question of God's existence is to be answered on the basis of a proof regarding certain properties, because if *a* has some property, then *a* does exist.

The physical approach arguing for the existence of a first mover is dropped. The existence of a first agent is argued for in terms of ontic causality. 'There is a being

> which is not eternal. For this reason, it is not from itself, nor from nothing, because it is not true that anything produces itself. Therefore, it is from another being. Therefore, either that being gives existence in virtue of something else, or this is not the case. If it is neither this way, nor that way – that is, it neither gives existence in virtue of something else, nor it takes existence from something else, then it is the first agent, because the notion of *first agent* comprises this. However, if it gives existence in virtue of something else, I ask the same question about that other being and there is no infinite regress. Therefore it is settled that a first effective agent does not cause in virtue of something else nor does it receives existence from something else. (*Lectura* I 2.41)

Duns interprets Richard's line of argumentation as answering the question of the philosophical explanation of temporal reality. There are entities which are not eternal. Possibly there is some time when they are not. According to the Christian faith, there was a time when they did not exist. Nothing is not productive. This necessary truth underscores Richard's argument. So, producing is producing something else. If something can be produced, then it is possibly produced by something else. Duns frames a series of exclusive disjunctions and with the help of the exclusion of an infinite regress it is concluded that there is a first causal agent. If there is an infinite regress, every being would have something producing it as a prior cause.[15] Duns summarizes his proof succinctly:

> Therefore, first, it is shown on the basis of effectivity that there is something which is first, because, as we have shown, there is something from

---

[14] *Lectura* I 2.38: 'In ente infinito sunt proprietates respectivae ad creaturas, et ex respectivo esse concluditur aliud esse. Ideo, proprietates respectivae Dei ad creaturas sunt propriae viae cognoscendi esse Dei et eius infinitatem, et huiusmodi proprietates oportet ostendere.'

[15] Duns' exclusion of an infinite regress is not to be understood here in terms of diachronic causality. He does not want to commit the fallacy of a *petitio principii*. The exclusion of a

which all that is possible can be. However, it is not possible that anything from which all that is possible can be is not of itself, since then it
would be from nothing. Therefore, it is necessary that it actually exists
of itself. This is the issue to be discussed.[16]

In rounding off this proof by concluding that a first effective agent
being of itself exists actually, it is not perfectly clear in *Lectura*
I 2.40–59 that the modality of divine existence arrived at is in fact the
possibility of such divine existence. The implicit transition from the
possibility to the actuality of God's existence is made explicit in
Reportatio Parisiensis I 2:

> If something *a* can exist while it is incompatible with the very notion
> of *a* that it be from something else, then it is possible that it exists of
> itself. However, *being from something else* is incompatible with the
> very notion of a first agent which is effective without further ado,
> since it is not an effect, nor does it have productive capacity from
> another agent. Nor is its ability to be productive, or its effectivity or
> its productivity due to something else. Furthermore, it is possible that
> it exists; therefore, it exists, for if it is possible that it exists, then it is
> either of itself, or from something else. However, it is not from some-
> thing else, because it is assumed to be first. If it is of itself, we have
> arrived at what is to be discussed, since it exists, if it is possible that
> it exists. Therefore, I conclude that it is the case that there exists an
> essential order in effective causes. Consequently, there is a first effect-
> ive agent without further ado.[17]

Finality

Agency requires direction, motivation, some purposiveness, and taking
into account a measure of achievement. The goal is that for the sake of
which an agent acts. So, action is tied to finality and purposiveness.

petitio principii requires a specific ordering of *causality*. Cf. O'Connor, 'Scotus's Argument
for the Existence of a First Efficient Cause,' *International Journal for Philosophy of Religion*
33 (1993) 17–32.

[16] *Lectura* I 2.59: 'Sic igitur primo ex efficientia ostenditur aliquod primum esse, quia, ut ostensum est, est aliquid a quo possunt omnia possibilia esse. Sed illud a quo possunt omnia possibilia esse non potest esse non a se, quia tunc esset a nihilo. Igitur oportet quod sit a se actu.
Et ita propositum.'

[17] *Reportatio Parisiensis* I 2, pars 1.ii (Frank and Wolter, *Duns Scotus. Metaphysician*, 50):
'Cuius rationi repugnat esse ab alio, illud si potest esse potest esse a se. Sed, rationi *primi
simpliciter effectivi* repugnat esse ab alio, quia non est effectum vel productivum ab alio, nec
virtute alicuius alterius est productivum vel effectivum vel producens. Et potest esse; ergo
est. Si enim potest esse, aut ergo a se, vel ab alio; non ab alio, quia ponitur primum. Si a se,
habetur propositum, quia si potest esse, est. Ergo concludo quod in causis efficientibus est
dare essentialem ordinem et per consequens aliquod efficiens primum simpliciter.'

Duns' proof for the existence of an agent acting for an ultimate goal is not spelled out in much detail in *Lectura* I 2 *part* 1 III A 2: from the viewpoint of *finality*. It is clear that, according to Duns Scotus, the argument is closely analogous to the proof for the existence of a first effective agent. His approach starts from the elementary nature of *agency* and is elaborated in terms of relational properties, for the basic relationship of agency is God being related to his creation. God is eminently good and uniquely active. His causality is effective and purposive. The second of the three main themes: causality or effectivity – finality – excellence, has to be paid attention to and this second proof based on *finality* reads as follows:

> Second, the thesis that a first agent exists is shown on the basis of *finality*. Something is suited to purposive agency. Therefore, either that agent directs to an end in virtue of itself, or in virtue of something else. If the first alternative is the case, then we have an end which is first. If it directs to an end in virtue of something else, then that second agent is suited to purposive agency. Since there is no infinite regress, we arrive at an end which is first.[18]

There are some agents and at least some actions are goal-directed and aim at an end. There can be a series of such goals. Something is done because of *a* and it is done because the goal *a* obtains for the sake of *b*. We cannot accept an infinite series of goals, because such an infinite regress blocks acting in terms of goals. So, there must be an ultimate goal, but Duns' finality proofs do not simply run in terms of goals themselves, but in terms of an agent directing to goals and an ultimate goal of activity. Eventually, it turns out to be that the first agent setting aims and an ultimate goal is God. *Setting an ultimate aim* is a possible attribute of God.[19]

> What Scotus wants to argue is that God is the ultimate goal of all actions. We normally think of goals as states of affairs, not as substances. But clearly, goals can be subsistent entities too: objects of our love. This is the sort of goal Scotus has in mind. The series of entities that we love for the sake of something else must be finite, headed by something that we love for its own sake.[20]

---

[18] *Lectura* I 2.60: 'Secundo, hoc ostenditur *ex fine*. Aliquid est aptum natum ad finem. Illud igitur aut finit in virtute sui, aut alterius. Si primum, igitur habetur propositum. Si in virtute alterius, igitur illud aliud est aptum natum ad finem, et non est processus in infinitum. Igitur, stabitur ad primum finem.'

[19] Duns Scotus does not present a possibility variant of his finality proof, but it is easily done.

[20] Cross, *Duns Scotus*, 23. Cf. *Ordinatio* I 2.60.

Excellence

The teleological argumentation links up well with the causal argumentation. If something is contingent and effected, then there is an activity of effecting and if there is activity, we may ask *why* it is done. Effective action presupposes the question: *why* are you doing so and so? If there is an infinite regress, this question cannot be answered. So, if we think there is a reasonable answer to be given, we escape from the infinite regress. In terms of the logic of finality, we are able to answer the question of the reasonableness of doing and effecting. In terms of the logic of excellence we are able to answer the question of the quality of doing so and so. The third of the three main themes: causality – finality – excellence, has to be paid attention to. The third proof based on *excellence* reads as follows:

> The third theory starts from *excellence*. Some good is excelled – or can be excelled (if you wish to argue in terms of *possibility*). Therefore, there is something which excels or can excel. Therefore, either that agent is excelled – or it can be excelled – or it is not. If not, then what is first in excellent goodness exists; if so, while there is no infinite regress, then the same follows as before.[21]

We meet again the same strategy. A possibility is assumed and if it proves possible to substantiate this possibility, it is reasonable to use this possibility as starting point. The crucial feature of this type of arguments for the existence of God is a recursive pattern, namely that it is assumed again and again that the property which is involved in the assumed possibility is essential for its bearer.[22]

Duns' analysis is based on the comparatives *better than* (excelling) and *less good* (excelled) and this comparative logic of *than* is exploited. The logic of *better than* leads to what is best and what is the best possible. Henry of Ghent and Duns Scotus apply this comparative logic to created reality and *excelling* and *better than* are seen as relations between God and creation. This realistic approach can also be transposed into an a priori argumentation which does not depart from creation. 'Its starting point is not what is good and commendable in creatures, because it is less good and defective, but aims

---

[21] *Lectura* I 2.61: 'Tertia via est *ex eminentia*. Aliquod bonum est quod est excessum vel natum excedi (si vis arguere cum possibilitate). Igitur est aliquid excedens vel natum excedere. Illud igitur vel exceditur aut natum est excedi, vel non. Si non, igitur est primum in eminentia bonitatis; si sic, et non est procedere in infinitum, igitur idem quod prius.'

[22] Regularly, Duns Scotus registers this pattern without paying much attention to the 'ontological' aspect of his own reasoning (Anselm). This dilemma shall be dealt with.

at what is completely and perfectly good and praiseworthy in the Creator.'[23]

The nature of the threefold primacy

We have looked at three lines of argumentation focusing on *causal agency, finality*, and *excellence*, respectively. The outcome is a three-fold primacy: an entity *a* which exhibits the property of *being a first effective agent*, an entity *b* which exhibits the property of *directing to an ultimate goal*, and an entity *c* which exhibits the property of *being maximally excellent*. Three logics – the logic of causal agency, the logic of *why?*-questions and the logic of *being better than* – show three first places, but how are *a*, *b*, and *c* related to each other? Duns' answer is simple and clear: *a*, *b*, and *c* are identical. Any entity which exhibits any of the three properties mentioned above must exhibit the other two as well:

> This threefold first agent is one and the same, because a first effective agent is most real and what is maximally excellent is the best of things. However, what is most real is also the best, with no mixture of evil or potentiality. Likewise, a first effective agent takes into account nothing but itself, for if it did not, the other agent would be better than itself. Therefore, it is the ultimate goal and so first in the order of goals. Therefore, they are identical.[24]

Effective primacy is a great-making property, for if a first effective agent is not present in a certain set of circumstances, it cannot function as a first agent. So, it must be the best of things if it is to do its job properly. Optimal goodness not only excludes evil, but it is also lacking potential goodness, as far as it is embodied in great-making properties. So, if the best is not real, its optimal goodness cannot work. So, it must be most real. Agents act for the sake of their goal, but the first effective agent cannot act for the sake of something else. If that were the case, there would be a rival which would excel the first effective agent which is the best agent. Therefore, the best effective agent is also the ultimate goal.

If *a* and *b* have the same properties in common, they are identical. Duns points out that the one property follows from the other and he

---

[23] See Henry of Ghent, *Summa* XXII 4 in the body of the article; cf. *Summa* XXV 2.

[24] *Lectura* I 2.62: 'Illud triplex primum est idem, quia primum efficiens est actualissimum et primum in eminentia est optimum. Sed quod est actualissimum, illud est optimum, nihil mali aut potentiae habens admixtum. Item, primum efficiens non intendit aliquid aliud a se, quia tunc illud esset nobilius eo. Igitur est ultimus finis, et ita primum im gradu finium. Sunt igitur idem.'

indicates only implicitly that we can also go the other way around.[25] The effectivity, the finality and the maximal excellence of the first agent which exists actually follow from each other. Finally, Duns connects this qualified agency with the nature of divine knowledge in *Lectura* I 2.63:

> We prove that God is his knowledge: if his knowledge be an accidental property, and not his nature, then there is a cause of his knowledge, because the first being is the effective cause of everything. However, God is a cognitive agent; therefore, He disposes of his knowledge before. About this knowledge we inquire as before. Either there is an infinite regress related to knowing anything so that He never knows anything, or we have the state of affairs that his actual knowledge is his essence.[26]

13.2.3 Infinity and unicity

Infinity

The next task Duns is committed to is proving that the first effective agent, acting for the sake of the ultimate goal and being maximally excellent, is infinite.[27] The temporal approach is rejected, and likewise Aristotle's concept of *eternity*. The divine nature is the foundation of God's infinity and the divine nature is also the foundation of God's knowledge:

> The thesis that God is infinite is shown on account of the divine essence which explains divine knowing. Just as an act of knowledge which is distinctly related to a number of things is more perfect than that act of knowledge which is only related to one thing, so also is the principle for knowing distinctly a number of things more perfect than

---

[25] As we may observe in many other cases, the sketchy argument of *Lectura* I 2.62 is elaborated on substantially in *Ordinatio* I 2.68–73. Cf. *Lectura* I 2.38–135 with *Ordinatio* I 2.39–190, a booklet on its own. See Prentice, 'The Evolution of Scotus' Doctrine on the Unity and Unicity of the Supreme Nature,' *De doctrina Ioannis Duns Scoti* II 377–408.

[26] *Lectura* I 2.63: 'Probatur Deus sit sua intellectio, quia si sua intellectio sit accidens et non natura eius, igitur cum primum ens sit causa efficiens omnium, erit causa suae intellectionis. Sed Deus est agens per cognitionem, igitur prius cognovit eam. Et de illa cognitione quaeritur [. . .], aut erit processus in infinitum ad hoc quod aliquid intelligat, et sic numquam aliquid intelliget, vel erit status, quod sua intellectio sit sua essentia.'

[27] In fact, Duns' starting point is the necessary truth: (x) (x is finite or x is not finite). Adding the premiss: 'it is not true that a is finite, we derive: a is not finite. As we have seen in §4.8 on negation, Duns' logic is familiar with both predicates and their complements, just as in modern logic: if a is not white, then a possesses the complement property *being not-white*. Compare Freitas, 'De argumentatione Duns Scoti pro infinitate Dei,' *De doctrina Ioannis Duns Scoti* II 427–434.

is the principle for knowing only one of them. Thus an essence which represents a number of things distinctly is more perfect than the essence which represents but one. However, the divine essence represents an infinity of things distinctly. Therefore, this essence possesses an infinite power of representation. Therefore, the divine essence itself is infinite.[28]

Analogously, Duns applies this pattern to divine knowledge in *Lectura* I 2.78:

A numerical plural requires greater perfection. So, an infinite number requires infinite perfection and an act of knowing related to a number of things is more perfect than an act of knowing related to only one item, as shall be proved. So, an act of knowledge knowing an actual infinity requires infinite perfection. However, the first cognitive and effective agent knows an infinity of things actually and distinctly with a single act of knowledge, as shall be proved. Therefore, it is actually of infinite perfection.[29]

The logic of superior, more reasonable and better knowledge entails the notion of an infinite act of knowledge.

Unicity

Assume that there is a necessary plurality of being divine. If there is necessarily a plurality of *being divine*, then there is at least a necessarily divine *a* and a necessarily divine *b*. If *a* and *b* have in common all possible properties, then *a* and *b* are identical. If they are identical, there is no plurality of necessarily divine beings. If there be a plurality of necessarily divine beings, then it must be possible to point out their differences, but it is not allowed that these differences concern the formal essentiality (necessity) under consideration, because then there is no formal essentiality of *being divine*. Therefore, there is no plurality of being divine:

---

[28] *Lectura* I 2.80: 'Hoc ostenditur ex parte essentiae divinae, quae est ratio intelligendi: sicut enim intellectio quae est distincte plurium, est perfectior illa quae est unius tantum, sic illud quod est principium intelligendi distincte plura, est perfectius illo quod est tantum principium intelligendi unum. Et essentia quae repraesentat distincte plura, erit perfectior illa quae tantum repraesentat unum. Sed essentia divina distincte repraesentat infinita, igitur habet virtutem infinitam repraesentandi. Est igitur infinita.'

[29] Ibid.: 'Pluralitas numeralis requirit maiorem perfectionem, et infinita infinitam. Sed intellectio plurium distincte est maioris perfectionis quam intellectio unius tantum, ut probabitur. Igitur, intellectio actu infinitorum requirit infinitam perfectionem. Sed primum intelligens et efficiens unica intellectione intelligit actu et distincte infinita, ut probabitur. Igitur, est actu infinitae perfectionis.' Cf. *De primo principio* IV 48–72 (Wolter). See also O'Connor, 'From First Efficient Cause to God,' *Metaphysics and Ethics*, 435–454.

If there is a plurality of necessary beings, then they are distinguishable in a certain respect. We assume that *a* and *b* are the components by which they are distinguished. Then, either *a* is an ontological necessity, considered from the formal point of view, and *b* likewise, or not. If so, then *a* and *b* are not distinguishable in this respect, since they share in a common necessity. If, from the formal point of view, they are not ontological necessities, then they are not necessary beings in a formal sense because of the components by which they are distinguished. The components by which they are distinguished, are possible entities and, consequently, both of them being a first effective agent and a necessary being, include contingency. So, they are not necessary beings.[30]

The hypothesis that there is a plurality of what exists necessarily is a contradictory one. So, there is only one necessary divine being. However, most arguments for the claim that there can be only one God numerically start from the idea that God is infinite in several respects. The argument from infinite power 'attempts to demonstrate that there cannot be two infinitely powerful agents. As Scotus understands infinite power, an agent is infinitely powerful if and only if it has the capacity to bring about any possible effect.'[31] The capacity of such an agent can explain any possible effect. So, it is a sufficient condition for any factual effect and there can be only one agent endowed with infinite power:

Two causes of the same order cannot both be the total cause of the same effect. But an infinite power is the total primary cause of every single effect that exists. Therefore, no other power can be the total primary cause of any effect. Consequently, no other cause is infinite in power.[32]

---

[30] *Lectura* I 2.121: 'Si sint plura necesse-esse, igitur *secundum aliquid* distinguuntur. Sint igitur illa in quibus distinguuntur *a* et *b* – aut igitur *a* est formaliter necessitas essendi et *b* similiter, aut non. Si sic, in illis non distinguuntur, quia conveniunt in necesse-esse; si non sunt formaliter necessitates essendi, igitur non sunt formaliter *necesse-esse* per ea quibus distinguuntur, quia illa quibus tunc distinguuntur erunt entitates possibiles, et per consequens utrumque quod est primum efficiens et necesse-esse, includet possibilitatem, et ita non erunt necesse-esse.'

[31] Cross, *Duns Scotus*, 27. *Omnipotence*, taken in its Christian sense, is a kind of infinite power to be specified as follows: an agent is *omnipotent* only if it has the capacity to bring about any possible effect *immediately*, that is 'without the activity of any causal chain between the agent and any of its effects' (ibid.).

[32] *Ordinatio* I 2.172 f. The English translation is Cross's (ibid.). On divine unicity, see Cross, *Duns Scotus*, 27–29, Wolter, 'The Existence and Nature of God,' in *The Philosophical Theology of Scotus*, 273–275, and Wainwright, 'Monotheism,' in Audi and Wainwright (eds), *Rationality, Religious Belief, and Moral Commitment*, 289–314.

13.2.4 Simplicity

The traditional characterization of the doctrine of *divine simplicity* ignores the classic theory which was developed in the Western tradition of theological scholasticism. On the negative side this theory lacks extravagant claims, and on the positive side it mainly comprises three distinctive points. These three points are to be seen as the kernel of the theory of Duns Scotus: there are no quantitative parts of God because God is not a material and corporeal being. For the same reason the distinction between *subject* and *accident* is not applicable to God. God does not have corporeal accidents because He does not have matter nor quantity in the material sense of the word. The notion of *accident* is built on the notions of *matter* and *passive potency*. Along the same lines, the distinction between *matter* and *form* (the so-called *essential parts* of an entity) is not applicable to God.[33] In sum, the apparatus of Aristotelian logic is not suitable as a conceptual foundation for the doctrine of divine simplicity, and, in general, for the doctrine of God.[34]

Thus Duns Scotus denied some kinds of distinctions, namely distinguishing between material parts and quantitative aspects of God. The striking fact is that these kinds of denials are lucidly reasoned. If God is not material and if God does not have a body in an essential way, then distinctions and separations which presuppose material and corporeal reality are out of place. However, the denials of kinds of composition pointed out by Duns are not only crucial, there are also denials which are conspicuous by their absence. Duns tries to create room for the presence of individual properties and strictly equivalent properties. Quite a lot of innovations are needed in order to avoid fideism and irrationalism when the opposition to Aristotelian semantics and logic is fundamental. When it is conceded that talk of God cannot be elucidated with the help of these theories, the consequence is a *sacrificium intellectus* if these theories are the only ones we have in our possession. The function of Duns' logical and ontological innovations is precisely to fill this gap and at the same time they constitute quite decisive contributions to the development of rational thought.

---

[33] *Lectura* I 8.8–9: 'Deus est omnino simplex. Et circa hoc sunt tria ostendenda: primo, quod in essentia sua non habet compositionem, ita quod ibi non sit compositio partium essentialium (quae dicitur esse compositio essentialis); secundo, quod non est ibi compositio partium quantitativarum, ita quod non habet quantitatem; et tertio, quod ibi non est compositio accidentis cum subiecto.' See *Lectura* I 8.10–47.

[34] See *Lectura* I 8.8–27. On divine simplicity, see Cross, *Duns Scotus*, 29 f. Cf. *KN* (1981) 341–351, and Immink, *Divine Simplicity*.

This observation may become clear when we compare Duns' approach with that of Thomas Aquinas.

Prima facie, *Summa Theologiae* I 3 may not seem to deliver much evidence that the stance of *Summa Theologiae* I 3 is incompatible with *Lectura* I 8.8–27. The simpler version of Duns turns on the same kind of ideas as Thomas' does. However, when we turn to *Summa Theologiae* I 14 and 18, we observe the intrusion of the basic ideas of *divine simplicity* into wider areas of the doctrine of God. *Summa Theologiae* I 14.2–3 and 5 are quite compatible with Scotus' point of view, but if we analyze *Summa Theologiae* I 14.4 and 8, we become aware of disagreements. The center of this theoretical storm is the relationship between God's essence and his knowledge. According to Thomas Aquinas, God's act of knowing is his essence and his being. In God his intellect, the known, the *species intelligibilis*, and the act of his knowing are one and the same.[35] Because God's essence is necessary, his one act of knowing is necessary and all the known must be necessary. Such a line of argumentation rests on ignoring the basic distinction between *subject* and *predicate*. According to Thomas, in no sense is God a body composed of extended parts. Neither is God composed of form and matter, because God cannot contain matter. The distinction between kind and specific difference is not applicable to God, nor is the distinction between substance and accidents. There can be no composition with other things. However, Thomas also defends the point that God has to be identified with his own essence or nature, since the individual does not differ from his own nature.[36] Duns Scotus' and Thomas Aquinas' theories of predication and individuality differ substantially from each other and these crucial differences also determine their doctrines of divine simplicity. Given Duns' theory of individual haecceity, it is quite clear that he disagrees with the following argument: 'The individuality of things not composed of matter and form cannot however derive from this or that individual matter, and the forms of such things must therefore be intrinsically individual and themselves subsist as things. Such things are thus identical with their own natures.'[37]

Modern theology still mirrors these disagreements as we see when Charles Hodges distinguishes between creaturely predicates to be said

---

[35] *Summa Theologiae* I 14.4 in the body of the text.

[36] See *Summa Theologiae* I 3.3 in the body of the text: 'Dicendum quod Deus est idem quod sua essentia vel natura. [. . .] Unde in eis non differt suppositum et natura.'

[37] *Summa Theologiae* I 3.3 in the body of the text. The English translation is taken from the Blackfriars translation. Cf. Hughes, *On a Complex Theory of a Simple God.*

of God, trinitarian properties, divine perfections, or attributes and accidents:

> The perfections of God [. . .] are attributes, without which He would cease to be God. [. . .] There are two extremes to be avoided. First, we must not represent God as a composite being, composed of different elements; and, secondly, we must not confound the attributes, making them all mean the same thing, which is equivalent to denying them all together. [. . .] The theologians were accustomed to say that the attributes of God differ from his essence *non re, sed ratione*. This is explained by saying that things differ *ex natura rei*.[38]

He realizes that the tradition of classic theology is not entirely homogeneous and that Schleiermacher enjoys some support from the past. However, Hodge prefers the way Turrettini and Hollaz have presented the matter.

13.2.5   Ontological aspects

Although in *Lectura* I 2 Duns' methodological strategy is not perfectly clear, we are able to see that his strings of arguments have an enormous potential. If arguments concerning the equivalence of properties hold water, then an argument for God's existence need not deliver a series of proofs pointing out that every property is instantiated by a bearer. If in only one case Duns Scotus succeeds in demonstrating that God exists, then the concatenation of equivalent properties allows us to infer quite substantial knowledge about God.

Short implicit lines of argumentation, which in fact are mere sketches of argumentation, abound in *Lectura* I 2 *part* 1. If we were to weave together the different strands of incomplete arguments, we could make such short sketches complete,[39] for example *quaestio* 3 deals with the issue whether there is only one God. In §116 Duns brings forward the element of *necessary existence*. If a great-making property entails necessary existence, not only is the strict equivalence of individual great-making properties proved, but also the existence of the unique bearer of these properties. Richard Cross designed a reconstruction of Duns' proof, composed of elements collected from the different treatments Duns wrote over the years.[40]

---

[38] *Systematic Theology* I 369. Cf. Ralph John Danhof, *Charles Hodge as a Dogmatician*, Goes 1929, 72: 'Hodge denied that the divine attributes differ either *realiter* or *nominaliter*.'

[39] See Cross, *Duns Scotus*, 25 f. (18–30).

[40] This series of 'treatises' is a fine illustration of the 'monographic' tendency, running from *Lectura* I 2.38–135 to the fully-fledged monograph *De primo principio* is.

Nevertheless, *Reportatio Parisiensis* I 2 delivers the missing link. The enigmatic nature of Duns Scotus' proofs for the existence of God is rooted in his actualism. Eventually, Duns takes necessary propositions as a starting point for his proof, but this modal necessity is dependent on possible propositions and, in their turn, the possibility which is inherent in these propositions derives from the possibility of contingent propositions but, with Duns, *contingency* entails *actual truth*. According to Weinberg, Duns Scotus' starting point is that something is effectible and 'as there can be no infinite regress in effective beings which are effective only by virtue of being effected by something else, we must come eventually to a first effective being. This proves that a first effective being is a *possibility*.'[41] Thus Scotus aims at deriving the actual existence of God from the possibility of a first effective being. This may hold for later Scotists, but not for the historical Duns Scotus.

Richard Cross has been aware of some missing link and his recent work on Duns Scotus' theology and philosophy has some remarkable features and qualities. He is one of only a few authors who engage directly in a debate with Scotus. Discussing Duns Scotus' *excellence* proof for the existence of God, Cross observes:

> Scotus oddly claims that this [i.e. the idea that there is a most perfect member in an essential ordering of causes] supports the thesis that there is a 'simply unexcelled being', by which he means one that cannot be excelled – a maximally excellent being.[42]

To my mind, *a maximally excellent being* or *the best possible Person* are excellent definitions of what it is to be *God*,[43] but it is a remarkable fact that, in general, Duns Scotus' proofs do not use the 'ontological' point of departure.

However, Cross saw what was missing and also recorded the missing link found in *Reportatio Parisiensis* I 2. Here, the point of contact is the notion of *being uncaused*. *Being uncaused* must be an essential property of *a*, because if it is not, it is possible that *a* is caused

---

[41] Weinberg, *A Short History of Medieval Philosophy*, 221, cf. 117.

[42] Cross, *Duns Scotus*, 24. See *Reportatio Parisiensis* (eds Wolter/McCord Adams) I 2.73; cf. 30 – the English translation is found in Frank and Wolter, *Duns Scotus. Metaphysician*, 65–67. Cf. *Ordinatio* I 2.138 and 64, and *De primo principio* (ed. Wolter) IV 65; cf. III 35–37.

[43] A concept like *being the best possible person* does not constitute a *definition* (*definitio*) according to the medieval theory of definition. So, if it is said '*D* is not a definition,' which concerns the *form* of something, then the conclusion that *D* does not constitute a *definition* – according to our theory of definition – is faulty. Anselm and Scotus offer excellent candidates for definitions of what is to be meant by *God*. Duns uses *IQM* as a *descriptio* in *Ordinatio* I 2.137.

by something else and, then, it is also possible that *a* does not exist. However, if *a* does not exist, then it is impossible that *a* is uncaused, for there is no *a* to enjoy the property of *being uncaused*. Anything that is essentially uncaused must exist necessarily, since it is impossible if it is not essentially uncaused. *Being essentially uncaused* is certainly a great-making property. So, if a being is maximally excellent, then it is uncaused, because a maximally excellent being does not lack any great-making property.[44]

Essentially, Cross observes that Duns Scotus' arguments defend a host of essential properties of God and also reveal an 'ontological' pattern which boils down to the following entailment for any great-making property *P*, given that God is the bearer of such properties:

3. If it is *possible* that God enjoys *P*, it is *necessary* that God enjoys *P*.

Cross also points out that 'if (13) can be shown to be true, Scotus's argument will look fairly compelling,'[45] for if God enjoys a necessary property, then God – the bearer of the property – is himself a necessary entity, because it is impossible that *a* enjoys a certain property *Q* in a possible world *W*, if it does not exist in the possible world *W*. However, if God exists in any possible world *W*, then God exists in *Actua*, the factual possible world.

We look in vain for an Anselmian styled version of demonstrating attributes of God in *Lectura* I 2. However, *Ordinatio* I 2.137–147 offers a long digression which picks up the thread of the references to Anselm's ontological argument in *Ordinatio* I 2.11 (cf. *Lectura* I 2.9) and in *Ordinatio* I 2.35 (cf. *Lectura* I 2.35).[46] Here, we find the coloring of the Anselmian argument, famous from its version in *De primo principio*. The following element lends color to the argument involved:

---

[44] The final line of argumentation runs as follows: a maximally excellent being exists, for if a being exists necessarily – and such a being exists necessarily, if it exists possibly – then it exists actually. We have already seen that an uncaused being exists necessarily.

[45] Cross, *Duns Scotus*, 25. With Cross, (13) is the following proposition: it is possible that something is maximally excellent. A set of great-making properties is consistent, for if it is not, then the conjunctive great-making property is an impossible one. However, an impossible property cannot be a great-making property. If a certain candidate of being a great-making property is excluded by some core of great-making properties, then such a candidate does not make these properties inconsistent, for it has to be abolished.

[46] It is added at the end of the systematic exposition before the last part of *Ordinatio* I 2.2 *quaestio* 1, §§148–156, dealing with the *obiecta* of this question. See §9.2.1.

The argument of Anselm on the highest good conceivable can be colored by this element and its definition has to be understood as follows:

> If God is known consistently, He is that greater than which nothing can be thought consistently.[47]

Duns comments that the addition of *consistently* (*sine contradictione*) is obligatory, because in a broad sense our thoughts may be inconsistent. However, if a contradiction is involved, there are two thought contents which exclude each other and, for this reason, they do not form *one* consistent thought content.

Just at this point Duns passes on from the epistemological to the ontological level: if the highest entity is consistently conceivable, it *can be* in reality. So, from the point of view of *quidditative being* or *essential being* (*esse essentiae*) the item of the highest being consistently conceivable enjoys the nature of being an epistemic object. This feature means that the definition of the transcendent term *being* (*ens*) is applicable, even in the highest sense, because it is the highest good. We can only conclude that it also shares in the *existential being* (*esse existentiae*). A reformulation which is nearer to Anselm's *Proslogion* 3 is added to this typically Scotian interpretation of the Anselmian argument: if something is conceivable, then either it is possible that it exists, or it is not possible that it exists. It is only impossible that it exists if some contradiction excludes its possible existence. This possibility is excluded by coloring the Anselmian argument. Actual existence excels purely possible existence ontologically. So, the highest entity consistently conceivable exists actually.[48]

Finally, the ontological *possibility-actuality* pattern, characteristic of *Proslogion* 3, is made perfectly explicit in *Reportatio Parisiensis* I 2.73:

> If something that is the highest entity conceivable is in the intellect, then it follows that it *can exist* in actuality. And if it *can exist*, it *does exist*, for if it cannot, it is not the highest entity conceivable.[49]

---

[47] *Ordinatio* I 2.137: 'Per illud potest colorari illa ratio Anselmi de summo bono cogitabili, *Proslogion*, et intelligenda est eius descriptio sic: Deus est quo cognito sine contradictione maius cogitari non potest sine contradictione.'

[48] See *Ordinatio* I 2.138: 'Non est autem hoc sic intelligendum quod idem si cogitetur, per hoc sit maius si exsistat, sed, omni quod est in intellectu tantum, est maius aliquod quod exsistit.' For Duns, the argument is compelling *in excelsis*, because his actualism does not accept the purely possible. *Ordinatio* I 2.139 underscores this point. An *Epilogue* (*Ordinatio* I 2.145–147) finely summarizes the whole argumentation. See also §7.5.

[49] *Reportatio Parisiensis* I 2.73 (Frank-Wolter, *Duns Scotus. Metaphysician*, 66): 'Si aliquid summum cogitabile est in intellectu, sequitur ergo: potest esse in effectu. Et si *potest esse*, *est*, quia si non, non est summum cogitabile.'

Cross's assessment that Scotus' arguments look fairly compelling has to be endorsed, but a difference between his analysis and the Scotian evidence also has to be noticed. We touch the root of the problem in interpreting Duns Scotus' ontology. Cross's reconstruction integrates the lines of Anselm's *Proslogion* 2 and 3 in a modern way. Statement (3) above basically represents Cross's insight that there is an Anselmian dimension to Scotus' proofs. 'There can be no doubt at all that something than which a greater cannot be thought exists both in the understanding and in reality.'[50] If something than which nothing greater can be thought can be thought to exist in reality, then we have to conclude that it exists in reality. However, it can be thought to exist in reality. So, something than which a greater cannot be thought exists in reality, but if so, it is not possible to think of something than which a greater cannot be thought not existing, for if it can be thought not to exist, it is not identical with that than which nothing greater can be thought. 'And that simply will not do. Something than which nothing greater can be thought so truly exists that it is not possible to think of it as not existing.'[51]

First, Anselm derives existence from conceivable existence and, second, he derives – theoretically – necessary conceivability of divine existence from existence. This approach can benefit from an ontological translation which runs from possible existence to actual existence and from actual existence to necessary existence or necessarily enjoying properties. When we coordinate these two entailments, we have the basis of Cross's appraisal. All this is right and sound.[52] This is certainly one of the ways Scotus' doctrine of God has to be extrapolated, but it is not the key to interpreting Duns' factual argumentation. Duns' underlying actualism is the key to interpreting both his ontology and his proofs for the existence of God. Duns Scotus' first premiss is a *fact* – the fact of something effectible. If we can prove that a certain instance explains this fact, then we have arrived at two results: this instance is an actual agent, for we cannot explain a fact in terms of a purely possible agent, and this instance must be consistent, because an inconsistent agent cannot do anything and, so, does not explain anything.

---

[50] Conclusion of *Proslogion* 2 (English translation by Benedicta Ward, *The Prayers and Meditations of Saint Anselm* (^{2}1979) 245).

[51] Conclusion of *Proslogion* 3 (English translation by Benedicta Ward, ibid.).

[52] Suppose we have: '($Mp \rightarrow p$), then we can derive: ($Mp \rightarrow p$) $\rightarrow$ ($p \rightarrow Np$). With the help of the so-called hypothetical syllogism, we arrive at: $Mp \rightarrow Np$, the pattern of Cross's reconstruction.

Now, along Scotian lines, we may prove that the wonderful agent *a* enjoys the essential properties *F*, *G*, and *H*. The next step is selecting an imposing but complicated property *I*. Does *a* enjoy *I*? Only if *I* is a great-making property, but *I* is only a great-making property, if *I* is a possible property. This approach finely illustrates Duns Scotus' method – for better or for worse: Duns does not start a priori from the possibility dimension, but when he moves to the level of explaining what is in fact the case, he realizes that his favorite candidate is only a candidate *if* it is a possible candidate. Here, the consistency questions come in – not on an a priori level, but as a tool for perfecting the primary actualist argumentation. Duns loves to do so and apparently such questions are to his logical taste, but such analyses do not betray his fundamental intentions. They do not mirror the structure of his ontology, nor the tenor of his theory of divine properties.

13.3   GOD'S KNOWLEDGE

13.3.1   The nature of divine knowledge

In *Lectura* I 39 and *Ordinatio* I 39, Scotus raises the crucial *quaestio* whether the contingency of reality be compatible with God's know-ledge.[53] A *quaestio* is a question which poses a dilemma: a *quaestio* does not ask whether a particular event *e* happened or not, or whether it happened in 1265 or in 1266, or how probable *e* was, but a *quaes-tio* asks whether *p* is possible or not, or whether *p* is possible, given *q*.[54] Thus the target of Duns' analysis is the theory which considers God's knowledge to be incompatible with the contingency of reality. According to the contending type of theological epistemology, divine knowledge entails necessary truth. Objections taken from Aristotle's *De Interpretatione* are adduced to confirm the view that knowledge entails necessity.[55] The view that God has no infallible knowledge of reality assumes the same epistemic conviction that *knowledge* entails *necessity*, for in this case the possibility of not-knowing *p* although God knows that *p* proves that God is fallible. Again, the fallibility or infallibility of God are not contingent properties of God – *being fallible* or *being infallible* is a necessary property of God. So, the whole of epistemology is at stake when the possible contingency of divine knowledge is to be discussed.

---

[53] See CF 18 ff.: 'on the consequences of God's knowledge of future and contingent states of affairs.
[54] A *quaestio* is a dilemma in the Rylean sense of the word – see Ryle, *Dilemmas*, chapter 1.
[55] See *Lectura* I 39.1–3. Consult CF 44–49.

Duns is not only critical of a necessitarian theory of knowledge and science, but he is also adamant to develop a true alternative to it. He does not accept a vague notion of (diachronic) *contingency* so that it could be granted verbally that something contingent can be known as being necessary: for us, the state of affairs *s* is contingent, but for God *s* is necessary. Duns does not agree:

> We answer that no intellect can know a contingent proposition as being necessary, unless it were to err. Therefore, it does not make sense to say that contingent states of affairs are necessary as they are known by God; He knows the contingent as contingent.[56]

The consequence of posing the problem in this Scotian way is that *necessity* and *contingency* exclude each other in a contradictory way. The necessity of *p* excludes the synchronic possibility of *–p* so that *necessity* itself becomes *synchronic* necessity. If necessity and contingency are related to each other in such a way, while both really obtain, we have to assume both *necessary knowledge* and *contingent knowledge* if both dimensions of reality are known completely.[57] So, Duns Scotus' fundamental thesis is that God knows necessarily what is necessary and that He knows contingently what is contingent.

13.3.2   Stages of divine knowing

From the logical point of view, Scotus' philosophy is a coherent elaboration of the distinction between contingent and necessary propositions. God possesses both contingent and necessary knowledge. The contingency of reality is reclaimed from entrenched philosophical fashions. Ontologically, reality is not one-dimensional; so, personal activities are not one-dimensional either. Therefore, God is not one-dimensional. God would be one-dimensional if He were only to act by his essence and his essence-based knowledge. If so, the whole of reality known to God were necessary. It is clear that the decisive point of Scotus' doctrine of God is that God acts by his knowledge and by his will. 'God works by *intellect* and *will*.'[58]

---

[56] *Lectura Prologus* 112: 'Nullus intellectus potest cognoscere *contingens* ut *necessarium*, nisi erret. Et ideo nihil est dicere quod contingentia ut cognoscuntur a Deo sunt necessaria, sed cognoscit *contingens* ut *contingens*.' Cf. *Ordinatio Prologus* 212: 'Cognoscere contingens ut necessarium, non est cognoscere contingens. 'See also Vos et al., *Duns Scotus on Divine Love*, chapter 1. Cf. Cross's treatment of divine knowledge according to Scotus: *Duns Scotus*, 48–55.

[57] In the case of incomplete knowledge, all knowledge is contingent. If we can forget anything – and we certainly are able to do so – then all human knowledge is synchronically contingent, because anything diachronically contingent is synchronically contingent.

[58] *Lectura* I 39.42: 'Deus autem est movens per *intellectum* et *voluntatem*.'

The pattern of *omniscience* is connected with the idea of *knowability*. God not only knows everything there is, but also everything knowable. However, what in fact is the case cannot be derived from the whole of what is knowable. The knowledge of *Actua* is not entailed by the whole of what is knowable, just as what is factual is not entailed by what is possible, although the factual is also possible. The logic of *structural priority* is at work. Duns Scotus expounds divine knowing in incomparable detail. How personal this frame of mind, on the one hand, may be, on the other hand, it is just what the universal Christian tradition needs to solve its internal dilemmas. The following stages or structural moments of God's knowledge can be discerned.

I God knowing his own essence

What enjoys the priority of the *first structural moment* is seen under the aspect of what is essential without any specifying qualification and, at the same time, most universal. This knowledge must be knowledge of the best possible Knower. God has first-rate knowledge and, so, from the epistemic point of view, God's self-knowledge is primary. The theory of the knowledge of God starts with the feature of divine identity:

> The divine intellect knows the divine nature at the first moment.[59]

God enjoys best possible knowledge, since He is God:

> The intellect of God, seeing his essence at the first moment [*in instanti primo* videns *essentiam suam*], sees all things according to their being knowable.[60]

II God knowing neutral propositions as alethically neutral propositions

From God's best possible self-knowledge flows what is the best possible knowledge of everything else:

> God *can* know whatever is knowable. He can only know what He actually knows, since there is no potency in Him. Therefore, He has everything knowable in his mind and, so, everything knowable is eternally known.[61]

[59] *Lectura* I 36.22: 'Intellectus divinus primo intelligit essentiam.'
[60] *Lectura* I 39.93: 'Intellectus divinus *in instanti primo* videns *essentiam suam*, videt omnes res secundum earum esse intelligibile.'
[61] *Lectura* I 35.15: 'Deus potest intelligere quodcumque intelligibile, non autem potest intelligere nisi quod actu intelligit, quia in ipso non est potentia. Igitur, habet omne intelligibile in intellectu suo aeternaliter cognitum.'

At the same time, Duns Scotus turns against the view that God's existence and nature, knowing and willing, follow naturally from each
other.[62] First, Duns lays the foundations in order to be able to distinguish between what is necessary and what is contingent, with respect
to both divine willing and divine knowing:

> The intellect of God, seeing his essence at the first moment, *sees all
> things according to their being knowable, since in terms of that
> moment they are constituted into their being knowable,* but still they
> have no being in being producible *before* they have *being willed* by
> the will. Therefore, when a thing has that status, the intellect of God
> sees it in seeing his own essence.[63]

Let us ponder a bit more on this second stage. Duns' crucial theory of
the *neutral proposition* comes in to elaborate the second structural
moment of divine knowledge, usually known as the moment of divine
knowledge knowing things in their *being knowable (esse intelligi-
bile/cognitum)*:

> The divine intellect, understanding a proposition not as true or false,
> presents it to the will as *a neutral one*, just as when we understand:
> *Stars are even in number.*[64]

The new theory of the *neutral proposition* had already been touched
on before:

> When the divine intellect understands *This can be done* before an act
> of the will, it understands it as *neutral*, just as when we understand
> *Stars are even in number.*[65]

Apart from the role of God's will, a proposition has no truth-value
and *neutral* propositions lack a truth-value. In *Lectura* I 39.62, Duns

---

[62] According to the alternative view, God's creative willing is the necessary unfolding (emanation) of his essence and his necessary self-knowledge. See note 88.

[63] *Lectura* I 39.93: 'Intellectus divinus *in instanti primo* videns essentiam suam, videt omnes
res secundum earum *esse intelligibile*, quia tunc constituuntur in *esse intelligibili*, sed adhuc
non habent esse in esse producibili *antequam* habeant *esse volitum* a voluntate; et ideo
quando habet res illam rationem, eam videt in videndo essentiam suam.' See §6.5 and §7.4.
At this point, the easiest thing to do would be to explain this basic type of divine knowledge in terms of the ontology of *possible worlds*, but Duns Scotus does not have a theory
of possible worlds. This place is taken by his theory of the neutral proposition.

[64] *Lectura* I 39.62: 'Intellectus divinus offert voluntati suae aliquam complexionem *ut
neutram*, non apprehendens ut veram vel falsam, sicut cum apprehendo *astra esse paria*.'
See *Ordinatio* I 38.5–6 and 9–12, *Ordinatio* I 39.22–24 and 30. For *Reportatio Parisiensis*
I 38, see Wolter, 'Scotus' Paris Lectures,' in *The Philosophical Theology of Scotus*, 288–294.

[65] *Lectura* I 39.44: 'Quando intellectus divinus apprehendit *"hoc esse faciendum"* ante voluntatis actum, apprehendit *ut neutram*, sicut cum apprehendo *"astra esse paria"*.'

makes the same point in terms of a human action: *I am sitting.*[66] It has still to be decided. Literally, all propositions of the type *This can be done* have to be decided at a following moment of divine epistemic activity.

III   God knowing what enjoys being knowable

Duns talks of *being knowable* (*esse intelligibile*) in *Lectura* I 39.93 and he includes this moment of divine knowledge in the first structural moment. In fact, he distinguishes between two tightly connected aspects of this first epistemic moment. I call them the first structural moment of God's self-knowledge, knowing his own nature, and the second structural moment of knowing what enjoys *being knowable* (*esse intelligibile*).[67] This second moment is clearly distinguished from the moment of having being in *being producible*, characterized by having voluntative being (*Lectura* I 39.93). Witness the fact that Duns explicitly stipulates that the divine intellect knows contingent propositions *before* the act of will as neither true nor false (*Lectura* I 39.62) or as neutral (*Lectura* I 39.44), *being knowable* can only be identified as the semantic contents of neutral propositions. This Scotian move is attacked in the objection Duns discusses in *Lectura* I 39.90 where its formulation reads as follows:

> The divine intellect which first understands something to be done does *not* understand it *as true or false, nor as to be done*, before it is constituted into *being willed* by the will.[68]

Here, the alternative view is also clearly stated. Duns' analysis running in terms of structural moments is criticized because

> for the divine intellect the divine nature is the source of knowing all things without any aspects determining God's nature.

It is God's nature which represents some *thing* according to every aspect of it. At one and the same first moment everything is known completely, 'before it is constituted into *being willed* by the will.' Precisely this model is rejected by Duns: 'This kind of contingency does not come from the divine intellect in so far as it shows something

---

[66] See §7.4: 'The neutral proposition.'
[67] See also *Lectura* I 35.20–22, 33, and 36, and *Lectura* I 36.22. Cf. *DS* 159 f.
[68] *Lectura* I 39.90: 'Intellectus divinus apprehendens primo aliquid operandum, *non* apprehendit illud *ut verum vel falsum, nec ut operandum* antequam statuatur in esse volito per voluntatem.' Cf. *CF* 182 f.

to the will' (*Lectura* I 39.43), because this model destroys the contingency of reality.[69]

IV   *God knowing what enjoys voluntative being (being willed)*

The conceptual tool of the *neutral proposition* is used by Duns Scotus to show God's knowledge of the contingency of reality. It creates ample room for the pivotal role of the will of God. In terms of the purely epistemic stages obtaining *before* the act of God's will there are only empty propositional place-holders, to be filled with contingent truth by the will of God. God's will is the only ontological instance which can do the job of identifying the factual truth of *Actua*. So, it is necessary that God's will fills the objects of his own knowledge of *being knowable* with actual truth. Of course, He knows his own voluntative objects by knowing his own will. God's power is just the executive of what He wills, including all essential structures of contingency and freedom, individuality and responsibility, so characteristic for our created reality.

13.4   THE CONTINGENT NATURE OF GOD'S IMMUTABLE AND PERFECT KNOWLEDGE

Both the impact of the theory under fire and what Duns is aiming at are clear when we look at the fourth question of *Lectura* I 39. This question asks whether God necessarily knows all changeable reality. Let us assume that God knows necessarily what is changeable. It is certain, in terms of this type of epistemology, that what is unchangeable is necessarily known by God. Because everything is changeable or unchangeable, everything is necessarily known by God. If everything is necessarily known by God, everything is necessary.[70] So, *necessity* and *immutability* are strictly equivalent. This view is precisely what the argument in favor of the involved theory of divine knowledge in *Lectura* I 39.10 implies:

> It seems to be so: *God immutably knows that a.*
> Therefore: *He necessarily knows that a.*[71]

---

[69] Cf. CF 104–107. In *Ordinatio* I 39, the different structural moments are even more tightly connected with each other, although the moment of the divine will bestowing contingency on the voluntative objects enjoys the same right of way. See §13.5.

[70] If everything is necessary, then everything any person knows is necessary. So, this theory of divine knowledge entails the epistemic necessity rule of knowledge: if *a* knows that *p*, then *p* is necessary. Cf. §16.5.

[71] Ibid.: 'Deus immutabiliter scit *a*. Igitur, necessario scit *a*.' See CF 56–59.

Both sides embrace the view that *necessity* entails *immutability*. Duns' opponent subscribes to the strict equivalence of *necessity* and *immutability*. If we were to accept that *necessity* does not entail *immutability*, then necessity and mutability may be compatible. Something does not allow for any structural variability. It does not allow for any variability if it is synchronically necessary. The entailment *necessity* entails *immutability* cannot be abandoned. However, ancient philosophy holds onto the strict equivalence of *necessity* and *immutability*. Therefore, the only way the bond between *necessity* and *immutability* can be untied is by denying that *immutability* entails *necessity*. If this could not be done, subscribing to the immutability of divine knowledge would entail the universal necessity of God's knowledge (*Lectura* I 39.10–14 and 77–79). So, Duns' position asks for this move which we meet in the *responsio* of *Lectura* I 39.77.[72]

13.4.1 Contingent immutability

From the outset, it astonished thinkers how Duns Scotus could untie absence of change and necessity, after ancient thought had linked them inextricably. The Scotian theory of synchronic contingency is the key to this conceptual puzzle. Scotus distinguishes between two kinds of contingency: if something is *diachronically contingent*, it is *synchronically contingent*.[73] For Duns, diachronic 'contingency' and synchronic contingency go hand in hand; in terms of Aristotle's view there is no real contingency at all. With Duns the counterpart of synchronic contingency is logical necessity (= *synchronic necessity*).[74] For Duns Scotus, change and mutability are positioned on the level of diachronic contingency. It characterizes the temporal world of creation. Immutability has to be applied to God knowing his creation in an essential way, but 'immutability is not the cause of necessity, for in immutability only succession is missing.'[75] In terms of the old

---

[72] If we accept only the entailment *necessity* → *immutability*, then we also lose the equivalence of *contingency* and *mutability*. Now, we may prove a missing link in Duns Scotus' approach: (diachronic) *mutability* entails (synchronic) *contingency*. Aristotelian ontology accepts the first type of 'contingency.' So, it has to accept the second type of *contingency*.

[73] See *Lectura* I 39.45–54 and CF 108–129. Cf. §7.3. On *contingent immutability*, see A. Vos, 'Always on Time. The Immutability of God,' in Van den Brink and Sarot (eds), *Understanding the Attributes of God*, 53–73. See also §§16.4–16.5.

[74] Formally, this kind of necessity amounts to logical necessity, with respect to content it amounts to synchronic necessity and, so, on the formal level *synchronic contingency* is contingency in its logical sense.

[75] *Lectura* I 39.77: 'Immutabilitas non est causa necessitatis, quia immutabilitas non privat nisi successionem.'

meanings of 'immutability' and 'necessity,' the concepts of *necessity* and *immutability* coincide, but this cannot be the whole story.

Changelessness and immutability have to be accounted for in a way different from the way *necessity* has to be accounted for: *absolute necessity* rests on the relationship of its own terms so that it is not possible that it be different, but *immutability* only denies diachronic occurrence, although it is possible that it does not occur. We meet this same move of Scotus in *Ordinatio* I 39.31:

> In the case of *immutability* only possible succession is missing, when one contradictory succeeds the other contradictory, but in the case of *necessity* without any ado, the possibility of the opposite is missing in an absolute sense, and not only the successive occurrence of the opposite. So, the following argument is not valid: the one contradictory cannot succeed the other contradictory. Therefore, the contradictory possibility cannot hold.[76]

> In terms of ancient philosophy, '*necessity*' means that there is no change in the course of time and history; so '*unchanging*' and '*unchangeable*' coincide. Moreover, this absence of change and changeability is necessary. [. . .] This particular meaning of 'changelessness' and 'unchangeability' also entails that unchangeable things are necessary. Scotus disconnects this close relationship between *immutability* and *necessity*, when he rejects that the assumption that *God immutably knows* entails *God necessarily knows*. By doing this he undermines the whole framework of ancient non-Christian philosophy.[77]

According to this model of synchronic contingency, God's acts of knowing and willing contingent reality are only said to be changeless and immutable, but not necessary. Thus, the new theory of *contingency* gives rise to a new theory of *immutability*.

13.4.2   Divine infallibility

The new theory of *contingency* also gives rise to a new theory of *being mistaken* and *infallibility*.[78] If someone claims to know that *p* will be the case in the future and it turns out to be that *p* is not the case, then

---

[76] Ibid.: '*Immutabilitas* non privat nisi possibilem successionem oppositi ad oppositum. *Necessitas* autem simpliciter privat absolute possibilitatem huius oppositi, et non successionem oppositi ad hoc. Et non sequitur "oppositum non potest succedere opposito". Ergo, oppositum non potest inesse.'

[77] CF 165. Cf. Scotus' affirmation that God's knowledge of contingent reality is itself contingent.

[78] *Lectura* I 39.4 ff. and 71 ff. Cf. *Ordinatio* I 39.3 and 27 f., CF 48–53 and 158–161.

he is mistaken. *Lectura* I 39.4 presents an example, applied to divine knowledge:

> God knows that *a* will be the case,
> And *a* will not be the case.
> *Therefore*: God is mistaken.

In fact, the argument seems to be a slip of the pen, since the premisses form a contradictory conjunction. Just as Duns himself points out, the premisses imply that God 'would know that something will be which will not be.' Just as *being mistaken* that *p* implies that *p* is false, *knowing* that *p* implies that *p* is true. Duns wholeheartedly rejects that *knowledge* implies *necessity*; likewise, he accepts that *knowledge* implies *truth*. However, the opponent needs this wording in order to frame his objection against the doctrine of divine infallibility. We read in *Ordinatio* I 39.3:

> God knows that I will sit tomorrow, and I shall not sit tomorrow.
> *Therefore*: God can be mistaken
>
> is valid. Therefore, likewise
>
> God knows that I will sit tomorrow, and I can not-sit tomorrow.
> *Therefore*: God can be mistaken
>
> is valid. The first inference is evident, because he who *believes* what is not the case in reality is mistaken. From this I prove that the second inference holds too, because a possible thesis follows from a categorical premiss and another possible premiss, just in the same way as a categorical thesis follows from two categorical premisses.[79]

In *Ordinatio* I 39.3 we observe a fine example of Duns Scotus' style of revising his *Lectura* texts. *Lectura* I 39.4 does not only define what it is to be mistaken, but it also offers a superfluous application of a hypothetical mistake on God's side: given the nature of a mistake, God is mistaken if He knows that *a* is the case, while in fact *a* is *not* the case, because 'if God knew that *a* will be, and *a* will not be, then He would know that something will be which will not be. Therefore, God is mistaken' (*CF* 48). The actual wording of *Lectura* I 39.4 is not correct, 'for one who *knows* that something will be which will not be is mistaken' (ibid.) is not true, for he who *knows* is not mistaken in

[79] *Ordinatio* I 39.4: 'Ad secundam quaestionem arguo quod non, quia sequitur: *Deus novit me sessurum cras, et non sedebo cras. Ergo, Deus potest decipi.* Igitur, a simili sequitur: *Deus novit me sessurum cras, et possum non sedere cras. Ergo, Deus potest decipi.* Prima est manifesta, quia credens illud quod non est in re, decipitur; probo – ex hoc – quod consequentia teneat, quia sicut ad duas de inesse sequitur conclusio de inesse, ita ex una de inesse et altera de possibili sequitur conclusio de possibili.'

his knowing so. In §7 of the *Ordinatio* text we read Scotus' correction: 'He who *believes* what is not the case is mistaken.' Moreover, the objection neatly illustrates the conceptual structure of the ontological stance of the opponent, because for him

'I shall not sit tomorrow' and 'I can not-sit tomorrow'

are analogous. His objection only holds, if *can* entails *shall*. Duns will be in a hurry to point out in his *responsio* that *can* (*possibility*) indicates a synchronic alternative and not a diachronic or temporal alternative. The same pattern is at work in the next section:

> Furthermore, if God knows that I shall sit tomorrow, and it is possible that I do not sit tomorrow – suppose that *I shall not sit tomorrow* is the case – it follows that God is mistaken. However, an impossibility does not follow from supposing that a possible proposition is the case. *Therefore*: the proposition *God is mistaken* is not impossible.[80]

Two conceptual structures are able to make this objection consistent. If *knowledge* entails *necessity* and both *God knows that p* and *It is possible that p is false* are accepted, then we have to drop the universal infallibility of God. Likewise, if *can* and the *possibility* of a future event entails its future actualization, then God can be mistaken, if both *God knows that p* and *It is possible that p is false* are accepted. However, it is to be concluded that dropping both '*Knowledge* entails *necessity*' and '*Can* entails *shall*' is by far preferable to abandoning divine infallibility. In contrast to the patterns *Knowledge entails necessity* and *Can entails shall* which would make life intolerable it is God's wise infallibility which makes life sound.

13.4.3   The eternity of divine knowledge

All this implies that Duns Scotus also rejects some kinds of theories which endorse the eternity of divine knowledge. It is not quite clear from which sources Duns derived the eternity theory of God's knowledge. The wording of *Lectura* I 39.23 seems clear enough: 'Those who hold this theory say that everything is present to God in eternity according to its factual existence [*secundum eorum actualem exsistentiam*].' The metaphor of the stick in the water is only used in a negative way: that is *not* the way the relationship between time and eternity

---

[80] *Ordinatio* I 39.8: 'Praeterea, si Deus scit *me sessurum cras*, et possibile est *me non sedere cras* – ponatur in esse *non sedebo cras* – sequitur quod Deus decipitur. Sed ex positione possibilis in esse non sequitur impossibile. Ergo, ista *Deum decipi* non erit impossibilis.'

is to be imagined. The *Ordinatio* puts the analogies at the center of attention and now the positive description runs as follows: 'An alternative theory states that God has certain knowledge of contingent propositions about the future on account of the fact that the entire flow of time and everything which is in time is present to eternity' (*Lectura* I 39.25). The element of *factual existence* is dropped and now everything turns on the analogy between *immensity* and *eternity*. Again, the stick plays an elaborate part, but, in fact, it cannot be of any help. All time is present to eternity and a stick cannot be present to the river as a whole. Of course not, for the stick is in the river and as such a part of the river, although it does not consist of drops of water, and eternity is not a part of time. The role to be played by the analogies is rather elusive. At any rate, the main idea seems to be that what is immense is present to every place, and what is eternal is simultaneously present to every time. The *eternal now* and the *temporal now* are paired. They go together, but they are not to be equated. The *eternal now* is joined with the *temporal now*, but, just in this quality of being a pair, it transcends and excels the temporal now. This transcendent nature of eternity must imply that eternity is to be joined with another time and temporal now, and with all times as well (cf. *Lectura* I 39.25). Simultaneity is incompatible with time, successive as it is, and succession is incompatible with eternity (see *Lectura* I 39.27).

13.5 GOD'S WILL

13.5.1 Duns Scotus' explanation of contingency

How can there be contingency? It is not difficult to understand the impact of Duns' statements that such and such factors cannot be the source of the contingency of reality. Duns' first step underlines that true *contingency* is possible. If the foundations of a way of thought exclude contingency, then the question where the source of contingency is to be located makes no sense.

> All causes would necessarily act, if the First Cause acts necessarily. For this reason, the source of contingency in what there is stems from the fact that the first Cause acts contingently, and not necessarily. (*Lectura* I 39.41)

Again and again, with Duns we meet the same line of argumentation. Contingency has to be accounted for, but if we try to account for contingency in such and such a way, we lose contingency. So we have to look for an alternative account. Arguing the other way around is also typical of Duns: we can only account for contingency in such and such a way. So, we have to accept this theory. These moves mark the Scotian construction of logic and semantics, epistemology and proof theory, anthropology and ethics, ontology and the philosophical doctrine of God.[81]

God works contingently and the reality of creation is contingent, but where is the source (*causa*) of contingency to be located? The theme of the *source* of contingency hosts a series of arguments which are one by one a *reductio ad absurdum*. The starting point of these inferences is the following disjunctive proposition:

> The source of contingency is *either* God's nature, *or* God's essence-based knowledge, *or* God's power (potency), *or* God's will.[82]

Of course, all divine activity is based on God's nature, if we understand all the involved terms properly. God's essential properties belong to God, since they are entailed by his nature. Nevertheless, when we say here that the source of contingency is God's nature, what is meant is that the nature of God's activity follows his nature in the sense that He acts precisely as his nature *is*, namely necessarily. This option boils down, as we saw, to the view that God must act necessarily, because his personal identity itself is necessary. If the necessity of God's nature directly determines his activity and causality, contingency is impossible. According to this interpretation, God's nature cannot be the source of contingency.[83]

The next point illustrates the same approach. When we say that the source of contingency is knowledge based on God's nature, the nature of God's knowledge follows the model status of his nature so that the whole of God's knowledge is necessary too. This option entails the view that everything is necessary. If the necessity of God's knowledge directly determines his activity and causality, contingency is impossible. However, contingency is a fact, so, God's essential and necessary knowledge cannot be the source of contingency.

The argument for the third move proceeds in a different manner:

> If another potency is assumed in God, for instance, the executive potency, it cannot be the source of contingency, for it acts uniformly.

---

[81] See *CF* 33–37 and Vos, 'The Theoretical Centre and Structure of Scotus' *Lectura*,' in *Via Scoti* I 455–473.

[82] See *Lectura* I 39.41–44. Cf. *CF* 102–109.

[83] We may also argue the other way around: God acts contingently and it is necessary that He acts contingently. So, the reality of creation is contingent. Because reality depends on God and his contingent activity, the option of necessitarianism must be wrong. Duns Scotus mainly follows the first strategy.

Hence, that potency only produces something if an act of the intellect and the will precedes.[84]

God's necessary nature and his necessary knowledge cannot explain contingency, but his active potency is superfluous in explaining contingency. It does not add to the inner structure of divine activity, although it adds to God's activity. Now, we have eliminated three disjuncts of our fourfold disjunction. Following the rule of disjunction elimination, we conclude that God's will is the source of contingency.

13.5.2 Will and knowledge

The intellect of God sees the divine essence *at the first structural moment*. In the light of this self-knowledge, God sees all things as far as they are knowable. Duns says: *they are known by God according to their being knowable*. This divine knowledge constitutes them into their *being knowable* in terms of the second moment, but how can *being knowable* be understood? Duns elaborates on this point of view in two ways: first, by presenting the solution of Henry of Ghent, and, second, by presenting his own alternative along with a mild criticism of Henry's solution. Later on, the solutions of Henry of Ghent and Duns Scotus would often be confused with each other. When the Scotian solution was discussed, it was often simply Henry of Ghent's theory which was at stake. In *Ordinatio* I 39 the description of Henry of Ghent's view is to the point:

> The divine intellect sees that an event will take place for time *a* by seeing the *decision* of the divine will, since the will of God decides that it will happen for that time. The divine intellect knows that the will is immutable and not liable to be impeded.[85]

Henry of Ghent distinguished between the primary object of God's knowledge – the divine essence itself – and secondary objects, including possibles, but Duns Scotus takes Henry's view as pointing to

---

[84] *Lectura* I 39.42. Duns concludes: 'Therefore, we have to inquire whether the source of contingency in what there is stems from the divine intellect or from his will.' Cf. *Ordinatio* I 39.14. See also Wetter, 'Die Erkenntnis der Freiheit Gottes nach Johannes Duns Scotus,' *De doctrina Ioannis Duns Scoti* II 477–517.

[85] *Ordinatio* I 39.22 (*Opera Omnia* VI 428): 'Uno modo per hoc quod intellectus divinus videndo *determinationem voluntatis divinae*, videt illud fore pro *a*, quia illa voluntas determinat fore pro eo. Scit enim illam voluntatem esse immutabilem et non impedibilem.' Cf. Henry of Ghent, *Quodlibet* VIII *quaestio* 2 in corpore. On the later reception of this view, see Hoenen, *Marsilius van Inghen* (d.1396) *over het goddelijke weten* I, 164–170. Cf. CF 144–146.

transitions between several different elements which are related to each other as discursive moments of deliberation in God's intellect being correlated with his will.[86] Because Henry of Ghent talks of a *decision* of God's will (*determinatio suae voluntatis*), Duns reconstructs these epistemic and voluntary moments as a discursive series. He objects to this model, since there is no discursivity in the life of the divine mind. Again, we observe the familiar pattern of Duns criticizing his famous predecessor, not in order to outlaw him, but in order to improve on his contribution. The improvement proposed by Duns takes away the discursive element by stressing that, in spite of the crucial role of the divine will, there is no particular moment at which a particular decision has been made. It is not a decision at a certain moment which matters, but, as it were, an 'eternal decision': a voluntary determinateness of an open proposition, *being determinate* by the will of God (*Lectura* I 39.64). Let us now offer Duns' point of view:

> When the will has decided for one component [of the disjunction *p or not-p*], then that component is such that it is to be done and to be brought forth. Then the intellect does not see that proposition by the fact that it sees a decision of the will, but the divine essence is for the intellect the immediate ground of representing then that proposition. [. . .] The divine intellect sees the truth of a proposition, a truth which is made and worked by the will and which his essence immediately represents to his intellect. This truth only reflects in the essence under the aspect of something to be done when it has been determined by the divine will. The same holds for something else.[87]

Both the key role of God's will and the meaning of *determinare* have to be observed

> for *determining* the truth-value of every proposition does not entail the *causation* of every denoted state of affairs – at least not in the modern sense of the word 'causation' – although it is on a par with

---

[86] On Henry of Ghent's theory of divine knowledge, see Wippel, 'The Reality of Nonexisting Possibles According to Thomas Aquinas, Henry of Ghent, and Godfrey of Fontaines' (1981), in *Metaphysical Themes in Thomas Aquinas*, 173–184 (163–189).

[87] *Lectura* I 39.65: 'Quando voluntas determinavit se ad unam partem, tunc illud habet *rationem* factibilis et producibilis. Et tunc intellectus non per hoc quod videt *determinationem voluntatis*, videt illam complexionem, sed essentia sua sibi est immediata ratio repraesentandi tunc illam complexionem. [. . .] Intellectus divinus videt veritatem alicuius complexionis factam et operatam a voluntate (quam veritatem immediate sibi repraesentat essentia sua), quae non relucet sub ratione factibilis in essentia nisi postquam determinatum sit a voluntate divina. Et sic de alio.'

God's direct or indirect willing that the denoted states of affairs obtain in actual reality, and with the production of corresponding things in *being willed*. '*Determinare*' has to be read in a rather weak sense, referring only to the definite character of the truth-value of a knowable proposition.[88]

In *Lectura* I 39.65, Duns had already stated the mysterious thesis that the intellect of God knows the truth of a proposition, made true by his will and directly represented to his intellect by his essence. God's essence immediately represents truth to his intellect. Although it is clear what the theory of the structural moments of the life of the divine mind is up to, yet it is not easy to see in what way God's essence can explain what is at stake.

However, in *Ordinatio* I 39 Duns elucidates precisely this point in an admirably clear series of theoretical steps. On the one hand, the divine essence is the ground of the divine intellect knowing open, or neutral, propositions, and, on the other hand, the same essence of God is the ground of God's intellect grasping all determinate truth. This runs paradoxically, to say the least, but Duns' retort is a splendid *reductio ad absurdum*. If the essence of God is not also the ground of God's knowledge of contingent truth, it is impossible that there is contingent truth, but this consequence is impossible. Hence, it is necessary that the essence of God also plays this epistemic role. Duns addresses the paradoxical relationship between determinate contingent truth and the divine essence in *Ordinatio* I 39.23:

> When this element of *determinate truth* exists, then the fact that the intellect of God knows this truth finds its ground in his essence, namely in a *structural* manner, as far as it originates in his essence. Just as the divine intellect structurally knows all necessary principles, as it were, *before* an act of the divine will, [. . .],[89] it is also true that the divine essence is the ground of knowing them *in that primary moment*, for then they are true, [. . .],[90] but the divine

---

[88] Beck, 'Scotus' Theory of the Neutral Proposition,' in Bos (ed.), *Scotus. Renewal of Philosophy (1265/66–1308)*, 131. There is little literature on the *neutral proposition*. This excellent contribution also offers a systematic analysis and an assessment of several interpretations of Scotus' doctrine of divine knowledge. Cf. §7.4.

[89] Necessary truth does not depend on an act of the will. Such truth would have been known by God's intellect, if God were not to be a willing God, although that is impossible. Cf. §12.3.

[90] Ibid.: 'Surely, it is not the case that these truths, nor their terms, guide the divine intellect in order to grasp that truth. In that case, the divine intellect would devaluate, because it would not be informed on the basis of the divine nature, but by something else'.

> essence is the ground of knowing both simple concepts and com-
> pound concepts.[91]

This inferential series makes the basic, though perhaps not self-evident, point that the one and the same essence of God must be able to explain the different essential types of divine knowledge, if it is essential to God to be omniscient and if there is not only one kind of truth. Duns starts with the indisputable epistemic point that God enjoys essence-based knowledge of what is necessary and self-evident. However, there are *simple concepts* and *compound concepts*. God is as such familiar with both of them, for what's sauce for the goose is sauce for the gander. If there is more in heaven and earth than neces-sary truth, then the divine knowledge of all possible truth must flow from one and the same essence, although this flow cannot simply show the pattern of a strict entailment. The basic point having been made though, it is still not clear in what manner God's knowledge of contingent truth is based on his essence. That is just the next point:

> So far, there are no true contingent propositions, since there is still nothing by which they have *determinate truth*. If a decision of the divine will is assumed, then they are true *in that second moment*, and the ground of knowing them for the divine intellect is the same as *in the first moment*.[92]

However, this is still not the end of the story:

> For the intellect of God, the same is the ground of knowing these propositions which now are true *in the second moment* and would have been true in the *first* moment, *if* they would have been in the *first* moment.[93]

The heart of the matter is that contingency gives depth to the area of activities. The monotony of necessities being strictly equivalent is abolished. The theoretical depth of this move is covered by Duns Scotus' tool of structural moments (*instantia*) of acts and *formalities*.

---

91 Ibid.: 'Hoc autem exsistente "*determinato vero*," essentia est ratio intellectui divino intelli-gendi istud verum, et hoc naturaliter (quantum est ex parte essentiae), ita quod sicut *natu-raliter* intelligit omnia principia necessaria quasi *ante actum voluntatis divinae* [. . .], ita essentia divina est ratio cognoscendi ea in illo priore, quia tunc sunt vera [. . .], sed essentia divina est ratio cognoscendi, sicut simplicia, ita et complexa talia.' For the distinction between *simple concepts* and *compound concepts*, see §4.5: 'Concepts.'

92 Ibid.: 'Tunc autem non sunt vera contingentia, quia nihil est tunc per quod habeant deter-minatam veritatem. Posita autem determinatione voluntatis divinae, iam sunt vera *in illo secundo instanti*, et idem erit ratio intellectui divino – quod et in primo – intelligendi ista.'

93 Ibid.: 'Idem erit *ratio* intellectui divino [. . .] intelligendi ista quae iam sunt vera *in secundo instanti* et fuissent cognita *in primo*, si tunc fuissent *in primo instanti*.'

His theory of divine knowledge and will is a fine specimen of this approach. In *Ordinatio* I 39.23, Scotus makes clear that the roots of a complicated structure are the same as when – *per impossibile* – everything would have been very simple.

Various interpreters think that it is not clear how Duns Scotus answers the question in what way God can have knowledge of the future in his 'commentaries' on *Sententiae* I 39. However, if divine knowledge of contingency can be accounted for, then divine knowledge of the future is also explained. They say that in Duns Scotus' theory God's knowledge of the future is based on the knowledge of his will. This is perfectly right, but sometimes they also tell that all future states of affairs are effectively predetermined by divine will. It is a necessary truth that the factual future is willed by God, but if the role of God's will is understood in terms of a necessitarian notion of *predetermination*, then a perfectly un-Scotian element is introduced. Human acts are contingent too and they belong to *Actua* created by God. However, *being determinate* with respect to knowing and willing does not imply *determinate causation* in the sense of ancient and modern philosophy.[94]

13.6 PERSPECTIVE

For quite different reasons, Augustinian theology and, in general, classic Christian thought, including Duns Scotus', have often been seen as a kind of determinism. Both friend and foe applied this tendency to Calvinism.

> Courageous and intellectually deep-probing thinkers have [. . .] not shrunk from looking at the alternative that perhaps the origin of sin might in one way or another be in God himself. The awareness of the true contents of the word *God* drives one as it were in this monistic direction. From him and through him and to him are all things. Could one of the greatest 'things,' sin, fall outside that confession? [. . .] Reformed Protestantism has ventured the furthest in this monistic direction, driven by strict theocentrism.[95]

Both Berkhof and Pinnock look upon the classic doctrine of God as the main force behind this tendency. Pinnock sketches his spiritual

[94] See Schwamm, *Das göttliche Vorherwissen bei Duns Scotus und seinen ersten Anhängern*, 29 f., Langston, *God's Willing Knowledge*, 39–52 and 119–128, Craig, *The Problem of Divine Foreknowledge and Future Contingents from Aristotle to Suarez*, 136–139 and 144 f., and Hoenen, *Marsilius van Inghen* (d.1396) *over het goddelijke weten* I 164–166. Cf. CF 142–145.
[95] Berkhof, *Christian Faith*, 197–198.

and theological pilgrimage as a process that broke the chain of
Calvinist logic, a logic inherited from ancient Greek philosophy. The
omniscience and immutability areas of the classic doctrine of God are
the epicenter of this explosive necessitarianism and both concepts are
linked with necessity.

> First of all, I knew we had to clarify what we meant by the *divine
> immutability*. I saw that we have been far too influenced by Plato's idea
> that a perfect being would not change because, being perfect, it would
> not need to change – any change would be for the worse. [. . .]
> Creatures can relate to God, all right, but God cannot relate to them.[96]

For different reasons, both atheology – atheological philosophy
claims to be able to prove that the monotheistic view is false – and
much modern theology condemn classic theology, viewed as God-
based determinism. This interpretation overlooks all of the new conceptual structures, characteristic for most classic Western theology.
This oversight leads to a mistaken description of its doctrine of divine
immutability and its ontology. Classic Western theology and its affiliated philosophy are not the victim of Greek *philosophia*, but they
overcame its dilemmas. In general, such criticisms are misguided,
because classic theology and the philosophy affiliated with the main
theological university tradition usually reject the views ascribed to
them by their critics. This fact is rather unsatisfactory both from the
ethical and the methodological point of view. Throughout these
studies in Duns' philosophy I suggest that his thought is the historical zenith of the main Augustinian tradition. The philosophical innovations of the eleventh, twelfth and thirteenth centuries paved the
way for Duns Scotus' philosophical revolution (*Vorgeschichte*) and
the five centuries between 1300 and 1800 cannot be assessed adequately without accounting for his contributions, positively or negatively (*Nachgeschichte*).[97]

From the theological point of view, the situation is even more
crucial. Atheology and most modern theology exclude each other. This
fact does not mean that one or both options is tenable. During the nineteenth and twentieth centuries, both modern philosophy and modern

---

[96] Pinnock, 'From Augustine to Arminius: 'A Pilgrimage in Theology,' in Pinnock (ed.), *The
Grace of God, the Will of Man*, 24. Analogously, God's timelessness and omniscience are
dealt with. See §7.6 and §§16.4–16.5.

[97] Compare Luther for the negative option and Jansenism and the centuries of reformed
scholasticism for the positive option (*Nachgeschichte*). Ignoring the philosophical and theological place of John Duns Scotus' contributions leads to a distorted historical mirror.

theology presented countless alternatives to classic Christian thought, embodied in the Augustine-Anselm line of Western thought which dominated for a millennium – between 800 and 1800. However, the many alternatives modern philosophy and modern theology have to offer are mainly incompatible with each other and, hence, from the statistical point of view, they must enhance the probability of untruth enormously. The alternative option concludes that classic Western thought is basically right. Terms like 'philosophy of religion' and 'philosophical theory of divine attributes' are not immediately applicable to Duns Scotus' doctrine of God. Even *De primo principio* is a specimen of faith searching for understanding, but Scotus utilizes a concept of *demonstration* which is derived from a strict theory of proof. The effect is that large parts of his doctrine of God can be transposed into a modern theory of divine nature. His high standards make introducing his results into a modern philosophy of religion viable. For the modern mind, the medieval aim of demonstrating truth is a door, although this helpful door is only an accidental one in the edifice of Duns Scotus' thought.

Part III

Background and foreground: ancient and modern philosophy

CHAPTER 14

John Duns, Aristotle, and philosophy

14.1 INTRODUCTION

> From Parmenides onwards, ancient and medieval thought had a
> special liking for metaphysical speculation. No doubt, speculative
> thought was most influentially outlined by Plato and Aristotle.
> However, what the Christian thinkers achieved in metaphysics was def-
> initely more than just applying and adapting what was handed down
> to them. No student of medieval speculative thought can help being
> struck by the peculiar fact that whenever fundamental progress was
> made, it was theological problems which initiated the development.
> This applies to St Augustine and Boethius, and to the great medieval
> masters as well (such as Anselm, Thomas Aquinas, Duns Scotus). Their
> speculation was, time and again, focused on how the notion of being
> and the whole range of our linguistic tools can be applied to God's
> Nature (Being).[1]

The originality of medieval philosophy and the creativity of its logic
and theory of knowledge make themselves felt in many contributions
without any counterpart in ancient philosophy. Its novelties possess
a tremendous cultural importance in general and great theoretical
interest for modern philosophy and current systematic theology in
particular.

In his important introduction to medieval philosophy L. M. de Rijk
lists four examples of original contributions that excel the inventions of ancient Greek, Hellenistic, and Roman philosophy:[2] (1) terminist logic (which is in fact to be seen as a part of the wider
phenomenon of the *logica modernorum*);[3] (2) the metaphysics of

---

[1] De Rijk, 'On Boethius's Notion of Being. A Chapter of Boethian Semantics,' in Kretzmann
(ed.), *Meaning and Inference in Medieval Philosophy*, 1.
[2] See *PMA* 69–71. Consult in particular chapters 3 and 4 of *PMA*.
[3] Consult De Rijk, *Logica Modernorum* I (1962) and II (1967). Cf. *PMA* 4.4–4.7. On De Rijk,
see §15.5.

Thomas Aquinas;[4] (3) the critical theory of knowledge of the fourteenth and fifteenth centuries; and (4) a way of thought which
markedly differs from necessitarian Greek philosophy.[5]

Our question is: how does John Duns look at Aristotle and how
does he assess his philosophy? At any rate, Aristotle was called *the
philosopher (philosophus)* by Duns, and most scholastics, but how is
this fact seen by Duns? He calls himself *a Christian (catholicus)* or *a
theologian (theologus)*. The critical tendencies of thirteenth- and
fourteenth-century thought provide the broader context of Scotism
and nominalism. These tendencies and *viae* have no counterpart in
contemporary Jewish and Islamic philosophy. In order to illustrate
this field of forces we successively deal with: the 'philosophers'
and philosophy (§14.2); Henry of Ghent/Duns Scotus versus
Aristotle/Avicenna (§14.3); *Lectura* I 8: the 'philosophical' way of
ideas (§14.4); *Theologia* against the philosophers (§14.5); proof theoretical comments (§14.6); 'Theology' and 'philosophy' (§14.7); an
auctoritates culture (§14.8); and, finally, the perspective of a dilemma
(§14.9).

14.2   THE 'PHILOSOPHERS' AND PHILOSOPHY

The characterization *philosophical way of thought* has a paradoxical
ring. This philosophical way of thought of *the philosophers* is something John Duns himself calls the thought of the *philosophi* or the
opiniones philosophorum. Duns uses the word *philosophus* in two
ways. *Philosophus* is for him a noun, in fact used as a name, like
Commentator (= Averroes), *Apostolus* (= Paulus), and *Veritas* =
Christus. In the second place, the plural *philosophi* denotes a specific
group of thinkers and in *Lectura* I 8 Duns explicitly numbers among
them Aristotle, Plato, Avicenna, and Averroes.[6] Moreover, we regard
the thought of Plato and Aristotle not only as the historical starting
point, but also as an invaluable symbol of what *philosophy* still has
to be. In spite of the historical limitations of their works, the value of

---

[4] See *PMA* chapters 6 and 7. Cf. Vos, 'Theologie, wetenschap en alwetendheid volgens
Thomas van Aquino,' *Jaarboek 1981*, 15–37.

[5] See *PMA* 70 (69–71: 'Les développements propres à la philosophie médiévale'). Consult also
PMA 3.2 and 3.4 and cf. *KN* II and VII.

[6] See *Lectura* I 8.215: 'communiter apud omnes philosophos excepto Platone.' Cf. *Lectura*
I 8.115, 120, 220, and 221, where the opposition between Aristotle and Plato is pointed out.
See Chenu, 'Les "Philosophes" dans la philosophie chrétienne médiévale,' *Revue des sciences
philosophiques et théologiques* 26 (1957) 27–40: a 'philosopher' is a non-Christian Greek
or Arabic thinker.

rationality is linked with them in a unique way and, for example, Cousin, Burnet, and Mandonnet even adhered to much stronger views. We may have the feeling that Duns' immense personal admiration for Aristotle and Avicenna confirms this historical consciousness. When we see Duns asking whether theology be a science, whether some religious belief can be demonstrated, or when he delineates his own position with regard to Aristotle, then we probably take this as evidence that Duns feels himself challenged and obliged to defend himself before the tribunal of Reason. It is easy to be deluded by simple expressions of philosophical Latin which function as systematically misleading expressions.

14.2.1 *Philosophi* and *philosophia*

There is another tiny but not unimportant detail. Duns spoke of the theories or the opinions of the *philosophers* and I have called this the *philosophical way of thought*. Starting from Duns' characterizations of the basic ideas of Aristotle, Avicenna, and Averroes, we are able to derive a coherent body of thought, characterized by the principle of necessity. So far, so good. But what does Duns say about *philosophia*? Of course, he is familiar with Aristotle's and later use of *philosophia*, denoting the whole of the sciences,[7] but does he speak of *philosophia* within the specific context of discussing the controversy, conflict, or clash (*altercatio*) between *theologians* and *philosophers*? On the one hand, there is talk of *theologi* and *theologia*, but, on the other hand, only talk of *philosophi*. Although Henri Krop agrees with Étienne Gilson that for Duns Scotus 'what Aristotle knew, is what *philosophy* can know,'[8] he also perceptively observed that the noun *philosophia* is hardly used by Duns. Then his guess is that Duns is not familiar with the modern concept of *philosophy* as an independent discipline which *rationally* investigates reality.[9] However, Duns is familiar with a body of thought which investigates 'philosophically' the whole of reality, but to his mind, this philosophy cannot be connected with something that the modern term 'philosophy' indicates, because for him *philosophy* is not the final answer; it is not even a valid approach.

Moreover, we may easily overlook the fact that Duns does not discuss the nature of *philosophia*, but only argues about the theories

[7] See *Lectura Prologus* 8 and 38: according to Aristotle, there are three parts of philosophy: metaphysics, physics, and mathematics.
[8] See Gilson, *Jean Duns Scot. Introduction à ses positions fundamentales*, 13, cf. 33.
[9] Krop, *De status van de theologie volgens Johannes Duns Scotus*, 7–8.

or *opinions* of the philosophers. Even more helpful than the sober facts that there is no talk of *philosophia* and that Duns does not discuss the nature of *philosophia* in itself is the strikingly different approach where he elaborately discusses whether theology be *scientia* and whether theology is *scientia practica*, but not whether *philosophia* be *scientia*. We have already reminded ourselves that for Duns – and his Augustinian tradition – *philosophia* lacks truth, while knowing (*scire*) implies truth. Precisely for this reason there is no room for discussing the *scientific* nature of philosophy. It is even worse – if it be true that the necessitarian type of philosophy cannot be true, then in this controversy the whole of Western philosophy is at stake.

We have to realize that words like *philosophy, science,* and *rationality* do now have a ring rather different from what they had for John Duns. Although Duns immensely enjoyed argumentation and debate, nevertheless he was not impressed by *rationality*, but rather by *love.* He was not impressed by *science*, but rather by *faith* and *hope.* He was not impressed by *philosophy*, but rather by *theology*, and the original theology is God's *theologia.* The mystery is that this person – and the whole of his tradition – mentally so far away from the modern mind – nonetheless has much to say which may satisfy the requirements of rationality cherished by the modern mind. When we reconstruct Duns' attitude as to what we believe philosophy to be, we learn much more from diagnosing the types of Duns' arguments than directly characterizing his thought with help of the modern notions of philosophy, theology, science, and rationality or fideism (or theologism).

We observe the well-known phenomenon that the occasion for a revision arises out of a theological dilemma, while the revision itself is executed by reconstructing the involved concept formation. The necessity condition cannot be reconciled with God's certain knowledge comprising the whole of reality. This theological dilemma leads to the discovery that the contingent cannot be known as necessary. The necessity of the act of knowing does not follow from the necessity of the epistemic object. The Aristotelian parallelism of *thought* and *being* erects the necessity of the one upon the necessity of the other. Duns disconnects both and breaches the parallelism of *thought* and *being*, of *epistemology* and *ontology* (*metaphysics*).[10] The epistemic

---

[10] On the innovation of Duns disconnecting the ontological and epistemological dimensions, see *KN* (1981) 77 (76–81) and Krop, *De status van de theologie volgens Duns Scotus*, 210–212. Cf. Chapters 8–9 and *CF* 1–3.

status of an act or a disposition of *knowing* and the ontological status of the epistemic object are not strictly equivalent, but have to be handled as different problems. With regard to the topic of the *subject of a science*, the same phenomenon is to be observed.[11]

Duns' thought is revisionary by renewing the innovations of the past. This process is going on in reading Aristotle. Although there is an immediate contact between Aristotle's texts and John Duns reading them, there is no immediate historical connection between Duns and Aristotle. Duns operates in a different world of thought. In the development of his 'theological philosophy,' he reinterprets Aristotle's sentences-in-Latin, if they can be reinterpreted, whereas he leaves them aside if this cannot be done. We find here a piece of philosophy of science, profoundly deviating from Aristotle but without any polemics.

We may notice the same phenomenon recurring in the interpretative parts of his works, operating according to the rules of *exponere reverenter*. Within this context Duns nowhere says that Aristotle is profoundly wrong. Nevertheless, it has to be quite clear from the theories Duns is developing here that this is precisely the case as he himself explicitly states in *Lectura* I 8 and *Ordinatio* I 8. Just as the whole of the tradition he is moving in, Duns knows this himself. If this *quaestio* is not raised, an *auctoritates*-culture is polite, and silent.

14.3   HENRY OF GHENT/DUNS SCOTUS VERSUS ARISTOTLE/AVICENNA

The second part of *Lectura* I 8 is an atypical piece of analysis in the whole of Duns' systematic works.[12] The main question of *Part* II is the exclusive question whether *only* God is immutable. The answer that *only* God is immutable has two sides: first, there is the *positive* truth that God is immutable and, second, there is the *negative* truth that nothing else is immutable. Duns' strategy of exploring these different aspects is rather unique: first, he deals with a certain interpretation of the basis of Aristotle's and Avicenna's ontologies by Henry of Ghent (*Lectura* I 8.201–235).[13] Second, the main theme is a criticism of

---

[11] *Ordinatio Prologus* 211–213 spells out the main idea of *Lectura Prologus* 118 in more detail.

[12] *Lectura* I 8.196–285. Cf. *DS* 258–263.

[13] *Lectura* I 8.200: 'Sed circa aliam partem – negativam – istius quaestionis, an nihil aliud a Deo sit immutabile, procedam. Primo ponam unam opinionem quam quidam doctor imponit Aristoteli, et secundo aliam opinionem quam imponit Avicennae, et declarabo quod non bene imponit eis; et tertio arguam contra opinionem Aristotelis et Avicennae.' The first part is to be found in *Lectura* I 8.201–226, the second in §§227–235 and the third in §§236–271 and 274–285.

Aristotle's and Avicenna's philosophies. The link with the main problem of the second part of *Lectura* I 8 is that the *philosophical* principle

1. Everything is necessary[14]

would demolish the thesis that *only* God is immutable and necessary if it be true, because Duns also defends

2. Everything except God is contingent.

14.3.1 Aristotle

How does Henry of Ghent survey and criticize the main lines of Aristotle's ontology? He ascribes to Aristotle the view that there are realities different from God which are formally necessary, for example intelligences. Henry concludes that, according to Aristotle, the formally necessary realities are not causally dependent on God because everything which is causally dependent on something else is not from itself (*de se*) and is not necessary. Duns embraces the same hermeneutical principle as Henry does in interpreting Aristotle: the Philosopher does not assert anything contradictory. Henry uses this principle in deriving deductively that no formally necessary reality is causally dependent on something else.

Henry of Ghent concludes that, according to Aristotle, no necessary reality is caused by something else. These realities are essentially dependent on God and, nevertheless, they do not have their being from God: they are dependent and they are not dependent. So, according to Henry, Aristotle's basic view boils down to a contradiction. However, this is incompatible with the principle that Aristotle's basic thought is not self-contradictory and the young John Duns is eager to point out this principle. His thesis is that Henry of Ghent is right in believing that according to Aristotle realities different from God are necessary, but wrong in concluding that formally necessary realities are not causally dependent on God. In turn, Duns delivers an alternative reconstruction of Aristotle's position. It is not inconsistent that something is necessary and still depends in its own necessity on something else so that it takes its necessity from something else.[15]

---

[14] Honnefelder, *Scientia transcendens*, 79: 'Aus der Naturnotwendigkeit der göttlichen Kausalität ad extra würde nicht nur ein nezessitaristisches, sondern auch ein monistisches Universum folgen.'

[15] *Lectura* I 8.210: 'Igitur repugnat aliquid esse necessarium et tamen quod dependeat in necessitate sua ab alio ita quod capiat necessitatem ab alio, sed haec est intentio Philosophi.' From

All philosophers, with the exception of Plato, agree that it is evident that everything which is necessary in itself is related to something in a necessary, immutable, and immediate way.

14.3.2 Avicenna

According to Henry of Ghent, Avicenna asserts that incorruptible substances are caused by God and are possible of themselves (*ex se*). 'Yet they are necessary, because they necessarily get their being from something else, since their cause necessarily causes them.'[16] Again, Henry of Ghent concludes that this view is self-contradictory, for if a reality is possible from itself, it is possible that it does not exist. So, let us assume that it does not exist. Then its cause does not cause it in a necessary way. If it is necessary as well, a contradiction is involved (*Lectura* I 8.228). The concept of *being* is 'outside' the concept of the form or essence of something.

> Now it is clear that on the basis of the fact that everything which is caused gets its *being* from something else, everything which is caused is from itself *possible being* and has a potency in order to be. Therefore, his [Aristotle's] view does not differ from the theory of Avicenna who asserts the same as we have said before.[17]

Henry of Ghent and John Duns read Avicenna in a different way. They ascribe the same two main theses to Avicenna: *Incorruptible substances are necessary, because they are necessarily caused* and *Such substances are possible of themselves.* Henry reads the second proposition within his own framework of concepts and interprets *possibilis ex se* in terms of the Christian ontology of contingency: *non-being* is structurally (*ordine naturae*) prior to *being* (see §§6.3–6.4). So, if something is possible as such, then it is possible that it does not exist, but if it is necessary too, then it is impossible that it does not exist. Therefore, Avicenna's view is refutable, for it is inconsistent.

However, the young John Duns takes a different proof theoretical stand, although he believes with Henry of Ghent that the views under

---

Metaphysica 1050b 6–8 Duns derives the principle that what is always is necessary: *Sempiterna esse necessaria* (*Lectura* I 8.209). The following thesis can be derived: 'Aliquod necessarium potest habere causam a qua est sua necessitas.'

[16] *Lectura* I 8.227: 'Tamen sunt necessaria quia capiunt necessario esse ab alio, quia causa sua necessario causat eas.'

[17] *Lectura* I 8.235: 'Nunc autem manifestum est quod ex quo omne causatum capit esse ab alio, omne causatum ex se est "possibile esse" et in potentia ad esse. Igitur sua sententia non differt ab opinione Avicennae, qui idem ponit, ut praedictum est.'

consideration are necessarily false. Duns interprets 'possible of itself' in terms of the framework of Avicenna's own logic and ontology. Avicenna distinguishes between *being* (*esse*) and *essence* (*essentia*). The essence (*quiditas*) being a horse (*equinity* = *equinitas*) *is*, but *being* as a property of the essence *equinity* is not a part of the *notion* or *meaning* of the essence *equinity* itself.[18]

Duns analyzes this theory in terms of his own *structural moments* tool. Because an essence does not include as such *esse*, it has a *potentia ad esse*. The *potentia ad esse* is the first structural moment of the essence, receiving *being* from its necessary cause the second structural moment (§230). This analytical instrument boils down to *conceptual analysis*. God grasps a certain essence which is, as such *potentially being*. Whatever there is, excepting God, *is*, but now *being* is understood as an additional moment, because such an essence is not *being* itself. If it *is*, it gets its *being* because it is necessarily caused. This potency to *being* does not entail the possibility that it does not exist, for it is formally an *ens necessarium*. In this light the logical distinctions of Avicenna turn out to be conceptual or semantic *aspects* (*rationes*) within a necessitarian framework. It is just this framework that both Duns and Henry of Ghent combat. The discussion of Henry of Ghent's account ends up in the conclusion that Aristotle and Avicenna basically agree: 'Therefore, his theory does not differ from the intention of Avicenna who asserts the same theory as he put forward. This we said before.'[19] So, there is only a difference in formulae and expressions between Aristotle and Avicenna.

14.4 *LECTURA* I 8: THE 'PHILOSOPHICAL' WAY OF IDEAS

Duns identifies the *philosophical* point of view on the basis of the contributions of the philosophers who are for Duns the masters of *philosophia*: Aristotle and Avicenna. He admires both philosophers from the bottom of his heart: they are unable to commit logical lapses and even in the *Ordinatio* Duns will persevere in this boyish kind of admiration.[20] Although he definitely does not cherish as high an

---

[18] *Lectura* I 8.239: 'Avicenna enim praecississime loquebatur de quiditate rei, in tantum quod dicit quod "esse" extra rationem quiditatis rei est et omne illud esse accidens rei quod est extra rationem quiditatis rei et quod non importatur per quiditatem formaliter.'

[19] *Lectura* I 8.235: 'Et haec non est alia sententia ab intentione Philosophi; nam Philosophus ponit unam primam causam, et omnia alia ordinari ad ipsam et sic omnia esse causata et dependere ab ipsa. [. . .] Igitur sua sententia non differt ab opinione Avicennae, qui idem ponit, ut praedictum est.'

[20] As to *Ordinatio* I 8, it cannot be decided whether it be Oxford 1300 or Paris 1302.

admiration for Averroes, he regularly cites him in order to articulate the philosophical position. Although the *opinio philosophorum*[21] concretely refers to the convictions of Aristotle and Avicenna, Duns places them in a wider disagreement between the philosophers and (Christian) theologians. What counts as a theological proof does not automatically constitute a proof *for* Aristotle (§251). There are different spheres of argumentation and Duns uses the *ars obligatoria* in order to pinpoint the kind of differences involved.

The third part of Duns' exposition deals with the pros and cons of the position of Aristotle and Avicenna.[22] First, the pros are discussed. Duns formulates some basic points in a clear and resolute way. He comments on the nature of the relationship between the philosophical and the theological view. The way Duns describes and analyses the *philosophical way of ideas* is fascinating because he starts by defending the philosophical approach (*Lectura* I 8.236–244). Second, it is also clear to Duns that the basic tenets of *philosophia* are false. He does not criticize Henry's pronouncement that the philosophers are wrong and that their principles are false, but he criticizes the charge that their fundamental tenets are logically incoherent. In effect, this is a remarkable intermediate position and the question arises how Duns himself tries to refute the philosophical principles. At any rate, there is a wrong foundation. Third, it is clear that, to Duns' mind, a refutation of *philosophia* is not an easy affair and it is no surprise that to his mind many Christian arguments are unable to convince philosophers, but Duns continues to argue against them.

14.4.1   The nature of the 'philosophical' point of view

Duns is convinced that Aristotle, Avicenna, and Averroes subscribe to the common core of *philosophia*. In *Lectura* I 8 and *Ordinatio* I 8 he makes perfectly clear that the options of *philosophia* and *theologia* are fundamentally different. The kernel of the debate is of a magical kind: according to the philosophers, their view follows from the *perfection principle* and this principle entails that the First Cause is

---

[21] See *Lectura* I 8.245, 246, 250, 251, 256, and 274. Cf. *Lectura* I 8.235–237. Cf. the parallel texts in *Ordinatio* I 8 and, in particular, §292.

[22] To the third part – *Lectura* I 8.236–271 – *Lectura* I 8.274–285: 'Ad rationes pro opinione Aristotelis et Avicennae' has to be added. Specifically, *Lectura* I 8.274–285 has to be linked with *Lectura* I 8.236–244, *Lectura* I 8.245–271, containing seven counter-arguments.

necessarily related to everything else.[23] According to Duns, it is the
very *perfection principle* which excludes the philosophical view and
entails that God works contingently. Duns again identifies this theoretical foundation, but in the meantime he also comments on the
logical status of this basic dilemma:

> There is a conflict only between us and them about their foundation.[24]

In *Lectura* I 8.236 the critical discussion of the content of this view
begins with a short summary:

> Therefore, the thesis they unanimously hold runs as follows: 'What
> is permanent and incorruptible is possible in itself and yet neces-
> sary, for there is a cause which necessarily causes and that cause is
> necessary'.[25]

Here, we have the philosophical thesis of necessary causation by the
First Cause that pops up again and again in Duns' analyses. Duns
underscores this position as follows: the First Cause works from itself,
its own nature. So, it is impossible that the first Cause sometimes
works and sometimes does not work. If it works it effects immediately and necessarily.

The kernel of the theoretical dilemma concerns the nature of divine
agency. The *immutable* nature of divine agency entails the *necessary*
nature of this divine agency governed by the principle of *perfection*
(§236 and §238). What does the philosophical foundation consist of?
It consists of:

3. What is necessary in itself can immediately act, only if it necessarily acts.
4. What is necessary in itself produces what is necessary

can be derived from (3), because (4) follows from (3) on the basis of
the underlying principle

5. Necessary agency entails necessary effects.[26]

---

23 *Lectura* I 8.235: 'Philosophus ponit unam primam causam, et omnia alia ordinari ad ipsam
   et sic omnia esse causata et dependere ab ipsa. [. . .] Igitur sua sententia non differt ab
   opinione Avicennae.'
24 *Lectura* I 8.237: 'Non igitur est altercatio inter nos et illos nisi in isto fundamento eorum.'
25 Ibid.: 'Ista perpetua et incorruptibilia sunt possibilia ex se, et tamen necessaria, quia est causa
   aliqua quae necessario causat, quae causa necessaria est.'
26 *Lectura* I 8.237: 'Necessarium ex se non potest immediate agere nisi necessario agat et
   necessarium producat, quia hoc sequitur ex primo.' *Primum* refers to the antecedent of the
   involved argument, and not to a principle to be identified from the *Ordinatio*, as the
   Commissio Scotistica suggests.

The axiomatic foundation of these of assertions had already been stated in *Lectura* I 8.236:

6. It is only possible that the First Cause acts sometimes and does not act sometimes, if it does change.[27]

The *philosophical way of doing theoretical thought* has a systematic identity and consists of (3)–(6) while the prominence of

5. Necessary agency entails necessary effects, and
3. What is absolutely necessary in itself does only act necessarily

shines out. The proposition being the answer to the first preliminary question is

1. Everything is necessary.

The axioms of both alternative options are, respectively:

1. *Everything is necessary*

and:

2. *Everything except God is contingent*

and (1) and (2) exclude each other. Duns reduces the philosophical viewpoint to a strict ontology. He notices that Aristotle and Avicenna (and Averroes) use semantically different concepts, but in the end the basic formula (1) can be derived from them.

14.4.2 The heart of the matter

Lectura I 8.256–257 offers the heart of the matter, but there is still an unexpected additional gift. There is a short intervention inserted by Duns himself. Among the pros confirming the *opinio philosophorum* Duns cites the thesis that the ontologically more impressive component *being necessary* of the disjunctive transcendent property *being necessary or non-necessary* must be the characteristic of divine agency.[28] At this point, Duns intervenes by distinguishing sharply between the level of *being* and the level of *agency*:

---

[27] *Lectura* I 8.236: 'Ideo ponunt quod causa prima non potest agere quandoque et non agere, nisi mutetur.' However, (1) is to be derived from (3)–(6).

[28] See *Lectura* I 8.238: 'Ens dividitur per *necessarium* et *possibile*; sed *necessitas* est nobilior differentia entis quam possibile. Igitur competit nobiliori causae, igitur illa causa quae est nobilior necessario aget, et sic prima causa quae est *perfectissima, necessario* aget.'

7. On the level of existence, necessity is entailed by a nature which is simply perfect, but on the level of acting perfect agency contradicts necessity.[29]

Here a remarkable reversal of basic arguments is at play. On the philosophical side the basic contention is: *perfect agency must be necessary.* According to Duns, on the theological side the basic contention must be: *perfect agency being only necessary is self-contradictory.* Perfect divine agency cannot be exclusively necessary. These basic formulae elucidate Duns' point that the difference itself is a basic one. The one view takes the connection under consideration to be necessary while the alternative view considers this connection to be inconsistent or contradictory. The roles of *necessity* and *repugnancy* are reversed. What is coherent in the one system or model is contradictory in the alternative system or model, and vice versa.[30]

14.5   THEOLOGIA AGAINST THE PHILOSOPHERS

The final question is how Duns himself assesses the demonstrative force of the arguments purporting to prove the theological view and is it possible to discern some development when we compare *Lectura* I 8 and *Ordinatio* I 8?

Against the background of Duns' strict interpretation of the philosophical way of ideas, an impressive set of counter-arguments is to be discerned. There is a series of seven arguments against the *philosophical way of ideas* in *Lectura* I 8.245–270. This series is rounded off in §271: 'So I grant the thesis that God necessarily causes nothing which is different from Him, but He willingly [causes everything which is different from Him].'[31]

The counter-arguments to the *philosophical way of thought* are to be classified into different groups by the aid of their different introductions. The *cons* of the first group, consisting of the first and second

---

[29] *Lectura* I 8.239: 'Et dicit quod necessitas est simpliciter perfectionis in quocumque in quo est, sed necessitas agendi repugnat causae primae. Ideo non tenet.' *Dicit* signalizes the dialogical style of the *Lectura*. Duns' exposition of the alternative, which he himself will refute, is interrupted by the opponent. The exposition itself is an ongoing discussion and, thus, an alternative voice (*dicit*) rebuts the view put forward. Systematically seen, it is Duns' personal voice: *The notion of divine agency being only necessary is contradictory.*

[30] These points are principally repeated in *Ordinatio* I 8. We may still ask ourselves, why Duns considers *necessary divine agency* to be self-contradictory.

[31] 'Concedo igitur hanc conclusionem quod Deus nihil aliud a se causat necessario, sed voluntarie.'

counter-argument, are introduced, e.g. by 'against the theory of the philosophers some scholars argue in the following way.'[32] These counter-arguments are distinctly introduced by the form-critical formula: *arguunt (quidam)*. These arguments are in fact arguments of Henry of Ghent. A second set of arguments is simply characterized by the form-critical device *arguitur/arguunt*. In both cases we cannot say in advance what Duns thinks of such arguments.

A third form-critical device of introduction is in terms of the formula *arguo*.[33] If he writes *arguo*, we may be sure that he himself endorses this argument. So, the third set is what Duns himself proposes as cons against the philosophical view.

In sum, part two of *Lectura* I 8 is about *divine immutability* and its questions and the answers to these questions are presented in §§196–200 and 272–273. Thus the answer to the initial question has been placed in the long-winded debate on *the philosophical way of ideas*.

We turn first to the arguments derived from the thought of Henry of Ghent, the first set consisting of the first two arguments (*Lectura* I 8.245–255). These arguments are clearly to be distinguished in a form-critical way and, moreover, they are proof theoretically interesting, for Duns does not comment that these arguments are wrong, but his comments are of a proof-theoretical nature: These arguments are not conclusive for the philosophers or they are not apt to convince the *philosophers*, although they are sound theologically.[34]

Now we are in possession of the specific key to open Duns' personal box of arguments. Here the decisive point is not the validity of the arguments under consideration, but the question for whom a specific argument has the power to 'prove' or demonstrate something. So, finally, we concentrate on the arguments which are able to perform this difficult job according to Duns himself: *Lectura* I 8.256–257, and *Lectura* I 8.265–270 are added for specific reasons.

14.5.1 The third argument

> Moreover, in the third place I argue against the philosophers as follows: in what is some effect contingently caused. Then the First Cause causes contingently, and not necessarily. (*Lectura* I 8.256)

---

[32] *Lectura* I 8.245: 'Contra hanc opinionem philosophorum arguunt quidam sic.'

[33] See *Lectura* I 8.256: 'Tertio *arguo* contra philosophos sic.' Consult also §257.

[34] See *Lectura* I 8.246: 'Ista ratio non concluderet philosophis,' and §251: 'Ista ratio, licet sic bona sit catholicis, non tamen convinceret philosophos.'

The theoretical target is (1). Showing that not everything is necessary suffices to refute that the First Cause acts necessarily. This economic move constitutes Duns' starting point: one thing or another is contingent. This antecedent is true, because not everything is necessary. Given that some contingency is granted, b is contingently caused by a.

Duns asks whether a acts by itself or by c. The first alternative leads to what has to be demonstrated: a is the First Cause and acts contingently. If the second alternative holds, again c may act in a necessary or a contingent way. The first alternative is incompatible with what has been granted before. So, at no stage in this line of argument a necessarily causing or acting cause can arise. On the basis of what has been granted no necessarily causing or acting First Cause can arise. The *propositum* cannot be barred, because there can be no regress of kinds or types of causes which is structurally infinite. If there is no contingently acting First Cause, nothing contingent can be explained at all and the hypothesis of a necessarily acting First Cause is definitely wrong.[35]

In terms of simplicity, the fourth argument is even more powerful.[36] Because there is evil in the world, God acts in a contingent way. Therefore, it is the other way around in comparison with the line of argumentation defended by David Hume. Because there is evil, there is contingency and because there is contingency, God contingently acts and so God exists. Ethics and evil require God acting contingently.[37]

In the first part of *Ordinatio* I 8 the same position is defended. Duns ascribes a definite ontology both to Aristotle and to Avicenna,

---

[35] The text of this splendid piece of argumentation in *Lectura* I 8.256 runs as follows: 'Antecedens verum est, quia non omnia fiunt necessario. – Consequentiam ostendo sic: b causatur ab a contingenter; quaero igitur utrum a movet b et causat ipsum a se vel in quantum movetur ab alio? Si a a se et ex se movet et causat b, igitur est prima causa, et habetur propositum quod prima causa movet et causat immediate aliquid contingenter.'

'Si a movetur ab alio ad hoc quod causat b (sit illud aliud c), quaero igitur sicut prius utrum c causat et movet a ad causandum necessario aut contingenter? Si necessario movet a ad causandum, cum a non causat nisi in quantum movetur a c, igitur a causat et movet b – quod est oppositum positi et praeconcessi. Si autem c movet et causat a contingenter, quaero sicut prius utrum a se habet quod movet et causat, an ab alio?'

'Si a se, habetur propositum quod prima causa immediate causat contingenter; si ab alio et non a se movet, quaero de illo sicut prius – et cum non sit processus in infinitum in moventibus et motis, stabitur aliquando quod prima causa causat immediate aliquid contingenter et movet aliud ad causandum contingenter.'

[36] *Lectura* I 8.257: 'Praeterea, quarto arguo sic: aliquod malum in universo est et aliquod malum fit in universo; igitur Primum non agit ex necessitate.'

[37] See *Lectura* I 8.258. Cf. Honnefelder's survey of these arguments, *Scientia transcendens*, 76 ff., §2a: 'Die Frage nach dem Ursprung der Kontingenz der veränderlichen Seienden: Die Ausandersetzung mit dem Nezessitarismus der "philosophi".'

but in ascribing a specific view to them he makes use of a radical hermeneutical condition:

> I do not want to ascribe to them more absurd propositions than they express explicitly or than the propositions which necessarily follow from what they say. I want to offer the most reasonable interpretation of what they say which I can give.[38]

In *Ordinatio* I 8.251, Duns formulates the basic ideas of the *philosophi*, like *Acting necessarily only produces what is necessarily produced* and *Divine agency is necessary*, and his personal answer (*opinio propria*) runs as follows:

> So, my answer is that Aristotle, like Avicenna, has stated the following: 'God is necessarily related to the other things outside Him. From this follows that whatever else is necessarily related to Him (that as it were enjoys an immediate relationship to Him).'[39]

According to Aristotle, it is impossible that there be a *First Cause*, if this *First Cause* does not work necessarily. Therefore,

8. *The First Cause necessarily acts in a necessary way.*

According to Duns, Aristotle stands on an untrue foundation when he asserts that the First Cause necessarily acts and causes what is necessary (*Ordinatio* I 8.252). Duns identifies what both Aristotle and Avicenna have stated: God is necessarily related to entities which are not identical with Him. Therefore, everything else is necessarily related to Him. This thesis that *the foundation of reality is a necessary cause*, is false and so is (1).[40]

Thus Duns concludes in *Ordinatio* I 8.255:

> So, Aristotle and Avicenna agree in what follows because of a false principle they share, namely that God is necessarily related to what is outside Him. He is immediately related to it or through the mediation of what is immutable.[41]

---

[38] *Ordinatio* I 8.250: 'Nolo eis imponere absurdiora quam ipsi dicant vel quam ex dictis eorum necessario sequantur, et ex dictis eorum volo rationabiliorem intellectum accipere quem possum.'

[39] *Ordinatio* I 8.251: 'Respondeo ergo quod Aristoteles posuit, et similiter Avicenna, *Deum necessario sese habere ad alia extra se*, et ex hoc sequitur quod quodlibet aliud necessario se habet ad ipsum (quod quasi immediate comparatur ad ipsum).'

[40] See §252: 'Tenendo illud falsum fundamentum, Aristoteles, ponendo *ipsum esse necessariam causam*, non videtur contradicere sibi ponendo *causatum necessarium*.'

[41] *Ordinatio* I 8.255: 'Itaque concordant Aristoteles et Avicenna in sequentibus ex uno principio falso – in quo concordant – scilicet quod Deus necesario se habet ad quidlibet quod est

14.6 PROOF-THEORETICAL COMMENTS

We are in possession of an impressive series of Scotian arguments against the *philosophical way of ideas*. Is *philosophia* refuted by this battery of refutations and proofs? I think so. Does Duns himself say so? The answer must be: *no*, but why does Duns not say so? Our question is a modern one, couched in sets of problematics from the Renaissance and Enlightenment which embrace rather different concepts of philosophy and theology. We cannot expect the young John Duns directly to answer our questions of faith, rationality, proof, and refutation. Nevertheless, we are able to derive his potential answer to our question from the terminology and conceptual structures of his thought.

14.6.1 Can Aristotle be refuted?

Here, the young John Duns wavers a bit: is it possible to refute the *opinio philosophorum* and to demonstrate the theological framework or not? The answer seems to be: *yes* and *no*! and some variants of Scotus' answer *no* have become rather well known, even notorious. It seems a rather surprising move on the part of the *magister rationum*. It has to be granted that the evidence still seems to be ambivalent. On the one hand, we meet conclusions as in *Lectura* I 41 and *Ordinatio* I 41: divine omnipotence cannot be demonstrated in the theological sense of the word and the long-winded argument on the eternity of the world is inconclusive.[42] On the other hand, we have Duns' personal assessment of the theory of the Trinity and his philosophical view on the status of the doctrine of creation.[43] The same kind of ambiguity we meet in *Lectura* I 8. Henry of Ghent believes that he can straightforwardly refute the philosophical point of view as being inconsistent in itself. The point is not that Duns disagrees regarding the truth of Henry of Ghent's view. He is certain that the arguments of Henry of Ghent are true, but do they constitute a strict proof? Henry of Ghent criticizes Aristotle in terms of his personal theory of contingency. Duns points out that this is all very true, but probably will not convince the philosophers.

---

extra se, ad quod immediate vel mediante immutabili comparatur.' Cf. §251. For comparing the parallel sections in *Ordinatio* I 8.259–306 and *Lectura* I 8.236–285, see Vos, 'Duns Scotus and Aristotle,' in Bos (ed.), *Scotus. Renewal of Philosophy,* 69.

[42] See *DS* 234–245 and *DS* 163–164, based on *Lectura* II 1 and *Ordinatio* II 1, respectively.

[43] See *DS* 217–234 and *DS* 161–163: 'Trinitarische creativiteit,' based on *Lectura* II 1, *quaestio* 1.

In *Ordinatio* I 8 Duns slightly refined his strategy. He improves on the arguments of Henry and concentrates in his personal arguments on what the philosophers also accept.[44] In *Ordinatio* I 8 he is more confident than in *Lectura* I 8, but there is still the question of how to explain the evidence.[45] What is a strict proof or *demonstratio* according to Duns Scotus?

A *demonstratio* is a *ratio naturalis* and a *ratio naturalis* is a rather specific type of argument. A *ratio naturalis* is liable to the following necessary and sufficient conditions:

1. the logical relation between premisses, intermediate propositions, and conclusion must satisfy deductive validity;
2. the premisses must be necessarily true;
3. the premisses must be self-evident (*per se nota*).

If an argument satisfies only the two first conditions, it is called a *necessary argument*. So, in such an argument, the intermediate propositions and conclusion are necessary too. No proof can be framed for a *self-evident* proposition. If a proof of it can be delivered, the proposition under consideration is provable and what is demonstrable is not *self-evident*: *the self-evident* cannot be *demonstrated* (§§9.3–9.4).

Is *the third argument* a strict proof in terms of these conditions? It is a deductively valid argument and, according to Duns, the antecedent is self-evident.[46] However, is the antecedent in its role as a premiss *necessarily true*? In terms of Duns' definition of *contingens*, this premiss is not necessarily true, because something contingent is concerned, for it is contingent that there is a world of creation. Nevertheless, the sheer contingency of this world is as contingency a necessary feature. So, even in terms of Duns' rigorously demanding requirements, for a *demonstratio* the third argument can count as a *demonstration*. This fits in remarkably well with the refutations in the last part of *Lectura* I 8. In terms of modern proof theory there is no problem at all. If an argument is deductively valid and it is sound, it can be welcomed as a proof. The technical key lies in the *ars obligatoria. Concedere*

---

[44] *Ordinatio* I 8.282: 'Antecedens [namely "aliquid contingenter fit in entibus" – *Ordinatio* I 8.281] concedunt philosophi,' and *Ordinatio* I 8.284: 'Antecedens concedunt philosophi, sc. aliquod malum fit in universo' – see *Ordinatio* I 8.283.

[45] *Ordinatio* I 8.292: 'Ad quaestionem, quantum ad exponentem negativam illius exclusivae, respondeo: concedo conclusiones istarum rationum, quarum licet forte aliquae non convincerent philosophos quin possent respondere, sunt tamen probabiliores illis quae adducuntur pro philosophis, et aliquae forte necessariae.'

[46] See *Lectura* I 39.39–40, and cf. *CF* 96–101.

(*granting*) is a key term in the theory of dialogue which the *ars obligatoria* in fact is. In dealing with an argument by Henry of Ghent, Duns observes: the argument as such is generally evident, but 'it seems to contradict certain propositions of the discussant.'[47] The point of view of the opponent is taken into account. This pattern is vital to the *ars obligatoria* (see Chapter 5). There are two points of view to be reckoned with. Duns' epistemological observations are in place. An argument may be convincing for one party, but not for another. Argument and proof are person related.

14.6.2   The proof-theoretical dilemma of a basic difference

What constitutes a real proof? Here, the axiomatic method governs the definition of a strict proof or *demonstratio*. The premisses have not only to be necessarily true, but also self-evident. In terms of such a notion of *demonstratio* a *basic difference* is an odd thing to have within the framework of dialogue and argument. If there is a *basic* difference, a basic premiss will be accepted by one party and rejected by the other. In terms of a rational modern theory of proof, Duns' arguments are simply proofs, because the old notion of eventually self-evident premisses has been replaced by the *hypothesis rule*: anything may be assumed if it is acknowledged as such and the defendant is prepared to defend this assumption in a rational way. The overarching argument is missing with Duns Scotus, but can be filled in by the ontology of possible worlds. Such an ontological framework is not only fit to absorb and to transform Duns' proposals and intuitions, but can also serve to prove that the possibility of contingency cannot be wiped out.

14.7   'THEOLOGY' AND 'PHILOSOPHY'

One traditional view of medieval thought looks on it as a valuable – or less valuable and at any rate unoriginal – repetition of ancient philosophy. However, Christian medieval thought sees itself rather differently. In contrast with the traditional view of modern times, it sees itself in radical opposition to ancient philosophy. Philosophy and theology are diametrically opposed to each other. What we may call

---

[47] *Ordinatio* I 8.270: 'Licet ista ratio sit aliqualiter apparens, tamen videtur contradicere quibusdam dictis *arguentis*.' According to the discussant, the divine will is necessary, but what he defends, is only self-contradictory in terms of contingency.

'Christian philosophy,' they called theology. Philosophy, on the contrary, is dated: it belongs to the past and that past was wrong, admirably wrong. Duns' view is a pointed variant on this theme. The philosophers represented an articulated body of thought.[48] The huge difference is expressed in a sentence of remarkable charm: there is only one fundamental difference, concerning (N). The other argumentative moves of the philosophers are coherent. So, according to the mainstream thought of Duns Scotus' days, their views present a coherent body of thought which we call *philosophy*.[49]

14.7.1 Parting ways

In his honorary speech at the great Duns congress of 1968, Fernand Van Steenberghen said much about the situation Duns found himself in at the beginning of his academic career, but not much on Duns himself, apart from remarks on the novelty and originality of his terminology and ideas.[50] In a sense, Duns' thought constitutes a litmus test for interpreting medieval philosophy. Duns and his tradition saw an enormous difference, and even a cleavage, between the heritage of the philosophers and Christian theology. In an *auctoritates* culture, one world quite different from another may lie *within* that other world, just as, during the Middle Ages, the world lay within the church, both being real.

14.7.2 The appearance of *Aristoteles dicit*

Two systematically misleading techniques of interpretation considerably complicate our understanding of medieval philosophy. One feature properly belongs to medieval intellectual culture as such which altogether is primarily an oral culture and secondarily a manuscript culture – the universe of medieval reading and thinking is a handwritten world. This world is not quite authoritarian, in contrast with early modern or Enlightenment culture. In this respect it is easily misunderstood. It is an intellectual culture based on *auctoritates*. These *auctoritates* are not used in precisely the same way in every area

---

[48] See Burr, 'Petrus Ioannis Olivi and the Philosophers,' *Franciscan Studies* 31 (1971) 41–71.

[49] Theology is to be characterized as *the fundamental alternative to philosophy*, cf. Chapters 15 and 16.

[50] See Van Steenberghen, 'La philosophie à la veille de l'entrée en scène de Jean Duns Scot,' *De doctrina Ioannis Duns Scoti* I (1968) 65–74.

and every period of medieval culture, but the theological style of *exponere reverenter* marked reading 'philosophical' texts. The 'philosophical' texts are understood within this framework. 'Philosophical' texts are not texts in the modern sense of philosophy as an academic subject, but texts written by the *philosophi*.

14.8   AN *AUCTORITATES* CULTURE

The scientific revolution not only improved upon the methods and methodology of science, it also revolutionized the understanding of nature. The historical revolution not only changed the rules of doing historiography, but it also revolutionized the understanding of history. There was no history before the historical revolution; there were only time, the past, and eternity. There were only stories to be told. Broadly speaking, in 'history,' there were only story telling and narrative thought (*historia*). The historical revolution made it possible to explore the past in a rational and methodical way, but, during the century of history – the nineteenth century – this was mainly done in a biased way. In spite of the historical revolution and the birth of the science of history, the past was still explored in an *a*historical manner because, just as easily as the past was applauded before the historical revolution, the past was now criticized and condemned.

The historical-critical revolution created a chasm between the liberals and the conservatives. Among the liberals there were the historical *critics*, but many of these did not try to discover and develop purely historical research. They assumed that they understood history and, understanding history in their way, they frankly disagreed with the past, they judged the past (*krinoo*, *kritès*) and condemned it.[51]

The first discovery consists of seeing that the past is strange and unknown to us. When we have grown old ourselves, we realize that we have not understood our grandparents, but now it is too late to talk with them. We do not know the past directly, because it strangely differs from the present, and doing history is like looking at monkeys in a zoo. The second problem consists of the difficulty that we have to be trained in historical method and thinking in a historical way, but, in overcoming the *ahistorical* way of looking at persons, ideas,

---

[51] In condemning the past, they assumed along with the conservatives that the past is clear. They did not realize that the historical revolution implies that we have to discover that we are not familiar with the past. When we discover that we do not know the past, we may start to rediscover the past.

and things, we build a barrier between ourselves and the past. We are estranging ourselves from our forbears. So while we have to study medieval thought in a historical way, the medieval thinkers did not. The expressions *Scriptura dicit*, *Augustinus dicit* and *Aristoteles dicit* had meanings very different from what they have for us.

Apart from being an ahistorical culture just as the culture of antiquity was, medieval culture was also an *auctoritates* culture, just as ancient culture was. However, medieval culture was an *auctoritates* culture in a different way. Unlike antiquity, the Middle Ages were the age of faith and the Church, not because everybody was among the faithful and everybody loved the Church or loved Christ, but because, in most countries, all schools and almost all thinkers were Christians, members of the Church. Antiquity did not have one creed, councils, and the phenomena of orthodoxy and of an organized church – eventually it created these, but it was not marked by them – but medieval culture did.

How 'authoritative texts' work in an *auctoritates* culture differently from the worship of intellectual and ideological authority in a modern culture we clearly see in the fact that *auctoritates* occur on both sides of the *quaestio*. So, the *quaestio* is not decided at all by *auctoritates* and cannot be simply decided by them, because the fact that *auctoritates* can be appealed to only creates the space where truth is to be found. When the teacher has made up his mind, the *auctoritas* enjoys a treatment different from an 'authoritative' modern author. When Duns proposed his contingency theory, his opponents appealed both to Aristotle and to William of Sherwood. It is quite clear that, to Duns' mind, William of Sherwood's *Obligationes* is an excellent textbook. However, the text of Aristotle is reinterpreted so that a very smart answer pops up, although it is certainly not a thesis endorsed by the historical Aristotle. As to William of Sherwood, the reply is simply that he is wrong, but his *Obligationes* is not an *auctoritates* text, although Duns expresses his high esteem.

The *auctoritas* texts were believed to be true. Therefore, according to the medieval presumption, the *auctoritates* do not only embody *truth*, but they also embody *one truth*.[52] The truth is essentially the one truth of Scripture and it is existentially *the Truth*, *Veritas*. *Theology* is basically reading and understanding the Bible. The starting point of

---

[52] I do not say that the academic texts of the medieval curricula all embody one universe of thought. In contrast with what I was taught to believe in my student days, they did not.

medieval intellectual culture is rather puzzling. They are studying texts they were unable to understand properly – 'properly', of course, in terms of modern standards. One was not familiar with the tools of discovering the meanings of old texts and the historical events which had happened in the past. They were pupils of their past, in the key of eternity. They possessed precious texts and they discovered more and more, but, to our mind, all these discoveries had to result in a continuous disruption of the consensus of the *auctoritates*.

The solution is hidden within the difficulty. The texts that were read in the schools could not deliver the solution, nor could the past. So, the medievals themselves had to deliver the solution and they were able to do so by virtue of their view of what an *auctoritas* was. An *auctoritas* was in fact not an *authority*, but a text, an *authoritative* text. Such an authoritative text was read in an *a*historical way.[53] What then were they assumed to find in such texts? *Truth!* They not only read and studied their texts as the texts of contemporaries, but also as texts embodying truth. In a sense, every authoritative text was read as the Bible was and the Bible was never wrong. We have to study medieval texts in a historical and critical way, and a main ingredient of our historical consciousness has to be that the medieval author does not have such consciousness. If his remarks make a historical impression upon us, then they are masked. They do not say what at first sight they seem to say. Historical consciousness had not then been invented – and it would be centuries before it was. Texts from the past are immediately absorbed in the personal frame of mind. There is only our own present. In this light, the judicial presence of Aristotle according to the nineteenth-century approach becomes a comical phenomenon. The historical Aristotle could not be present, because he was not known. It was just the medieval thinker who mattered, driven by a passion for *truth*.

The impact of the *auctoritas* way of reading texts was reinforced by specific theological and legal developments. In *sacra pagina* one started to assume that the Fathers spoke with one voice, essentially the same voice as the voice heard in the Bible. When more and more sources became available, it was discovered that prima facie not everybody spoke with one voice. Sometimes even the same author did not speak with one voice, as is even testified to by Saint Augustine, judging by his *Retractationes*. All this produced a sea of deep semantic and logical

---

[53] See *PMA* §§4.3–4.4. Cf. §9.3.

analyses, but it also promulgated the method of *exponere reverenter*. The theologians introduced this method into reading non-Christian philosophical texts, and, in particular, the books of Aristotle. For example, the conflict around Siger of Brabantia and his followers was – among other things – a clash which was also elicited by the different approaches of theologians and *artistae*: the *artistae* may not have studied their texts in a historical way, but they were still inclined to read them more literally, because they were less used to the method of the *exponere reverenter* than the theologians were.

14.8.1 Synthesis or reconciliation?

Medieval culture was an ahistorical culture and also an *auctoritates* culture, as were ancient Semitic, Greek and Roman cultures. Nevertheless, medieval Western thought profoundly differed from ancient thought, just as it also differs distinctly from modern thought. The modern concepts of -isms and 'schools' are scarcely applicable. Modern 'schools' read themselves back into the past of medieval and Renaissance thought. Heiko Augustinus Oberman (1930–2001) challenged traditional views in his now classic *The Harvest of Medieval Theology* (1963). Traditional Protestant histories of theology emphasized the discontinuity between Reformation thought and late medieval developments. Analogously, these same centuries were routinely regarded as a period of decline and disintegration of the Thomistic synthesis in catholic histories of medieval philosophy. The great names of those who studied medieval philosophy at Paris – Cousin, Hauréau, Renan – started with ascribing a pivotal role to *Aristotle*. Van Steenberghen still called the thirteenth century *the century of Thomas Aquinas* in 1991, moving within the framework of the same parameters, and virtually all thirteenth-century philosophy is seen as broadly Aristotelian.[54] If this were true, there would not have been much philosophy in the thirteenth century. However, from the purely historical point of view, there was scarcely truly Aristotelian philosophy in the Christian West in the Middle Ages, although not every thinker contributed substantially to developing an alternative, just as the Church was by no means a pagan institution, although not every member contributed to her reform program or was even in sympathy with it.

---

[54] See Van Steenberghen, *La philosophie au XIIIe siècle*, 474–480, cf. chapter 1. Van Steenberghen started his research into medieval philosophy in Louvain in 1921!

Nevertheless, the differences between the great thinkers of these centuries are real and important and have everything to do with the ways of thought inherited from the past. However, inheritance is not the same as influence. Stating that the early industrial developments in the West in the twelfth and thirteenth centuries would be caused by the technical abilities of the Greeks would be pure fantasy. It is a strict truth that inventions not yet made cannot offer any solutions. This holds for thirteenth-century thought too. New theories are needed to solve the paradoxes. Puzzles in theology cannot do their jobs before they are invented. We cannot use a barrow before the invention of the wheel.

We have to discover the theories thirteenth-century authors held from the independent systematic parts of their expositions. The *ratio* parts of their *quaestio* literature independently argue for the truth they discern in the *auctoritates*. Van Steenberghen insisted that the scientific solution was only Thomas', while, according to Gauthier, Bonaventure saw the *Ethics* of Aristotle as a bad book and, thus, he mercilessly attacked false philosophy in his *Collationes in Hexaemeron*.

> The truth is that the philosophers – even those noble philosophers, those clear minds who, like Plotinus and Cicero, had admitted the ideas and the immortality of the soul – could not reach the truth because they did not have the light of faith. They were all plunged in darkness.[55]

Gauthier even accused both Albert the Great and Thomas Aquinas of having failed to see the flagrant inconsistency between Aristotelian and Christian ethics, overlooking the historical sense of Aristotle's teaching.[56] Such an accusation does not make any sense, because nobody interpreted historically, for quite the same reason that nobody cycled in the thirteenth century. Albert and Thomas deserve neither Gauthier's blame nor Van Steenberghen's praise.[57]

14.9 THE PERSPECTIVE OF A DILEMMA

Walter of Bruges and William of la Mare show no desire to trace the errors of philosophy to Aristotle, but even perceptive observations can easily mislead when we are not aware of the ways the observed

---

[55] Gauthier, 'Trois commentaires "averroïstes" sur l'*Éthique à Nicomaque*,' *Archives d'histoire doctrinale et littéraire du Moyen Age* 16 (1947–1948) 330 (187–336) ; English translation by Bonnie Kent, *Virtues of the Will*, 47.

[56] Gauthier, 'Trois commentaires,' op. cit., 304–318. Cf. his editions of Robert Grosseteste and Thomas Aquinas, and Gauthier and Jolif, *Aristote. L'Éthique à Nicomaque* I–II.

[57] Even Bonaventure's stance is enigmatic. Ferdinand Delorme published an alternative edition of the *Collationes* in 1934, differing considerably from the Quaracchi edition.

phenomena were affected by the *a*historical way of thinking and the *auctoritates* nature of the texts, both in antiquity and in the Middle Ages. Bonnie Kent discovered that Walter of Bruges emphasized the harmony between Aristotle and Christian authorities.[58] How are we to explain this curious phenomenon? The answer must be that if the *corpus aristotelicum* belongs to the set of *auctoritates* texts, the works of Aristotle are considered to be in harmony with the original *auctoritates* texts of the Christian tradition. After all, the world of thought of an *auctoritates* culture starts from a pre-established harmony of the *auctoritates*. It is assumed that they present one world of truth.[59] For this reason, statements within this framework do not concern historical reality. They are related to the intended truth of the texts.

How do we explain that William of la Mare showed no inclination to trace the great errors of philosophy to Aristotle? Again, the answer must be that if the *corpus aristotelicum* has been taken into the heaven of the *auctoritates* texts, they are virtually free from error and errors are not traced to 'infallible' *auctoritates*. This is also the reason why Aristotle was shown mercy but Aquinas was not. Aquinas was a *modernus* and one felt free to criticize contemporary authors, but Aristotle's writings had become Scripture-like texts. They were institutionally 'infallible,' but they were only invulnerable as far as they were held to be *auctoritates* texts and as far as they were interpreted as *auctoritates*.[60]

In this respect, the history of the *corpus aristotelicum*, unofficially accompanied by works of Avicenna and even by those of the 'damned' Averroes, enjoyed a remarkable career. Originally, they could not be accounted for as *auctoritates* texts, for they were books shrouded in darkness, but within half a century they joined the ranks of the *auctoritates* texts. Kent's narrative on 'Aristotle among the Christians'

Kent acknowledges both sides of the coin – see her *Virtues of the Will*, 58: Bonaventure did not simply reject Aristotle's authority in ethics and 'his object is not to attack Aristotle's ethics or even those contemporaries who discuss ethics philosophically. It is to attack those who pursue philosophy as if they were pagans.' She also points at the importance of different genres.

[58] See Kent, *Virtues of the Will*, 84 (81–84: 'William de la Mare').

[59] It is not helpful to say that Aristotle agreed with Church authorities. Such *Church* authorities did not exist, because such *authorities* did not exist. They were not needed because of the spiritual dynamics of Church and society. See Southern, *The Making of the Middle Ages*, 163 ff.

[60] Cf. Kent, *Virtues of the Will*, 81 ff. Special problems between the interdiction of Gregory IX (1231) and the generations of Olivi and Scotus' *magister* Gonsalvo of Spain have to be accounted for.

becomes a fascinating story read through *auctoritates* lenses, for this story tells us how the *corpus aristotelicum* was adopted into the family of mostly Christian *auctoritates*, even in circles which were most critical of the 'historical' Aristotle, as the Franciscans were.

In general, the expositions in Bonnie Kent's chapters culminate in presenting Duns Scotus' views as the last summit in a chain of mountains.[61] Duns Scotus was spellbound by Aristotle as an individual writer. If we did not know explicitly how he assessed the real truth-value of Aristotle's philosophy, then we would not have the slightest idea of his personal stance by going over endless pages of *exponere reverenter Aristotelem*. We meet a combination of phenomena perfectly unimaginable for the modern mind: immense admiration for an individual from a dim past and his oeuvre, a strong conviction that the involved philosophy is wrong, just as, in general, the *philosophi* were basically wrong (see §§14.4–14.5), and a reading method which bewitches Aristotle's texts into texts of eternal truth.

We can only see the logic of such phenomena against the common background of the *ahistorical* way of thinking, the *auctorita(te)s* character of medieval – and ancient – culture, in combination with the method of *exponere reverenter*, especially practised by theologians and jurists. On the one hand, the *exponere reverenter* is a common ingredient of understanding texts in an *auctoritates* culture, but the theologians transformed this method by also applying it to texts which were literally incompatible with the original canon. The common flexibility was even more drastically transformed into an immense flexibility when they applied this method to texts which were simply at variance with the original tradition of the *corpus auctoritatum*. The crucial difference in comparison with modern interpretations is that Duns Scotus and his followers simply knew what they were doing, although they themselves did not in any historical sense. The whole of this transformation was even successful where the condemnations and decisions of 1231 failed: to amend and to purify Aristotle. It deluded numerous interpreters into believing that these thinkers were Aristotelians. They definitely were not; they were themselves.

The paradoxical upshot of an intellectual *auctoritates* culture is the virtual absence of academic authority and authorities, although a book may enjoy an enormous existential authority for some

---

[61] In Kent, *Virtues of the Will*, for Duns Scotus, see chapter 3: 'Voluntarism' (94–149): 143–149, chapter 4: 'Moral Weakness and the Problem of Sin' (150–198): 193–19, and chapter 5: 'Virtues of the Will' (199–245): 238–245, respectively.

individual, as the Bible did for many theologians, and a certain oeuvre may be very special, as Augustine's and Anselm's works were for Duns Scotus. Of course, there were authorities in a different sense: parents and priests, bishops and princes. However, generally speaking, the place of the modern phenomenon of ideological authority is taken by the *auctoritates* and these *auctoritates* are texts. If we call these texts *authoritative texts*, we have to remind ourselves that the authoritative character of these texts is founded on *truth*, i.e. truth as it is perceived by the author who reads them within the context of his personal world. The harmony of these sources is a harmony which is presupposed to be there, but it is neither a historical achievement, nor, a priori, a historical fact. Of course, *auctoritates* are in harmony with each other. Otherwise, they are no *auctoritates*. Surely, to the medieval mind, they had probative value, but what did they affirm? The duality of *auctoritas* and *ratio* delivers both a hermeneutical key to what is meant and a systematic key to the philosophical strength of the position at stake. The questions of Walter of Bruges are critical of Aquinas, but they reveal no animus against Aristotle. The author makes no special appeal to Augustine's authority in arguing for freedom of the will, for he strives to reconcile Aristotle with Augustine. What views do the Aristotle passages aim at? Not at Aristotle's. There is no historical Aristotle present in the writings of the great thirteenth-century writers if they interpret Aristotle by *exponere reverenter.* They do not read *Aristotle*, they read *texts of* Aristotle. At bottom, *auctoritates* texts of ... Aristotle, like *auctoritates* texts of Augustine, Boethius, and Anselm, are texts of ... Truth.

14.9.1 The *auctoritates* status of the *corpus aristotelicum*

It has already been pointed out that, in the case of Aristotle, there was a special difficulty. Even in the Franciscan world, there is no monolithic use of the *auctoritates* taken from the *corpus aristotelicum*. Bonnie Kent summarizes the debate on Peter Olivi as follows:

> Ferdinand Delorme, Orazio Bettini, and David Burr have all insisted that Olivi was not, in fact, anti-Aristotelian – or at any rate, not totally and consistently anti-Aristotelian. Delorme argues that Olivi opposed all non-Christian philosophers: he had no greater respect for Avicenna or Plato than for Aristotle. Besides, Olivi's student days at Paris – in 1260s, when masters of arts had just made the joyous discovery of 'philosophical' method – do much to explain why he became a bitter opponent of pagan philosophers and their influence.

[...] Burr argues that Olivi was not consistently hostile to pagan philosophy and that many of the references to Aristotle in Olivi's works
are reasonably straightforward appeals to Aristotle's authority.[62]

So, might we say that the most anti-Aristotelian theologian from the
last quarter of the thirteenth century is not anti-Aristotelian? Most
scholars agree that most Franciscans are strongly opposed to Thomas
Aquinas, but there is also rather little hostility to Aristotle, although
Delorme acknowledges that Olivi opposed all 'non-Christian philosophy.' The interesting fact is that, from the historical point of view,
this holds for all Christian thinkers of the thirteenth century, including, of course, Albert the Great, Aquinas and Godfrey of Fontaines,
as well as Siger of Brabant. The fact that there is plain opposition to
Thomas Aquinas and little hostility to Aristotle cannot imply that
these authors are less 'Thomistic' than 'Aristotelian.' The disagreements with Aquinas are 'inner-Christian' peanuts in comparison to
the real convictions of the historical Aristotle. The evidence adduced
does not point to very different attitudes towards Aristotle, but to the
not yet rigidly fixed phenomenon of the *auctoritates* character of the
corpus aristotelicum.

14.9.2   Conclusions

There is a paradoxical conclusion to be drawn: an academic *auctoritates* culture like the medieval one is hardly familiar with the phenomenon of *authority*. Authors of *auctoritates* texts have in fact no
'authority' just because their writings are *auctoritates* texts – texts
which are accepted as set books and are held to be true. Of course,
most books are not *auctoritates* texts. Their authors do not enjoy
authority either. The scholar is not a 'critic.' In the first centuries of
the university this is generally true and so it is also true of Thomas
Aquinas, although in this regard we have to add that his works soon
enjoyed *auctoritates* status within his own order.[63] When Thomas'
Summa Theologiae replaced the *Sententiae* of Peter Lombard in the
course of the sixteenth century, all this has also to be applied to the
early modern Thomas Aquinas. This view has also to be the key in

---

[62] Kent, *Virtues of the Will*, 84 f. See also Burr, 'Petrus Ioannis Olivi and the Philosophers,'
Franciscan Studies 31 (1971) 41–71, and idem, *The Persecution of Olivi*, 25–35, and especially 27 f. Cf. §1.5, §6.3 and §§16.2–16.3.

[63] We see this confirmed by the duality of *bishop* and *master of divinity* in matters religious.
The fine thing was that most bishops 'criticized' and 'judged' asking advice from the masters.

reading sixteenth-century authors criticizing (Luther) or endorsing (Cajetan) medieval books. The Thomas Aquinas of Utrecht's great theology in the seventeenth century is reformed.

Within the factual context of the medieval evolution of philosophical and theological knowledge the medieval voices get their own meaning and interest. *We* have to concentrate on the thought world of the individual medieval thinker himself, apart from his *Aristoteles dicit*, and if the historical Aristotle incidentally appears in these texts, these appearances are just flashes of the historical Aristotle in the light of modern discovery, just as in theology appearances of the historical biblical contents are just flashes of the old Semitic or Hellenistic world. The messages may nearly coincide, but this conclusion is only to be drawn because we discover that there are such agreements – in a contingent manner. *We* have to concentrate on the nature and the contents of the individual works and their individual authors who did not produce *auctoritas* texts themselves at the time of writing. The system seems to be rather anti-individualistic, but *we* have to concentrate on the individuals and their individual development. The dynamics of discovery and explanation is the natural *Sitz im Leben* for understanding and interpreting systematic texts – not in terms of -isms, but in terms of personal contributions and, in particular, of individual theories – in an ongoing process of emancipation from the thought patterns of ancient thought and philosophy. They started anew in a rather simple manner in the tenth and eleventh centuries and through the development of the *logica modernorum* they marched into the century of the university creating a new universe of systematic thought.

CHAPTER 15

Historical dilemmas concerning Duns Scotus' thought

15.1 INTRODUCTION

According to the Renaissance view of the development of Western philosophy there is a 'breakdown of traditional thought' around 1500. This approach leads to the paradoxical view that English and French, German and Italian, Spanish and Dutch, Scandinavian, Middle and Eastern European philosophy start only *after 1500* and that modern European philosophy is not much older than American thought. Moreover, modern history of modern philosophy pays a great deal of attention to the great individual philosophers outside the universities. Hobbes and Descartes, Locke and Berkeley, Spinoza and Leibniz are those so privileged.

However, this approach begs some questions: can systematic thought of the sixteenth, seventeenth and eighteenth centuries be understood without taking into account university thought? Can the thought of the universities be understood without interpreting it in the light of the thirteenth-, fourteenth- and fifteenth-century universities? Can a realistic approach to the history of Western philosophy ignore the continuity of thought from about 1200 to about 1800? The European university shows a remarkable continuity between its birth in around 1200 till around 1800. The six first centuries of the Western university ($\pm 1200-\pm 1800$), consisting of two sets of three centuries, form one specific whole.[1]

The traditional view overlooks medieval thought and the philosophical contributions of its Augustinian main line. The separation of modern languages from Latin and the separation of modern philosophy from medieval philosophy are linked with the separation of philosophy from theology, but what we now call *theology* is the key to understanding the dynamics of Western and medieval thought in an

---

[1] The development of philosophy and theology up to 1800 has to be studied as a whole. Only the nineteenth-century university takes a different route.

alternative way. When we block out medieval thought and Duns Scotus' philosophy, we miss the most original facet of Western thought. In this light, our point of departure is the dilemma of the earliest modern studies in medieval philosophy which did not acknowledge the phenomenon of *medieval philosophy* (§15.2). §15.3 deals with the rebound of the 'historiens croyants'. The views of Étienne Henri Gilson (1884–1978) are dealt with in §15.4 while §15.5 focuses on Lambertus Marie de Rijk (b.1924), because his teaching and oeuvre are the *sine qua non* of understanding the approach developed in this study. The paradox of Western philosophy is softened by its perspective (§15.6).

15.2 THE DILEMMA OF MODERN STUDIES IN THE HISTORY OF MEDIEVAL PHILOSOPHY

According to De Wulf and Van Steenberghen, the Renaissance and Reformation sounded the death knell for medieval scholasticism and contributed badly to a regrettable leap over the Middle Ages, but it is not as bad as that.[2] Not only did Reformational thought during the sixteenth, seventeenth and eighteenth centuries, but even much orthodox Protestant thought during the nineteenth and twentieth centuries have to be included in the whole scholastic tradition. In particular, Reformed scholasticism of the seventeenth and eighteenth centuries followed the main path of Scotism.[3]

15.2.1 Cousin, Hauréau, and the *historiens rationalistes*

Scholastic thought went into paradoxical obscurity around about 1800 after a wonderful career of almost a millennium. The traditional university collapsed and suffered from an institutional disaster which came along with the oblivion of scholastic thought. The historical revolution of Niebuhr and Ranke (in around 1825) also led to the investigation of medieval philosophy according to new historical methods and to the creation of the history of medieval philosophy as an independent subject. Like its demise, the birth of the history of

---

[2] De Wulf, *Histoire de la philosophie médiévale* I, Louvain (⁶1934) 9 f., and Van Steenberghen, *Introduction à l'étude de la philosophie médiévale*, 36–39.

[3] See Vos, 'De kern van de klassiek gereformeerde theologie,' *Kerk en Theologie* 47 (1996) 106–125, idem, 'Ab uno disce omnes,' *Bijdragen* 60 (1999) 173–204, and Van Asselt and Dekker (eds), *Reformation and Scholasticism* (2001).

medieval philosophy led to a paradox. Its start was a *Fehlstart*, a failure, to be compared to the origins of critical and historical biblical research in the nineteenth century.

The first quarter of the nineteenth century had simply forgotten what scholastic thought consisted of. The effect was that medieval philosophy became a kind of mystery. Scholastic thought is a very complex and detailed phenomenon which requires a lot of effort and time to master. One generation of negligence may mean the end of it. During the last stages of the eighteenth century and the troubled two first decades of the nineteenth, the rich technicalities of scholasticism were no longer mastered because the continuity of training collapsed. The so-called defeat of scholasticism consisted of oblivion.

Nevertheless, rescue was near and it came from quite an unexpected corner. The history of medieval philosophy was born in the second quarter of the nineteenth century – in the same period that history itself was born as an independent branch of critical learning. This unexpected rebirth was the more paradoxical because the first historians of medieval philosophy did not believe that there was genuine *philosophy* in the Middle Ages. The Middle Ages were the Age of Faith and the Age of Faith was unable to think rationally because it did not know what the Age of Reason would reinvent: *scientific thought* and *rational philosophy*.

15.2.2   Victor Cousin (1792–1867)

Cousin, born at Paris, was educated at the École Normale where he started his teaching career as an assistant in courses on the history of philosophy at the University of Paris in 1815. In the 1820s Cousin, being out of work, spent his time in writing and editing the works of great philosophers. He edited Proclus (1820–27) and Descartes (1826) and started translating Plato (1822–40). This Parisian world of historical scholarship produced the first critical editions, the first monographs and the first textbook of the history of medieval philosophy. Apart from his general work in the history of philosophy, Victor Cousin published two text editions of Abelard: *Ouvrages inédits d'Abélard* (1838) and *Petri Abaelardi Opera* I–II (1849–59). In the same spirit, Charles de Rémusat (1797–1875) wrote his *Abélard* in two volumes (1845) and his *Saint Anselme* (1853). Ernest Renan's doctoral thesis *Averroès et l'Averroïsme* dates from 1852. The so-called 'rationalistic' origins of the history of medieval philosophy as an academic enterprise antedated Christian initiatives for investigating historically medieval philosophy by more than a generation. Certainly, the neoscholastic revival, particularly the revival of Neothomism in Italy, is older, but this development stood outside the borders of the new historical scholarship. The Parisian scholarly thinkers, critical of the Catholic Church and Christian religion, were the fathers of searching for and discovering manuscripts, editing medieval texts critically, investigating historical connections and initiating comparative philosophy. Paradoxically, they were also driven by admiration for scholasticism. 'I am an avowed friend of scholasticism' (Cousin).

The master of the Cousin tradition was the keeper of the manuscripts of the Parisian *Bibliothèque Nationale* (from 1848): Jean-Barthélémy Hauréau (d.1898). In 1850 Hauréau published the first history of medieval philosophy: *De la philosophie scolastique*. It might easily mislead us to conclude that, according to Hauréau, there existed philosophy in the Middle Ages. Certainly, it did, but as a legacy which could not be digested, because it was alien to the Age of Faith and its *patrimonium fidei*. Nevertheless, Hauréau was the author of the standard history of medieval philosophy of the second half of the nineteenth century: *Histoire de la philosophie scolastique* I–III (1872–80). Even more important are his *Notices et extraits de quelques manuscrits latins de la Bibliothèque Nationale* I–VI (1890–93).[4] Likewise, Maurice De Wulf was responsible for the standard history of medieval philosophy in the first half of the twentieth century: *Histoire de la philosophie médiévale* I–III (^{6}1933–47 (^{1}1900)). After Gilson's *History of Christian Philosophy in the Middle Ages* (1955) nobody dared any longer to write a history of medieval philosophy on the grand scale.

15.2.3 Émile Bréhier (1876–1952)

Bréhier continued the Hauréau tradition of Paris. His *La philosophie du moyen âge* (1937) was published in the series *L'évolution de l'humanité*, directed by Henri Berr. The intellectual evolution centers on the Greek genius, the paradigm of rationality. Here, *human reason* was constituted. The significant title of Léon Robin's contribution was: *La pensée grecque et les origines de l'esprit scientifique*. In late

---

[4] Van Steenberghen, *Introduction à l'étude de la philosophie médiévale*, 47 f., and Inglis, *Spheres of Philosophical Inquiry and the Historiography of Medieval Philosophy*, 55–57, 93–95, 109–112, and 159 f. Cf. Jolivet, 'Les études de philosophie médiévale en France de Victor Cousin à Étienne Gilson,' in Imbach and Maierù (eds), *Gli studi de filosofia medievale fra otto e novecento*, 1–20.

antiquity, philosophy and science were immersed in religion and mysticism. The Middle Ages were the period when philosophical teaching was the business of the clergy. It was a period of conflict between reason and faith and attempts to reconcile them, but Christianity and non-Christian ancient culture, faith and rationality are incompatible realities. So, the medieval project which tried to reconcile the irreconcilable was bound to fail.[5]

The formative eleventh century was studied in this light. J. A. Endres saw eleventh-century thought dominated by the controversy between the 'dialecticians' (for example, Berengar of Tours) and the 'antidialecticians' (for example, Peter Damian).[6] According to Bréhier, this conflict between dialectics and theology had to result in a synthesis at the end of the century and this synthesis is to be found in the thought of Anselm. Anselm tried to elucidate the faith from within. He only dealt with theological themes and there was no room for reason except as applied to matters of faith. Still, this type of theology is far removed from rational theology. In *Cur Deus homo?* we see Anselm trying to prove the necessity of incarnation. He had to reconcile the freedom of divine decisions and necessity. Completely overlooking Anselm's discovery of several kinds of necessity, in particular the distinction between *necessitas praecedens* and *necessitas sequens*, Bréhier decreed that Anselm did not show how they could be compatible. For him, without any doubt, this 'fissure' led eventually in the fourteenth century to the collapse of the scholastic edifice Anselm had founded.[7] It was Albert the Great and Thomas Aquinas who completely separated philosophy from theology. They defended that *reason* is linked with *nature* against the Augustinians.

15.2.4 Bréhier on Duns Scotus

La philosophie du moyen âge is to be characterized as an introduction which is 'clair et distinct.' The first chapter of its fifth part focuses on the dissolution of scholasticism. However, Bréhier did not concentrate

---

[5] Henri Berr, in É. Bréhier, *La philosophie du moyen âge*, III ('Avant-propos': I–XVIII): 'Il [= Bréhier] suit l'effort pour unifier deux données irréductibles: le christianisme et ce qui subsiste de la civilisation gréco-romaine; il met en vive lumière [. . .] *les conflicts de la raison et de la foi*.'

[6] See Endres, *Petrus Damiani und die weltliche Wissenschaft* (1910), and idem, *Forschungen zur Geschichte der frühmittelalterlichen Philosophie* (1915). This view has been definitively refuted by Holopainen, *Dialectic and Theology in the Eleventh Century*.

[7] *La philosophie du moyen âge*, 125–126 (121–129: 'Saint Anselme').

on the methodology of scholasticism but looked on scholasticism as the balance between reason and faith, or at any rate as an attempt at reconciliation. Because the project was an impossible one, it was doomed to failure and the vibrant meaning of the fourteenth century was considered precisely as the collapse of scholasticism. In the fifth part, the last part of his overview, only Duns Scotus, Ockham, the Ockhamists, skeptics and mystics are treated.[8] Many thinkers of the fourteenth century were convinced that Aristotle could not be used in theology and Ockamism had to end up in skepticism.

Bréhier rounded his moderate portrait of Duns' philosophy off with the verdict that Duns suppresses order and synthesis and that all his principles tend to dissolve the unity of faith and reason. However, this verdict does not follow from the bare letter of Bréhier's description of Duns' philosophy. In fact, the only wonder in Bréhier's exposition is this last unwarranted verdict. He does not even attempt to underscore it by evidence, nor to prove his own premises. His 'atheology' seems to make such a project superfluous. Perhaps, however, this is a bit unfair to Bréhier. He simply believed that Greek philosophy had not only invented rationality, but embodied reason. The idea of *fides quaerens intellectum* is simply a square circle. Along this line Bréhier was able to combine a rather fair description of Duns' views with an absolute verdict. However, Bréhier's approach is yet more paradoxical. The fourteenth century was a creative period, but this creativity was ignored. Can such an approach be adequate?[9] Van Steenberghen summarized this 'rationalist' movement in medieval studies as follows: the Parisian line does not acknowledge a positive *philosophical value* in medieval thought. These historians did not even look at the distinctive medieval contribution to philosophy *as* philosophy. The Middle Ages were only a tool. The philosophical sterility of the Middle Ages is due to Christianity and church.[10] The destruction of medieval scholasticism was what our culture needed and is what the Enlightenment achieved, for philosophy requires unbelief.

---

[8] Ibid., 375–432. See chapter II: Ockham (392–413) and chapter III: the ockhamists (414–422). Bréhier opted for a reversed ideology of decline. Just as the Neothomists complained of this decline, Bréhier welcomed it as the liberation Western thought longed for.

[9] Creative thinkers like Scotus and Ockham are seen as witnesses of the dissolution of scholasticism and causes of the dissolution of philosophy.

[10] Just as the state had to fight in order to regain its independence from the church, so philosophy had to reconquer its independence from theology.

15.3   THE REBOUND OF *THE HISTORIENS CROYANTS*

The second quarter of the nineteenth century saw the birth of the history of medieval philosophy as a scientific enterprise with the help of so-called rationalist historians; its second half saw the subject cared for by 'historiens croyants' (Fernand Van Steenberghen). What did the Catholic rebound consist of?

The neoscholastic revival reached back to the beginning of the nineteenth century when Vincenzo Buzzetti (1777–1824) succeeded in arousing new interest in the philosophy of Thomas Aquinas, introducing many talented students into training still styled along seventeenth- and eighteenth-century lines. His important student Serafino Sordi (1793–1865) taught, among many others, Guiseppe Pecci, the brother of the future Pope Leo XIII (1878–1903), and Gioacchino Pecci (b.1810), who himself had taught philosophy at the Jesuit German College in Rome. The Jesuit Order was restored in 1814 and flourished again in the nineteenth century. During the eighteenth century Thomas Aquinas' complete works were reprinted half a dozen times and the first volume of the first nineteenth-century reprint appeared in Naples in 1846 where Gaetano Sanseverino (1811–65) founded the Academy of Thomistic Philosophy.[11]

15.3.1   Kleutgen and Stöckl

The young Joseph Kleutgen (b.1811), born in Dortmund (Germany), became acquainted with Catholic Enlightenment Christianity, but he was converted to pre-Enlightenment theology and philosophy, studying in Munster in 1832–33. He joined the Jesuits in 1834 and in these early years he was convinced that reason and revelation can be reconciled only if one steps back from modern philosophy. Kleutgen's first work against the Enlightenment was *Über die alten und die neuen Schulen* (1846) and he continued to publish: *Die Theologie der Vorzeit vertheidigt* I–III (Munster 1853–60) and *Die Philosophie der Vorzeit vertheidigt* I–II (Munster 1860–63). Kleutgen was convinced that the revolutionary destruction of the first half of the nineteenth century proved the evil nature of modern philosophy and theology.

---

[11] See Coreth, Neidl, and Pfligersdorfer (eds), *Christliche Philosophie im katholischen Denken des 19. und 20. Jahrhunderts* I–III, and chapters 1 and 2 of Inglis's excellent *Spheres of Philosophical Inquiry and the Historiography of Medieval Philosophy*.

John Inglis perceptively discovered that Kleutgen changed his theoretical program in the third volume of his *Die Theologie der Vorzeit vertheidigt* (1860).

> He no longer discusses the various theological doctrines that he had originally set out to treat. Having already considered God, creation and grace, if he were to remain faithful to the order of Aquinas, he should have discussed Christ, the sacraments, and the last things. Instead Kleutgen begins his investigation anew and states that he must now clarify the relation of philosophy to revelation.[12]

His guiding question was whether the medieval use of Greek philosophy was fatal to theology. His own answer was that faith requires the use of reason. In spite of Kleutgen's stern criticisms of Descartes' philosophy, he followed the epistemological turn of modern philosophy stating that epistemology plays the foundational role in philosophy.

However, Kleutgen claimed that Thomas Aquinas' theory of knowledge was superior to modern thought. His criterion was that good philosophy logically leads to the moral good. The three medieval philosophical schools were those of realism, nominalism, and formalism. Thomas Aquinas' philosophy is the crown of the project for reconciling reason and revelation, but Ockham destroyed this achievement.

> Kleutgen implies that since Protestants are members of many churches and not united in one church they have a predilection to agree with Ockham's view of the importance of multiplicity. There are only particulars in the universe and no forms shared by individuals. In general, Protestants are unable to evaluate correctly the philosophy of Aquinas.[13]

Kleutgen's treatment of Duns Scotus is even more enigmatic. Scotus does away with actual individual subjects because of his idea of individuality. Because there are no subjects in Scotus' philosophy, there is only an endless number of predicates. 'Formalism' leads to the conclusion that the entire world is a single subject and this means that Duns Scotus implicitly ends up in pantheism. This early form of decline ideology is rather highly spirited. At the end of the century,

---

[12] Inglis, *Spheres of Philosophical Inquiry*, 81 (62–104: 'Kleutgen and the Spheres of Philosophical Inquiry').

[13] Ibid., 97. Nevertheless, the Protestant neoscholastic revival also followed the footsteps of Aquinas. If a Protestant thinker took into account medieval Christian thought, he mainly opted for Thomas Aquinas.

De Wulf judged that such an approach was not historical, but its historical character had already been questioned in 1861.

Albert Stöckl (1823–95) followed the footsteps of Kleutgen. He went to school in Eichstätt (Bavaria, South Germany), became a priest of the diocese of Eichstätt and studied and taught at its Seminary. He started as an Old Testament scholar, but from the 1850s he devoted himself to patristic and medieval studies. During the years 1864–66, he published a full-scale three-volume *Geschichte der Philosophie des Mittelalters* of almost 2,300 pages.[14]

Just as the books of Kleutgen show, the point of view is the reconciliation of reason and revelation. He dealt with more authors than Kleutgen and consistently applied the useful method of dividing philosophy into modern subjects. He discussed, for example, Abelard and the Victorines, including Peter Lombard, by surveying epistemology, metaphysics, psychology, ethics, and so on. Kleutgen's and Stöckl's histories linked up well with each other. Stöckl published his first mighty volume in 1864, while Kleutgen had finished his first series in 1863, but Stöckl also adopted Kleutgen's models of the reconciliation of faith and reason and the threefold picture of realism, nominalism, and formalism.

John Inglis discovered the important role Kleutgen and Stöckl had played in defining the dominating model of neoscholastic philosophy, studying the history of scholasticism which was identified with medieval scholasticism. Van Steenberghen fairly mentioned them in his mighty *Introduction à l'étude de la philosophie médiévale*. When he paid attention to the 'Catholic historians,' two considerable works are immediately mentioned: Joseph Kleutgen's *Die Philosophie der Vorzeit vertheidigt* I–II (1860–63) and *L'aristotelismo della Scolastica nella storia dela filosofia* (1873) by Salvatore Talamo. Albert Stöckl's *Geschichte der Philosophie des Mittelaters* I–III (1864–66) is honored as the first great history of scholasticism, written by a Catholic author. The rationality and independence of philosophy are stressed.[15] Nevertheless, in general, it is true that there was a strange oversight of Kleutgen's and Stöck's role in the twentieth century, although Gilson did mentioned Stöckl. Probably, twentieth-century historiography underestimated the importance of *Aeterni Patris* and did not try to explain this intervention. Moreover, the research of the second half of

---

[14] See ibid., 109–131 (105–136: 'Albert Stöckl's *Geschichte der Philosophie des Mittelalters*').
[15] Van Steenberghen, *Introduction à l'étude de la philosophie médiévale*, 55 f. Scholasticism is seen as a kind of Aristotelianism, a view dear to Van Steenberghen.

the twentieth-century tried valiantly to discover a broader importance and meaning of medieval philosophy, but John Inglis's anatomy of the body of historical scholarship is indispensable.

However, we may also see the point of the Louvain criticisms at the end of the nineteenth century. Kleutgen and Stöckl had read and studied medieval texts, but they had never tried to conquer the new canons of text critical and historical critical research. They simply condemned them.[16] Neither early neoscholasticism, nor the new approach of Kleutgen and Stöckl was rooted in the new 'scientific' Parisian approach. Nevertheless, Kleutgen tried to answer it. Hauréau and Bréhier may have been mistaken in identifying medieval thought patterns, but paleography, textual research, chronology, philology, and so on make quite a difference in interpreting scholastic texts. In fact, before the generations of Mandonnet and De Wulf, medieval texts still were not considered historical texts for Christian medievalists, but texts for eternity. *Mirabile dictu*, nineteenth-century historical research was often rather *a*-historical.

In fact, Kleutgen and Stöckl did not *discover* what they thought of medieval philosophy, but they imposed an a priori model on it. So, we may appreciate the criticisms of the young De Wulf that their studies were not histories. The same assessment holds for the early 'histories' of Protestant scholasticism, dating from the 1830s and the 1840s. Although their authors were more prudent than Kleutgen and Stöckl were, their reconstructions were speculative and not based on an adequate grasp of scholastic Latin. Although they were liberal theologians, they wholeheartedly believed in the truth of their tradition, but according to their own interpretation and not allowing for an alternative.

When we look at Kleutgen's interpretation of medieval philosophy, it is evident that it is basically mistaken, apart from considering Thomas Aquinas as the center of the medieval development of philosophy and apart from his ideology of decline. The reconciliation of faith and reason cannot have been the center of this development because there was no battle or even tension between them for the simple reason that the modern concept or reality of reason did not exist, to be compared with the fact that there was no state in the

---

[16] In general, nineteenth-century orthodoxy was rather critical of the methods and the outcome of liberal scholars who condemned old kinds of traditional Christianity in a very relaxed manner. In the Netherlands, there were ministers of the Reformed Church, who were atheists ontologically but still ministers of the church.

modern sense in the Middle Ages, only Church and society. The problem did not exist. So, the solution is an improbable phenomenon. This is one thing. It is a remarkable fact that the model endured in the next century.[17]

15.3.2   Maurice De Wulf (1867–1947)

In 1893, Maurice De Wulf was appointed to hold the first Catholic chair in the history of medieval philosophy and it was no coincidence that this occurred at Louvain. His *Histoire de la philosophie médié-vale* became the leading history of medieval philosophy, from the first edition in 1900 to the sixth edition in three volumes (I 1934, II 1935, and III 1947), which was the last.[18] De Wulf proposed an intrinsic def-inition of what is essential to scholastic philosophy. Scholasticism is also a system of thought, characterized by the dualism of God and creation, for God is pure act and his creatures are a mixture of act and potency. Pantheism is out of the question. God is a personal God and scholastic philosophy is as such creation thought. Its ontology stresses the contingency and the dynamic character of reality. It also stresses the existence of individuals and the spiritual nature of the human soul. It rejects subjectivism and idealism. Its ethics is an ethics of freedom (*libertaire*).[19]

The logic of scholastic philosophy is both analytical and synthetic. Albert the Great and Thomas Aquinas closely followed Aristotle, the uncontested master, but Duns' excessive realism and Ockham's exces-sive subjectivism destroyed the Aristotelian balance. The scholasticism of the fourteenth and fifteenth centuries is degenerate scholasticism.[20] In spite of his success and influence, De Wulf met widespread criticism for his views on the essence of scholastic philosophy, especially after the fifth edition of *Histoire de la philosophie médiévale* I–II (1924–25).

---

[17] Inglis's 'biography' is breathtaking reading. See also §§15.5 ff. and Chapter 16.

[18] *Histoire de la philosophie médiévale* I and II were translated into English by Ernest C. Messenger: *History of Mediaeval Philosophy* I (1935) and II (1937).

[19] *Histoire de la philosophie médiévale*, Louvain (¹1900), 288 f. The first history published by De Wulf (1894) is called: *Histoire de la philosophie scolastique dans les Pays-Bas et la Principauté de Liège*. Cf. the title of Hauréau's important history: *Histoire de la philosophie scolastique*.

[20] De Wulf, *Histoire de la philosophie médiévale* II 287 f. For a striking memoir by his star pupil and successor Fernand Van Steenberghen, see Van Steenberghen's 'Maurice De Wulf (1867–1947)' (1948), *Introduction à l'étude de la philosophie médiévale*, 287–313, cf. 61–63. Cf. Wielockx, 'De Mercier à De Wulf. Débuts de l'École de Louvain,' *Gli studi de filosofia medievale fra otto e novecento*, 89–95.

In De Wulf's mind there is a distinctive philosophy to be discovered and to be uncovered during the Middle Ages and the great Christian masters of medieval thought share a set of substantial theories. So, real philosophy does exist in the Middle Ages and, over and against ancient and modern philosophy, there is also a deep consensus which is called by De Wulf *philosophie scolastique*.

The criticisms De Wulf sought to deal with consisted of the charge that he assumed a relevant consensus, but also equated this consensus to the 'Aristotelian' orthodox philosophy of the great Dominican masters Albert the Great and Thomas Aquinas. Many critics considered his real definition of 'scholastic philosophy' too restrictive, the more so because, in the first edition, he appended his analysis of scholastic philosophy to his exposition of Thomas Aquinas' philosophy. However, another observation has also to be made: De Wulf's definition of scholasticism was too general. Not only Reformational thought during the sixteenth, seventeenth and eighteenth centuries, but even much orthodox Protestant thought during the nineteenth and twentieth centuries have to be included according to his definition, although this fact does not square with De Wulf's Thomist-styled definition.

Moreover, we have to note that, in contrast to his personal statements made on principle and in contrast to the impression De Wulf's doctrine made on some minds, from the start, De Wulf included not only the old Franciscan doctors of theology (the line of Alexander of Hales, Bonaventure and Richard of Middleton) in his denotation of 'scholastic philosophy', but also Duns Scotus and the Scotists, and Ockham and the nominalists. In fact, his definition is quite consistent with this broad set of thinkers. His examples of 'anti-scholastic' and deviant philosophies in the Middle Ages form a rather limited part of medieval thought and perhaps it was even more limited than De Wulf realized himself: John Scottus Eriugene and some twelfth-century thinking, associated with Scottus Eriugene, and, from the thirteenth century onwards, his examples are mainly so-called Latin Averroists.[21]

During the third period which comprises the fourteenth century and the first half of the fifteenth century, the main supporters of

---

[21] De Wulf, *Histoire de la philosophie médiévale* II (⁵1925) 90: 'Au XIIIe siècle, c'est l'averroïsme (sc. l'averroïsme latin) qui est, par excellence, le système antiscolastique': see §325 (90–91): 'Son caractère antiscolastique.' Cf. ibid., 216: 'C'est toujours l'averroïsme qui demeure le grand rival de la scolastique.'

'anti-scholastic' philosophy are again Latin Averroists, this time in the company of a few theological determinists (Bradwardine)[22] and the skeptical 'nominalists' (223–229: Nicholas of Autrecourt and John of Mirecourt).[23]

15.3.3   De Wulf on Duns Scotus

Against this background, De Wulf wrote on the life, works, and thought of Scotus. He opted for an English Duns, born in 1274 (!) – according to De Wulf, Duns died at the age of 34. He was a pupil of William of Ware (*doctor profundus*) and was influenced by Roger Bacon. Duns reveled in mathematics, taught by Bacon. He went to Paris in 1304 and died at Cologne in 1308. Richard of Middleton was the last representative of the old Franciscan school in the style of Alexander of Hales and Bonaventure. Duns created a new orientation.[24] His was a critical, though always courteous, mind. He distinguished between theology and philosophy. Rational and natural truth is the subject matter of philosophy. On the contrary, theology is a practical science. Reason veils her face before the mystery of faith in obedience to the Word of God. De Wulf was afraid of a rationalistic tendency in Duns' options.

Scotus' *distinctio formalis a parte rei* was a new distinction invented by Duns.[25] It endangers the unity of God. In spite of his theory of the univocity of *being* Duns Scotus gave in with regard to the demonstrability of several attributes of God, for example his

---

[22] In §419 De Wulf tells us about the re-edition of Bradwardine's *De causa Dei* in 1618 (London). This re-edition was related to the coming Synod of Dordt (1618–19), several parties preparing themselves for their debates. For that matter, Thomas Bradwardine was not a determinist, nor was Wycliffe. In their own independent ways, both followed contingency thought, influenced as they were by Duns Scotus.

[23] See De Wulf, *Histoire de la philosophie médiévale* II (⁵1925) 90–105: 'Averroïsme latin,' including Siger of Brabant (95–99), and 216–219: 'L'averroïsme à Paris. Jean de Jandun.' Nicholas Cusanus (230–235), like the Latin neoplatonists (106–126), Roger Bacon (126–143) and Raymond Lulle (143–146) in the thirteenth century, belongs to independent minds, and not to 'anti-scholasticism.' De Wulf is more appreciative than his fundamental considerations allow him to be.

[24] De Wulf, *Histoire de la philosophie médiévale* II 308 f. The Dominicans only knew of one philosophical style – Thomism, but the Franciscans had 'deux fractions philosophiques.'

[25] Ibid., 316: 'A la différence de la *distinctio realis* qui existe entre deux choses réellement diverses, de la *distinctio rationis* qui multiplie les concepts d'une même chose, pour la considérer sous des points de vue différents (*d. rationis cum fundamento in re*) ou identiques (*d. rationis sine fundamento in re*), la "*distinctio formalis aparte rei*" porte dans une même substance individuelle, sur les formalités objectives, qui y sont réalisées, indépendamment de tout acte intellectuel.'

omnipotence.[26] Freedom is essential both to divine and human will. Duns subscribed to Avicebron's hylomorphism.[27] According to Thomas Aquinas, will is a passive faculty; according to Henry of Ghent and Duns Scotus, will is an active one. Virtues are placed in the theory of will. Duns' doubts resulted in Ockham's philosophy, fourteenth-century Averroism and later Renaissance philosophy.[28] In the fourth edition of De Wulf's *Histoire de la philosophie médiévale*, P. Minges was considered to be the outstanding authority on Scotus scholarship. Between 1922 and 1924 Longpré published the contents of his *La philosophie du B. Duns Scot* and in the fifth edition De Wulf accepted Longpré as the great expert.

In sum, the second quarter of the nineteenth century saw the birth of the history of medieval philosophy as a scientific enterprise with the help of 'rationalist' historians. The third quarter saw the subject cared for by faithful historians, 'historiens croyants' (Fernand Van Steenberghen), followed by a century of intense historical research, mainly under neoscholastic inspiration, resulting in many editions and monographs. De Wulf revised his Scotus picture by doing justice to Minges' and Longpré's discoveries.

15.4 ÉTIENNE HENRI GILSON (1884–1978)

On the one hand, it was clear to Gilson that there was no common philosophy present within the many theologies developed during the Middle Ages. Rather, there were different authentic philosophies. On the other hand, Gilson's *The Spirit of Medieval Philosophy* shows that the Christian faith and its theology have produced an independent kind of metaphysics and have also transformed philosophy itself. Here two major theses come in: there is the phenomenon of *Christian philosophy* as a matter of historical fact.

> The Thomism of Thomas Aquinas, rather than that of his interpreters, is the unique instance of a Christian philosophy that best mirrors Catholic thinking and that grounds the truths achieved by all

---

[26] Ibid., 310–311. Here, De Wulf's basic stance colors his description. Cf. *PMA* 4.2.

[27] Ibid., 313: 'Il prend probablement (Avicebron) pour un philosophe chrétien.' De Wulf's exposition of Duns' theory on *matter* and *form* heavily rests on *De rerum principio* (ibid., 313–315).

[28] De Wulf did not commit the howlers sometimes ascribed to him: in De Wulf's eyes, Duns was no pantheist, neither was Ockham. In the company of Thomas Aquinas, both belong to *scholastic philosophy*, although De Wulf does not posses a theory which backs this treatment of the Franciscan and other orders and sympathizing secular masters.

other Christian philosophies. Thomism is the philosophy of a theologian and is characterized both by its metaphysics of being, which holds that what is real and intelligible is so by virtue of its act of existing.[29]

Gilson accepted Thomas' distinction between philosophy and theology, but opposed their separation as practised by Renaissance theology. There is a tension between the thesis of a philosophical plurality of the Middle Ages and the thesis of Thomism as the unique core of Christian philosophy. Moreover, what does Christian philosophy consist of? The major event was the publication of *La philosophie de Saint-Bonaventure*.

Gilson was a phenomenon in the world of historical scholarship and systematic thought. The first quarter of the twentieth century was the era of De Wulf, the second was Gilson's, and the third Van Steenberghen's. Gilson's output lasted over sixty years, extending from Dante to Descartes. In reviews he has often been called a Thomist. What matters most, however, is the fact that as a student he was already gripped by philosophy and, when he prepared his theses on Descartes, gripped by Christian philosophy in its quality as a distinct historical reality.[30] Like Cousin, Hauréau and Bréhier, Gilson was born in Paris and studied at its university. It was due to the great Jewish thinker Lucien Lévy-Bruhl that Gilson's start in historical scholarship was highly original. In 1905 Lévy-Bruhl advised Gilson to investigate the historical origins of Descartes' philosophy in a new way by turning to its medieval sources. He learned to read Aquinas and it was an encounter for life. The fruits were *Index scolastico-cartésien* (1913) and *La liberté chez Descartes et la théologie*.

In 1818, Cousin expressed his views on the dynamics of the history of Western philosophy in his *Cours de philosophie*. There are only two distinct periods in the history of philosophy and these periods are parallel to the main periods of the history of mankind: antiquity and the modern age. In between, the light of the Greek genius had gone down in the night of the Middle Ages. The fifteenth and sixteenth centuries are only the infancy of the seventeenth century: the age of modern philosophy starts with Descartes. 'Philosophy' before Descartes is in fact theology. This thesis played a vital role in the metaphilosophy of, for example, Mandonnet and, in a transformed way, in Gilson's. These views were not considered to be hypotheses or theories to be checked.

---

[29] According to the fine wording of Thro, 'Étienne Gilson,' *ER* V 560.
[30] See Laurence K. Shook, *Étienne Gilson*.

In fact, they functioned as axioms. Here, the revolution of Gilson's theses comes in. The 'merveilleusement intelligent' Lévy-Bruhl suggested to Gilson a topic for his future research: *Descartes and scholasticism*, in 1905. At that time, Gilson (b.1884) had not read one line of Thomas Aquinas, but Lévy-Bruhl knew that the young Gilson was a Catholic and assumed that he was familiar with scholasticism.

Gilson's first books on medieval philosophy were published in Strasbourg. In the meantime, Gilson had succeeded Picavet at the Sorbonne (1921) and his *La philosophie au moyen âge* I–II appeared in Paris in 1922. According to Gilson, Thomas Aquinas' philosophy was an original synthesis. Because of the creative dynamics of their faith and theology, the two extraordinary geniuses Albert the Great and Thomas Aquinas not only discerned the enormous value of Aristotle's philosophy in presenting Christian dogma, but, being free from Aristotelian docility and non-Christian errors, they also immediately achieved the ideal adaptation of Aristotle's philosophy to that dogma.[31]

Again, we see here operating the Parisian axis of Aristotle's philosophy defined as philosophy and as natural reason or light as such. Gilson read Albert's and Thomas' reading Aristotle as a historical reading, steering the middle course between two wrong extremes of reading Aristotle: (Latin) Averroism on the one hand and Christian traditionalism on the other. It was also difficult for Gilson to explain why the Bonaventure line did not accept this kind of innovation. His explanation was that the synthesis of the two Dominican geniuses was too new for the conservative Augustinians, but this solution, already put forward by Mandonnet and De Wulf, is not consistent with Gilson frankly recognizing the independent genius of Oxford and the value of the Oxonian contributions to scientific thought.

According to Van Steenberghen, Gilson defended from the start of his postwar career two theses which are simply complementary in Gilson's eyes: the Middle Ages produced authentic philosophies some of which were distinctly Christian.[32] Gilson has become famous through these theses. Nevertheless, the notion of an original system of

[31] *La philosophie au moyen âge* II, 36, cf. 31–35 and 3–6. In his prewar period (World War II), Gilson cherished two assumptions: a great medieval thinker has a personal system (Hamelin) and he enjoys a unique intuition (Bergson). Both assumptions are not quite medieval. See Alain de Libera, 'Les études de philosophie médiévale en France d'Étienne Gilson à nos jours,' in *Gli studi di filosofia medievale fra otto e novecento*, 21–33 (21–50).

[32] See 'L'oeuvre d'Étienne Gilson': Introduction (64–68), in *Introduction à l'étude*, 63–77.

philosophy within the borders of Christian thought is only applied to the doctrines of Albert the Great and Thomas Aquinas. Bonaventure only ascribed to Aristotle a subordinate place without changing the character of traditional philosophy.[33] The historically most important discovery took place when Albert of Bollstädt (1206/7–80) introduced the decisive distinction between philosophy and theology. It was not Luther, Calvin, or Descartes liberating Western philosophy. No, independent philosophy is due to the patient efforts of medieval thinkers. The history of *medieval philosophy* is the history of a *rationalist movement* continuously developing itself. This definitive discovery is in fact the foundation on which modern philosophy rests. The Middle Ages are progressively on the way towards a complete separation of philosophy from theology. The essential characteristic of modern thought is due to Albert the Great. His is the cradle of the albertino-thomistic philosophy.[34]

The medieval philosophers of the preface of *Le thomisme* (1919) are thinkers within the Thomist tradition and the philosophical nature of the thought of these theologians is dependent on the nature of philosophy itself which is par excellence the philosophy of the *Philosophus*. In this stage of his development, Gilson stood squarely within the new Catholic tradition in the rebound against the Parisian approach, defending the presence of philosophy in medieval thought in perfect harmony with the faith and theology of the church. Gilson's stance was near to Mandonnet's and De Wulf's. As to Oxford's scientific thought and Duns Scotus, Gilson was more tolerant than many of his colleagues, but the notion of Christian philosophy was not a vital question before his course on the philosophy of Bonaventure (1923–24). Even his philosophical rhetoric was rather similar to Mandonnet's in 1899. Bonaventure had his successors: John Pecham, Matthew of Acquasparta, Roger Marston, and Richard of Middleton. Even after the triumph of the Aristotelianism of Thomas Aquinas there are the philosophical rights of Duns Scotus' great synthesis which we shall meet with Malebranche.[35]

---

[33] *La philosophie au moyen âge* II 3: 'Jamais l'aristotélisme n'y était autorisé à se développer pour lui-même et conformément à ses exigences propres. C'est bien l'aristotélisme [. . .] qui va passer au premier plan dans la synthèse doctrinale que nous allons examiner.'

[34] *La philosophie au moyen âge* II 10 (8–13): 'C'est pourquoi le moment où nous sommes arrivés peut être considéré comme décisif, non seulement dans l'histoire de la philosophie médiévale, mais encore dans l'histoire de la pensée humaine.'

[35] *La philosophie au moyen âge* II 158–160, where also Olivi, William of La Mare, and Henry of Ghent are added to this same tradition line.

All this changed when Bonaventure came in. Gilson came forward with a personal interpretation of Bonaventure while Mandonnet's views are discussed in a different vein. This approach might be underscored from the viewpoint of a certain conception of *philosophy* in general and of *scholastic philosophy* in particular.

> Looked at from the rationalist point of view of modern philosophy, St. Bonaventure's doctrine does undoubtedly appear as the most mediaeval of mediaeval philosophies; and so, in certain aspects, it is. No thirteenth century thinker set himself more systematically to reduce the sciences to theology. [. . .] Looked at from the point of view of Thomist philosophy, St. Bonaventure's doctrine would seem to be disqualified for an analogous reason. Assuredly, Thomism was modern from the moment of its birth – in this sense, that, established of set purpose on the common ground of the human reason, it professed to resolve philosophical problems by methods common to all.[36]

How is Bonaventure's *philosophy* to be viewed in terms of such a universe of rational demonstrations? If you set Bonaventure's doctrine against these philosophies, it is for them not a *philosophy*. For Gilson, it constituted an independent alternative.

Eventually, Gilson published his massive *Jean Duns Scot* in 1952. In 1955 he devoted twenty pages to Duns in his masterwork on the history of Christian philosophy which aimed at providing an introduction (845 pages) to the history of Christian philosophy from Justin Martyr up to Nicholas of Cusa. The way Gilson defined 'Christian philosophy' is not 'Scotian' in style. Christian philosophy is not philosophy in the strict sense, nor is it philosophy in a broad sense – as Van Steenberghen again and again interpreted Gilson – but a *use* of philosophy: 'We call *Christian philosophy* the *use* made of philosophical notions by the Christian writers of those times.'[37] At this sensitive point, John Wippel introduces an important distinction:

> It is one thing to suggest that in a given case a medieval thinker may have moved from prior religious belief in a certain point to philosophical inquiry concerning the same. It is something else to suggest that he must have moved from his theology to philosophical investigation of the same.[38]

---

[36] Gilson, *The Philosophy of St Bonaventure*, Paterson 1965 ([2]1943), 437 f.

[37] *HCPMA* V, cf. Van Steenberghen, *Introduction à l'étude*, 63–77: 'Gilson,' cf. 85–92.

[38] Wippel, 'Thomas Aquinas and the Problem of Christian Philosophy,' *Metaphysical Themes in Thomas Aquinas*, 24. On Gilson, see part 1: 'Étienne Gilson and Christian Philosophy,' ibid., 2–22, cf. John M. Quinn, *The Thomism of Étienne Gilson. A Critical Study*.

To Wippel's mind, the later Gilson adopted both proposals, while only the first is acceptable for Wippel. Wippel sees Gilson's view on Thomas Aquinas refuted by the fact that Thomas devoted so much time and energy to writing the philosophical *opuscula*, for instance *De unitate intellectus* and *De aeternitate mundi*, and the philosophical 'commentaries.'[39] Gilson downgraded the importance of these philosophical writings, while Weisheipl and Van Steenberghen regarded these works as important sources for discovering Thomas' personal thought.[40] Gilson charged Duns Scotus with 'theologism,'[41] but Wippel judges that Gilson underestimated the independent philosophical drive of Thomas Aquinas' thought. Thomas was well aware of the nature and method of metaphysics and philosophy and it is a challenging and fertile task to reassemble the elements of Thomas' philosophical thought 'according to the philosophical order outlined by Thomas himself, not according to the theological order proposed by Gilson.'[42]

15.5 LAMBERTUS MARIE DE RIJK (B.1924)

We have met rivals in understanding the nature of medieval philosophy and immensely different alternatives. Moreover, there are excellent introductions to medieval philosophy, but many philosophical faculties offer only courses on the history of ancient and modern thought. Having said goodbye to Augustine we immediately join René Descartes. *In academicis* we are not fair to the whole of Western philosophy's past.

The fact that the academic past is an enigmatic part of the history of our culture is mirrored in the quite different interpretations found in the history of researching medieval philosophy. The old Paris line claimed to discover only *non-philosophy* in the Middle Ages. The Christian rebound acknowledged only true medieval philosophy as far as it was thought to be basically in line with Greek philosophy. Many Protestant theologians held that medieval thought offers

---

[39] On these philosophical works, see Weisheipl, *Friar Thomas d'Aquino*, 272–285.

[40] See Van Steenberghen, *La philosophie au XIII* siècle ([2]1991), 280 (280–283) and 294–297. Cf. Wippel, 'Metaphysics and *Separatio* in Thomas Aquinas,' *Metaphysical Themes in Thomas Aquinas*, 69–104.

[41] This charge was effectively refuted by Wolter, 'The "Theologism" of Duns Scotus' (1947), in *The Philosophical Theology of Scotus*, 209–253. Cf. §9.6.

[42] Wippel, 'Thomas Aquinas and the Problem of Christian Philosophy,' *Metaphysical Themes*, 32.

profound evidence that man was corrupted by nature, especially Christians before 1517. Likewise, most Marxist philosophers considered medieval philosophy to be useless.

For opponents of Gilson, Gilson was the great exception to this rule, but he also put medieval contributions in the wider context of a harmony of reason and faith, where the synthesizing power of Thomas Aquinas is seen as the high point of medieval philosophy and Ockham as the bête noire, bringing about the dissolution of medieval philosophy. John Inglis analyzed piles of introductions and introductory materials and, eventually, he stressed the significance of 'Franciscan philosophy,' the exception to the old-fashioned rule.

The axis of the rule of understanding medieval philosophical thought is most easily illustrated on the basis of the traditional Catholic interpretation, because this interpretation did not originate in caricature or contempt but was dictated by admiration and love. This approach historicized the duality of *nature* and *super nature.* The super nature of faith and Church is considered to rest on the fundamental order of nature. Medieval thought is seen to rest on ancient *philosophia* just as super nature is founded on nature.

We meet a variant of this type of view in the metaphilosophy of Professor Cornelia Johanna de Vogel (1905–86). She taught the history of ancient philosophy at Utrecht University (1947–74) in combination with the history of medieval philosophy. *Greek Philosophy* I–III (1950–59) shows her formidable scholarship. She was *amicissima Platonis* and a devoted Catholic convert. She acknowledged the great importance of the medieval period. According to her, the importance of medieval philosophy was due to the Christian acknowledgement and purification of the sublime truth, already present in Greek philosophy, in particular in Plato.

> She always maintained that Greek philosophy and especially Platonism had prepared the way to Christian mediaeval thought and that is why she hardly noticed the unique development within mediaeval culture. People like Abelard and Ockham she viewed with suspicion, and even a figure such as Duns Scotus did not seem to fit in with her ideas.[43]

The Plato and Aristotle scholar De Rijk revolutionized the scholarly investigation of medieval logic and philosophy by changing

---

[43] De Rijk, 'In Memoriam Cornelia Johanna de Vogel,' *Vivarium* 25 (1987) 1 (1 f.). She contributed much to *Phronesis*, but also supported De Rijk in founding *Vivarium*. See also Mansfeld, 'De Centrale Interfaculteit,' *De Utrechtse Universiteit 1936–1986*, 493–496.

essentially the point of view in examining scholastic thought: medieval thought is not good, or bad, because it simply repeats ancient thought; on the contrary, it is interesting because many of its important tendencies and theories cannot be traced back to ancient thought. It is not true that it is not interesting as being quite unoriginal; it is just interesting because of its originality, based on its past, in a fruitful interaction of *tradition* and *renewal*. De Vogel's star pupil De Rijk started as a classical scholar and historian of ancient philosophy. His first book dealt with Aristotle and his *Aristotle* I–II date from 2002.[44]

De Rijk was born in Hilversum, in North Holland, in November 1924, forty years after the birth of Gilson. In the prewar period, many Dutch theological students preparing for the priesthood profited from a profound schooling in philosophy before passing on to theological studies, and the young De Rijk studied philosophy at the Archdiocesan Seminary of Utrecht before passing on to studying classical philology and philosophy at the University of Utrecht, where he received his doctorate in 1952. Having switched to medieval philosophy he published his first critical text edition in 1956, when he also became a member of the Senate, the Upper Chamber of the Dutch Parliament. He also acted as Vice-President of the Senate (1980–91).[45]

De Rijk was Professor of the History of Medieval Philosophy at the Catholic University in Nijmegen (1961–69), the first chair in the history of medieval philosophy in the Netherlands, and lecturer and part-time Professor (1967–83: 'professor extraordinarius') of Medieval Philosophy at Utrecht University (1963–83). After his Nijmegen years, he taught ancient and medieval philosophy at the University of Leiden (1969–88). For the last two decades De Rijk has again paid much attention to the great Greeks: *Plato's Sophist* and *Aristotle* I–II,[46] and he still teaches as 'honorary professor' at Maastricht University (Limburgia). His activities follow three

---

[44] *The Place of the Categories of Being in Aristotle's Philosophy* (PhD thesis Utrecht, 1952). Cf. idem, 'Aristoteles en de eleatische bewegingsantinomieën,' *Tijdschrift voor Filosofie* 9 (1947) 171–202.

[45] It was only due to an extraordinary political constellation in the House of Commons that De Rijk was not the President of the Upper Chamber in the 1980s.

[46] *Plato's Sophist. A Philosophical Commentary* (1986), and *Aristotle* I–II (2002). The following editions are among the rich harvest of the years of his retirement: De Rijk (ed.), *Nicholas of Autrecourt* (1994), idem (ed.), *Giraldus Odonis Opera Philosophica* I (1997), and idem (ed.), *Johannes Buridanus. Summulae de demonstrationibus* (2001).

tracks: original research, academic teaching, and politics. Being critical 'to the inch,' he has conducted himself as a socially motivated politician, an inspiring friend, and an exemplary editor and interpreter.[47]

His international fame is based on his creative investigations of medieval semantics and logic and, in particular, on his discovery of the origins of the *logica modernorum*. 'L. M. de Rijk's *Logica Modernorum* [. . .] opened the gates to all subsequent research.'[48] 'For the twelfth and thirteenth centuries, De Rijk (1962–1967) is again invaluable.'[49] In 1956, he published his first critical text edition: the edition of the final logical work – *Dialectica* – of Abelard, a logician and philosopher he admires very much. This splendid edition was followed by an impressive series of crucial text editions.[50] His contributions to the discovery of the origins of the *ars obligatoria* also comprise fascinating editions. In Paris, we meet a quite remarkable collection of three works on *obligationes* from the second quarter of the thirteenth century: *Tractatus Emmeranus de falsi positione* together with the twin treatise *Tractatus Emmeranus de impossibili positione*, and *Obligationes Parisienses*.[51] These works show a kind of family resemblance and are testimonies to the same academic

---

[47] See Mansfeld, 'De Centrale Interfaculteit,' in *De Utrechtse Universiteit 1936–1986*, 494, and Bos, 'Curriculum vitae' and bibliography 1947–84 in Bos (ed.), *Mediaeval Semantics and Metaphysics*, VIII f. and IX–XXIV, respectively.

[48] Jacobi, 'Logic: the Later Twelfth Century,' in Dronke (ed.), *A History of Twelfth-Century Western Philosophy*, 248 note 106.

[49] Spade, 'Recent Research on Medieval Logic,' *Synthese* 40 (1979) 7, cf. 5. This volume, edited by Simo Knuuttila (!), contains most of the papers read at the Helsinki Symposium (1976) on medieval philosophy.

[50] For example, *Petrus Abaelardus. Dialectica* ([1]1956, [2]1970); idem, *Garlandus Compotista. Dialectica* (1959); idem, *Logica Modernorum. A Contribution to the History of Early Terminist Logic* I (= *Logica Modernorum* I, 1962), and II (= *Logica Modernorum* II, 1967) – the second volume contains the text critical edition of fifteen important logical and semantic treatises, dating from the twelfth century. Cf. De Rijk, 'The Early Origin of the Theory of Supposition,' *CHLMP* 161–173, and idem, *Peter of Spain (Petrus Hispanus Portugalensis) Tractatus* (1972).

[51] 'Some Thirteenth Century Tracts on the Game of Obligation. I: Two Separate Tracts on *falsi positio* and *impossibilis positio*,' *Vivarium* 12 (1974) 94–123; idem, *Tractatus Emmeranus de falsi positione*, ibid., 103–117, and *Tractatus Emmeranus de impossibili positione*, ibid., 117–123; idem, 'Some Thirteenth Century Tracts on the Game of Obligation. II: The *Obligationes Parisienses* Found in Oxford, *Canon. misc.* 281,' *Vivarium* 13 (1975) 22–54 (critical edition, ibid., 26–54); idem, 'Some Thirteenth Century Tracts on the Game of Obligation. III: The Tract *De petitionibus contrariorum*, Usually Attributed to William of Sherwood,' *Vivarium* 14 (1976) 26–49. The crowning contribution in this tradition is by De Rijk's pupil and Nijmegen successor H. A. G. Braakhuis, 'The *Obligationes* of Nicholas of Paris (?),' *Vivarium* 36 (1998) 152–233.

milieu. The historically interesting tract *De modo opponendi et respondendi* has to be added to all this.[52]

The second half of the nineteenth century saw the first newly styled editions, Cousin and his followers having paved the way. However, assessing critically the first generations of critical editions is a complex task accompanied by mixed feelings. Even the concept of *criticism* enjoys a complicated biography. Apart from the use of manuscripts and the issues of spelling and quotations, the editors often corrected their texts at liberty. Both the Bible and the Bonaventure of the old editions are the Bible and the Bonaventure of the editors.[53] Jacqueline Hamesse recently formulated what is advisable concerning spelling, quotations, inventories of manuscripts (also needed in order to solve authenticity problems), a *stemma codicum* (if possible), and the critical apparatus.[54] I think it will be absolutely revealing to look at De Rijk's editions from 1956 to 2001 in the light of Jacqueline Hamesse's *pia desideria*: all have already been fulfilled already. This fact is a striking example, because De Rijk's editions run over forty-five years. Fortunately, splendid editions appear in many countries, against a background of a history of textual criticism of two centuries, in the wake of biblical and classical scholars.

However, De Rijk's splendid teaching on medieval thought had a much broader scope than his editorial work suggests. It covered the whole of medieval philosophy and culture and offered special interpretations of the dynamics of medieval scholasticism and the development of theology which, in general, are not found in his critical editions in English. Trained in classical philology and ancient philosophy De Rijk is very sensitive to the elements of medieval thought which have no counterpart in ancient philosophy.[55] The results of the

---

[52] L. M. de Rijk, *Die mittelalterlichen Traktate De modo opponendi et respondendi*, in *Beiträge zur Geschichte der Philosophie und Theologie des Mittelalters* NF 17 (1980) 89–95. His preface is dated April 1975. Compare pp. 26–29.

[53] When I was a second-year student of theology I added about seventy-five textual emendations (so-called conjectures) to my interpretation of a prophetical chapter from the Old Testament, gaining praise from my tutor.

[54] See Hamesse, 'New Perspectives for Critical Editions of Franciscan Texts of the Middle Ages,' *Franciscan Studies* 56 (1998) 173–179 and 184–187. Cf. B. Distelbrink, *Bonaventurae scripta*, Rome 1975, I. Brady, 'The Edition of the *Opera Omnia* of Saint Bonaventure (1882–1902),' *AFH* 70 (1977) 352–376, and Louis-Jacques Bataillon, 'Le edizioni di *opera omnia* degli scolastici e l'Edizione Leonina,' in *Gli studi filosofia medievale fra Otto e Novecento*, Rome 1991, 141–154.

[55] De Rijk's *Middeleeuwse wijsbegeerte. Traditie en vernieuwing* (1977) is of crucial importance; it was translated into French, unfortunately not into English: *La philosophie au moyen âge*. See Imbach's review of *PMA* in Fr. Cheneval, Th. Ricklin, Cl. Pottier, Silvia Maspoli and

research of the so-called Dutch school, which basically is the De Rijk school, led to a new interpretation of the nature of medieval logic and semantics against the background of De Rijk's approach of the phenomenon of scholasticism.

15.5.1 The problem of the scholastic method

Within the context of the history of the university, scholasticism is not restricted to the Middle Ages. In around 1800 the history of *reformational scholasticism* ended abruptly. In the *catholica*, scholasticism continues up to the present, but when and where did scholasticism arise? On the one hand, it is clear that there was no scholasticism in antiquity, and, on the other hand, the generations of Garlandus Compotista, Lanfranc and Anselm were familiar with it. After the Dark Ages, the *scholastic method* was already developing in the tenth century:[56] what, however, is meant by 'scholastic method'? The scholastic method is a method applied in philosophy and theology which is characterized, both on the level of *research* and on the level of *teaching*, by the use of an ever recurring system of concepts, distinctions, definitions, propositional analyses, argumentational techniques, and disputational methods, which had originally been derived from Aristotelian-Boethian logic, but later on, on a much larger scale, from indigenous terminist logic

De Rijk's approach to the phenomenon of scholasticism distinctly differs from the old Paris and Louvain approaches which view scholasticism as a total view in terms of the relationship between reason and faith. On the contrary, De Rijk examined the origins of scholasticism. In the tenth and eleventh centuries the study of elementary grammar of medieval Latin went through such a creative stage that twelfth-century linguistics were already seeing a mature semantic and syntactical theory of Latin. Theory of language (*grammatica*) and logic (*dialectica*) met. This development of combining logical and grammatical analyses led to one dynamic river of analytical thinking. Scholastic thought is simply to be characterized as critical and precise thinking to be developed in the schools

---

Marianne Mösch (eds), *Ruedi Imbach. Quodlibeta. Ausgewählte Artikel/Articles choisis*, Fribourg 1996, 1–19. On the problem of the periodization of medieval philosophy and the originality of medieval philosophy, see *PMA* 8–22 and Chapters 3–4, and *DS* 1–8. Cf. Bos (ed.), *L.M. de Rijk. Through Language to Reality*.

[56] See *PMA* 68–80 and Chapter 4: 'La méthode scolastique' (82–105). Cf. Grabmann, *Geschichte der scholastischen Methode* I, Graz ²1957.

(*scholasticus* = scholar) and then maturing as analytical thinking *pur sang*. The confluence of grammar and logic in the eleventh and twelfth centuries created a method of logical and semantic analysis of language.

At the same time, theology and (canon) law opened their gates to all these powerful tools. Logical analysis of language especially flourished in theology, starting as *sacra pagina*. In this period *theology* originally was an academic endeavor aimed at interpreting the sacred pages of Scripture. The contextual approach of the functions of words in Latin sentences was the cradle of *terminist logic*: the logic of properties of terms and the uses of terms in propositions.[57]

Here, not so much a *scientific revolution* was at stake, but a revolution of an entire *thought form*. At the center of this intellectual storm is *ontology*.

> At the end of the thirteenth century the impact (of typically Christian ideas) got such a decisive momentum, particularly in the Franciscan schools, that it fundamentally changed both metaphysics and epistemology through the theory of *radical contingency* of creation.[58]

Following Gilson, Boehner and Wolter, De Rijk baptized the central notion of this type of ontology as 'radical contingency'.[59] Bert Roest puts the change in the development of studies in medieval philosophy which many scholars of the previous generation brought about in a wider perspective.

> In the field of history of philosophy, it was caused by the logical and scientific interests of modern scholars such as Jan Pinborg, Norman Kretzmann, Paul Vignaux and Lambertus de Rijk (main protagonists of the so-called modern analytical approach). As a result, the picture of the late medieval period is no longer solely depicted in autumn colors.[60]

De Rijk's discovery of the true origins of the *logica modernorum* revolutionized researching the dynamics of medieval philosophy. Against the background of the work of Moody and Boehner, De Rijk,

---

[57] *Logica Modernorum* IIA 95–130. Cf. De Rijk, 'The Early Origin of the Theory of Supposition,' *CHLMP* 161–173.

[58] *PMA* 72. Unfortunately the French translation has 'twelfth century' instead of 'thirteenth century.'

[59] KN II identified *radical or un-Aristotelian* contingency as *synchronic* contingency.

[60] Roest, *A History of Franciscan Education*, 177. The French theologian Vignaux does not fit in this list, but his analyses are of rare clarity. For Roest's label, see Marenbon, *Later Medieval Philosophy*, 85–87.

Kretzmann, and Pinborg put studying medieval philosophy on a new foundation, while De Rijk was also familiar with the Paris and Louvain traditions. He put all this on a new foundation in the Netherlands, judging by the considerable output of his pupils.[61]

Due to the initiatives of Gilson and Boehner new contributions on Duns Scotus' philosophy poured in from the United States after World War II.[62] In particular, we have to acknowledge the outstanding merits of Wolter's sustained efforts over more than fifty-five years to produce a continuous series of interpretative contributions and translations, culminating in Girard Etzkorn's and Allan Wolter's *Questions on the Metaphysics of Aristotle by John Duns Scotus* I–II (1997–98) and Wolter's *John Duns Scotus. A Treatise on Potency and Act* (2000). Allan Bernard Wolter (b.1913) is second to none in interpreting and translating Duns Scotus throughout the twentieth century, through an impressive series of works running from his Boehner dissertation *The Transcendentals and Their Function in the Metaphysics of Duns Scotus* (1946) to *A Treatise on Potency and Act* (2000).[63]

De Rijk and the Dutch De Rijk School enabled me to see thirteenth-century philosophy in a new light. Gilson added the viewpoint of theological creativity to that of logical and semantic originality and creativity, although his work foundered on Scotus' complicated writings. However, in addition to the important contributions of Parthenius Minges and Timotheus Barth, only the 'Boehner-Wolter School' supplied a continuous flow of publications on Duns Scotus' thought. Boehner and his pupils were also instrumental in rehabilitating William of Ockham. Moreover, the momentous decision of the team of Ockham editors in the mid-1980s to edit Duns Scotus' *Opera Philosophica* averted the impending disaster threatening the future publication of Duns Scotus' philosophical works (cf. §§3.6.2–3.6.3, §§3.6.7 and §3.7).

---

[61] See Ebbesen, 'Doing Philosophy the Sophismatic Way. The Copenhagen School, with Notes on the Dutch School,' in Alfonso Maierù (ed.), *Gli studi di filosofia medievale fra Otto e Nove cento*, Rome 1991, 331–359. Cf. Ebbesen, 'Opening Speech,' in Ebbesen and Freedman, *Medieval Analyses in Language and Cognition*, 8ff. De Rijk invented the name 'Copenhagen School.'

[62] Cyril L. Shircel (Washington 1942), Maurice J. Grajewski (Washington 1944), Wolter (St Bonaventure 1946), Evan Roche (1949), Peter C. Vier (1951) and Damascene Webering (1953).

[63] See Martin Wolter, 'The Life and Times of Allan B. Wolter O.F.M.,' in Frank and Etzkorn (eds), *Essays Honoring Allan B. Wolter*, 7–20.

15.6   ON THE PARADOX OF WESTERN PHILOSOPHY

John Inglis's discoveries are remarkable. There are continuities and discontinuities in the understanding medieval philosophy from the middle of the nineteenth century to the middle of the twentieth century. The discontinuities are less clear in Inglis's diagnosis, because, in general, he leaves aside most liberal and Protestant, atheist and Marxist authors, but he may have had profound reasons for doing so. The history of philosophical studies in medieval thought in the traditionally Catholic countries and neoscholastic circles is fascinating in itself. The success of the Kleutgen-Stöckl model was so impressive because it fitted in with the Western way of understanding philosophy and the identity of the theology of the Counter-Reformation. Modern Enlightenment philosophy departed from the main patterns of ancient Greek and Roman philosophy which had also defined the canons of rationality. One adhered to the myth of a *philosophia perennis*. Even our teacher Professor De Vogel did so (§15.5). The presumption of modern philosophy and the theological *duplex ordo* way of thinking, operating in terms of the duality of *nature* and *super nature*, fit in with each other. The battle between Louvain and Paris took place within the same metaphilosophical parameters, but these parameters belonged also to the identity of the philosophical culture of the Roman languages speaking countries. Here again Louvain comes in, because there is another side to Louvain theology and philosophy, being sensitive to the Augustinian dimension of Western thought, to Jansenism, Pascal and the Reformation, to the results of the *théologie nouvelle* research and De Lubac.[64]

15.6.1   The analytical 'turn'

In her fine book *Virtues of the Will*, Bonnie Kent observes that roughly throughout the 1970s and 1980s research in the history of medieval philosophy turned way from metaphysics and toward problems of logic, language, physics, and mathematics, 'away from "Christian philosophy" and toward less theological concerns; even to

---

[64] J. H. Walgrave, *Geloof en theologie in de crisis*, Kasterlee 1966, *KN* III and VII, and Veldhuis, *Ein versiegeltes Buch*, 1–59 and 381–430. Cf. H. Veldhuis, *Geen begrip voor de ander*, Utrecht 1990. Louvain scholarship combining the 'Aristotelian' and 'Augustinian' pictures of Western philosophy, sensitive both to the culture of Southern Europe and to the Continental Reformation, forms the background of Dutch studies in medieval philosophy.

some extent, away from thirteenth-century thought and toward fourteenth-century developments.'[65] Be this as it may, in the light of the history of the *logica modernorum* between the middle of the twelfth and the middle of the thirteenth centuries, the recent turn in philosophical medievistics can be seen in an alternative way. Familiarity with the *logica modernorum* helps in the reading of systematic texts of those centuries. The reason is rather simple: by starting with the issues attended to in the logical and semantic turn of studying medieval philosophy, we start precisely where the medieval thinkers started themselves, both linguistically and philosophically.[66]

The riddle of the history of the Western ways of ideas rests on the problem of the relationship between ancient and medieval 'philosophy.' Is medieval philosophy a christianized form of ancient philosophy, slightly tarnished in a Christian way and marked by an essential continuity with ancient philosophy, or is it an original and independent type of philosophy, standing on the didactic shoulders of the old Greek and Hellenistic philosophers? The modern view on this dilemma deviates from the medieval view itself. Admittedly, the medieval view was not a historical one. Its thought was deeply *ahistorical* because of the simple fact that *historical thought* did not exist at all before the time of Niebuhr and Ranke.[67] However, the modern view is not historical either in spite of historical research flourishing at modern universities. The modern view simply ignores the original and creative impact of the philosophy of the medieval university and, in particular, of philosophy as it was developed in the medieval faculties and schools of theology. If such a decisive period in the development of Western rationality is ignored, then such a view is rather arbitrary.

The main mystery of Western philosophy consists of the illegitimate marriage of two paradoxes: the paradox of a rather Christian interpretation of Greek philosophy as wedded to a rather non-Christian interpretation of medieval thought. Both lines of interpretation are not correct. The first line is especially popular with Catholic and secular scholars and thinkers, while the second line is especially favorite with Protestant scholars. The existence of the *AA*-line of medieval thought – the long chain of tradition from Augustine and Anselm through the Victorines and the mendicant orders to the

---

[65] *Virtues of the Will*, 19 (19–34: 'The Golden Age Revisited: Scholastic Ethics').

[66] See De Rijk, '*Glossary*,' in *Nicholas of Autrecourt*, 39–43.

[67] See Mackay, *Geschiedenis bij de bron*, 122–138.

scientific revolutions by Duns Scotus and William of Ockham to nominalism – refutes the idea of a *philosophia perennis*. On the contrary, Western thought shows two types of philosophy, one created in antiquity and one in the Middle Ages, and not only one. The paradox of the traditional approach is mirrored in the characterizations of Christian philosophical movements like Augustinianism as a kind of Platonism and Thomism as a kind of Aristotelianism. The most astonishing effect of the traditional approach was the exclusion of Duns Scotus' philosophical contributions from the domain of philosophy. They were only seen to belong to theology, or even only to mysticism (Mandonnet). Acknowledging the philosophical structure of Duns Scotus' thought requires a permanent renewal of the study of the history of Western philosophy.

John Wippel sees the Condemnations of 1277 as evidence of a crisis within the Universities of Paris and Oxford over the relations of faith and reason; both Giles of Rome and Thomas Aquinas, and not just Siger of Brabant and Boethius of Dacia, were targets of the Paris condemnations.[68] Calvin Normore linked the involved dilemmas with the general debate between philosophy and Christian theology, already begun in late antiquity. Late ancient non-Christian philosophy saw Christianity as both irrational and impious, but we may also point at the philosophical dimension of the theology of the Fathers and the glorious presence of converted philosophers such as Justin the Martyr and John Philoponus.

> One of the cornerstones of late Greek philosophical 'theology' was the doctrine of the necessary and eternal existence of a kosmos which was unchanging in its fundamental aspects. Philoponus challenged every aspect of this picture. In works directed against Proclus and against Aristotle he insisted on the philosophical respectability of the position that the world was created in time from nothing by the free act of a being subject to no necessity.[69]

This insight results in the nice Normorian phrase that the Condemnations of 1277 can be seen as a victory for the 'Philoponeans,' who are simply the representatives of mainstream Western thought in these centuries. They were convinced, as Thomas Aquinas was not, that the fundamental structure of Aristotle's philosophy was wrong. This was

---

[68] Wippel, *Medieval Reactions to the Encounter Between Faith and Reason*. Cf. Ingham, *Ethics and Freedom*, 62–67, 102–106, and 132–134.

[69] Normore, 'Who Was Condemned in 1277?,' *The Modern Schoolman* 77 (1995) 274.

precisely the point of view of Duns Scotus: since the principles are mistaken, the conclusions share the same fate (Chapters 10 and 14).

From the start, Gilson rejected Harnack's theory of a progressive Hellenization of Christian thought. 'In this view, the whole body of Christian dogmas appears as a construction of Greek inspiration erected upon the soil of the Gospel.'[70] According to Gilson, 'Christianity did not become "a religious philosophy" at all, but, precisely because it always remained a religion, and the very same religion, it did become an abundant *source* of theological and philosophical speculation' (ibid.). Philosophy was unable to kill faith; Christianity does not only save souls, it even saves philosophy. According to Harnack, the Christian faith lost its case; according to Gilson, it simply won. However, the possibility of a non-dependent Christian philosophy is hardly defended at all. According to Mandonnet and Van Steenberghen, there is no need of a specifically Christian philosophy; according to Barth and Brunner, it is simply impossible. Even more striking is the fact that, even according to Gilson, there is no Christian philosophy in its role as an alternative to Greek and Hellenistic philosophy and its modern derivatives. The whole fascinating – Paris and Louvain – debate on the status and the possibility of Christian philosophy does not recognize the suggestion that the Augustine-Anselm line of thought and Duns Scotus' philosophy may be the key to an alternative view.

The first step to be taken in order to place Duns Scotus' development in its proper perspective is to interpret the archaic ancient world in a realistic way. Just as theologians usually interpret the world of the Old Testament in a too Christian way, historians of ancient intellectual Greek culture and philosophy usually look on ancient Greek *philosophia* in a too modern and Christian way, and medieval scholasticism is seen in a too pagan way. Such an approach takes away the sensitivity needed to spot the special dynamics of the development of Western thought.

When we pay attention to the role religion might play in doing philosophy we meet the paradoxical fact that one often assumes that the Christian faith has to be put in brackets in order to reach rationality, but that the Greek religion does not endanger rationality. Van Steenberghen calls the pagan speculations of Neoplatonism 'purely rational,' but the Christian faith does not lead to *philosophy*

---

[70] *HCPMA* 5, referring to Harnack's *Das Wesen des Christentums*, where a reference to his massive and extremely influential *History of Dogma* I–III is expected.

properly.[71] We observe an *a*-historical application of the Renaissan-
cist pattern of *nature* and *super nature* to the history of Western philosophy. We have to subtract *super nature* in order to arrive at *nature*.
So, we have to subtract the Christian faith in order to arrive at *reason*,
but, in the case of the non-Christian Greek religion, we spontaneously
get pure *reason* in spite of the presence of Greek religion. However,
old Greek religion is no more a path to responsible thinking and ethics
than old Semitic religion is.

When we see that the way of thought of ancient Greek philosophy
simply excludes the Christian innovations of the Middle Ages
between Anselm and Duns Scotus, there are two possible conclusions
to be drawn: either this result demonstrates the utterly irrational
nature of theology, or here we meet the summit of intellectual creativity, never mind the issue of truth. Ancient Greek and Hellenistic
philosophy did not include the notion of *synchronic contingency*. The
important branches of ancient philosophy embody the *one (possible)*
world model and this model excludes both *synchronic contingency*
and the possible truth of the Christian faith. The non-Christian
philosophers who were acquainted with the Christian faith were quite
clear about this (Celsus, Plotinus, Porphyry). However, not only was
a collision of truth claims at stake, but the formal and logical aspects
of the Greek *logos* were also shaped by this type of worldview.
Because these aspects were not neutral, the Christian opposition had
to conquer an alternative rationality or lose its case. When we start
to study medieval thought we have to become aware of a continuous
flow of theoretical innovations and discoveries. The story of medieval
philosophy between Augustine and Duns Scotus and his successors is
the story of the birth of a basic alternative: *contingency* thought
developed by the *philosophia christiana* in a long process of ongoing
emancipation (see Chapters 4–14).

The present approach starts from De Rijk's discovery of the origins
of the *logica modernorum* (in the second quarter of the twelfth
century).[72] John Duns was also every inch an Oxford man and he
stood squarely in the international Franciscan movement. In this
world the Parisian headquarters and the Parisian problems and
perspectives were continuously hot news in Oxford. Duns Scotus'
philosophy is the philosophical account of the Christian faith and,

---

[71] Van Steenberghen, *Introduction à l'étude de la philosophie médiévale*, 334. The *riddle* – it
is said – is how to pass on *reason* to *faith*; cf. chapter 2: 'Les leçons de l'histoire.'
[72] See §15.5 and cf. §§1.4–1.5, §§3.6.2–3.6.5 and Chapters 4 and 5.

specifically, the Parisian and Oxonian Condemnations (1277 and 1284), just as Aristotle's thought is also a philosophical account of old Greek religiosity.

Two of De Rijk's viewpoints were especially instrumental in shaping my approach: we need the *trivium* treatises in order to become familiar with the systematic language the theologians utilized too. Referring to contributions by Gillian Evans on Peter the Chanter (1982) and by Giusberti on Alan of Lille (1982), Jacobi pointed out that in the second half of the twelfth century the work of theologians was powerfully influenced by the procedures characteristic of logic.[73]

The primary suggestion is: learn the conceptual language of the *trivium* subjects for the benefit of reading theological and philosophical texts. In reading theological texts through these eye glasses a second eye opener presents itself: the most interesting philosophy is to be found in the works of the great theologians. Artificially, from the works of the greatest theologians we are able to abstract an alternative philosophy. This procedure is artificial in the way that what we call *the philosophy of Duns Scotus* is usually neither called *philosophy* during the thirteenth and fourteenth centuries, nor in the nineteenth and twentieth centuries, interwoven with theology as it was. Nevertheless, if the procedure of abstracting is related to the main subjects of modern systematic philosophy (semantics, logic, epistemology, ontology, theory of divine attributes, and so on), we discover a coherent and comprehensive web of philosophical beliefs, sharply focusing on new philosophical contents of the thought of these theologians.

15.6.2 Duns Scotus

In this light, Duns Scotus' thought is seen as the culmination point of a general development in the specific new – semantic and logical – key of *synchronic contingency* which is not the driving force or central inspiration of his work, but the tool the whole of the Christian faith is asking for, if it is understood consistently. The new start provided by Duns Scotus is not only a fresh beginning for ontology (Kluxen, Honnefelder), but a fresh start for the whole of systematic philosophy and theology. In fact, it is classic Christian thought in a new theoretical key. The greatest thinkers of the Middle Ages were after all

---

[73] See Jacobi, 'Logic: the Later Twelfth Century,' in Dronke (ed.), *A History of Twelfth-Century Philosophy*, 250 f.

theologians. They worked with a concept of systematic thought rather different from what we now acknowledge as systematic thought. Their concept of theology was rather different from the Renaissance and Enlightenment concepts of theology.

Then it is also clear that their concept of philosophy must have been rather different from what we usually consider philosophy to be. In all parts of *Lectura* I–III and *Ordinatio* I–IV Duns Scotus speaks as a theologian. However, because many parts of his theology belong to necessary theology (*theologia necessaria*), his systematic theology can be extrapolated in a *philosophical* way in the modern sense of 'philosophical'. Revelation creates a new philosophy, because in medieval thought a specific *theological model of thought* molds the conceptual structures of a philosophy which is philosophy in a new theoretical key. Systematic philosophy shows a scientific revolution. In the fourteenth century, this approach to epistemological problems is more and more refined by a subtle criticism of the ancient philosophical theory of knowledge. The evidentialist principle is purged in many ways. After Scotus the whole of this process was linked with a specific stress on individuality, self-knowledge, and will as conscious intellectual endeavor, put in the center of philosophical attention.

This factor is crucial to the theme of 'Christian philosophy' elicited by theological concerns. Seen in this light, 'Christian philosophy' is not an edifying variant of philosophy, to be compared with the philosophies of a Nietzsche, Bolland, or Jaspers, nor *philosophy*, still taken in an absolute sense, corrected and enriched by theological interventions, but just *philosophy*. In a nutshell, the theoretical upshot is very simple: Christian philosophy is just an alternative type of philosophy, precisely diametrically opposed to the answers of ancient Greek and Hellenistic *philosophia*. A parallel phenomenon is found in the Old Testament religion, diametrically opposed to old Semitic religions as it is. Once we have a clear idea of the main common structures of Greek *philosophia*, we may derive the main positions of Christian philosophy from those taken by *philosophia*, by denying them consistently.

CHAPTER 16

Philosophy in a new key – extrapolations and perspectives

16.1 INTRODUCTION

Modern secular philosophy has often objected to theology that Christianity is loaded with paradoxes. The paradoxical situation of our Western theoretical culture is that its philosophy is itself a paradox, for modern philosophy cannot know *itself* if it ignores its own history. Apart from the fact that there is flourishing research in the history of medieval philosophy, general philosophy still widely ignores the decisive continuity between sixteenth-, seventeenth-, and eighteenth-century thought, on the one hand, and theology and philosophy in the twelfth, thirteenth, and fourteenth centuries, on the other. The effect of this pattern is that the discontinuity between Western thought at the eighteenth-century universities and philosophy at nineteenth-century universities is usually misunderstood. This misinterpretation specifically has the result that the medieval way (*via*) of Scotism, which was still very important at the universities of the seventeenth and eighteenth centuries, plays only a marginal role in the historical literature on seventeenth- and eighteenth-century thought.

The outcome is that the great philosophical individuals (Hobbes, Descartes, Locke, Berkeley, Hume, Leibniz, Wolff) are considered to be the main figures and that the impact of university philosophy and theology is somewhat overlooked. 'Modern students of theology have often been frequently encouraged to believe that significant theological thinking is a product of the nineteenth century.'[1] Philosophy students enjoy the same myth. That was the trick of nineteenth-century academic culture, intensified further by the historical revolution of the 1820s. However, the university of the sixteenth, seventeenth, and eighteenth centuries is the updated medieval university – Catholic and reformational. Scholasticism of the early modern university can only

---

[1] Brian Davies, 'Series Foreword,' in Cross, *Duns Scotus*, vii (vii–x).

be understood in continuity with the history of the learning of the medieval university, where the main line of *contingency-will* thought shines out. Duns Scotus' philosophy is its rather early culmination point.

As to Scotus, we have now reached the end of a long journey. Although we have not paid attention to all the philosophical subjects Duns Scotus dealt with – for instance, we left out his philosophy of law and his political and economic philosophy – we have met a long series of specific contributions.[2] When I was preparing *Johannes Duns Scotus*, I was continuously struck by the fact that, again and again, it appeared to me that a very long series of theological dilemmas – though not all – had already been solved in principle by Scotus.[3]

Again and again, Duns Scotus utilizes *necessity–contingency* based tools and insights to actualize his problem-solving program. Thus, the new question arose: might his philosophical contributions enjoy the same kind of coherence? If so, coherent philosophy would turn out to be a possibility – in companion with the coherence of theism. Thus every new chapter and every subject occasioned an exciting adventure: would this hypothetical point of view substantiate itself, again and again? Because I was already impressed by the remarkable depth of coherence of Duns Scotus' thought, for many years I cherished my hopes. Nevertheless, this kind of mountaineering was excting and exacting too. The wonderful view at the top is that Duns Scotus' life and works show the same pattern of ongoing emancipation from ancient thought patterns as medieval thought itself shows in general (Chapters 1–2 and 14–15). However, we have still not reached the end of another story. Is this remarkable heritage a possible starting point for a process of elaborating, improving on and proving of what Duns Scotus had offered over the years? This last chapter offers comments on a wide variety of Scotian subjects and theories. These comments look upon Scotus' thought as a central focus and ingredient of a main tradition of Western thought, not as an idiosyncratic –ism or movement.

Understanding early modern philosophy cut off from *university* training and learning is a rather *a*historical enterprise which blocks understanding the dynamics of Western thought itself. This also turns out to be so in the dilemma of the history of medieval philosophy itself (§16.2). §16.3 deals with some characteristics of Duns Scotus' oeuvre and §16.4 with the dilemma of two types of philosophy. The deep

---

[2] See Parisoli, *La philosophie normative de Jean Duns Scot*; cf. Harris, *Duns Scotus* II.
[3] *DS* surveys almost the whole of Duns Scotus' theology.

structure of Duns Scotus' way of thinking is expounded, both by explaining some specific terminological points and by reviewing Duns Scotus' explanation of contingency (§16.5). A broad range of extrapolations follow: logic and semantics (§16.6), knowledge and proof (§16.7), the ontology of reality (§16.8), an ethics of dignity and love (§16.9), and the philosophical theology of God (§16.10), while §16.11 rounds off by looking at the perspective of a *philosophia christiana*, in the surprising sense of tenable academic philosophy *tout court*. Idealistic qualifications cannot promote philosophy, just as they cannot promote science. Only results count. What matters is true philosophy.

16.2   THE DILEMMA OF THE HISTORY OF MEDIEVAL PHILOSOPHY

The Parisian approach to medieval thought was a vital moment in the tradition of studies in medieval philosophy. According to the great Parisian founders of philosophical medievistics (Cousin, Hauréau, Renan), Duns Scotus was by no means a philosopher (§15.2). He did not take part in philosophy, for the position of Duns Scotus and Ockham demonstrated that the medieval interaction between faith-based theology and philosophy was doomed to failure. This type of medieval studies mirrors the starting point of secular nineteenth-century thought. It influenced the history of medieval philosophy and also marked the Neothomist approach where Louvain excelled (§15.3).

Certainly, there are splendid fruits to be acknowledged. The Parisian approach led to the sources and, thanks to the Catholic rebound, we now have a wealth of fascinating texts in critical and semi-critical editions. This is a wonderful harvest. The Parisian and Louvain traditions have been prevalent for a long time in researching the history of medieval philosophy. They share a fundamental conviction: in the Age of Faith, philosophy is only to be found in the tradition of *Philosophus*. So, the phenomenon of philosophy is marginal and destined to fail (Paris), or essential and vital but quantitatively still marginal (Louvain). Their joint impact is paradoxical from the viewpoint of medieval philosophy itself.

We recognize Comte's and Cousin's division of the history of ideas. After the era of mythology we have the era of theology to be replaced in due course by philosophy and the sciences. In 1931 Émile Bréhier gave rise to a fierce debate on the issue of the possibility of Christian philosophy: *Y a-t-il une philosophie chrétienne?* Brehier's personal answer is a definite *no*. However, our conceptions of *philosophy* and *theology* are not equipped to do justice directly to medieval 'philosophical' thought (§§15.1–15.3). Thirteenth-century terminology is itself quite helpful. The terms *philosophia* and *theologia* are not used in the way they were used in ancient Greek thought and patristic theology, nor in the modern way. *Philosophia* and *theologia* do not indicate subjects or sciences, nor academic professions or faculties, but *ways of thought* or *ways of ideas*. According to both Thomas Aquinas and Duns Scotus, *philosophia* was a dated way of thinking, and it was not only dated but also basically wrong. The future was not in philosophy. *Theologia* was the way of thinking of the future, basically and mainly right (see Chapter 14).

Modern secular thought acknowledges the phenomenon of theology, or is at least acquainted with it, but does not see theology *as* philosophy, for theology must be irrational and invalid. It is incompatible with Greek philosophy and Enlightenment thought. All these views are understandable in themselves, but the historian of Western thought cannot operate reasonably with such a prejudice, because it excludes the main part of Western thought (800–1800) and its riches. In fact, it overlooks the main source of philosophical originality, embodied in the works of the great theologians. However, the parallel answer of important Christian scholars and theologians is even more remarkable. According to Bréhier, the expression 'Christian philosophy' is a square circle and, for quite different reasons, this atheological assessment was shared by such different Christian thinkers as Mandonnet, De Wulf and Van Steenberghen, and Barth and Brunner and their followers: philosophy and faith are quite different, just as medieval thought tells us. The position of Gilson is even more striking. According to his oppnents, Gilson was the great defender of the presence of an alternative Christian medieval philosophy, but he only stressed the fruitful influence of faith and theology on distinct philosophical theories.[4]

16.2.1 The case of Duns Scotus' philosophy

Which authors do historians of medieval philosophy read? Especially, *theologians*. Why? From the viewpoint of most modern history of medieval philosophy, there is no natural answer to this question. That is a riddle. In fact, most modern philosophers still adhere to some

---

[4] See Inglis, *Spheres of Philosophical Inquiry and the Historiography of Medieval Philosophy*, chapter 7: 'Étienne Gilson and the Historiography of Medieval Philosophy.' So, doing justice to Western thought requires reconstructing teaching its history.

variant of the Parisian approach: *modern philosophy* originated only in the seventeenth century or during the Renaissance. Medieval thought is *pre-philosophical*. So, the 'Parisian' approach fails in the face of Duns Scotus.

Modern interpretations of medieval philosophy get deadlocked if they collide with Duns Scotus' philosophy and what is vital to this line of philosophical development. Acknowledging Duns Scotus and his philosophical environment as a philosophical power wrecks the traditional 'modern' presumption as to what Western philosophy consists of. The so-called second Augustinian 'school' is the environment of Duns Scotus' life work, and the whole of eleventh-, twelfth-, and mainstream thirteenth-century thinking is simply the natural habitat of this school. The 'early Dominican school' was even more voluntarist than the 'early Franciscan school.'

Duns Scotus merely completed temporarily what the Franciscan and other mendicant thinkers and their predecessors had started with. It is difficult to understand the *philosophical* impact of the early contributions without the contributions of later tradition, delivered at the end of the thirteenth and the beginning of the fourteenth centuries. It is not helpful to place Henry of Ghent under the umbrella of fourteenth-century scholasticism, and the same obtains for Duns who made his major discoveries around 1297–99. We meet the puzzling situation that the great antagonists (Mandonnet, Gilson, and Van Steenberghen) all leave out Henry of Ghent and Duns Scotus in their attempts to describe and to reconstruct the dynamics of thirteenth-century philosophy and theology.

Such a metaphilosophy does not view the history of philosophy as a historical and philosophical problem. If history does not embody truth a priori, the assessment of a philosophical position cannot be *pre*supposed in a philosophical way in our descriptions. A historian is not a judge *qua* historian. Bréhier simply *assumed* that Duns and his theoretical outlook were wrong. Of course, an adequate answer does not lie in the parallel assumption that Duns be right, but Bréhier and his like forgot that it is unreasonable simply to outlaw a thinker or a tradition. The traditional approach outlawed the main tradition of medieval thought.

The issue is a decisive one. The one possible world model of Greek and Hellenistic philosophy does not yield enough room to the conceptual needs of the Christian faith. Early medieval culture had already rendered harmless much of what was unacceptable to the requirements of the Christian faith, but Anselm points out new ways, based on tradition. The twelfth century saw battle, but both the necessitarian-ism of John Scottus Eriugene and Abelard's thesis that it was only the best possible world God could create are rejected. The line of Hugh of St Victor and Bernard of Clairvaux becomes the legacy of the Victorines miraculously bearing fruit in the works of Alexander of Hales and John of La Rochelle, Bonaventure and Pecham, Henry of Ghent and Duns Scotus.[5]

16.3   SOME CHARACTERISTICS OF DUNS SCOTUS' OEUVRE

The true challenge of Duns Scotus' philosophical development is given in the brute fact that his biography itself points to this dilemma. There is a tension in Western philosophical thought itself which is mirrored in Duns' personal decisions and chances. The typical struc-ture of the medieval university gave birth to two groups of authors producing two fundamental sets of medieval texts: 'commentaries' on Aristotle's works, and 'commentaries' on Peter Lombard's *Sentences*, because these works were the primary pedagogical tools for the two major faculties of Europe's universities and the academic schools of the religious orders. 'Students and masters alike were expected to show their familiarity with and elaborations upon both Aristotle and the *Sentences*.'[6] Steven Livesey built an admirable biographical data-base focusing on these two groups of authors and their philosophical and theological works, and, a few years ago, possessed some 37,000 records covering more than 1,500 commentators including 214 Franciscan authors. When the focus is on Duns and the Franciscans in contradistinction to scholars of a different background, some illus-trative comparisons can be offered.[7]

First, we look at the general pool. 'Within the wider pool of com-mentators, 848 (54.9%) commented on the *Sentences*; 859 (55.6%) on at least one of Aristotle's works; and 206 (13.3%) on both the *Sentences* and Aristotle' (ibid.).

---

[5] Cosmological determinism, monopsychism, and the theory of the eternal world were already condemned in 1270. All kinds of philosophical and theological theories were rejected in 1277 and 1284 (see Chapters 14 and 15).

[6] Livesey, 'De viris illustribus et mediocribus,' *Franciscan Studies* 56 (1998) 205.

[7] Looking at the textual population of the database is interesting too. See Livesey, ibid., 219: 'Among the general population in the database, in decreasing order, the most popular genre was commentaries on Aristotle [2,287 texts (13.5%)], followed by sermons [1,916 texts (11.3%)], commentaries on the Bible [1,826 texts (10.7%)], theological works other than commentaries on the *Sentences* [1,812 texts (10.7%)], commentaries on the *Sentences* [1,072 texts (6.3%)], epistolae [905 texts (5.3%)], and quaestiones disputatae [712 texts (4.2%)].'

Second, in order to compare the Franciscan authors with the wider pool of commentators, we look at the Franciscans: 'Of the 214 Franciscan authors in the database, 170 (82.1%) wrote commentaries on the *Sentences*; 83 (40.1%) wrote at least one commentary on one or more of Aristotle's works; 46 (22.2%) commented on both the *Sentences* and Aristotle' (ibid.).

Third, 38.6 per cent of all texts of the Franciscan authors are theological works, against 27.7 percent in the general pool. 'Similarly, Franciscans seem to have preferred disputed and quodlibetal questions (13.7% compared with 6.5% of the general pool). The reverse of this is the emphasis on Aristotle in the general pool (13.5%) compared to the Franciscan pool (8.6%).'[8]

Fourth, Duns wrote about eight logical and philosophical works, discussing problems passed on by the works of Porphyry and Aristotle. He wrote also about eight theological works, all unfinished. While the emphasis on Aristotle in the Franciscan pool is the reverse of this emphasis in the general pool, according to the ratio of 1 : 2, the proportion of Duns' emphasis on Aristotle compared to this emphasis in the Franciscan pool is many times larger.

All Duns' logical and philosophical works discussing the writings of Aristotle and Porphyry belong to his first Oxonian period – the *Quaestiones Metaphysicae* being the exception to this rule – if we divide his Oxonian years of writing into two periods: before about 1296 and from about 1296–97 onwards.

Fifth, Duns' emphasis on Aristotle in terms of the quantity of his works is matched by the quantity of his works on the *Sentences*, four in all. A general characteristic of systematic authors during the centuries of the university focusing on the *corpus aristotelicum* and on the *Sententiae* is mirrored by Duns' works in a remarkable way. The two focuses of his oeuvre are works on Aristotle and works on the *Sentences*, while Duns also shared the Franciscan preference for disputed and quodlibetal questions.

Sixth, another noticeable aspect of the writings of Duns which we have had in our possession since 1538 is the absence of biblical monographs.

Duns Scotus is the primary example of this phenomenon. He was a magisterial thinker whose early death shocked Europe's academic youth and frustrated the development of Western philosophy.

---

[8] Livesey, ibid., 220. Unfortunately, many 'commentaries' on the *Sentences* by outstanding *secular* masters of theology are missing in the manuscript tradition.

However, what matters is the philosophical interest the academic youth of the fourteenth century invested in his legacy. In a sense, it was an impossible legacy. No work was finished, because of his early death and his impossible career. A typical example in point is *Opus Oxoniense* II. His personal copy showed many lacunae. Because of the intense interest that was taken in it, many scholars then desperately tried to fill in the lacunae. Fourteenth-century culture was still a manuscript culture. Duns' legacy was also a handwritten world and a handwritten world is complicated. Many interested researchers created their own manuscripts. So it was the very philosophical popularity and the enormous interest Duns intellectual legacy enjoyed which caused the complicated state of affairs present textual criticism still wrestles with.

It has to be concluded that Duns Scotus embodies the bipolar tension of medieval theological and philosophical teaching. Within the context of his studies, he starts with Aristotle and takes him utterly seriously. In reconstructing systematic theology, he also concentrates on eliciting philosophical answers from faith and from theological viewpoints and dilemmas. This movement from logical and philosophical answers through theological questions and challenges to new philosophical answers mirrors the dvelopment of medieval theology and philosophy. The upshot is exceptional. It was Duns Scotus himself, standing amid the collision of *fides* and *intellectus*, who contributed most to the articulation of alternative thought.

16.4   THE PHILOSOPHICAL DILEMMA OF TWO PHILOSOPHIES: IMMUTABILITY IN A NEW KEY

In terms of the history of the ontological theory of immutability there seem to be two distinct ways of handling the concept. Most literature on the subject is only familiar with one concept of immutability according to which immutability and necessity coincide. Thus the history of the theory of immutability is plagued by distortion. Let us designate the Aristotelian type of immutability *immutability* I and the Scotian type of immutability *immutability* II. Immutability II presupposes *contingency* and because of the consequences of immutability I the relevant propositions of the classic doctrine of God on the immutability of divine knowing and willing must be interpreted in exactly the reverse way. The systematic dilemma is clear. If a philosophical view subscribes to

(N) All states of affairs are necessary

one is obliged to accept that there is only one possible world.[9] The dilemma of *necessitarianism* versus *contingency ontology* has articulate consequences for developing concepts of *(im)mutability*. According to the first and oldest theoretical framework, *immutability* and *necessity* must be strictly equivalent. If one drops (N), then the strict equivalence must be canceled. Let us see why all this is so. Wherever we take a stand in ontology, either holding on to necessitarianism or convinced that such ontologies are inconsistent, we have to analyze and to compare both

1. If p is necessary, then p is immutable, and
2. If p is immutable, then p is necessary.[10]

Within the (N) model of only one possible world, everything is necessary and every state of affairs is synchronically necessary. So, if *being necessary* is a trait of the factual world, then if anything is necessary, will it then also be immutable? Because everything is necessary, even what does in fact change and is changeable, according to a Platonist, Aristotelian or Neoplatonist worldview *necessity* in the modern sense does not entail *changelessness*. That can only be said of Eleatism. This paradox can be solved. Although these philosophies are *necessitarianisms* in the modern sense of necessary, they are not familiar with this notion of necessity. Here, we meet the riddle of the evolution of knowledge. Key concepts of later developments are to be applied to earlier theories, although they do not occur in these theories themselves.

Only the birth of a fundamental rival can give rise to a new kind of analysis of these old Greek and Hellenistic ways of thought and it would take many centuries before the *philosophia christiana* of medieval thought – and in particular of medieval theology – could perform this job. Only explicit alternatives can drive away the bewitchment of absolute naivism. Without relevant alternatives we may be deeply naive without being able to see it ourselves. Here I only touch on this intrinsic problem of philosophical description. Descriptions which restrict themselves to the conceptual systems of the philosophies to be described give the impression of historical

---

[9] *Lectura* I 30.60: 'Philosophi ponunt aliud a Deo esse necessarium, quia a Deo necessario producitur aliud, ita quod fecunditas naturae divinae includit "creaturam produci" (unde secundum eos non potest esse Deus secundum infinitam perfectionem suam nisi sit aliquid necessario creatum ab eo).'

[10] This is also true of individuals. If a is necessary, then a is immutable. A necessary being has to exist for every time of every possible world.

meticulousness. Nevertheless, they delude us, because the deep truth of what is under scrutiny will not be revealed in this way. In terms of (N), *contingency* is purely *diachronic* contingency, that is contingency which cannot be linked with *synchronic* contingency. The state of affairs *s* is only contingent, if there is a time t_m when *s* does indeed obtain and a time t_n when *s* does not obtain. Of course, according to this conceptual structure, s_{tm} itself is necessary, but the fact that both what is immutable and what is changing is necessary, does not mean that, according to the necessitarian viewpoint itself, the notions of *necessity* and *immutability* do not coincide. Although, according to this view, changes are necessary – in terms of the synchronic notion of *necessity* – they are not in terms of the necessitarian notion of *necessity*. In this case, (2) is crucial. If the state of affairs *s* obtains at every time t and if proposition *p* is true at every time t of *Actua*, then we have arrived at the *necessary always* and the necessitarian notion of *necessity* precisely amounts to this idea of *necessary always*.

The alternative option we see at work with Duns Scotus disconnects *necessarily* and *always* so that *always* and *changeless* can also be linked with *contingency*. From the outset, it has astonished thinkers how Duns Scotus could untie absence of change and necessity when Aristotle had linked them very tightly. The Scotian theory of synchronic contingency is the key to this conceptual puzzle. Duns Scotus distinguishes between two kinds of contingency: something is diachronically contingent and something is synchronically contingent.[11] For Duns, diachronic contingency and synchronic contingency go hand in hand; for the rival approach, diachronic contingency excludes synchronic contingency. There is no real contingency at all.

In this model of contingency, we say that God wills and knows something contingently, *immutably* – in the sense of without any change and eternally. For about half a millennium – between about 1300 and about 1800 – it is characteristic of the theological language of the doctrine of God that the existence and essence of God are said to be immutable and necessary, but that God's acts of knowing and willing are only said to be immutable – not necessary. However, is this option consistent? Is it possible that one drops (2) and still adheres to (1)? And what about dropping both (1) and (2)? How many alternatives are viable if we analyze the possible relationships between

---

[11] See *Lectura* I 39.45–54 and CF 108–129, and especially *Lectura* I 39.77 and CF 164–167. Cf. §13.4.

1. If p is necessary, then p is immutable

and

2. If p is immutable, then p is necessary?

From a purely speculative viewpoint, we may think that both of them hold or neither, or that only (1) is valid or only (2).[12] Both have to be distinguished clearly from the modern concept of *being contingent*:

3. It is possible that p and it is possible that $-p$.

16.5   The structure of Duns Scotus' way of thinking

16.5.1   An analytical explanation of the 'neutral proposition'

Scotus's thought marks a turning point in the exercise of ontology. The originality of many of his theories has ensconced itself among the commonplaces of recent history of medieval thought, but confusion still reigns about exactly *what sort of change* he brought about. His most creative innovations are a conceptual minefield. We cannot get at the heart of this minefield if we stick to describing the web of his positions. If we directly replace analysis by assessment, we are unfair to what Duns achieved in his time. Duns Scotus' way of ideas is basically a coherent elaboration of the fundamental distinction between *contingency* and *necessity* and the necessity and contingency of propositions and states of affairs. So, God must possess both contingent and necessary knowledge.[13] The contingency dimension of reality has to be reclaimed from entrenched modes of thinking. From an ontological point of view, reality cannot be one-dimensional nor can personal activities. So, ontologically, God cannot be one-dimensional. God would be one-dimensional if He were only to act by his essence and by his essence-based knowledge. If so, the whole of reality known by God would be necessary.

Terminological facts may have far-reaching consequences. The semantical facts that *contingent* entails *being true* and that *possible* entails *being false* are understandable enough.[14] In general, medieval

---

[12] Historical analysis yields systematic homework. The truth question will be discussed in §16.8 where the untenability of necessitarianism is shown.

[13] This crucial thesis entails that God exists necessarily. See also Barth, 'Die Notwendigkeit Gottes,' *De doctrina Ioannis Duns Scoti* II 409–425.

[14] Eleatic philosophy denies diachronic alternativity: contingency is illusion. Kinds of necessitarianism are related to true reality, true in an absolute sense, in one way or another.

philosophy links *contingency* with what is the case now (while it shall *not* be the case later on) and *potency* with what is *not* the case at the present (while it shall be the case later on). In fact, philosophy is a kind of extended theory of negation, and theology likewise. Scotus sees necessitarianism as the root of all philosophical evil. Understandably enough, he also keeps *actual truth* as a component of *contingency*. Duns Scotus' theology turns on the thesis that God's will bestows contingency on reality. This will reigns semantically: if a certain proposition *p* is true contingently, then *p* is so *after* (*post*) an act of God's will. When we abstract from this act of the divine will and consider *p* *before* (*ante*) an act of God's will, our proposition *p* lacks both *truth* and *contingency*. According to Duns, there is no contingency to be discerned in terms of the two first structural moments of divine knowledge, but contingency has to be introduced. It is introduced by the will of God. *After* the relevant act of God's will, there is contingency and since *contingency* includes *truth*, there is truth, or falsity. *Before* the act of God's will there is no contingency, but since contingency includes truth, there is no truth, or falsity, either. So, *before* the relevant act of God's will, the propositions known to God are neither true nor false: they have no truth value at all – *propositiones neutrae*.[15]

Conclusion

The theory of the *neutral proposition* follows from acknowledging synchronic contingency, including truth, being dependent on God's will. Because it is common Christian wisdom that contingent creation depends on the will of God, Duns' starting point is understandable enough. However, this approach leads to a complex network of theories because of the conflation of *contingency* and *truth*. This result sheds new light on the famous issue of a Scotian ontology of possible worlds. The ontology of possible worlds does not originate with Duns Scotus; it is precisely the absence of such an ontology which explains the complicated structure of Duns Scotus' thought. When we replace his theory of neutral propositions by an S_5–styled ontology of possible worlds, we can host all of Duns Scotus' crucial insights and theories by eliminating in particular his crucial theory of the neutral propositions which is virtually absent in the history of Scotist studies.

Then, we get the following ontological picture: at the second structural moment of divine knowledge, God knows the whole of all

---

[15] On neutral propositions, see §7.4, and on God knowing them, see §13.4.

possible worlds. Since He knows all possible states of affairs, He knows all maximal states of affairs, including the contingent ones. The vulnerable assumption that God does not know contingencies apart from the divine will is avoided, and likewise the conflation of *contingency* and *truth* is eliminated. Nevertheless, there is still the pivotal role of the will of God, because there is no other instance which is possibly able to select *Actua*. The two operations of disconnecting *contingency* and *truth* and of introducing the link between what is *actual* in any possible world and what is *factual* in the unique possible world *Actua* simplifies the foundations of Duns Scotus' theory of reality and makes it intelligible and consistent.

Is there a (possible) source of contingency?

When we consider *p before* an act of God's will, according to Duns Scotus, *p* lacks both *truth* and *contingency*. However, this move is an unhappy one, since *truth* and *contingency* are modally different, for *p* is contingently true or contingently false – in the modern sense of *contingency*, if *p* is contingent – but the contingency of *p* itself is necessary.[16] Within the Scotian theoretical framework, the analytical operation of the involved structural moment, namely *before divine volition (ante actum voluntatis divinae)*, takes away both the truth value *being true* and the ontological status of *being contingent*. The first – crucial – step is simply right, but the second step is tricky.

In spite of some inadequate terminological aspects, Duns Scotus' argument that it is God's will which accounts for contingency is basically right. Nevertheless, it invites confusion and the history of their interpretation is a story of confusion, attributing to Duns Scotus proposals he never made.[17] Actual truth can only depend on God's *voluntas beneplaciti*, but *contingency* cannot. We face here the dominating factor of misinterpeting Duns Scotus' ontology and way of thought. However, his actualism accounts for his idiosyncratic theory of neutral propositions: a proposition enjoys no truth value *before divine volition (ante actum voluntatis divinae)*. So, originally, it has no truth value at all, which defies the axiom that a proposition is true or false.[18] Scotus is not a Plantingian Platonist.[19] *Before divine volition (ante actum voluntatis divinae)*, there is no articulate ontological

---

[16] See *KN* VII–VIII and 408–411: *p* is contingent $=_{def} p$ is possible and $-p$ is possible.

[17] See Tobias Hoffmann, *Creatura intellecta*.

[18] At the end of the sixteenth century, Suarez will be critical of this move.

[19] See Chapters 7 and 13. Cf. Plantinga, *The Nature of Necessity*, chapter 1.

dimension: it only consists of *propositions* without any truth value. God's intellect is familiar with these neutral propositions and offers them to the divine will to be filled with *truth* (or *falsity*). In sum, Duns' thesis that God's will bestows contingency on *p* is true within its own terms – Duns does not assert that *contingency* in the modern sense of the term can be bestowed on propositions, for necessity cannot be given contingently.[20] If we disconnect *contingency* and *actual truth*, we see that there cannot be a *source* (*causa*) of the contingency of reality. There is no *source* of the contingency of reality, since *contingency* itself is a necessary feature of contingent propositions. If not, it is contingent that something is contingent which is impossible.[21]

16.5.2 Duns Scotus' explanation of contingency

It is not difficult to understand the impact of Duns' statements that some factors cannot be the source of the contingency of reality. Duns' first step underlines, of course, that true *contingency* must be possible. If the foundations of a way of thought exclude contingency, then the question where the source of contingency is to be located does not make any sense.

> All causes would necessarily act, if the First Cause acts necessarily. For this reason, the source of contingency in what there is stems from the fact that the first Cause acts contingently, and not necessarily. (*Lectura* I 39.41)

With Duns Scotus, we often meet this line of argumentation. Contingency has to be accounted for, but if we try to account for contingency, we lose contingency. So, we have to look for an alternative account. Arguing the other way around is also typical of Duns Scotus: we can only account for contingency in such and such a way. We have to accept this theory. These moves mark the Scotian construction of logic and semantics, epistemology and proof theory, anthropology and ethics, ontology and the philosophical doctrine of God.[22]

God works contingently and the reality of creation is contingent, but where is the source (*causa*) of contingency to be located? The theme of the *source* of contingency hosts a series of arguments which

---

[20] We are able to cope with this semantic confusion in an alternative manner, without concessions to a non-contingency type of ontology. See §16.8. Cf. *KN* VIII.

[21] See §16.8. Cf. *KN* VII 1.2, VIII 2, and IX 1–2.

[22] See *CF* 33–37, and Vos, 'The theoretical centre and structure of Scotus' *Lectura*: philosophy in a new key,' in Sileo (ed.), *Via Scoti* I 455–473.

are one by one a *reductio ad absurdum*. The starting point of these
inferences is this disjunctive proposition:

> The source of contingency is *either* God's nature, *or* God's essence-
> based knowledge, *or* God's power (potency), *or* God's will.

Of course, all divine activity is based on God's nature, if we understand the involved terms properly. God's essential properties belong to
God, since they are entailed by his nature. Nevertheless, when we say
that the source of contingency is God's nature, what is meant is that
the nature of God's activity follows his nature in the sense that He acts
precisely as his nature *is*, namely necessarily. This option boils down
to the view that God acts necessarily, because his personal identity
itself is necessary. If the necessity of God's nature directly determines
his activity and causality, contingency is impossible. According to this
interpretation, God's nature cannot be the source of contingency.[23]

The next point is cut from the same cloth. When we say that the
source of contingency is God's nature-based knowledge, the nature of
God's knowledge follows his identity so that the whole of God's
knowledge is necessary. This option again entails the view that everything is necessary. If God's knowledge is necessary, it structures his
activity in a necessary way. Therefore, this option also entails that contingency is impossible. However, contingency is a fact; so, God's essential and necessary knowledge cannot be the source of contingency, just
as simply essence-based activity cannot account for contingency.

The third move is argued for in a different manner:

> If another potency is assumed in God, for instance, the executive
> potency, it cannot be the source of contingency, for it acts uniformly.
> Hence, that potency only produces something if an act of the intellect
> and the will precedes.[24]

So, God's necessary nature and necessary knowledge cannot explain
contingency and his active potentiality adds nothing to the inner
structure of divine activity, although it adds to God's deeds. God's
nature itself, his first-rate necessary knowledge, and his power cannot
be the source of the contingency of reality (see §13.5). So, it must be

---

[23] God acts contingently and it is necessary that He acts contingently. So, the reality of creation
is contingent, for reality depends on the contingent activity of God. For this reason, necessitarianism is wrong. Scotus mainly follows the first strategy. See note 20.

[24] *Lectura* I 39.42. Duns concludes there: 'Therefore, we have to inquire whether the source of
contingency in what there is stems from the divine intellect or from his will.' Cf. *Ordinatio*
I 39.14.

concluded that God's will is the source of contingency. This elucidation of the basis of Duns' stance with respect to the origin of contingency is not the end of our story. Although we understand Duns' mind
working, we have still to face some complications and we do so in
two rounds.

First, we deal with the thesis that *contingency* has to be explained
philosophically in the sense that a *source (causa)* has to be indicated –
the source of *contingency* has to be the will of God. Second, the will
of God is the item involved so that more attention has to be paid to
the issue that God's knowledge cannot be the source of contingency
(*Lectura* I 39.41–44).

Contingency does not have its origin in God's intellect as far as it
presents something to God's will. Anything God's intellect knows
before the act of his will, God's intellect knows *p before* the act of his
will, God's intellect knows *necessarily*.[25] In order to understand the
Scotian *model of philosophical constructs* we have to focus on the
interplay of *knowing* and *willing*. In order to understand this interplay of knowing and willing we have to realize that Scotus' actualism
presupposes that an *M*-modeled (or *L*-modeled) ontology is responsible for the drive of his thought. What is actually true in the past,
present, and future is seen as contingent, but this contingency is not
discussed apart from its actual truth. Because God's knowledge
cannot give rise to what is true in the actuality of the past, present,
and future, two substantial consequences follow from this approach:
the first function of knowledge must be necessary and the first function of knowledge must also precede the fact of a particular truth
value. So, knowledge of particular truth values must be based on
another divine property, namely the will of God. Along these lines,
we understand Duns Scotus' thesis that contingency is will based.
However, this option has nothing to do with voluntarism and voluntarist interpretations are missing the point. Of course, relativizing the
role of the will is likewise missing the point. The crucial role of the
will is related to factual reality, not to contingency as such, for contingency in itself is necessary too (see §16.8). The necessity of contingency is already intelligible on the level of God's necessary
knowledge, for God knows all possible propositions and, so, He also
knows all possible contingent propositions. The nature of a contingent proposition or state of affairs is not constituted by divine will.

---

[25] See *Lectura* I 39.43 (42–44). Cf. CF 104 ff.

Duns Scotus solves his dilemmas, elicited by the intrinsic connection of *contingency* and *factuality* in medieval thought, in his own idiosyncratic way with the help of the theories of the *neutral proposition* and *will-based contingency*. We can perfectly sound their impact and, therefore, rephrase and repair the infelicities of Scotus' solutions. So, can we accept – in modern terms – his move that God's essential knowledge cannot be the source of the contingency of reality? We cannot do so, since – in modern terms – contingent knowledge is not knowledge of *Actua qua Actua*. Such divine knowledge knows every possible world in its own actuality, containing contingent states of affairs, without identifying *Actua qua Actua*. *Actualism* cannot account for the accessibility properties of the possible worlds. Duns accepts $N\,p \to p$, $N\,p \to NN\,p$ and $M\,p \to NM\,p$. However, his ontology has no room for reflexive relations and although he accepts $M\,p \to NM\,p$, it has no room for symmetric relations either. The decisive point of Duns Scotus' doctrine of God is that God acts by his knowledge and his will (cf. §16.5.1).

16.6 LOGIC AND SEMANTICS

In spite of the fact that the context of doing logic and semantics had already changed fundamentally, the early logical writings of John Duns still offer many ideas and theories which are much more akin to Aristotelian views than the theological *baccalaureus* would be prepared to accept a few years later on. In this stage of his development Duns started from a rather strict idea of the *universal* in the sense of a form embodied in matter which accounts for singularity but cannot be the object of true knowledge. A word signifies the *species intelligibilis* which is also the object of the knowing mind (see §§4.4–4.6).

Duns Scotus eventually cherished a quite different view of speech and language. Nouns enjoy a double function. The spoken words are both signs of outside things and signs of internal thoughts. However, these functions show a specific priority. The primary function is to specify things in reality directly. The way he sees the relationship between words on the one hand and things and thoughts on the other hand is highly interesting. Spoken words also signify directly mental concepts.[26] So, there is a definite priority of the real over the mental or conceptual dimension and Duns leaves aside the medieval Aristotelian preference for the mentalist structure of abstraction.

---

[26] See *Lectura* I 27.2 where Duns mentions a *magna altercatio*, a big clash of opinions.

The contrast with the Aristotelian type of theory is striking: in this view spoken terms directly signify mental phenomena and these signs of the mind directly signify things and facts. The mind is the passive counterpart of reality and language is mind-dependent in a realist way. Duns also rejects the view that a word is not a sign of a concept. Both significations are direct, but the semantic relationship between speech and reality is the only proper and primary one. Maurer succinctly filled in a wider context.

> St Thomas claims that a general word like 'man' directly signifies a concept and not a reality, for it designates human nature in abstraction from individual men. Scotus, on the contrary, argues that general words can directly signify realities, for in his view there are real common natures.[27]

We may suggest that Ockham took his lead from Duns, radicalizing mentalism, while Duns overcame it.

From his point of view, Duns rebuts the old empiricism. A wall or a window can be experienced in itself; there is no need for them to be white just as it is now in order to be experienced, but in fact they are white, although their whiteness at the moment is different from their whiteness some time ago. In order to be able to say veritably of *both* that they are white, I need a third meaning which I impose on both. Then, what I am saying is still perfectly meaningful and true, but absolutely annoying to the semantic empiricist whether he be a medieval or a modern one, because there is no picture or image (*species*) of something white we do not see, although the language involved is perfectly meaningful. Even the meaningfulness of the famous example 'golden mountain' cannot be accounted for according to abstractionist lines, because we cannot abstract an image or picture of a golden mountain from a golden mountain, for golden mountains are nowhere to be found. However, we can expand the area of meanings of language by analyzing and combining and thus we are able to construe meaningful talk of golden mountains and meaningful talk of God.

The impact is simply to drive out mentalism and abstractionism from the philosophy of language by starting from the semantic phenomena of words and sentences themselves. Let us frame an example

---

[27] Maurer, 'William of Ockham on Language and Reality,' in Zimmermann (ed.), *Sprache und Erkenntnis im Mittelalter*, 797 f. Cf. Kluxen, 'Bedeutung und Funktion der Allgemeinbegriffe in thomistischem und skotischem Denken,' *De doctrina Ioannis Duns Scoti* II 229–240.

in a Scotian vein. I plan to write an article on Scotian semantics. In the meantime I become so impressed by his semantics that I decide to change the words and sentences as bricks in the wall of my article in order to produce a personal contribution to semantics and not a historical article. There is neither a common idea or picture, nor even a possible common idea or picture, because the common element is itself a set of words and sentence meanings. Nevertheless, both articles form a genre and the genre itself is different from the first kind of Scotist contributions.

There is no understanding in terms of sense images, but talk in terms of symbols and nouns is still perfectly meaningful in terms of a *reality-language* based approach and Scotus' theories of concept and proposition, truth and negation, possibility and relation are *necessity-contingency* based theories (§4.12).

Medieval thought has to be read within the broad context of medieval culture. In particular, the concrete achievements in medieval logic and semantics have to be understood and explained within the parameters of their intellectual culture. The culture of medieval intellectuals and scholars is a culture of *manuscripts* and it is a culture of *auctoritates*. Everything comes from a handwritten world and this handwritten world is a universe of *texts*. In this vein they ascribe all good things and all good thinking to the 'holy' texts and to the masters of the past. In logic, they put all good logic to the account of the father of logic: *Aristotle*.

> The schoolmen of the Middle Ages were too deeply convinced that they were the perpetuators of a long-standing tradition in which they lived and which they consciously kept alive. This statement applies to logic too. [. . .] In their opinion, Aristotle had invented logic as a science in its basic form, and posterity had only to continue, to develop and to carry to completion what he had founded.[28]

Boehner aptly quotes from an anonymous fifteenth-century introduction to logic – the *Copulata tractatuum parvorum logicalium* – when the author rebuts the charge of original invention, for Aristotle has, in principle, invented the whole body of logic: 'First it is to be stated that he [Aristotle] sufficiently completed Logic inasmuch as the being of logic is concerned.'[29]

---

[28] Boehner, *Medieval Logic*, 16.
[29] Ibid., 17. Boehner offers an English translation of the preface of this treatise (ibid., 17–18). For the Latin text, see De Rijk, *Logica Modernorum* I 15.

We meet again this medieval and Renaissance view with Immanuel Kant.

> That logic has already, from the earliest times, proceeded upon this sure path is evidenced by the fact that since Aristotle it has not required to retrace a single step. [. . .] It is remarkable also that to the present day logic has not been able to advance a single step, and is thus to all appearance a closed and completed body of doctrine.[30]

De Rijk's *Logica Modernorum* I–II simply destroy this view by showing that the logic of fallacies and the theory of supposition are truly original and authentic innovations of twelfth-century logic. Terminist 'logic developed as a result of the fact that, to a much greater extent than it had been done by Abailard and his contemporaries, the proposition was beginning to be subjected to a strictly linguistic analysis.'[31] Medieval logicians and grammarians, theologians and philosophers continuously poured new wine into old skins. The historical analysis of medieval philosophy aims to rediscover that these old wine skins were in fact new ones by removing the 'history' fiction of the traditional self-interpretation. Duns Scotus' logic and semantics form an ample illustration of this phenomenon. The *logica modernorum* not only comprises the theory of the properties of terms, but also the theory of the syncategorematic terms and the practical exercise of obligations.[32]

The impact of Duns Scotus' semantic and logical theories on the historical development of these theories is to say goodbye to 'abstractionism,' 'universalism,' and 'factualism' and their underlying world-views. We are far away from the logophoric semantics of ancient philosophy. On the other hand, the formalism of contemporary approaches in logic and semantics lies at a far distance too. The main factors are still actualism and the dominance of constants, in the logical sense of the word. Nevertheless, what Duns has to offer can easily be restated in modern terms. The innovations are limited in historical detail, but enormous in scope.

In thirteenth-century semantics we may discern the main lines of two semantic approaches, as Braakhuis has pointed out several times. Duns is opposed to the 'empiricist' criterion of meaning and truth of all sorts.[33] The impact of his approach is to drive out mentalism and abstractionism by putting language on its own footing, when we

---

[30] Norman Kemp Smith, *Kant. Critique of Pure Reason*, 17.
[31] *Logica modernorum* I 22.
[32] See the doctoral theses of Green (1963) and Braakhuis (1979).
[33] Fregean options fit adequately Duns' way of developing logic.

compare his approach with that of his predecessors William of Sherwood and Roger Bacon.[34] Duns starts from the semantic phenomena of words and sentences in medieval Latin.

16.7 KNOWLEDGE AND PROOF

In Duns Scotus' thought, the parallelisms of *knowledge* and *necessity* and of *thinking* and *being* disappear. The emancipation from ancient philosophical foundations culminates in his philosophy. Duns elaborates an ontology of contingency and draws the epistemological consequences from it.[35] The achievement of critical epistemology in the thirteenth and fourteenth centuries constitutes a paradigm change of epistemic structures. Epistemological logic is a powerful instrument in analyzing the concepts of traditional philosophies. Jaakko Hintikka's *Knowledge and Belief* presents an impressive set of techniques in order to facilitate the analysis of philosophical concepts. A specific epistemic principle dominates the scene of Hintikka's epistemological logics, in particular his logic of knowing:

(C.KK) If *a* knows that *p*, then *a* knows that *a* knows that *p*.

I call this principle *the epistemic principle of certainty*. It also plays an important role in Hintikka's historical survey of epistemic logic,[36] but there is still another principle dominating traditional thought: *the epistemic principle of necessity*:

(C.KN) If *a* knows that *p*, then it is necessary that *p*.[37]

(C.KN) is as conspicuous by its absence in Hintikka's piece of the history of epistemic logic as it is absent in his analysis and evaluation. It is a dominant feature of the history of epistemology. Ancient Greek and Hellenistic epistemology is characterized by a specific connection

---

[34] We notice a parallel phenomenon in the transition from the semantics of logical positivism before World War II to philosophies of language like Alston's and Searle's. For alternative accents, see Perler, 'Things in the Mind: Fourteenth-Century Controversies over "Intelligible Species",' *Vivarium* 34 (1996) 231–253, and idem, 'Duns Scotus's Philosophy of Language,' in Williams (ed.), *The Cambridge Companion to Duns Scotus*, 161–192.

[35] See *KN* II, VI and VII. Cf. Chapters 8 (esp. §8.9) and 9 (esp. §§9.5 ff.).

[36] *Knowledge and Belief*, 22 ff., and chapter V: 'Knowing that One Knows.'

[37] For the career of (C.KN) during the whole of the history of Western thought, see *KN* chapter I (1–38): ancient philosophy, chapter II (39–104): medieval philosophy and theology, and chapter III (105–134): modern philosophy.

between *knowledge* and *necessity*: knowledge *entails* necessity. What is not necessary cannot be known. Modern philosophy also delivers ample evidence for the dominance of (C.KN). Only the necessary can be known. Real knowledge must be knowledge of reality and really rational knowledge (*epistème*, *scientia*) can only have necessary objects. If both principles obtain in a system, the consequences are far-reaching, since (C.KK) and (C.KN) entail (C.K,NK):

(C.K,NK) If *a* knows that *p*, then it is necessary that *a* knows that *p*.[38]

(C.K,NK) is the more important, since the principle of necessitarianism:

(N) All states of affairs are necessary

can be derived from (C.K,NK), and vice versa.[39]

The *principle of epistemic necessity* can be blocked in three ways: either by dropping (C.KK), by dropping (C.KN), or by dropping both. Duns Scotus drops (C.KK) as an essential ingredient of the notion of *knowing* in *Lectura Oxoniensis* III 27. There are more exceptions to subscribing to (C.KK) in the fourteenth century and in the seventeenth century. In contrast to ancient and modern thought, medieval theology and philosophy show a wealth of exceptions to (C.KN). The situation was the more pressing for medieval Christian thought, for (C.KK) cannot be dropped in the case of divine knowledge. The vulnerability of (C.KN) and (N) is crucial for adequate systematic thought.

Another striking principle of epistemic logic, very characteristic for Hintikka's approach, is:

(C.KH) *aKq* follows from: if *p*, then *q* and *aKp*.

---

[38] The following formulae have to be introduced: $aKp =_{def} a$ knows that p and $Np =_{def}$ it is necessary that p. In terms of these formulae and standard logic, (C.K,NK) is derived from (C.KK) and (C.KN) as follows:

(1)	aKp	HYP
(2)	$aKp \rightarrow aKaKp$	(C.KK)
(3)	$aKaKp$	1, 2, MPP
(4)	$aKaKp \rightarrow aKp$	3, (C.K)
(5)	$aKaKp \rightarrow NaKp$	4, (C.KN)
(6)	$NaKp$	3, 5, MPP
(7)	$aKp \rightarrow NaKp$	1, 6, II.

[39] See KN 248–257.

It is clear from Duns Scotus's *ars obligatoria* (§§5.5–5.6) that he also rejects the Hintikkian approach evidenced in (C.KH).

Dropping (C.KN), (C.KK), and (C.KH) gives free passage to a new epistemological style. Knowledge of different sorts of contingent propositions has to be analyzed independently. These patterns also structure Duns Scotus' theories of intuitive knowledge and memory.

16.7.1 Time and deductive knowledge

Some propositions are necessary truths in virtue of the meanings of their terms. Eventually, the certainty of a deductive thesis depends only on the certainty of self-evidently known principles and the demonstrative power of the inference. The point of Duns' analysis is that the degree of reasonableness of a necessary thesis is not diminished if we derive it step by step deductively. We may say that we know such a theorem a priori. Thomas Aquinas and Descartes, Locke, Kant and Chisholm were in the same epistemic league, subscribing to a logic of *time* and time-bound *knowledge*. Duns Scotus dropped this time-bound model and disconnected *deductivity* and *time*, just as he disconnected *certainty* and *time*, *time* and *necessity*, and *knowledge* and *necessity*. If a type of thought is able to withstand such a tradition, it must enjoy mighty resources in itself.[40]

16.7.2 Provability and the hypothesis rule

We have to rewrite the development of Western epistemology in the light of an ongoing emancipation over centuries, but we may also amend on some epistemic patterns. We can only understand Scotus' comment: 'We are unable to *demonstrate* that *p*,' if we realize that demonstrations have to start eventually from what is self-evident. According to Scotian terminology, the self-evident cannot be demonstrated and the demonstrable cannot be self-evident. However, what we grant the opponent, we may also grant ourselves. The rule of granting which the *ars obligatoria* adheres to is an epistemically democratic rule. We may assume whatever (hypothesis rule), if we are prepared

---

[40] The epistemic logic of *KN* 194–197 builds further on the basis of Chisholm's logic of knowing, but drops the Chisholmian pattern that certainty decreases at new deductive steps. This pattern is replaced by the epistemic rule of vincible risks. In terms of such an epistemic logic *a priori propositions* can be *certainly known* just as Duns proposes in *Ordinatio* I 3. See also §8.4 and §9.7.

to defend it and to try to prove it, possibly from varying starting points. It is preferable to replace the old *self-evidence-demonstration* covenant by the *hypothesis rule*: standard logic teaches that we may *assume* everything if we add the modest comment: *hypothesis*, and continue to defend it as well as we may.

16.7.3   Contingent certainty

In contrast to Chisholm's epistemic assessment of *I know that Duns was called John*, I propose to ascribe the epistemic *iudicium certain* to this piece of knowledge.[41] If this intuitive knowledge lacks the same certainty that abstractive knowledge has, the reason is that, here, more epistemic risks have to be coped with. John knows that he is called John and John knows that Peter is called Peter. Scotus does not decree a priori that certain kinds of propositions cannot be known certainly. He assesses them in terms of epistemic risks. John knows that $1 + 1 = 2$, but in the case of *John knows that he (John) is called John* we have to overcome more risks. *If* we overcome them, then everything is all right, but, from the viewpoint of epistemic appraisal, the credentials of $1 + 1 = 2$ are more easily satisfied than those of *John knows that he is called John* and *John knows that Peter is called Peter*. *I know that Duns was called John* is still more complicated.

16.8   The ontology of reality

In logic at work in the basic conceptual structures of ontology, the heart of Western philosophy is at stake.[42] The history of medieval thought shows an enormous cultural and philosophical battle (see Chapters 7 and 14). The riddle is that it seems utterly improbable that the philosophical newcomer which *philosophia christiana* was might win, because the place of *philosophical rationality* was already taken by the opponent. We see this historical field of force mirrored in the fact that the great non-Christian philosophers of the second and third centuries were not worried at the rise of Christianity and its thought, if they were interested in it at all. They simply believed that this sad madness would soon pass away.

---

[41] Cf. Chisholm's *Theory of Knowledge* (^{2}1977), chapter 3, and the epistemic logic of *KN* V.

[42] For a clear and traditional approach to Duns Scotus' ontology, see King, 'Scotus on Metaphysics,' in Williams (ed.), *The Cambridge Companion to Duns Scotus*, 15–68.

We may think of a cultural analogy: the battle of faith evidenced by the Old Testament. There, we observe a desperate struggle. We understand its tension and despair much better when we realize that the Old Testament is not the fruit of a political and cultural unity, because the people of the Israelite kingdoms themselves were polytheistic. There is no people, no culture, no nation standing behind the Old Testament. Only the voice of God their Lord stands behind the Old Testament where we also hear the voice of those who listened to his voice. Nevertheless, the Old Testament is a historical datum. The new ways of medieval thinking were excluded by their ancient philosophical alternatives as much as Old Testament faith was excluded by the polytheistic religions of ancient Palestine.

Nevertheless, the new medieval way of ideas won, but it did not do so in the same way as the Old Testament won. Schools are no prophets. In contrast to faith and discipleship, Christian *philosophy* is not revealed. The alternative theories of Christian theology and philosophy are discovered on the basis of faith – *fides quaerens intellectum* – and within the realm of Revelation, but they are not revealed themselves. They were invented and developed in a profound process of emancipation from ancient thought patterns ongoing for centuries and this ongoing emancipation temporarily culminated in the life and works of John Duns Scotus who died at the age of forty-two. Nevertheless, miraculously, it did not fall dead to the ground. The conceptual structures which his theory of *synchronic contingency* embodied and developed were just the elements Christian thought was desperately in need of in order to be able to integrate hosts of innovations worked out in the centuries before. It was the master stroke needed to infuse coherence into the whole fabric.

Duns realized that there was a problem, although there was no problem at all for Bonaventure and Henry of Ghent. For them, it was evident that the alternative of Aristotle and Avicenna was inconsistent, but Duns did not begrudge that the opponent enjoyed his own self-evident starting point – in the vein of the *ars obligatoria*. The question remained whether Aristotle could be beaten. Duns Scotus hesitates, but he thinks that the Aristotelian option has to yield to the change argument: there is change, so there is contingency. However, the *a*historical way of thinking is playing tricks on Duns when he writes: 'I argue against the *philosophers* as follows: some effect is caused contingently in what there is' (*Lectura* I 8.256), for *contingency* and *change* have different roles in both models. The philosophers do not mean by *contingency* what Duns means by it, as he himself expounds extensively in *Lectura* I 8 and *Ordinatio* I 8. If we cannot prove that purely *diachronic contingency* entails *synchronic contingency*, then Duns Scotus' option does not refute the necessitarian alternative when we stick to this premiss of *diachronic contingency*. Of course, *diachronic contingency* in its Aristotelian sense excludes *synchronic contingency*, since what is *diachronically contingent* in this sense is in itself necessary.[43] Several courses are open to us in order to decide the battle. First, we may steer a strict course by attacking fundamental hypotheses and patterns of thought espoused by the opponent. Second, we may try to prove the contingency stance by departing from a premiss the opponent also accepts. The third course consists of proving directly that the contingency position is reasonable.

16.8.1   The untenability of necessitarianism

Most ancient and modern philosophical systems join the necessitarian club – from Parmenides to Foucault and Hawkins. If we can refute the logical kernel of the necessitarian position, the philosophical field of force differs substantially from what most systems claim. We focus on the necessitarian notion of *necessity*. The impossibility of this notion can be shown. If this notion were to hold, then all structural variability would be excluded. Something can change over time, but if something does *not* happen, then it *cannot* happen. So, accordingly, the meaning of the symbol of *negation* boils down to *impossibility*:

4. If it is *not* true that *p*, then it is *not* possible that *p*.

However, it is impossible that *not* only means *impossibly*. If Duns Scotus is not a bishop, then this negative fact does not entail the impossibility of Scotus being a bishop. Many masters of theology became a bishop in the thirteenth century and their common essential properties do not exclude becoming a bishop. So, there is the possibility that Duns Scotus is a bishop and this possibility is not barred by the fact that he was not. We argue that the fact that he was *never* a bishop does not entail that it is impossible for him to be a bishop.

If *not* entails *impossibility* and *being the case* entails *necessity*, then *p* is necessarily true or necessarily false and –*p* is also necessarily true

---

[43] Duns Scotus is quite aware of this fact, but he neglects it when he frames his crucial counterarguments in *Lectura* I 8.257–259 (see §14.5). We have to focus on purely diachronic change in order to reach *synchronic contingency*, for *synchronic contingency* can be derived from *purely diachronic change/contingency*. Cf. the last paragraph of §16.5.1.

or necessarily false. We may remember the truth tables of non-modal propositional logic. If necessitarianism were to hold, then only truth tables containing columns of T(rue) or F(alse) are possible. We are familiar with the philosophical dilemma whether modal thinking is acceptable – some philosophers do not think so. However, the necessitarianist is bound to hold that *only* modal thinking is possible.

Necessitarian conceptual structures not only exclude contingency, but they also exclude the *possibility of contingency*. If the possibility of contingency is excluded, *necessity* and *impossibility* are the only viable modal notions. Then, the conjunctive property *not being necessary and not being impossible* is an impossible property, although *being necessary* and *being impossible* are acceptable in themselves. However, if P is an acceptable and possible property, then $-P$ is also an acceptable and possible property. A transcendent term like *being* is a universal term, but this datum does not entail that *not being* is an impossible notion. So, according to necessitarian lines, *being contingent* must be impossible. If necessitarianism is right, the ontological opposition square collapses and is transformed into a line:

5. *necessary* * _____ * *impossible.*

However, *contingency* itself is a necessary trait of reality. If *contingency* itself is not a necessary trait of contingent reality, then it is possible that it is necessary. However, the necessary cannot be contingent, because it is as such not contingent, and the contingent cannot be necessary, because it is as such not necessary.[44] If not, the modal opposition square would collapse into a line and the modal *possibility* operator M in Mp would collapse into the modal *necessity* operator N in Np. On the one hand, only modal thinking is possible, but, on the other hand, modal theory formation is impossible. So, we can only conclude that necessitarianism cannot be maintained. Necessitarianism entails the impossibility of *true contingency*, but modal logic demonstrates the possibility of contingency. The whole of modern elementary logic is based on contingency and modern elementary logic is taught all over the world. This logic symbolizes a rare worldwide consensus, but, intrinsically, it only agrees with types of ontology and theology which incorporate the Scotian innovations. The possibility of *synchronic* contingency is necessary and what is necessary cannot be abolished or eliminated.

---

[44] For the modal opposition square, see *KN* 408–411. Cf. *KN* 142 ff., 174 ff., and 211 ff.

16.8.2   The untenability of a necessitarian law of M-distribution

Another crucial difference seems to be a tiny one:

$$N\,(p \to q) \to (Np \to Nq)$$

and

$$(Np \to Nq) \to N\,(p \to q)$$

so

$$N\,(p \to q) \leftrightarrow (Np \to Nq)$$

are valid, both in the traditional model of ancient philosophy and in the new one.

Not only entailments, but also conjunctives show the same pattern:

$$N\,(p\ \&\ q) \to (Np\ \&\ Nq)$$

and

$$(Np\ \&\ Nq) \to N\,(p\ \&\ q)$$

so

$$N\,(p\ \&\ q) \leftrightarrow (Np\ \&\ Nq)^{45}$$

For ancient philosophy, reality is a great chain of being. The great chain of being not only holds onto the parallelism of *thought* and *being*, but also rests on parallelisms. If laws of distribution hold for some logical key concepts, they must hold for all. According to these lines, the *possibility* operator M is treated in precisely the same way:

$$M\,(p\ \&\ q) \leftrightarrow (Mp\ \&\ Mq)$$

Indeed, the crucial difference seems to be a tiny one, for

$$(M1)\qquad M\,(p\ \&\ q) \to (Mp\ \&\ Mq)$$

---

[45] On these distribution laws, see Hughes and Cresswell, *A New Introduction to Modal Logic*, 25–31, where they deal with K, K1, K2, and K3.

is acceptable for everyone.[46] So, the only logical space available for divergence of opinion is to be found in (M2), the converse of (M1):

(M2) $(Mp \ \& \ Mq) \rightarrow M \ (p \ \& \ q)$

We have to notice that (M2) fits into the system of necessary diachronic contingency, because here contingency is enclosed in only one possible series of events. Real possibilities are possibilities, joined in one and the same maximal set of events, which is the only possible one.

It is just (M2) which is used by Duns' opponent in *Lectura* I 39.89 and 92, *Reportatio Parisiensis* I 39,[47] and *Ordinatio* I 39.20, in order to refute his ideas on synchronic contingency. Here, we have a distinctive difference between two ways of systematic thinking. (M2) aptly illustrates the big clash of the two philosophies, because both parties subscribe to (M1) and to the same kind of claim: both claim that the opponent commits a logical blunder. What is to be said on

(M2) $(Mp \ \& \ Mq) \rightarrow M \ (p \ \& \ q)$

and can this dilemma of two opposite logical claims be decided?

We assume the conjunction: $Mp \ \& \ Mq$. Mp yields that there is an alternative possible world W' which has p. The same goes for Mq which delivers that there is a possible world W'' which contains q. However, the given does not *entail* that p and q meet in the same possible world W'''. This conjunction is not excluded, but neither is it entailed. So, we are not allowed to conclude: $M \ (p \ \& \ q)$. It is easily to be seen why this is so. If we replace q by $-p$ in (M2), then the antecedent $Mp \ \& \ M\text{-}p$ is perfectly acceptable. Nevertheless, the consequent is necessarily false, since the contradiction: $p \ \& \ -p$ is necessarily false and it is impossible that what is necessarily false is a possible truth. At this moment, we also comprehend why modern modal logic does not extend a warm welcome to (M2), for (M2) is simply inconsistent. So, the necessitarian opponent has been refuted.[48]

---

[46] For (M1), see Hughes and Cresswell, *A New Introduction to Modal Logic*, 35 f., on K8, and their thesis: 'In contrast with K6, the converse of K8 is not a theorem of K' (ibid., 36).

[47] Cf. Wolter, 'God's Knowledge of Future Events,' *The Philosophical Theology of Scotus*, 307, and note 58, running parallel to *Lectura* I 39.92. See §6.4.

[48] Did Duns Scotus himself do so? Duns used nicely convincing examples in *Lectura* I 39 and in *Reportatio Parisiensis* I 39, but he offered no proof.

16.8.3   Diachronic contingency entails synchronic contingency

We have seen that Duns Scotus argued against the *philosophers* that some effect is caused contingently in what there is, so (N) must be false (*Lectura* I 8.256). However, this argument fails according to Duns Scotus' own metholodological principles, for *contingency* and *change* have different meanings in both models and Aristotle does not grant the decisive premiss *Some effect is caused contingently*, if *contingently* is understood along Scotian lines. The philosophers could not do so, because they were not familiar with the Scotian meaning of *contingent*. The Scotian meaning of *contingent* had not yet been invented.[49] We ask now whether *dia*chronic contingency entails *syn*-chronic contingency. We look again at:

1. If p is necessary, then p is immutable.

Is it possible that (1) is shown to be true? If p is necessary, then p is the case in every possible world W. If p is necessary, then it is also excluded that $-p$ belongs to any possible world W where p is true. If p and $-p$ belong to some possible worlds, then we have the conjunction

3. It is possible that p and it is possible that $-p$.

However, (3) is precisely the definition of what it is to be *contingent*. So, if p is necessary, then $-p$ is excluded from any possible world W. If we accept that p is necessary and that p is true in every possible world W, it has to be concluded that $-p$ is barred from any possible world W. So, if p is *necessary*, then the truth-value of p cannot vary over other possible worlds and it can neither change in one and the same possible world. We are bound to:

1. If p is necessary, then p is immutable.

Necessity and *diachronic contingency* are irreconcilable and, there-fore, we have arrived at:

6. If p is necessary, then p is not *dia*chronically contingent.

With the help of *modus tollens* and the elimination of double negation:

7. If p is *dia*chronically contingent, then p is not *syn*chronically necessary

---

[49] By the same token, we cannot say that Thomas Aquinas rejected the Scotian notion of con-tingency. We cannot reject what we do not know.

can be deduced from (6). Now, we have arrived at the missing link. *Synchronic contingency* can be derived from *diachronic contingency*, which is crucial for diachronic necessitarianism:

8. If *p* is *dia*chronically contingent, then *p* is *syn*chronically contingent.

We have seen that we cannot drop both (1) and (2), since we are not allowed to drop (1), but can we drop

2. If *p* is immutable, then *p* is necessary

alone? (2) is only valid if (N) is true. However, (N) has been refuted, so (2) is false. By now, we have also solved the *immutability* dilemma.

2. If *p* is immutable, then *p* is necessary

is not acceptable according to modern logic and the alternative way of doing ontology.[50] Duns Scotus replaced the diachronic framework of a plurality of times by a synchronic framework of *one and the same time* (*in eodem tempore*) and a full-fledged ontology can be derived from this move.[51]

16.8.4 Triumphant contingency

We have to disconnect *contingency* and *actuality* – *pace* Duns Scotus and the whole of the – old and new – traditions of Christian actualism, because the actual is either necessary or contingent. If what is actual is not necessary, then it is contingent. We are also able to prove that, but it is also true that *contingency* itself is a necessary feature of both contingent propositions and contingent states of affairs.[52] True *contingency* cannot be abolished. In spite of the limitations of Duns Scotus' own theory formation, his *auctoritates* culture, and its ahistorical way of ideas, we are able to demonstrate that, in principle,

---

[50] Again, first we have to face a problem of meaning. Both in the Aristotelian tradition and in the tradition of Christian dogmatics, we see that both *changing* and *changeable/mutable* and *unchanging/changeless* and *unchangeable/immutable* are equivalent, but are they indeed according to the family of contingency ontologies? They are not, since the logic of events differs from the logic of possibilities.

[51] *Ordinatio* I 39.17 (*Opera Omnia* VI 420): 'Et istae duae propositiones verificantur, quia significantur attribuere praedicata sua subiecto *pro eodem instanti*; et hoc quidem verum est, nam voluntati isti *in eodem instanti* convenit *non velle a* cum possibilitate ad oppositum pro *a*, sicut significatur inesse cum illa de possibili.'

[52] Let us assume the opposite hypothesis: $- (Cp \rightarrow NCp)$. If $- (Cp \rightarrow NCp)$, then Cp & CCp is possibly true. However, Cp means: Mp & $M-p$. Therefore: $CCp \rightarrow (MCp$ & $M-Cp)$. However, $M-Cp \rightarrow MNp$, and the following entailment also holds: $MNp \rightarrow Np$. We have arrived at the conclusion: Cp & Np, which is contradictory, because it entails: $-Np$ & Np. See *KN* VIII.

his approach is right. We did so by proving that *diachronic contingency* entails *synchronic* contingency. So, what ancient philosophy and the old-Semitic cultures share cannot be true and this impossible truth entails the Christian point of view. True *contingency* cannot be eliminated. The necessitarian coalition – from Parmenides to Foucault and Hawkins – is not philosophically tenable. Necessitarianism cannot be true, since it entails the impossibility of *true contingency*.

16.8.5   The moral of modal thinking

Dropping the diachronic approach to the *nature* of what happens boils down to introducing a new and strict concept of *the nature of . . .* What happens, happens as such at a certain time. Suppose that the *same* event could have happened at another time, then it is evident that it is not time that determines the ontological identity of that event. This timely revolution adds up to much more conceptual changes. If the paradigm changes, then old specific rules disappear and new rules conquer the stage. New concepts of *possibility*, *contingency*, and *necessity* are introduced. A new logical language arises. The inference from *necessarily* to *always* goes in both models. If only this entailment holds, we might already surmise that it is not *time* that defines structure. If something obtains for every time, it obtains for a certain time. We may get from this pattern the logical glimpse that time does not define the nature of *nature* – in the alternative sense of *nature*. Not only the ontological principle of *necessity* has to be dropped, but also the principle of *plenitude*.

If we see that necessitarianism is untenable, Duns Scotus' philosophical revolution and the conceptual moves contingency thought requires are now seen in a broader perspective. Disconnecting *nature* and *time*, no matter how strange it might have been to Aristotle's sense of logic, is decisive in itself. Disconnecting *Being (Sein)* and *Time (Zeit)* decides the contest between the conceptual structures, regardless of how odd it might have been to Heidegger's mind. When, in contradistinction to Aristotle and to Ecclesiastes, we essentially distinguish between *nature (structure)* and *time*, we drop the model of the *only one possible world*. If we leave aside this model, we distinguish contingent propositions and states of affairs from necessary ones while we see that temporally indexing does not change the logical and ontological status of a proposition or a state of affairs.

The impact of John Duns Scotus' basic innovations is clear. Duns Scotus prematurely rounded off what Christian thought had prepared in the course of more than a thousand years, rooted in a religious revolution grounded in Old Testament revelation. Duns Scotus' way of doing philosophy shows a wealth of ramifications derived from the notion of synchronic contingency. However, he does not have the concept formation of *possible worlds*. Therefore, we have to add to his tools *modal logic* and the theory of *possible worlds*. Moreover, Duns Scotus' tools have to be enriched and implemented by modern *elementary logic* and Georg Cantor's theory of *infinite sets*. The upshot is that the notion of a *maximal set of states of affairs* is wedded to the Scotian idea of synchronic contingency. If we drop Duns Scotus' tool of the neutral proposition and the actualist weft of his ontology, we conclude that the philosophical needs of the Anselmian and Scotian orientation are served best by an S_5 modeled ontology.

However, is a possible worlds translation of the synchronic contingency view in reality a valid one? In his excellent *The Worlds of Possibilities* (1998), Charles Chihara pays special attention to the ontological realisms of Lewis and Plantinga and to the anti-realist ontology of Graeme Forbes. Although some philosophers deny any serious role to the notion of a *possible world*, David Lewis has defended a rather robust interpretation of it: possible worlds are concrete totalities, things of the same sort as the whole actual universe. In addition to this concrete interpretation of what is meant by possible worlds, there is also Plantinga's defense of an abstract view. Chihara's choice is exquisite, but somewhat misleading too, because the opposition against such strong realisms as Lewis's and Plantinga's and Forbes's deviation from them is unfortunate. A more safe starting point is the idea of a maximal set of states of affairs, in combination with necessary modal truths. It is preferable to start with necessary truths about *Actua* as a maximal set of states of affairs and its S_5 styled accessibility, instead of offering initial speculative intuitions, couched in informal language.

In spite of Chihara's understandable criticisms of modal realism, his possible worlds semantics paves the way for a realistic version of modal realism, based upon Duns Scotus' notion of synchronic contingency, which is just logical contingency from the formal point of view.[53] The foundation of such a realistic realism consists of the insight that the whole of actual reality – *Actua* – is a maximal set of states of affairs, including necessary truths. So, *Actua* is a possible

---

[53] See Chihara, *The Worlds of Possibilities*, chapter 1: Possible worlds semantics. Compare Plantinga, *The Nature of Necessity*, chapters 1–4, Robert Stalnaker, *Inquiry*, David Lewis, *The Plurality of Worlds*, and Graeme Forbes, *Languages of Possibility*.

world and this truth is a necessary one. However, if what is contingently not true in *Actua* is not related to *Actua*, being a maximal set of states of affairs in terms of possible alternatives, then what is not true in *Actua* does not constitute possible alternatives for *Actua*. Then, what is not true is impossible and contingency is abolished. Since this conclusion is necessarily false and is also excluded by what Chihara himself grants – in company of most other ontologists – one cannot coherently object to a realistic version of modal realism of possible worlds – on the basis of the alternatives which are referred to.

16.9   An ethics of dignity and love

According to ancient epistemology, only what is necessary is scientifically knowable. *Epistèmè* is certain and unshakable knowledge of true things which can only be just as they are. Knowable reality cannot be otherwise. Only what is necessary can be known. Analogously, only what is universal can be known. An *act-potency* framework does not rehabilitate the individual, nor matter. Just as we have to look for a rehabilitation of matter in a theology of creation, in the same way we have to look for regard for the individual in a different corner. When we read in the Decalogue that God is a jealous God, punishing the children for the sins of the fathers to the third and the fourth generation of those who hate Him, but showing love to a thousand generations of those who love Him and keep His commandments (Exodus 20: 4), we may realize that the notion of individuality is far removed from the ancient mindset. Ezekiel quotes a proverb: 'The fathers eat sour grapes, and the children's teeth are set on edge' (Ezekiel 18: 2).

The individual is only born in the fiery proclamation of John the Baptist that every individual has to start anew, looking for the heavenly kingdom, and even this birth is still implicit. Regard for the individual is born when a vulnerable and wounded man is only looked for and cared for in narrative reality, because the merciful and good Samaritan only existed in the heart and the language of the storyteller.

In terms of the history of the thought of mankind, it is a long way to Duns Scotus' ontology of the haecceity of the individual, promoted to higher ontological glory (see §§11.2–11.4). Ethical dignity presupposes ontological dignity. The ontological hierarchy is turned upside down: reality is primarily the world of the individuals which also enjoy common and universal properties. In a sense, the contrasts between ancient philosophy and philosophy in a new key are lucid and uncomplicated: the individual enjoys ontological priority. The new ethical perspectives are along the same lines. If something *a* is not something in itself and by itself, it cannot be appreciated as something being itself *a*. If anybody *b* is not an individual in himself or in herself, she or he cannot be treated, appreciated, and loved as someone being just *b* and *b* must be somebody in order to be able to be a good *b*.

16.9.1 The reasonableness of goodness and love

Goodness in terms of will does not belong to the goodness of 'the law of nature.' 'When we completely leave out the act of will and the intellect of God grasps the terms of those principles, then it grasps the power and correctness of those principles before an act of will' (*Lectura* III 37.13). Basically, a truth is 'naturally' true, if it is true in terms of the intrinsic nature or structure of the proposition involved, and not in terms of an absolutistic concept of nature derived from cosmology. Natural truths are truths which are true in terms of their own nature and contents. The crucial ethical principles are derived from philosophical theology in the style of faith searching for understanding. The self-evident basis is constituted by the specific identity or essence of God's personal character. Theology is a theology of love. Analogously, Duns Scotus' ethics is an ethics of love. Meta-ethics shows teleological and deontological approaches, naturalist, intuitionist, and emotive viewpoints, and command theories, but Duns Scotus' ethics belongs to a select company. Love for God, neighbor-love and self-love are connected as tightly as possible. The life of love rests upon the life and identity of God. Thus, the Anselmian type of goodness is decisive: the correct goodness is good, because the objective goodness of the other appeals to us, absorbs us, and invites us to absorb it by loving it. Ethics can only be based on moral goodness which focuses on the other who is our neighbor, and the Other, in a contingent world.

There is a shift from the ego to orientation on the other and the neighbor. *Being free* is also a central notion of Scotian ethics and anthropology. Freedom is not primarily freedom from sin. Even *sinning* presupposes freedom and so *being free* in the sense of freedom based on alternative choices is essential to a person.[54] *Being free* is

---

[54] See Dekker and Veldhuis, 'Freedom and Sin. Some Systematic Observations,' *European Journal of Theology* 3 (1994) 153–161. Cf. Noone, 'Universals and Individuation,' in Williams (ed.), *The Cambridge Companion to Duns Scotus*, 100–128, and Bonnie Kent, 'Rethinking Moral Dispositions: Scotus on the Virtues,' in Williams (ed.), *The Cambridge Companion to Duns Scotus*, 352–376.

also essential to God being impeccable. The interplay of goodness and, on the other hand, of contingency and freedom in Scotian ethics requires a much more elaborate role for deontic logic. Duns Scotus' ethics focuses on actual goodness, just as his epistemology and ontology are dominated by actual truth. However, what is the case is not only determined by what is the case, but is also constituted by what can be the case and by what has to be done. Duns Scotus' point of view waits for a creative role for deontic logic and deontic ethics, analogous to the role of renewal the *ars obligatoria* played in his theory of demonstration. His theories of goodness and divine will have to be extended by preferential logics of divine and human willing and this can be done in a natural way.[55]

The ontological reorientation of the philosophy of the individual waits for the crucial role of the dignity of the individual, in search for understanding, goodness, and love, just as the ontological reorientation of contingency thought waits for the crucial role of will and freewill.[56]

16.10 GOD

> O Lord, our God, you have proclaimed yourself to be the first and the last. Teach your servant to show rationally what he holds with faith most certain, that you are the first effective agent and most eminent and the last goal.[57]

Duns Scotus looks upon himself as a servant, waiting for his master to teach him in his quality as the most true Doctor (*De primo principio* §1.2) who has to be acknowledged as unique, simple, infinite, wise, and endowed with will (*De primo principio*, chapter 4). What Duns looks for mostly is love, for the more we know Him, the more we love Him:

> The blessed who know Him more, do love Him more. So, he who is more acquainted with the mighty deeds of God, is more directed to praise and to love God.[58]

---

[55] For this option, see Chapter 13.

[56] See Smith, 'John Duns Scotus and Ecumenical Dialogue: The Dignity of Man,' *De doctrina Ioannis Duns Scoti* III, 769–772, and Doyle, 'Duns Scotus and Ecumenism: Duns Scotus and the Dignity of the Individual,' *De doctrina Ioannis Duns Scoti* III 638–643.

[57] *De primo principio* (ed. Wolter), chapter III section 2. Cf. §1.2 and §4.2.

[58] *Lectura Prologus* 163: 'Beati qui plus cognoscunt, plus diligunt. Et hic qui plura magnalia Dei cognoscit, magis ordinatur ad laudandum et diligendum Deum.' Cf. §164: 'Intellectus, perfectus habitu theologiae, apprehendit Deum ut amandus et secundum regulas ex quibus potest elici praxis. Ideo, est habitus practicus.'

It is a natural perception that love is a basic category of Christian life. The spiritual world Duns Scotus is at home with radicalized this attitude of love, existentially and theoretically. 'The disposition by which God is loved is a theological disposition' (*Ordinatio* III 28). The word Duns uses to express this virtue is *caritas* ('charity'), for 'the disposition by which we hold God to be dear [*carus*] is called *caritas* [charity, love]' (ibid.). He is dear to us and we are dear to Him. It is primarily directed towards God and we ought to love our neighbor and ourselves as well. Worship and faith mark the daily existence of Duns Scotus. His theology is a theology of love, including his philosophical theology. For Duns, such theological demonstrations are a matter of prayer. There is no skeptical or fideist dualism of heart and mind, faith and reason. He prays that he shall believe and he prays that he can prove his faith. Faith and rational philosophy go hand in hand.

Duns Scotus' concept of contingency, understood as synchronic contingency, gives rise to a precise concept of *synchronic necessity* as well. Basically, Duns Scotus' thought is structured by the powerful distinction between necessary and contingent propositions. In terms of this basic distinction the young Duns was already distinguishing between *necessary theology* and *contingent theology*:

> Not only belongs knowledge of necessary propositions to this doctrine, but also knowledge of contingent propositions. Indeed, for the major part of theology deals with contingent propositions.[59]

Although the major part of theology consists of contingent propositions, the dimension of the necessary propositions is the decisive one, because necessary theology formulates the preconditions of what can happen and ought to be done in the world of contingency. This structure is illustrated by an *ethical* example in *Prologus* 172 of Duns' *Lectura* I–II:

> *I love God* is contingent. Yet there can be a necessary truth about it, for example, that I must love God above all. This thesis can be proved as follows: *God is the greatest one we can think of.* Therefore, He is most lovable and I ought to love Him most. [. . .] It concerns necessary truths which can be concluded about what is contingent.

In terms of the basic distinction between *necessary theology* and *contingent theology*, it is seen that Duns' theology is a theology of love.

---

[59] *Lectura Prologus* 111. Cf. *Lectura Prologus* 114 and 118. For the theme of philosophy, theology, and scientia, see §12.4, Chapter 14 and §§16.2–16.4.

Reality is open and just as open reality it must be ordered. Ordering reality requires a center and this center has to be personal, because it cannot act without knowledge and will. Therefore, the center of contingent reality has to be God. He is not only the ontological, but also the existential and ethical center. God is the best possible Person and *not loving God* is deontically impossible. We ought to love God and *loving God* takes pride of place in Scotus' necessary theology:

> I say that to love God above all is an act which follows from a correct and a priori argument which prescribes that what is best must be loved most of all. Consequently, it is an act which is right of itself; nay, it is self-evident that it is right, just as a first principle of ethics is right. What ought to be loved most of all is nothing but the highest good, just as nothing but the highest good must intellectually be held to be true most of all.[60]

In his philosophical theory of what God is, Duns starts with an axiomatic basis and in his necessary theology what is valid is either self-evident, or axiomatic, or a priori and provable. Philosophy and revelation, logic and faith go hand in glove. We have already met the proof, a revelation which coincides with Revelation:

> This is confirmed by the fact that moral commandments belong to the law of nature, and, consequently, the commandment: *Love the Lord, your God*, and so on, belongs to the law of nature. Therefore, it is evident that this act is right. It follows from this that there can be a virtue which directs essentially towards this act, and this virtue is theological, for it concerns God immediately. (Ibid.)

We ought to love God and this love is a primary preference which can be proved theoretically, but it is also an existential preference:

> The virtue of *love* is distinct from faith, for its act is one neither of knowing nor of believing. It is also distinct from hope, for its act is not one of desiring a good for the lover as far as it fits the lover himself, but it directs towards its object for its own sake and it would do so – to assume the impossible – even when its benefit for the lover were excluded. So, I call this virtue which perfects the will as far as it appreciates justice: *love*. (Ibid.)

Because this love of God entails the rule that we ought to love our neighbor, and to love ourselves as well, it orders the whole of our behavior on an axiomatic basis. The style is that of Anselm's

---

[60] *Ordinatio* III 27 *articulus* 1 (Wolter, *Duns Scotus on the Will and Morality*, 424). Cf. §§12.4–12.5 and §9.3.

philosophia christiana. I do not know of a philosophical alternative which can compete with this option, based on divine and human love, integrating revelation and philosophy in manner without compare. Duns Scotus' proofs of the existence of God brought him much more fame, but the approach of these masterpieces have to be integrated into the structure of the whole of his thought. In his philosophy of religion, the task of demonstration is central. So, following the basic rules of the *ars obligatoria*, the opponent states the starting points. For this reason, the Anselmian style of a *God is the best possible Person* philosophy cannot be used. However, the hypothesis rule of modern theory of argumentation accepts any assumption, if we are prepared to try to prove anything we assume. Duns Scotus' method was extremely polite towards Aristotle and Avicenna who espoused principles incompatible with his own. However, we are able to refute Aristotle's and Avicenna's necessitarianisms, just as we can refute any kind of necessitarianism adhering to a *one possible world* model. On the one hand, we have the crucial interplay of God's necessary and contingent knowledge and his necessary and contingent willing; on the other hand, we have an S_5-styled ontology, delivering the fabric for a consistent philosophical theory of God's attributes.[61]

From the time of Lanfranc and Anselm until the last years of the eighteenth century (Christian Wolff, Christian Crusius, and Bernhardinus de Moor), the doctrine of God constituted the systematic epicenter of Western university thought. The model of Duns Scotus' doctrine of God set the agenda for centuries. Later alternative models – for example, the Nominalist model, the *scientia media* model of the great Jesuit thinkers such as Fonseca and Molina, Suarez and Bellarmine, and the Socinian, Arminian, and Cartesian models – were all dependent on the Scotist model. Even Spinoza derived his system from the Reformed doctrine of God by abolishing all shades of contingency. In particular, the history of Reformed scholasticism delivers impressive illustrations. In the sixteenth, seventeenth, and eighteenth centuries, this tradition shows dozens of universities, all adhering to the Scotist model. Paul Helm suggests that interpreting Reformed scholasticism does not need the notion of synchronic

---

[61] See Scapin's excellent contribution: 'Il significato fondamentale della libertà divina secondo Giovanni Duns Scoto,' *De doctrina Ioannis Duns Scoti* II 519–566. Cf. Ross and Bates, 'Duns Scotus on Natural Theology,' in Williams (ed.), *The Cambridge Companion to Duns Scotus*, 193–237.

contingency,[62] although he grants that 'God's knowledge of the contingent must itself be contingent.'[63]

The modern doctrine of God is beset with paradoxes. I like to suggest that the systematic alliance of *necessity-contingency*-based methods in philosophy and theology can cope with the old and new dilemmas of philosophical theology. The issue is that we are still in two minds about doing philosophy and about doing philosophy of religion, ignoring the consistent reconstruction of Western thought in its classic tradition and mixing contradictory models of thought. For many centuries, the doctrine of God was the central area of Western academic activity. Its creativity is still the hermeneutical key to understanding the development of Western philosophy, and not only of theology. It also delivers the key for contributing to the consistency of philosophy and the coherence of theism.

What matters is a philosophical theology which presents a consistent elaboration of crucial essential and contingent properties of Him who is the best possible Person, for ever and ever.

16.11 A PERSPECTIVE: *PHILOSOPHIA CHRISTIANA*

Modern philosophy and modern theology show a bewildering variety of different movements mostly incompatible with each other. However, the whole of the history of Western thought presents an alternative to this confusion. A handful of alternative points of view may be proposed.

1. We have to take account of the whole of the history of Western thought, including medieval thought.[64]
2. If we take account of the medieval history of our thought, we discover that it is not true that there is only one *philosophia perennis*. The general idea that we are taught *philosophically* that something is such and such is misguided. From a purely historical point of

---

[62] Helm believes that the main stamp of classic Reformed thought is necessitarian, but the decisive roles of the notion of *potentia ad oppositum* and the *necessity-contingency*-based Reformed doctrine of God, the heart of this way of thinking, have to be taken into account – witness the central roles of the distinctions between God's necessary and free knowledge and his necessary and contingent will. See Helm, 'Synchronic Contingency in Reformed Scholasticism,' *Nederlands Theologisch Tijdschrift* 57 (2003) 207–222, and Beck and Vos, 'Conceptual Patterns Related to Reformed Scholasticism,' ibid., 223–233.

[63] Helm, 'Synchronic Contingency,' ibid., 218. This concession suffices, if we build upon it consistently.

[64] Likewise, we can only explain the plan and the most famous buildings of an old city in the northern part of Europe, e.g. the city of Dort (NL), from its medieval history, and not from antiquity.

view, we observe *two philosophies*: before 1800, we meet the well-known legacy of archaic thought and ancient Greek, Hellenistic, and Roman *philosophia*, on the one hand, and the philosophical legacy of the Augustinian-Anselmian line culminating in the heritage of Duns Scotus' philosophy and theology, and, since the Renaissance, a wealth of mixtures of the two main tendencies.

3. The Christian alternative was elicited by theological dilemmas and solutions. So, we have to undo the separation of philosophy from theology. This separation is incompatible with the facts of the history of ideas, because in patristic and, in particular, in medieval thought theology is the key for discovering the alternative contingency type of philosophy.

4. Only after the fall of scholasticism in around 1800 was philosophy separated from theology. We have to study the previous six centuries as a whole.

5. At the end of the thirteenth century, Oxford and Duns Scotus come in. Duns Scotus summarizes and remolds the creative contributions of the thirteenth century and the upshot of this development is the hidden fact that Scotus is still a big power in seventeenth-century philosophy. What is called the *consensus philosophorum et theologorum* in the seventeenth century was a way of thought constituted by systematic innovations which were rooted in the medieval contingency and will tradition. Originally they were mainly Scotian.

6. Responsible examination of the whole of Western thought including its Christian stages requires that modern philosophy and theology restore the study and analysis of crucial Latin texts which reach far into the nineteenth century.

7. Western thought cannot overcome its irrational lack of consensus if it continues to ignore points (1)–(6). If we skip the dualisms mentioned above, we arrive at a rather different picture of Western philosophy and theology. An alternative philosophical way of thought came about during the millennium between about 800 and about 1800.

8. Of course, we also have to start where we are, with the fields of forces in which we find ourselves, but we also have to redirect them in the light of the overarching viewpoints inherited from the *Enlightenment* before the 'Enlightenment.'

There are no essential differences between the metaphilosophies of Jacques Maritain and Gilson. For Gilson, the Christian character of much medieval thought is a historical fact, but to Gilson's mind, *philosophy* and *revelation* are still two different worlds apart, although they are not two ships passing in the night. There is a rational juxtaposition, just as Maritain's characterization runs: Christian faith changes the philosopher, but it does not deliver a new philosophy.[65] So, there is a profound difference between Maritain and Gilson, on the one hand, and, on the other, the Christian philosopher Maurice Blondel who aims at a philosophy which spontaneously agrees with the Christian faith. The views of Gilson would not satisfy Blondel according to whom philosophical unrest leads to faith. De Lubac and Blondel agree and their views are modern counterparts to the ancient religious thought of Justin the Martyr and Augustine.

Much modern theology considers the nature of Duns Scotus' philosophy in quite a different way. Traditional theology, which was in fact based on Scotist innovations, is seen as a kind of determinism. Pinnock sensed that parallel shifts of interpretation had taken place in Dutch Reformed circles during the middle of the twentieth century.[66] The main point is that, on the hermeneutical level, classic Reformed doctrine is interpreted along determinist lines. However, the determinist interpretation of Reformed scholasticism is a rather modern phenomenon.[67] Nineteenth-century orthodox theology furiously rejected liberal dogmatics, but adopted the determinist interpretation of Reformational scholasticism developed by the first-generation analysts of the historical revolution. The history of the concept of *immutability* shows what was taking place. There was hardly any Protestant determinist theology and philosophy before 1800. The consequences of not being familiar with the main lines of classic theology wedded to philosophy are rather serious, because it leads to mistaken pictures of early modern Western thought. By misinterpreting our heritage, theology and philosophy become haunted houses. If we are unable to draw from tradition we suffer from weaker alternatives.

---

[65] See Maritain, *De la philosophie chrétienne*, and idem, 'De la notion de la philosophie chrétienne,' *Revue Néo-scolastique* 43 (1932) 153–186. On the debate of the 1930s, see Renard, *La querelle sur la possibilité de la philosophie chrétienne*.

[66] Pinnock referred to Berkouwer and Berkhof's *Christian Faith*, but he probably overlooked the fact that Berkhof not only rejected the doctrine of double predestination and limited grace, but also the doctrines of the Trinity and God's incarnation in Christ.

[67] It developed during the 1840s by thinkers such as the Swiss theologian Schweizer and the Dutch theologian and philosopher Scholten, the founder of Dutch 'modern theology,' a movement far more liberal than German liberal theology. See Vos, 'Protestant Theology: The Netherlands,' in McGrath (ed.), *Blackwell Encyclopedia of Modern Christian Thought*, 511–515.

16.11.1   Old Testament faith

We have to free ourselves from contemporary polarizations by taking seriously what has already happened. Historical alternatives of thinking, feeling, and willing have been developing so that things can no longer be the same. The history of mankind is basically a story of David and Goliath. The Old Testament is a book written in a culture which was diametrically opposed to it. In a sense, it is a book without an author. For this reason, it is called the Word of God. In terms of purely historical understanding, we cannot understand the birth of the Old Testament and its faith, apart from its own confession: *The Word of the Lord came to me.* Nevertheless, we have the book in our possession, although there is no simple cultural explanation of the Old Testament and its faith. It is a tremendous historical fact, because it embodies a way of life entirely excluded by the ways of life mankind was familiar with before. It was the faith of a lonely community which made no idols, in contrast to the majority of the nation. Their heaven was no place of bearing and birth. They did not write cosmogonic and theogonic myths. They believed in the Creator of heaven and earth. He who has no beginning guides the history of salvation and our everyday life. We become the more aware of the unimaginable differences between the Old Testament and its historical background when we realize that most old-Israelite believers were convinced that the Fall of Jerusalem at the beginning of the sixth century BC was caused by neglecting the worship of the goddess Astarte and her friends. Serving the one true God is simply unimaginable to the pre-Old Testament believer. Although it is an impossible possibility, this faith was generally accepted in the Israelite life of the Persian period, and, of course, in Jesus' time.

16.11.2   New Testament faith

The New Testament and the early Church tell the same kind of story. Rediscovering the true impact of the great past of an ongoing emancipation over thousands of years on the basis of the entire tradition of Western thought and of a long-standing tradition of biblical and Christian faith simply amounts to discovering what the philosophical translation is of the mysterious fruits of Revelation, introducing itself into worlds which were only able to look upon it as madness. This madness was the cradle of a new way of life elicited by a profound process of conversion leading to a new way of thinking. The Church broke into the ancient world with an impossible Gospel. To the mind of the ancient philosophers, this Gospel was sheer madness. However, this madness (Paul) gave rise to a new way of thought opposed to old Greek religion and ancient philosophy as well. It was a faith which created a new type of understanding by searching for understanding.

16.11.3   Christian philosophy

According to Greek thought, the order and the logical that is not personal is higher than what is personal. Fate is above the gods and the tragic reigns. Biblical faith does not know of the phenomenon of fate, rising higher than God, and does not accept the tragic. Creation belief is incompatible with both Greek religion and philosophy, but Christian thought is creation thought. Even the Platonist *kosmos noètos* is seen as creation. It is just the other way around: God is necessary and creation is contingent. The necessity of God and the Logos (the Gospel of John) absorbs what is necessary and sets the world and human existence free. In this process of *Umwertung aller Werte*, contingency replaces necessity, freedom replaces fate and determinism, the individual is rehabilitated and universals turn out to be properties and, eventually, matter does matter. Language and thought are decosmologized and ethics and anthropology turn around divine presence, for man is an image of God who creates his own image in the Man of sorrows.

From the logical point of view, these matters religious look simple: from the viewpoint of coherence, the Old Testament is easily understood simply by denying the main positions of Canaanite polytheism. In a parallel way, Christian philosophy is just the opposite of non-Christian ancient philosophy. However, historical matters tell us a complicated story and the story is drama, just as the history of physics is more complicated than physics itself.

David beats Goliath and this process of conversion and emancipation from old thought patterns leads to a newly styled life and a newly styled thinking, uniquely represented by the philosophy of John Duns Scotus, following the footsteps of *il poverello*.

Bibliography

Opera Omnia

Opera omnia Ioannis Duns Scoti, Lyons 1639, in 12 volumes (reprint Hildesheim 1968).

Opera omnia. Editio nova iuxta editionem Waddingi, Paris: L. Vivès 1891–1895, in 26 volumes.

Critical Editions

Commissio Scotistica, *Doctoris subtilis et mariani Ioannis Duns Scoti Ordinis Fratrum Minorum Opera Omnia* I. Critical introduction to the *Ordinatio* I manuscripts, including the list of the manuscripts, containing the authentic writings, and the *Prologus* of the *Ordinatio*, Rome 1950.

Opera Omnia II, *Ordinatio* I 1–2, Rome 1950.

Opera Omnia III, *Ordinatio* I 3, Rome 1954.

Opera Omnia IV, *Ordinatio* I 4–10, Rome 1956.

Opera Omnia V, *Ordinatio* I 11–25, Rome 1959.

Opera Omnia VI, *Ordinatio* I 26–48 Rome 1963.

Opera Omnia VII, *Ordinatio* II 1–3, Rome 1973.

Opera Omnia VIII, *Ordinatio* II 4–44, Rome 2001.

Opera Omnia XVI, *Lectura Prologus* and I 1–7, Rome 1960.

Opera Omnia XVII, *Lectura* I 8–45, Rome 1966.

Opera Omnia XVIII, *Lectura* I 1–6, Rome 1982.

Opera Omnia XIX, *Lectura* II 7–44, Rome 1993.

Opera Omnia XX, *Lectura* III 1–17, Rome 2003.

Opera Omnia XXI, *Lectura* III 18–40, Rome 2004.

Opera Philosophica I: R. Andrews, G. Etzkorn, †G. Gál, R. Green, T. Noone and R. Wood (eds), *B. Ioannis Duns Scoti Opera Philosophica* I. *Quaestiones in librum Porphyrii Isagoge et Quaestiones super Praedicamenta Aristotelis*, St Bonaventure, NY 1999.

Opera Philosophica II – general editors: Girard Etzkorn, Romuald Green and Timothy B. Noone. R. Andrews, G. Etzkorn, †G. Gál, R. Green, T. Noone, R. Plevano, A. Traver, and R. Wood (eds), *Quaestiones in libros Perihermenias Aristotelis*. R. Andrews, O. Bychkov, S. Ebbesen, G. Etzkorn, †G. Gál, R. Green, T. Noone, R. Plevano, and A. Traver (eds), *Quaestiones super librum Elenchorum Aristotelis*. M. Dreyer and H. Möhle, in cooperation with G. Krieger (eds), *Theoremata*, St Bonaventure, NY: St Bonaventure University and Washington, DC: Catholic University of America 2004.

Opera Philosophica III–IV: R. Andrews, G. Etzkorn, †G. Gál, R. Green, †F. Kelley, †G. Marcil, T. Noone and R. Wood (eds), *Quaestiones super libros Metaphysicorum Aristotelis* I–V and VI–IX, St Bonaventure, NY 1997.

Opera Philosophica V: general editor: Timothy B. Noone. C. Bazan, K. Emery, R. Green, T. B. Noone, R. Plevano and A. Traver (eds), *Quaestiones super libros De Anima Aristotelis*, Washington, DC: Catholic University of America 2006, forthcoming.

BIBLIOGRAPHIES

Bochenski, I. M. (ed.), *Bibliographische Einführungen in das Studium der Philosophie* 22: Odulfus Schäfer, *Johannes Duns Scotus*, Bern 1953, 1–34.

Schaefer, Odulfus, *Bibliographia de vita, operibus et doctrina Iohannis Duns Scoti, doctoris subtilis et mariani*, Rome 1955, listing 4,506 titles. Additions to Schäfer's bibliography are to be found in Odulfus Schäfer, 'Conspectus brevis bibliographiae scotisticae recentioris,' *Acta ordinis fratrum minorum* 85 (1966) 531–550, and in Servus Gieben, 'Bibliographia scotistica recentior (1953–1965),' *Laurentianum* 6 (1965) 492–522.

STUDIA SCOTISTICA

Commissio Scotistica, *De doctrina Ioannis Duns Scoti* I–IV, Acta Congressus Scotistici Internationalis Oxonii et Edimburgi 11–17 sept. 1966 celebrati, Rome 1968.

Societas Internationalis Scotistica, *Deus et Homo ad mentem I. Duns Scoti*. Acta Tertii Congressus Scotistici Internationalis Vindebonae, 28 sept.–2 oct. 1970, Rome 1972.

Societas Internationalis Scotistica: Camille Bérubé (ed.), *Regnum Hominis et Regnum Dei* I–II. Acta Quarti Congressus Scotistici Internationalis, Rome 1978.

Sileo, Leonardo (ed.), *Via Scoti methodologica ad mentem Joannis Duns Scoti* I–II, Rome 1995.

LATIN

Introduction to medieval Latin

Sidwell, Keith, *Reading Medieval Latin*, Cambridge 1996, including the sections 'Grammar' (362–372), 'Orthography' (373–375), and 'Note on vocabulary' (376–377).

Dictionary

Latham, R. E., *Revised Medieval Latin Word-List*, Oxford ²1980 (¹1965).

GLOSSARIES

Alluntis, Felix and Allan B. Wolter, *John Duns Scotus. God and Creatures. The Quodlibetal Questions*, Princeton, NJ 1975, 493–540: Glossary.

De Rijk, L. M., *Nicholas of Autrecourt. His correspondence with Master Giles and Bernard of Arezzo*. A critical edition from the two Parisian manuscripts with an introduction, English translation, explanatory notes and indexes, Leiden 1994, 39–43: *A glossary*.

BIBLIOGRAPHY OF WORKS CITED

Abate, Giuseppe M., 'La tomba del Ven. Giovanni Duns Scoto, o.min. nella chiesa di S. Francesco a Colonia. Note e documenti,' *Miscellanea Franciscana* 45 (1945) 29–79.

Abelson, Raziel, 'History of Ethics,' *EP* (1967) III 81–117.

Alanen, L. and S. Knuuttila, 'The Foundations of Modality and Conceivability in Descartes and his Predecessors,' in S. Knuuttila (ed.), *Modern Modalities. Studies of the History of Modal Theories from Medieval Nominalism to Logical Positivism*, Dordrecht/London 1988, 1–69.

Albuquerque, Luis de, 'History of Sciences in Portugal,' in *Symposium Hooykaas, Janus* 64 (1977) 1–13.

Alluntis, Felix, *Dios uno y trino. Obras del Doctor Sutil Juan Duns Escoto*, Madrid 1960.

Alluntis, Felix and Allan B. Wolter, *John Duns Scotus. God and Creatures. The Quodlibetal Questions*, Princeton, NJ 1975.

Alluntis, Felix, Celestino Solaguren, Bernardo Aperribay, and Antonio Eguiluz (eds), *Obras del Doctor Sutil Juan Duns Escoto. Edicion bilingüe. Cuestiones cuodlibetales*, Madrid 1968.

Amorós, L., *Fr. Gonsalvi Hispani O.F.M. Quaestiones disputatae et de Quodlibet*, Quaracchi 1935.

Andrews, Robert, 'The *Notabilia Scoti in libros Topicorum*, An Assessment of Authenticity,' *Franciscan Studies* 56 (1998) 65–75.

Andrews, Robert, 'Andrew of Cornwall and the Reception of Modism in England,' in Ebbesen and Friedman (eds) (1999) op. cit., 105–115.

Anscombe, G. E. M. and P. T. Geach, *Three Philosophers. Aristotle. Aquinas. Frege*, Oxford 1973.

Ashworth, E. J., 'Jacobus Naveros (fl. ca. 1533) on the Question: "Do Spoken Words Signify Concepts or Things?",' in De Rijk and Braakhuis (eds) (1987), op. cit., 189–214.

Baeumker, Clemens, 'Erinnerungen an P. Ignatius Jeiler. Mit Briefen von P. Ignatius an den Verfasser,' *Franziskanische Studien*, Munster 1923, 33–49.

Balic, Carlo, *Les commentaires de Jean Duns Scot sur les quatre livres des Sentences. Étude historique et critique*, Louvain 1927.

Balic, Carlo, 'De *collationibus* Ioannis Duns Scoti, doctoris subtilis ac mariani,' *Bogoslovni Vestnik* 9 (1929) 185–219.

Balic, Carlo, 'Erwiderung' (to F. Pelster, 'Antwort'), *Theologische Revue* 28 (1929) 449–52.

Balic, Carlo, 'Une question inédite de J. Duns Scot sur la volonté,' *Recherches de théologie ancienne et médiévale* 3 (1931) 191–218.

Balic, Carlo, *Ioannis Duns Scoti Theologiae Marianae Elementa*, Sibenik 1933.

Balic, Carlo, 'Alte Handschriften der Dominikanerbibliothek in Dubrovnik (Ragusa),' *Aus der Geisteswelt des Mittelalters* III A, Munster 1935, 3–18.

Balic, Carlo, 'Die Frage der Authentizität und Ausgabe der Werke des J. Duns Skotus in Vergangenheit und Gegenwart,' *Wissenschaft und Weisheit* 2 (1935) 136–158.

Balic, Carlo, 'Bemerkungen zur Verwendung mathemathischer Beweise und zu den Theoremata bei den scholastischen Schriftstellern,' *Wissenschaft und Weisheit* 3 (1936) 191–217.

Balic, Carlo, 'Henricus de Harcley et Ioannes Duns Scotus,' *Mélanges offerts à Étienne Gilson*, Paris 1959, 93–121.

Balic, Carlo, 'The Life and Works of John Duns Scotus,' in Ryan and Bonansea (eds) (1965) op. cit., 1–27.

Balic, Carlo, 'The Nature and Value of a Critical Edition of the Complete Works of John Duns Scotus,' in Ryan and Bonansea (eds) (1965) op. cit., 368–379.

Balic, Carlo, *John Duns Scotus. Some Reflections on the Occasion of the Seventh Centenary of his Birth*, Rome 1966, 1–57 (13–44: 'The Life and Literary Activity of John Duns Scotus' = 'The Life and Works of John Duns Scotus' in Ryan and Bonansea (eds) (1965) op. cit., 1–27; and 45–57: 'The Nature and Value of a Critical Edition of the Complete Works of John Duns Scotus' = 'The Nature and Value of a Critical Edition of the Complete Works of John Duns Scotus,' in Ryan and Bonansea (eds) (1965) op. cit., 368–379).

Balic, Carlo, 'Where Was Duns Scotus Born,' in *John Duns Scotus. Some Reflections on the Occasion of the Seventh Centenary of his Birth*, Rome 1966, 5–11.

Balic, Carlo, 'John Duns Scotus,' *New Catholic Encyclopedia* IV, New York 1967, 1102–1106.

Balic, Carlo, 'Note per la Storia della Sezione e poi Commissione Scotista per l'Edizione Critica delle Opere di Giovanni Duns Scoto,' in R. St Almagno and C. L. Harkins (eds), *Studies Honoring Ignatius Charles Brady Friar Minor*, St Bonaventure, NY 1976, 17–44.

Barth, Timotheus, 'Die Notwendigkeit Gottes und seine Begründung bei Duns Scotus,' *De doctrina Ioannis Duns Scoti* (1968) II 409–425.

Basly, Déodat Marie de, 'Les *Theoremata* de Scot,' *AFH* 11 (1918) 3–31.

Bataillon, Louis-Jacques, 'Le edizioni di *opera omnia* degli scolastici e l'Edizione Leonina,' in Imbach and Maierù (eds) (1991) op. cit., 141–154.

Beck, Andreas J., ' "Divine Psychology" and Modalities: Scotus' Theory of the Neutral Proposition,' in Bos (ed.) (1998) op. cit., 123–137.

Beck, Andreas J., 'Gisbertus Voetius (1589–1676): Basic Features of His Doctrine of God,' in Willem J. van Asselt and Eef Dekker (eds), *Reformation and Scholasticism. An Ecumenical Enterprise*, Grand Rapids, MI 2001, 205–226.

Beck, Andreas J. and A. Vos, 'Conceptual Patterns Related to Reformed Scholasticism,' *Nederlands Theologisch Tijdschrift* 57 (2003) 223–233.

Beck, Lewis White, *Early German Philosophy. Kant and His Predecessors*, Cambridge, MA 1969.

Beckmann, J. P. et al. (eds), *Sprache und Erkenntnis im Mittelalter. Miscellanea Mediaevalia* 13/1, Berlin 1981.

Bendiek, J., 'Die Lehre von den Konsequenzen bei Pseudo-Scotus,' *FS* 34 (1952) 205–234.

Berkhof, Hendrikus, *Christian Faith*, Grand Rapids, MI 1979.

Berr, Henri, in É. Bréhier, *La philosophie au moyen âge*, Paris 1937 (²1949), I–XVIII.

Bérubé, Camille, *La connaissance de l'individuel au moyen âge*, Montreal/Paris 1964.

Bérubé, Camille, 'Antoine André, témoin et interprète de Scot,' *Antonianum* 54 (1979) 369–446.

Beth, E. W., *De wijsbegeerte der wiskunde van Parmenides tot Bolzano*, Antwerp/Nijmegen 1944.

Beth, E. W., 'Metafysica en wetenschap,' in *Door wetenschap tot wijsheid. Verzamelde wijsgerige studiën*, Assen 1964, 28–36.

Beth, E. W. 'Algemene beschouwingen over causaliteit,' in *Door wetenschap tot wijsheid. Verzamelde wijsgerige studiën*, Assen 1964, 74–81.

Bettoni, Efrem, *Duns Scotus. The Basic Principles of his Philosophy*, Greenwood, CT ²1979 (¹1961).

Biller, Peter and Barrie Dobson (eds), *The Medieval Church: Universities, Heresy, and the Religious Life: Essays in Honour of Gordon Leff*, London 1999.

Bocheński, Joseph M., *Formale Logik*, Fribourg/Munich ²1962 (¹1956).

Boh, Ivan, 'Consequences,' *CHLMP* (1982) 300–314.

Böhner, Philotheus (ed.), *Walter Burley. De puritate artis logicae*, St Bonaventure, NY 1951.

Böhner, Philotheus (ed.), *William of Ockham. Summa totius logicae*, St Bonaventure, NY 1951.

Böhner, Philotheus, *Medieval Logic. An Outline of Its Dvelopment from 1250 to c.1400*, Manchester 1952.

Böhner, Philothius, *Collected Articles on Ockham*, St Bonaventure, NY 1958.

Boler, John F., *Charles Peirce and Scholastic Realism*, Seattle, WA 1963.

Bonansea, Bernardino M., 'Duns Scotus and St. Anselm's ontological Argument,' *De doctrina Ioannis Duns Scoti* II (1968) 461–475.

Bos, E. P., 'Curriculum vitae' and 'Bibliography 1947–1984,' in E. P. Bos (ed.), *Mediaeval Semantics and Metaphysics. Studies dedicated to L. M. de Rijk, Ph.D., on the occasion of his 60th birthday*, Nijmegen 1985, VIII f. and IX–XXIV.

Bos, E. P., 'The Theory of the Proposition According to John Duns Scotus' Two Commentaries on Aristotle's *Perihermeneias*,' in De Rijk and Braakhuis (eds) (1987) op. cit., 121–139.

Bos, E. P. (ed.), *L. M. de Rijk. Through Language to Reality*, Northampton: Variorum Reprints 1989.

Bos, E. P., 'A Contribution to the History of Theories of Induction in the Middle Ages,' in Jacobi (ed.) (1993) op. cit., 567–570.

Bos, E. P. (ed.), *John Duns Scotus. Renewal of Philosophy (1265/66–1308)*, Amsterdam 1998.

Boudri, J. Chr., H. Floris Cohen, and Valerie MacKay (eds), *R. Hooykaas. Fact, Faith and Fiction in the Development of Science*, Dordrecht 1999.

Boulnois, Olivier, *Duns Scot. Sur la connaissance de Dieu et l'univocité de l'étant*, Paris 1988.

Boulnois, Olivier, 'Représentation et noms divins selon Duns Scot,' *Documenti et studi sulla tradizione filosofica medievale* 6 (1995) 255–280.

Boulnois, Olivier, *Duns Scot. La rigueur de la charité*, Paris 1998.

Boulnois, Olivier, *Etre et représentation*, Paris 1999.

Braakhuis, H. A. G., 'The Views of William of Sherwood on Some Semantical Topics and Their Relations to Those of Roger Bacon,' *Vivarium* 15 (1977) 111–142.

Braakhuis, H. A. G., *De 13de eeuwse tractaten over syncategorematische termen. Inleidende studie en Uitgave van Nicholaas van Parijs' Sincategoreumata* I–II, Meppel 1979 (DPhil thesis, Leiden University).

Braakhuis, H. A. G., 'English Tracts on Syncategorematic Terms from Robert Bacon to Walter Burley,' in Braakhuis, Kneepkens, and De Rijk (eds) (1981) op. cit., 131–165.

Braakhuis, H. A. G., 'Kilwardby versus Bacon? The Contribution to the Discussion on Univocal Signification of Beings and Non-Beings found in a Sophism attributed to Robert Kilwardby,' in E. P. Bos (ed.), *Medieval Semantics and Metaphysics*, Nijmegen 1985, 108–142.

Braakhuis, H. A. G., 'Obligations in Early Thirteenth Century Paris: The *Obligationes* of Nicholas of Paris (?),' *Vivarium* 36 (1998) 152–233.

Braakhuis, H. A. G. and C. H. Kneepkens (eds), *Aristotle's Peri Hermeneias in the Latin Middle Ages. Essays on the Commentary Tradition*, Groningen-Haren 2003.

Braakhuis, H. A. G., C. H. Kneepkens, and L. M. de Rijk (eds), *English Logic and Semantics. From the End of the Twelfth Century to the Time of Ockham and Burleigh*. Acts of the 4th European Symposium on Medieval Logic and Semantics, Leiden-Nijmegen, 23–27 April 1979, Nijmegen 1981.

Brady, I., 'The Edition of the *Opera Omnia* of Saint Bonaventure (1882–1902),' *AFH* 70 (1977) 352–376.

Brampton, C. K., 'Duns Scotus at Oxford, 1288–1301,' *Franciscan Studies* 24 (1964) 5–20.

Breda, Herman Leo Van, 'La preuve de l'existence de Dieu dans la *Lectura*,' *De doctrina Ioannis Duns Scoti* II (1968) 363–375.

Bréhier, É., *La philosophie au moyen âge*, Paris [1]1937 ([2]1949).

Broadie, Alexander, *The Circle of John Mair. Logic and Logicians in Pre-Reformation Scotland*, Oxford 1985.

Broadie, Alexander, *Introducton to Medieval Logic*, Oxford [2]1993.

Broadie, Alexander, *The Shadow of Scotus. Philosophy and Faith in Pre-Reformation Scotland*, Edinburgh 1995.

Brown, Patterson, 'Infinite Causal Regression,' in Anthony Kenny (ed.), *Aquinas. A Collection of Critical Essays*, London 1970, 214–236.

Brown, Stephen F., 'Robert Cowton, O.F.M. and the Analogy of the Concept of Being,' *Franciscan Studies* 31 (1971) 5–40.

Brown, Stephen F., 'Matthew of Aquasparta (c.1238–1302),' *REP* VI (1998) 201–203.

Brunn, E. Zum, Z. Kaluza, and A. de Libera, *Maître Eckhart à Paris. Une critique médiévale de l'ontothéologie. Études, textes et introductions*, Paris 1984.

Burr, D., 'Petrus Ioannis Olivi and the Philosophers,' *Franciscan Studies* 31 (1971) 41–71.

Burr, D., *The Persecution of Olivi*, Philadelphia 1976.

Buytaert, Eligius M. (ed.), *Philotheus Boehner O.F.M. Ph.D. Collected Articles on Ockham*, St Bonaventure 1958.

Callebaut, André, 'La patrie du B. Jean Duns Scot,' *AFH* 10 (1917) 3–16.

Callebaut, André, 'L'Écosse: Patrie du Bienheureux Jean Duns Scot,' *AFH* 13 (1920) 78–88.

Callebaut, André, 'Le B. Jean Duns Scot étudiant à Paris vers 1293–1296,' *AFH* 17 (1924) 3–12.

Callebaut, André, 'Le Bx Jean Duns Scot. Bachelier des *Sentences* à Paris en 1302–3,' *La France franciscaine* 9 (1926) 293–317.

Callebaut, André, 'La maîtrise du Bx. Jean Duns Scot en 1305; son départ de Paris en 1307 durant la préparation du procès contre les Templiers,' *AFH* 21 (1928) 206–239.

Callebaut, André, 'Le Bx. Jean Duns Scot à Cambridge vers 1297–1300,' *AFH* 21 (1928) 611.

Callebaut, André, 'Les séjours du B. Jean Duns Scot à Paris,' *La France franciscaine* 12 (1929) 353–373.

Callebaut, André, 'A propos du Bx. Jean Duns Scotus de Littledean. Notes et recherches historiques de 1265 à 1292,' *AFH* 24 (1931) 305–329.

Capkun-Delic, P., 'Commissio omnibus Operibus Ioannis Duns Scoti critice edendis,' *De doctrina Ioannis Duns Scoti* I (1968) 361–373.

Carmody, F. J. (ed.), *Alpetragius. De motibus caelorum*, Berkeley, CA 1952.

Carreras y Artau, J., *Ensayo sobre el voluntarismo de J. D. Scot*, Gerona 1923.

Catto, J. I. (ed.), *The History of the University of Oxford* I: *The Early Oxford Schools*, Oxford ²1986 (¹1984).

Catto, J. I., 'Theology and theologians 1220–1320,' in Catto (ed.) (²1986) op. cit., 471–517.

Chadwick, Henry, 'Christian doctrine,' in J. H. Burns (ed.), *The Cambridge History of Medieval Political Thought c.350–c.1450*, Cambridge 1988, 11–20.

Cheneval, Fr., Th. Ricklin, Cl. Pottier, Silvia Maspoli, and Marianne Mösch (eds), *Ruedi Imbach. Quodlibeta. Ausgewählte Artikel/Articles choisis*, Fribourg 1996.

Chenu, M. -D., 'Les "Philosophes" dans la philosophie chrétienne médiévale,' *Revue des sciences philosophiques et théologiques* 26 (1957) 27–40.

Chihara, Charles S., *The Worlds of Possibility. Modal Realism and the Semantics of Modal Logic*, Oxford 1998.

Chisholm, Roderick M., *Theory of Knowledge*, Englewood Cliffs, NJ ²1977 (¹1966).

Chisholm, Roderick M., *Person and Object. A Metaphysical Study*, London 1976.

Chisholm, Roderick M., *The Foundations of Knowing*, Brighton 1982.

Clagett, Marshall, *The Science of Mechanics in the Middle Ages*, Madison, WI 1961.

Clagett, Marshall, 'Some General Aspects of Physics in the Middle Ages' (1948), in *Studies in Medieval Physics and Mathematics*, London 1979, chapter I.

Clagett, Marshall, 'Richard Swineshead and Late Medieval Physics. The Intension and Remission of Qualities' (1950), in *Studies in Medieval Physics and Mathematics*, London 1979, chapter III.

Clagett, Marshall, *Studies in Medieval Physics and Mathematics*, London 1979.

Clark, Andrew (ed.), *Survey of the Antiquities of the City of Oxford composed in 1661–6, by Anthony Wood*, Oxford 1890.

Cobban, Alan B., *The Medieval Universities: Their Development and Their Organization*, London 1975.

Cobban, Alan B., *The Medieval English Universities: Oxford and Cambridge to c.1500*, Aldershot 1988.

Copi, Irving M., *Symbolic Logic*, London ⁵1979.

Copleston, Frederick C., *A History of Philosophy* II. *Augustine to Scotus*, London 1950.

Coreth, Emerich, Walter M. Neidl, and Georg Pfligersdorfer (eds), *Christliche Philosophie im katholischen Denken des 19. und 20. Jahrhunderts* I–III, Vienna 1987–90.

Courtenay, William J., *Adam of Wodeham. An Introduction to his Life and Writings,* Leiden 1978.

Courtenay, William J., 'The dialectic of omnipotence,' in T. Rudavsky (ed.), *Divine Omniscience and Omnipotence in Medieval Philosophy,* Dordrecht 1985, 243–269.

Courtenay, William J., *Schools and Scholars in Fourteenth-Century England,* Princeton, NJ 1987.

Courtenay, William J., 'Programs of Study and Genres of Scholastic Theological Production in the Fourteenth Century,' in Hamesse (ed.) (1994) op. cit., 331–336.

Courtenay, William J., 'The Parisian Franciscan Community in 1303,' *Franciscan Studies* 53 (1993) 155–173.

Courtenay, William J., 'Scotus at Paris,' in Sileo (ed.), *Via Scoti* I (1995), 149–163.

Courtenay, William J., 'Between Pope and King. The Parisian Letters of Adhesion of 1303,' *Speculum* 71 (1996) 577–605.

Courtenay, William J., 'The Instructional Programme of the Mendicant Convents at Paris in the Early Fourteenth Century,' in Biller and Dobson (eds) (1999) op. cit., 77–92.

Courtenay, William J., 'Study Abroad: German Students at Bologna, Paris, and Oxford in the fourteenth Century,' in William J. Courtenay and Jürgen Miethke (eds), *Universities and Schooling in Medieval Society,* Leiden 2000, 7–31.

Craig, William Lane, *The Cosmological Argument from Plato to Leibniz,* London 1980.

Craig, William Lane, *The Problem of Divine Foreknowledge and Future Contingents from Aristotle to Suarez,* Leiden 1988.

Crombie, A. C., *Robert Grosseteste and the Origins of Experimental Science 1100–1700,* Oxford 1953.

Cross, Richard, *The Physics of Duns Scotus. The Scientific Context of a Theological Vision,* Oxford 1998.

Cross, Richard, *Duns Scotus,* Oxford 1999.

Cross, Richard, ' "Where Angels Fear to Tread": Duns Scotus and Radical Orthodoxy,' *Antonianum* 76 (2001) 7–41.

Cross, Richard, *The Metaphysics of the Incarnation. Thomas Aquinas to Duns Scotus,* Oxford 2002.

Cunningham, F., 'The "Real Distinction" in John Quidort,' *Journal of the History of Philosophy* 8 (1970) 9–28.

Dahlstrom, D. O., 'Signification and Logic: Scotus on Universals from a Logical Point of View,' *Vivarium* 18 (1980) 81–111.

Daniels, A., *Quellenbeiträge und Untersuchungen zur Geschichte der Gottesbeweise im dreizehnten Jahrhundert. Beiträge zur Geschichte der Philosophie des Mittelalters* VIII 1–2, Munster 1909.

Danhof, Ralph John, *Charles Hodge as a Dogmatician,* Goes 1929.

Day, John, *Intuitive Cognition a Key to the Significance of the Later Scholastics,* St Bonaventure, NY 1947.

Dekker, Eef and Henri Veldhuis, 'Freedom and Sin. Some Systematic Observations,' *European Journal of Theology* 3 (1994) 153–161.

Delorme, Ferdinand -M., 'Autour d'un apocryphe scotiste: Le *De rerum principio* et Godefroy de Fontaines,' *La France franciscaine* 8 (1925) 279–295.

Delorme, Ferdinand -M., 'L'oeuvre scolastique de maître Vital du Four d'après le *Ms.* 95 de Todi,' *La France franciscaine* 9 (1926) 421–471.

Delorme, Ferdinand -M., 'Le Cardinal Vital du Four. Huit questions disputées sur le problème de la connaissance,' *Archives d'histoire doctrinale et littéraire du moyen âge* 2 (1927) 151–337.

Delorme, Ferdinand -M., *Vitalis de Furno SRE. Card. Quodlibeta tria*, Rome 1947.

Denifle, H. and A. Chatelain, *Chartularium Universitatis Parisiensis* II 1, Paris 1891.

Denifle, H. and Fr. Ehrle, *Archiv für Litteratur- und Kirchengeschichte des Mittelalters* VI, Berlin 1892.

Denifle, H. and A. Chatelain, *Auctuarium chartularii Universitatis Parisiensis* I, Paris 1894.

Dermott, A. C. S., 'Note on the Assertoric and Modal Propositional Logic of the Pseudo-Scotus,' *Journal of the History of Philosophy* 10 (1972) 273–306.

Derrett, J. Duncan M., 'The Parable of the Profitable Servant (Luke XVII.7–10),' *Studies in the New Testament* IV, Leiden 1986, 157–166.

Distelbrink, B., *Bonaventurae scripta*, Rome 1975.

Docherty, Henry, 'The Brockie Forgeries,' *The Innes Review* 16 (1965) 79–129.

Docherty, Henry, 'The Brockie Mss. and Duns Scotus,' *De doctrina Ioannis Duns Scoti* I (1968) 327–360.

Doucet, Victorin, 'L'oeuvre scolastique de Richard de Conington O.F.M.,' *AFH* 29 (1936) 396–442.

Doucet, Victorin, *De editione Operum omnium Ioannis Duns Scoti*, Ad Claras Aquas 1937.

Doyle, Eric, 'Duns Scotus and Ecumenism: Duns Scotus and the Dignity of the Individual,' *De doctrina Ioannis Duns Scoti* III (1968) 633–652.

Dronke, Peter (ed.), *A History of Twelfth-Century Philosophy*, Cambridge 1988.

Duhem, Pierre, 'Sur les Meteorologicorum libri quattuor, faussement attribués à Jean Duns Scot,' *AFH* 3 (1910) 626–632.

Dumont, Stephen D., 'The Necessary Connection of Prudence to the Moral Virtues According to John Duns Scotus – Revisited,' *Recherches de théologie ancienne et médiévale* 55 (1988) 184–206.

Dumont, Stephen D., 'The Origin of Scotus's Synchronic Contingency,' *The Modern Schoolman* 72 (1995) 149–167.

Dumont, Stephen D., 'The Question on Individuation in Scotus' *Quaestiones super Metaphysicam*,' in Sileo (ed.), *Via Scoti* I (1995) 193–227.

Dumont, Stephen D., 'William of Ware, Richard of Conington and the *Collationes Oxonienses* of John Duns Scotus,' in Honnefelder et al. (eds) (1996) op. cit., 59–85.

Dumont, Stephen D., 'John Duns Scotus (c. 1266–1308),' *REP* III (1998) 153–170.

Ebbesen, Sten, *Incertorum auctorum Quaestiones super Sophisticos Elenchos*, Copenhagen 1977.

Ebbesen, Sten, 'Ancient Scholastic Logic as the Source of Medieval Scholastic Logic,' *CHLMP* (1982) 101–127.

Ebbesen, Sten, 'Doing Philosophy the Sophismatic Way. The Copenhagen School, with Notes on the Dutch School,' in Imbach and Maierù (eds) (1991) op. cit.

Ebbesen, Sten and Russell L. Friedman (eds), *Medieval Analyses in Language and Cognition*, Copenhagen 1999.

Eco, Umberto, 'Denotation,' in Eco and Marmo (eds) (1989) op. cit., 43–77.

Eco, Umberto and Costantino Marmo (eds), *On the Medieval Theory of Signs*, Amsterdam/Philadelphia 1989.

Effler, R., *John Duns Scotus and the Principle 'Omne quod movetur ab alio movetur'*, St Bonaventure, NY 1962.

Ehrle, Franz, *Der Sentenzenkommentar Peters von Candia, des Pisaners Papstes Alexanders V. Ein Beitrag zur Scheidung der Schulen in der Scholastik des vierzehnten Jahrhunderts und zur Geschichte des Wegestreites*, Munster 1925.

Eijnden, J. G. J. van den, *Poverty on the Way to God. Thomas Aquinas on Evangelical Poverty*, Louvain 1994.

Emden, A. B., *A Biographical Register of the University of Oxford to A.D. 1500 I*, Oxford 1957.

Emden, A. B., *A Biographical Register of the University of Oxford to A.D. 1500 III*, Oxford 1959.

Endres, J. A., *Petrus Damiani und die weltliche Wissenschaft*, Munster 1910.

Endres, J. A., *Forschungen zur Geschichte der frühmittelalterlichen Philosophie*, Munster 1915.

Ermatinger, Charles J., 'John of Tytynsale (d. ca.1289) as the Pseudo-Scotus of the Questions on *Metaphysics* X and XII,' *Manuscripta* 23 (1979) 7 ff.

Esser, Dietrich, 'Das Grab des seligen Johannes Duns Scotus in Köln,' in Dietrich Esser and Gioacchino D'Andrea (eds), *Johannes Duns Scotus. Untersuchungen zu seiner Verehrung*, Mönchengladbach 1986, 165–204.

Esser, Dietrich, *Johannes Duns Scotus. Leben, Gestalt und Verehrung*, Mönchengladbach 2000.

Estermann, Josef, *Individualität und Kontingenz. Studie zur Individualitätsproblematik bei Gottfried Wilhelm Leibniz*, Bern 1990.

Etzkorn, G. J., 'Roger Marston,' *EP* V (1967) 168 f.

Etzkorn, G. J., 'John Peckham,' *EP* VI (1967) 69 f.

Etzkorn, G. J. and I. C. Brady (eds), *Fr. Rogeri Marston O.F.M. Quodlibeta Quatuor*, Grottaferrata ²1994.

Etzkorn, G. J., 'Review of L.M. de Rijk, *Nicholas of Autrecourt*, Leiden 1994,' *Franciscan Studies* 56 (1998) 367–370.

Fanna, Fedele Maddalena da, *Ratio novae collectionis omnium operum sive editorum sive anecdotorum Seraphici Ecclesiae Doctoris S. Bonaventurae proxime in lucem edendae manuscriptorum bibliothecis totius Europae perlustratis*, Madrid 1874.

Felici, Angelus Cardinal, *Decretum* of Duns' Beatification by the *Congregatio de Causis Sanctorum*, in *Opera Omnia* XIX, Rome 1993, IX–XII.

Ferchio, Matteo, *Discussiones Scoticae*, Padua 1638.

Ferguson, Sinclair B. and David F. Wright (eds), *New Dictionary of Theology*, Leicester/Downers Grove, IL 1988.

Finnis, John (ed.), *Natural Law* I–II, Aldershot/New York 1991.

Finnis, John, 'Natural Law,' *REP* VI (1998) 685–690.

Fischer, H., *Meister Eckhart*, Fribourg-Munich 1972.

Fleig, P., 'Um die Echtheit von Duns Scotus' *De Anima*,' *FS* 16 (1929) 236–242.

Frank, William A., *John Duns Scotus' Quodlibetal Teaching on the Will*, Washington, QC 1982.

Frank, William A. and Girard J. Etzkorn (eds), *Essays Honoring Allan B. Wolter*, St Bonaventure, NY 1985.

Frank, William A. and A. B. Wolter, *Duns Scotus. Metaphysician*, West Lafayette, IN 1995.

Freitas, Emmanuel, 'De argumentatione Duns Scoti pro infinitate Dei,' *De doctrina Ioannis Duns Scoti* II (1968) 427–434.

Gál, G., 'De I. Duns Scoti "Theorematum" authenticitate ex ultima parte confirmata,' *Collectanea Franciscana* 20 (1950) 5–50.

Gál, G., 'Gonsalvus Hispanus,' *New Catholic Encyclopedia* VI, New York 1967, 608–609.

Gardener, W. H. (ed.), *Poems of Gerard Manley Hopkins*, London ³1948, 84 – sonnet 44: 'Duns Scotus's Oxford.'

Gauthier, R.-A., 'Trois commentaires "averroïstes" sur *l'Éthique à Nicomaque*,' *Archives d'histoire doctrinale et littéraire du Moyen Age* 16 (1947–48) 187–336.

Gauthier, R. -A. and J. Jolif, *Aristote. L'Éthique à Nicomaque* I–II, Louvain/Paris 1970.

Geach, Peter T., 'Aquinas,' in Anscombe and Geach (1973) op. cit., 65–125.

Gilson, Étienne, *La liberté chez Descartes et la théologie*, Paris 1913.

Gilson, Étienne, *La philosophie au moyen âge* II, Paris 1922.

Gilson, Étienne, *The Spirit of Medieval Philosophy*, New York 1936.

Gilson, Étienne, *The Philosophy of St. Bonaventure*, Paterson ²1965 (¹1943).

Gilson, Étienne, *Jean Duns Scot. Introduction à ses positions fondamentales*, Paris 1952.

Gilson, Étienne, *History of Christian Philosophy in the Middle Ages*, London 1955.

Glorieux, Palémon, *Répertoire des maîtres en théologie de Paris au XIIIᵉ siècle* II, Paris 1933.

Glorieux, Palémon, *La littérature quodlibétique de 1260 à 1320* I, Paris 1925, and II, Paris 1935.

Glorieux, Palémon, 'Pour en finir avec le *De rerum principio*,' *AFH* 31 (1938) 225–234.

Glorieux, Palémon, 'Notations brèves sur Godefroid de Fontaines,' *Recherches de théologie ancienne et médiévale* 11 (1939) 168–173.

Glorieux, Palémon, 'Où en est la question de quolibet?,' *Revue du moyen âge latin* 2 (1946) 411 ff.

Glorieux, Palémon (ed.), *Jacques de Thérines. Quodlibets I et II. Jean le Sage. Quodlibet I*, Paris 1958.

Gölz, B., 'Die echten und unechten Werke des Duns Scotus nach dem gegenwärtigen Stand der Forschung,' in *Sechste und siebte Lektorenkonferenz*, Werl 1934, 53–60.

González, C., *Historia de la filosofía* II, Madrid 1886.

Goorbergh, Edith A. van den and Theo H. Zweerman, *Light shining through a veil. On Saint Clare's Letters to Saint Agnes of Prague*, Louvain 2000.

Goorbergh, Edith A. Van den and Theo H. Zweerman, *Yours Respectfully. Signed and Sealed: Saint Francis*, St Bonaventure, NY 2001.

Grabmann, Martin, *Geschichte der scholastischen Methode* I, Graz ²1957 (volume I: Freiburg im Breisgau ¹1909).

Grabmann, Martin, 'De Thoma Erfordiensi auctore *Grammaticae* quae Ioanni Duns Scoto adscribitur *speculativae*,' *AFH* 15 (1922) 273–277.

Grabmann, Martin, 'Die Entwicklung der mittelalterlichen Sprachlogik IV: Die *Tractatus de modis significandi*,' *Philosophisches Jahrbuch* 35 (1922) 132–135 and 199–202; also in *Mittelalterliches Geistesleben. Abhandlungen zur Geschichte der Scholastik und Mystik* I, Hildesheim ²1975 (Munich ¹1926), 104–146.

Grabmann, Martin, 'Das Bonaventurakolleg zu Quaracchi in seiner Bedeutung für die Methode der Erforschung der mittelalterlichen Scholastik,' *Franziskanische Studien. Festnummer zur Hundertjahrfeier des P. Ignatius Jeiler 1823–1923*, Munster 1923, 62–78 (= Grabmann, *Mittelalterliches Geistesleben* I, Hildesheim ²1975 (= ¹1926) 50–64).

Gracia, Jorge J. E., *Introduction to the Problem of Individuation in the Early Middle Ages*, Munich ²1984.

Gracia, Jorge J. E. (ed.), *Individuation in Scholasticism. The Later Middle Ages and the Counter-Reformation 1150–1650*, Albany, NY 1994.

Grajewski, M. J., *The Formal Distinction of Duns Scotus. A Study in Metaphysics*, Washington, DC 1944.

Grant, Edward, *Physical Science in the Middle Ages*, New York/London 1971.

Green, Romuald, *An Introduction to the Logical Treatise 'De Obligationibus,' with Critical Texts of William of Sherwood (?) and Walter Burley* I–II, Louvain 1963.

Green-Pedersen, Niels J., *The Tradition of Topics in the Middle Ages*, Munich 1984.

Guthrie, W. K. C., 'The Development of Aristotle's Theology,' *Classical Quarterly* 27 (1933) 162–171, and *Classical Quarterly* 28 (1934) 90–99.

Guthrie, W. K. C., *A History of Greek Philosophy* I: *The Earlier Presocratics and the Pythagoreans*, Cambridge 1962.

Guthrie, W. K. C., *History of Greek Philosophy* II: *The Presocratic Tradition from Parmenides to Democritus*, Cambridge 1965.

Guthrie, W. K. C., *A History of Greek Philosophy* VI. *Aristotle. An Encounter*, Cambridge 1981.

Hamesse, Jacqueline, ' "Collatio" et "reportatio": deux vocables spécifiques de la vie intellectuelle au moyen âge,' in Olga Weijers (ed.), *Terminologie de la vie intellectuelle au moyen âge*, Turnhout 1988, 78–82.

Hamesse, Jacqueline (ed.), *Manuels, programmes de cours et techniques d'enseignement dans les universités médiévales*, Louvain-la-Neuve 1994.

Hamesse, Jacqueline, 'New Perspectives for Critical Editions of Franciscan Texts of the Middle Ages,' *Franciscan Studies* 56 (1998) 169–187.

Harris, C. R. S., *Duns Scotus* I–II, Oxford 1927.

Hart, H. L. A., *The Concept of Law*, Oxford 1961.

Hartshorne, Charles, and Paul Weiss (eds), *The Collected Papers of Charles Sanders Peirce* I, Cambridge, MA 1931.

Hauréau, Jean-Barthélémy, *Histoire de la philosophie scolastique* I–III, Paris 1872–80.

Hedwig, Klaus, 'Das Isaak-Opfer. Über den Status des Naturgesetzes bei Thomas von Aquin, Duns Scotus und Ockham,' *Miscellanea Mediaevalia 21/2. Mensch und Natur im Mittelalter*, 645–661.

Heidegger, Martin, *Die Kategorien- und Bedeutungslehre des Duns Scotus*, Tübingen 1916.

Helm, Paul, 'Synchronic Contingency in Reformed Scholasticism. A Note of Caution,' *Nederlands Theologisch Tijdschrift* 57 (2003) 207–222.

Hempel, Carl G., *Philosophy of Natural Science*, Englewood Cliffs, NJ 1966.

Henninger, Mark G., *Relations. Medieval Theories 1250–1325*, Oxford 1989.

Henry, Desmond Paul, *The Logic of St. Anselm*, Oxford 1967.

Henry, Desmond Paul, 'Predicables and Categories,' *CHLMP* (1982) 128–142.

Hintikka, Jaakko, 'Necessity, Universality, and Time in Aristotle,' *Ajatus* 20 (1957) 65–90.

Hintikka, Jaakko, *Knowledge and Belief. An Introduction into the Logic of the Two Notions*, Ithaca, NY 1962.

Hintikka, Kaakko, 'A.O. Lovejoy on Plenitude in Aristotle,' *Ajatus* 29 (1967) 5–11.

Hintikka, Jaakko, *Time and Necessity. Studies in Aristotle's Theory of Modality*, Oxford 1973.

Hintikka, Jaakko, Unto Remes, and Simo Knuuttila, 'Aristotle on Modality and Determinism,' *Acta Philosophica Fennica* 29, Amsterdam 1975.

Hodge, Charles, *Systematic Theology* I–III, Grand Rapids, MI ²1977.

Hoenen, Maarten J. F. M., *Marsilius van Inghen* (†1396) *over het goddelijke weten* I–II, Nijmegen 1989.

Hoenen, Maarten J. F. M., *Marsilius of Inghen. Divine Knowledge in Late Medieval Thought*, Leiden 1993.

Hoenen, Maarten J. F. M. 'Scotus and the Scotist School. The Tradition of Scotist Thought in the Medieval and Early Modern Period,' in Bos (ed.) (1998) op. cit., 197–210.

Hoenen, Maarten J. F. M., J. H. J. Schneider, and G. Wieland (eds), *Philosophy and Learning. Universities in the Middle Ages*, Leiden 1995.

Hoffmann, Tobias, *Creatura intellecta*, Munster 2002.

Holopainen, Toivo J., *Dialectic and Theology in the Eleventh Century*, Leiden 1996.

Honnefelder, Ludger, *Ens inquantum ens. Der Begriff des Seienden als solchen als Gegenstand der Metaphysik nach der Lehre des Johannes Duns Scotus*, Munster 1979.

Honnefelder, Ludger, *Scientia transcendens. Die formale Bestimmung der Seiendheit und Realität in der Metaphysik des Mittelalters und der Neuzeit*, Hamburg 1990.

Honnefelder, Ludger, Rega Wood, and Mechthild Dreyer (eds), *John Duns Scotus. Metaphysics and Ethics*, Leiden 1996.

Hooykaas, Reijer, *Religion and the Rise of Modern Science*, Edinburgh ²1973 (¹1972).

Hooykaas, Reijer, *Geschiedenis der Natuurwetenschappen. Van Babel tot Bohr*, Utrecht ⁴1983.

Hooykaas, Reijer, *G. J. Rheticus' Treatise on Holy Scripture and the Motion of the Earth*, Amsterdam 1984.

Hughes, Christopher, *On a Complex Theory of a Simple God. An Investigation in Aquinas' Philosophical Theology*, Ithaca, NY 1989.

Hughes, G. E. and M. J. Cresswell, *A New Introduction to Modal Logic*, London 1996.

Huning, Hildebert Alois, 'Petrus de Trabibus: ein Vorläufer des Johannes Duns Scotus in der Lehre vom Formalunterschied,' *De doctrina Ioannis Duns Scoti* I (1968) 285–295.

Imbach, Ruedi and Alfonso Maierù (eds), *Gli studi di filosofia medievale fra otto e novecento*, Rome 1991.

Imbach, Ruedi and François-Xavier Putallaz, *Duns Scot. Traité du premier principe*, Paris 2001.

Immink, F. Gerrit, *Divine Simplicity*, Kampen 1987.

Ingham, Mary Elizabeth, *Ethics and Freedom. An Historical-Critical Investigation of Scotist Ethical Thought*, Lanham/New York 1989.

Ingham, Mary Elizabeth, *The Harmony of Goodness*, Quincy, IL 1996.

Inglis, John, *Spheres of Philosophical Inquiry and the Historiography of Medieval Philosophy*, Leiden 1998.

Innocenti, B., 'Il *De perfectione statuum* del B. Giovanni Duns Scoto (Saggio storic-ocritico),' *Luce e amore* 6 (1909) 498–508.

Ishiguro, Hidé, *Leibniz's Philosophy of Logic and Language*, London 1972.

Jacobi, Klaus, 'Logic II: the later twelfth century,' in Peter Dronke (ed.), *A History of Twelfth-Century Philosophy*, Cambridge 1988, 227–251.

Jacobi, Klaus (ed.), *Argumentationstheorie. Scholastische Forschungen zu den logischen und semantischen Regeln korrekten Folgerns*, Leiden 1993.

Jammer, M., 'Motion,' *EP* V (1967) 396–399.

Jansen, B., 'Beiträge zur geschichtlichen Entwicklung der *Distinctio formalis*,' *Zeitschrift für Katholische Theologie* 53 (1929) 317–344 and 517–544.

Jolivet, Jean, 'Les études de philosophie médiévale en France de Victor Cousin à Étienne Gilson,' in Imbach and Maierù (eds) (1991) op. cit., 1–20.

Kemp Smith, Norman, *I. Kant. Critique of Pure Reason*, London 1953.

Kent, Bonnie, *Virtues of the Will. The Transformation of Ethics in the Late Thirteenth Century*, Washington, DC 1995.

Kent, Bonnie, 'Rethinking Moral Dispositions: Scotus on the Virtues,' in Thomas Williams (ed.), *The Cambridge Companion to Duns Scotus*, Cambridge 2003, 352–376.

Kestell Floyer, J., *Catalogue of mss preserved in the Chapter Library of Worcester Cathedral*, Oxford 1906.

King, Peter, 'Scotus on Metaphysics,' in Thomas Williams (ed.), *The Cambridge Companion to Duns Scotus*, Cambridge 2003, 15–68.

Kirby, Gerald J., 'The Authenticity of the *De perfectione statuum* of Duns Scotus,' *The New Scholasticism* 7 (1933) 134–152.

Kirschner, Stefan, 'Oresme on Intension and Remission of Qualities in His Commentary on Aristotle's *Physics*,' *Vivarium* 38 (2000) 255–274.

Klibansky, R., *Commentarium de Eckardi magisterio. Magistri Eckardi Opera Latina* XIII, Leipzig 1936.

Kluxen, Wolfgang, 'Bedeutung und Funktion der Allgemeinbegriffe in thomistischem und scotischem Denken,' *De doctrina Ioannis Duns Scoti* II (1968) 229–240.

Kluxen, Wolfgang, *Johannes Duns Scotus. Abhandlung über das Erste Prinzip*, Darmstadt 1974.

Kneale, William and Martha, *The Development of Logic*, Oxford ²1968 (¹1962).

Knijff, H.W. de, *Tussen woning en woestijn. Milieuzorg als aspect van christelijke cultuur (On Environmental Ethics)*, Kampen 1995.

Knowles, David, *The Religious Orders in England* I, Cambridge 1948.

Knudsen, Christian, 'Intentions and impositions,' *CHLMP* (1982) 479–495.

Knuuttila, Simo, *Aika ja modaliteetti aristotelisessa skolastiikassa*, Helsinki 1975.

Knuuttila, Simo, 'The Statistical Interpretation of Modality in Averroes and Thomas Aquinas,' *Ajatus* 37 (1978) 79–98.

Knuuttila, Simo, 'Scotus' Criticism of the "Statistical" Interpretation of Modality,' in Beckmann et al. (eds) (1981) op. cit., 441–450.

Knuuttila, Simo (ed.), *Reforging the Great Chain of Being. Studies of the History of Modal Theories*, Dordrecht/Boston 1981.

Knuuttila, Simo, 'Time and Modality in Scholasticism,' in Knuuttila (ed.) (1981) op. cit., 163–257.

Knuuttila, Simo, 'Modal Logic,' *CHLMP* (1982) 342–357.

Knuuttila, Simo, *Modalities in Medieval Philosophy*, London/New York 1993.

Kraml, H., 'Beobachtungen zum Ursprung der *"distinctio formalis"*,' in Sileo (ed.), *Via Scoti* I (1995) 305–318.

Kraus, Johannes, *Die Lehre des Johannes Duns Scotus von der natura communis*, Freiburg 1927.

Krebs, Engelbert, *Studien über Meister Dietrich. Genannt von Freiburg*, Freiburg i. Br. 1903.

Krebs, Engelbert, *Meister Dietrich*, Munster 1906.

Kretzmann, Norman, 'History of Semantics,' *EP* VII (1967) 358–406.

Kretzmann, Norman (ed.), *Meaning and Inference in Medieval Philosophy*, Dordrecht 1988.

Kretzmann, Norman, Anthony Kenny, and Jan Pinborg (eds), *The Cambridge History of Later Medieval Philosophy*, Cambridge 1982.

Krop, Henri A., *De status van de theologie volgens Johannes Duns Scotus. De verhouding tussen theologie en metafysica*, Amsterdam 1987.

Lagerlund, Henrik, *Modal Syllogistics in the Middle Ages*, Leiden 2000.

Langston, D. C., *God's Willing Knowledge. The Influence of Scotus' Analysis of Omniscience*, University Park, PA/London 1986.

Lauriola, Giovanni, *Giovanni Duns Scoto. Antologia*, Alberobello 1996.

Leader, D. R., *A History of the University of Cambridge*, Cambridge 1988.

Leclercq, Jean, François Vandenbroucke, and Louis Bouyer, *A History of Christian Spirituality* II: *The Spirituality of the Middle Ages*, London and Tunbridge Wells ²1982.

Lecq, Ria van der, 'Duns Scotus on the Reality of Possible Worlds,' in Bos (ed.) (1998) op. cit., 89–99.

Leff, Gordon, *Paris and Oxford Universities in the Thirteenth and Fourteenth Centuries. An Institutional and Intellectual History*, New York ²1975 (¹1968).

Leijenhorst, Cees, Christoph Lüthy, and Johannes M. M. H. Thijssen (eds), *The Dynamics of Aristotelian Natural Philosophy from Antiquity to the Seventeenth Century*, Leiden 2002.

Lemmon, Edward J., *Beginning Logic*, London 1965.

Lewry, Osmund, 'The Oxford Condemnations of 1277 in Grammar and Logic,' in Braakhuis and De Rijk (eds) (1981) op. cit., 235–278.

Libera, Alain de, 'The Oxford and Paris Traditions in Logic,' *CHLMP* (1982) 174–187.

Libera, Alain de, 'Les "Raisons d'Eckhart",' in Brunn et al. (1984) op. cit., 109–140.

Libera, Alain de, 'Les études de philosophie médiévale en France d'Étienne Gilson à nos jours,' in Imbach and Maierù (eds) (1991) op. cit., 21–50.

Little, Andrew G., *The Grey Friars in Oxford*, Oxford 1892.

Little, Andrew G., 'Chronological Notes on the Life of Duns Scotus,' *English Historical Review* 47 (1932) 568–582.

Little, Andrew G., *Franciscan Papers, Lists, and Documents*, Manchester 1943.

Little, Andrew G., 'The Franciscan School at Oxford,' in Little (1943) op. cit., 55–71.

Little, Andrew G., 'Documents I. Licence to hear confessions under the Bull *Super cathedram*,' in Little (1943) op. cit., 230–243 and 262.

Little, Andrew G., 'The Friars and the Foundation of the Faculty of Theology in the University of Cambridge,' in Little (1943) op. cit., 131–138.

Little, Andrew G. and F. Pelster, *Oxford Theology and Theologians c. A.D. 1282–1302*, Oxford 1934.

Livesey, Steven J., '*De viris illustribus et mediocribus:* A Biographical Database of Franciscan Commentators on Aristotle and Peter Lombard's *Sentences,*' *Franciscan Studies* 56 (1998) 201–237.

Lobato, Abelardo, 'La metafísica cristiana de Duns Escoto,' *De doctrina Ioannis Duns Scoti* II (1968) 76–80.

Locke, John, *An Essay concerning Human Understanding*, ed. Peter H. Nidditch, Oxford 1975.

Lohr, Charles, 'Medieval Latin Aristotle Commentaries: Authors Jacobus-Johannes Juff,' *Traditio* 26 (1970) 135–216.

Lohr, Charles, 'The Social Situation of the Study of Aristotelian Natural Philosophy in the Sixteenth and Early Seventeenth Centuries,' in Leijenhorst, Lüthy, and Thijssen (eds) (2002) op. cit., 343–348.

Longpré, Anselme, *Éphrem Longpré*, Richilieu 1974.

Longpré, Éphrem, 'Les *Conclusions métaphysiques* de Gonzalve de Balboa,' *La France franciscaine* 5 (1922) 432 f.

Longpré, Éphrem, 'Gauthier de Bruges O.F.M. et l'augustinisme franciscain au XIIIᵉ siècle,' *Miscellanea Francisco Ehrle* I, Rome 1924, 199–218.

Longpré, Éphrem, 'Gonzalve de Balboa et le B. Duns Scot. Nouveaux documents pour l'histoire du voluntarisme franciscain,' *Études Franciscaines* 36 (1924) 640–645.

Longpré, Éphrem, *La philosophie du B. Duns Scot*, Paris 1924.

Longpré, Éphrem, 'Le primat de la volonté. Question inédite de Gonzalve de Balboa, O.F.M.,' *Études Franciscaines* 37 (1925) 170–181.

Longpré, Éphrem, 'Pour la défense de Duns Scot,' *Rivista di filosofia neoscolastica* 18 (1926) 32–42.

Longpré, Éphrem, 'Le B. Jean Duns Scot. Pour le Saint Siège et contre le gallicanisme (25–28 juin 1303),' *La France franciscaine* 11 (1928) 137–162.

Longpré, Éphrem, *Quaestiones disputatae du B. Gauthier de Bruges*, Louvain 1928.

Longpré, Éphrem, 'L'ordination sacerdotale du Bx Jean Duns Scot. Document du 17 mars 1291,' *AFH* 22 (1929) 54–62.

Longpré, Éphrem, 'Nouveaux documents franciscains d'Écosse,' *AFH* 22 (1929) 588 f.

Longpré, Éphrem, 'Philippe de Bridlington, O.F.M. et le Bx Duns Scot,' *AFH* 22 (1929) 587–588.

Longpré, Éphrem, 'Duns Scot,' in *Catholicisme hier, aujourd'hui, demain* III, Paris 1952, 1174 ff.

Losee, John, *A Historical Introduction to the Philosophy of Science*, Oxford 1972.

Lottin, Odon, 'Une question quodlibétique inconnue de Godefroid de Fontaines,' *Revue d'Histoire Ecclésiastique* 30 (1934) 852–859.

Lottin, Odon, 'L' "Ordinatio" de Jean Duns Scot sur le livre III des *Sentences*,' *Recherches de théologie ancienne et médiévale* 20 (1953) 102–119.

Lottin, Odon, *Psychologie et morale aux XII et XIII siècles* IV, Louvain/Gembloux 1954.

MacIntyre, Alasdair, *A Short History of Ethics*, London ¹1966.

MacIntyre, Alasdair, *After Virtue. A Study in Moral Theory*, London 1981.

MacIntyre, Alasdair, *Whose Justice? Which Rationality?* London 1988.

MacIntyre, Alasdair, *Three Rival Versions of Moral Enquiry*, London 1990.

MacKay, Donald M., 'Religion and the New Mechanics,' *Symposium Hooykaas, Janus* 64 (1977) 119–129.

Mackay, Ewald, *Geschiedenis bij de bron. Een onderzoek naar de verhouding van christelijk geloof en historische werkelijkheid in geschiedwetenschap, wijsbegeerte en theologie*, Sliedrecht 1997.

McCord Adams, Marilyn, 'Universals in the Early Fourteenth Century,' *CHLMP* (1982) 411–439.

McCord Adams, Marilyn, *William Ockham* I–II, Notre Dame ²1989 (¹1987).

McCord Adams, Marilyn (ed.), *Allan B. Wolter, O.F.M. The Philosophical Theology of John Duns Scotus*, Ithaca, NY and London 1990.

McCord Adams, Marilyn, 'Scotus and Ockham on the Connection of the Virtues,' in Honnefelder et al. (eds) (1996) op. cit., 499–522.

McGrath, Alister E., *Christian Theology. An Introduction*, Oxford 1994.

McInerny, Ralph, 'Scotus and Univocity,' *De doctrina Ioannis Duns Scoti* II (1968) 115–121.

Mahoney, Edward P., 'Duns Scotus and the School of Padua around 1500,' *Regnum Hominis et Regnum Dei* II (1978) 215–219.

Maier, Anneliese, *Zwei Grundprobleme der scholastischen Naturphilosophie. Das Problem der intensiven Grösse. Die Impetustheorie*, Rome ³1968.

Mansfeld, Jaap, *Heraclitus. Fragmenten*, Amsterdam 1979.

Mansfeld, Jaap, 'De Centrale Interfaculteit,' in *De Utrechtse Universiteit 1936–1986. Tussen ivoren toren en grootbedrijf*, Maarssen 1986, 492–496.

Mansfeld, Jaap, *Studies in Later Greek Philosophy and Gnosticism*, London 1989.

Manzano, Guzmán Isidoro, 'Das An-sich-Sein der Freiheit nach J. D. Scotus (Ansätze zur Freiheitslehre des J. D. Scotus),' in Herbert Schneider (ed.), *Fons Salutis Trinitas – Quell des Heils Dreifaltigkeit*, Kevelaer 2002, 79–100.

Marenbon, John, *From the Circle of Alcuin to the School of Auxerre. Logic, Theology and Philosophy in the Early Middle Ages*, Cambridge 1981.

Marenbon, John, *Early Medieval Philosophy (480–1150). An Introduction*, London 1983.

Marenbon, John, *Later Medieval Philosophy (1150–1350)*, London ²1991 (¹1987).

Maritain, Jacques, 'De la notion de la philosophie chrétienne,' *Revue néoscolastique* 43 (1932) 153–186.

Maritain, Jacques, *De la philosophie chrétienne*, Paris 1933.

Marmo, Costantino, 'Ontology and Semantics in the Logic of Duns Scotus,' in Eco and Marmo (eds) (1989) op. cit., 143–193.

Marmo, Costantino, 'The Semantics of the Modistae,' in Ebbesen and Friedman (eds) (1999) op. cit., 83–104.

Marti de Barcelona, P., 'Fra Antoni Andreu, OFM, *"doctor dulcifluus"* (s. XIV),' *Criterion* 5 (1929) 321–346.

Marrone, Steven P., 'The Notion of Univocity in Duns Scotus's Early Works,' *Franciscan Studies* 43 (1983) 390 ff.

Marrone, Steven P., 'Duns Scotus on Metaphysical Potency and Possibility,' *Franciscan Studies* 56 (1998) 265–289.

Marrone, Steven P., 'Henry of Ghent (early 13th century–1293),' *REP* IV (1998) 354–360.

Maurer, Armand A., 'Esse and Essentia in the Metaphysics of Siger of Brabant,' *Mediaeval Studies* 8 (1946) 68–86.

Maurer, Armand A., 'Henry of Harclay (*c*.1270–1317),' *EP* III (1967) 476 f.

Maurer, Armand A., *Master Eckhart. Parisian Questions and Prologues. Translated with an Introduction and Notes*, Toronto 1974.

Maurer, Armand A., 'William of Ockham on Language and Reality,' in Albert Zimmermann (ed.), *Sprache und Erkenntnis im Mittelalter. Miscellanea Mediaevalia* II, Berlin and New York 1981, 797 ff.

Mavrodes, George, *Belief in God. A Study in the Epistemology of Religion*, New York 1970.

Meier, Ludger, 'Erfurter Schulen,' *Antonianum* 5 (1930) 57–94, 157–202, 333–362, and 443–474.

Meier, Ludger, 'Erfurter Franziskanerschule,' *Franziskanische Studien* 18 (1931) 109–150.

Merton, Thomas, 'Figures for an Apocalypse' (1947), in *The Collected Poems of Thomas Merton*, New York ¹1977, 133–193.

Messenger, Ernest C., *Maurice De Wulf. History of Mediaeval Philosophy* I (1935) and II (1937).

Minges, Parthenius, *Ist Duns Scotus Indeterminist?*, Munster 1905.

Minges, Parthenius, 'Die Skotistische Litteratur im XX. Jahrhundert,' *FS* 4 (1917) 49–67, 177–198.

Minges, Parthenius, *Joannis Duns Scoti doctrina philosophica et theologica*, Quaracchi 1930.

Modric, Luka, 'Rapporto tra la *Lectura* II e la Metaphysica di G. Duns Scoto,' *Antonianum* 62 (1987) 504–509.

Möhle, Hannes, *Ethik als scientia practica nach Johann Duns Scotus. Eine philosophische Grundlegung*, Munster 1995.

Molland, George, 'Henry of Harclay (*c*.1270–1317),' *REP* (1998) III 360–363.

Moody, Ernest A., 'William of Ockham,' *EP* (1967) VII 306–317 (= idem, 'William of Ockham,' in Lynn White (ed.) (1975) op. cit., 409–439).

Moody, Ernest A., 'Medieval Logic,' in *History of Logic, EP* IV (1967) 528–534.

Moorman, John R. H., *The Grey Friars in Cambridge. 1225–1538*, Cambridge 1952.

Moorman, John R. H., *A History of the Franciscan Order from Its Origins to the Year 1517*, Oxford 1968.

Müller, Marianus, 'Stand der Skotus-Forschung 1933. Nach Ephrem Longpré, O.F.M.,' *Wissenschaft und Weisheit* 1 (1934) 63–71.

Müller, Marianus, *Joannis Duns Scoti Tractatus de Primo Principio*, Freiburg i. Br. 1941.

Muller, Richard, 'The Problem of Protestant Scholasticism – A Review and Definition,' in Willem J. van Asselt and Eef Dekker (eds), *Reformation and Scholasticism. An Ecumenical Enterprise*, Grand Rapids, MI 2001, 45–64.

Noone, Timothy B., 'Scotus's Critique of the Thomistic Theory of Individuation and the Dating of the *Quaestiones super libros Metaphysicorum* VII q. 13,' in Sileo (ed.), *Via Scoti* I (1995) 391–406.

Noone, Timothy, B., 'Individuation in Scotus,' *American Catholic Philosophical Quarterly* 64 (1995) 527–542.

Noone, Timothy B., 'Appreciation of Girard J. Etzkorn,' *Franciscan Studies* 56 (1998) IX f.

Noone, Timothy B., 'Universals and Individiuation,' in Thomas Williams (ed.), *The Cambridge Companion to Duns Scotus*, Cambridge 2003, 100–128.

Normore, Calvin G., 'Future contingents,' *CHLMP* (1982) 358–381.

Normore, Calvin G., 'Who Was Condemned in 1277?,' *The Modern Schoolman* 77 (1995) 274 ff.

Normore, Calvin G., 'Scotus, Modality, Instants of Nature,' in Honnefelder et al. (eds) (1966) op. cit., 161–174.

Nuchelmans, Gabriël, *Theories of the Proposition. Ancient and Medieval Conceptions of the Bearers of Truth and Falsity*, Amsterdam 1973.

Nuchelmans, Gabriël, *Wijsbegeerte en Taal. Twaalf studies*, Meppel 1976.

Nuchelmans, Gabriël, *Late Scholastic and Humanist Theories of the Proposition*, Amsterdam 1980.

Nuchelmans, Gabriël, *Judgment and Proposition. From Descartes to Kant*, Amsterdam 1983.

O'Connor, D. J., 'Substance and Attribute,' *EP* (1967) VIII 36–40.

O'Connor, Edward D., 'The Scientific Character of Theology According to Scotus,' *De doctrina Ioannis Duns Scoti* III (1968) 3–50.

O'Connor, Timothy, 'Scotus's Argument for the Existence of a First Efficient Cause,' *International Journal for Philosophy of Religion* 33 (1993) 17–32.

O'Connor, Timothy, 'From First Efficient Cause to God: Scotus on the Identification Stage of the Cosmological Argument,' in Honnefelder et al. (eds) (1996) op. cit., 435–454.

Oliger, Livarius, 'P. Ignatius Jeiler in Quaracchi,' *Franziskanische Studien. Festnummer zur Hundertjahrfeier des P. Ignatius Jeiler 1823–1923*, Munster 1923, 50–61.

Parisoli, Luca, *La philosophie normative de Jean Duns Scot*, Rome 2001.

Pater, C. de, 'Petrus van Musschenbroek (1692–1761). A Dutch Newtonian,' *Symposium Hooykaas, Janus* 64 (1977) 77–87.

Pattin, Adrien and Émile Van de Vyver (eds), *Auguste Pelzer. Études d'histoire littéraire sur la scolastique médiévale*, Louvain and Paris 1964.

Pauli Papae VI, *Epistula Apostolica 'Alma Parens'* (1966), in *De doctrina Ioannis Duns Scoti* I (1968) 33–39.

Paulus, J., *Henri de Gand. Essai sur les tendances de sa métaphysique*, Paris 1938.

Pelster, Franz, 'Handschriftliches zu Skotus mit neuen Angaben über sein Leben,' *FS* 10 (1923) 1–32.

Pelster, Franz, 'Heinrich von Harclay, Kanzler von Oxford und seine Quästionen,' *Miscellanea Francisco Ehrle*, Rome 1924, 307–356.

Pelster, Franz, 'Duns Scotus nach englischen Handschriften,' *Zeitschrift für katholische Theologie* 51 (1927) 65–80.

Pelster, Franz, 'Roger Marston O.F.M., ein englischer Vertreter des Augustinismus,' *Scholastik* 3 (1928) 526–556.

Pelster, Franz, 'Zur Scotus-Forschung,' *Theologische Revue* 28 (1929) 145–152.

Pelster, Franz, 'Eine Münchener Handschrift des beginnenden vierzehnten Jahrhunderts mit einem Verzeichnis von Quaestionen des Duns Scotus und Herveus Natalis (*Cod. lat. Monac. 8717*),' *FS* 17 (1930) 253–272.

Pelster, Franz, 'Handschriftliches zur Überlieferung der *Quaestiones super libros Metaphysicorum* und der *Collationes* des Duns Scotus,' *Philosophisches Jahrbuch* 43 (1930) 474–487 and 44 (1931) 79–92.

Pelster, Franz, 'Review of C. Balic, "Die Frage der Authentizität und Ausgabe der Werke des I. Duns Skotus," *Wissenschaft und Weisheit* 2 (1935),' *Scholastik* 11 (1936) 133.

Pelster, Franz, 'Theologisch und philosophisch bedeutsame Quästionen des W. von Macclesfield O.P., H. von Harclay und anonymer Autoren der englischen Hochscholastik in *Cod. 501* Troyes,' *Scholastik* 28 (1953) 222–240.

Pelzer, Auguste, 'A propos de Jean Duns Scot et des études scotistes,' *Revue néoscolastique de philosophie* 25 (1923) 410–420; also in Pattin and Van de Vyver (eds) (1964) op. cit., 411–421.

Pelzer, Auguste, 'Le premier livre des *Reportata Parisiensia* de Jean Duns Scot,' *Annales de l'Institut Supérieur de Philosophie* 5 (1924) 447–492; also in Pattin and Van de Vyver (eds) (1964) op. cit., 422–467.

Pelzer, Auguste, 'Étude sur les manuscripts des Quodlibets de l'Italie et de la Cité du Vatican,' in Odon Lottin (ed.), Jean Hoffmans and Auguste Pelzer, *Le Quodlibet XV et trois Questions ordinaires de Godefroid de Fontaines. Étude sur les manuscripts des Quodlibets. Les Philosophes Belges* XIV, Louvain 1937, 231–244.

Perler, Dominik, 'Things in the Mind: Fourteenth-Century Controversies over "Intelligible Species," ' *Vivarium* 34 (1996) 231–253.

Perler, Dominik, 'Duns Scotus's Philosophy of Language,' in Thomas Williams (ed.), *The Cambridge Companion to Duns Scotus*, Cambridge 2003, 161–192.

Peters, W. A. M., *Duns Scotus. Het eerste beginsel*, Baarn 1985.

Pinborg, Jan, *Logik und Semantik im Mittelalter*, Stuttgart 1972.

Pinborg, Jan, 'The English Contribution to Logic before Ockham,' *Synthese* 40 (1974) 19–42.

Pinborg, Jan, 'Logik der Modistae' (1975), in Sten Ebbesen (ed.), *Jan Pinborg. Medieval Semantics*, London 1984, V 39–97.

Pines, Shlomo, 'Jewish Philosophy,' *EP* (1967) IV 261–277.

Pini, Giorgio, 'Una lettura scotista delle *Metafisica* di Aristotele: l'*Expositio in libros Metaphysicorum* di Antonio Andrea,' *Documenti e studi sulla tradizione filosofica medievale* II 2 (1991) 529–586.

Pini, Giorgio, 'Scotistic Aristotelianism: Antonius Andreas' *Expositio* and *Quaestiones* on the *Metaphysics*,' in Sileo (ed.), *Via Scoti* I (1995) 374–389.

Pini, Giorgio, 'Duns Scotus' Literal Commentary on the *Metaphysics* and the *Notabilia Scoti super Metaphysicam* (Milan, Biblioteca Ambrosiana, C 62 Sup., ff. 51r–98r),' *Bulletin de philosophie médiévale* 38 (1996) 141–142.

Pini, Giorgio, '*Notabilia Scoti super Metaphysicam*: una testimonianza ritrovato del'insegnamento di Duns Scoto sulla *Metafisica*,' *AFH* 89 (1996) 137–180.

Pini, Giorgio, 'Critical Study. Duns Scotus's *Metaphysics:* The Critical Edition of His *Quaestiones super libros Metaphysicorum Aristotelis*,' *Recherches de théologie et philosophie médiévales* 65 (1998) 353–368.

Pini, Giorgio, 'Duns Scotus' Commentary on the *Topics*: New Light on His Philosophical Teaching,' *Archives d'histoire doctrinale et littéraire du moyen âge* 66 (1999) 225–243.

Pinnock, Clark H., 'From Augustine to Arminius: A Pilgrimage in Theology,' in Clark H. Pinnock (ed.), *The Grace of God, the Will of Man. A Case for Arminianism*, Grand Rapids, MI 1989, 15–30.

Plantinga, Alvin, *The Nature of Necessity*, Oxford 1974.

Pou y Marti, Ioseph M. (ed.), *Bullarium Franciscanum II (1455–1471)*, Quaracchi 1939.

Powicke, F. M., *The Thirteenth Century 1216–1307*, Oxford 1953.

Quine, Willard Van Orman, *Philosophy of Logic*, Englewood Cliffs, NJ 1970.

Quinn, John M., *The Thomism of Étienne Gilson. A Critical Study*, Villanova 1971.

Quinton, Anthony, 'British philosophy,' *EP* I (1967) 369–396.

Read, Stephen, 'Self-reference and Validity Revisited,' in Yrjönsuuri (ed.) (2001) op. cit., 183–196.

Renard, Alexandre, *La querelle sur la possibilité de la philosophie chrétienne. Essai documentaire et critique*, Lille 1941.

Richter, Vladimir, *Studien zum literarischen Werk von Johannes Duns Scotus*, Munster 1988.

Rijk, Lambertus M. de, 'Aristoteles en de eleatische bewegingsantinomieën,' *Tijdschrift voor Filosofie* 9 (1947) 171–202.

Rijk, Lambertus M. de, *The Place of the Categories of Being in Aristotle's Philosophy* (PhD thesis Utrecht), Assen 1952.

Rijk, Lambertus M. de, *Petrus Abaelardus. Dialectica. First Complete Edition of the Parisian Manuscript*, Assen ¹1956 (²1970).

Rijk, Lambertus M. de, *Garlandus Compotista. Dialectica. First Edition of the Manuscripts with an Introduction on the Life and Works of the Author and on the Contents of the Present Work*, Assen 1959.

Rijk, Lambertus M. de, *Logica Modernorum. A Contribution to the History of Early Terminist Logic* I. *On the Twelfth Century Theories of Fallacy* (= *Logica Modernorum* I), Assen 1962.

Rijk, Lambertus M. de, Part II volume one: *The Origin and Early Development of the Theory of Supposition* (= *Logica Modernorum* II A), Assen 1967.

Rijk, Lambertus M. de, 'Die Bedeutungslehre der Logik im 13. Jahrhundert und ihr Gegenstück in der metaphysischen Spekulation' (1970), in Bos (ed.) (1989) op. cit., VII.

Rijk, Lambertus M. de (ed.), *Peter of Spain. Tractatus called afterwards Summulae Logicales. First Critical Edition from the Manuscripts with an Introduction*, Assen 1972.

Rijk, Lambertus M. de, 'Some Thirteenth Century Tracts on the Game of Obligation. I: Two Separate Tracts on *falsi positio* and *impossibilis positio*,' *Vivarium* 12 (1974) 94–123.

Rijk, Lambertus M. de, 'Some Thirteenth Century Tracts on the Game of Obligation. II: The *Obligationes Parisienses* found in Oxford, *Canon. misc.* 281,' *Vivarium* 13 (1975) 22–54.

Rijk, Lambertus M. de, 'Some Thirteenth Century Tracts on the Game of Obligation. III: The Tract *De petitionibus contrariorum*,' *Vivarium* 14 (1976) 26–49.

Rijk, Lambertus M. de, *Die mittelalterlichen Traktate De modo opponendi et respondendi. Einleitung und Ausgabe der einschlägigen Texte*, in *Beiträge zur Geschichte der Philosophie und Theologie des Mittelalters* NF 17, Munster 1980.

Rijk, Lambertus M. de, *Middeleeuwse wijsbegeerte. Traditie en vernieuwing*, Assen ²1981 (¹1977).

Rijk, Lambertus M. de, 'The early origin of the theory of supposition,' *CHLMP* (1982) 161–173.

Rijk, Lambertus M. de, *Het ongure individu. Uitdager èn spelbreker van het denken* (*The Disreputable Individual. Challenger and Spoilsport of Philosophical Thought*), Leiden 1983.

Rijk, Lambertus M. de, *La philosophie au moyen âge*, Leiden 1985: French translation of De Rijk (1981).

Rijk, Lambertus M. de, *Plato's Sophist. A Philosophical Commentary*, Amsterdam 1986.

Rijk, Lambertus M. de, 'In Memoriam Cornelia Johanna de Vogel,' *Vivarium* 25 (1987) 1 f.

Rijk, Lambertus M. de, 'On Boethius's Notion of Being. A Chapter of Boethian Semantics,' in Kretzmann (ed.) (1988) op. cit., 1–29 (= Bos (ed.) (1989) op. cit., I).

Rijk, Lambertus M. de, 'Un tournant important dans l'usage du mot *idea* chez Henri de Gand,' in *Idea*. VI Colloquio Internazionale. Atti a cura di M. Fattori e M. L. Bianchi, Rome 1990, 89–98.

Rijk, Lambertus M. de, *Peter of Spain. Syncategoreumata. First Critical Edition with an Introduction and Indexes and with an English Translation by Joke Spruyt*, Leiden 1992.

Rijk, Lambertus M. de, 'A Special Use of *ratio* in 13th and 14th Century Metaphysics,' in *Ratio*, VII Colloquio Internazionale. Atti a cura di Fattori e Bianchi, Rome 1994, 197–218.

Rijk, Lambertus M. de, *Nicholas of Autrecourt. His Correspondence with Master Giles and Bernard of Arezzo. A Critical Edition from the Two Parisian Manuscripts with an Introduction, English Translation, Explanatory Notes and Indexes*, Leiden 1994.

Rijk, Lambertus M. de, *Giraldus Odonis O.F.M. Opera Philosophica*. Volume I: *Logica. Critical Edition from the Manuscripts*, Leiden 1997.

Rijk, Lambertus M. de, *Johannes Buridanus. Summulae de demonstrationibus*, Groningen 2001.

Rijk, Lambertus M. de, *Aristotle. Semantics and Ontology* I–II, Leiden 2002.

Rijk, Lambertus M. de and H. A. G. Braakhuis (eds), *Logos and Pragma. Essays on the Philosophy of Language in Honour of Professor Gabriël Nuchelmans*, Nijmegen 1987.

Roche, Evan, *The* De Primo Principio *of John Duns Scotus*, St Bonaventure, NY 1949.

Rodd, Cyril S., *Glimpses of a Strange Land: Studies in Old Testament Ethics*, Edinburgh 2001.

Roest, Bert, *A History of Franciscan Education (c.1210–1517)*, Leiden 2000.

Rosier, Irène, 'Henri de Gand, le *De Dialectica* d'Augustin, et l'institution des noms divins,' *Documenti e studi sulla tradizione filosofica medievale* 6 (1995) 145–191.

Rosier-Catach, Irène, ' "Modisme, prémodisme, proto-modisme": vers une définition modulaire,' in Ebbesen and Friedman (eds) (1999) op. cit., 45–81.

Ross, James F. and Todd Bates, 'Duns Scotus on Natural Theology,' in Thomas Williams (ed.), *The Cambridge Companion to Duns Scotus*, Cambridge 2003, 193–237.

Roth, B., *Franz von Mayronis. Sein Leben, seine Werke, seine Lehre vom Formalunterschied in Gott*, Werl 1936.

Ruler, A. A. van, *Theologisch Werk* V, Nijkerk 1972 (*Theologisch Werk* I–VI (II–VI (ed.), J. A. van Ruler-Hamelink) Nijkerk 1969–73).

Ryan, John and Bernardine M. Bonansea (eds), *John Duns Scotus. Studies in Philosophy and the History of Philosophy* III, Washington, DC 1965.

Ryle, Gilbert, *Dilemmas*, Cambridge 1954.

Saint-Maurice, Béraud de, *Jean Duns Scot. Un docteur des temps nouveaux*, Rennes and Paris ²1953.

San Cristóbal-Sebastián, A., *Controversias acerca de la volundad desde 1270 a 1300*, Madrid 1958, 109–118.

Santogrossi, Ansgar, 'Scotus' Method in Ethics: Not to Play God – a Reply to Thomas Shannon,' *Theological Studies* 55 (1994) 314–325.

Sbaralea, H., *Supplementum et castigatio ad Scriptores trium Ordinum S. Francisci* II, Rome 1921.

Scapin, Pietro, 'Il significato fondamentale della libertà divina secondo Giovanni Duns Scoto,' *De doctrina Ioannis Duns Scoti* II (1968) 519–566.

Scapin, *Il primo principio degli esseri*, Rome 1968.

Schmidt, Axel, *Natur und Geheimnis. Kritik des Naturalismus durch moderne Physik und scotistische Metaphysik*, Freiburg 2003.

Schmidt, M. A., 'Theologen des Übergangs,' in Carl Andresen (ed.), *Handbuch der Dogmen- und Theologiegeschichte* I, Göttingen 1982.

Schmitt, Charles B., 'Filippo Fabri's *Philosophia naturalis Io. Duns Scoti* and its relation to Paduan Aristotelianism,' *Regnum Hominis and Regnum Dei* II (1968) 305–312.

Schmücker, R., *Propositio per se nota, Gottesbeweis und ihr Verhältnis*, Werl 1941.

Schneider, Herbert, 'Die Aktualität des seligen Duns Scotus,' in Herbert Schneider (ed.), *Johannes Duns Scotus. Seine Spiritualität und Ethik*, Kevelaer 2000, 76–83.

Schwamm, H., *Das göttliche Vorherwissen bei Duns Scotus und seinen ersten Anhängern*, Innsbruck 1934.

Searle, John R., *Speech Acts*, Cambridge 1968.

Seeberg, Reinhold, *Die Theologie des Johannes Duns Scotus*, Leipzig 1900.

Serene, Eileen, 'Demonstrative science,' *CHLMP* (1982) 496–515.

Sessevalle, F. de, *Histoire générale de l'Ordre de Saint François* I, Paris 1935.

Shannon, Thomas A., 'Method in Ethics: A Scotistic Contribution,' *Theological Studies* 54 (1993) 272–293.

Shannon, Thomas A., *The Ethical Theory of John Duns Scotus*, Quincy, IL 1995.

Sharp, D. E., *Franciscan Philosophy at Oxford*, London 1930.

Sheenan, M. W., 'The Religious Orders 1220–1370,' in Catto (ed.) (^{2}1986) op. cit., I 193–221.

Sheldon-Williams, I. P., 'The Greek Christian Platonist Tradition from the Cappadocians to Maximus and Eriugena,' in A. H. Armstrong (ed.), *The Cambridge History of Later Greek and Early Medieval Philosophy*, Cambridge 1970, 421–533.

Shook, Laurence K., *Étienne Gilson*, Toronto 1984.

Sidwell, Keith, *Reading Medieval Latin*, Cambridge 1996.

Sileo, Leonardo (ed.), *Via Scoti methodologica ad mentem Joannis Duns Scoti* I–II, Rome 1995.

Smith, Eustace, 'John Duns Scotus and Ecumenical Dialogue: The Dignity of Man,' *De doctrina Ioannis Duns Scoti* III (1968) 667–676.

Solaguren, Celestiono, 'Contingencia y creación en la filosofía de Duns Escoto,' *De doctrina Ioannis Duns Scoti* II (1968) 297–348.

Somerset, Fiona, 'Dietrich of Freiberg (*c.*1250 – after 1310),' *REP* (1998) III 69–71.

Somerville, Robert, 'Leo I,' *ER* (1987) VIII 514 f.

Sondag, Gérard, *Duns Scot. Le principe d'individuation*, Paris 1992.

Sondag, *Duns Scot. La théologie comme science pratique (Prologue de la Lectura)*, Paris 1996.

Spade, Paul Vincent (ed.), 'Robert Fland's *Insolubilia. An Edition, with Comments on the Dating of Fland's Works*,' *Mediaeval Studies* 40 (1978) 56–80.

Spade, Paul Vincent, 'Recent Research on Medieval Logic,' *Synthese* 40 (1979) 5 ff.

Spade, Paul Vincent (ed.), 'Robert Fland's *Obligationes*. An Edition,' *Mediaeval Studies* 42 (1980) 41–60.

Spade, Paul Vincent, 'Obligations: B. Developments in the Fourteenth Century,' *CHLMP* (1982) 335–341.

Spade, Paul Vincent, *Five Texts on the Mediaeval Problem of Universals: Porphyry, Boethius, Abelard, Duns Scotus, Ockham*, Indianapolis, IN and Cambridge 1994.

Spade, Paul Vincent and E. Stump, 'Walter Burley and the *Obligationes* Attributed to William of Sherwood,' *History and Philosophy of Logic* 4 (1983) 9–26.

Spijker, Willem van 't, 'Reformation and Scholasticism,' in Willem J. van Asselt and Eef Dekker (eds), *Reformation and Scholasticism. An Ecumenical Enterprise*, Grand Rapids, MI 2001, 79–98.

Spruyt, Joke, 'Thirteenth-century Positions on the Rule "*Ex impossibili sequitur quidlibet*," ' in Jacobi (ed.) (1993) op. cit., 161–193.

Spruyt, Joke, 'Duns Scotus's Criticism of Henry of Ghent's Notion of Free Will,' in Bos (ed.) (1998) op. cit., 139–154.

Stannard, Russell, *Grounds for Reasonable Belief*, Edinburgh 1989.

Stella, Prospero, 'L'Ilemorfismo di G. Duns Scoto,' in *Testi e studi sul pensiero medio-evale* II, Turin 1955, 147–163.

Steenberghen, Fernand Van, 'Maurice De Wulf (1867–1947)' (1948), in Steenberghen (1974) op. cit., 287–313.

Steenberghen, Fernand Van, *La philosophie au XIIIe siècle*, Louvain and Paris ²1991 (¹1966).

Steenberghen, Fernand Van, *Introduction à l'étude de la philosophie médiévale*, Louvain and Paris 1974.

Steeenberghen, Fernand Van, *Maître Siger de Brabant*, Louvain and Paris 1977.

Stump, Eleonore, 'Obligations: A. From the Beginning to the Early Fourteenth Century,' *CHLMP* (1982) 315–334.

Stump, Eleonore, 'William of Sherwood's Treatise on Obligations,' in E. F. Konrad Koerner, Hans-J. Niederehe and R. H. Robins (eds), *Studies in Medieval Linguistic Thought, dedicated to Geoffrey L. Bursill-Hall: Amsterdam Studies in the Theory and History of Linguistic Science – Studies in the History of Linguistics* 26, Amsterdam 1980, 249–264 (= *Historiographia Linguistica* VII 1/2 (1980) 249–264).

Sturm, Douglas, 'Natural law,' *ER* (1987) X 318–324.

Sylla, Edith D., *The Oxford Calculators and the Mathematics of Motion 1320–1350. Physics and Measurement by Latitudes*, New York 1991.

Thijssen, J. M. M. H. and H. A. G. Braakhuis (eds), *The Commentary Tradition on Aristotle's De generatione et corruptione. Ancient, Medieval and Early Modern*, Turnhout 1999.

Thijssen, J. M. M. H. and Jack Zupko (eds), *The Metaphysics and Natural Philosophy of John Buridan*, Leiden 2001.

Thro, Linus J., 'Étienne Gilson,' *ER* (1987) V 560.

Thro, Linus J. and Charles J. Ermatinger, 'Questions on Aristotle, *Metaphysics* X and XII, by Master John Dymsdale,' *Manuscripta* 36 (1992) 71–124 and 37 (1993) 107–167.

Tonna, Ivo, 'The Problem of Individuation in Scotus and Other Franciscan Thinkers of Oxford in the 13th Century,' *De doctrina Ioannis Duns Scoti* I (1968) 257–270.

Bibliography 641

Torrance, J. B. and R. C. Walls, *Duns Scotus*, Edinburgh 1992.
Torrance, Thomas F., 'Intuitive and Abstractive Knowledge from Duns Scotus to John Calvin,' *De doctrina Ioannis Duns Scoti* IV (1968) 291–305.
Toulmin, Stephen E., 'Matter,' *EP* (1967) V 213–218.
Treharne, R. F., 'Edward I of England,' *Encyclopaedia Britannica. Macropaedia*, Chicago and London 1976, VI 434–436.
Veldhuis, Henri, *Geen begrip voor de ander*, Utrecht 1990.
Veldhuis, Henri, *Ein versiegeltes Buch. Der Naturbegriff in der Theologie J. G. Hamanns (1730–1788)*, Berlin 1994.
Veldhuis, Henri, 'Ordained and Absolute Power in Scotus' *Ordinatio* I 44,' *Vivarium* 38 (2000) 222–230.
Verbeek, Theo, *Descartes and the Dutch*, Illinois 1992.
Verdenius, W. J., 'Hylozoism in Early Greek Thought,' *Symposium. Hooykaas and the History of Science* (Utrecht), *Janus* 64 (1977) 25–40.
Veuthey, L., 'Alexandre d'Alexandrie, maître de l'Université de Paris et ministre général des Frères Mineurs,' *Études Franciscaines* 43 (1931) 145–176 and 319–344, and 44 (1932) 21–42, 193–207, 321–336, and 429–467.
Vier, Peter C., *Evidence and Its Function According To John Duns Scotus*, St Bonaventure, NY 1951.
Vignaux, P., 'Pour situer dans l'école une question d'Eckhart,' in Brunn et al. (1984) op. cit., 141–154.
Vogel, C. J. de, *Wijsgerige aspecten van het vroeg-christelijk denken*, Baarn 1970.
Vos, Antonie, 'Middeleeuwse Wijsbegeerte. Traditie en vernieuwing,' *Nederlands Theologisch Tijdschrift* 34 (1980) 66–72.
Vos, Antonie, *Kennis en Noodzakelijkheid. Een kritische analyse van het absolute evidentialisme in wijsbegeerte en theologie (Knowledge and Necessity: A Critical Analysis of Absolute Evidentialism in Philosophy and Theology)*, Kampen 1981, I–XVIII and 1–456.
Vos, Antonie, 'Thomas van Aquino en de gereformeerde theologie. Een theologiehistorische impressie,' *Jaarboek 1982. Werkgroep Thomas van Aquino*, Utrecht 1982, 114–119.
Vos, Antonie, 'Logical Aspects of the Concept of Sin,' *The Third European Conference on Philosophy of Religion* (acta of the congress), Munich 1982, 62–68.
Vos, Antonie, 'Procesfilosofie versus Plantinga. Een repliek,' *Nederlands Theologisch Tijdschrift* 37 (1983) 326–333. Reply to Prof. Dr H. G. Hubbeling: 'Procesfilosofie versus Plantinga. Een kritische bespreking van het werk van Dr. A. Vos: *Kennis en Noodzakelijkheid*,' *Nederlands Theologisch Tijdschrift* 36 (1982) 238–245.
Vos, Antonie, 'Almacht volgens Thomas van Aquino en Duns Scotus,' *Thomas-Jaarboek 1984*, Utrecht 1984, 39–67.
Vos, Antonie, 'De ontologische argumenten,' *Wijsgerig Perspectief* 24 (1984) 158–163.
Vos, Antonie, 'On the Philosophy of the Young Duns Scotus,' in Bos (ed.) (1985) op. cit., 195–220.
Vos, Antonie, 'Johannes Duns Scotus,' *Kerk en Theologie* 36 (1985) 177–195.
Vos, Antonie, *Confitemur. Een symbolische oriëntatie*, Utrecht 1989.
Vos, Antonie, 'Voetius als reformatorisch wijsgeer,' in J. van Oort, C. Graafland, A. de Groot, and O. J. de Jong (eds), *De onbekende Voetius*, Kampen 1989, 220–241.

Vos, Antonie, *Het is de Heer!*, Kampen 1990.

Vos, Antonie, 'De ethische optie van Duns Scotus,' *Kerk en Theologie* 44 (1993) 17–32.

Vos, Antonie, 'Protestant Theology: The Netherlands,' in Alister E. McGrath (ed.), *Blackwell Encyclopedia of Modern Christian Thought*, Oxford and New York 1993, 511–515.

Vos, Antonie, *Johannes Duns Scotus*, Leiden 1994, I–X and 1–284.

Vos, Antonie, 'The Theoretical Centre and Structure of Scotus' *Lectura*: Philosophy in a New Key,' in Sileo (ed.), *Via Scoti* I (1995) 455–473.

Vos, Antonie, 'Moments of the Ars Obligatoria according to John Duns,' in Gordon A. Wilson and Timothy B. Noone (eds), *Franciscan Studies. Essays in Honor of Dr. Girard Etzkorn* 56 (1998) 383–422.

Vos, Antonie, ' "Always on Time". The Immutability of God,' in Gijsbert van den Brink and Marcel Sarot (eds), *Understanding the Attributes of God*, Frankfurt and Bern 1999, 53–73.

Vos, Antonie, 'Ab uno disce omnes,' *Bijdragen* 60 (1999) 173–204.

Vos, Antonie, 'Hauptlinien der Scotischen Ethik,' in Herbert Schneider (ed.), *Johannes Duns Scotus. Seine Spiritualität und Ethik*, Kevelaer 2000, 21 (3–38).

Vos, Antonie, 'Scholasticism and Reformation,' in Willem J. van Asselt and Eef Dekker (eds), *Reformation and Scholasticism. An Ecumenical Enterprise*, Grand Rapids, MI 2001, 99–119.

Vos, Antonie, Ilse N. Bulhof, and Kees Stam, *Geschiedenis van de middeleeuwse filosofie*, Utrecht 1986.

Vos, Antonie, H. Veldhuis, E. Dekker, N. W. den Bok, and A. J. Beck, *Duns Scotus on Divine Love*, Aldershot 2003, I–X and 1–235.

Vos, Antonie, H. Veldhuis, A. H. Looman-Graaskamp, E. Dekker, and N. W. den Bok, *Johannes Duns Scotus. Contingentie en vrijheid. Lectura* I 39, Zoetermeer 1992, 1–208.

Vos, Antonie, H. Veldhuis, A. H. Looman-Graaskamp, E. Dekker, and N. W. den Bok, *John Duns Scotus. Contingency and Freedom. Lectura* I 39, Dordrecht/Boston 1994.

Waal, Cornelis de, 'Peirce's Nominalist-Realist Distinction, an Untenable Dualism,' *Transactions of the Charles S. Peirce Society* 34, 1 (1998) 183–202.

Wainwright, William J., 'Monotheism,' in Robert Audi and William Wainwright (eds), *Rationality, Religious Belief, and Moral Commitment*, Ithaca, NY 1986, 289–314.

Wald, 'Die Bestimmung der *ratio legis* bei Thomas von Aquin und Duns Scotus,' in A. Zimmermann and Andreas Speer (eds), *Miscellanea Mediaevalia 21/2. Mensch und Natur im Mittelalter*, Berlin and New York 1992, 662–681.

Walgrave, J. H., *Geloof en theologie in de crisis*, Kasterlee 1966.

Ward, Benedicta, *The Prayers and Meditations of Saint Anselm*, Harmondsworth ²1979 (¹1973).

Wéber, Édouard, 'Eckhart et l'ontothéologisme: histoire et conditions d'une rupture,' in E. Brunn et al. (1984) op. cit., 13–83.

Webering, D., *Theory of Demonstration According to William Ockham*, St Bonaventure, NY 1953.

Weinberg, Julius R., *A Short History of Medieval Philosophy*, Princeton, NJ 1965.

Weinberg, Julius R., *Abstraction, Relation and Induction. Three Essays in the History of Thought*, Madison, WI and Milwaukee, WI 1965.

Weisheipl, James A., 'Roger Swyneshed O.S.B. Logician, Natural Philosopher, and Theologian,' in *Oxford Studies Presented to Daniel Callus*, Oxford 1964.

Weisheipl, James A., *Friar Thomas d'Aquino. His Life, Thought and Works*, Oxford 1975.

Wetter, Friedrich, 'Die Erkenntnis der Freiheit Gottes nach Johannes Duns Scotus,' *De doctrina Ioannis Duns Scoti* II (1968) 477–517.

White, Lynn (ed.), *Ernest A. Moody. Collected Papers 1933–1969*, San Francisco 1975.

Wielockx, Robert, 'De Mercier à De Wulf. Débuts de l'École de Louvain,' in Imbach and Maierù (eds) (1991) op. cit., 75–95.

Williams, Thomas, 'The Unmitigated Scotus,' *Archiv für Geschichte der Philosophie* 80 (1998) 162–181.

Winden, J. C. M. van and A. H. Smits, *Bonaventura. Itinerarium. De weg die de geest naar God voert*, Assen 1996, edited by the Research Group *Bonaventura*: A. H. Bredero, P. G. J. M. Raedts, A. H. Smits, A. Vos, J. C. M. van Winden, and Th. H. Zweerman.

Wippel, John F., 'Godfrey of Fontaines: the Date of *Quodlibet* 15,' *Franciscan Studies* 31 (1971) 300–369.

Wippel, John F., *The Metaphysical Thought of Godfrey of Fontaines. A Study in Late Thirteenth-Century Philosophy*, Washington, DC 1981.

Wippel, John F., 'Essence and existence,' *CHLMP* (1982) 385–410.

Wippel, John F., *Metaphysical Themes in Thomas Aquinas*, Washington, DC 1984.

Wippel, John F., 'Essence and Existence in the *De ente*,' in John F. Wippel (1984) op. cit., 102–132.

Wippel, John F., 'Essence and Existence in Other Writings,' in John F. Wippel (1984) op. cit., 133–161.

Wippel, John F., 'The Reality of Nonexisting Possibles According to Thomas Aquinas, Henry of Ghent, and Godfrey of Fontaines' (1981), in John F. Wippel (1984) op. cit., 163–189.

Wippel, John F., *Medieval Reactions to the Encounter Between Faith and Reason*, Milwaukee, WI 1995.

Wollheim, Richard, 'Natural law,' *EP* (1967) V 450–454.

Wolter, Allan B., *The Transcendentals and Their Function in the Metaphysics of Duns Scotus*, St Bonaventure, NY 1946.

Wolter, Allan B., *John Duns Scotus. A Treatise on God as First Principle*, Chicago ²1983 (¹1966).

Wolter, Allan B., *Duns Scotus. Philosophical Writings*, Edinburgh and London ¹1962 (Latin/English), Indianapolis, IN ²1975 (English).

Wolter, Allan B., 'John Duns Scotus. Life and Works,' in Alluntis and Wolter (1975) op. cit., XVIII–XXVII.

Wolter, Allan B., 'John Duns Scotus,' *The New Encyclopaedia Britannica. Micropaedia* IV, London ¹⁵1997, 278 f. (= *Macropaedia* V (1976) 1083–1085).

Wolter, Allan B., *Duns Scotus on the Will and Morality*, Washington, DC ¹1986 (²1997).

Wolter, Allan B., 'John Duns Scotus,' *ER* (1987) IV 513–515.

Wolter, Allan B., 'The Realism of Scotus' (1962), in McCord Adams (ed.) (1990) op. cit., 42–53.

Wolter, Allan B., 'Scotus' Individuation Theory,' in McCord Adams (ed.) (1990) op. cit., 68–97.

Wolter, Allan B., 'Duns Scotus on Intuition, Memory, and Our Knowledge of Individuals' (1982), in McCord Adams (ed.) (1990) op. cit., 98–122.

Wolter, Allan B., 'Native Freedom of the Will as a Key to the Ethics of Scotus' (1972), in McCord Adams (ed.) (1990) op. cit., 148–162.

Wolter, Allan B., 'Duns Scotus on the Will as Rational Potency,' in McCord Adams (ed.) (1990) op. cit., 163–180.

Wolter, Allan B., 'The "Theologism" of Duns Scotus' (1947), in McCord Adams (ed.) (1990) op. cit., 209–253.

Wolter, Allan B., 'Duns Scotus and the Existence and Nature of God' (1954), in McCord Adams (ed.) (1990) op. cit., 254–277.

Wolter, Allan B., 'Scotus' Paris Lectures on God's Knowledge of Future Events,' in McCord Adams (ed.) (1990) op. cit., 285–333.

Wolter, Allan B., 'Reflections on the Life and Works of Scotus,' *American Catholic Philosophical Quarterly* 67 (1993) 1–36.

Wolter, Allan B., 'God's Knowledge: A Study in Scotistic Methodology,' in Sileo (ed.), *Via Scoti* I (1995) 165–182.

Wolter, Allan B., 'Duns Scotus at Oxford,' in Sileo (ed.), *Via Scoti* I (1995) 183–192.

Wolter, Allan B., and Girard J. Etzkorn, *Questions on the Metaphysics of Aristotle by John Duns Scotus* I–II (translation), St Bonaventure, NY 1997.

Wolter, Martin M., 'The Life and Times of Allan B. Wolter O.F.M.,' in Frank and Etzkorn (eds) (1985) op. cit., 7–20.

Wood, Rega, 'Scotus's Argument for the Existence of God,' *Franciscan Studies* 47 (1987) 257–277.

Wulf, Maurice De, *Histoire de la philosophie scolastique dans les Pays-Bas et la Principauté de Liège*, 1894.

Wulf, Maurice De, *Histoire de la philosophie médiévale* II, Louvain ⁵1925.

Wulf, Maurice De, *Histoire de la philosophie médiévale* I–III, Louvain ⁶1933–47.

Yrjönsuuri, Mikko, *Obligations. 14th Century Logic of Disputational Duties*, Helsinki 1994.

Yrjönsuuri, Mikko (ed.), *Medieval Formal Logic. Obligations, Insolubles and Consequences*, Dordrecht 2001.

Yrjönsuuri, Mikko, 'English translation of *Question* X of Pseudo-Scotus' *Questions on Aristotle's Prior Analytics*,' in Yrjönsuuri (ed.) (2001) op. cit., 225–234.

Yrjönsuuri, Mikko, 'English translation of the Emmeran treatises on *falsi positio* and *impossibilis positio*,' in Yrjönsuuri (ed.) (2001) op. cit., 199–215.

Zavalloni, Roberto, *Richard de Mediavilla et la controverse sur la pluralité des formes. Textes inédits et étude critique*, Louvain

Index